What is Language Development?

What is Language Development?

Rationalist, empiricist, and pragmatist approaches to the acquisition of syntax

JAMES RUSSELL

Reader in Cognitive Development
Department of Experimental Psychology
Cambridge University

OXFORD
UNIVERSITY PRESS

OXFORD
UNIVERSITY PRESS

Great Clarendon Street, Oxford OX2 6DP

Oxford University Press is a department of the University of Oxford.
It furthers the University's objective of excellence in research, scholarship,
and education by publishing worldwide in

Oxford New York

Auckland Cape Town Dar es Salaam Hong Kong Karachi Kuala Lumpur
Madrid Melbourne Mexico City Nairobi New Delhi Shanghai Taipei
Toronto

With offices in

Argentina Austria Brazil Chile Czech Republic France Greece
Guatemala Hungary Italy Japan South Korea Poland Portugal Singapore
Switzerland Thailand Turkey Ukraine Vietnam

Oxford is a registered trade mark of Oxford University Press
in the UK and in certain other countries

Published in the United States
by Oxford University Press Inc., New York

A catalogue record for this title is available from the British Library

ISBN 0 19 2632485 (Hbk)

ISBN 0 19 8530862 (Pbk)

10 9 8 7 6 5 4 3 2

Typeset by Cepha Imaging Pvt. Ltd, Bangalore, India
Printed in Great Britain
on acid-free paper by Biddles Ltd, King's Lynn

Preface

Why was this book written, and what kind of book is it? It was written in order to put between two covers (I'm sure, for the first time) the *three* psychologies of language development, and to do so whilst tilting the exposition towards the Rationalist, nativist (i.e., Chomskyan) position, with the further intention of redressing an imbalance within contemporary developmental psychology. From where I sit, developmental psychologists, if they teach language development at all (and they are *very* unlikely to teach syntactic development unless it happens to be their area of research), seem to regard the Chomskyan approach as something to be shunned; a kind of scholasticism with implausible, untestable, and inappropriate scientific pretensions. They might tell their undergraduates about connectionist work on past tense learning, and, very likely, they will have warm words to say about, and if not actually evangelise in favour of, the approach that I call in the book 'pragmatist', within which the child is assumed to 'construct' syntax from what she apprehends of the conceptual and the social domains. This approach, it would be said, is 'truly developmental'; as if something cannot be formalist, nativist and 'truly developmental' at the same time.

I wrote the book then, as a way, I admit a *long* way, of saying 'not so fast': consider the possibility that in thinking, not to mention telling your undergraduates, that language development is no more than associative learning or that each child heroically constructs human syntax *de novo* by listening to what is being said and making some simple cognitive moves, you may be deluded. Moreover, in opting for one of the three psychologies of language development you are also opting for an *epistemology* - Rationalist, Empiricist, or Pragmatist. That is to say, if you believe *that (e.g.,* syntactic categories emerge from statistical learning, or language development is a species of socio-cultural learning) then you must assent to *this* – being some venerable but maybe vulnerable view of human nature and knowledge. I try to spell out in the book, the *that-this* linkages.

This then is the 'why', out of which the 'what kind of' naturally grows. Needless to say, the kind of book that has resulted would never be mistaken for a monograph. That's to say, I do not pretend that the book includes any ideas about syntactic development that are original to me. I present, rather, a panoramic but opinion-coloured perspective on established ideas and on data mostly in the journals. A central aim throughout is exposition. The book might, in fact, be read as a *lecture*. In keeping with this, I have tried to adopt a prose style, which, while not being conversational in tone, involves frequent addresses to the reader-as-audience, in which there is much referring back and forwards, much reminding about where we are, plus some metaphor-infused reflections along the way.

But while not being original as *science*, this book is original as a *book*. Not only is it original in its range of reference and its synthesis, as we have seen, but in its constructing a frame in which a provocative theory of the relationship between conceptual development and syntactic development is enabled to emerge as a plausible, testable, alterative to some tired antitheses. This is Martin Atkinson's *dynamic minimalism*. This analogises Chomsky's most recent theory, the Minimalist Programme (1995), to the process of language acquisition. Chomsky argued that we can suppose, as a conjecture for linguistic research, that the human language faculty came into being as the 'optimal' solution to conditions for mutual 'legibility' imposed at the 'interface' between verbalisation and two 'external' systems: for articulation/hearing and for thinking. Atkinson further supposes that we can view language development, to put it in my own terms, as the process whereby the innate language capacity produces optimal solutions to conditions for language-thought legibility imposed by conceptual development. (Explicating these metaphors will take a good deal of work of course; and there will need to be some hedging around the 'optimal' when applied to development.) On this perspective, one can both give conceptual development its proper due whilst avoiding one of Piaget's grimmest legacies, which is the view that syntactic development is essentially cognitive development *tout court*.

Finally, with regard to my description of the book as being like a 'lecture', I would like to give, for the first time, a quotation to which, as readers will see, I have become somewhat addicted. It is Louis Menand's description of the appeal of pragmatism as a philosophy. Encountering it, he writes, makes readers feel

> 'as if some pressing but vaguely understood obligation has suddenly been lifted from their shoulders, that some final examination for which they could never have been properly prepared had just been cancelled'.

Well, there will be no examination after the course of lectures, so readers can take what they will from the wealth of neutral exposition on offer among the editorializing and tendentious commentary, pumping their intuitions as they wish.

J.R.
Cambridge,
September, 2003.

Acknowledgements

I would like to thank Vanessa Whitting, who, shortly before she left OUP, encouraged me to submit a proposal based on my unformed, hesitant ideas for a book on 'the problem of language acquisition'. Martin Baum of OUP gave my project firm and patient support, and to him also I am very grateful.

However the book in its present form would not even have conceived had I not, in the spring of 1999, attended a meeting of the Cambridge University Linguistics Society in King's College at which Martin Atkinson spoke on Chomsky's minimalist programme, also briefly describing his own ideas on 'dynamic minimalism'. This seminar was an inspiration to me. My further gratitude goes to Martin Atkinson for answering so fully the plethora of questions I emailed to him over a two-year period. I must also thank Martin's University of Essex colleague, Andrew Radford, for giving me permission to quote from his unpublished paper on minimalism and development.

Heather van der Lely helped me hone my discussion of specific language impairment, provided me with much reading, and was marvellously generous with her time. Thanks too to Helen Goodluck for reading a portion of the book, for sending papers, and for useful email correspondence. Stephen Butterfill read Parts 1 and 2 and provided invaluable discussion – challenging but supportive – over beer-and-sympathy in the *Baron of Beef*. Rainer Spiegel and Lisa Saksida provided valuable comments on Part 3. Thanks to Rainer additionally for wonderfully stimulating discussion. Thanks to Tony Wells for his comments on Part 2 and for his *invaluable* help with proofreading. Jaideep Prabhu, Charlotte Russell, and Kate Plaisted were good enough to comment on Part 1. For help with references and for miscellaneous advice I thank: Nicky Clayton, Selvino de Kort, Roz McCarthy, Nick Mackintosh, Helen Moss, Brian Moore, Ilona Roth, Paddy Russell, and Sabine Trebbich.

Julian Pine's advice about what to read was simply invaluable. I'm grateful in particular for his pointing me towards the recent, to-be-published work of Franklin Chang. My discussion of Julian Pine's important work benefited enormously from his keeping me up to date with it. Email discussions with Julian also helped to focus my own position on a number of matters.

I am grateful to Robert Fishwick for holding back a tide of administration, towards the end, so I could get the book finished. Wantao Song's help with computing was tireless and good humoured. I also acknowledge his advice about Chinese.

However my deepest gratitude is due to Dr. Maria Angeles Gallego-Garcia. Witnessing at close hand her work in an area of linguistics (Semitic philology) far removed from the concerns of this book, gave me a model of remorseless scholarship, control of mind-boggling detail, and sensitivity to linguistic nuance that it has been impossible for me to emulate; though I have tried. But more than this, she gave me the kind of support, during the writing, that it is simply impossible to acknowledge adequately. This book is dedicated, in love and friendship, to her.

J.R.
Cambridge,
September, 2003.

Contents

Introduction:
'temper temper'

The question in the title is, of course, rhetorical – no less than Mailer's *Why are we in Vietnam?* The reason for asking it is to spur the thought that theories of how children acquire the grammar of their native language are so profoundly divergent as to seem to be addressing three different kinds of phenomenon. Indeed the rationalist, the empiricist and the pragmatist do see different kinds of phenomenon, by virtue of the philosophical goggles through which they view the developing child. The intention behind this book is to describe what the world looks like when wearing the different kinds of goggle and to describe how the acquisition of syntax looks through each of them. There will also, of course, be some evaluation taking place – along the way.

Would it be better simply to remove these artificial aids in the hope of seeing language development plain? What a grim, descriptive exercise that would turn out to be. When psychologists ask questions about what makes us human they do so, willy nilly, with certain philosophical presuppositions in mind. To struggle against this fact would be to produce something bloodless, dull, and superficial. This is a truism to most of us; but truisms do have the clear merit of being true. And like many truisms it is often rendered invisible by virtue of its very familiarity. It is obvious, for example, that empirical investigation alone could never decide between the views of Noam Chomsky, on the one hand, and those of Jeffrey Elman or Michael Tomasello on the other.

Another way of describing the current situation is by saying that in this area we have three coexisting Kuhnian paradigms. Three paradigms then for what is to count as a theory, what is to count as data, and three answers to the question posed in the title:

Rationalism: It is the experientially canalised maturation of innate, domain-specific knowledge, manifested as the ability to carry out formal operations of increasing complexity on linguistic data. Human beings have innately specified *sui generis* apparatus for moving between speech and thought. The 'moves' are not learnable.

Empiricism: It is a species of associative learning. There is in the speech input to the child sufficient structure, stochastically mediated, to inform the child of the kinds of rules and representations she requires to crack the linguistic code. Children recruit domain-general mechanisms of associative learning; and connectionist models serve as the existence proofs that this kind of learning can do the job.

Pragmatism: It is something that the child *does*, not something that happens to her by virtue of maturation or of the automatic associative calculus. The other two approaches undersell the child's active construction of her knowledge. Syntactic development is not something the child *undergoes*, but something she achieves by virtue of recruiting her cognitive and social capacities. This position rejects both the blank-slate views of the empiricist and the syntactic nativism of the rationalist.

As we shall see, one of the many elegant phrases coined by William James was 'the empiricist temper regnant'. Well, most of us have one kind of temper or another regnant within us. When it comes to language, I must admit that mine is rationalist. (Though when it comes to the child's developing knowledge of the external world and self-awareness, I still – as in Russell [1996] – think that Piagetian pragmatism has some of the best tunes.) Given this rationalist temper, there will be in the book quite a bit of editorialising broadly on behalf of the Chomskyan approach. But at the same time I strive to let the other positions have their say in full. This is why it has taken nearly a quarter of a million words to address this rhetorical question. But *should* there not be a lot to be said about what makes us human?

PART 1

Three psychologies: rationalist, empiricist, and pragmatist

Explaining language development is a job for psychology, and how you undertake that job will depend upon the kind of psychology you decide – as if it were a matter of free decision! – to operate within. In this part of the book I describe the three main kinds of on offer. Although some of the details set out here will be far removed from the material of language acquisition they will – I hope – deserve their place, because it is not just in poetry that 'showing' is better than 'telling'. In any event, I have tried to arrange things so that readers will be able to let details wash over them whilst retaining the main points. As I warned in the introduction, there will also be a good deal of editorialising on behalf of the rationalist approach; but that should not interfere with the 'showing'. It will be seen that the resources of the three approaches are about as different from one another as it is possible to be.

It is fair to say that the connectionist (empiricist) and the socio-cognitivist (prag-matist) paradigms define themselves in relation to the Chomskyan position rather than in relation to each other. For the connectionist, the aim is to demonstrate that linguistic categories and rules can be constructed from the speech input by systems that not only lack rules of any kind but which operate without symbols; while the socio-cognitive theorist regards the apparatus of Chomskyan theory as no more than a descriptive enterprise whose arcane principles tell us nothing about how the child 'breaks into' language. The Chomskyan position is the common enemy. Unless I have missed something recently, connectionists and socio-cognitivists are far more likely to ignore, rather than square up to, each other.

Why? What are they rejecting? They are not simply rejecting nativism. In the first place, connectionists not only object to the idea that children start off with tacit knowledge of a universal grammar (UG): they object to the very idea that the cognitive-linguistic capacities of adults (not to mention the cleverer animals) are explicable in terms of their manipulation of symbols and rules. In the second place, despite its emphasis on the process of 'cultural learning' (Tomasello, 1999), the socio-cognitivist position itself makes some strong assumptions about innate capacities – about infants' skill at reading the intentions of other people, for example.

Given this, it is clear that we are not looking at three competing theories – let alone three competing hypotheses – offering different accounts of a single phenomenon.

The level at which these two approaches reject the Chomskyan is epistemological. It can be seen that the connectionist epistemology is empiricist while the socio-cognitivist one is pragmatist (Tomasello, personal communication October 2000, is comfortable with this label). By the same token, Chomsky's position is first and foremost a rationalist one, not merely nativist – though it is certainly that.

In this Part I will examine how these three epistemologies canalise three kinds of research on syntactic development. Readers will have to forgive me if expressions like 'as we shall be seeing in section so-and-so' keep cropping up, as the idea is to signpost the paths towards the theories. What I will be doing is taking a broad view of why there can be such fundamental disagreement as to what a 20-month-old is manifesting when she says, for example, 'Allgone sticky'.

Although this will be the shortest Part of the book it will still be on the long side; and this is because we will be comparing three systems of thought. This takes a long time. My general approach to these matters is, then, distinct from that of Steven Pinker. In his book *Words and Rules*, Pinker (1999a) concentrates his discussion of nativist versus empiricist ideas about language development around the question of how they explain the mastery of the English past tense, because, Pinker writes, this study 'is the only case I know in which two great systems of Western thought may be tested and compared ... like ordinary scientific hypotheses'. Perhaps. But another way of doing it is to look at the 'systems of Western thought' themselves – as well a taking a much more inclusive view of syntax development.

1.1 Rationalism

It will immediately emerge that rationalist psychology is a highly linguistic and philosophical affair.

I will first outline the respects in which Chomsky's theory is indeed rationalist, and then describe the explanatory goals of his linguistic theory and how he makes the transition from theoretical linguistics to theoretical developmental psychology. We will also consider the arguments fielded by J. A. Fodor in favour of the view that the conceptual system on which language depends is not only innately represented but must itself have a language-like format (the 'language of thought' doctrine). This would seem to suggest that the interaction between the linguistic and the conceptual faculties is thereby made easier to understand. But – as I end by saying – even Fodor has some highly sceptical things to say about whether the so-called 'computational theory of the mind', which is an intimate associate of the language of thought doctrine, is capable of describing everyday thought, as opposed to thought sequestered within a single domain. So if the computational theory of the mind does not offer a complete account of thought, then either (1) even more is demanded of a linguistic theory by way of explaining how the linguistic and the conceptual are mutually 'legible' or (2) the computational theory of mind – despite its being a cornerstone of rationalist psychology – is of no particular relevance to Chomsky's ideas; or (3) a bit of both.

1.1.1 A 'god-like reason' and its armature

It would be difficult, if not impossible, to capture a single set of tenets which all the philosophers usually classed as rationalists hold in common. But one can at least

sketch out the link between being a rationalist and being a nativist. As the name suggests, rationalism is the view that reason, and not sense experience or learning or the
regnant cultural norms or divine revelation, makes the central contribution to our
acquisition of knowledge.

Reason is normally conceived of by rationalists as being distinct from sensory
experience and – inevitably – as being irreducible to it. It is a faculty whose content
does not emanate from some source external to the individual but which
autonomously determines – in the 'god-like' way Hamlet evoked – the way our experience must be. If the faculty of reason is independent from external sources (not
counting God among these), then it must be internal; it must be innate (implanted
by God for the seventeenth-century rationalists, by biology for us).

For Descartes, the innate (as opposed to the 'adventitious' ideas like that of the
colour blue) were ones like the idea of God, extended matter, and certain geometric
ideas. In modern times however, we are more likely, whether philosophers or psychologists, to think of them as being representational formats that ground our use of
logical principles in thought, our possession of a basic conceptual system, and – the
topic of this book – our having the armature of reason, which is syntax. A rational
creature will have structured thoughts (on which more later) and if this creature is
also a thinker in a public language then the form of its sentences is likely to be well
adapted (Chomsky: optimally adapted) to expressing that structure. The rationalist
believes that sensory experience, and what experimental psychologists typically mean
by 'learning' are not sufficient to serve as the foundations for capacities of this kind.

The idea that knowledge requires foundations at all is debated; but there are a
number of considerations in favour of the view that something must serve as an
unconditional bedrock for our concepts. Martin Hollis (1973) puts it like this.
Suppose that I make a list of all the propositions I believe – the known truths. Some
of these will require inference (Hollis's example: that there were once dodos on
Mauritius) and so my belief in them will be only conditional on my belief of other
propositions. I then star all the conditional ones. Well, what justifies my retaining a
starred entry or retaining a subset of starred items complete in itself but depending
upon one another? Nothing: it would follow that I knew none of these entries. 'For',
Hollis writes, 'if I know the truth of P, only if I know the truth of Q and if, moreover,
my warrant for claiming to know Q is P itself (or else R, whose warrant is P), then
I know the truth of neither P nor Q' (Hollis, 1973, p. 33).

One who is a nativist about syntax is likely to believe that our knowledge of how
the lexicon constructs phrases and how phrases construct clauses is unstarred. And
because it is unstarred children must bring this knowledge with them to the task of
interpreting the speech they hear and of acquiring knowledge of the target language's syntax sufficient to frame sentences of their own.

Yet there are a number of respects in which the rationalism of Chomsky looks
quite different from that of thinkers such as Descartes. We'll encounter some in the
next subsection, but this for now. As Martin Braine (1994) has pointed out, whereas
the seventeenth-century rationalist philosophers thought of innate ideas as propositions (*veritées innées* not just *idées innées*) usually of a metaphysical and religious
nature – whereas these ideas had content – the innate knowledge proposed by Noam

Chomsky comes closer to being knowledge of structure and mechanism – attributes, default tendencies, and grammatical principles. In fact, for Braine, Chomsky has essentially abandoned the distinction between content and structure/mechanism, so that in effect:

> The nativists have won by capturing the political centre, so to speak, by expanding the term 'idea' so that the distinction between content and structure/mechanism became irrelevant to it, with the result that it covered virtually every terrain of cognition.
>
> (Braine, 1994, p. 12)

But ten years after this was written, few would so confidently say that the nativists have 'won' in the field of syntactic development. For we have witnessed the continuing rise of connectionist modelling since the mid 1980s and the growing influence of empirical work on language development – heavily influenced by Braine's own ideas, as we shall be seeing – purporting to show that children construct syntax bit by bit without any prior knowledge apart from that within the social and cognitive domains.

There is indeed something in what Braine says, but he underestimates the degree to which proposals about innate structure and mechanism depend upon further claims about content – about innate symbolic capacities.

1.1.2 Noam Chomsky – a somewhat unconventional rationalist

While the term 'radical nativist' certainly characterises Chomsky, and while Chomsky's way of proceeding surely has a strongly a-prioirist flavour, his rationalism is not of a purely philosophical kind. While he places himself within the rationalist tradition in philosophy – notably with Descartes – he does not ground his theories by explicity philosophical analysis, let alone advance particular claims with the kind of step-by-step argument-building that characterises analytical philosophy; indeed he implicitly rejects the idea that one can get from A to B by reason alone. Moreover, Chomsky's attitude to the work of the philosophers he finds unsympathetic is one of impatient dismissal, treating them as not so much in error as misguided, as if they were engaged in the wrong kind of enterprise rather than doing the right kind of thing not well enough. In the late 1960s,[1] for instance, Chomsky would dismiss the Wittgenstein idea that language is fundamentally a social practice in which meaning is grounded in function and context with an anecdote about the occasion on which he gave an address to students at an anti-Vietnam-war rally before a heavily-armed contingent of National Guardsmen. His sentences carried meaning, he pointed out, despite the fact that his social mind was elsewhere. A similar spirit is present in his latest non-technical book (Chomsky, 2000a). In a review of this book Fodor (2000a) captures this spirit well: 'some philosopher sticks his head out of a hole,[2] and Chomsky whacks him. Quine, whack! Davidson, whack! Dummett, whack! Searle, Dennett, Burge, Putnam, whack, whack, whack, whack!'

---

[1]   I am thinking here of his John Locke lectures in Oxford, given in 1968.

[2]   In the game Whack-a-Mole the idea is to bash with a mallet as quickly as possible 'moles' which pop up from different trapdoors on a board.

These hammer blows are frequently not so much philosophical arguments as 'killer facts' about the English language. Thus, when Chomsky turns his attention to Quine and Dummett he illustrates the poverty of (1) the Quinean view that a sentence's semantic interpretation is ultimately relative to our total belief system and (2) Dummett's defence of the language-as-social practice position by reference to two sentences.

  1) Mary expects to feed herself.

  2) I wonder who Mary expects to feed herself.

He points out that the different possibilities for co-reference between 'Mary' and 'herself' in these two apparently similar sentences rest upon *language-internal* facts, quite encapsulated from 'belief systems' and 'social practices'.

This brings me to a second respect in which Chomsky's practice is somewhat removed from that of the philosophical a-priorist: he uses data, and he regards data about our 'intuitions' regarding the grammaticality of sentences as being of a scientific status by no means inferior to that collected in the psycholinguistic or the developmental laboratory. Despite the clear philosophical resonance of his work then, what he is doing – Chomsky insists – is science, not conceptual analysis-cum-linguistics. He (1980, pp. 189–192) draws a parallel between his kind of theoretical psychology and theoretical physics, especially the kind of theoretical physics which, for practical reasons, has no recourse to direct experiment. Solar physics in a case in point. Astrophysicists cannot examine the thermonuclear reactions taking place deep within the sun and so have to collect data 'at the periphery' – evidence about the nature of light emissions and about the neutrinos released by reactions 'at the periphery'. Well, just as physicists do not dismiss such data by reason of their 'indirect' nature, psychologists should not regard Chomsky's data as too tightly bound within the hermeneutic circle of language itself to be taken seriously – demanding evidence from 'within' our own particular 'sun' (the brain). Furthermore, Chomsky (2000a, e.g. pp. 116–117 , p. viii, 82) is predictably sceptical about the authority that the brain sciences nowadays claim for themselves on all matters psychological, including questions about linguistic meaning and structure. It is naive to believe, he argues, that linguistic theories of his kind can be 'reduced to' data about (say) electrical activity in the brain, because the only plausible reduction is the other way about – neuroscientific data to a coherent linguistic theory. After all, we have no 'theory' of event-related potentials or neuroimaging; and one does not try to reduce the theory-rich to the theory-lite.

There is a further sense in which Chomsky's rationalism is not of the traditional kind. While nativism is at the core of rationalism, Chomsky's nativism is not one that would be easily recognised by Plato, Leibniz or Descartes. He writes:

> Furthermore [I] support what might fairly be called a rationalist conception of the acquisition of knowledge if we take the essence of this view to be that the general character of knowledge, the categories in which it is expressed or internally represented, and the basic principles that underlie it, are determined by the nature of the mind. In our case the schemativism that is assigned as an innate property to the language acquisition device determines the form of knowledge ... The role of experience is only to cause the innate schemativism to be activated.

(Chomsky, 1975a, p. 129)

Commenting on this passage, Cottingham (1984, pp. 123–124) recalls the parallel that Chomsky himself draws between this view and the Leibnizian view that experiental stimuli are like the hammer blows of a sculptor that do no more than uncover a pre-existing form in the marble. But he goes on to say that Chomsky's notion of innate knowledge is significantly different from that of Plato, Descartes or Leibniz in so far as these philosophers took innate knowledge to consist in either explicit awareness of certain conceptual truths (e.g. about geometry) or in the ability to achieve such awareness after exposure to the right kind of stimulation. It might be said – against this – that Chomsky's use of grammatical intuitions as data was surely a kind of acknowledgement that innate capacities carry us forward to explicit awareness of certain truths about language. But this would be a mistake. Obviously enough, we do not have innate ideas about the rules that determine grammaticality in English; and still less is something akin to 'a concept of the well-formed sentence' innate. Rather, what Chomsky intends by innate knowledge is closer to the notion of innate machinery than to that innate conceptual content (cf. the position of Braine, discussed above). Indeed, we shall see that in his most recent work Chomsky is in the process of abandoning some of the claims about innate representations and replacing it with the idea that we have innate abilities for performing certain foundational linguistic operations – a more bottom-up view of syntax, in fact. This may seem a far cry from the traditional rationalist concern with innate capacities for reasoning. For Chomsky, the language faculty is 'optimally designed' for relating the purely linguistic to the rational faculties.

However, before we become carried away with the idea that Chomsky's rationalism is less than full-blooded, it is time to redress the balance and focus on the respects in which it is entirely four-square.

1.1.3 Competence

It is one thing to be caused, in virtue of a history of training or in virtue of being 'programmed' in a certain way, to behave such that one's behaviour can be described as rational, and another thing to *be* a 'rational animal'. The difference consists, essentially, in the fact that in the former case the individual produces behaviour that can be said to be *governed* by certain kinds of rules (as can the behaviour of the planets!), while in the latter case the individual is *following* rules, rules that, in this domain, she takes to be inviolable – and which we take to be formalisable as axioms. The degree to which an individual will be able to state the rules, the degree to which she is conscious of them, will be a moot point; but she will certainly enjoy what might be called 'intuitions' about such things as what is a good or fallacious argument or inference. In short, she will *know* a rule-system. When it comes to mounting a psychological theory of this capacity, two things will have to be included: (1) an account of what is known; (2) an account of the representations and the operations on them – the system of information-processing – that serves as the substrate of this knowledge, this being a theory of *use*. For the past twenty of a so years the most influential account of the latter has been Philip Johnson-Laird's (1983) theory of mental models (Stenning, 2002, for a critique). In the domain of reasoning, the theory of what knowledge is being computed is not a significant area of controversy; but this is not the case when we come to syntax.

When the rationalist turns to language, a similar distinction will be taken to hold between the theory of knowledge and the theory of use: Chomsky's famous distinction between *competence* (knowledge) and *performance*. The performance theory is psycholinguistics, and no doubt

> A reasonable model of language use will incorporate, as a basic component, the generative grammar that will express the speaker-hearer's knowledge of the language; but this generative grammar does not, in itself, prescribe the character or functioning of a perceptual model or a model of speech production.
>
> (Chomsky, 1965, p. 9)

What is a generative grammar? Chomsky (1965, pp. 8–9; emphasis added) writes:

> An interesting generative grammar will be dealing, for the most part, with mental processes that are far beyond the level of actual or potential consciousness; furthermore, it is quite apparent that a speaker's reports and viewpoints about his behaviour may be in error. Thus *a generative grammar attempts to specify what the speaker actually knows not what he may report about his knowledge*.... When we speak of a grammar as generating a sentence with a certain structural description, we mean simply that the grammar assigns a structural description to the sentence. When we say that a sentence has a certain structural derivation with respect to a particular grammar, we say nothing about how the speaker might proceed, in some practical or efficient way, to construct such a derivation ... The term 'generate' is familiar *in the sense intended here in logic*. Furthermore, 'generate' seems to be the most appropriate translation of Humbold's term *erzeugen*.

(I will discuss *erzeugen* in section 2.4.2.) Many deny the need for any such division between competence and performance, and wonder in what kind of frictionless atmosphere a competence theory is supposed to be floating. Why indeed must theories of *rationality* be the explanatory template? On such an anti-rationalist view, the theory of knowledge is no more than – this is a phrase beloved of empiricists and pragmatists – 'an empty formalism'. A theory of language capacity and its acquisition should be a theory of performance *tout court*!

The rationalist asserts, by contrast, the autonomy (in the sense of the irreducibility to processing mechanisms) of both reason and grammar. Indeed we might even say that she regards a grammar as being something like 'reasons' why speaker-hearers behave as they do. There is no more prospect for reducing this to information-processing capacities and dispositions than there is for reducing our knowing the truth of $p \rightarrow q$, p, therefore q to neural processes. More recently, as we shall immediately see, Chomsky has come to speak in terms of the 'I-language' rather than competence; but the story is just the same.

Finally, how plausible is the view that we use knowledge of language (competence) *consciously* when speaking? Very plausible. As Higginbotham (1987, p. 125) puts it:

> Suppose that I am on the point of speaking and that – recognising that what I am going to say would be ambiguous and therefore liable to misinterpretation – I switch at once to a more precise way of expressing myself. Then I have used my knowledge of language, even though nothing has happened that the auditors can detect.

1.1.4 Individualism and internalism

Rationalism is based upon an *individualist* and *internalist* conception of mental capacity, mental life, and human nature. Chomsky is certainly no exception here. Perhaps the most famous instance of individualism/internalism in the history of rationalism is Descartes' 'cogito' in which he seeks to establish, on the basis of introspection alone, his own existence and from this foundation goes on to deduce, by a series of arguments, the existence of the external world. While Chomsky's individualism/internalism does not take this form, he certainly shares with Descartes the assumption that the materials for approaching truths and for attaining competence within a given domain lie within each of us and take essentially the same form in each of us. How this works for Chomsky is perhaps best appreciated through the parallels he draws between the mind as an objective entity and the body as an objective entity. Both of them are, by necessity, organised. That is to say, for them to be effective, responsibility for functioning must be shared between a set of quasi-autonomous organs. Accordingly, just as we are *not* born with bodies that are undifferentiated and equipotential, bodies possessed of certain domain-general principles of environmentally-guided change (the physiological analogues to, say, classical and instrumental learning) that enable us to learn to digest food, regulate temperature, and so forth, no more are we born with undifferentiated and equipotential minds that develop towards the adult state by 'learning'.

Given this, mental organs are organs in much the same sense as that in which the liver and the heart are organs. And, while each organ interacts with others, each has its own *sui generis* structure that can be studied more or less independently from that of other organs. But more centrally, mental organisation inheres in the individual in much the same way as does physical organisation. This is my arm and it has essentially the same nature as your arm; likewise my kidneys, medulla, and so forth. These organs had much the same starting state as yours and they all developed in the same way. Similarly, this is my language faculty, my cognitive faculty and my sensorimotor capacity. You have them too, and the fact that you may be quite a different kind of person with a completely different life history does not alter the fact that these mental organs take the same form in both – in all – of us.

For this reason, mental organs are 'internal' to each of us, and one individual organism is exemplary of all. It is this quintessentially rationalist starting-point that has led Chomsky to replace his famous notion of 'competence' with that of the I-language ('internal' and 'individual'[3]) in his linguistic theory.

It is important to reflect here upon what internalism/individualism about the mental leads one to abandon. The abandonment of empiricism is obvious enough, but the abandonment of any form of social or cognitive relativism about language is no less central. (More will be said on this topic when we discuss pragmatism.) On internalism/individualism, the language organ is distinct from whatever cognitive and social organs we might have; and by the same token language comprehension and production cannot be understood as a set of performances mutually infused with human intelligence more generally. This is the symmetrical opposite of what a philosopher of language such as Donald Davidson takes to be the case. For Davidson, a listener manages to construct a model of a speaker's meaning by a process of *interpretation*, in the service of which a 'passing theory', derived from the

---

[3]   Note that it is also 'intensional' (see p. 77 below); but I won't go into this.

context of utterance and from current ideas about the speaker, will need to be constructed. (Cf. Quine's holism about linguistic meaning and also work in relevance-theory by Sperber and Wilson, 1986). On such a view, the 'the concept of language' has no utility, says Davidson, in so far as it is understood as 'a portable interpreting machine set to grind out the meaning of an arbitrary utterance'; indeed we 'abandon ... not only the ordinary notion of language, but we have *erased the boundary between knowing a language and knowing our way around the world generally'.* Since there are no rules for arriving at passing theories we 'must give up the idea of a clearly defined shared structure which language users acquire and then apply to cases' (Davidson, 1986, p. 446, emphasis added). In short 'There is no such thing as language' (quoted in Chomsky, 2000a, p. 29).

The internalist/individualist, of course, believes the exact opposite: that the task of linguistics within theoretical psychology is to 'isolate coherent mechanisms that are amenable to naturalistic enquiry and wholeheartedly to accept the idea that there is a generative procedure that "grinds out" linguistic expressions' (Chomsky, 2000a, p. 29) that will interface with other ('performance') systems in the cognitive and sensorimotor domains to produce adequate comprehension and production. Chomsky diagnoses what lies at the heart of this misguided rejection of internalism/individualism is the idea of language use being dependent upon speakers and hearers having 'shared meanings' – a notion that opens up the endless panorama of all human social and intellectual life (the undifferentiated and equipotential 'body cognitive' of which I spoke earlier). No:

> Successful communication between Peter and Mary does not entail the existence of shared meanings or shared pronunciations in a public language (or a common treasury of thoughts or articulations of them) any more than physical resemblance between Peter and Mary entails the existence of a public form that they share.

Note the use of the bodily parallel here. Chomsky goes on to say that for communication to work in this case Peter assumes that, give or take a bit, Mary is like him and that (unreflectively, as a rule) he 'understands what Mary says as being what he means by his comparable expression' (Chomsky, 2000a, p. 30).

This position is, of course, easily recognised as being Cartesian; and so it will, for some, have to answer the charge of solipsism that Cartesian positions inevitably attract. Be that as it may, such a position brings with it the substantial advantage of rendering the scientific study of human language tractable. In contrast, imagine a Davidsonian 'anatomy' in which the structure of the liver could not be understood without reference to that of every other organ in the body – and indeed to what the body happened to have ingested that day.

This, then, is Chomsky's famous 'modularity'. And note how it is more a matter of circumscribing domains of enquiry (and of framing questions about how the different mental organs interface) than of 'discovering' mental modules.[4] Indeed, Chomsky cautions (ibid., p. 117) that his conception of the module – as a mental faculty or organ – should not be confused with Jerry Fodor's use of the term to refer

---

4 On the fashion for 'discovering' modules in developmental psychology, see Russell (2002).

to 'input systems'. In fact, within the Fodorian architecture, the language faculty, as opposed to sentence parsing, might have to be located within the central systems of the mind.

From within a project of this kind, cognitive–developmental psychology is construed as the study of a *sui generis* human nature becoming manifest. Human nature is something that children bring with them into the world; it does not emerge from 'interaction' with the social or physical environment. Moreover, the passage from Chomsky I quoted earlier (directed against the idea that successful communication depends upon finding 'shared meanings') also stands in stark contrast to the developmental ideology (fashionable in the 1970s, rather less so today) which holds, after Vygotsky, that mental development is carried forward by a kind of socialisation process in which children and 'caretakers' 'construct meanings' as dyads, with the very idea that 'meaning' (eliding all kinds of meaning together here) is something that can be said to inhere in a single mind being anathema.

Finally in this section, I want to point up an apparent irony, by way of illustrating the width and depth of Chomsky's commitment to rationalism – despite his somewhat insecure place in the 'great tradition'. The social-constructivist picture of mental development just mentioned, in so far as it is relativist, and indeed collectivist, is naturally hospitable to the political left. But the seeming irony of where this leaves Noam Chomsky – who is at least as well known as a left-libertarian thinker and polemicist as he is as a linguist – is easily and fruitfully dissolved.

The rationalist, as we have seen, takes the view that we own our minds in a similar way to that in which we own our bodies, believing that the elements of mentality (the 'organs') have an endogenously determinate, inner character. The physical organs need nutrient to develop and the language faculty needs speech and a social life, with the structure of the latter being no less of biological fact than the structure of the former. By the same token, human beings can be said to possess a capacity for reason as well as a capacity for moral sentiment. We owe these capacities to nothing outside ourselves (they are internal) – certainly not to families, schools, or to public structures and to ideologies. Accordingly, the rationalist is likely to take her own reason as a touchstone, just as she will trust her own bodily reports about whether she is sated or in pain. And so she will feel competent to think for herself, withstanding any consensus about whether it is right to (say) destabilise, or collude in the bullying of, a distant state at the cost of endless misery to its inhabitants in order to bolster the interests of the American empire. The materials for coming to a different view are her own and no external authority need gift her confidence in her intellectual autonomy.

It is not, therefore, difficult to appreciate why rationalism, in so far as it is internalist/ individualist, can encourage an instinctive distrust of authority – in the sense of those who take it upon themselves to 'socially construct' our political reality. Which gives us the means to understand, as Chomsky's biographer puts it, 'Chomsky's frequent claim, that, despite his loathing of labels, he would be satisfied to be labelled a contributor to *an anarchist (if properly defined)* or an eighteenth-century rationalist tradition' (Barsky, 1997, p. 106, emphasis added). My point is that these two traditions are not just contingently related. Indeed, in his fervent anti-empiricism combined with anti-authoritarian radicalism (not to mention the system-building), and in his intellectual audacity, I like to think of there being a parallel between Noam Chomsky and William Blake.

1.1.5 Explanatory adequacy: how to get from linguistics to developmental psychology

It is now time to tackle more substantive questions about how Chomsky's rationalist mindset determines the moves he makes from linguistics to theoretical psychology – to claims about the course and nature of development.

We have already discussed the nature of his data: our (in practice, the linguist's) intuitions about whether certain sentences are well-formed – whether they are grammatical, ungrammatical, ambiguous, or uninterpretable.[5] But children are unable to provide such data, as metalinguistic awareness emerges many years later than the acquisition of syntax itself. So what kind of data are relevant to Chomsky's developmental proposals? The question must be answered in terms of Chomsky's distinction between two levels of 'adequacy' for a linguistic theory: 'descriptive' and 'explanatory'.

The goal of descriptive adequacy is that of characterising the underlying rules of a particular language in such a way that its classifications of sentences in the language as 'grammatical', and so forth, are in line with those made by the native speakers of the language. Given any sentence judged to be grammatical, the theory can describe in virtue of which kind of rule-following it is grammatical; and given any sentence judged ungrammatical, it can describe what has gone wrong in terms of these same principles. Such an enterprise is certainly empirical in so far as critics of the grammar are free to seek examples of sentences that, according to that grammar, should be judged to be grammatical/ungrammatical, but are not.

In Chomsky's terms, such a grammar finds 'a way to account for the phenomena of a particular language' (1995, p. 5). Contrasted with this is the goal of 'explanatory adequacy' where the linguist tries to 'explain how knowledge of these facts arises in the mind of the speaker-hearer' (ibid, p. 3 emphasis added).

More explicitly:

> To attain descriptive adequacy for a particular language, L, the theory of L (its grammar) must characterise the state attained by the language faculty. To attain explanatory adequacy, a theory of language must characterise *the initial state of the language faculty* and show how it maps experience to the state attained.

Here Chomsky cites with approval the judgement of Otto Jespersen that it is only 'with regard to syntax' that we would expect 'that there must be something in common to all human speech … no one ever dreamed of a universal morphology'.

Viewed in this light then, we can see that data on linguistic intuitions are indeed indirectly relevant to the assessment of Chomskyan claims about syntactic development. For the linguist cannot move directly towards the goal of explanatory adequacy without being armed with some descriptively adequate account of the language

---

[5] An example of such a sentence: *Which guy did you meet Mary and Sue.*

within which the theory is being developed. However, the goal of explanatory adequacy is, as we have seen, explicitly developmental: to produce a theory of (1) the initial state of the child's syntax organ that also explains (2) how speech input to the child enables this knowledge to be exploited such that competence – an I-language for that particular language – will be acquired.

Over the years (as I shall describe in Part 2), Chomsky's linguistic theories have posited fewer and fewer rules while (not at all paradoxically) it has required progressively more imagination, if not actual suspension of disbelief at some points, to understand. The reason is that, with each new theoretical development, the goal of descriptive adequacy was gradually replaced by one of explanatory adequacy. For achieving descriptive adequacy requires the linguist 'to enrich the format of permissible systems' (Chomsky, 1995, p. 24), whereas achieving explanatory adequacy requires their *stripping back*. If we are to characterise the tool kit ('Human') that enables children to acquire any human language then we should not be providing them with tools that mesh only with the contours of English or Swahili.

But it is important not to lose sight of the fact that a descriptively adequate theory – a theory of the end state – is necessary to the explanatory enterprise. For if the linguist is not operating with a theory of what this English (or Korean or ...) child is developing towards he or she will never be able to characterise what is developing. Development is viewed – this is a further feature of rationalism – *from the perspective of its end point*. (Thus, the rationalist will keep in mind that the toddler who says 'allgone sticky' might one day be saying things like 'The accountants are suggesting to widows that Lloyds is a safe place for their inheritance, while the commission touts work the dinner tables'). In contrast to this, the empiricist and the pragmatist stand alongside the child and, with a narrow-angle lens, pan across the course of development, stopping at certain points to present the most 'parsimonious' account of how the child managed to get this far.

Chomsky's conception of explanatory adequacy has evolved somewhat over the years (see Greene, 1971, for his earlier views), and one would be guilty of oversimplifying if one left the impression that the descriptive/explanatory distinction is a clean and straight one. Moreover, we need to look more closely at what explanatory adequacy amounts to if we are to gain a clear idea about how developmental data operate in this area.

The complexity is evident from Andrew Radford's (1997a, pp. 4–6) four-way taxonomy:

1) Descriptive adequacy;

2) A theory of grammar;

3) Explanatory adequacy;

4) Learnability.

With regard to (2), the linguist is aiming towards a grammar that is sufficiently general to describe the well-formedness of sentences in any language. This is a theory of universal grammar (UG). What constitutes the step from (2) to (3)? For Radford it is, rather than listing a set of universal properties (as does UG), a matter of asking: 'Why do natural language grammars have the properties they do?' (ibid., p. 5)

Now this would immediately appear to conflict with Chomsky's own characterisation of the explanatory goal in terms of a study of the child's initial state and of how linguistic experience maps onto this. However, when we come to examine Chomsky's 'minimalist programme' we shall see why this conflict is more apparent than real. To anticipate: in answering questions about why syntactic rules must take the form they do if they are to interface adequately with cognitive structures (be 'legible' by them) one is inevitably answering questions about how such a process can get underway and continue in the child. That is: what is it about innately represented UG that enables it to interact with the process of cognitive development?

Turning to (4) – learnability – one encounters a condition on explanatory adequacy itself, namely, that any rules that the linguist includes in the (purportedly) explanatory adequate grammar must be learnable by human children given what we know about the kind of speech data available to them and given that they have a finite amount of time to converge upon the correct I-language. Note the relation between this and Radford's definition of explanatory adequacy: that one reason (if not the central reason) why innately represented UG takes the form it does it that any language must be learnable by human children.

In fact, since the early 1960s (Chomsky, 1963; Miller and Chomsky, 1963), questions about learnability have had almost no role to play in the development of Chomsky's theory. One reason for this is that such questions can be posed, not only without regard to actual data from children, but also without regard to the grammars that linguists actually produce.[6] 'Learnability theory' (a branch of mathematics) concerns, instead, 'the logical problem' of language acquisition. In this area, one asks questions about the kind of speech input and the kind of initial hypothesis-bank a notional child requires to learn a grammar of a certain kind. The most influential work in this area is that of Gold (1967) who proved (in the mathematical sense) that a child who begins with a set of candidate languages (in the form of sets of sentences) will fail to identify which of these is the target language to which she is being exposed unless, in addition to exposure to grammatical sentences, she is also exposed to ungrammatical ones which are tagged as such. The general goal here is to discover the abstract conditions (on starting hypotheses and on kind of speech input) that have to be met if the child is ever to internalise the grammar of the language to which she is being exposed in a finite amount of time – or 'in the limit' as Gold calls it.

So one obvious question to ask next about rationalist theories of syntactic development is: If the goal of explanatory adequacy is not significantly constrained by formal theories of what is learnable by the notional child[7] what *does* constrain such theories? How, that is, do we select between descriptively adequate theories in order to get closer to the holy grail of explanatory adequacy? The linguist selects between grammars on the criterion of '*simplicity*'. I will use this term as the synecdoche for

---

6   See Atkinson (1992) pp. 16–21.

7   See Atkinson (1992, p. 21) on drawing conclusions about learnability from the formal properties of grammar.

Chomsky's 'elegance, simplicity, and economy'. The descriptive grammar that explains the largest number of features of the language using the smallest number of generalisations – and with fewest ad hoc assumptions – is the preferred one. Chomsky admits that the notion of simplicity is vague; but there is nothing remotely vague in the way in which his rationalism infuses his practice here. We might indeed call it 'methodological rationalism'. He notes that descriptive adequacy:

> is justified on purely *external* grounds, on grounds of correspondence to linguistic fact. On a much deeper and hence a much more rarely attained level (that of explanatory adequacy) a grammar is justified to the extent that it is a *principled* descriptively adequate system, in that the linguistic theory with which it is associated selects this grammar over others, given primary linguistic data with which all are compatible. In this sense, the grammar is justified on *internal* grounds of its relation to a linguistic theory that constitutes an explanatory hypothesis about the form of language as such. The problem of internal justification – of explanatory adequacy – is essentially the problem of constructing a theory of language acquisition, an account of the specific innate abilities that make the achievement possible.
>
> (Chomsky, 1965, p. 27, emphasis in original)

It would be difficult to find a passage that illustrates rationalist psychology more graphically. Far less important than correspondence to 'linguistic fact' are the qualities that the theory of grammar has as a linguistic theory. We will pass over awkward questions about the criteria for simplicity itself (e.g., is a grammar with a small number of long rules more economical than one with a large number of short rules?) and get to the nub of the issue: What justifies the parallel drawn between an explanatory adequate theory and a theory of the child's 'innate abilities'? Here is how one might think about this claim.

The first logical step is the assumption that the child does indeed possess innate formal knowledge of Human (the universal human language). Note that this assumption arises directly from the rationalist framework. It is not something derived from Chomsky's famous claims about the 'poverty of the stimulus'. In fact it is made prior to the devising of a descriptively adequate theory, because claiming that the speech input is too impoverished to support the acquisition of a grammar is something that can only be done relative to a particular descriptively adequate theory. Let us suppose that there is not yet one in place, because right now we are thinking only about the explanatory adequacy as a goal in developmental psychology.

The next step is to suppose that children, in acquiring the I-language of their mother tongue, will end up with two kinds of grammatical rule internally represented. One of these is the set of rules specific to that language, capturing facts about (say) what is marked on the verb (e.g., tense and subject number, but not addressee status in English) or about whether verbs must appear at the beginning or at the end of verb phrases. Call these kinds of rules *ABC* rules. Children will also have in their I-language, of course, a set of rules – perhaps 'operating principles' is a better term – that are common to all the 'dialects' of Human. These will be more general in nature and will determine such matters as how elements are combined to make up phrases and what kind of procedures are followed to ensure that agreement (e.g., in number, case, tense) is achieved between the elements of sentences. Call these *xyz* rules. Now, on the assumption we have already made that some formal principles are innate, it must surely be the case that the *xyz* rules are innate – given that children can learn any human language. But it is also a very plausible assumption that *xyz* rules will be *simpler* than *ABC* rules. We have already noted that in seeking descriptive adequacy (a grammatical theory for a particular language) linguists find themselves, in Chomsky's words, having 'to enrich the format of permissible systems'. In contrast to this, *xyz* rules will make fewer ad hoc assumptions (e.g., what happens to be marked on the verb is an ad hoc fact) and they will be applicable to more sentences. Take, for example, the rule that when operations are performed on sentences to change their status from affirmative to interrogative, the elements of the sentence are always moved from the end towards the beginning, never from the beginning towards the end. In fact this generalisation appears to hold universally in the case of question-forming (Comrie, 1988). Contrast this with the *ABC* rule that the canonical word-order in English is subject-verb-object (SVO). This generalisation does not even hold for commands (e.g., 'Catch the ball Peter', which is VOS); it is not a simple generalisation about all English sentences comparable with the simple generalisation about movement.

In the light of this, it becomes clear why the harder linguists try to simplify the rules in their descriptively adequate grammars, the closer they get to *xyz* rules – the rules that (by hypothesis) are innate in human children. If the innate rules/operations/representations that the infant brings to the task of learning a particular language are in the infant's mind in virtue of the fact that they are simple (i.e., in relation to ad hoc rules of particular languages) and if the linguist adopts simplicity as her criterion for selecting between descriptively adequate grammars then – it can reasonably be expected – the rules/operations/representations in question will be more or less the same ones in child and linguist.

(By the way, readers who immediately think that Chomsky's background assumption here is that natural selection has caused us to evolve the most economical rule system must be warned to abandon all such thoughts! Viewing syntactic rules in terms of selective fitness belongs to the pragmatist, not to the rationalist tradition. To put it mildly, Chomsky has always backed away from this line of thought. His ideas about how the syntax evolved are characteristically audacious – as we shall see in 2.3. His more measured views are reported in Part 4.5.3.)

Does this mean that we can construct theories about the nature of innate syntactic knowledge by doing linguistics *alone* – without any reference to how and when children actually acquire language? Certainly not. Returning to the analogy that Chomsky (1980b) drew between his kind of linguistics and solar physics, just as the physicist is dependent on data regarding the behaviour of light waves and neutrinos outside the sun so the Chomskyan linguist depends upon data 'at the periphery' – from the child's behaviour. He himself cites developmental data in support of his views;[8] and we will, of course, be discussing such data when we come to a detailed assessment of the theory. But for now, here are both and real and fanciful examples of developmental data that conflict with claims about innate knowledge.

----

[8]   He did so, most notably, in his debate with Piaget (Chomsky 1980b).

In the first place, Chomsky's so-called Standard Theory (developed around the mid 1960s) claimed that passive sentences like 'The ball was caught' are more computationally complex (because they require a further, 'deletion' transformation from their deep structure) than passives like 'The ball was caught by John'. In which case then, we should we expect the first to be observed later than the second kind of sentence. But the first is actually observed earlier rather than latter type.

In the second (fanciful) case, let us return to the putatively innate assumption (*xyz* rule) that movement of sentential elements is always from the end to the beginning of a sentence. If we found English-learning children who were able to frame affirmative sentences but who routinely made errors in imperative-framing such as '*Johnny ball catch!' (i.e., moving the verb to the right) then this would tend to undermine the claim of explanatory adequacy on behalf of a grammar that said all movement is from end to beginning.

This, then, is what a rationalist approach to language acquisition amounts to. Its practice may be 'internalist' through and through but it makes claims that are corrigible 'at the periphery'.

1.1.6 The nature of the cognitive organ

Here the discussion will centre around Fodor's doctrine of the 'Language of Thought'.

In terms of the mind–body analogy, the relation between the syntax and the cognition organs is surely more similar to that between the heart and the bloodstream than it is between, let's say, the auditory system and the pancreas. In the former case, life would not be sustained unless the basic features of one did not mesh with those of the other. If, for example, blood were a gas or a powder the heart could not do its job, and if the heart functioned, like the brain, electrochemically rather than hydraulically then blood would never be distributed round the body. So we need to say what it is about the cognitive organ that makes it liase successfully with the syntax organ – that makes sentences expressive of thoughts, as well as (perhaps) enabling language development to take place in harmony with cognitive development.

By its very name, the doctrine of the 'Language of Thought' (LOT) is clearly what we need to make sense of this meshing. There are two aspects to this doctrine: one, on which we focus first, concerns the content of concepts and the second, more relevantly to our interests, concerns the structure of propositions.

In the first, Fodor (1975, 1980) was expressing the kind of scepticism about the possibility of acquiring concepts by learning that has been around since ancient times. The idea is that concept acquisition requires 'inductive generalisation', meaning a process of hypothesis-testing and confirmation enabling the individual to make inferences about the range of items a concept covers from experiencing feedback about whether something is or is not an exemplar of that concept. But if such a process is going to work, individuals must already be in possession of – they must have mentally represented – the very features that are definitive of that concept. Therefore what actually takes place, says Fodor, is something that is more appropriately called 'belief fixation' than learning, in the sense that individuals' experiences lead them to believe that a certain set of criterial features of a concept (that are already represented in the mind) constitute that concept.

> In short no theory of learning that anybody has ever developed is, as far as I can see, a theory that tells you how concepts are acquired; rather, such theories tell you how beliefs are fixed by experience – they are essentially inductive logics. That kind of mechanism which shows you how beliefs are fixed by experiences makes sense only against the background of radical nativism.
>
> Fodor (1980, p. 144)

Let us take it a little more slowly, and extend it toward the 'language' element.

1) Concept learning boils down to inductive extrapolation by hypothesis formation and confirmation.

2) The child will have hypotheses of the kind 'X is a chair iff[9] it is a portable seat for one', 'X is a bucket iff it is a portable seat for one'.

3) The environment will inform the child about the truth or falsity of these hypotheses.

4) Where do these hypotheses come from? Ultimately, it must be from the child.

5) If they are innately present then they must be in a representational format of some kind.

6) As the format must comprise elements standing for sets of data it must be symbolic.

7) So there must be an innate language of thought.

Fodor applied this line of thought to Piagetian theories of mental development, which, while they do not claim that concepts are acquired by associative or by stimulus response learning, do deny that the logico-mathematical complexity of the child's cognition develops because more complex systems of thought are innately represented in the mind, with their development being 'triggered' or 'fixed' by experience. Piaget claimed that (to use Fodor's terminology) 'stronger logics' develop by a process called 'reflective abstraction' in which children bootstrap themselves onto a higher cognitive level by abstracting from the structures of action and internalising these, which will themselves in turn be abstracted from later in development – and so on. Fodor insists that this is tantamount to admitting that 'each successive one [logic] has the former as a proper part' which means that Piaget's account of mental development has to be regarded as nativist if it is to work at all. 'Piaget must not, in point of logical necessity (not empirical necessity) be a *non*-nativist about changes of stage, that is, about the mechanisms that take you from one stage to another.' (Fodor, 1980, p. 147; original emphasis).

Fodor argued further, as we saw in (5)–(7) above, that one cannot say that cognitive development is a matter of an innate representational formats for human concepts leading to belief fixation by experience unless one also accepts that this innate format is *in the form of a language*. This is so because there is no other way to conceptualise a representational format than by saying that it consists of symbols that

---

9   Iff = if and only if.

stand for data. Thus, children will never learn the meaning of the word 'chair' unless they have a representational format for {portable seat for one} – two concepts in a semantic relation to a third, each of which can be decomposed into finer grain concepts; *but at some point we reach bedrock*. The bedrock is the language of thought, a symbol system that Fodor analogised to the digital machine-code of a computer. In this sense then, Fodor famously concluded, 'all concepts are innate'. Certainly, this conclusion looks as rationalist as you might wish.

Developmental psychologists tended to respond to what became known as 'Fodor's paradox' (most regard the conclusion *as* paradoxical) in one of four ways. In the first place – and this was the response of Jean Piaget himself, one acknowledges with some regret – Fodor's argument is too strong because it entails that minds could not evolve. But a moment's thought tells us that this is wrong. As Fodor put it, the implication is no more that viruses know about set theory than that viruses have legs; it does not follow from the fact that viruses don't have legs that legs don't evolve by natural selection. Fodor is concerned, that is to say, with development in the individual; his argument does not deny that that the human conceptual system was all implicit in the primordial slime. A second response was to swallow the argument whole and replace Jean Piaget with Jerry Fodor as the cynosure. In retrospect, it is not difficult to see why this was an attractive option; for while this forced developmentalists to abandon the very idea of mental development as 'construction'; at least they could avert their gaze from the implausible Piagetian picture of children having within them an homunculus with prodigious reflective abilities able to derive the rules that generate meaningful sentences from the formal 'structures' expressed through negotiating the physical world, imitating and pretending. What's more, allying LOT to Fodor's (*The modularity of mind*, 1983) conception of modules as innately specified and encapsulated input systems that parse perceptual inputs and pass them up, in splendid isolation, to 'the central systems' (where the thinking goes on) licences one to invent any number of innate modules written in LOT. (This was how the gang of TOM, TOBY, EDD and SAM came to have their fifteen minutes of fame.[10]) But for a number of us this was an unattractive option. For one thing it ignored the fact that Fodor's *The modularity of mind* is best read as a sceptical essay on the *limitations* of modular theorising in cognitive psychology, given that its being unable to explain domain-*general* thinking and everyday action is quite a falling-short (to be discussed in 1.1.7). Moreover, the kind of developmentalising that resulted seemed to be as unconstrained as looking for faces in the clouds.

The third response to Fodor's paradox involved trying to show why it was a bad argument, why it was no more than a *reductio* of radical nativism rather than proof of its necessity. There were a number of attempts; and I went into print with three.[11] But (in retrospect again) metaphors of tar babies and windmill-tilting spring to

---

[10] These are some sub-modules of theory of mind proposed by Simon Baron-Cohen and by Allan Leslie. The '15 minutes' dig refers to the fact that their popularity did not really survive into the new millennium.

[11] My three attempts at refuting Fodor: in Russell, 1984, 1988, 1996.

mind here. For the hard question in all this is whether it is possible to explain the development of symbolic thought (whose onset Piaget timed at around 18 months) *in creatures that have no innate symbolising capacities,* capacities it is hard to envision without symbols themselves. This brings us to the fourth kind of response. In this case, the developmentalist accepts that, even if one wants to reject Chomsky's syntactic nativism and argue that children's acquisition of syntax is founded upon semantic capacities, one still has to buy in to at least a limited form of LOT, in which concepts such as 'agent', 'action' and 'event' are innate. This was the position of Martin Braine, which will be examined in detail in 4.4.

Fodor's (1987) argument for the second aspect of the LOT doctrine (about the structure of propositions) springs from a different, though clearly not unrelated, set of concerns; and it does not take a developmental form. The starting assumption is that, on pain of being a behaviourist, we are obliged to regard the process of thinking in terms of individuals taking up mental orientations (*'propositional attitudes'*: think that, hope that, expect that etc.) to mental contents. In that sense, one is a 'realist' about mental states ('intentional realism'): mental states are computational states with causal powers rather than explanatory fictions – nets thrown over behaviour by the social conventions of 'folk psychology'. (Note the internalism/individualism here.) Moreover, these mental contents are complex. I might think (or hope or expect …) that Jane will catch the bus – a composite object containing the concepts of a woman called Jane, of buses, and of catching them. But where LOT goes beyond plain intentional realism is by saying that not only is the 'intentional object' of the thought complex (i.e., what is being thought about – the object of the thought) but so too is the mental state that makes that thinking possible. The mental state has, like a sentence of a natural language, *constituent structure.* That is to say, just as noun phrases and verb phrases are constituents of sentences while verbs and noun-phrases can be constituents of verb phrases, so concepts, represented symbolically are the constituents of thoughts. Mental states have, then, a *syntax* in this sense.

There are two claims here, the second of which will need some expansion: 'The LOT story amounts to the claims that (1) (some) mental formulas have mental formulas as parts; and (2) parts are 'transportable': the same parts can appear in lots of mental formulas.' (Fodor, 1987, p. 137; original emphasis). Transportable?

> … they can share the constituents they contain, since, presumably, the subexpression that denotes 'foot' in 'I raise my left foot' is a token of the same type as the subexpression that denotes 'foot' in 'I raise my right foot'. Similarly (*mutatis mutandis*) the 'P' that expresses the proposition P in the formula 'P' is a token of the same type as the 'P' that expresses the proposition 'P' in the formula 'P and Q'.

As is the case, then, for the words and sentences of natural language, in LOT we have to make the distinction between types and tokens.[12] Only symbols (and symbol strings) have this property of transportability. Moreover, if we factor in the claim (from the argument for innate semantic atoms in LOT) that symbols cannot be acquired within a lifespan then the conclusion must be that the states of any empiricist-style computational model will fail to have the property of transportability.

....

[12] Type = a kind of lexical item; token = a single occasion of its use.

As yet, however, we do not really have an argument for LOT as a kind of mental syntax, but only a parallel between mental properties and linguistic properties. (Showing up a parallel is not enough: both language and skilled action on objects have the property of recursion, but this does not of itself demonstrate that all action requires LOT.) So Fodor went on to present three arguments for LOT as structured with a kind of syntax. These were intended to show, and I think we should accept that they do show, that a theory of thinking without LOT is doomed to fail. I shall discuss two of them.

The first argument is that a theory of thinking requires an account of how we move from thought to thought, and that this cannot be achieved without reference to symbols moving across parse trees.

Take the case of question formation. You are told 'John bit —'. But you don't catch the final word, so you think that somebody has been bitten but don't know whom. You may tell a friend that John bit somebody. The parse tree for this is shown in Figure 1.1 (taken from Fodor, 1987, p. 124). But if you want to find out who was bitten, you will frame the next thought and will express it as the sentence 'Who did John bite?', the parse tree for which is given in Figure 1.2. (This is *not*, in fact, a technically correct parse tree – as we shall see in Part 2 – but it will do for this illustration.) In moving from one sentence to the other you have moved elements in the first sentence from the end to the beginning: the element corresponding to *somebody/who*.

But sentences express thoughts. And unless one wants to insist that mental representations are unstructured while sentences are structured (thereby giving oneself the task of explaining how something structured is supposed to mesh with something unstructured) one has to admit that this linguistic characterisation is capturing something significant about the computations carried out when we move from

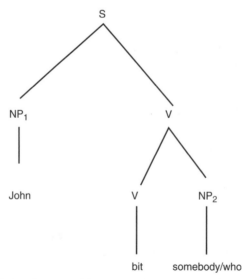

Figure 1.1 Fodor's (1987) structural description of an initial thought.

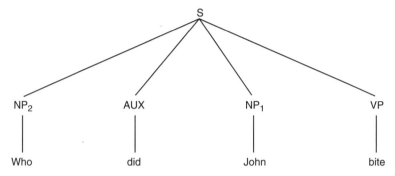

Figure 1.2 Fodor's (1987) structure description of the subsequent thought.

one *thought* to another. We move pieces of parsing trees in LOT – elemental states that have constituent structure.

Fodor's second argument for LOT as mental syntax begins in a manner reminiscent of one of Chomsky's famous arguments against behaviourist views of the language capacity: linguistic competence is creative/productive. That is to say, while the resources of any language are finite, speakers are able to generate and to comprehend an infinite number of sentences. Every moment of our lives we are speaking and comprehending sentences for the first time. Jackendoff (1993) illustrates this fact in a vivid way. There are tens of thousands of nouns in English – 10^4 at a conservative estimate. Now, just taking one kind of grammatical frame 'An X is not a Y' we have $10^4 \times 10^4$ possible sentences ($= 10^8$). If we then pair these possible sentences using a clause of the form 'Since an X is not a Y, a ...' we then have $10^8 \times 10^8 = 10^{16}$ sentences. Given that there are somewhere around 10 billion (10^{10}) neurons in the brain, this 'divides out to 10^6, or one million sentences per neuron' (Jackendoff, 1993, p. 12); and this is just restricting ourselves to a single grammatical frame. Thus, *while the brain is finite, our competence is not,* suggesting that the competence takes the form of a set of rules for generating sentences, not sets of possible sentences. Not an *inventory*, as the pragmatists of Part 4 call it.

These rules for generating sentences have, then, a *combinatorial semantics*, or *compositionality*: a lexical item must make the same semantic contribution to each expression in which it occurs. That is to say, sentences are made by combining meaningful elements in a rule-bound manner; they have individually-meaningful component parts that can be combined in different ways to make different sentences; and there is no limit to this process. But on LOT, thought too has combinatorial semantics, so it is unsurprising that thinking has the same kind of creativity/productivity as syntax: novel thoughts are constantly being entertained by us. Fodor is, however, reluctant to take this 'productivity' argument as decisive. This is because it is vulnerable to the critic who says that productivity is (a) a mere idealisation of human competence and (b) is something that anti-representational theorists like J. J. Gibson (1979) would explain in terms of experiences causing us to have a large but finite number of independent mental dispositions which we exercise in response to different kinds of perceptual input. But there is, conceivably, some property shared by language and thought that does not rely on idealisations of competence and perhaps explains the productivity of both. In any event, the general form of Fodor's argument is this:

(a) There's a certain property that linguistic capacities have in virtue of the fact that natural languages have a combinatorial semantics.

(b) Thought has this property too.

(c) So thought too must have combinatorial semantics.

Before pressing on, however, it would be well to pause to consider this general form of argument, as it is one that will reoccur (more implicitly) throughout this book. In fact, it can be regarded as an example of the logical fallacy of 'affirming the consequent'. Its bare form is:

(a) Having combinatorial semantics makes possible a certain property.

(b) Thought has this property.

(c) So thought has combinatorial semantics.

Which formalised is:

(a) $P \rightarrow Q$,

(b) Q,

therefore:

(c) P.

But if we accept this form then we must accept the following:

(a) Being a dog entails being an animal.

(b) This (cat) is an animal.

(c) So it is a dog.

Are things as bad as this? Fodor is breezily confident that they are not. If one can take this as an example of fallacy of affirming the consequent (i.e., deriving P by affirming Q) then 'So be it: one man's affirmation of the consequent is another man's inference to the best explanation?' (Fodor, 1987, p. 149). Making 'inferences to the best explanation' is what philosophers do when they stop doing philosophy and start to do theoretical psychology (see Carruthers, 1997, for a recent example). Inference to the best explanation means choosing the hypothesis or theory that best explains the available data, looking for features such as simplicity, depth, comprehensiveness and heuristic power (Harman, 1965).

As Fodor has insisted since he first coined the phrase 'Language of Thought', LOT is an empirical hypothesis in theoretical psychology established, via philosophical considerations of various kinds, from everyday and laboratory-based facts about cognition. The existence of LOT is not derived by a series of watertight logical deductions. When doing theoretical psychology we run with the explanation that is 'better' (simplest, most general) than the alternatives; and this, recall, is what Chomsky was doing with 'explanatory adequacy'.

(a) If something is a dog it will look, act, and smell like one.

(b) This looks, acts and smells like a dog.

(c) So it's a dog.

Not logically valid, but the best inference (in the circumstances, perhaps) to what the creature is.

What then is this mysterious property that is shared by linguistic and cognitive capacities – if it is not productivity? This leads us to the third argument for LOT.

> The property of linguistic capacities that I have in mind inheres in the ability to understand and produce sentences. That ability is – as I shall say – *systematic:* by which I mean that the ability to produce/understand some of the sentences is intrinsically connected to the ability to produce/understand many of the others.
>
> (Fodor, 1987, p. 249; original italics).

Compare the situation of the speaker of a natural language with that of somebody who is learning a new language by using an enormous phrase book. In the latter case, there need be no connection between the individual's ability to say/understand one sentence and to say/understand another one. Thus the phrase book user might be able to say/understand 'John's car is in Mary's garage' while being unable to say/understand that 'Mary's car is in John's garage'. This is because the phrase-book user, unlike the speaker of a natural language, did not acquire the ability to produce/comprehend sentences by generating them via combinatorial principles. The person who has acquired a language has acquired general procedures for deriving the meanings of sentences from their constituent structure (from their constituting elements); and the upshot must be systematicity because the same kind of combinatorial mechanisms that determine the meaning of any of the sentences determine the meaning of all the rest. Fodor does add 'give or take a bit', presumably because it is an empirical matter just how much of the I-language an individual has grasped in being able to generate a certain kind of sentence or set of sentences, and thus how generalisable is the ability. But that said, we would surely expect somebody who could understand (to take a much discussed example of Fodor's) the sentence 'John loves the girl' to be able to understand the sentence 'The girl loves John'.

It is important to bear in mind that combinatorial semantics cannot exist unless sentences have consistent structure – unless they consist of elements related to one another in a rule-governed fashion. For now at least, we can think of these constituents as lexical elements and phrases. Fodor concludes:

> OK, so here's the argument. Linguistic capacities are systematic, and that's because sentences have constituent structure. But cognitive capacities are systematic too, and that must be because *thoughts* have constituent structure. But if thoughts have constituent structure then LOT is true.
>
> (Fodor, 1987, pp 150–151; original emphasis)

Fodor remarks immediately that what is being defended here is the idea that cognitive capacities are *systematic*: that what has been attributed to language must be attributed to thought. Thus, to understand 'John loves the girl' is to have the thought that (not necessarily the *belief* that) John loves the girl, and if one can think *that* then one must also be able to think that the girl loves John. Broadly speaking, a capacity for thought must be at least as systematic as linguistic capacities, since the function of language is to express thoughts.

Before winding up this section it would be well to compare Fodor's argument from systematicity to LOT with an argument, owing to Gareth Evans, which would appear to be attending to just the same property of cognition, but which backs off from the conclusion that cognition requires LOT. Making this comparison will – one hopes – serve to sharpen the definition of systematicity and to point up crucial differences between human language and the 'languages' of formal logic. (We will need the latter when we come to consider Chomsky's minimalist programme.)

Evans points out that '[t]he thought that John is happy has something in common with the thought that Harry is happy, and the thought that John is happy has something in common with the thought that John is sad'. (1982, p. 100). But cautions:

> This might lead immediately to the idea of a language of thought, and it may be that some of the proponents of that idea intend no more by it than I do here. However, I certainly do not wish to be committed to the idea that having thoughts involves the subject's using, manipulating, or apprehending symbols – which would be entities with non-semantic as well as semantic properties,[13] so that the idea I'm trying to explain would amount to the idea that different episodes of thinking can involve the same symbols, identified by their semantic and non-semantic properties. *I should prefer to explain the sense in which thoughts are structured, not in terms of their being composed of several distinct elements, but in terms of their being composed of several distinct abilities.*
>
> (Evans, 1982, p. 101; emphasis added)

In the present example, the individual exercises the ability to apply the 'concept of happiness' to two people, and, separately, the ability to apply two different emotions to two different people. This captures, argues Evans, the way in which thought is structured, a notion that he formalises in the following way: the ability to attach predicate F to argument[14] a and predicate G to argument b is intrinsically related to the further ability to think Ga and Fb. That is to say, predicates can be 'detached' from one argument and 'moved' to another (cf. Fodor's transportability); and *mutatis mutandis* for arguments from predicates. Evans calls this *the generality constraint*.

Evans adds that what he has just said about thinking is also true of understanding sentences: the ability to understand one sentence entails the ability to understand a complex of other sentences. So why does he not make the 'inference to the best explanation' that this is so because thinking possesses a similar kind of representational format to that of language, and that it is this which accounts for the fact that the both involve structured abilities?

While the language case 'yields useful analogies', Evans writes, there is a 'crucial difference' between the structured nature of language and of thought. In language, he argues, the structuring is a *contingent* feature of human language; while in the domain of thought it is a conceptually necessary feature. Accordingly, language is *not essentially structured*, because any meaning expressed by a structured sentence could be expressed by an unstructured sentence. For example, one could invent a language containing a certain one-word sentence which is stipulated to have such-and-such a complex meaning. By contrast it is impossible for a *thought* like *Fa*

---

[13] A symbol has non-semantic properties in the sense that it is individuated by formal properties it does not share with its referent. For example, the word 'cat' has these, but a picture of a cat does not. 'Cat' and 'dog' differ formally as well as in virtue of what they refer to (their semantics).

[14] See footnote 8 in Part 2 and associated text.

not be to structured, that is, for its not to be the exercise of two distinct abilities for (1) predication and for (2) picking out an argument. Thus, possessing the concept of happiness (F) must be to possess the knowledge that the fact of being happy is not tied to one individual alone. The thinker must be in a position to dissociate predicates from arguments and apply them to different arguments, and likewise for the arguments *vis-à-vis* the predicates. As Evans points out, this is the same feature of thought that Strawson (1959) was alluding to in his much-discussed anti-cogito argument – an argument against Descartes' assumption that the hero of the cogito's starting state could have the ability to apply the predicate 'think' to himself but to nobody else.

> The idea of a predicate is correlative with that of a range of distinguishable individuals of which the predicate can be significantly, though not necessarily truly, affirmed.
>
> (Strawson, 1959, p. 99).

It would appear, then, that the generality constraint has application (beyond the kind of systematic cognitive capacities with which Fodor was concerned) to any kind of referential thought. For this reason, I (Russell, 1996, Part 2) once borrowed it in order to explicate the Piagetian sense of 'object concept' (as contrasted with the much looser and thinner sense employed by those who assess infants' knowledge of objects using the 'violation of expectation' paradigm). In this (Piagetian) case, one takes the arguments (such as a and b) to be analogous to objects and the predicates (such as F and G) to be analogous to actions on objects, and then takes Piaget's characterisation of the actions of an infant 'with' an object concept in terms of mathematical group theory as being a characterisation of how structured actions make object-directed thoughts possible. But in this case – I argued – no assumption has to be made that infants require LOT to achieve such structured cognition.

So why are Fodor and Evans ending up with different positions if they are both 'working upwards' from the structured nature of thought? The way to resolve this apparent paradox is to make a clear distinction between what Fodor calls 'systematic' and what Evans calls 'structured'. The meanings of the terms are not as similar as they appear to be. Doing this will require the spotlight to be turned upon the essential differences between natural language and the formal languages of logic and mathematics.

Systematicity is the result of the subject's possessing a *sui generis* piece of mental machinery which ensures that her thinking one thought will ('give or take a bit' again) entail her ability to think other thoughts. Thus, the thought that John loves Mary is carried forward in some syntactic format which (for the sake of convenience) we will call a subject-verb-object (SVO) format. Well, if a person can think John (S) loves (V) Mary (O), then one would expect this same syntactic format to be capable of yielding Mary (S) loves (V) John (O). Similarly, if the subject can construct a mental question ('wonder to himself') about who John loves, having had the thought that John loves somebody implanted in him by a speaker, then he will be able achieve the same when the contents are 'Mary' and 'hates'.

Let us at this point reconsider the long quotation from Evans on page 24. Note the contrast made between 'distinct elements' and 'distinct abilities' at the end of it: Evans is concerned with distinct abilities. Contrast this with the case of natural language, by way of approaching this difference between Fodor's and Evans' concerns.

The ability to represent something as the subject of a verb is *not* a 'distinct ability' from representing something as the object of a verb; and this because *the character of each syntactic category/operation exists only in relation to that of other syntactic categories/operations*. Similarly, the ability to represent the syntactic element labelled 'somebody' as the object of a sentence is *not* a distinct ability from representing the same element as the determiner ('who') at the start of a question. Meanwhile, we have seen that regarding thoughts as being composed of several distinct *elements* (as contrasted with representing distinct *abilities*) enables us to give a plausible account of how we move from thought to thought (see Figures 1.1 and 1.2).

But regarding thoughts as 'being composed of distinct elements' is exactly what Evans does not want to do, as we see in the quotation. Also note the passage in which Evans says 'it may be that some of the proponents of that idea [LOT] intend no more by it than I do here'. Well I hope it is clear that Fodor *does* intend more than Evans intended by the generality constraint. And the reason he did was that he was concerned with the language-like features that we must ascribe to human thought if we are to give an adequate account of mental processes (the transitions between thoughts) and of the systematic nature of cognition, whereas Evans was concerned with more austere, metaphysical issues about the nature of referential thought. *Evans was interested in the conceptual abilities themselves, rather than with the format in which these are realised in human cognition.*

To focus this point then, the abilities invoked by the notion of systematicity are indeed related rather than distinct. They are related in much the same way in which linguistic categories and operations are related. Evans, meanwhile, emphasises their independence. The elements over which systematic mental operations range are, however, distinct, in much the way in which words are distinct. Evans, by contrast, is concerned with abilities rather than elements.

It is also necessary to guard against the idea that because Evans describes the kind of cognitive abilities he is concerned with using formal logic – the predicate calculus in fact (*Fa* and *Gb* etc.), – he has thereby committed himself to something like a syntactic format. Now it is wrong to say that the predicate calculus has no syntax at all, but it is a trivial syntax compared to that of natural language. By 'trivial' I do not mean only that its complexity is small compared to that of a language such as English and so its expressive power is relatively small; though it is certainly that. Rather the 'syntax' of formal logics and mathematics is trivial in a principled sense: its triviality arises from the fact that it is stipulated by us: it is purpose-built. As Higginbotham (1998) points out, even if we elaborate predicate calculus by adding higher-order operators it would still be trivial in this sense because 'it would be specifiable in terms of a simple inductive definition of notions like term and formula … No human language is like that …' (1998, p. 217). So what is special and non-trivial about human syntax? To anticipate a long discussion that will happen in Part 2, and to do so in a necessarily elliptical and metaphoric way, the syntactic systems of human languages are full of features that seem to have no utility and that are not motivated directly by semantics. Thus the rules which determine how questions (see Figures 1.1 and 1.2 again), passives etc. are formed are certainly not motivated by considerations of semantic transparency and parsimony; whereas the construction of a system of formal logic is motivated entirely by such considerations: *the semantics exhausts the syntax*, with the result that the latter becomes very dissimilar to human syntax.

These considerations go some way towards explaining why Evans is able to say that while sentences need not be structured, thoughts are structured in their essence, and that any meaning expressed by a structured sentence can be expressed by an unstructured one. Recall that he illustrates the latter claim by saying that there might be a one-word sentence 'introduced by stipulation to have such-and-such a meaning'. But this only serves to highlight the fundamental difference between formal languages, which get whatever structure they have *by a similar process of stipulation*, and natural languages, which are biologically designed to express thoughts.

Issues of this kind will be at the forefront when we discuss Chomsky's minimalist programme. We will see then that while natural languages have all kinds of Heath Robinson features which formal logical languages lack, *it may be these very properties that make language so well designed* – perhaps 'optimally' designed – to express thoughts. In any event, we shall see that the coherence of Chomsky's ideas about the relation between the syntax of Human and 'the conceptual-intentional' or 'thought' systems may depend upon his subscribing to the notion of a language of thought – which is why I have spent so long discussing it.

1.1.7 The language of thought and the computational theory of the mind: Could the former exist without the latter?

Despite this section being about rationalism, I have had almost nothing to say about thought *qua* reasoning. We shall see that when we do consider thought in that sense we find that the LOT doctrine does rather less for us than we want it to. This fact does not threaten the Chomskyan project, though it does complicate, to the point of weakening, a popular rationalist doctrine about thought being carried forward by a context-independent logico-mechanical process.

First, what Fodor calls the 'computational theory of the mind' (CTM) is something much stronger than a simply-stated analogy between the digital computer and the mind and between LOT and natural language. For the CTM is supposed to explain how we move from thought to thought, not (as in the illustration in Figures 1.1 and 1.2) in the sense of moving elements in mental syntax from one symbol-string to another, but with regard to how we move from thought to thought so as to preserve semantic relations between these thoughts – just as the move from premises to conclusions is truth-preserving. The somewhat paradoxical fact is that semantic (or justificatory) relations between thoughts are preserved in virtue of what Fodor calls the 'syntax' of thought: the form takes care of the meaning, and does so mechanically.

To illustrate, the thought 'John drinks and Mary smokes' has the syntactic form *P and Q*, and it is true if and only if *P* and *Q* are both true, while also entailing the truths of both *P* and *Q* separately. On the CTM, what is claimed is that the semantic/justificatory relation between *P and Q* and (say) *P* ('John drinks') comes about because the mind computes over symbols that stand for *P and Q* and *P*, so as to guarantee mechanically that *P* is entailed by *P and Q*. This 'mechanical' is cashed in terms of Turing machine, given that Alan Turing showed that a computing machine will recognise any argument (a thought to thought transition in this context) in virtue of its syntax. As Fodor (2000b, p. 13) puts it, 'it's only if the sufficient conditions for an inference to be truth preserving are syntactic that Turing guarantees that a machine is able to recognise its validity'.

But note – along the way – that the use of the term 'syntactic' here is one that no linguist would recognise. It is essentially a metaphor meaning 'in virtue of form'. In any event, for Fodor (2000b, p. 14), the cornerstone of a 'rationalist psychology' is that

> beliefs, desires, thoughts, and the like have logical forms, and that their logical forms are among the determinants of the role they play in mental processes [...] the causal role of a mental state depends (at least inter alia) on what logical form it has.

This much is also true of the 'thought' of digital computers.

It is the CTM, then, which is advertised as the solution to the problem of how the mind–brain makes everyday inferences: it does so by virtue of the syntax of the mental states having the kind of well-understood causal relations to one another that exist between the states of a digital computer. The relationship of LOT to CTM, meanwhile, has been much discussed. Some philosophers argue that LOT can be true independently of CTM, while others take the view that LOT-minus-CTM errs on the side of vagueness, telling us no more than that mental operations must be syntactic, without committing itself to the transitions between states being computational in the Turing sense.

Anyway, is CTM true? Well, Fodor (2000b) has recently decided that it is not. One reason he gives for this abandonment springs from the fact that much of our thought takes the form of (as alluded to above) 'inference to the best explanation', which is also called 'abduction' and 'evidential' reasoning. The problem resides in the fact that CTM only holds for modular mental processes, and – as Fodor (1983) pointed out some time ago – the central cognitive systems are domain-general and global[15] rather than modular. Here is an example taken from Fodor, concerning how something other than the syntax of a thought can influence practical reasoning. The thought is *no wind tomorrow*. Consider the way in which adding this thought to a plan could complicate it. If the plan was to drive or fly to Chicago tomorrow then it will probably not complicate it at all. But if it was to sail a yacht to Chicago it complicates it greatly. Moving a thought from one context to another does not affect the thought's inherent syntax, so it must be having these differential effects because of the contexts in which it becomes embedded. In short, the feature of the embedding 'theory' affects the inferential-cum-causal roles of the constituent beliefs. This is,

---

[15] Global cognition is 'Quinean' and 'isotropic'. Quinean (after W.V.O. Quine) = in the confirmation of scientific theories (or in the fixation of everyday beliefs) the confirmation assigned to any given hypothesis is sensitive to properties of the whole belief system. Isotropic = facts relevant to the confirmation of a scientific hypothesis (or to any everyday belief) can be drawn from anywhere in the field of established empirical truths.

then, the sense in which central cognition is 'global'.[16] We can see this emerging just as clearly when we consider how we gather evidence for our beliefs – when we infer to the best explanation. I borrow the following example from Stephen Butterfill. Peter notices that a bottle of red wine is missing and comes to suspect that Patsy drank it. For one thing, she has some red stains on her shirt. But on reflection Peter also knows that Patsy does not like red wine and said she would be having some grapes with her lunch. Well, the significance of these stains (their inferential-cum-causal roles) will be significantly affected by the nature of Peter's other epistemic commitments – by the context – despite the fact that the thought about the stains has the same syntax in different contexts.

Indeed, one *might* go so far as to say that, $P \rightarrow Q$, Q, therefore P could be a warranted inference to make against the right kind of epistemic background. Thus, 'if it is a dog then it's an animal, it's an animal, therefore it's a dog' does not look so shaky in the context of what is on a lead at Cruft's dog show.

This then in how things now stand with CTM. For some, Fodor's admission of the shortcomings of CTM is tantamount to saying that rationalistic psychology is fundamentally limited. But for Fodor, as a rationalist, any apparent shortcoming of rationalist psychology is taken to be a shortcoming *of cognitive psychology itself*. Are things really this bad? Take analogical reasoning and our attempts to explain how it works. Fodor (1983) had earlier argued that this is a quintessentially central-system/global ability; and indeed it shares with inferring-to-the-best-explanation the property that no answer to a problem of that kind is definitively wrong or right. Accordingly, we may not have spotted the analogy that the tester had in mind but we drew a justified one; we may have made the wrong 'inference' but only because of things we were in no position to know about the world (Patsy was in reality a secret drinker, in the above example). Well, there has been some progress in recent years in modelling analogy-making (Mitchell, 1993; in press), although the mechanisms (mini-agents operating in parallel and in a probabilistic fashion) are undreamed of in Turing's philosophy. (These ideas will be discussed at the end of Part 3.)

Be that as it may, and for our purposes at least, the relevance of these matters to Chomsky's programme would seem to be slight. The syntax of natural language is not designed to fix the truth-preserving nature of our inferences: agreement, word order, 'height' on the parse tree, and so forth, are formal facts of a different order to facts about logical forms.[17] (And recall what I said earlier about the differences between the 'languages' of logic and natural language.) So if we lose CTM there still remains much that is language-like about thought. Indeed the legibility of thought to the language faculty would seem to be impossible to understand if this were not so.

----

[16] Fodor also adds the property 'holistic' (ibid., p. 28). But this does not entail an abandonment of his long-held opposition to meaning holism. He still believes that mental symbols gain their meaning atomistically, and that it is possible for a creature to have only one thought. On the threat of meaning holism to the LOT doctrine, see Russell (1996).

[17] Chomsky – as some readers may know – does refer to 'logical form', but it means something quite different from its use in this context. See Part 2.

We will be returning to these matters in Part 3, when we consider whether the systematicity and combinatorial semantics of thought sets limits on connectionist attempts to explain how language can be the expression of it.

1.2 Empiricism

Here we will witness the historical progression from the work of the seventeenth and eighteenth century British empiricists towards present-day associative experimental psychology and developmental connectionism. David Hume will emerge as the dominant figure.

I will be assuming a clean and profound division between mental processes that are 'associative' and those that are 'cognitive'. This is by no means a rationalistic eccentricity of my own. If one looks, for example, at up-to-the-minute developments in the field of human sequence learning (an area with some relevance to language learning, see end of Part 3) one frequently sees 'hybrid' models with two distinct components – one associationist and stochastic and the other rule-following, explicit and cognitive (e.g., Spiegel and McLaren, 2003). This division did not come about from reading Chomsky and Fodor!

I shall be 'assuming' the division rather than arguing for it, because a principled argument for its existence would be a major operation indeed. In any case, much of Part 3 will be devoted to the question of whether there is something about cognition and language that resists associative theories. This is another way of testing the reality of this division, in fact.

For some readers, the word empiricism – suggestive as it is of 'empirical'– will arrive as a breath of fresh air after the stiflingly formal cloisters of rationalism. To them it might have seemed a staggering fact that Chomsky constructs his account of language acquisition with almost no reference to what children actually say and how they say it. From this perspective, the Chomskyan mode of thought would exemplify the kind of sterility that the founders of The Royal Society of London for the Improving of Natural Knowledge in 1660 were reacting against when they trumpeted a new era of 'Natural Philosophy' based upon observation and experiment. And indeed Chomsky does place himself within the tradition of the Cambridge Platonists, who championed reason as a route to knowledge and who were operating some 30 years before the founding of the Royal Society.

But etymology is a bad guide here; and so these readers will be disappointed. Although John Locke ('the father of English psychology'[18]) was elected to a Fellowship of the Royal Society in 1668, his experimental work was minimal,[19] and his case against the rationalist doctrine of 'innate ideas' was pursued from an entirely philosophical basis, with its aim being to underpin theoretically what the observers and experimenters were doing. Descartes, by contrast, conducted ground-breaking experiments in sensory physiology. (Devising the arguments for the cogito proved to be no impediment to dissecting cows' eyes.) And be aware that it is

---

[18] See Aaron (1965, p. 128).

[19] Locke helped Robert Boyle with his experimental studies (see Aaron, 1965, p. 13).

Chomsky's theory – no other – that has driven empirical research in language develop-ment since the 1960s, in the sense that everything has been done in relation (support-ive or oppositional) to his syntactic nativism. Most pertinently, current empiricist ideas about language acquisition are typically carried forward by computer simulations, not by observing childrens' speech or by running experimental studies with them.

Indeed, with specific regard to research on language acquisition, empiricism pro-vides far more than a Lockean 'theoretical underpinning' to enquiries based upon observation and experiment: it provides very strict epistemological limits within which the theorising can be done. That is to say, contemporary empiricism about language development does not represent a Baconian let-the-data-speak kind of open-mindedness; but represents an unshakeable commitment to the Lockean idea that the starting state of the mind is as empty of content as (in his metaphor) a sheet of white paper, plus an equally strong Humean commitment to the idea that mental processes are associative through and through. These ideas are alive and well today.

But whatever the philosophical commitments of contemporary empiricism, it is clear that rationalism pays scant regard to the respects in which the acquisition of language is a perceptually-based process. Empiricism roots mental life in perception. ('To hate, to love, to think, to feel, to see; all this is nothing but to perceive' wrote David Hume.) All concepts and mental operations are taken to have a perceptual basis. The empiricist will say that it is all very well furnishing the mind with innate ideas about nouns, verbs, phrase structures, and so forth but somehow or other the English-acquiring child has to learn that the past tense of 'bring' is 'brought'; and at some level it *must* be right to say that he achieves this by perceiving people's speech. That said, this leaves intact the big questions about whether (1) there is any mileage in, or even coherence to, the idea that children learn the syntax of their native tongues without the support of innate knowledge, and whether (2) the thoughts that our sentences express can be characterised in terms of agglomerations of perceptually-based categories cemented by association and habit.

I should own up that one of the not-so-hidden agendas of this section is to show just who the intellectual forebears of developmental connectionism were and to say loud and clear that it was not the (anti-empiricist) Jean Piaget – despite what the developmental connectionists themselves (e.g., Elman *et al.*, 1996) say.

1.2.1 The empiricist legacy

We begin with a dispute that took place among the British empiricists, in which Hume sided with Berkeley against Locke. The issue was this. If you decide to believe that all mental contents are derived from perceptual experience you will have no trouble explaining how we are able to attach the label, say, 'cat' to this animal, because you will think that all that is involved is the pairing of a sound with some visual impression – perhaps recorded as a visual image. All names for things are like proper names on this view. You will, however struggle with explaining our ability to form what were called in the seventeenth century *abstract ideas*, and what today would be called concepts. In any event, the view that words refer to abstract ideas is generally called *conceptualism*.[20]

---

[20] As contrasted with realism and nominalism. This will be dealt with below, on p. 37.

Few would dispute that, after a certain age at least, calling a class of objects 'cat' is achieved on the basis of our having the concept CAT, and that while having this concept will require us to know what cats look like, the concept CAT will include all kinds of contents that are not directly traceable to perception, such as being an animal, being a living thing, being sensitive to pain, being motile, facts about what cats are disposed to do, and so forth. Possessing the concept CAT will entail that some abstraction away from particular cats has been achieved, and that this abstractive ability will be in evidence in somebody who has never had perceptual experience of Lois but can reason that 'if Lois is cat then she is an animal'. Locke believed that we do indeed have abstract ideas and that these ideas are grounded entirely in perceptual experience. However, the issue becomes more urgent when we consider the kinds of abstractions found in mathematics and geometry. With reference to our knowledge that all wholes are greater than the sum of their parts, a contemporary of Locke's, Henry Lee, pointed out that such

> general propositions ... [are] certainly true ... yet we can come to no knowledge of them merely by our senses; because they cannot reach to all the particulars included in the subjects of them. Our senses may inform us that any single whole is equal to all its parts; but not that all wholes in the world are so, unless we could suppose, that we had seen or felt them all.[21]

What Lee says about wholes and parts, one might equally well say about the fact that – as children acquiring English tacitly know – the form classes in English (nouns, verbs, adjectives, prepositions etc.) appear at the beginning of the phrases which they govern, while Japanese children tacitly know that they appear at the end. They learn this 'by perceiving how people talk', but they have ended up with an abstract and infinitely generalisable principle.

Berkeley's response was to reject the very notion of abstract ideas. With heavy irony he said:

> Whether others have this wonderful faculty of abstracting their ideas, they best can tell ... [I cannot] abstract one from another or conceive separately, those qualities which it is impossible should exist so separated ... [I cannot] form the idea of extension as such, which is neither line surface, nor solid, nor has any figure or magnitude but is an idea entirely prescinded from all these.

More famously, he argued that he could not form an idea of a triangle as such, meaning one that was not equilateral, right-angled, isosceles etc. – but abstract.

In modern parlance Berkeley might be said to have been proposing a 'stereotype'[22] theory of concepts, in which an individual's idea of a triangle might be an equilateral one, his idea of an even number might be four. But what's wrong with this? After all, subjects in experiments are perfectly happy to say what is a 'good' even number or a good plane geometric figure (Barsalou, 1987). But the question is whether we are happy to accept that having a stereotype in the mind's eye captures all that it

----

21   Quoted in Woodhouse (1988, p. 77).

22   This is distinct from a from prototype representation, in the sense of central tendency (on which see Shanks, 1995). Prototypes will be discussed shortly.

means to have a concept, and whether it is possible to explain all we can do with concepts (e.g., employ them in inferences) while abandoning the idea of concepts as being abstract entities.

While Hume agreed with Berkeley's rejection of abstract ideas, his own account was distinctively different – indeed different in its very aim. In the first place, one might say that he replaced Berkeley's stereotype theory of concept-formation with an exemplar, or instance-based, theory. That is to say, he focused on the fact that when we use a word like 'cat' correctly we are manifesting the ability to group a number of particular ideas of cats under a common label, and that thinking of one cat under this label will evoke ideas of other particular cats. But what is truly distinctive about Hume's account, what proved to be enormously influential, and what marked Hume out among the British empiricists as a theoretical psychologist, was the fact that he offered a mechanism by which the grouping of instances was achieved. This was the association of ideas. He argued that customary association between many particular instances constituted, as it were, the mental adhesive necessary for using general terms. Indeed the more diverse individuals' mental representations of particular (say) cats (recalled or imagined) the richer will be their understanding of the meaning of the word 'cat'. This enables them better to record what features the exemplars have in common. To give one of Hume's examples of this process, a globe of white marble and a cube of white wood are diverse in feel, visible shape and in substance though alike in colour; and they together illustrate the kind of resemblance we require there to be between things to which we attach the label 'white'.

This would seem to most readers to be abstraction by another name; and if it is not then how does one account for the ability – one we surely have – of thinking of the meaning of the word 'white' without its being attached to, say, snow. But what Hume was trying to achieve here is more relevant to our present purpose than the success of the endeavour. He was trying to explain our ability to use words meaningfully in terms of dispositions within us to make links between instances based upon resemblance. All that the mind 'contains' on this view are mental representations of particular instances plus a capacity for associating them. Accordingly, in the above example, our ability to reason 'if Lois is a cat then she is an animal' would be explained in terms of our disposition to assent to the proposition that any cat one cares to evoke is an animal, and so howsoever Lois is imagined (e.g., as a black cat, as tabby ...) the same would be true.

It is worth stressing that Hume was endeavouring here to establish an empirical principle 'based on observation' rather than, like Locke, trying to refute the doctrine of innate ideas and put in its place a taxonomy of perceptually-derived mental representations ('simple ideas' versus 'complex ideas', with 'modes' 'substances' and 'relations' being sub-types of the latter). (For Locke, association was not an explanatory principle but a disease of the mind – like a bad habit.) In fact, rather than Locke, Hume's intellectual mentor was his near-contemporary Newton; and indeed he tried to follow Newton's example in being 'cautious of admitting no principles but such as were founded on experiment; but resolute to adopt every such principle, however new and unusual'. Indeed, just as Newton formulated his inverse square law to explain the gravitational attraction between bodies, a principle which accounted for a number of diverse observations, so Hume's ambition was to do the same with mental phenomena. He made the link explicit in saying that he was positing a form of mental attraction that 'is a kind of attraction which in the mental world will be found to have as extraordinary effects as in the natural, and to show itself in as many and various forms'. Moreover, it is strange to note that he applauds Newton for not speculating about the ultimate causes of gravitational attraction, as this parallels his own refusal to speculate about possible mechanical principles which might underlie the 'gentle force' between ideas – perhaps some formulation at the similar level as that of classical conditioning or Hebb's law. Instead, like Locke, he produced a taxonomy of kinds of association – 'resemblance' (which we have been considering), 'proximity' (or 'contiguity in space and time'), 'cause and effect' (e.g., the idea of pain being the 'effect of the idea of a wound'.

All that is represented in the Humean mind, therefore, are impressions with a perceptual character – a kind of multiple mirroring, with verbal judgement being explained in terms of dispositions born of custom and habit. With regard to the latter, some of Hume's claims are reminiscent of the 'logical behaviourism' of mid-twentieth-century philosophers such as Gilbert Ryle. (For example, Ryle characterised the mental state of enjoying doing something in terms of our disposition to be upset at being disturbed when doing it.) The motivation behind logical behaviourism is to explain cognition with as few commitments to mental representation as possible: the aim is representational continence. Which returns me to Fodor – by way of an interim taking stock.

In his book *The language of thought* (1975) Fodor began by clearing the ground of logical behaviourism, following up on themes from his previous book (*Psychological explanation*, 1968). It is not difficult to see why he took such ground-clearing to be necessary. For, if conceptual abilities can be analysed in terms of dispositions (perhaps with an associative basis, though Ryle did not add this) then the case for LOT is fatally weakened. Fodor's starting assumption is that we do indeed have concepts represented in our minds, concepts that cannot be analysed away in terms of dispositions to act, and which are more than agglomerations of images. A Humean would insist that such a commitment should be abandoned because really it is associations 'all the way down'.[23]

But Hume's radical dismissal of abstract concepts comes with costs. There are a number of these and they will emerge. But for now: If you wish to argue that all there is to thinking is the operation of associative mechanisms then all our beliefs about the world are reduced to images with greater or lesser power and to links between these with greater or lesser strength. (Yes one can sneak in the analogy prematurely and call the former 'activations' and the latter 'connection strengths'.) Critics of Hume have insisted that a theory of this kind lacks the resources to explain belief. Of course our ideas do indeed vary in power ('force' and 'vivacity' were terms

---

[23] In his recent book on David Hume (Fodor, 2003), Fodor is more sympathetic, in so far as he stresses Hume's commitment to representationism, following in the Cartesian tradition, as contrasted with Wittgenstein and the pragmatist tradition.

that Hume used), but the power of an impression will vary independently from our beliefs. For example, I may have a very powerful, lucid, and unshakeable image that I know to be derived from a movie I recently saw and so it is not taken to be true; whereas I may believe, looking into the garden, that the ivy could damage the cherry tree, a belief that has only a dim and desultory phenomenology that fades immediately. But what did Hume actually say about belief?

Hume claimed that of the three kinds of association it was causation that grounded belief. In our everyday beliefs the 'vivacity' of a current impression (e.g., of an unsupported object) is causally carried forwards to an associated impression (of falling), with the result that the idea of falling is picked out and rendered vivid, in relation to other ideas – which transforms it to an expectation or belief. How would this work in the case of well-ingrained factual (rather than folk-physics) knowledge such as my belief about the effects of ivy on tree trunks, our beliefs about Hitler being the leader of Germany in the last world war, and so forth? Having distinguished between the everyday Joycean flux of associations based on resemblance and contiguity Hume proposed a set of stable beliefs which, by their settled order and regular causal links to impressions and memory make it a relatively permanent fact about the person that propositions of a certain kind are assented to. He gives the example of his own beliefs about the city of Rome. Hume was, on his account, 'disposed to assent to' certain propositions about the history and geography of the city.

> All this and everything else which I believe are nothing but ideas, though by their force and settled order, arising from custom and the relation of cause and effect, they distinguish themselves from the other ideas, which are merely the offspring of the imagination.
>
> (Hume 1739/1962, p. 142)

MacNabb (1966, p. 77) unpacks what he calls this 'somewhat loosely worded passage' in the following way. (The term 'realities' is used to refer to stable beliefs.)

> The ideas called realities are marked by 'force and settled order'. This means that they are assented to with some promptness and vigour ('force') as a matter of habit 'settled' provided they occur in a certain pattern of spatio-temporal relations ('order'); e.g., I habitually assent to a certain representation of the city of Rome, which represents it on the banks of the Tiber and south of the Alps. A similar representation of the city, which, however, placed it north of the Alps would not command my assent in the same way. Such beliefs then are habitual beliefs, habits of assent, even if they are (as in this case) particular as opposed to general beliefs.

This then is what Hume's associative account of belief amounts to; and perhaps it is the best that any associative account of belief can amount to. It is nothing if not representationally continent, using as it does only the raw materials of what I will (tendentiously) call the 'level of activation' of individual ideas and the habit-forged 'strength of connections' between them.

The reason I have illustrated Hume's associative psychology is to suggest how unconvincing an account of belief it yields, certainly one that is unlikely to 'be assented to with promptness and vigour' even by a contemporary experimental psychologist working on associative learning. What are its main shortcomings?

In the first place, it fails to capture the fact that a belief is a mental orientation towards a content – a propositional attitude. Thus, the differences between the belief that P, the hope that P, the hope that not-P, the expectation that P, the fear or desire that P are hardly of a kind that can be explicated in terms of notions like activation level ('vivacity' etc.) and habit. Perhaps the alternative metaphor for the attitudes, offered by supporters of a representational/LOT view of thought (Field, 1978) as being 'boxes' in the mental architecture into which 'sentences' are put may seem to many to be equally unappealing, but at least it captures the fact that the attitudes give the same proposition different roles within the mental life, roles which might be analogised as different 'locations' lending different causal powers.

Turning to the object of the attitudes (the 'content'), it is clear that an account of belief rooted in perception is unable to capture the compositional nature of mental content (see pp 19–23 above). (It is illuminating that MacNabb, above, chooses a *picture* of Rome in his example.) The thought that 'Jane will catch the bus' is a composite of a conceptual elements, elements that can be decomposed and recomposed (cf. the generality constraint) in different ways – 'John will catch the bus', 'Jane will catch the train', 'Mike will catch the ferry' … Given this, a Humean machine for simulating thought could be able to 'think' (aka 'assent to') 'A and B' but not to 'A' – more of which in part 3.5.

How might this Humean machine simulate syntactic knowledge? If we take the view – though a Humean might not in fact – that framing and comprehending sentences requires us to utilise representations of at least the class of words 'noun' and 'verb', then one might speculate that these grammatical notions would be treated as perceptually-derived categories. First, words like 'man', 'dog', 'tree', 'party', 'experiment', and so forth, would be grouped together (by the 'gentle force' of association) in terms of the associative principles of proximity and causation – not similarity, as nouns only share syntactic roles, rather than extra-syntactic properties. They can all be preceded by words like 'a' 'the' 'by' 'for' and so forth, they frequently precede wh-words (like 'who', 'which' etc.) and they frequently begin sentences. They also frequently precede words like 'run', 'sleep' 'expire' etc., which in turn can be preceded by words like 'could' 'will' 'to' and so forth and often end with '-s' and '-ed'. But what of the 'closed class' (or 'function') words themselves, the articles, prepositions, and auxiliaries? These in turn will be categorised by their associative links to particular words. At which point the utility of positing abstract representations whose character does *not* have to reduce to their associative role becomes immediately apparent. And if we tried to move to grammatical properties like case and agreement – not to mention phrase structure – things would get even muddier.

It would be unfair to suggest, however, that the British empiricists were invariably happy to saddle themselves with the view that all types of words and all grammatical categories are traceable to perceptually-derived ideas. Locke, for one, was not. He wrote of words like 'is', 'not' and 'of' 'and', 'therefore' and 'of' (what he called 'particles') as words that are 'made use of to signify the connection that the mind gives to ideas one with another'. Moreover:

> To think well it is not enough that a man has ideas clear and distinct in his thoughts, nor that he observes the agreement or disagreement of some of them; but he must think in train and observe the dependence of his thoughts and reasonings on one another.
>
> (Locke, quoted in Aaron, 1965, p. 211)

He pointed out that the distinction between such words and the rest had scarcely been mentioned before and illustrated their linguistic peculiarities with the example of the word 'but'. However, what would have become a discussion of enormous originality was cut short with 'I intend not here a full explication of this sort of sign'.[24] As we saw from his acceptance of abstract ideas then, it seems that Locke's commitment to the principle that all mental characteristics are directly traceable to perceptual experience was not full-hearted.

Finally in this subsection, I will discuss the related issues of Hume's (also Berkeley's) nominalism and his ideas about what constitutes the difference between human and animal cognition. The latter will serve as a bridge to the next section in which I will draw as clear a line as possible between human associative learning (whose study imports methods and concepts from learning in laboratory animals) and human cognition, by which I mean that which language expresses, which is structured in a language-like manner, and whose development interfaces with language development.

First nominalism. Philosophical views about the nature of concepts have traditionally fallen into three types: realism, conceptualism, and nominalism. In the Middle Ages, not only ink but blood was spilt between the protagonists for the three views. Realists (after Plato) held that we are able to make sense of general words like 'cat' because, through experiencing each cat, we gain access to a real and independent world in which resides the universal cat, the ideal 'form' of cathood, felinity at its core. Conceptualists rejected this as piece of mysticism, proposing instead that we can name cats because we have in our minds an abstract idea of cathood – what a contemporary psychologist would call an 'internal representation'. Contemporary logicians and formal semanticists might treat these abstract representations as 'sets' of real or possible objects, whereas contemporary philosophers offer a number of views of how concepts are individuated in the mind – symbols (the LOT view), functional roles, capacities for discrimination, and so forth. Nominalism, meanwhile, is the view that conceptual capacity is split between words and the sensory conditions (e.g., Humean ideas) for their application – with nothing between. Our concern is with whether nominalism, which would appear to be the only view of concepts that is consistent with classical empiricism, is a coherent position to apply in studying the development of thought and language.

A nominalist could say (bracketing awkward questions about how syntactic categories arise) that language acquisition is the process of labelling the stored sensory impressions of groups of objects. And he might add that thinking is no more than the manipulation of these labels. Accordingly, thinking that the cat sat on the mat is a kind of inner speech in which one says the sentence to oneself, thereby evoking a sensory image of a cat sitting on a mat. In other words, thinking is something children learn to do by becoming adept at keeping data on their articulatory loop – data that trigger series of images. The nominalist neuroscientist would predict that during thinking there will be simultaneous activation of Broca's area and the sensory cortex and that pathways will be found between them. So far so good, but the nominalist has also to claim that unless a word evokes a sensory impression it has no meaning. If he does not wish to saddle himself with this view, however, he might say that 'cat' is only a proxy token (after Luria's 'secondary signalling system') for

---

[24] See Aaron (1965, p. 211).

a sensory impression, and that what happens in the skilled thinker is that the inner speech sound 'cat' gains the power to interact with other inner speech sounds like 'sat' and 'mat' so as to produce a visual image of a cat sitting on a mat. But if so, the mental token 'cat' is being individuated not by its power to evoke a sensory impression but by its *shape* (Fodor, 1987). The *sui generis* shape of a mental symbol is both arbitrarily related to its referent and gives that symbol a specific causal power to interact with other symbols. The auditory contours of the sound '[kat]' will interact with the contours of other mental sounds to compute a thought, but will not do so in virtue of the image that 'cat' evokes. In this case then, the token has acquired an abstract status; and so we have ended up with a position that it is difficult to distinguish from LOT. The moral of the story is that, if the pristine purity of a nominalist theory of thinking is to be retained, the thinker's mind must be regarded as a kaleidoscope of ever-shifting sensory contents and their labels. A child who understands the word 'no' does so by evoking an image of his being told not to do something. (In Part 3 we will discuss a passage from Dennett in which a view not a million miles from this one is proposed.)

Given his nomimalism, it will probably come as no surprise that Hume assumed 'the reason of animals' to be no different in kind to the reason of humans: the fact that humans cloak their reason in language adds nothing of significance. He wrote that 'no truth appears to me more evident, than that the beasts are endowed with thought and reason as well as men. The arguments in this case are so obvious, that they never escape the most stupid and ignorant'. The inference an animal draws from 'the present impression is built on experience, and on his observation of the conjunction of objects in past instances. As you vary his experience he varies his reasoning'. Having said this (*Treatise on human nature, Book 1*, 1739/1962, p. 229) Hume set out a challenge to any philosopher who cares to explain 'that act of the mind that we call belief' without reference to 'the influence of custom on the imagination … and let his hypothesis be equally applicable to beasts as to the human species'. That this cannot be done, he says, and that Hume's own view of the commonality that exists between animal and human reasoning in virtue of the role of custom in both is the correct view 'is evident almost without any reasoning'.

It almost goes without saying that, whatever Hume's views about human language being the mere expressive medium of mental mechanisms that are thoroughly associative in nature, recent work on human associative learning is thoroughly Humean in character. In the next two subsections I will discuss this work.

1.2.2   Human associative learning and the learning of artificial grammars

While there is an unbroken thread of British associationist thought from Locke to the present day, winding sometimes beyond the academic world to such figures as William Wordsworth and S. T. Coleridge, the influence of associationist ideas in psychology has fallen and risen again quite precipitously in the past 100 years. Associationist theory certainly went into decline in the wake of the Chomskyan 'revolution'; but now it is enjoying a rebirth due not only to the 'thought experiments' of connectionist modelling but also to recent experimental work showing deep commonalities between animal and human learning. We need to touch on this work because there are those who would argue in the following way: If human thought is an associative process, as Hume claimed, and if thought has to interface with syntax (as it surely does) then we had better run with associative (i.e., broadly connectionist) theories of syntax. What I shall be arguing is that while some kinds of human performance (discrimination and categorisation, in particular) can be explained in much the same way as that in which we explain the performance of laboratory animals in classical conditioning experiments, and by recruiting specifically Humean ideas (e.g., about spatio- and temporal contiguity), such performances fall far short of anything that can reasonably be called 'thinking'. I will be suggesting that the distinction between the two kinds of mental process is, to borrow Hume's phrase, 'evident almost without any reasoning'.

To set all this more securely in context – and to convince the reader that there are no straw figures in sight – David Shanks, the author of a monograph on associative learning, begins with a credo shared by many experimental psychologists working on human associative learning: 'I might as well come clean and confess that I believe empiricism is the basic starting point from which learning should be viewed' (Shanks, 1995, p. i). This is, in fact, an almost uncontroversial statement when applied to the phenomena his book covers. But a little later he extends it thus:

> but I should mention that I believe that the ability to explain language learning is the touchstone of any theory of learning, and I would be surprised if language learning turns out to rely on mechanisms radically different from those discussed here.
>
> (Shanks 1995, p. 5)

– associative mechanisms, in other words.

But if the language that is 'learned' is something we employ to express our thoughts then this fact – so I shall be assuming – had better be extended to the further claim that thinking too can be explained by associative mechanisms. So what is the modern face of associationism and what kind of phenomena in human performance does it cover?

Most often, human subjects in associative learning experiments have to judge the degree of contingency between two events or decide which of two categories a stimulus belongs to. As one would expect, the three forms of Humean association are well represented here: causality (in contingency judgements), spatial and temporal contiguity (in contingency judgements), and similarity (categorisation). With regard to contingency, humans and all other animals would quickly succumb if they were poor at estimating the chances of a subsequent event occurring after an initial event. This, it has been argued, is what animals are doing in conditioning experiments: they are detecting contingencies between stimuli, responses, and reinforcers. In the human case, however, researchers are more concerned with our conscious judgements about the degree of covariation between a signal and an outcome as expressed on a rating scale (e.g., Allan and Jenkins, 1983), or in their judgements about whether a signal indicates one outcome or another (e.g., whether a certain symptom or combination of symptoms indicates illness A or B) (e.g., Shanks, 1991). Less often, response rate is used as the dependent measure (Chatlosh et al., 1985), but here one assumes that the rate at which subjects have decided to press a key to make a light come on (and thus to earn points) depends, at least to some degree, on conscious judgements about contingencies.

While comparisons are made in this area between human and animal performance – (e.g., about the influence of additional cues that do not alter the contingency (Durlach, 1983) – the main interest is in how good humans are at doing the necessary intuitive statistics. Thus, given a signal and an outcome there are four possibilities: signal followed by outcome, signal not followed by outcome; no signal but the outcome; neither signal nor the outcome. Can they utilise such a contingency matrix in a 'rational' or 'normative' manner? Experiments set probabilities for each of the four cells and ask how sensitive subjects are to what appears in all of them. While there are biases in judgement, and while subjects can be heavily influenced by the way in which the trials are presented (e.g., blocked versus mixed), people are in general remarkably good at such tasks. It will come as no surprise that subjects are also sensitive to both temporal (Shanks, 1989) and spatial (Shanks, 1986) contingencies between two events.

It is as well to bear in mind however, that only in some studies – such as the medical diagnosis studies and the 'video games' in which shells are fired and tanks explode (e.g., Shanks, 1986) – are subjects being called upon to judge causality. This does not really weaken the analogy with Hume's principle of causality however, because this associative principle essentially concerns our expectations about what happens next given our experience of contingencies; indeed Hume famously argued that causal links have no 'necessity' beyond psychological facts about what we expect to happen. There is, however, a significant sense in which the associative concerns of Hume and the issues raised by the 'rational analysis of human learning' diverge. Where Hume was concerned with the way in which the mechanism of 'custom' makes us subject to certain expectations, the studies touched upon here require explicit judgements of statistical likelihood. In contrast to this, as we shall see immediately, the term 'associative learning' is often taken to refer to 'implicit' and non-cognitive mental processes. This raises the issue of whether the term 'associative' acquires its application here mainly because parallels can be drawn between the performance of laboratory animals and of humans (Shanks, 1995, p. 54).·

In the case of categorisation experiments however, there is no room for scepticism about the purity of the Humean legacy, because here we are clearly seeing the working of simple associative principles in human learning. And in this case there is a direct influence also from the results of animal experiments to human studies. Mackintosh (1995, p. 211) states this linkage in the following way. If we wish to study human associative learning (i.e., learning that is 'incidental or implicit' and is not 'based on rules, strategies and other "cognitive" processes') then we need the right theory of associative learning. Furthermore, because many connectionist architectures are based on incorrect assumptions[25] the correct theory will be derived

----

[25] That is, applying the standard form of the connectionist delta rule leads to failures to explain latent inhibition, perceptual learning, and retrospective revaluation; see discussion of perceptual learning to follow very shortly (e.g. p. 41).

from conditioning experiments with animals, as these display 'the rules of associative learning in their basic form, often untouched by other complex processes'. From this it follows, argues Mackintosh, that the way to look for associative processes in human learning is to compare our performance with that of pigeons. (Pigeons, rather than rats, because of their visual abilities.)

While it goes well beyond the scope of this book to summarise more than a tiny amount of this work, two phenomena at least deserve mention – *perceptual learning* and *the peak shift*. The first is about categorisation and discrimination and the second is about – what seems to be – relational learning. In the first, subjects (pigeons or people) who have learned to classify or categorise a set of variable exemplars into two categories – all As into one category, all Bs into another – will, as a result of that experience alone, find it easier to discriminate between two new As or two new Bs. Similarly, as William James noted with reference to wine tasting, the more one has to discriminate between clarets and burgundies the better one is able to discriminate *within* each of the categories.

In the second (peak shift), the pigeon or person has to make an initial discrimination between two stimuli which differ in (say) brightness and then has to make a further discrimination between two stimuli along the same continuum. The initial discrimination might be between 550 nm (positive) versus 560 nm (negative). It is found that, after training on the initial discrimination, subjects will then respond more readily to lights of 540 nm and 530 nm than to another light of 550 nm. It is as if (but only 'as if', as we shall see later) they had initially learned to respond to a relation – to the dimmer light of two rather than to an absolute brightness of 550 nm.

If the assumptions are made that (1) stimuli consist of elements and (2) the degree to which two stimuli share common elements determines how well they will be discriminated, both phenomena can be explained in the same terms – in terms of prototype effects. With regard to perceptual learning, the associative model of perceptual learning developed by McLaren, Kaye and Mackintosh (1989) makes the assumption that the associative strength of the elements *common* to, say, A-exemplars is *reduced* with experience. (These common elements can be regarded as constituting the prototype from which the stimuli were generated.) Note that this is the *opposite* assumption to that made by McClelland and Rumelhart's connectionist (1985) model of categorisation, which claims that categorisation is achieved by the elements constituting a prototype having *greater* levels of activation. In any event, the McLaren *et al.* model predicts, on this basis, that the stimuli *unique* to A and those *unique* to B will have greater salience the more the associative value of the common elements has been *lowered*. Moreover, any new pair of exemplars from within A will benefit from this exhaustion of the associative value of the prototypical elements – which is perceptual learning.

Similar processes are taken to account for the peak shift. In this case, the initial pair of stimuli (550 nm and 560 nm in value) will have elements in common, while the positive stimulus (550) will have a set of unique elements, with a relatively high associative value, on the theory. However, stimuli of 540 nm and 530 nm will inevitably (as they exist along a continuum and nearby) have not only such unique elements, but will have them 'uncontaminated' with the elements common to the negative stimulus with a value of 560 nm – with the result that they will attract higher associative values.

This might be seen, then, as the mechanism underlying Hume's principle of similarity. But is not the idea of a prototype, in the sense of the statistical 'central tendency', as a kind of abstract representation quite distant from particular perceptual experiences, a very un-Humean notion? (Recall that Hume's theory of categorisation bore stronger similarities to an exemplar or instance-based theory, with each exemplar having a distinct mental representation.) Not necessarily, for Mackintosh argues (1995, p. 202) – the details need not detain us – that, although the central tendency is playing a role, what also may be responsible for the prototype effects mentioned here and for other effects[26] is the fact that the prototype has fewer elements in common with members of other categories than do most of its own exemplars, and so it forms weaker associative links with members of other categories. In the latter case the prototype is the set of elements farthest from the category boundary, and is therefore not only something abstracted away from sets of elements present in the numerous positive exemplars. While the idea of stimuli consisting of elements was undreamed of in Hume's philosophy, at least his notion of atomic perceptual experiences is being retained here.

It might be said, then, that the spirit of David Hume has found a secure home in human associative learning laboratories, especially those where categorisation studies are run. But it is one thing to say this and quite another to insist that whenever people seem to be learning by applying rules what we are really witnessing is associative learning of the kind just described. Shanks (1995, Chapter 5), for one, does not take this line. What's more, one does not find students of associative learning (at least not in print and in seminar rooms, rather than in pubs) saying that in time all explicit (aka conscious) and strategic cognition will yield to an associationist analysis. ('Connectionists', however, are quite likely to do just this.) Moreover, explicit cognition by subjects is likely to *interfere* with the kind of simple associative mechanisms we have been discussing. As Mackintosh (1995, p. 211) notes:

> One experimental secret is probably to present stimuli or problems at a relatively rapid rate so as to overload working memory and so that subjects do not have the time to start wondering what the experimenter has in mind or what the experiment is really about. Another is to reduce the probability that subjects will label the stimuli, both by using stimuli that are not obviously nameable and by varying them in random ways from trial to trial. Perhaps what we are doing in all these cases is to make it difficult for subjects to generate and test appropriate hypotheses about the structure of the task – the absence of hypothesis testing being the reason why incidental or automatic learning can also be characterised as simply associative.

And it goes without saying – it is, as I promised, 'evident almost without any reasoning' – that these wonderings, labellings and hypothesis-framings are just what concerns one who wishes to characterise the kind of cognition that interfaces within syntax.

We now turn, however, to the linguistic side of the fence, and find a harder nut to crack: the claim that artificial grammar learning by laboratory subjects is associative

---

[26] For example, that an unseen prototype will be categorised more accurately than exemplars of its category.

in nature and that, given this, we are well on the way to explaining grammar learning by children in associative terms. A maker of such a claim might add that my above denial that cognition can be explained associatively is no more than a turning away from real and tractable empirical issues towards the comfort blanket of folk psychology, to indefinable distinctions between rules and associations, and to soft and fluffy notions like 'thinking'. The fact is – such a person will say – that there is a distinction between thinking as we take it to be and the processes that underlie our ideas about thinking; and that for all we know the latter may well turn out to be associative in nature. And by the way (he adds) you have taken care to stick to what Mackintosh qualifies as 'simple' (i.e., pigeonesque) associative learning. If you looked at the far-from-simple forms of associative learning found in connectionist networks it would be a different story.

On this view we should forget about how something we hardly understand at all (thought) interfaces with something we do at least understand a little (grammar), and exploit the fact that grammar learning is something amenable to study in the laboratory by using adult subjects and inventing simple grammars. If we make the grammar sufficiently dissimilar to that of the subjects' own language then it is unlikely that they are learning by exploiting syntactic knowledge they already possess; and so we can ask questions about how these artificial languages are learned, and then generalise the answers back to children. In general, if it can be shown that grammars simpler than those of the natural language, while still being the same kind of thing, can be learned by essentially associative processes, then it has been demonstrated that something structured (in so far as all grammars are structured in some sense) has been learned associatively; after which we can argue in a Whorfian-cum-nominalist style that the now-learned grammar can structure (in some sense) thought.

Some of the earlier studies of artificial grammar learning were motivated by questions about whether subjects were learning the rules of the grammar unconsciously or 'implicitly' (Reber, 1989). In fact, it is unlikely that truly implicit rule learning had been demonstrated (Shanks and St John, 1994); but it is certainly the case that subjects' ability to articulate what they have learned is very limited. We will not, however, be concerned with questions of conscious access, but with the question of what has been learned. That is to say, have subjects learned an abstract rule system (perhaps automatically) or have they learned sets of associations and facts about particular instances? In a typical study of this kind, people are presented with sets of letter strings that have been 'generated' by a 'grammar' of the kind shown in Figure 1.3. Initially, subjects have to read a series of 'grammatical' strings such as MXRVXT and are told that their task is to memorise them. Next they are told that the strings they have been reading were generated from a set of rules, and that their task is now to assess, for new strings they have not seen before, whether each is a legal product from that set of rules. Typically, people perform at above-chance levels on this kind of task, while their ability to explain how they did it is typically found to be poor (Mathews *et al.*, 1989).

One reason, of course, why subjects are so bad at reporting on the rules they appear to be using is that they are not in fact using rules at all, but are instead encoding

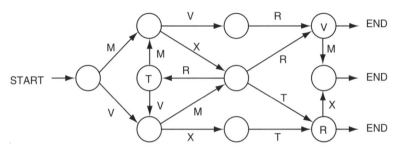

Figure 1.3 Brooks and Vokey's (1991) artificial grammar. If a node contains a letter then that letter can be added repeatedly at that point. Reproduced from Shanks, *The psychology of associative learning* (1995), with permission from Cambridge University Press.

in memory a set of strings as complete items and then judging the grammaticality of the new strings on the basis of their similarity to these stored items. A good Humean strategy! A study by Brooks and Vokey (1991) suggested that this is what people are indeed doing. They varied the 'grammaticality' of the items against their similarity to the initially exposed items in such a way that a test string might share either one or four letters with an initially exposed item. These authors found a very substantial effect of perceptual similarity, with only a minority of dissimilar grammatical strings being judged grammatical.

Moreover, Whittlesea and Dorken (1993) were able to show that the way in which subjects store the strings, and thus the basis of the similarity judgements they make, is heavily influenced by the way they were initially encoded. In their experiment, half of the study items had to be spoken aloud (they were pronounceable strings like ENROLID) and the other half had to be spelled out. At test, each item was either spoken or spelled out, so that mode of encoding could either match or mismatch with the mode or test. The outcome was that judgement of grammaticality was efficient if the two matched, but if they mismatched it was bad. As Shanks concludes in his discussion of this work, it appears then that what is being encoded are not sets of rules but rather very specific items, in the sense that what is stored in memory

> is a 'snapshot' that not only preserves those structural relationships, but also many of the relationships pertaining at the moment between the elements of the stimulus and the mental operations performed upon them, as well as, perhaps such things as the experimental context and the emotional state of the subject.
>
> (1995, pp. 91–2)

Something, in fact, that is not a million miles from Humean 'ideas'.

What seems, however, to argue against the conclusion that all the subjects were engaged in here was instance (or 'exemplar' learning) is that when generalisation tests are run in which subjects are tested with strings constructed according to the same rules but with a completely different set of letters, performance was still above chance; although, as one would expect, it was not as good as when the letter set was the same. More impressively, Altmann, Dienes and Goode (1995) were able to show that when not only the letter set changed but also the modality of the items, from letter strings to tones (and vice versa), that grammaticality judgements were superior to those of a control group which has not seen or heard the training set. (In their study, each letter had a tonal counterpart, such as M with middle C.)

So, do studies of this kind show that subjects were learning abstract rules after all? Not necessarily. In the first place, whether subjects transfer to new letter strings depends upon the instructions they are given at presentation, in a way that it does not when the letter set remains the same. Returning to Whittlesea and Dorken (1993). There were three types of instructions here: (a) the subjects were simply told to memorise the initial list, (b) the letter strings were a distractor from a primary task and (c), subjects were instructed to count the repetitions of particular letters in each string. At test, they either had to assess novel strings from the original set of letters or novel strings using novel letters. In the first case, there was no effect of instruction conditions; but there was a clear effect in the second (novel letters) case. In (a), as is usual, the subjects were above chance with the novel letters but worse than with familiar letters, in (b) they were at chance with the novel letters, in (c) – the repletion-counting condition – however they performed as well with the novel letters as with the familiar ones. The authors conclude that in condition (b), then, they were simply encoding the surface features; in condition (c) they were encoding the relations between items; while in (a) they were probably doing a bit of both. This adds further weight, then, to Brooks and Vokey's conclusion that what is learned depends upon what is asked of subjects at encoding and test. Mackintosh concludes in a discussion of such work:

> When Whittlesea and Dorken's subjects were asked to note repetitions, they did not suddenly learn the rules of the artificial grammar; they learned about the relations between items. What psychologists often describe as the abstraction of rules (whether by people or other animals) can often be understood as learning about the relations between events.
>
> (Mackintosh, 2001, p. 136)

Of course it all depends on what one takes to be a 'rule'. One might say that subjects abstract the rule 'if the second and fourth letter are the same then the string is grammatical'. But one might more cautiously say that they notice a similarity that they cannot put their fingers on between KRBBBYK on the one hand and MQKKKHM or AGF#F#F#BA on the other. Mackintosh argues that while we need not say that the subjects are using abstract rules in this case we do have to concede that they are noting second-order relations holding between relations (noting where repeated items are relative to their number, in this example). Alternatively, might they be perceiving a perceptual gestalt? The Wittlesea and Doren (1993) finding of excellent transfer between letter sets when subjects were told to count the repetitions suggests that success depends upon something deliberated rather than something perceptual; but gestalt-like processes may be operating in some cases. In any event, attributing the learning of abstract rules to subjects would seem generally to be unwarranted.

(For readers impatient about the relevance of all this to syntactic acquisition, I should point out that questions of this kind become urgent when we come to assess empirical work on 'the algebraic infant', in 3.3.3).

At this point, a supporter of empiricist theories of grammatical development could say that if it is the case that what appears to be the learning of abstract rules is really no more than learning about relations between items (if not instance learning), *then so much the better for empiricism*. For the same may turn out to be true of grammatical development in children. How successful is this strategy?

First, if this argument is successful, the victory would be a somewhat Pyrrhic one, as it would be won at the cost of asserting that the ruleboundness of language use is illusory. This is at odds with the claim made by the developmental connectionists that associative mechanisms enable the child to *extract rules and categories from the input with associative means alone*. Moreover, denying the ruleboundness of language use forecloses any options on the Whorfian/nominalist line that language structures thought. At this point, the option of denying that thought *is* structured, at bottom, might become attractive. This is a position favoured by philosophers such as Andy Clark, as we shall be discussing in Part 3.

In any event, it would appear to be difficult to draw strong parallels between artificial 'grammars' and the grammars of human languages. A grammar of a language is obviously more than a set of rules for sequencing elements. Natural language grammars have classes (nouns, verbs, adjectives etc.), sub-sentential rule-bound groupings of elements (phrases) and rules of agreement (e.g., in number between subjects and main verbs), not to mention features like 'movement' (see Figures 1.1 and 1.2). Moreover, what is learned by the developing child is not how to differentiate legal from illegal sequences *but how to express thoughts* (or, if you like, 'semantic representations' or 'propositions') with the grammar of a particular language. So at this point the question becomes: How do subjects fare when the artificial grammar consists of natural language properties of the kind just listed? The only one of these properties that has been studied to date is that of classes – analogous to grammatical classes like noun, and so forth.

The literature on learning artificial grammars that consist of more than sequential rules has been usefully reviewed by Martin Braine (1987), who was also among the first, if not the first, to do this kind of work. Braine pointed out that while subjects easily learn, as we have seen, co-occurrence between individual morphemes,[27] the absolute position of an item in a string (e.g., first or last), the position of items or groups of items to a marker word (analogous to function words like wh-words, articles etc.), they find it *impossible to learn the privileges of occurrence of classes of words that have nothing perceptually in common* (as do all nouns, verbs, prepositions etc.[28]). For example, Smith (1966) constructed a miniature system with four grammatical classes, arbitrarily labelled M, N, P, and Q. Their privileges of occurrence were given by the following two rules: string → M + N; string → P + Q. In other words all strings were two words long, with the class of M and the class of P words always coming first and with the class of N and Q words always coming second and

---

[27] Sometimes these were English nonsense words rather than letters of the alphabet.

[28] In addition, many nouns do not refer to things, many verbs do not refer to actions, and so forth. We will deal with this issue later.

with the proviso that N words only followed M words and Q words only followed P words. The string lists were repeatedly presented (Smith, 1969) until they had been rote learned. While the subjects achieved rote recall there was no point between the initial exposure and learning at which they registered the dependencies between the four classes of words. They did notice the M and P words tended to come first and that N and Q words tended to come second, but no more; with the result that they would falsely remember the ungrammatical strings MQ and PN as readily as MN and PQ strings they had not heard. 'In sum,' Braine concludes, 'laboratory work indicates that there is a huge gap between the ease with which subjects register simple positional properties and inter-morpheme co-occurrences, and the difficulty of registering the class dependencies of the MN/PQ structure' (Braine, 1987, p. 69).

Class learning is not, however, impossible if the items within each class all refer to a distinct set of entities in a constructed set of objects (Moeser and Bregman, 1972); that is, when semantic cues are given to subjects. One might object that this is a situation far divorced from natural grammar acquisition because all nouns do not refer to things, all verbs do not refer to actions, and so forth. But Braine (1987) himself demonstrated in an artificial grammar learning study that class dependencies of the MN/PQ type can be learned by college students if the correlation between semantic features of the reference set (the visible genders of dolls) and the arbitrary class is at least *partial* – as it is in the acquisition of natural languages (e.g., not all, but many nouns refer to physical objects).

What should be concluded from this? For Braine, it is that subjects can indeed learn classes so long as they have some, at least partial, correlate to distinguish one class from others. In his own study, this correlate was semantic (the visible cues to dolls' genders) but, as he says, it could equally well have been that some of the dolls had stripes and some had spots. In other words any semantically-arbitrary cue will do (e.g., a phonological one) to serve as the partial correlate of a class.

What general moral can be derived from this work – one that can be applied to the questions with which we began about the role of associative processes in grammar learning? For Braine it is one with an empiricist flavour. He argues explicitly for the role of 'associative learning (i.e., the learning of contingencies and co-occurrences, especially with phonological elements)' (1987, p. 85) in the child's acquisition of grammatical classes and other syntactic features. But this is an account of how children (who *might* have no innate representations of syntactic classes) could be bootstrapping themselves into syntax. It is not the view that syntactic rules and categories *will on closer analysis reduce entirely to associations* – a 'Humean' view. In other words, accepting that children utilise what Braine calls 'associative foci' (semantic or phonological) of various kinds is a million miles from claiming *that abstract linguistic categories and rules do not exist.* (In any event, we shall be looking more closely at bootstrapping theories of this kind in 4.4, and we will also be considering a connectionist model of learning the German definite articles (which change with gender, case, and number). Here, associative learning (as Braine intends it) would appear to be the only option.)

To sum up this subsection, it is clearly the case that some kinds of human learning are no less associative than is the learning of pigeons, and that essentially

Humean concepts can be put to work to explain such learning. But this fact in no sense erodes the anti-empiricist credo that thinking requires the non-associative deployment of abstract rules and categories. Furthermore, the fact that subjects' ability to learn artificial grammars can be explained by simple forms of sub-rulebound learning cannot be generalised to the view that children's learning of natural grammars is a sub-rulebound process. That the learning of arbitrary classes within artificial grammars becomes possible with the provision of associative cues may provide hints about how such cues function in the developmental process; but none of this entails that what is being acquired is associative *tout court.*

1.2.3 Beyond associations: two developmental examples and Piagetian theory

In this section I will illustrate the pressure that developmental data can put upon associative theories of human learning – sufficient, for some, to squeeze out further thoughts in favour of LOT. Along the way I will make some observations about where Piaget stands in relation to the rationalism–empiricism axis in order to prepare the ground for a discussion of why Piagetian theory is really no friend to connectionist-style empiricism that will be discussed in the subsequent section.

First, back to the peak shift. This time I will describe the procedure in a more schematic fashion, taking size as the dimension rather than brightness, as this is the dimension commonly used with children. Consider the following stimulus values:

1″ 2″ 3″ 4″ 5″ 6″ 7″ 8″ 10″ 12″ 14″ 16″ 19″

    − +   ? versus ?

Imagine that the stimuli are squares. The children are reinforced for picking the 3″ square over the 2″ square, and when they are faced with a choice of 3″ versus 4″ or 5″ the latter two stimuli are found to attract more responses – which is the phenomenon definitive of the peak shift, whether or not the associative process is the same. This might immediately lead one to think that they are doing the task by coding the relation 'bigger'. But if so, then they should choose the bigger of *any* two stimuli, say 12″ versus 14″ or 16″ versus 19″, this being known as a *transposition* task. However if the subjects are animals or young children they do not; and this is called the *distance effect.* Broadly speaking, adults do not show the distance effect – they can pass the 'far test' – and often report that they are choosing on the basis of a relation ('bigger', 'dimmer' 'the taller, thinner ones' etc).

How do associative theories deal with data of this kind? We have already seen that Mackintosh's elemental theory can explain the peak shift. (And indeed this associative theory explains it more successfully than does the first attempt at such a theory, owing to K. W. Spence (Bryant, 1974, for discussion). But how do associative theories deal with transposition? They have done so – it will come as no surprise – by adopting a form of nominalism: the theory that abstract concepts are nothing over and above verbal labels for recording stimuli (or 'ideas' in the seventeenth and eighteenth centuries).

Margaret Kuenne (1946) found that there was a relationship between failing transposition (i.e., showing the distance effect) at around age 4 and passing transposition at around age 6 and overt use of verbal labels for the relation (e.g., 'the big one').

In accordance with the behaviourist ethos of the time, she argued that the relational terms that the older children had had time to acquire served as 'verbal mediating responses'. The details need not detain us, but the general idea is that inner speech provides a chain of covert stimulus-and-response when the 6-year-old is faced with the 16″ and the 19″ squares. But there is a deep conceptual flaw in this nominalist attempt to explain how subjects utilise abstract relations with no more than associative resources, that Peter Bryant (1974, chapter 2) put his finger on: How were they able, with only associative resources, *to learn the meaning of relational terms in the first place?* And remember that for the verbal mediation theory to work the child must have grasped the meaning of the terms, rather than simply attaching a sound to a stimulus. Fodor cites this passage in Bryant's book with approval when setting out his argument that nothing can be expressed in natural language that can't be expressed in the language of thought and that if something could we could not learn the word or phrase in natural language that expresses it.

> I know of only one place in the psychological literature where this issue has been raised. Bryant (1974, p. 27) remarks: "the main trouble with the hypothesis that children begin to take in and use relations to help them solve problems because they learn the appropriate comparative term like 'larger' is that it leaves unanswered the awkward question of how they learned these words in the first place". The argument generalises, with a vengeance, to any proposal that the learning of a word is essential to mediate the learning of a concept that the word expresses.

> (Fodor 1975, p. 84)

It does indeed, and it is the perfect pocket-sized developmental argument – or 'intuition pump' to sceptics – for the necessity for LOT.

But this is not – or at least not yet – an argument for LOT being *innate*. As is well known, Jean Piaget argued that at around the age of 6 years children acquire the ability to code reflexive relations (i.e., A > B; B < A) and that this manifested itself in their passing tests of transitive reasoning (e.g., A > B; B > C; A ? C). Indeed, the age of around 6 years was supposed, more generally, to herald the beginning of the 'concrete operational' stage, in which children's thought attained a 'structure' that Piaget described in terms of mathematical 'group' theory. These 'groupings' were supposed to describe the mental structures necessary for thinking about classes and relations. Now while there was certainly an executive element in Piaget's account of concrete operational thinking (Russell, 1999), it is fair to say that he was also describing a kind of representational format (for thinking about classes and relations) that was applicable across domains. And one would not be slipping too far into metaphor to say that these 'logico-mathematical' structures would have to be represented in some form of logical symbolism; in any event his account of the domain-general changes at adolescence in terms of 'the 16 binary propositions' makes explicit reference to logical symbolism. My point is this. Although Piaget held that mental structures of this kind were not innately specified, but developed through interaction with the physical world in infancy (infants' actions described in terms of group theory, Piaget, 1948), there is an important similarity between his 'constructivist' ideas and those of rationalists like Fodor and Chomsky. Both approaches posit formal structures (formats) that are not learned in any of the ways posited by empiricism, and which certainly are not based on associative processes. Piaget's account of how mental structures developed was more Kantian than empiricist, if we take Kant to be saying that certain forms of thought are a priori in the sense of being necessary to coherent experience without making the further claim that 'a priori = innate'.

Let us now look closer at transitive reasoning tasks, in order to put further pressure on associative theories of how they come to be solved. The claim has been made that pigeons (Fersen *et al.*, 1991) can solve transitive puzzles, not to mention rats (Davis, 1992) and monkeys (McGonigle and Chalmers, 1977). Now the fact that pigeons can do something does not in itself tell us that they are doing it associatively! But it does raise questions about whether the mechanism underlying humans' ability to draw the inference may be associative in nature. How might such a theory work? The story begins with Bryant and Trabasso's (1971) critique of Piaget's original experiments.

Telling the child that A > B and that B > C and then asking them about the relation between A and C can lead, argued Bryant and Trabasso (1971) to both false negatives and to false positives. There may be false negatives because children may have forgotten the premises when the question is asked; and so one must train their memory before questioning them. There may be false positives, because all the child has to do to succeed is to remember that A is big and C is small (ignoring B) to get the right answer. To circumvent this problem one must give children a five-term series problem of the following kind: A > B, B > C, C > D, D > E, and ask them about the relation between B and D once we have ensured that they have learned the premises. (The stimuli were coloured sticks and the only feedback the children received was verbal: they never saw the sticks' complete length.) When these steps are taken, the authors demonstrated, children much younger than 6 years pass the test, suggesting that what develops between (roughly) 3 and 6 years is memory rather than logical ability. Be that as it may, how would an associative account of their success work?

While they did not call their theory associative, this is the essence of de Boysson-Bardies and O'Regan's (1973) model. As did Kuenne, they suggested that the children's success might be attained via verbal labelling. In the first place, it is worth bearing in mind that young children are only able to learn the premises when they are trained on adjacent pairs (i.e., not on pairs like A > C; Halford, 1984). According to de Boysson-Bardies and O'Regan children will tend to label the sticks as 'big' and 'little'. The upshot is that the only sticks that receive a consistent label will be end sticks A and E:

A	B	C	D	E
'big'	'little'	'big'	'little'	
	'big'	'little'	'big'	'little'

Remember that it is the B and D sticks that children are asked about at test. We can forget about stick C, which is not needed for an associative (unlike a logical) solution and note that while B and D never acquire a consistent label, B is invariably presented alongside A and D is invariably presented alongside E. Now, because the assumption is that it is associations rather than relations that the child is learning, we can argue that presenting a stick that has received no consistent label alongside a stick that has received a consistent label will cause the former to gain that label by association, and so B will have the proxy label 'big' and D will take the proxy label 'little'.

The success of animals on this task can be explained in much the same way, when we replace 'big' with the fact of the animal obtaining a food reward (+) and 'little' with the fact of the animal obtaining no food reward:

A	B	C	D	E
+	−	+	−	
	+	−	+	−

Accordingly, because B is paired half the time with A, which is consistently rewarded, it becomes more strongly associated with reward than does D which is paired half the time with the consistently unrewarded E. So the animals chose B over D when they are presented together. Clearly then, the warrant for saying that pigeons etc. can reason transitively dissolves under this analysis.

But the fact that we have an associative explanation of success on this task does not entail that de Boysson-Bardies and O'Regan were correct about how children succeed. If children are behaving associatively rather than coding relations then they should perform just as well on a task in which they simply receive verbal reinforcement for picking one stick over another as on a task in which they are told about a (say) size relation. We made this comparison (Russell *et al.*, 1996), giving one group of 5- to 6-year-old children a task in which there was no transitive continuum (one coloured box contained a ball, the comparison box was empty) and another in which there was a transitive relation of size (one box contained a bigger ball than the other). Controlling for premise memory in the two tasks, we showed that children found the latter (genuinely transitive) task the *easier*, suggesting that they were indeed utilising knowledge about transitive relations.

It is when we consider a possible objection to this conclusion that issues germane to LOT return to the agenda. For it is possible to argue that the 'transitive' task employed with animals was actually doing more than building associative strengths to different stimuli (with the same applying to the child version of this task). The argument runs that reinforcing A over B, B over C etc. down to D over E is actually training the animals to *prefer* A to B, B to C, and so forth (see McGonigle and Chalmers, 1992). In his influential book on animal cognition Ewan Macphail (1982, p. 308) says with reference to the idea that monkeys are utilising a preference algorithm of this kind:

> Unless … we believe that the monkey is saying to itself B is better than G, G is better than R and so on (and no alternative account has been proposed), it is difficult to see what is meant by transitive inference. The derivation of the inference relies on there being formal (or at least formalisable) rules for the use of words or symbols involved, for the ordering of words within each string, and so on.

That is to say, the very idea of preference is relational, and if relations are to be encoded as such (transitive or otherwise) then they must be encoded in some symbolic medium: associative machinery cannot be sufficient. (This, by the way, is a further consideration in favour of the view that Piaget's 'groupings' of relations and classes is something that would require representation in a formal medium.)

Finally, it would appear to be conceptually impossible, rather that just practically difficult, to present a transitive task to infra-verbal creatures without reinforcing them for choosing A over B, B over C etc. Remember that what is required of the experimenter here is *telling*, rather than showing, the creature what the relation is. (If we showed the animal that A is longer/heavier/etc. than B, all the animal will need to do is to associate certain absolute stimulus values with the colour of A, B etc.) It would appear that there is simply no other way to get facts about relations 'into a creature's head' other than by using a symbolic medium of some kind. Of course it is trivially true that we cannot make it known to an infra-verbal creature that Granny is coming to tea the second week in September without using language; but the fact of being unable to express a relation in anything other than language is far from being a trivial fact, in so far as relations are the very warp and weft of logico-mathematical cognition. And if the immediate thought here is that this fact speaks to the importance of *natural* language (rather than LOT) to adequate cognition then we must remember Bryant's statement that this 'leaves unanswered the awkward question of how they learned these words in the first place'.

1.2.4 Connectionist developmental theory: new connectionism, old empiricism

In Part 3, I will deal in detail with connectionist models of language and cognitive development, but for now all I wish to do is to make the case for saying that connectionist ideas about mental and syntactic development are empiricist through and through.

1.2.4.1 Networks

Neural networks consist of 'units' (or 'nodes') and the connections between them, whose strengths ('weights') are usually randomly seeded before learning (which, like the connectionists, I will equate with 'development' – for the time being). By far the most common kind of architecture used in connectionist developmental work is the three-layer feedforward network (see Figure 1.4). In this, data are presented at the input level, which determine the connection weights leading up to a bank of 'hidden' units , which in turn determines the connection strengths to a bank of output units. Data are presented in terms of patterns of activations over input units, with the modeller fixing the 'meaning' of the input in terms of these patterns. Learning takes place by the network's computing the difference between the achieved output and a target output emanating from a 'teaching signal' and adjusting the connection weights accordingly (making the degree of adjustment relative to the degree to which a connection was 'responsible' for the error – called *back-propagation*). Other kinds of architectures, such as simple recurrent networks (SRNs) (Elman, 1990) and cascade correlation (Mareshal and Shultz, 1996) are variations on this basic theme.

However the task of a network is not merely to achieve correlation between the pattern of input activation and the pattern of output activation, but also to do so in such a way as to reflect underlying patterns of regularity between the two sets of patterns. The acid test for this is whether the net can generalise what has been learned to a new set of data. If this has been achieved, it will have been done at the level of the hidden

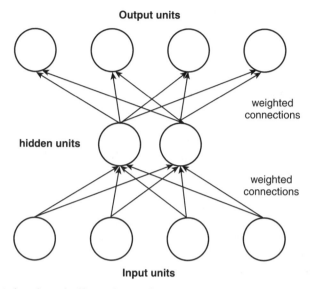

Figure 1.4 A three-layer, feedforward network.

units, which can be viewed as computing representations in n-dimensional 'state space', with 'n' being equal to the number of input units. Mathematically, the value of each input to a row of units is a vector, as it is a pattern of numbers (see Jordan, 1986, on the linear algebra underlying connections); and if there are, say, 20 input units then the hidden units' state space will be 20-dimensional. When learning has been achieved, the modeller can examine the state space to see how it has been partitioned in order to solve the task – known as *principle component analysis*. It is of course impossible to visualise space beyond three dimensions, but what can be imagined is state space in which each variable in the data set represents a dimension. Note that in the successful network only the variables that are distinctive to the domain are responded to. It has come to reflect the fundamental sources of variance in the data.

What is the status of these representations? They are Humean in nature. Recall that for Hume, as for Berkeley, it was a betrayal of the fundamental empiricist tenet that all knowledge derives from perception to ascribe to us abstract or 'universal' concepts. We think with ideas that are determinate and image-like, and they only function 'as if [they] were universal'.[29] But many of the concepts we possess do appear to have an abstract or universal character. Recall that Hume's answer to the challenge of maintaining the central tenet of empiricism whilst accounting for behaviour that seemed to be generated by abstract knowledge was to propose a version of an instance-based theory of concept learning in which the thinker is taken to exercise a natural disposition to link instances together by the associative principle of similarity. In this sense then, we cannot be said to have any 'central'

[29] *Treatise on Human Nature,* I, I, 7.

representation of (say) the colour white or of cats above and beyond our associative mechanism of linking recorded instances via similarity. The essence of the similarity itself is not itself represented – as it was for Locke. One way of describing Hume's solution is to say that in the Humean mind, as in the connectionist mind, there is no distinction between data and their processing. That is to say, seeing a cat (or having an activation pattern of a certain kind on the input units) is part and parcel of the mental mechanism of thinking 'cat' (or of producing a certain activation pattern on the output units). So where the rationalist regards the perceptual experience of a cat as being assimilated to a pre-existing and central conception or schema of cathood (the percept is one thing and what the mind does with it is another), for Hume and the connectionists knowledge really is nothing more than the associative links between data.

There would, however, seem to be one respect in which the Humean-connectionist analogy does not hold; and it is one in which the Humean view would appear to come out as *more* representational than the connectionist. For the Humean, an instance would count as a particular representation (like a snapshot of a cat), whereas there are of course no individual instances represented in networks. On my analogy, however, a connectionist instance is a *single input pattern*, and what corresponds to the Humean 'vivacity' of this pattern/instance is the frequency with which the net 'sees' it. That said, the role of the instance in the two views of mind is the same, in so far as, in both, the character of the representation is exhausted by the frequency/vivacity of the instances. Each instance contributes to what is represented in much the same way as each grain of sand in an egg-timer contributes to the length of time it takes for the sand to run through. In fact one might say that instances in Hume and in connectionism approximates to Leibniz's notion of unconscious *petites perceptions*. We hear the roar of sea, said Leibniz, and for that roar to have the character it does the barely audible sound of countless tiny wavelets each contribute – each a *petite perception*. No single one of them would be missed, but the roar of the sea is nothing over and above the sum of them: the character of the perceived whole is exhausted by its minuscule parts, just as in the Humean-connectionist picture, the character of the cognised whole is exhausted by the *petite perceptions* that constitute it. And this is inevitable on a radically empiricist view of thought.

The Humean and the connectionist theories of mind are also alike in being potentially nominalist. Recall that empiricism and nominalism are conceptually linked in the sense that both deny the existence of semantic essences, that is, of representations that are not derivable from perceptual experience alone. As I characterised it earlier, the nominalist view of semantic development is as a process of labelling stored sets of sensory impressions. And so, to return to my analogy, the label might correspond to the teaching signal fed to the network. The point to stress here is that there is no sense in which this signal names a representation that is already 'in' the network. Rather, it is the 'teaching signal + label linkage' that determines how a 'representation' in the hidden units will be constructed from the input patterns. This would appear to capture the essence of nominalism: the idea that a concept is nothing beyond the mental upshot of labelling agglomerations of instances.

Let us now consider what it means to say that connectionist networks have 'representations'. There is a clear sense in which the hidden units do indeed have representations. This is so in the sense that input–output links are not direct ones: associations are 'squeezed through' gateways – hidden units – that force the computation of the fundamental sources of variance in the data – representations of the regularities. In this sense then, what is being represented on the hidden units are statistical properties of the data. For example, in a simulation we shall be discussing in 3.3, the network had to predict a possible next word in a string of words, such that given a sequence like 'girls chase' the next word had to be selected from the training set of nouns, and given 'who dogs ...' the next word had to be selected from the training set of verbs. Principle component analysis showed that the noun set clustered together in one area of state space while the verb set clustered together in another. It might seem churlish to deny here that the noun set was receiving a 'representation' distinct from that of the verb set.

But there is also a sense in which connectionist representations are so different from symbolic and iconic representations that they need their own term to distinguish their kinds of representation – 'records' perhaps. What principle component analysis reveals, on the representations-as-records view, are not so much the network's representations of categories (e.g., nouns) but rather *the records of the processes that it underwent to correlate input with output*. They show a record of what has happened to the network, what it has *undergone* in solving the task. Given this, it makes no sense to anthropomorphise the learning process by saying that the net has 'extracted the noun and the verb categories *in order to* solve the correlational task', because extracting the noun set versus the verb set as a principle source of variance just *is* solving the task. The structure of state space does not show us the representations that were 'constructed' as a means of solving the correlational task: they show us a *record of the task's being successfully solved*.

Here is another example of how easy it is to slide between talking about the records of the hidden units' activity and talk about the network's representations of a domain. Munakata *et al.* (1997) ran similations to explore the process of 'predicting' when an object passing before the network's 'eye' would re-emerge from behind an occluder. When the hidden unit activation levels of successful networks were examined it was found that when the object was temporally invisible, some of the fifteen hidden units maintained as high a level of activation as when the object was visible. This, the authors concluded, was a primitive form of object permanence, in the sense of the networks' maintaining a representation of a datum when no perceptual input was being received from it. But this kind of representational talk is not mandatory. All we need to say is that activity on some of the hidden units had to be maintained if the correct prediction was to be made. *We are seeing a record of the network doing its job.* And all this would appear to be a consequence the fact that, as just noted, a connectionist representation is exhausted by the process it underwent – that data, process, and representation are one.

If this analysis is correct, it would appear that there is a conceptual linkage between adopting a 'connectionist' (*à la* Elman *et al.* see below) perspective on development and being an empiricist. In other words, the situation is not that connectionists of the Elman *et al.* kind[30] just happen to develop their ideas in an empiricist style but that the very rationale behind a certain kind of connectionist modelling of development is empiricist through and through. For if a connectionist representation is better viewed as a record of what the successful network has undergone, and *as there cannot be a record of something that has yet to happen*, there simply cannot be innate representations of a connectionist kind.

That said, it is possible to construct kinds of networks that do not have to learn how to do a task. The success of these networks, however, is not due to their having innate representations of a domain but due rather to their having purpose-built architectures. Consider, in illustration, the network shown in Figure 1.5, taken from Rumelhart and McClelland (1986). This network solves the 'exclusive or' problem ('XOR': respond to A or to B, but not to A and B) because its units act as thresholds and because its connection weights are fixed; that is the way the machine works. This shows that hard-wiring a mechanism can obviate the need for learning and it can do so without having representations of data. But such a network no more has representations than a colander represents garden peas *vis-à-vis* petits pois or a bridge represents vehicles lower than 20 feet. But does this not suggest that connectionism need not be empiricist? It does so only if you take 'empiricism' to entail a rejection of innate *mechanisms* as well as innate ideas (aka innate 'contents' or 'representations'; see Martin Braine on innateness in 1.1.1). But Hume himself proposed innate mechanisms (the associative principles of similarity, temporal continuity and causality); so on this reading David Hume himself would not be counted as an empiricist!

This fact is worth bearing in mind when we consider some of the claims made by Elman *et al.*, in the developmental connectionist 'bible' *Rethinking innateness: A connectionist perspective on development* (1996). The authors hotly deny that there is anything empiricist about their approach because – they point out – what they are opposed to is '*representational* nativism' rather than innate mechanisms or processes. Well, as we have just seen, this is a view they share with David Hume. They say that 'there is no logical incompatibility between connectionism and nativism' – only between connectionism and 'representational nativism'. 'In neural networks, it is possible to actually explore various avenues for building in innate predispositions, including minor biases that have major structural consequences across a range of environmental conditions' (Elman *et al.*, 1996, p. 48). And later:

> All connectionist models necessarily make some assumptions which must be regarded as constituting innate constraints. The way in which stimuli are represented, the parameters associated with learning, the architecture of the network, and the very task to be learned all provide the network with an entry point to learning.
>
> (Elman *et al.*, 1996, p. 100)

But there must be no truck with 'representational nativism'.

---

[30] See the beginning section of Part 3 for connectionist modellers who are less ideologically committed and more eclectic.

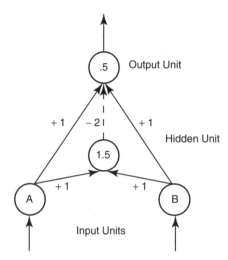

Figure 1.5 A network 'innately wired' to perform exclusive or (from Rumelhart and McClelland, 1986, permission sought).

What do Elman *et al.* have against representational nativism? Surprisingly, there are no attempts in the book to tackle head-on the arguments of Chomsky and Fodor and the data of developmental nativists such as Spelke (e.g. Spelke *et al.*, 1992). It is more a matter of fastidiously averting the gaze. What attempts there are to undermine representational nativism in the book are made entirely at the *neural* level. Representational nativism is, they say, 'expressed at the neural level in terms of direct constraints on fine-grained patterns of cortical connectivity'. But while this is 'plausible on theoretical grounds … the last two decades of research on vertebrate brain development force us to conclude that innate specification of synaptic connectivity at the cortical level is highly unlikely' (ibid., p. 361). The adult brain is the outcome of many complex interactions between neurochemical and other forms of constraint.

But none of the issues surrounding representational nativism (Chomsky-style or Fodor-style) are touched by the fact of neural plasticity. The plasticity or otherwise of the human nervous system is beside all the points being discussed in this book. Why?

A child may have all of his left hemisphere removed to prevent severe epilepsy, with the result that his language capacity comes to be represented on the remaining right brain (Devlin *et al.*, 2003). The appropriate inference from this and from other findings of this kind would appear to be that innate structures are not represented at the level of individual neurons and their connections, and that the organisation of the brain is at a level higher than the synaptic. As Fodor (1998a) puts it in a review of Elman *et al.*:

> That one brick is like another is not a reason to doubt that the structure of brick buildings is, by and large, pre-planned. All it shows is that, if planning did go on, you have to look at *aggregates* of bricks to see the effects.

> (Fodor, 1998a, p. 145)

Moreover, if we insist with Elman *et al.* that, because knowledge is encoded in the nervous system, our failing to find 'the right kind of neural connectivity when we look at the infant's brain shows there is no innate content there' (in Fodor's words) then this should force us to conclude further that there is no *learned* content in the adult brain either. Because we simply have no idea how cognitive content is realised in terms of neural connectivity – innate or learned – we will be forever finding ourselves failing to relate synaptic wiring diagrams to cognitive contents. The upshot is that arguing against representational nativism by keeping the discussion at the synaptic level is doomed to futility, because nobody understands how the cognitive and the neural level are related: 'Nobody knows how to make a brain-like cognitive model, classical or connectionist, because nobody knows how the cognitive brain works' (Fodor, 1998a, p. 145).

In any event, by the end of the book Elman *et al.* (p. 365) are still insisting:

> We are neither behaviourists nor radical empiricists. We have tried to point out throughout this volume that the tabula rasa approach is doomed to failure, but that in reality, all connectionist models have prior constraints of one kind and another. What we reject is representational nativism.

But I hope enough has been said to convince the reader that radical empiricism is *exactly* what developmental connectionism is. They are correct, however, in saying that they are not behaviourists (if by that they intend 'Skinnerians'). Their position is not a behaviourist one because the behaviourists were concerned, however bizarrely, with action: the organism produces 'operants' which the environment shapes – action then its consequence. While neural networks can model the way in which feedback and feedforward improves motor skill (Jordan, 1990), connectionist models typically – and throughout Elman *et al.* – do not produce actions (qua changes in their perceptual input) but passively extract regularities from the perceptual input. And this is one of the reasons why their position is not a Piagetian one either, though Piagetians (a modernised version at least) is what they want to be.

They take their position to be Piagetian rather than empiricist because they, like Piaget, are concerned with 'interaction'. But Piaget's interactionism depended fundamentally on the child's being an agent. While agency could conceivably be modelled on networks (Russell, 1996, 1.4 (iii)) this is not Elman *et al.*'s concern. What they call 'interactionism' is either something that exists at the level of synaptic development or it is the common denominator of *all* developmental theories: 'our major thesis is that while biological forces play a crucial role in determining our behaviour, those forces cannot be understood in isolation from the environment in which they are played out' (ibid., p. 356). Neither Chomsky nor J. B. Watson would have any trouble with *that*.

This is not to deny, of course, that there are similarities between Piagetian theory and developmental connectionism. Piaget too was opposed to representational nativism (at least as much as he was opposed to empiricism), and he too stressed cognitive plasticity. One also finds in his writings approving references to 'neural networks' – though of a kind that predated connectionist models (Piaget in Piatelli-Palmarini, ed, p. 280) . Moreover, as McClelland (1989) pointed out, one can construct an analogy between the process of back-propagation and Piaget's concept of accommodation; though, as he also points out, there is a more direct parallel with the Rescorla-Wagner model of classical conditioning.

There is one major respect, however, in which Piagetian theory is symmetrically opposed to the connectionist perspective on development: the Piagetian concern with cognitive structures. True, he regarded these as being derived from action, but once derived, they had – as I argued earlier – a status not a million miles from that of a language of thought. That is to say, Piaget held in common with the rationalists the aim of explaining the adequacy (or otherwise) of cognition in terms of the way it was structured; and while he did not have the same kind of structuring in mind as did Chomsky, Fodor, and Evans, there is a broad similarity of aim.

There is, in any case, no real need to push the parallel between Piagetian mental structures and those discussed earlier in 1.1. The more urgent question is whether connectionism has the resources to model the structured (in Evans' sense) and systematic (in Fodor's) nature of human cognition. The fact that networks do not perform computations over syntactically composed representations would suggest that they cannot. However this does not worry Elman *et al.* who say that, while Fodor and Pylyshyn (1988) are correct to deny that networks cannot (say) infer 'A' from 'A and B', to require that they should be able to do so if they are to be adequate cognitive models 'seems to reflect a profound misunderstanding of what human cognition is like.' (ibid., p. 103)

Similarly, Andy Clark (1993, p. 227) puts down the rationalists' concern with systematicity to a kind failure of the imagination – a failure to imagine what might lie beneath the language of thought:

> What seems increasingly clear is that the language of thought is, at best, the symbolic problem-solving tip of a large and developmentally extended iceberg. Beneath the symbolic waters, and reaching back across our individual developmental histories, lie the larger, less well-defined shapes of our basic cognitive processes. To understand these is to address the fundamentals of cognition.

Those who agree with this will ascribe my undercurrent (to stick with Clark's oceanic metaphor) of scepticism about the claims of developmental connectionism to no more than (changing the metaphor) the mumblings of a dogmatic slumberer. We will reawaken these big issues in Part 3.

1.3 Pragmatism

At this point it is necessary to say loudly and clearly what rationalists and empiricists hold in common: they both assume that mentality must be explained by reference to our capacities for achieving and manipulating *representations*. Thus, when they debate the need to postulate innate rules and representations they are at least *symmetrically* conflicting over the same basic question. Pragmatists, though, have a different set of explanatory priorities. For them, knowledge and rationality do not have to begin either with a capability for acquiring representations nor with a prior representational repertoire. Rather it begins with what John Dewey (1938, p. 12; original emphasis) called 'ways of action' (to which he added 'sufficiently general as to be properly called *habits*'). These ways of action begin by being 'biological' and by affording only punctate conscious access ('we are aware at most of particular acts and particular consequences') until they evolve into consciousness, with attention to action leading to its control. As they generalise 'we discover that if we draw our inferences in a certain way we shall, all things being equal, get dependable conclusions', until eventually 'the idea of a method of inquiry arises as an articulate expression of the habit that is involved in a class of inferences'.

Here I shall have more to say about the historical background than I did in the case of rationalism and empiricism, on the assumption that the readership will be relatively unfamiliar with it. I shall also, however, work harder, as I go along, to point up the relevance of these ideas to theories of language development, as the relevance emerges less plainly in this case. In the survey I shall contrast the pragmatism of C. S. Peirce (its founder) with that of a major contemporary philosopher, Richard Rorty. The former is marked by an attempt to replace our representationist ideas about the nature of belief with something more sceptical and dynamic and by an essentially Kantian view of knowledge, while in the latter we see a radically nominalist view of human knowledge which seeks to erode our faith in language as the expression of thoughts about an objective universe bleached of theory and 'text'. I also show what a radically pragmatist view of syntax looks like (more Rorty than Peirce) in the hands of a philosopher: the work of Robert Brandom. Finally, I parallel Peirce's pragmatism with Alison Gopnik's 'theory theory' view of mental development.

1.3.1 The historical background

Anybody dipping in to William James's article 'What pragmatism means'[31] might be forgiven for thinking that it is, in fact, a sub-species of the empiricism we have just finished discussing.

> Pragmatism represents a perfectly familiar attitude in philosophy, the empiricist attitude, but it represents it, as it seems to me, both to a more radical and in a less objectionable form from than it has yet assumed. A pragmatist turns his back resolutely and once for all upon a lot of inveterate habits dear to professional philosophers. He turns away from abstraction and insufficiency, from verbal solutions, from bad a priori habits, from fixed principles, closed systems, and pretended absolutes and origins. He turns towards concreteness and adequacy, towards facts, towards action, and towards power. This means the empiricist temper regnant, and the rationalist temper sincerely given up. It means the open air and possibilities of nature, as against dogma, artificiality and the pretence of finality in truth.

And a little later James says: 'It agrees with nominalism for instance, in always appealing to particulars'.

But don't be misled. Pragmatism is not a kind of empiricism, despite the fact that it makes appeals to the deliverances of experience in the way in which rationalism does not. For these appeals *are not made in the name of the empiricist tenet that all our concepts are derived from perceptual experience*. Rather they are appeals to what experience shows us about the results of *doing* something. Accordingly, the meaning of a concept and the truth of a belief are analysed by the pragmatist not through asking whether they represent the world (a reality 'beyond' or 'behind' human habits and conventions – beyond human language) adequately, but by asking about the result of taking this

---

[31] Passage taken from L. Menard (ed.) 1997, pp. 86–97.

concept or belief to be true. (James famously analysed the notion of truth in terms of its 'cash value'.) Perhaps the most important phrase in this James passage is that in which he says that the pragmatist turns 'towards action'. A concept is the concept it is, and has the adequacy it has, in virtue of its practical results. After all, the term 'pragmatism', derives, as he reminds us, from the Greek *pracma*, meaning 'action'.

What pragmatism seeks to do – as pointed out at the start of this section – is to undermine the seeming cogency of the basic goal that rationalism and empiricism share: that of describing the origins of our mental representations. It is a radically different kind of philosophy, a radicalism that is evident from the fact that its principal contemporary exponent, Richard Rorty, takes the view that a truly pragmatist programme will ultimately replace philosophy with something else, with a hermeneutic discipline indistinguishable from literary criticism – sometimes, indeed, indistinguishable from turning one's back on the academy altogether. Indeed James seems to be anticipating this current in the final sentence of the quotation (about the open air and nature). For there is no denying that reading some of the pragmatist texts (Rorty most notably) can be a liberating experience. Menard (1997, pp. xi–xii) captures this, when he writes that it feels to readers 'as if some pressing but vaguely understood obligation has suddenly been lifted from their shoulders, that some final examination for which they could never have been properly prepared had just been cancelled'. Instead of cramming for a future inquisition, we get engaged in something to the immediate point. Instead of knitting our brows over the latest text beamed down from the Chomskyan Olympus or adding another dozen hidden units to see if our language-learning network will generalise to a new data set we do an experiment to see what two-year-olds know about the verb class. As one of the founding fathers of pragmatism, Oliver Wendell-Holmes, put it, while philosophically-based theories and formal methodologies are certainly part of the intellectual wardrobe, they are the dinner jacket and bow tie we instinctively take off when it is time to change the tyres. In 1899 he wrote:[32]

> All the pleasure of life is in general ideas, but all the use of life is in specific solutions – which cannot be reached through generalities any more than a picture can be painted without knowing some rules of method. They are reached by insight, tact and specific knowledge.

Many researchers in developmental psycholinguistics would see these words – summing up the pragmatist stance – as expressing fine advice.

It is evident then that pragmatism has a number of facets. Before I take a bird's-eye view of these – and in order to help the reader track the relevance of the issues they reflect – I will say something of a synoptic nature about pragmatism and about the approach to language development that the pragmatist stance inspires.

1) One consequence of pragmatism's anti-representationalist position is an anti-internalist and anti-individualist (see pp. 7) view of mentality. That is to say, if you swing the intellectual spotlight away from the content of a concept towards its implications for action then you will tend to say that, if there is no useful sense in which concepts can be analysed in terms of what is represented in the individual mind, then they might be analysed in terms of sets of collective practices.

---

32 From L. Menard (ed.) 1997, pp. xxi–xxii.

This is because much of the intellectual action that we engage in – deciding, justifying, and so forth – is social in nature. Thus, the truths inherent in my belief that the stuff that comes out of the tap is 'water' or of my belief that the feeling I get when a cigarette burns me is 'pain' are manifested in terms of how the holding of these beliefs allows my life to go in relation to others. The content of these concepts should be understood in terms of networks of social practices.

2) A consequence of this will be, in turn, a collectivist view of human consciousness and an undermining of the notion of the ego as an entity to be understood as distinct from social experience. As John Dewey and (definitively) G. H. Mead argued, the origins of first-person thoughts are in children's experiences of others in relation to themselves:

> The mere presence of affective experience, of imagery, or organic sensations, does not carry with it consciousness of a self to which these experiences belong. Nor does the unitary character of the response which tends to synthesise our objects of perception convey that same unitary character to the inner experience until the child is able to experience himself as he experiences others.
>
> (G. H. Mead, 1912, reprinted in Menard, 1997, p. 293)

In Rorty this collectivist view of consciousness takes the following form. He poses the traditional question of what is the mark of the mental – in the sense of individuals' reports on their subjective lives as opposed to their judgements of objective fact – and answers 'its incorrigibility'. Incorrigibility is not the same as infallibility; for we might be mistaken when we say that we are 'in pain' or have a 'sanguine' attitude to something. Rather, incorrigibility *is the status that human culture has given to mental reports*: the fact that we allow a person first-person authority on his or her subjective reports is the *socially-grounded rule* for picking out the mental.

3) Pragmatism is the natural bedfellow of Darwinism, so it is no surprise that James and Dewey both tried to reconcile pragmatism with Darwinism by analysing human beings' pursuit of the good and the true as being continuous with the drives and habits of the lower animals (see the quotation from Dewey at the head of this section), and by paralleling biological evolution with cultural evolution. These two ways of viewing human nature spring from a common interest in analysing human competencies in terms of their social functions. Indeed the 'evolutionary psychology' so popular today is thoroughly pragmatist in spirit. What could be more pragmatist than analysing our difficulties with testing rules by looking for counter-instances in terms of our evolved tendency to detect cheaters, and of doing this instead of looking for the rules and representations that subjects actually use?[33]

In Part 4 we will discuss empirical hypotheses and studies that the pragmatist stance has inspired, but for now it would be well to present a summary view of what a pragmatist approach to language development will amount to. Some looking ahead at this point may be useful.

---

[33] I am alluding to Cosmedes and Tooby's (1992) 'evolutionary' account of the Wason Selection task – to be discussed in Part 3. See footnote 4 in Part 3.

1) *Syntax*: A pragmatist theory of language development might regard syntax in one of two ways. The first way would be Piagetian. Piaget famously proposed that syntactic structures develop from structures of action. For example, the embedding of one phrase within a sentence or within a phrase higher on the parse tree derives from the child's ability to embed one action within another, such as embedding the means act of pulling a towel inside the higher-order action of retrieving the out-of-reach toy sitting on its far corner. As we shall be seeing, this approach received some support from the work of Patricia Greenfield (Greenfield, Nelson and Saltzman, 1972). The pragmatist strain in Piaget's theory hardly needs to be spelt out. In fact one of Piaget's earliest (and unpublished) papers was called 'Sketch for a neo-pragmatism' in which he first set down his idea that there is a logic of action.[34] In the second place, a pragmatist theory of language development will ground syntax – unsurprisingly – in pragmatics. Syntax is structure, semantics is meaning, pragmatics is use. But this need not imply that the nature of the first cannot be explained in terms of the exigencies of the last. Where rationalists emphasise the arbitrariness of syntactic rules (something which can go hand in hand with scepticism about theories of syntactic evolution by selective advantage), the pragmatist will say that each bit of syntactic machinery takes the form it does because of the need to communicate effectively. For example, the particular syntactic rules in English that determine how questions can and cannot be framed might become explicable in terms of the need to foreground the semantic 'focus' of the question in such a way that this is rendered plain to the hearer.

2) *Representational agnosticism*: It is not uncommon for linguistic theory to pass without mention in the papers of (what I will be calling) pragmatist students of language development. And while there is certainly a sense in which the pragmatist approach is assuming syntax to be learned by the developing child, connectionist models too receive little or no attention. This is unsurprising, given that at the very core of pragmatism lies the notion that the ideas we have are *not* best explicated in terms of the character of the mental representations that ground them. Similarly, pragmatist students of language development extend this to the assumption that the syntactic capacities expressed in the child's language are not explicable in terms of abstract syntactic representations of which the child is in possession. Accordingly, while it makes sense to ask, within this research programme, whether children generally have (say) the category 'noun' or 'verb' at a certain age, the question is framed in terms of the *processes* through which children have come to bring their language *use* in line with that of adults – bracketing questions about the status of these categories from the point of view of theoretical linguistics. These acquisitional processes are deeply social. The concern with processes – social processes, social goals, social meanings and conventions – is intended to result in a theory that has no essential commitments either to representational nativism or to representational empiricism.

---

[34] For extensive discussion of this idea see Russell (1996).

3) *Social processes*: Where rationalism explicitly downplays the contribution of communicative function and where *empiricists* do so implicitly, pragmatists place them at the very heart of the enterprise. A truly pragmatist student of language development will pull away from the idea that the developing child is coming to be able to express her thoughts in language in so far as these thoughts are taken to be about an objective world set apart from any interests or engagements that humans might have in relation to it; and will reject the idea that speaking enables the child to share the representations of her individual mind with other people. Thinking is, on this view, a fundamentally intersubjective affair; and so we can only understand what children come to do with language in the light of their ability to share social meanings with others. This stress on the intersubjective can be seen at work not only in Mead but also in J. M. Baldwin (who is primarily referred to in histories as an influence on Piaget). Baldwin worked harder than did Mead to ground mental development in shared meaning, although the resulting system does inspire the oxymoronic description 'brilliantly cloudy' (see Russell, 1978, for a thorough assessment of Baldwin's developmental theory).

4) *Darwinism*: This will lead the researcher to look for continuities between the linguistic capacities of children and animals. It does not determine the view that there is nothing special about human communication, only an interest in the comparative question.

1.3.2 Two kinds of pragmatism: from Peirce and from Rorty

I now return to pragmatism as a philosophical movement. The pragmatist's sceptical views about explicating mentality in terms of mental representations deserve at least as much attention as I gave to the rationalist and empiricist worrying-away at the nature and origin of these representations. Readers who suspect that this anti-representationalism is just a piece of ideology – no more than a decision to change vocabulary, focus, and intellectual stance – will, I hope, have their minds changed. Anti-representationism was, in hands of C. S. Peirce, a substantive thesis, which continues to be taken seriously by analytical philosophers today.

That said, there is to be found, in the more modern, Rortyan form of pragmatism at least, a strong ideological strain – a kind of gung-ho nihilism – that needs to be distinguished from the Peircean programme. I'll differentiate these two forms of pragmatism in the next subsection, which should be read with the following two *possibilities* in mind.

1) To the extent that the pragmatist programme of explicating notions like truth and belief in terms of use (rather than representation) is successful, attempts to give a scientific account of linguistic and mental development by assuming the existence of innate formats or by assuming that formats are learned by exploiting statistical regularities in the input until they are represented on the mental network will both be undermined.

2) To the extent that the project of modern, radically nominalist, pragmatism has validity, the distinction between cognitive and linguistic abilities – as we see the distinction drawn by Chomsky – evaporates.

1.3.2 Pragmatism as epistemology and as ideology

William James was the populariser and public champion of pragmatism, but Charles Sanders Peirce was its founder. James introduced the world to pragmatism in a public lecture at Berkeley in 1898 … 'the principle of Peirce, the principle of pragmatism' he said. He was, in fact, doing a favour for an old friend; and for him to do so was characteristic.

Peirce was one of the triumvirate of founding fathers of American psychology and philosophy whose academic career was ruined by a sexual scandal. (The other two were J. B. Watson and J. M. Baldwin.) Indeed, during much of the decade before James' lecture Peirce, on the lam from creditors and assault charges, had been sleeping on the streets of New York City and cadging food from the Century Club before being evicted. (Set beside this, Baldwin's exile in Mexico was Arcadian.) But whether or not Peirce was grateful to James for this notice, he did not approve of what pragmatism had become in James' hands, seeking to distance himself from the alien doctrine by contriving the term 'pragmaticism', 'a term' he said, 'ugly enough to be safe from kidnappers'.

In this section I will distinguish between the Peircean version of pragmatism and later elaborations of the pragmatist doctrine owing to Rorty and derived from James and Dewey rather than from Peirce. One way of drawing this distinction is by saying that Peirce had problems in mind that were recognisably Kantian whereas Rorty repudiates even the kind of inquiry associated with Kant (1787/1933). But before describing what it means to adopt and not to adopt a Kantian approach in this context let us begin with Peirce's non-representational theory of truth as a route towards that distinction.

The two great, competing philosophical theories of truth – the correspondence theory and the coherence theory – are both representational in nature. According to the correspondence theory, a proposition is true if and only if anyone who entertains such a proposition has a mental representation that corresponds in some to-be-explicated way to a situation in the world. In the twentieth century this view has become most strongly associated with the early Wittgenstein, in philosophy, and with Philip Johnson-Laird in psychology (as a theory of reasoning). This theory is realist, in the sense that the existence of objective states of affairs persisting whether or not anybody makes judgements about them is presupposed. The coherence theory is less friendly to common sense. What makes a belief true on this view is not how it corresponds to an extra-mental reality but how it relates to other beliefs: the only thing that can make a belief true is another belief or a network of them. To retain plausibility, coherence theories must assume that mental representations are holistic in the sense that they do not individually have *sui generis* characters of the kind that could correspond to anything extra-mental: that to have a belief is to configure our whole network of beliefs in a certain way. (Note how holism carries a natural threat to LOT in so far as this is an atomistic theory.) If a proposition can be assimilated into this network in such a way as to cohere with other beliefs then it is true; if not, not. Such a theory is anti-realist in so far as it presupposes, at least, scepticism about our being able to bring our thoughts into line with an extra-mental reality; or, at most, denies that there *is* an extra-mental reality. These two theories share the assumption, however, that for a belief to be true it must be – either atomistically or holistically – a *representation* of the right kind.

Peirce's view, by contrast, is non-representationist in the sense that he denies that we will ever achieve a satisfactory analysis of truth if we continue to think of it in terms of the individual's mind being in the right kind of representational state. He does not have to deny that there are such things as mental representations; but he does deny that these are truth bearers essentially. And he begins from a different starting-point from that of the correspondence and coherence theories, by asking about the role that the concept of truth plays in our intellectual life. Truth, he says, is a concept that cannot be prised apart from concepts of belief, assertion, and inquiry.

In one of his earliest and most anthologised papers called 'On the fixation of belief', Peirce argues that a true belief is one that that does not let us down – does not lead to disappointment. Such a belief would not be defeated were inquiry to be pursued as far as it could possibly go. The process of inquiry takes, for Peirce, the following form: it begins with settled belief which is then challenged by unexpected experiences and argument, which leads to the 'irritation' of doubt, which in turn stimulates the thinker to attain a new, settled (or 'fixed') belief. A belief will be judged to be true in so far as it cannot be improved upon by further inquiry. Thus, our concept of truth might be said to be exhausted by the role it plays in inquiry, in the sense that the process of inquiry provides the practical context in which the concept of truth can be rendered coherent.

This view certainly attracted critics, many of whom dismissed it as a piece of psychological generalising masquerading as philosophical analysis. Some pointed out that so much depends upon how we analyse the notion of doubt. In this early paper it seemed to have the character of a psychological itch, with inquiry having the character of scratching – corresponding to what Peirce calls 'a state of satisfaction'. In this vein, Frankfurt (1958, p. 590) objected that if coming to the satisfaction of 'true' belief is a *psychological* affair – that if inquiry is no more than the process of converting doubt into settled belief – then why should we not grant that an individual who 'invited some subtle psychologist or advertising wizard to induce him to believe some proposition' was thereby engaged in an inquiry. But, as Migotti (1999, p. 79) points out, Peirce can be defended here by tightening up the claim that to inquire is to seek to convert doubt into settled belief in the following way: 'To inquire is to seek that settlement of belief that would be found if the pursuit of settled belief were pushed to its indefeasible limit'.

In this way, the possibility of what Frankfurt calls 'capricious' methods of fixing belief are avoided. For it is difficult to imagine somebody whose beliefs were prompted and sustained by non-intellectual causes having the goal of seeking the settlement of inquiry that *would* be found if the pursuit of settled belief were pushed to its limit. For other recent (qualified) defences of Peirce's view of truth and belief see Wiggins (1999), Wright (1999), and Hookway (1995).

If something along the lines of the Peircean analysis of truth can be sustained, the prize will be a theory of truth that does not require extravagant metaphysical commitments to views about the ultimate nature of reality – as do the two main representational theories. Or as Peirce himself put it:

> You only puzzle yourself by talking of this metaphysical 'truth' and metaphysical falsity that you know nothing about. All you have any dealings with are your doubts and beliefs … Your problems would be greatly simplified, if, instead of saying that you know the Truth, you were simply to say that you wanted to attain a state of belief unassailable by doubts.[35]

This deflationary attitude has led to what is known as the disquotational theory of truth in which the schema ['*p*' is true if and only if *p*] is taken to capture the entire content of the predicate 'is true'. This has, in turn, led Rorty to propose that the notion of truth should be jettisoned in favour of that of warranted assertion relative to a particular group of inquirers. In the wake of truth, concepts like validity and reason also dissolve, and, in so far as we operate with a concept of objectivity, this will come to mean intersubjectivity or (Rorty's term) 'solidarity'.

This is, needless to say, an anti-metaphysical route – if not an anti-philosophical one; but it was not Peirce's route. Peirce did not found the form of pragmatism that holds that the limit of human language marks the limit of reality. In fact he endeavoured to marry a form of realism – though not of the kind offered by correspondence theories of truth – with the pragmatist view of truth understood as the fixation of belief as the end of inquiry. As Christopher Hookway expresses it in his book on Peirce:

> He appears to be concerned with familiar problems about truth and verification, attempting to reconcile the view that reality has an objective character which is independent of our view of it with the claim that this character is available to us if we conduct our inquiries efficiently or correctly.
>
> (Hookway, 1985, p. 1)

Migotti (1999) calls these the 'independence' and the 'accessibility' thesis:

1) Independence from thought: truth is independent from thought in the sense that 'it is so, whether you or I or anybody think it is so or not … [and] no matter if there be an overwhelming vote against it' (Peirce, 1868, quoted in Migotti, 1999, p. 89).

2) Accessible to thought: this is so in so far as honest inquiry, carried out sufficiently far, is fated to arrive at truth. 'Fated' was in fact the term Peirce used:

> Fate means that which is sure to come true, and can nohow be avoided. It is a superstition to suppose that certain sorts of event are ever fated, and it is another to suppose that the word fate can never be freed from its superstitious taint.
>
> Quoted in Migotti (1999, p. 90)

But before we enter too far into the metaphysical jungle, let us return to developmental base camp for a while to consider a feature of Pierce's form of realism. Peirce's ideas about the development of selfhood in children illustrate this neatly: reality is that which constrains the nature of our concepts by being that which is responsible for the element of refractoriness in our experience. It is, indeed a form of constructivism, familiar from the work of Baldwin and Piaget (Russell, 1996, Part 3) Peirce (1868, quoted in Migotti, 1999, p. 88) gives the following example.

....

[35] Quoted from Misak (1999, p. 1).

> A child hears it said that the stove is hot. But it is not, he says; and indeed, that central body (which it finds especially important) is not touching it, and only what that touches is hot or cold. But he touches it, and finds the testimony confirmed in a striking way. Thus he becomes aware of ignorance, and it is necessary to suppose a self in which this ignorance can inhere.

As Migotti (1999, p. 87) insightfully says, this claim that the development of a conception of self depends upon, as Peirce put it, drawing distinctions between 'my believing that *p*' and 'its being the case that *p*' bears a strong resemblance to the claim that children acquire a 'theory of mind' (in the sense of an explicit conception of their own and others' mental states as being representations of reality[36]) when they gain a conception of false belief (Wimmer and Perner, 1983).

Thus refreshed, we can strike on to higher ground: a discussion of the sense in which Peirce's position was Kantian.

One might (ahistorically!) regard Kant as constructing a metaphysical cure for the maladies inherent in correspondence and coherence theories of truth. (The cliché is that Kant attempted to reconcile empiricism and rationalism; and, to the extent that correspondence theories are empiricist in nature and coherence theories are rationalist, this is a way of spinning that cliché.)

Correspondence theories of truth founder in so far as they give us no warrant for saying that there is a mind-external world to which our judgements can or cannot correspond. How can this be known if we only have our faculty of judgement itself to go by? Coherence theories have the opposite kind of difficulty: a lack of faith in mind-external reality. In coherence theories of truth there is no elbow-room for the possibility that while some propositions may cohere wonderfully with our network of beliefs, our network as a whole might be misrepresenting the way things really are. Kant sought to avoid being impaled on the horns of this dilemma by distinguishing between two kinds of reality: a noumenal reality which we posit but which is ultimately unknowable by us (the world of God and the 'thing in itself'), and phenomenal reality which is the reality that we confront in our everyday experience.

Kant, then, asked about *the form that our phenomenology had to possess if it was to be that of a mind-external world*. Broadly speaking, he argued that judgements must possess a certain kind of logical form, which he described in his table of 'judgements': four triads of features. For example, a judgement has a given 'quantity' (either universal, particular, or singular), and it will express a 'relation' (categorical, hypothetical or disjunctive). From the judgements, Kant was able to 'deduce' the fundamental 'categories' of thought. (A further 'base-camp' thought, by the way: drawing a parallel between this Kantian project and Piaget's project of explicating mental development in terms of logico-mathematical 'groupings' and 'INCR' groups should not be resisted.)

These forms of thought were a priori, in the sense of being logically necessary for there to be any experience at all, while they are used in *synthesising* the 'manifold'

---

[36] This 'theory' is distinct from the one that Peirce opposed: that the notion of *truth* should be analysed in terms of a representation of reality.

(sensory input) to yield objective experience so that the judgements we make in using the categories are *synthetic* – synthetic a priori then. A priori does not mean, for Kant, innate.[37] Rather, the categories are constitutive of objective experience, or presupposed by it. Our knowledge of the categories is not knowledge of empirical fact, but knowledge of them is gained when we are occupied not so much with objects as with the mode of our knowledge of objects in so far as this mode of knowledge is to be possible a priori (Kant, 1933/1787, B. 25). This is, for Kant, transcendental knowledge: knowledge about the necessary forms of objective experience.

Peirce was a Kantian in the sense that he too constructed a system of judgements and deduced categories of experience from these; although he was critical of Kant's system of categories and developed his own (Hookway, 1985, chapter 3). But what is more to the present point is that in some respects Kant anticipated Peirce's pragmatism. He did so in so far as he regarded the synthesising activity of the mind as something that yields a practical result (experience as objective and coherent) but which does not *represent reality* – whose ultimate nature is noumenal. The categories were not taken to be *that which we have to employ if we are to possess a coherent phenomenology.*

In short, what the synthetic a priori yields is an heuristic system for giving experience a form as of a mind-external reality. Moreover, there are certain 'ideals', for Kant, that are a priori notions to which nothing in experience can correspond and whose application is justified pragmatically, such as the concept of one's own mind. In this regard, it is very useful

> to connect all appearances, actions, and the receptivity of the mind … as if it were a simple substance, which endowed with personal identity (at least during life) permanently exists, while its states, to which those of the body belong only as external conditions continuously change.
>
> (Kant, quoted in Körner, 1955)

Accordingly, we sustain a mental life by treating certain concepts which may in fact be empty as if they were applicable. 'We should,' writes Körner, 'then be methodological pragmatists. We might easily then be led to go further and consider the *usefulness of a concept as the criterion of its applicability*. Our pragmatism would then be 'epistemological or metaphysical' (1955, p. 124; emphasis added) before going on to describe Peirce's debt to Kant. Some commentaries have claimed that Peirce took the term 'pragmatic' from Kant's use of the term *pragmatisch* to refer to rules of thought that have their application in experience.[38]

Kant's pragmatism is also in evidence in his remarks on religion. Knowledge of God is unattainable because, if He exists, He must exist in the noumenal world; while this should not weaken our religious faith. Kant's actual position on religious

---

[37] Strawson (1966) describes a 'crude innatist psychology' which can be – illegitimately – derived from Kant.

[38] It seems, however, that Kant reserved the actual term *pragmatisch* to refer to sanctions that concern 'the general welfare' rather than the laws of natural science, on the one hand, and of morality on the other. I am grateful to Edward Craig for pointing this out and for his translations.

faith is much debated, but essentially he held that we have good reason to believe in God, because certain features of human nature and human motivation make it more or less mandatory.[39] There is a pragmatist strain in this, in the sense of reading 'upwards' from human life to transcendent reality, rather than the other way round; while it is a far cry from James' full-bloodedly pragmatist view that we should ask not whether God exists but what difference to our lives believing in Him would bring about.

Peirce himself summed up his philosophy by saying that it was Kant 'without the thing-in-itself'. That is to say he tried to further Kant's project of describing what was practically necessary for our mental life to be as it is and for our concepts to be as they are while jettisoning reference to a noumenal, mind-independent reality.

Rorty would say that this is too soggy a position, reflecting a thoroughly un-pragmatist failure to see through our inquiry to a settled end. If the only sense that can be made of the active, subjective capacities by which the thinker structures, for cognitive use, the information that the world provides is an as-if sense, and if the notion of an objective but ultimately unknowable world is infinitely problematic, then we should stick to our pragmatist guns and jettison the notion of objective reality altogether, accepting that reality is nothing beyond the community of human practices. Moreover, the Kantian and the Peircean 'categories' should not be regarded as abstract necessities for adequate cognition but rather as an outgrowth of human linguistic conventions.[40] They are nothing beyond talk and text.

That said, while Rorty rejects the Kantian programme there is a distinction owing to Kant upon which Rorty's pragmatism entirely depends: the distinction between the causation of beliefs by the world and their justification by reference to norms of validity, rationality, and so forth. For Rorty, all our beliefs are caused by the environment and none can be justified from the vantage point of pure reason. There is no doxastic higher ground, within the system of human beliefs thus caused, from which someone might exercise epistemic authority over the correctness of beliefs: they simply are the beliefs we have been caused to have. Beliefs are regarded as natural phenomena; and Rorty's position is therefore a radical form of naturalism. Languages are tools that creatures use to live their lives, and the environment causally configures our belief system entirely through the medium of language, as there is no other: 'The world can, once we have programmed ourselves with language, cause us to hold beliefs' (Rorty, 1982). Robert Brandom (2000, p. xiv) comments on this:

> And to understand the sense in which we are 'in touch with reality' all we need to understand is that causal contact with the world, the sort of contact describable in the language of afferent and efferent physiology (underlying perception and action), in the context of an account of how we are (naturally) wired up and (socially) trained ... notions of authority and responsibility don't get a grip until we are already in the conceptual space opened up by the applicability of a vocabulary.

---

[39] I am grateful to Edward Craig for elucidation on this point.

[40] Peirce's categories had more linguistic character than Kant's: they were concerned with such things as signs and predication.

It goes without saying that Rorty's position is at least as nominalist as it is naturalist – nominalist in so far as he assumes that everything we choose to say about reality is said within a certain vocabulary and cannot by evaluated from any perspective outside of that vocabulary. He cites with approval Hans-Georg Gadamer's epigram 'Being that can be understood is language'[41] (*Sein, das verstanden werden kann, ist Sprache*), adding that the essence of nominalism is the claim that 'no description of an object is more true of the nature of that object than any other'. To take this view is, for Rorty, to jettison a number of venerable distinctions and metaphors:

1) The distinction between how an object is 'for us' and 'in itself' – and thus the notion of 'privileged descriptions'. This distinction 'is misleading as it suggests, as does the correspondence theory of truth, that words can be checked against non-words in order to find out which words are adequate to the world'.

2) The metaphor of 'moving closer' to an understanding of reality through science and philosophy.

3) The 'phallocentric' metaphor of depth. 'The deeper and more penetrating our understanding of something, so the story goes, the further we are from appearance and the closer to reality'.

4) The metaphysical distinction between appearance and reality itself.

5) Replacing the metaphor of depth by one of breadth, resulting in the view that the wider the range of descriptions we have the more we know.

6) The notion that 'reason' and 'imagination' describe distinct and special relations to reality.

7) Abandoning 'the scientistic, problem-solving, model of philosophical activity with which Kant has burdened our discipline'.

In the Rortyan scheme of things we will abandon reverence for science as a discipline that can deliver us messages from the world as it is, untainted by human discourse and interests, because science is itself just another mode of discourse. Does this not mean that any old mode of discourse is as good as any other – that no forms of intellectual activity are inherently admirable and productive of wisdom? Not really. Rorty has spoken of the central role of 'the strong poet'.[42] He is not very explicit on this point, but I take him to mean poets who demonstrate in their work a conscious acknowledgement that no aspect of human life is fundamental to or more serious than any other (such as John Ashbery) or who exploit in the verse tensions between different modes of discourse (scientific/personal; microscopic/astronomic; biological/epistemic) (such as J. H. Prynne).

Having reached this point we might seem to have travelled very far away from the study of language and thought development. But we have not. This is so for two reasons – the second being much more important for our purposes than the first.

---

[41] From the *London Review of Books*, 16 March 2000. All subsequent quotations on this page from Rorty will be from that piece, unless otherwise stated.

[42] Tanner Lectures, Clare Hall, Cambridge, 1992.

In the first place, Rorty himself – it is inevitable from his position – certainly does not have a neutral position on how mental and linguistic development take place.

> I should be unperturbed if the offers currently made by the human sciences were withdrawn: if Chomsky's universalistic ideas about communicative competence were repudiated by a connectionist revolution in artificial intelligence, if Piaget's … empirical results proved to be unduplicatable, and so on.
>
> (Rorty, 2000, p. 14)

Later (p. 29) he expands on the connectionism comment; and I think that this quotation should be read in the light of his view that beliefs are naturalistically caused rather than embedded in formal, rational structures:

> The 'MIT' notion, associated with Chomsky and Fodor, of 'communicative competence' is gradually being displaced, within the field of artificial intelligence, by the 'connectionist' view favoured by those who see the brain as containing no hard-wired flow-chart of the sort constructed by 'cognitivist' programmers. Connectionists urge that the only biologically universal structures to be found in the brain are ones which cannot be described in terms of flow-charts labelled with the names of 'natural kinds' of things and words. So the notion of 'communicative competence', as something common to all human linguistic communities, drops out in favour of the notion of 'enough neural connections to permit the organism to be made into a language user'.

One detects here the undercurrent that facts about which view is currently in favour or out of favour are sufficiently significant to foreclose further thought about which views should or should not be favoured.

In the second place – and central to the issues that this book is airing – if nominalism as radical as the Rortyan kind is embraced, then the Chomskyan assumption that there is thought (the 'conceptual-intentional' systems) that is distinct from the linguistic system and that interfaces with it will be deemed to be incoherent. Thought is a system of linguistic judgements caused to be as it is by the environment – the social environment especially.

But it is now time to consider in detail, rather than at a near-metaphysical level of abstraction, what philosophically pragmatist approaches to language look like. We will consider the work of Robert Brandom.[43]

1.3.3 A recent pragmatist approach to syntax by Robert Brandom

A thoroughly pragmatist account of language will reject the following picture of the relationship between natural language and thought – one that is cognate to the rationalist position. Thought is structured/systematic, and partly in virtue of this fact we are able to represent the world mentally in a pre- or non-linguistic mode. Thoughts are that which natural language expresses. For something to be a thought, it must contain a representational element; and indeed the fundamental function of thinking is to construct representations – perhaps even 'theories' – of reality. No matter how many anomalies a representationist view of mind gives rise to,[44]

----

[43] At least one philosopher, friendly to connectionism, has applauded this view of language, as against the Chomskyan – van Gelder (1990).

[44] I am thinking of the Wittgensteinean point that representations do not come complete with their interpretations. This is discussed, in relation to rule-following in 3.2, below.

it is the only one we've got and we are stuck with it. If we give up on the notion of representation we must also abandon the notion of truth. One thing the linguistic system does is interface with the cognitive systems, and so it must be understood as a system designed to expedite the expression of mental representations in this public medium. The syntax of natural language provides armatures around which 'publicisable' thoughts can be constructed; and in so far as these armatures support possible thoughts with content, language too is fundamentally representational. None of the pragmatic functions of language – joking, fantasising, promising, phatic forms, and so forth – would be possible unless language had this representational character. Partly for this reason, we can regard the sentences of a particular language as having a canonical form (e.g., subject–verb–object in the case of English), a form that can be regarded as a canonical representational format. The price of regarding the thought–language relationship in this way is subscription to the LOT doctrine – or to something like it. For unless we accept that thought is (a) symbolic and (b) systematic the prospects are dim for explaining how it can interface with language.

In his substantial and ambitious book *Making it explicit* (1994) Robert Brandom paints an alternative picture to this one, using all the colours in the pragmatist paintbox. He does not attempt to undermine the Chomsky-Fodor position by directly confronting it; indeed in his 716 pages Chomsky only gets one brief and noncommittal mention. Instead, Brandom begins from an entirely different point from Chomsky in order to build up an account of even the compositional nature of language in pragmatist terms.

Where the rationalist begins with the mind as a device for constructing representations and builds a theory of language on this basis, Brandom begins with language as a fundamentally social process and tries to show how our talk about representations, conceptual contents, propositional attitudes and truth are a secondary product of this. The implicit and fundamental character of language, he argues, consists of social performances – speech acts of asserting, giving and demanding reasons, expressing commitment to certain consequences of our assertions and the audience being entitled to those commitments. There is a system of implicit norms of what can and cannot be done in language which he calls deontic – i.e., related to the obligations of speakers and hearers, to what the former ought to do and ought to be committed to and to what the latter are entitled to expect. Representation talk is really the second-order and explicit realisation of these pragmatic processes. There are no representational primitives.

Before giving a brief description of Brandom's attempt to account for the compositional nature of language, using these materials, and of how he describes this process of 'becoming explicit', we need to take account of his so-called deontic scorekeeping model of pragmatics.

> Competent linguistic practioners keep track of their own and each other's commitments and entitlements. They are (we are) *deontic scorekeepers*. Speech acts, paradigmatically assertions, alter the deontic score, they change what commitments and entitlements it is appropriate to attribute, not just to the one producing the speech act, but also to those to whom it is addressed.

> (Brandom, 1994, p. 142; original italics)

Brandom tends not to illustrate his claims with examples, so I have constructed this one.

MARY: {*He is entitled to an acknowlegement of my being late.*}

Sorry I'm late.

JOHN: {*I am entitled to an explanation.*}

What happened?

MARY: The train was late.

{*I am committed to having travelled by train.*}

JOHN: {*I am entitled to the reason why she came by train when she had earlier committed to coming by car.*}

Why didn't you come by car?

MARY: This panic-buying of petrol. Too much risk.

{*I am committed to there being long tailbacks outside petrol stations, to various other scenarios, and to the journey being too long to undertake on a single tank.*}

JOHN: Of course.

{*This commits me to the petrol crisis being sufficiently grave to warrant that behaviour.*}

More simply, saying that 'John's car is red' commits the speaker to John's car being coloured, while entitling the hearer to an account of why he is being told that fact.

We can also see this in play in the kind of conversations in which young children engage. A real conversation this time:[45]

As mother pours water on Sarah's head...

SARAH (2;11): What that? What you doing?

MOTHER: I put some water on your head.

SARAH: {*She is committed to the view that pouring water onto heads is permissible.*}

I pour you some.

MOTHER: No I don't want any.

SARAH: {*I am entitled to an explanation for her making herself an exception.*}

Why?

MOTHER: Because I don't like to get wet.

SARAH: Huh? Don't like ... go wet ... swim? You want you swim.

{*She is still committed to giving a reason, because in some circumstances she is happy to get her hair wet.*}

On this view then, what lies beneath the level of the sentence is the speech act, with the paradigmatic form of speech act being the assertion. Moreover, subsentential

---

45   From Bartsch and Wellman (1995, p. 127).

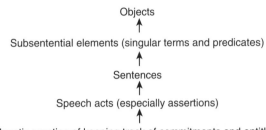

Objects

↑

Subsentential elements (singular terms and predicates)

↑

Sentences

↑

Speech acts (especially assertions)

↑

The deontic practice of keeping track of commitments and entitlements

[where ↑ = grounded by]

Figure 1.6 A schematic representation of Brandom's view of how language and reference are grounded in 'deonotic storekeeping'.

elements as such singular terms[46] only exist in virtue of the sentence, which is coupled to the nominalist assumption that the objects to which the singular terms refer can only be conceptualised by way of singular terms see Figure 1.6. Does Brandom's account have the resources to explain the way in which the subsentential elements depend upon the sentences and these upon the speech act?

His account is a traditional one at least in the sense that it is based, as was that of Frege and of modern theoretical linguistics, on the notion of substitution.

> Two subsentential expressions belong to the same syntactic or grammatical category just in case no well-formed sentence (expression that can be used to perform one of the fundamental kinds of speech act) in which the one occurs can be turned into something that is not a sentence merely by substituting the other for it.

(For example, the sentence 'The cat escaped my attention' cannot be changed into a syntactically ill-formed sentence if any noun is substituted for 'the cat', and any transitive verb is substituted for 'escaped', and so forth. This is, as we shall see in Part 2, a good acid test for whether two terms belong to the same syntactic class.) To continue the quotation:

> Two subsentential expressions of the same grammatical category share a semantic content just in case substituting one for the other *preserves the pragmatic potential* of the sentences in which they occur.

(Brandom 1994, p. 368; emphasis added)

There is nothing particularly noteworthy about this view, as applied to syntax. But what is distinctive to Brandom's account is that he asks the (what he takes to be deeper) question of why there are any subsentential expressions at all. He answers that without them the *implicit commitment-makings described above could never be made explicit*. To explain. Brandom draws a distinction between the singular terms which can be substituted and the sentence frame – the 'remainder' – into and from which they are substituted. Thus, we substitute 'the dog' for 'the cat' in 'The cat escaped', with the frame being 'α escaped'. What remains, then, are predicates.

---

[46] Meaning words for objects broadly construed - including events, abstract entities, emotions etc.

Predicates also can be substituted; but with different consequences for meaning, as we shall see. With regard to singular terms, if meaning and 'pragmatic potential' are to be preserved over substitution then the substitution will be symmetrical if the terms refer to the same object; but this is not guaranteed in the case of predicates because predicates refer to properties, relations, and actions, not to objects. Thus, if 'Rex' and 'John's pet' co-refer, the latter can be substituted for the former and vice versa in the sentence 'α is a dog' with no effect on the meaning. In the case of predicates like 'is a dog', however, the substitution may only work in one direction because different predicates have different breadths of reference: the substitution relationship is asymmetrical. For example, in the sentence 'John's pet is a dog', one can substitute 'is a mammal' and retain the meaning. However if we tried to do this the other way round and substituted '– is a dog' for '– is a mammal' we might end up with a false sentence; because John's pet might refer to a cat in the sentence 'John's pet is a mammal'.

This is regarded by Brandom as a difference between two kinds of *commitment*; and, because of this, the notion of symmetrical commitment to substitution is taken to be logically prior (this is not, in fact, how Brandom expresses it) to the notion of two singular terms co-referring. It is part of his pragmatist strategy to explicate the idea of reference to objects not in terms of a relation between a representing mind and a mind-external object, but rather in terms of whether a community of language users applies the symmetrical commitment principle. Similarly, a term is a predicate, not if it refers to a property, relation, process or state, but if the community of language users sets restrictions on substitution such that only the asymmetrical kind is possible. Talk about co-reference and the scope of predicates is a 'making explicit' of these different kinds of commitment.

There is a further sense in which the existence of subsentential expressions is supposed to be explicable in terms of their roles in rendering explicit the kinds of pragmatic commitments and entitlements that are primary and implicit – according to Brandom. He discusses the role of logical operators like the conditional (if … then …) and negation. To return to the example just used, a speaker who says 'Rex is a dog' is implicitly committing himself to the claim that a Rex is a mammal; whereas his saying 'John's pet is a mammal' is not to commit oneself implicitly to the claim that it is a dog, though certain claims about the animal's physiology are implicitly being made. It is clear that these claims could never be rendered explicit unless (a) singular terms and predicates were made the focus of the assertions and (b) logical operators were employed. Thus, what underlies the implicit commitment in the first sense is 'if α is a dog then α is a mammal' (α = the singular term and 'is a mammal' the predicate) and in the second 'α's being a mammal does not entail it's being a dog'. For Brandom, it is the existence of logical operators that carves out singular terms and predicates as tokens in the social process of giving and asking for reasons.

In all this, recall, Brandom is not only trying to explain in pragmatist terms how subsentential expressions function within sentences, but is asking 'Why are there singular terms at all, given that pragmatic commitments and entitlements could be made without them?' This in turn, as we have seen, narrows to the question of why there are the kind of symmetrical and asymmetrical commitments described above.

We now have, then, the answer:

> The strategy pursued in answer to this question is to focus on the use of logical vocabulary to permit the explicit expression, as the content of sentences, of relations among sentences that are partly constitutive of their being contentful. To say that subsentential expressions are used by a community as substituted-for and substitution-structural frames is to say that the contents conferred by the practices of the community on the sentences in which those expressions have primary occurrence are related systematically to one another in such a way that they can be exhibited as products of contents associated with the subsentential expressions, according to a standard substitutional structure.
>
> (Brandom 1994, p. 401)

Whatever else this illustrates, it certainly illustrates how the pragmatist feels duty bound to conceptualise the compositional machinery of human language not in terms of some I-represented (internal, individual) formal knowledge but in terms of entirely external, collective practices. In Brandom's case it is the practice of keeping the score of commitments and entitlements.

It is also worth considering how Brandom is able to explicate, in terms of the social tally of commitments and entitlements, a linguistic idiom whose entire point is the rendering explicit of how subsentential elements (complement phrases in this case) capture how an individual is representing reality. This is the idiom of *propositional attitude* sentences, sentences in which we refer to the individual's mental orientation to a content, whose precise verbal expression tells how reality is being represented by the individual. In sentences of this kind there can be no symmetrical substitution of singular terms, because this can alter the sentence's truth value. Indeed lack of such substitutability is their logical hallmark. To explain.

1) Jocasta was the wife of Oedipus

2) Oedipus's mother was the wife of Oedipus.

In these sentences, symmetrical substitution of the singular terms 'Jocasta' and 'Oedipus's mother' does not affect the truth value of the sentences. However, if we substituted the latter for the former in the following sentence the sentence would be judged to be false.

3) Oedipus thought that Jocasta was the wife of Oedipus.

4) Oedipus thought that Oedipus's mother was the wife of Oedipus.

Sentence (4) would naturally be taken to be false because Oedipus did not represent Jocasta under that description – as he did not know she was his mother. So-called 'intensional' (sic) or 'referentially opaque' contexts of this kind are created by all mental verbs (hope, expect, etc.,) in addition to 'think'; and they can also be created in other ways.[47]

I say that sentence (4) 'would naturally be taken to be false' rather than 'is false', because there is a reading of it under which it would be true. The sentence is in fact true as a description of the object that the sentence is about, just as long as we don't think of that object (Jocasta) under any particular description. This is called a *de re* (literally 'about the thing') or 'extensional' reading; and it goes without saying that

---

47 See Fauconnier (1985) on these.

the very existence of such readings is a challenge to the nominalism espoused within the pragmatist account – one reason why Brandom spends so long on this topic, perhaps. Sentence (4) is, however, intensionally false or *de dicto* (literally 'of the saying'): it must be judged to be false if is reporting a sentence ('My mother is my wife') to which the individual would assent.

What then would be a deontic scorekeeping account of *de re* and *de dicto* contexts? In brief, they are taken to illustrate ways in which the community of language users makes explicit the different kinds of doxastic (= about beliefs) commitments attributed to people by speakers. If the belief is ascribed to Oedipus that Jocasta is his wife then the content of the *de dicto* 'that' clause 'is limited to what, according to the ascriber, the one to whom the commitment is ascribed would (or in a strong sense should) acknowledge as an expression of what the individual is committed to' (Brandom 1994, p. 506).

It is possible, however, to force a *de re* reading of the belief by expressing it in the following way: 'Oedipus believes of his mother that she is his wife' or 'Oedipus's belief regarding Jocasta being his wife is about his mother'. In this case it is the ascriber who endorses his *own* commitment to the possibility of the symmetrical substitution of 'Jocasta' and 'Oedipus's mother'. But with regards to the target of the ascription:

> The part of the content specification that appears within the scope of the *de re* 'of' includes what, according to the ascriber of the commitment, but not necessarily according to the one to whom it is ascribed, is acknowledged as an expression of what the target of the ascription is committed to.
>
> (Brandom, 1994, p. 507)

It renders explicit the fact that commitments may be unwitting, and quarantines these from the normal case in which speakers know (whether or not their locutions make this explicit) what they are committed to.

How then is the nominalist purity of the pragmatist view of language supposed to be retained for *de re* contexts? It is done so by assuming that *de re* locutions and interpretations of ambiguous locutions are not in fact an attempt to say what is the case in the mind-external universe irrespective of how it is talked about (per impossibile for the pragmatist!), but are instead ways of saying what dicta the target of an ascription is committed to willy nilly. And so everything can stay safely within the hermenuetic circle of social processes.

On Brandom's analysis, the *de re* reading of an intentional context might be thought to be the more complex of the two, given that it involves more qualification of the ascriptions to its target. Strange then that children move – around age 6 – from preferring *de re* readings to preferring *de dicto* ones, of contexts that adults interpret *de dicto* (Russell, 1987a, for the original demonstration[48]).

On the subject of developmental implications, it might seem that we have travelled very far from such concerns. But in fact, as Brandom points out, the view that the primary linguistic unit is the sentence used as a speech act does suggest a developmental account of how children break into language as a

---

[48] This might suggest, *pace* Pragmatism, that it is the real-world referential reading that we find the more natural, rather than one in terms of speech events.

productive system consisting of subunits that can be combined in an infinity of ways. Indeed, immediately after his brief mention of Chomsky's position, Brandom considers how one might explain language learners' ability to use and understand novel sentences if their basic unit of understanding is the sentence as yet unanalysed into singular terms and predicates – the fact of what he calls 'projection' and Chomsky calls 'creativity'. I shall quote what he says in full because it provides a good illustration of the developmental position one is likely to adopt – perhaps is forced into – if one's premises are thoroughly pragmatist: if, that is, one rejects the idea that what determines linguistic creativity is the possession (internalist, individualist representation) of formal (not socially-grounded) rules.

> A two-stage compositional strategy for the explanation of projection would take it that what is settled by properties of use governing the smaller, sample set of sentences, which is projected, is the correct use of the subsentential components into which they can be analysed or decomposed. The correct use of these components is then to be understood as determining the correct use also of further combinations of them into novel sentences. The linguistic community determines the correct use of some sentences, and thereby of the words they involve, and so determines the correct use of the rest of the sentences that can be expressed using these words. *By learning to use a relatively small initial sample of sentences, the individual learns to use the words they involve and thereby can learn to use all the sentences that can be formed out of those words by recombining them.*

(Brandom, 1994, p. 366; emphasis added)

As Brandom gives no examples of this process, one can only guess at how this is supposed to work in practice. My reading of it is that the learner is assumed to be able to note the recurrence of certain singular terms and predicates both across different sentences and across different contexts. In any event, one is irresistibly reminded here of the view of researchers, such as Julian Pine (see 4.3.3), who argue that the child begins by using unanalysed strings of words, which gradually become decomposed into elements. For example, she might use 'Assa [that's a] clever girl' but never use any of the component words in the company of other words.

Brandom's theory can, then, be seen to have developmental implications. But how convincing is it as an alternative to representationalist views of language – whether rationalist or empiricist? My summary of the theory has doubtless done some violence to its subtleties, and it has certainly failed to capture its full sweep, but it will be evident from it that rationalists and empiricists must still feel entitled to an account of how asserting rather than representing can be foundational when there can be representings without assertings but not assertings without representings (the relation is asymmetrical). Moreover, the notion of syntactic well-formedness remains unanalysed within the theory, while meat-and-potatoes syntactic properties such as phrase structure and agreement are not even touched upon.

1.3.4 Pragmatism within contemporary developmental theory – one Peircean legacy

If you are a developmental psychologist who, following Peirce, wishes to replace the conception of coming to believe as bringing one's mental representations into line with a mind-independent reality with that of a process of continuous inquiry in which something is believed only to the extent of its having survived ever-applicable doubt, and in which a state of undefeasible belief settlement is not achievable, then you will likely be a subscriber to the 'theory theory' view of cognitive development. This position is most strongly associated with Alison Gopnik.

According to the theory theory (TT), children develop their everyday knowledge of the world by using the same cognitive devices that adults use when they do science. Like the theories of scientists, children's theories are abstract and coherent systems consisting of causal entities and rules. Children regard their theories as being infinitely revisable and replace them when their predictions are falsified. This retains, of course, Peirce's dynamic, open-ended picture of knowledge acquisition.

This approach has been applied across many domains of development, even to object permanence (Gopnik and Meltzoff, 1997). But paradoxically, while Gopnik (2003, p. 242) calls TT one of the 'empiricist alternatives' to nativism she notes that 'We have suggested, in particular, *that infants are born with initial innate theories*, and that they begin revising these theories even in infancy itself' (ibid, p. 241; emphasis added). (Ceasing to make the A-not-B error in object search is taken to be the outcome of a theoretical advance.) (See Gopnik and Meltzoff, 1997, p. 51.) But the paradox is resolved thus. First, she claims that 'the very patterns of representation that occur can alter the representational system itself. This is what makes theory formation a kind of learning.' In other words, starting theories – indeed later ones too – are like ladders that can be thrown away. 'Eventually,' she writes, 'we may end up with a system with a completely new set of representations and a completely different set of relations between inputs and representations than the system we started out with' (Gopnik, 2003, p. 241). Borrowing a metaphor from Neurath's, she sees human knowledge as being like a boat that we perpetually have to keep rebuilding as we sail it, so that we (child and scientist) may end up with not a single plank or rivet from the original structure. Second, the difference between TT's nativism and the Chomskyan kind is that the former is *starting-state nativism* as contrasted with Chomsky's 'classical' nativism in which the end state of the system is innately represented in its essentials.

But what makes the child-scientist analogy so compelling for Gopnik? It is that scientific theory formation is a '*demonstration proof* that there are learning mechanisms in the universe powerful enough to generate the kinds of representations we want from the kinds of input we know we have' (Gopnik, 2003, p. 245; emphasis added). In other words, scientific advances constitute evidence against classical nativism. For nobody (she jabs: 'except perhaps Jerry Fodor') would say that scientific theories are innately determined and triggered by the evidence.

Setting to one side questions about how fruitful the child-scientist analogy is when applied to general cognitive development (Harris, 1994, for a sceptical assessment) does it work at all plausibly in the case of syntax? 'It is', Gopnik accepts, 'possible that syntax is simply not the sort of thing you can have theories about' (ibid., p. 251) essentially because syntactic representations do not represent nature: there is 'nothing out there' (p. 251) that representations are representations of.[49] But this, she says, will come as cold comfort to Chomskyans because the special status of syntactic knowledge tells us that it is not really knowledge at all, at least in the following sense: it is more like 'certain kinds of social abilities, or perhaps motor abilities, or musical abilities, than scientific knowledge of our everyday understanding of the world' (ibid., p. 251).

Gopnik does not, in fact, point up the Peircean nature of TT. Chomsky however, does (Chomsky, 2003). He himself posited the so-called 'science forming faculty' or SFF some time ago (Chomsky, 1968). And so with regard to TT – which claims that SFF is also responsible for cognitive development – Chomsky says 'I have no opinion, lacking relevant information about SFF (hence about TT)' (Chomsky, 2003, p. 322). That is to say, the nature of the mental processes responsible for scientific hypothesis-testing are essentially unknown to us, so what TT is doing is seeking to explain something about which we know at least a little (cognitive development) in terms of something about which we know next to nothing. Chomsky then reminds us that the classic model of SFF is Peirce's notion of abduction, which he tended to equate with a 'guessing instinct' that provides us with hypotheses to test. Peirce recognised that abduction is a mystery; and recall that in 1.1.6 we saw the consequences for the CTM of Fodor's parallel recognition.

> As far as I can see, TT adopts the Peircean framework with no substantive change, except to hold that these capacities suffice to account for cognitive development generally, a conclusion that cannot be evaluated until the mysteries of abduction are unravelled.
>
> (Chomsky, 2003, p. 323)

1.4 Taking stock

Despite the numerous twists and turns and undergrowths of detail, I hope certain themes have emerged on the resources that these three ways of doing psychology have for explaining language development.

The resources on display within rationalism are rich and well-adapted in fairly obvious ways. For it is, after all, the formal structure of human knowledge that rationalism emphasises, and it is formal structure that is definitive of syntax. But where rationalism is rich in form and formalisms it is poor in psychological mechanism. It might be thought that Chomsky's linguistic theory posits mechanisms aplenty; but these are not of course mechanisms of information processing (relegated to the 'performance systems'), but are formally necessary steps in the characterisation of competence (or the I-language). For many years (e.g., Johnson-Laird, 1977) however, psychologists have been objecting that psycholinguistics should not be the handmaiden of theoretical linguistics but that it should proceed from known psychological mechanisms upwards, being constrained or inspired by linguistics where it needs to be. For Chomsky, of course, the opposite is the case: linguistic theory constructs the frame in which psychologists can operate. Applied to the study of language development this means – at least to the sceptical onlooker – that the states

---

49 I admit that this whiff of scientific realism does not seem very Peircean, but recall my discussion of what Migotti (1999) calls these – the 'independence' and the 'accessibility' theses.

and transitions in syntactic development must be characterised in terms of whatever theoretical position Noam Chomsky happens currently to hold. Coupled with this, and barely dissociable from it, we find a deeply pessimistic attitude towards the progress of and prospects for scientific psychology – from Chomsky with regard to the neuroscience of language and from Fodor with regard to the psychology of general cognition.

But within rationalism we do find a serious and thorough attempt to characterise the nature of what will be acquired, both syntax and thought, and how these two might interact. It is unique in that.

Empiricism is of course mechanism-rich and structure-poor. The mechanism is associative learning. As we saw however, the kind of phenomena that associative models pure-and-simple can explain – perceptual learning and perceptual categorisation more generally, pseudo-relational learning (the peak shift), transitive performance in so far as this is associative rather than logical, sequence ('grammar') learning in so far as this is associative rather than rule-based – are just not language-like. Connectionism is certainly not associationism 'pure-and-simple', but it is a form of associative learning right enough. (As we shall see in Part 3, there is also a distinction to be drawn between connectionism pure-and-simple and a less ideologically driven kind that admits symbolic elements where necessary.) And indeed there is a self-styled 'connectionist' way of doing developmental psychology, exemplified by Elman *et al.* (1996), that is empiricist and associationist. This sets itself a mighty challenge: to explain that which is symbolic and rule-bound at its very heart using only materials bleached of both symbols and rules.

That said, connectionism does give us learning mechanisms; and only an intellectual Luddite would say that connectionist models of learning are simply irrelevant to all aspects of syntactic development.

Finally, it is exactly rationalism's strength (explaining development by keeping in mind a model of the end state) that pragmatism takes as a weakness. That mental development has an end is a contingent fact, like our current historical state, not a fact that necessarily constrains how we characterise the early mind of the child. Mental development is the process of the child constructing for herself a series of models of social and physical reality, and we should view the syntax-acquiring child as somebody who has constructed a reasonable working theory from the available evidence, a theory that need not contain the seeds of adult grammar. But when we shift our gaze from language as sociocultural action to language as the medium for expressing thoughts we find what looks like a very un-nutritious position: language as being on a par with 'certain kinds of social abilities, or perhaps motor abilities, or musical abilities' in Gopnik's words.

But pragmatism's very lack of commitment to whatever is the currently regnant linguistic theory and computational theory of learning frees developmental psychologists with this cast of mind to ask any empirical questions they will about what children at a certain stage of syntactic development actually know and how they have come to know it. For there is something to be said for William Jame's call to 'the open air and possibilities of nature, as against dogma, artificiality and the pretence of finality in truth'.

Finally, I will be assuming henceforward that one condition on being an adequate theory of syntactic development is that the theory have the resources to explain how the course of cognitive development makes contact with the course of syntactic development.

PART 2

Syntactic nativism: language development within rationalism

We have discussed the philosophical and methodological assumptions underlying Chomsky's ideas at some length. It is now time to examine the nuts and bolts of the theory itself and to assess it against the developmental evidence. Because this kind of enterprise has been attempted many times in the past thirty or more years, the reader is entitled to expect that this review will contain some provocative or novel elements – to justify its existence. I can't promise much provocation, but there will be two novel features, novel at least to the developmental audience. In the first place, I will spend some time describing Chomsky's Minimalist Programme, which, at the time of writing, has received no attention from developmental psychologists. Second, as the final sentence of Part 1 foreshadowed, I shall be keeping to the fore questions about the relation between linguistic and cognitive development rather than assessing the theory as a theory of syntactic development alone. Indeed one of the reasons that the minimalist programme is so intriguing is that it is *designed* around questions about how language and thought interface.

Here then is the order of business.

1) *The psychological reality of syntactic level of representation.* This will be a very basic discussion of English phrase structure. What justification is there for looking at *English,* especially in the light of the fact (if it *is* a fact) that human languages exist in which there are *semantic* regularities where English has syntactic rules. The answer is that English (not to mention other Indo-European languages similar to English) is learnable by all human children. So humans are capable of learning languages with syntactic rules; this fact stands in need of explanation; *we need to look at how these rules operate at least in one language;* and it is highly debatable whether anti-Chomskyan developmental psychologists can or should take comfort from the existence of human languages whose rules seem to be 'more' semantically motivated than those of English, as I shall be discussing.

2) *The road to minimalism.* In this section I will sketch in the main lineaments of Chomsky's 1957 and 1965 theories before discussing the 1981 (Principles and Parameters – P & P) theory in some detail. *The reader needs to be fairly conversant with this if he or she is to be able to assess the empirical work that it inspired.*

3) *The minimalist programme.* This will be described, with most attention being paid to Chomsky's ideas about how the design of a syntactic system must be 'legible' at its interface with the 'cognitive intentional systems'. We will also discuss the empirical claims that the theory inspires about the course of syntactic development and, more generally, about the developmental relationship that one should expect to find with cognitive development.

4) *Empirical work inspired by Chomskyan theory.* The demonstrations of English-speaking children's remarkably early acknowledgement of some of the 'constraints' proposed by P & P will be discussed. We will also consider whether the existence of Specific Language Impairment (SLI) does indeed provide evidence for an autonomous syntactic module of the kind proposed by the P & P.

2.1 The 'psychological reality' of the syntactic level of representation: from phrase structures to X-bar grammar[1]

This section has a dual purpose: to introduce readers who are not familiar with it to standard analyses of sentence structure and to introduce two entities which play a central role in much of Chomskyan theory – *X-bar grammar* and the *inflection phrase.*

We can begin by asking why it is necessary to describe the constituents of English sentences in term of units that are larger than the word – phrasal units. Why does Figure 2.1 fail to represent even our most basic intuitions about the constituents of the sentence?

The first reason is that there would appear to be a natural break between *cabinet* and *outshone*. This is because the first string of words (*Few of the jewels on the cabinet*) might be regarded as containing the 'subject' of the sentences in the sense

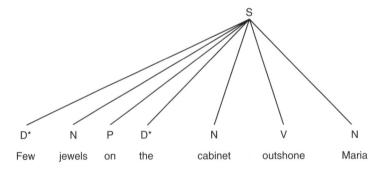

* = determiner

Figure 2.1 A sentence parse with only lexical items as the sub-sentential elements.

---

[1] In this section, my treatment up to page 96, will stay quite close to that to be found in Weisler and Milekic's *Theory of Language* (2000).

(semantically) that it is what the sentence is about, while (syntactically) it is the noun plus qualifying words which precedes the verb and agrees with it in number. The phase *outshone Maria* is the 'predicate' in the semantic sense of telling us something about the items referred to in the 'noun phrase' (as we shall see) and in the syntactic sense of consisting of a verb plus (possibly) its complements and modifiers (*Maria* is the complement of the transitive verb to outshine). A sentence without these sub-sentential structures could only exist in what Bickerton (1990) has called a *protolanguage*, meaning the kind of language that early humans might have spoken or that can be seen in the early stages of pidgins. In a protolanguage each word is simply added to others in the hope, as it were, that the hearer will pick up the meaning.

This results in the parse shown in Figure 2.2.

The next step is to find ways to justify our analysis of the subconstituents of the subject and the predicate. As we saw in the discussion of Brandom's pragmatist approach, we can establish that two items belong to the same syntactic category if free substitution of one by another results in a sentence whose meaning is different but which is no less grammatically correct. As Radford (1988, p. 52) puts it: 'Does a word or phrase have the same distribution (i.e. *can it be replaced by*) a word or phrase of a known type? If so, then it is a word or phrase of that type'.

In our example, it is possible to swap *Maria* and *few of the jewels on the cabinet*. But in what sense are these two 'within the same category'? In terms of analyses by subjects, predicates etc. they are *not* in the 'same category' because, under the analysis

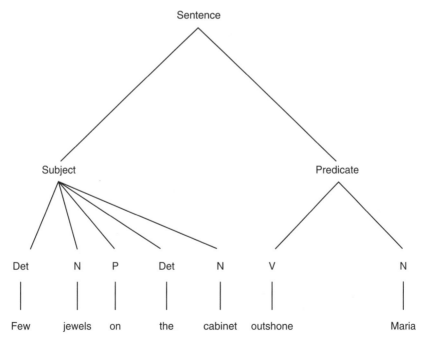

Figure 2.2 A parse with a subject-predicate split.

shown in 2.2, we would either say that *Maria* was an object or (as we have seen) 'the complement of transitive verb', while *few jewels* etc. clearly is not either of these. We must therefore propose, more neutrally, that both *Maria* and *few jewels in the cabinet* are *noun phrases* (NPs), the somewhat counterintuitive move here being that of referring to a single noun as a noun *phrase* (see Figure 2.3).

What we have assumed here is that a NP is the phrasal node that immediately *dominates* the noun, but which can also include determiners (e.g., *few*) and modifiers (e.g., *on the table*). But on this criterion *the cabinet* is also a NP because it consists of a determiner ('the') and a noun. Given this, we should also be able to swap *Maria* and *the cabinet* to produce *Few jewels on Maria outshone the cabinet* (see Figure 2.4).

We next turn our attention to questions about why a seeming-phrase such as 'on Maria' cannot be considered to be a noun phrase, despite the fact that it contains a noun. Is it sufficient to say that the phrase fails the substitution test with true noun

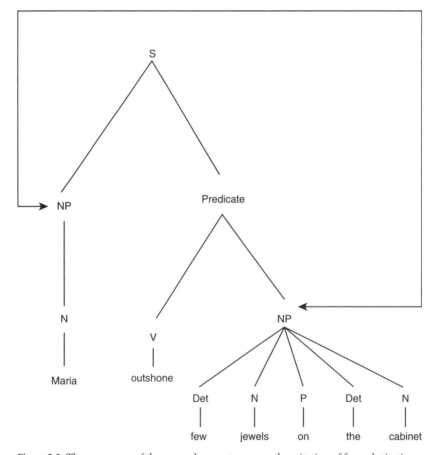

Figure 2.3 The emergence of the noun phrase category on the criterion of free substitution.

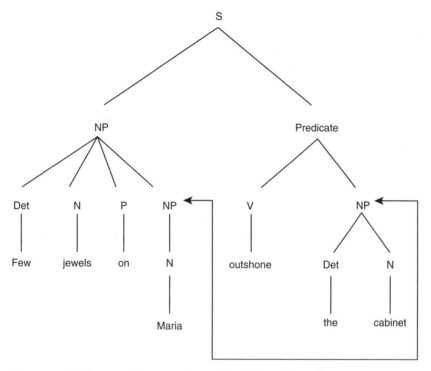

Figure 2.4 A further noun phrase emerging on the criterion of free substitution.

phrases? Here are two further tests for sentence constituency. This second test is called, by Weisler and Milekic (2000), the *incredulity test*. The following expressions of incredulity all make sense by virtue of the fact that they express predicates or NPs.

– Maria?
– Outshone Maria?
– The jewels on the cabinet?
– The cabinet?
– The jewels?

On the other hand, only the final one of the following expressions of incredulity invite meaningful replies. Bear in mind that these are supposed to be expressions of incredulity about the information given, not a request to repeat an inaudible word (*= ill-formed).

– *The jewels on?
– *On the?
– *Jewels on the?
– *The jewels outshone?
– *On the cabinet outshone Maria?
– On the cabinet?

On the cabinet is a well-formed expression of incredulity because it is a prepositional phase (PP) – a preposition followed by a NP complement.

In the closely related *interrogation test* (Weisler and Milekic, 2000) we see that only properly formed constituents can serve as answers. For example:

1) Who did few jewels in the cabinet outshine?

2) Where were few jewels that outshone Maria?

3) What did few of the jewels in the cabinet do?

Non-constituents like *in the* and *jewels outshone* cannot function as meaningful answers to such questions.

Our final move in establishing the constituents of a parse is motivated not by the three tests (substitution, incredulity, and interrogation) but by the familiar Chomskyan criteria for descriptive adequacy of elegance, simplicity, and economy. Why, specifically, are we retaining the category of predicate in which to house the verb when nouns and prepositions are housed within their own phrases? Accordingly we replace the category of predicate by that of *verb phrase* (VP). Note too, by the way, that in English (though not, as we shall see, in a number of other languages) the element whose name is given to the phrase *begins* the phrase: it is the *head* of the phrase, making English a *head-first* language. This results in the parse shown in Figure 2.5.

This process has resulted in our now being armed with a set of *phrase structure rules* (also called 'rewrite rules) for English, meaning rules for generating a new syntactic structure from another higher in the analysis tree. These are (parentheses mean 'optional'):

S → NP VP
NP → (Det) N (PP)
VP → V (NP)
PP → P NP

It might then be said that competent speaker-hearers of English know ('tacitly' for Chomsky) sets of rules of this kind and have the ability to insert items from their lexicon in the terminal nodes. (This is a portion of the 'competence' described in 1.1.3.) This means that they can also understand sentences such as *Many people in the room admire Maria, Most items in the catalogue please John* – assuming of course that they also know what lexical items *are* nouns, verbs etc. in English. We can say indeed that generating grammatical sentences is a matter of (1) constructing a phrase structure and (2) the lexical insertion of the appropriate classes of words into the terminal nodes of the tree. (We shall see later that the constraints on lexical insertion amount to more than knowing whether a word is a verb, noun and so forth.)

There are, however, further complications, centring around the structure of the noun phrase. Note that the NP 'mother' node has three 'daughter' nodes ('mother–daughter–sister' terminology is standard) whereas all the others have two. Does this not suggest that the number of branches from a node is unconstrained, this being something that violates the criterion of elegance, simplicity and economy? In fact, if we attempt to restrict the daughters of NP to two we come up against an ambiguity, which reveals that there is indeed more structure in the NP than first appeared. Do we adopt the first interpretation in Figure 2.6 or the second?

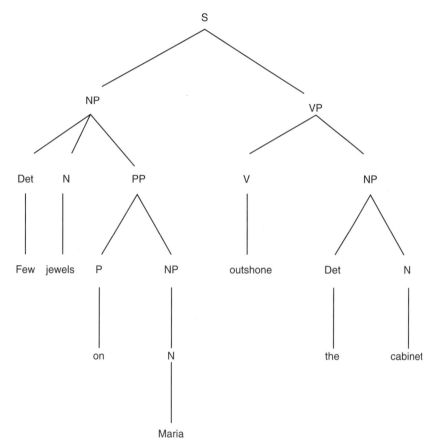

Figure 2.5 The result of replacing 'predicate' by 'verb phrase'.

There are two problems with the first parse. In the first place, if we treat *few jewels* as a NP then we will come up against failures of substitution. Thus, if we replace it with another NP *they* what results is the ungrammatical sentence *They on the cabinet outshone Maria*. Second, the idea of there being a structural break between *jewels* and *on* does not make good semantic sense – for the following reason. Intuitively, *few* does not just qualify *jewels* but *jewels on the cabinet*; for what the speaker is clearly not doing in this phrase is picking out few of the jewels *in the universe* and separately qualifying them by saying they are on the cabinet. For reasons such as these, the second parse in Figure 2.6 is to be preferred.

Note that this introduces a new syntactic category – N′ (pronounced 'noun-bar'). N′s are not full noun phrases (they fail the substitution test, for one thing), but they are daughters of NPs. The N′ level is a level *intermediate* between bare nouns and full noun phrases.

N′s can in turn have daughter N′s (see Figure 2.7). Without this innovation, phrase structure rules would be rewriting themselves as NP→NP. (NPs can be

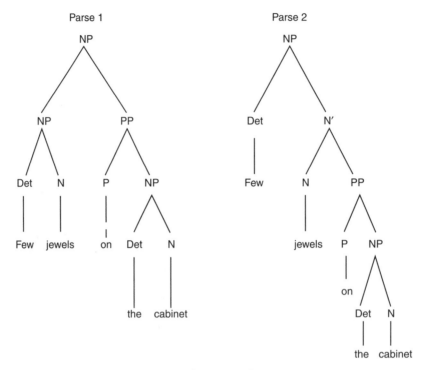

Figure 2.6 Two possible ways to parse within a noun phrase.

written N″ to capture the fact that they must be higher in the tree than N's.) Note, by the way, from Figure 2.7 that the parse captures our intuition that the PP *of bridge* is more closely related to *player* than the PP *from Bristol*: it is represented as the 'sister' (i.e., on the same level of the tree as another daughter of the N′) of the N. The two PPs are not equivalent in status because, if we switched them, a phrase would result that might be judged to be ill-formed: *A player from Bristol of bridge*. The difference is due to the fact that the lower PP is a complement of a N whereas the higher PP is a modifier of a N′.

Turning now to verbs and VPs, we encounter reasons for introducing the syntactic category V′(verb bar) which parallel, to some extent, those for introducing N′. Consider the necessary constraints on the kind of verbs that can be inserted into the terminal nodes of a parse tree. Merely categorising a word as a verb is not sufficient to ensure that lexical insertion will result in a grammatical sentence. For one further constraint is on whether the verb is transitive or intransitive and whether or not it takes a that-clause as a complement. Thus 'John *verbed* the bus' requires a transitive verb and blocks an intransitive verb. Intransitives cannot occur with NP objects; while 'John *verbed* that Mary was late' will block the insertion of both transitive verbs like *caught* and intransitive verbs like *sleep*. What must be done, then, is to fix, for each verb in the lexicon, the kinds of complement it can take – if any. Linguists call

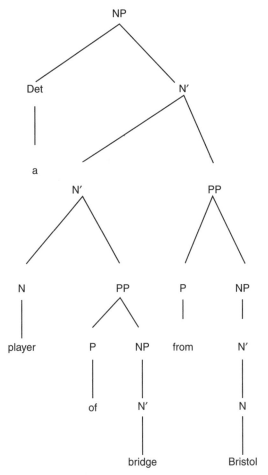

Figure 2.7 Noun-bars (N's) as daughters of noun-bars.

this fixing the *valence* of the verb (after the usage in chemistry). Accordingly, verbs like *think* and *expect* take sub-sentences (S's) after the so-called complementiser *that*, whereas transitive verbs like *bring* require a NP object as their complement. Intransitive verbs, however (because they can stand alone as complete predicates) take *null* complements.

So how then do we account for the well-formedness of a sentence like *Jomo arrived at the village in style?* The phrase *in style* would appear to be a complement, but *arrive* is an intransitive verb, which should not be taking a complement. What linguists do to resolve this seeming anomaly is to deny that a phrase like *in style* is a complement of a VP and say instead that it is the *modifier* of a V' phrase of a similar status to the modifiers within N' phrases (see Figure 2.7). This allows us to insert as many PP modifiers of intransitive verbs as we like. We can also insert them in any

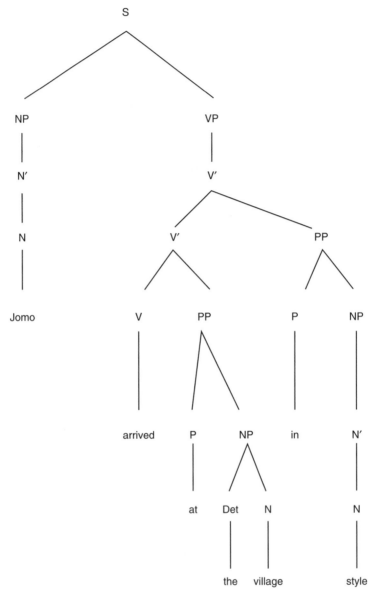

Figure 2.8 Illustrating the verb-bar (V′) category and the prepositional phrase as modifier of the verb phrase.

order, as they have a similar status. Thus *Jomo arrived in style at the village* is no less well formed than *Jomo arrived at the village in style* (see Figure 2. 8).

Note now the parallels between the bar structures in Figures 2.8 and 2.9 – one for verbs and one for nouns. Indeed these parallels only have to be noted for it to be clear that the interests of elegance, simplicity, and economy to dictate that rather than

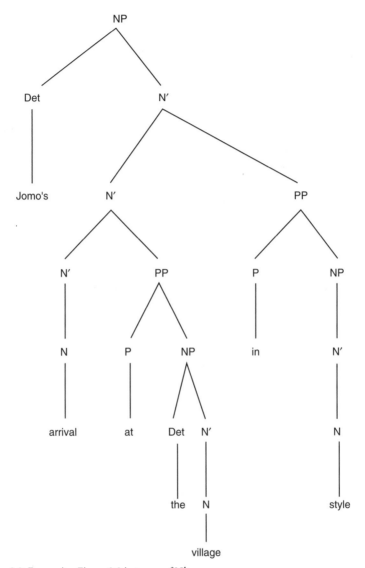

Figure 2.9 Expressing Figure 2.8 in terms of N's.

having separate rules for NP→N' and VP→V' we might say more generally and simply that for any kind of phrase XP, be it NP, VP, PP, adjectival phrase, and so forth,
that XP (or X″) dominates X', which dominates X. (We can also apply a V' analysis
to all kinds of verbs, not just to intransitives.) This is the X-bar grammar (Jackendoff,
1977), utilised, as we shall see in the next section, by Chomsky in his P & P theory.

Generally speaking then, X-bar syntax requires and allows (optional elements in
parenthesis) the following.

XP → Specifier X′ (modifier)
The player of bridge (from Bristol)
X′ → X′ (modifier)
player of bridge (from Bristol)
X′ → X⁰ (complement)
player (of bridge)

It is worth elaborating further on X′ grammar because of the central role it has played in theoretical linguistics in the past thirty or so years. As we did for other subsentential elements, we can apply tests for whether a phrase is of the intermediate, X′ kind. Here are some from Radford (1988). The test is: Can the string serve as the antecedent of a pronoun or, more generally, a proform? For example, the proform *one* can have the italicised strings of words as antecedents in the following sentences.

> The *big leather briefcase* Jane bought was perfect, so I got one for myself.
> The big *leather briefcase* weighed a ton, so I got a little one.
> The big leather *briefcase* cost a mint, so I got a plastic one.

There are then three structural levels beneath that of the NP *the big leather briefcase*. Note two things which were implicit in what has gone before: (1) that full NPs are headed by specifiers like *the*, and (2) even the bare noun is conceptualised as having a N′ node above it.

Finally, we might consider how X-bar grammar leaves the relationship between XPs and sentences. If elegance, simplicity and economy are the touchstones, this qualitative division between phrases and sentences might seem to be poorly motivated, as it leaves us with no principled way of describing the relation between the two levels. Chomsky's proposal was that the sentence can itself be regarded as a form of XP – an *inflection phrase*. There is a *functional category* called *inflection* or *INFL* (later plain *I*), which I will describe immediately below. A sentence then, can be conceptualised as an inflection phrase or IP, *with the subject filling the role of specifier*.

The I category captures how the verb is inflected and what information it carries about tense, person and number (agreement properties), aspect[2] and modality; while it can be represented by an affix (indirectly) or by an auxiliary (directly, see Figure 2.10a). It does this by assuming that the I category is either filled (with an auxiliary) or unfilled. This gives the somewhat counterintuitive analysis of plain finite verbs shown in Figure 2.10b. The assumption is that the tense and agreement properties of the V heading the VP will 'percolate up' to INFL.[3]

---

[2] The aspect of a verb represents whether the action or event being referred to is discrete or continuous (e.g., *chopped* versus *chopping*).

[3] The term INFL obviously stands for 'inflection' but it also stands for the *INFinitivaL* particle *to*. Why, in passing, are these two being elided? Chomsky (1981) noted the following parallel between auxiliary forms like *should* and the infinitival particle *to*. In the first place they often behave the same way. Thus
It's vital that John should attend;
It's vital for John to attend.
Just as *should* requires the subsequent verb to be in the infinitive form so does *to*; only the form *attend* is grammatical, while *attended* or *attending* etc. are not. Furthermore, these

(a)

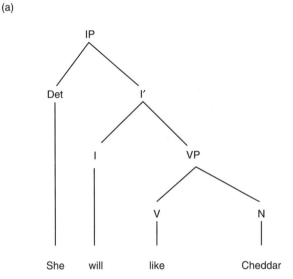

(b)

Figure 2.10 The inflection phrase (IP) reading of a 'sentence'.

Continued

two forms show what is called 'ellipsis of the complement'. Accordingly the following two are both acceptable:

I don't want to go to the lecture but I know I should [go]

I know I should go to the lecture but I don't want to [go]

But the following is not:

*I know I should go to the lecture but I don't want.

This then is the motivation for positing the functional category of I. There are two further kinds of motivation for claiming that clauses which do not have overt auxiliaries in fact have unfilled auxiliaries (as in Figure 2.10b), and thus for the broader claim that all sentences are IPs. One of these is 'theory internal' (i.e., determined by the desired form of a linguistic theory) and the other is 'empirical' (i.e., justified by observations of grammatical and ungrammatical sentences). Radford (1997a, p. 91) describes the former succinctly. (We need to bear in mind, by the way, that the term 'clause' in the following quotation means an expression that contains both a subject and a predicate and that a sentence is a freestanding clause, meaning one that is not contained within some larger expression. Given this, we can read 'sentence' for 'clause'):

> 'But why on earth should we want to pretend that clauses which obviously don't contain an auxiliary actually contain an unfilled auxiliary?' you might wonder. Well, from a theoretical point of view, an obvious advantage of the IP analysis is that it provides a unitary characterisation of the syntax of clauses, since it allows us to say that all clauses contain an IP projection, and that the subject of the clause is always Spec-IP (i.e., always occupies the specifier position within IP), that INFL in a finite clause always has a nominative subject, and always agrees with the subject.
>
> (Radford 1997a, p. 91)

Turning now to the empirical evidence in favour of the idea that finite verbs have unfilled INFL, Radford cites such facts as the following. If auxiliaries are heads of IPs while finite verbs are heads of VPs then they should behave differently. Compare the verb *have* as used either as a perfective auxiliary heading an IP (e.g., in *They have gone home*) and used as a causative finite verb (e.g., *I'll have them check the brakes*) or experiential finite verb (e.g., *John has the audience walk out [on him]*) heading VPs. In the auxiliary case, because it is in the head position, it can undergo inversion in the framing of questions. Thus:

> Have they gone home?

is acceptable. But the following two are not:

> *Have you them check the brakes?
> *Has John the audience walk out?

Furthermore, why can *have* as an auxiliary be cliticised into (say) *They've* where *have* as a finite verb cannot? For example, we can say *They've seen the cat* but not *They've their brakes checked*. Examination of the sentence structure gives the answer, and illustrates the covert operation of the empty I category.

> [$_{IP}$ They [$_I$have][$_{VP}$ [$_V$seen] the cat]]
> [$_{IP}$ They [$_I$____][$_{VP}$ [$_V$ have] their brakes checked]]

Note that in the second case above the possible cliticization *is blocked by the intervening but imperceptible constituent [$_I$____], which serves as evidence for the psychological reality of the empty I category.* (We will later encounter other examples of covert syntactic elements blocking verb reduction of this kind, and also developmental evidence for children's early recognition of this blocking.)

The case of the IP illustrates, then, the way in which both theory-internal and empirical considerations lead to the establishment of grammatical categories. The former are, of course, the considerations of elegance, simplicity and economy which – recall – are intended ultimately to lead to the construction of a theory that is not only descriptively adequate but explanatorily adequate. That is to say, if we continue to simplify and simplify the rules for generating well-formed sentences we will ultimately have a plausible account of the rules that children are using, given that children too must be motivated by considerations of simplicity. (They are unlikely to hit upon a complex way of parsing the input if a simpler one is available.) Well, X-bar syntax can be regarded as a simplifying heuristic for learning the phrase structures of languages like English. While X-bar syntax may not be part of universal grammar (UG), the challenge is nonetheless extended to non-nativists to explain how children exposed to languages like English are able to acquire it without some prior assumptions about phrases and their possible constituents.

2.2 The road to minimalism – transformational grammars

It might appear that much of what I will be saying in this section is only of historical interest, given that Chomsky's theory has evolved at a pace in the past 45 years. However, a review of this kind can, at least, help the reader to appreciate what it means in practice for linguistic enquiry to be motivated by considerations of *simplicity* (henceforward short for 'elegancy, simplicity and economy'). Undertaking such a review is also a good way of explaining Chomsky's ideas about the 'autonomy' of the syntactic level.

Before I begin this review, I will (literally – Figure 2.11) sketch out how one might regard Chomsky's early theories from a psychological perspective. If we do indeed take linguistics to be providing a theoretical psychology of how the thought systems and the sensorimotor systems for communication interrelate then Figure 2.11 represents how things stood early in the development of Chomskyan theory. The text that follows will colour it in.

2.2.1 Assigning structure – the 1957 theory

Immediate constituent (IC) analysis (the idea that, at each syntactic level of analysis, units are classified as the immediate constituents of a higher level) originated not with Chomsky but with Bloomfield (1933). However, one of the innovations contained in Chomsky's book *Syntactic structures* (1957) was the attempt to explain why IC analysis – resulting in the production of phrase structure or 'rewrite rules' of the kind described in section 2.1 – was *insufficient* to produce a descriptively adequate theory of English. What made the book so influential was Chomsky's proposals for supplementing the IC analysis.

One obvious limitation of a simple IC analysis is that many additional rules have to be added if lexical insertion is to be successful. We have just been considering an example of this in the context of different kinds of verb (e.g., transitive versus intransitive). But more fundamentally, constraints on agreement cannot be met if lexical insertion is *context free*. For example the existence of a plural subject determines that the verb must have a plural form and the existence of a feminine singular subject constrains the selection of the pronoun *she*. Considerations of simplicity

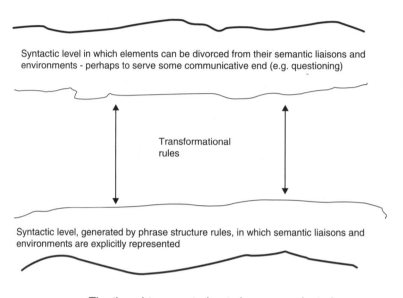

The sentence spoken or heard

Syntactic level in which elements can be divorced from their semantic liaisons and environments - perhaps to serve some communicative end (e.g. questioning)

Transformational rules

Syntactic level, generated by phrase structure rules, in which semantic liaisons and environments are explicitly represented

The thought generated or to be communicated

Figure 2.11 A sketch of Chomsky's early psychological theory of the thought/language relationship.

suggest that *multiplying ad hoc context-sensitive rules for each item in the string is not the best way of doing this.*

Second, IC analysis only works adequately on a limited number of sentences. Finally, Chomsky's aim, unlike Bloomfield's, was not that of developing a descriptive account of how English sentences can be adequately parsed but was, rather, an attempt to develop an account of how speaker-hearers can *generate syntactic representations for an infinity of English sentences.* He wished to devise a *dynamic* account of how production and comprehension are achieved, not a static description of it.

Chomsky replaced the notion of context-sensitive rules operating on individual lexical items with that of rules which operate *on an abstract representation of the whole sentence string.* These are the famous transformational rules. Again this concept did not originate with Chomsky, but with his mentor, Zellig Harris.

Chomsky illustrates the inadequacy of context-sensitive rules through the case of the passive. Without going into details, he demonstrated that the various elements that make up a passive form cannot be slotted in independently of one another – that the interlocking of contexts is very cumbersome to achieve.

A simpler way of generating a passive is by specifying the structure of strings underlying *active* sentences and then applying a transformational rule to them of the following kind.

$NP_1 + aux + V + NP_2 \Rightarrow$
$NP_2 + be + en + V + by + NP_1$

Thus, *The boy is chasing the girl* becomes *The girl is being chased by the boy*. It is important to note here that the passive transformation (like all transformations) does not apply to a particular English sentence but to a *formal representation of a kind of sentence.*

This analysis suggests that the simplest grammar for English is one in which phrase structure rules directly generate a limited set of underlying strings, together with transformational rules which perform operations of permutation, addition and deletion in order to generate all possible sentences in the language. Three kinds of transformational rules were proposed. First, *obligatory* transformations are those which produce the various forms of agreement, which insert the word *do* into negatives and questions, and which insert word boundaries. The subset of sentences that are produced by applying only obligatory transformations Chomsky called *kernel* sentences. These are active, affirmative and declarative. Second, there are the *optional* transformations. These are necessary when we take the option of putting a sentence in the passive voice, of negating a sentence, or of asking a question or issuing a command. The final type of transformational rule is that of the *generalised* transformation. These are necessary for the production of compound sentences such as those generated by joining two strings with *and* or *but* or by linking, say, *The boy is impatient* and *The boy went home* by embedding one in the other to produce *The boy who is impatient went home.*

This then was Chomsky's first attempt at setting a descriptively adequate grammar of English on the road to explanatory adequacy. We need to note some of its features before passing on. First, it pays minimal regard to semantics, in the sense that the operations apply mechanically to abstract syntactic structures with the meanings of the lexical items broadly being bleached out. Chomsky does not, however, ignore the difference between kinds of noun, of abstract versus proper, for example. Take, for example the difference between the following two kinds of sentence: ones like *John plays golf* or *Sincerity frightens John* as compared with *Golf plays John* or *John frightens sincerity*. Chomsky says that ideas about the 'degree of grammaticalness' should be applied with regard to such distinctions.

> I believe that this approach is correct, and that there is a clear sense in which [the first kind of sentence] is more grammatical than [the second kind], which are themselves more grammatical than 'sincerity admires eat' etc. Any grammar that distinguishes abstract from proper nouns would be subtle enough [to draw the distinction], and surely linguistic theory must provide the means for this distinction.
>
> (Chomsky, 1957, p. 78)

What motivates this idea, however, is not only a desire to capture our intuitions about which kinds of sentence make sense but also to block the production of passives like *Sincerity is frightened by John* in the simplest way. This is achieved by the blocking of certain $NP_1 + V + NP_2$ representations at the *kernel* level. If, instead of a system in which passivisation was achieved by specifying *the nature of the strings that underlie all active sentences* and then transforming them, passives were generated 'directly' by a set of phrase-structure rules then these selection restrictions would have to be stated again in the opposite direction for passives – a duplication of effort. Once again, simplicity is the motivating factor. Of course, speakers aim to speak meaningfully and extract meaning from speech, but these aims cannot be achieved, on the Chomskyan view, without speaker-hearers being armed with a set of formal procedures whose internal coherence is as strong as that which we find in mathematics and logic – a deeply rationalist assumption.

Next, as we noted in Part 1, a linguistic theory should not only be capable of generating all grammatical sentences of a language, but should also account for speaker-hearers' *intuitions* about the status of sentences – about their grammaticality of course, but also about whether a sentence is ambiguous. Transformational grammar can, for example, account for why we judge a sentence like *The shooting of the hunters was terrible* to be ambiguous: it is one sentence derived from two kernels containing strings such as *The hunters shoot* and *Someone shoots the hunters*. It can also account for our intuition that the following all have something *structurally* in common: *John kisses Mary, Mary is being kissed by John, Kiss Mary John, John is not kissing Mary.*

Finally, to the extent that this theory aims at an explanatory account of universal competence it can be undermined by cross-linguistic evidence showing that languages exist for which a transformational analysis is otiose – as sets of context-sensitive, or even context free, rules might be sufficient for the grammar to achieve descriptive adequacy. In the aftermath of the *Syntactic structures* theory one of Chomsky's co-workers, Paul Postal, applied the theory to Mohawk, one of the surviving Iroquoian languages (Postal, 1964). Postal demonstrated, first of all, that well-formed sentences of Mohawk cannot be enumerated by context-free rules. More important, he was able to show that the situation cannot be improved by making the phrase structure rules context-sensitive because doing so would result in a combinatorial explosion: 'Since the relevant vocabulary in Mohawk is probably about a thousand, it follows that even this wholly unacceptable grammar requires on the order of six million rules mentioning thirty-six million grammatical symbols' (Postal, 1964, p. 150). He interprets this result as showing that, first, phrase structure grammars suggest an incorrect theory of human languages and second that, as transformational grammars are the only ones that can circumvent the limitations of phrase structure, the evidence from Mohawk can be taken as 'indirect evidence for the claim that natural languages require transformational grammars' (ibid., p. 146).

It could be claimed on behalf of the *Syntactic structures* theory then, that it demonstrated transformational rules not only to be capable of generating an infinity of well-formed sentences in English and no ill-formed ones but also of assigning structural descriptions to sentences that match native speaker's intuitions about ambiguity and about how sentences are related. The further claim was floated that explanatory adequacy was also being approached by transformational grammar in so far as it provided the simplest taxonomy of rules for generating human languages – not just English.

A point to which I will return (in 2.4.2) is that the term 'generate' is somewhat ambiguous, in so far as it hints at a productive psychological process while really being intended formally (cf. πr^2 'generating' circles). But for the rationalist it is an enabling ambiguity, in the sense that ideas about the formal, mathematical generation of sentences by rules can be expected to inform us about the actual biological processes that take place when we frame our thoughts into sentences. That assumption lies at the heart of Chomsky's rationalism. Recall the discussion of competence versus performance in 1.1.3.

2.2.2 The 'Standard theory' – 1965

The theory set out in *Aspects of the theory of syntax* (1965) was at once the same kind of theory as the 1957 theory, modified through considerations of simplicity, and a radical expansion of it to encompass semantics. It therefore approached a complete theory of language competence. We will discuss the purely syntactic modifications first.

While Chomsky still refers to kernel sentences in the *Aspects* theory (these involve 'a minimum of transformational operations in their generation') the fundamental distinction between kernel and complex sentences has now gone, to be replaced by a distinction between the *deep structure* of a sentence and its *surface structure*. The final surface structures (the sentences we speak or hear, plus their superficial grammatical features) of all kinds of sentence are determined by markers in deep structure which determine the transformations that will be applied. Thus negatives, questions etc. are not generated by applying optional transformations to kernels but are generated from deep structures that contain negative, interrogative etc. markers. As before, however, the components of the underlying structures are generated by phrase structure rules. The distinction between optional and obligatory transformations remains; but does so without the 1957 assumption that there is a class of sentences that have been produced by only obligatory transformations. (In fact, the obligatory/optional transformation remains until the 1981 theory; so we will return to it later.)

This move simplifies the generation process in a number of ways. First, with regard to compound sentences (containing embedded elements) there is less generative work to be done, as separate strings no longer have to be combined by optional transformations. This is because the deep structure contains not only the embedded elements but also information to indicate the structural relations that will hold between the sub-elements in the final sentence. To return to the example of *The shooting of the hunters was awful*, instead of having a set of kernel strings in the underlying structure (*The hunters shoot; the shooting is awful*) there is now one underlying string which is generated by rules of the following kind: $NP \rightarrow that + S$. This gives us the (*simplified*) deep structure in Figure 2.12 (taken from Greene, 1972).

Moreover, the inclusion of obligatory transformational markers within deep structure means that in many cases one rule will do the work that had previously been done by two. Thus, the 1957 theory would have needed one rule to specify which kinds of verbs can be passivised (e.g., *kiss* can and *resembled* cannot) and another to determine which kinds of verbs can take adverbs of manner (e.g., *walk*) and which cannot (e.g., the verb *to be*). The fact is that only passivisable verbs can take adverbs of manner, a fact which can now be captured by a single element of deep structure. Again I'll take the example from Greene (1972). Only the first of the following two sentences can be passivised and only the first can take an adverb of manner (e.g., *carefully*):

John weighed the baby.
John weighed 12 stone.

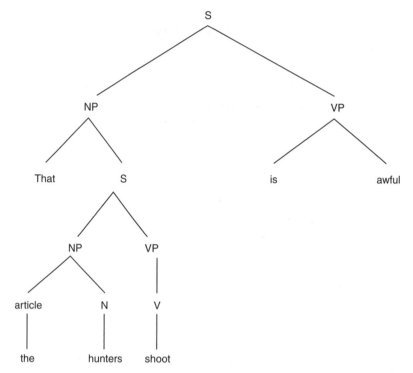

Figure 2.12 A simplified deep structure for 'The shooting of the hunters is awful'. From *Psycholinguistics: Chomsky and psychology*, Greene (Penguin Books, 1972), Figure 4, p. 58. Copyright © Judith Greene, 1972. Reproduced by permission of Penguin Books Ltd.

These regularities can be encompassed within one rule by putting a node in the deep structure that can either be rewritten as an adverb of manner or as a passive marker or both, as in Figure 2.13. A similar kind of simplifying motivation underlies the introduction of other kinds of marker into deep structures.

It may, in passing, help the reader to think about deep structure in the following way. Note that in the Figure 2.11 sketch I said that the level closer to the thought represents the 'semantic liaisons and environments' of the sentential elements. One way of doing this is by bracketing. Thus (example borrowed from Lyons, 1970) – the phrase *young men and women* can express two different thoughts: about people who are all young or about a group of people that can contain women who are not young. In other words: *young (men and women)* versus *young (men) and women*. Where we put the brackets determines meaning just as it does the computed value in arithmetic and algebra. The brackets, then, are the 'syntactic' elements, analogous to phrase structures, which determine the semantic interpretation.

I now turn to Chomsky's introduction of a semantic component into the *Aspects* theory. In order to put this into perspective I should mention a feature of the 1957 theory that was not discussed earlier: the morphological rules that generate the phonetic structure of the spoken words. In the *Aspects* theory this has become the *phonological component*. The result is the surface structure generated by transformational rules.

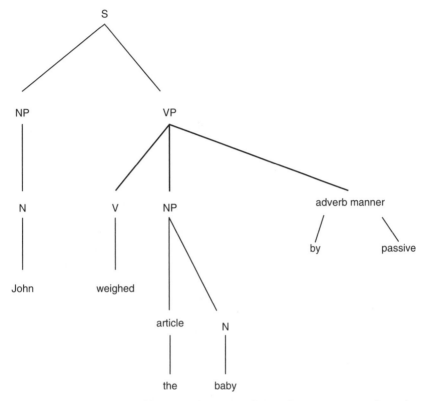

Figure 2.13 An illustration of how introducing a node into deep structure can determine whether a sentence can both be passivised and take an adverb of manner. (Compare 'John weighed 12 stone'.)

But sentences also have semantic representations. Recall from Part 1 that Chomsky denied that assigning meanings to sentences is something achieved via the pragmatic processes of 'interpretation' and 'context of utterance'. Rather, on the rationalist view, semantic interpretation is no less of an *internal, individualist,* computational matter than syntax itself. Accordingly, in the *Aspects* theory, Chomsky conceptualised deep structure rules as rules operating on the *base* (phrase structure) together with the lexicon in order to produce the semantic representation. In this way, the rules of the syntactic component *provide the structural information necessary for semantic interpretation,* while the rules within the semantic component conduct a semantic analysis to produce the meaning of the sentence. As Fodor (2000a, p. 4) writes:

> Chomsky has always liked the syntactic picture according to which syntax generates the structures that belong to a language and phonology and semantics interpret them; the former as instructions for pronunciation, the latter as instructions for drawing inferences.[4]

----

[4] E.g., inferences based on meaning such as 'if it's a red ball then it's a coloured three-dimensional object'.

This picture is just as vivid today as it was in 1965.

It is worth pausing to consider the parallel that is assumed to exist here between the phonological products of syntactic generation and the semantic products. Phonology is described in terms of sets of features and distinctions such as voiced/voiceless, aspirated, alveolar and so forth. In addition, native speakers utilise sets of rules by which they move from their phonemic representation of a word to its phonetic representation – how it is actually said. For example, in English we have the rule that if a vowel precedes a voiced consonant then it is lengthened; which is why *bit* has a short vowel and *bid* has a long one. For Chomsky, semantics is constituted in a similar way, with word meaning (as is speech) being determined by sets of features possessed by the word. Thus, the reason that *John frightens sincerity* (see above) is meaningless is explained, not in terms of the fact that there is no conceivable situation in the real world to which this sentence can refer, but in terms of the fact that the *selectional features* on the component words have been ignored. The selectional features of *John* would include [N, + animate, + human]. Those of *sincerity* would include [N, abstract]. Those for *frighten* would include not only features like '+ causative' but also a list of the kinds of NP it can link: (+ animate ... +animate), (+ abstract ... + animate), omitting (+ animate ... + abstract) and (+ abstract ... abstract +). Thus, the generation of sentences like *John frightens sincerity* and *Sincerity frightens relativism* would be blocked.

These selectional rules, in the *Aspects* theory, are features of the lexicon, which is included in the base of the syntactic component in which phrase structure rules are generated. It belongs here because, where phrase structure rules rewrite symbols into other symbols (e.g., S → NP + VP) the lexicon rewrites terminal symbols into words (V → *frightens*). What Chomsky was doing here was assimilating ideas about meaningfulness into those of ungrammaticity. And so his famous sentence *Colourless green ideas sleep furiously*, is not meaningless because it necessarily fails to refer to something in the real world; in fact it is not so much meaningless as ungrammatical by virtue of the fact that it violates selectional restrictions existing at the base level. *Chomsky was, then, an internalist about meaning from the early days.*

In fact, Chomsky's understanding of the term 'semantics' is so radically internalist as to be widely at variance with its usual philosophical sense – in which notions like truth and reference are taken to be paradigmatic semantic properties. For many people using the word *chair* to refer to a chair is not merely to express semantic features like '+ inanimate', in the way in which saying the word aloud necessarily involves the expression of phonological features and nothing more: it is mentally to represent something in the world. As Fodor puts it: 'Referring to a chair is like seeing one, and both processes have got chairs on the far end, and chairs are "things in the world"' (Fodor, 2000a, p. 4).

To zoom forward briefly, Chomsky (in *New Horizons in the study of language and mind*, 2000a) has recently defended his meaning internalism on the grounds that once we give house-room in linguistics to notions like truth and reference we are abandoning all prospects for a science of meaning, and this because there is supposed to be no satisfactory way in which referents can be adequately captured by criteria tight enough for science. (What, for example, are the necessary and sufficient criteria for a something's being 'near the Thames'?). But this is in many ways a paradoxical view for a rationalist to adopt, as it *suggests a kind of nominalism.* That is to say, on this view, the only thing that makes a word have the meaning it does is the set of *constraints on its relations to other words.* This results in a position that is not a million miles from that of Rorty (see pp. 69–72). As Fodor put it, it reminds one of 'a familiar sort of postmodern Idealism according to which science speaks only of itself … There are traces in *New Horizons* of incipient sympathy with this Wittgenstein-Goodman-Derrida sort of picture, but it is one which a respectable Realist should entirely abjure' (ibid., p. 4). (A further – more historically anchored – paradox, however, is that it was the semantic theory of Katz and *Fodor* [1963], in which word meaning is broken down into atoms called *semantic features,* that heavily influenced Chomsky in the construction of the 'semantic component' in the *Aspects* theory.)

2.2.3 Principles and parameters theory – the early 1980s

The *Aspects* theory, with its deep-surface distinction and its complex and extensive armoury of transformational rules, became known as the 'standard' theory, partly in order to mark the way in which the theory that Chomsky began to articulate around the late 1970s and early 1980s broke from the past – was *non*-standard (Chomsky, 1981). There was, in fact, a more substantial theoretical advance between the *Aspects* theory and the *Principles and Parameters* theory (P & P; also called 'government binding') theory than there was between the *Syntactic structures* theory and the *Aspects* theory (henceforth ST for standard theory). (Strictly speaking, government binding theory is one of the approaches that falls with the P & P family of theories. I will use the term P & P to cover both.)

Figure 2.14 is supposed to capture what, for the psychologist, became especially distinctive to Chomsky's view of the thought-language relationship in the 1980s. This centres around the notion of *logical form* (LF). I will describe what this means at a more technical level in a little while, but for now we can approach it by contrasting two ways of thinking about thoughts. In one sense (a particularly psychological one) a thought exists in the mind–brain, and it is this which gives rise to a sentence and which is given rise to by our perceiving one. But in a particularly linguistic sense the sentence itself just *is* a formalised thought. It is not merely something that happens to have the right configuration for *causing* thoughts, but it is one – in a sense. To revisit our example of *young men and women,* the ambiguity of the phrase is not a psychological fact about how potential audiences might interpret it; it is a formal fact about how the *scope* (the technical term) of the word *young* necessarily affords two interpretations. It is a linguistic fact. Scope and many other determinants of sentence interpretation are now dealt with via LF. And *it is here that Chomsky now locates the interface between the thought systems and the computational system for language.* That is to say, he regards the sentence itself as something that contains a covert archaeology of its derivation from deeper systems; it wears its thought on its invisible (except to the linguist) sleeve. For the linguist – for one whose goal is an explanatorily adequate account of the I-language – this is a tractable way of conceptualising the language – thought interface; for linguists do not – none of us do – hold the key to the mysteries of how thoughts give rise to sentences.

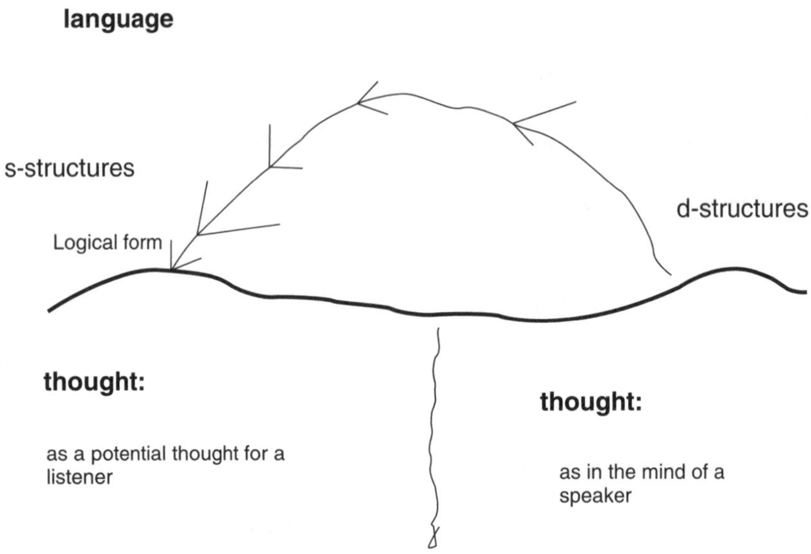

language

Figure 2.14 A sketch of the Chomskyn thought/language relationship in the early 80s.

I will spend some time on P & P, because not only is it arguably the most elegant and ingenious of Chomsky's theories but it is the one which best illustrates how the pressure towards simplicity impacts upon theory construction. It is also the Chomskyan theory which is the most testable by developmental experimentation, as the claims for early competence it inspires are so specific. My treatment will, however, omit much, and so readers who feel short-changed can be directed to a number of useful sources[5].

P & P was not a *complete* break with the past, as two distinctively Chomskyan features remain: the distinction between lower and higher syntactic levels (now called *d-structures* and *s-structures* rather than deep and surface), and the claim that the generation of sentences requires the application of transformational rules to the lower level. However it can be seen from Figure 2.16 (compare with Figure 2.15) that in at least two respects the order of generation has been inverted. In the first place, rather than lexical items being inserted into syntactic structures that had been generated by phrase structure rules, *the construction of lexical representations is the first step* (this assumption has remained to the present day), with these directly determining how phrases will be put together. Indeed, while some accounts of P & P, have it that both 'phrase structure rules' and the 'lexicon' contribute to the formation of d-structures, it is more accurate to say that phrase structure rules (at least of the kind that we saw operating in the 1957 and 1965 theories) have been jettisoned and replaced by the X′ structures, described in section 2.1. The second kind of inversion

---

[5] These are: Stevenson (1988), Goodluck (1991), Atkinson (1992), Haegeman (1994). I have been most reliant upon Atkinson (1992).

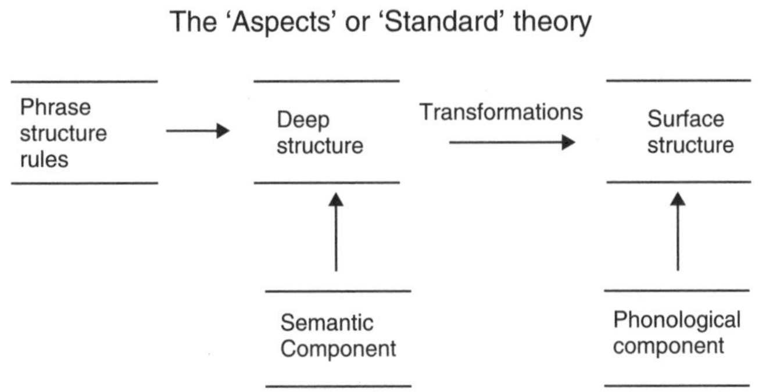

The 'Aspects' or 'Standard' theory

Figure 2.15 The 'aspects' or 'standard' theory.

concerns the semantic component. In ST the semantic component was based on deep structure (and determined by selectional restrictions); in P & P it is based on s-structures. As just described, logical form (LF) is the syntactic essence of the semantic interpretation, 'logical' because it makes explicit the logical structures that determine meaning.

(1) Everyone hoped that he would win.

To illustrate the latter claim, the sentence in (1) can be interpreted to mean either that everyone wanted a particular contestant to win, or that each of the contestants hoped that he-himself or she-herself would win. It has two potential LFs. LF is derived via a transformation (to be discussed) from s-structure, and must be formalised not by the syntactic apparatus of the theory but by the apparatus of predicate calculus. A reading of a sentence as intensional or extensional (see pp. 77) is also something that would be represented at the level of LF. We will return to the topic of LF shortly.

It might be useful here to reprise an earlier remark about the fundamental difference between formal logic and natural languages: 'the syntactic systems of human languages are full of features that seem to have no utility and that are not motivated directly by semantics' (p. 2–6). Formal logic, by contrast, is constructed by humans in order that every semantic distinction and relation is *transparently and without ambiguity* formalised. Now it might be said that the thought a sentence expresses is closer in form to formal logic than to human syntax, and this because *for the speaker* the thought that her sentence expresses is transparent and unambiguous to her, though not to her audience. So this is one sense in which LF is the *interface* between the syntax and the thought (i.e. for the audience).

LF is complemented by a further level called 'full semantic representation', determining the pragmatic inferences that can be drawn from the sentence. We shall see, however, that semantics, in the sense of word meaning, rather than sentence meaning, can be injected into the system at the lexical level.

One substantial difference between the two theories, which is only implicit in Figures 2.15 and 2.16, is that far less syntactic work is now done by transformational

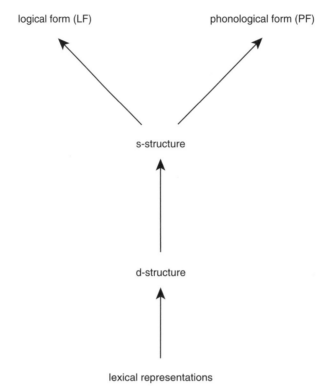

logical form (LF)

phonological form (PF)

s-structure

d-structure

lexical representations

Figure 2.16 The architecture of Principles and Parameters Theory.

rules. In ST these transformations took responsibility for both semantic interpretation and for the well-formedness of the surface structure. In P & P the many kinds of transformations, each tailor-made to produce a specific deep-surface transformation, are replaced by a single kind of transformation called *movement*, or move-α, meaning *move anything anywhere*. The obvious question then becomes: What mechanism is responsible for ensuring that the generative journey from lexical representations to s-structure, including the appropriate operation of the seemingly open-ended movement rule, does not result in ill-formed sentences? This is taken care of by a set of *principles*. These are a set of *semi-autonomous modules* that are designed to interact with one another. Some of these – X′ theory is a case in point – operate in the generation of d-structures, some operate on movement, and some operate at the generation of LF out of s-structures.

This then is why the word 'principles' appears in the title of the theory. But why *parameters*? The fact is that some principles are parametised, such that they are free to vary between languages. Two examples. First, different languages have different canonical word orders – subject-verb-object (SVO) and verb-subject-object (VSO) are the most common – and these are determined to some extent by how the elements in an X′ phrase are ordered in constructing d-structure. Given this, d-structure might be said to represent the canonical word order of the particular language.[6] Second, different languages, as we will later discuss, vary around the degree of liberality with which they apply the principles that constrain movement. For the first time then, Chomsky was presenting a theory that took account of linguistic variation, something that is obviously necessary for any explanatorily adequate theory.

Indeed, given the goal of explanatory adequacy, the motivation for discarding the multiplicity of transformational rules is not difficult to appreciate. In the current system there are fewer rules but they have more general application and they are mutually motivating – in the sense that each answers a need created by another. Also, the more specific and ad hoc the rules are (1) the smaller will be the scope for applying the system to languages unlike English and (2) the more complex will be the child's learning task. With regard to (2), the developmental implication to be drawn from ST was that children know innately the deep-surface distinction and the fact that these levels are related by transformational rules, with their task being to discover what *are* the transformational rules in the language to which they are being exposed. Well, it is difficult to see how the child could do this without embarking on a process of hypothesis testing; and this immediately raises questions of how this could work without their having certain hypotheses disconfirmed. But we know that children do not receive negative evidence, in the sense of a pairing of the ill-formed result of a transformation with its tagging as being ill-formed, e.g., *Who did John see who?* – wrong. Indeed, we know that when children speak ungrammatically they tend not to be corrected by adults (Brown and Hanlon, 1970; Hirsh-Pasek *et al.*, 1984). But even if they *did* receive negative evidence we would still be faced with the kinds of problems raised by Fodor (see p. 17) in the context of semantic development, namely: What other source could this pool of correctible hypotheses have other than an endogenous one? In other words, ST inspired the ascription of too much *highly specified* innate knowledge, such as of the passivisation and the pronominalisation transformations of *English*.

Chomsky's construal of syntactic development as *parameter setting* brilliantly circumvents this set of problems. As we have seen, some principles of P & P are paramaterised, in the sense that they can take more than one value, with the value they take varying from language to language. Given this, what the child needs to know is that there *is* such a parameter and the directions in which it can vary; and so all that is required from the input is *positive* evidence about how the parameter is set in the language being learned. The metaphor frequently used to illustrate this idea is that

---

6   The existence of so-called *non-configural* languages in which there is almost free variation in word order (such as Walpiri and Latin) does not imply that these languages lack d-structures! This is because, while d-structure will carry order information in configural languages, the purpose of the d-structure is not only to encode order information but more fundamentally to encode how arguments [see footnote 8] are related to predicates. Clearly, this needs to be done in non-configural languages.

of a parameter being a switch (in the child's mind–brain) that is initially set to an upright neutral position. Hearing sentences of a certain kind will throw the switch in one direction or another. One of the most discussed parameters is that of *head first* versus *head last* languages. To explain, English and other western-European languages are *right branching*, which means that their phrase structures branch to the right, given that the head (V in VP, N in NP etc.) is to the left of the phrase with the modifying material being built up to the right of this (Figure 2.17a). Japanese, by contrast, is a *left branching* language. In Japanese, the material modifying the head is placed to the left (Figure 2.17b); both figures taken from Baker (2003, p. 350) (Additionally, in Japanese, a complement sentence (S') is placed to the left of the verb and relative clauses precede the noun). Accordingly, an English-learning child has merely to hear sentences of a certain kind for the switch to be thrown 'to the right', while the Japanese-learning child's switch will be thrown 'to the left'. (Note, however, how much children will need to know about syntactic categories and structures for them to *perceive* the sentence type; plus, the fact that children can acquire English and Japanese at the same time suggests that parameter-setting is language specific.)

A second and narrower motivation for abandoning the ST system of transformations hinges on the distinction (lingering from the 1957 theory) between obligatory and optional transformations. As Chomsky (Chomsky and Lasnik, 1977) was the

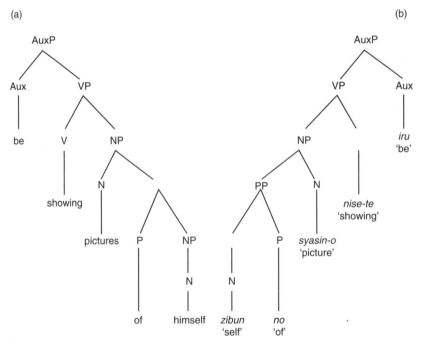

Figure 2.17 An illustration of the difference between a right-branching (a-English) and a left-branching (b-Japanese) language. Reprinted from *Trends in Cognitive Sciences*, 7, M. C. Baker, Linguistic differences and language design, pp. 349–53, Copyright (2003), with permission from Elsevier.

first to point out, a child would be unable to know that certain transformations *were* obligatory without negative evidence. He or she must find out that certain sentences in which a transformation has not been applied are not grammatical. Chomsky's solution was that all transformations should now be optional. (As Grimshaw [1981, p. 166] points out, however, the problem could also be avoided by having only obligatory transformations.)

A further motivation for radically overhauling the ST system of transformations was empirical (in the linguistic sense of 'empirical'). For some transformational rules did not yield the desired result. We can return to a previously-discussed sentence to illustrate a problem with the pronominalisation transformation. In ST, the sentence (2a), as meaning that all contestants wanted to win, would have been derived from an underlying structure similar to (2b).

> (2) (a) Everyone hoped that that he would win.
>
> (b) Everyone hoped that everyone would win.

But of course what the sentence means is not this, but that each individual covered by the term *everyone* hoped that he himself or she herself would win; if it is not intended to mean that they all wanted a particular person to win. There seemed to be no satisfactory means of accounting for this by a system in which pronouns were created in the very process of transformation. The solution was to have the pronouns already present in d-structure, with the mapping to LF taking care of the interpretive question. To anticipate, this arrangement meant that there had to be principles in the theory to constrain how proforms were interpreted in relation to co-referents.

Before embarking on an account of the principles/modules, it would be well to present three important concepts which are utilised at all levels of the theory. These are (1) *levels of projection*, (2) *c-commanding*, (3) *government*. First, the notion of projection level has already been encountered in the context of X′ grammar:

$X'' = XP$ (e.g., NP, VP, PP)
$X' =$ intermediate level
$X^0 =$ word level

X'' is the *maximal projection* of an item, with X^0 being the minimal projection and X' the intermediate projection. The contrast with ST derives from the fact that, under that theory, phrase structure rules resulted in only one level of projection (e.g., N→NP), whereas here we have the intermediate X′ level. The motivation for introducing X′ has already been discussed in section 2.1 in a theory-neutral way. Later we will discuss Chomsky's own motivation for introducing X′ as a module/principle within P & P.

Next, *c-commanding* (constituent-commanding) can be regarded as one of the 'principles' of P & P, although the generality of its application makes the term 'module' somewhat inappropriate to it. This formalises the conditions under which one node in a parse tree can be said to be 'higher' than another; and the notion of height-on-tree is essential to the articulation of the modular principles of P & P. There are a number of definitions of c-commanding, but the following will do for our purposes:

> Node A c-commands node B if and only if the first branching node above A dominates B and neither A nor B dominates the other.

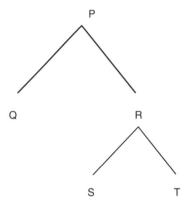

Figure 2.18 An abstract illustration of c-commanding (see text, this page).

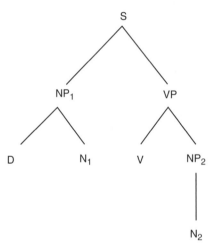

Figure 2.19 Government: NP_1 c-commands V, NP_2 and N_2 but does not govern them. V, though, does govern NP_2.

Accordingly, in the Fig. 2.18 node Q c-commands nodes R, S and T; node R c-commands node Q, node S commands T and T c-commands S. This means that a node c-commands all of its sister nodes together with all the nodes dominated by its sister.

Finally, we combine the concepts of maximal projection and c-commanding to arrive at the concept of *government*:

> Node A governs node B if and only if (1) it c-commands B and (ii) no maximal projections intervene between A and B.

Accordingly, because the maximal projection VP, in Figure 2.19, intervenes between NP_1 and V, NP_2 and N_2, NP_1 c-commands these nodes but does not govern them. V, on the other hand, not only c-commands NP_2, it also governs it, given the absence of an intervening maximal projection. So government, unlike c-command implies that both governor and governee share dominating maximal projections. Again, we shall see that some of P & P's modular principles are defined in terms of the notion of government.

We shall now encounter the apparatus of the theory itself by working 'upwards' from the level of *lexical representation* (LR). In ST, lexical representations were no more than the lexicon plus selectional restrictions – intimately related to deep structures via lexical insertion. In P & P, however, the properties of lexical items have a greater role to play in the formation of d-structures. Indeed one might say that while in ST words are inserted into deep-structures in terms of their particular properties, in P & P these properties play a major role in constructing the d-structures themselves. The term that Chomsky uses to describe the relation between lexical representation and d-structure is (confusingly, given its use in the quite different notion of 'maximal projection') is *projection*. The lexicon projects its properties onto d-structure. Indeed this exemplifies a general feature of the theory, called the *projection principle*, which states that

> Syntactic representations must be projected from the lexicon, in that they observe the lexical properties of the items they contain.

This marks a major break with the past in the sense that, for the first time, substantial syntactic features are carried forward from the level of the word. Words are no longer just the idiosyncratic terminal nodes of phrase structures. As we shall see in the next section, this process reaches its apotheosis in the Minimalist Programme.

A lexical representation comes complete with two kinds of properties: *categorical features* and a *subcategorisation frame*. For example, the word *help* will have the categorisation feature $[+V, -N]$. Its subcategorisation frame will mark the kind of complements, if any, that the verb can take. In this case it can appear both with a complement NP and without any complement, so the frame is

> *help* $[-\text{NP}]$, $[-\emptyset]$

A verb like *think*, on the other hand, can take a subsentential (S') complement: think that (= complementiser) then a sub-sentence.

> *think* $[-\text{S}']$

Verbs like *defer* and *rely* must take PP complements, and in these cases the preposition must be specified:

> *defer* $[-[\text{PP to NP}]]$
> *rely* $[-[\text{PP on NP}]]$

Given the projection principle introduced above we can say that:

> Representations at the syntactic level are projected from the lexicon, preserving the subcategorical properties of lexical items.

However, it may not have escaped the reader's attention that the question of how the child comes to find out that (say) *think* is V and *tree* is N – how, that is, the categorisation is achieved at all – has been glossed over. Syntactic nativism by itself is no help here, for the following reason. It is all very well ascribing to human children innate knowledge of the category (say) N; but this is not sufficient for them to find out that, say, *tree* is a noun. A solution to this crucial issue for syntactic nativism was offered in an important paper by Jane Grimshaw (1981). Her paper fell into three parts; and in the third she proposed a solution to the problem raised above: that while Chomsky's theory of UG simplifies the learning task considerably and while X-bar grammar seems able to project the categorisation of phrases from the level of lexical representation 'upwards', 'UG does not provide a universal structural defini-tion for lexical categories'. That is to say, there is no evaluation metric for deciding on the lexical category of a particular word.

Having dismissed the view that children's ability to derive a word's lexical category arises from their recording facts (in a connectionist-like manner) about its distribu-tional properties within sentences (see Maratsos and Chalkey, 1980, for such a sug-gestion), Grimshaw suggests that *semantic* assumptions must play the crucial role in fixing the category. For while there is no perfect one-to-one mapping between the semantic and the syntactic – while, for example, all nouns are not object words and all verbs are not action words – there is a partial mapping, in the sense that many nouns are object words and many verbs are action words, especially in the kind of speech that young children can understand. Accordingly, at a first approximation, the child can assume that if it is an object word then it is a noun; if the word describes an action then it is a verb. Doing this will enable a huge number of words to be correctly categorised, after which X-bar grammar will to begin its work. Grimshaw writes:

> Thus certain cognitive categories have what I call a *Canonical Structural Realisation* (CSR): CSR(object) = N, CSR(action) = V. LAD [the Language Acquisition Device] employs a CSR principle: a word belongs to its CSR, unless there is evidence to the contrary. Of course, the data [i.e., input to child] will include many examples that cannot be analysed this way, but they are likely to occur in relatively complex sentences that probably do not form part of the real data base at this point. In any event, should a sentence like 'NP *belongs to* NP' occur, *it will just have to be ignored.* LAD can construct phrase structure rules for NP and VP by drawing on example sentences whose lexical items can be assigned category labels by CSR principles.

> (Grimshaw, 1981, p. 174–175, first and final italics mine)

This solution to the categorisation problem is one approved of by Chomsky (1986). This idea will be re-encountered in section 4.4 when it will be discussed under its more familiar label of the *semantic bootstrapping hypothesis*. But for now what needs to be appreciated is the way in which such an injection of semantic knowledge at the level of categorisation projects semantics throughout the syntactic system like a spreading stain, and does so without undermining the principle of syntactic autonomy.

Viewed in a semantic light, therefore, the child, in learning a word like *kiss,* also learns a frame of the kind:

  kiss: V; Agent, Patient

and applies the assumption that:

  CSR (Agent) = NP
  CSR (Patient) = NP

This process (together with some principles to be discussed later) means that the pro-jection from lexical representations to d-structures (without, note, recourse to phrase-structure rules) results in the d-structure carrying canonical information about the syntactic structures which lexical items frame. Thus, a d-structure containing the lexical item *kiss* will include a place for the Patient (the kissee) as well as for the Agent (kisser). But if this is so – this an issue familiar from the 1957 theory – we need a transformation of some kind to get us from this canonical form of representation to non-canonical forms – such as questions. This serves to introduce a preliminary description of the operation of the sole transformational rule in P & P – move α.

The d-structure of the question *Who did John kiss?* will (respecting the fact that a transitive verb like *kiss* needs to have a patient or *theme*[7] after the verb) will be:

John [$_{VP}$ kissed who]

Note that this d-structure is in the canonical word order of English (SVO), and that *who* is within the same semantic environment as the verb to which it is the complement – while this is not so in the question surface structure.

As the move-α transformation allows anything to be moved anywhere, it is a simple matter to move *who* to the beginning of the sentence. This is unproblematic in a sentence as simple as this; though, as we shall see later, the solution is not so simple in more complex kinds of sentence, and so constraints are required to ensure that a grammatical form results. In any event, the movement of *who* to the beginning will leave a *trace* (sometimes called a 'gap') – a co-indexed empty category (*e*) within the VP. This is the resulting s-structure with its derivational 'archaeology' indicated.

who$_i$ did [$_S$ John [$_{VP}$ kiss e_i]]

Traces, empty categories and co-indexing play a central part in the theory, and without them, the operation of constraints (expressed as 'principles') cannot be understood. Neither can the notion of LF (logical form), to which we now return. The first thing to note is that move-α not only mediates between d-structure and s-structure, moving not only *wh*-elements (*what, where, who*, etc.) but other kinds of element; *it also mediates between s-structure and LF*, in a way I am about to describe. Move is not only overt but also covert (see Figure 2.20).

LF is not a representation of the surface form of the sentence. It is a representation of the syntactic structure of the thought – the sentence plus its archaeology of traces – to which that sentence can give rise (or be framed to express), and it is necessitated by the fact that sentences do not map 'directly' onto thoughts. Usually, of course, any change in *phonological form* (PF) will result in the sentence's generating a different thought – changing, for example the final phoneme of *Seize the day* results in *Seize the dad*. But consider an example like (3).

(3) John likes his mother.

The word *his* may or may not refer to John. So both of the following interpretations are acceptable. The subscripts indicate co-reference.

(4) a. John$_i$ likes his$_i$ mother.
    b. John$_i$ likes his$_j$ mother.

---

[7] The entity undergoing the effect of some action.

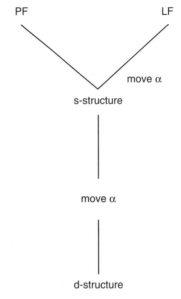

Figure 2.20 An illustration of the roles of overt and covert 'move α'.

The following three interpretations are, however, not acceptable:

(5) a. *He$_i$ likes John$_i$'s mother.
    b. *Who$_i$ does his$_i$ mother like?
    c. *His$_i$ mother likes everyone$_i$.

The postulation of LF arose, in part, out of an attempt to formulate a principle which would explain at a stroke why (5a) (5b) and (5c) are all unacceptable. Before tackling this point, however, it would be well to consider why it is that *wh*-elements and quantifiers like *everyone* create difficulties of interpretation. To put it loosely, such expressions seem to behave like arguments[8] syntactically, but they are not arguments in the sense that they do not pick out specific referents. Indeed, they exist at a higher level of abstraction than do arguments and predicates. For example in

Who did John see?

an effective way of capturing the referential role of *who* is to express the sentence as in (6).

(6) For which x, x is human, is it the case that John saw x?

Similarly, for the sentence

John saw everyone.

---

[8] The name of the entity within a proposition of which something is predicated. In generative grammar, an 'argument slot' is the noun phrase position within a sentence.

We can formalise the interpretation in terms of (7).

(7) For all x, it is the case that, if x is human, then John saw x.

There are other, more colloquial, expressions that, while appearing to refer to specific entities in fact do not. The *his* in (8), for example, does not refer to a particular son, but to any son you care to mention; and so it is in fact *functioning more like a logical quantifier* (see below).

(8) His mother is a boy's best friend.

The kind of representations exemplified in (6) and (7) are very close to those employed in the *predicate calculus* (see below) some of whose basic apparatus I will now briefly introduce. The symbol $\forall$ is the *universal quantifier* meaning *all* and the symbol $\exists$ is the *existential quantifier* meaning *one* or *some*. The symbols x and y are arguments and capital letters are predicates (e.g., H = human and S = sees). Thus the representation of (7) in predicate calculus is given in (9).

(9) $\forall x (Hx \rightarrow Syx)$.

The relation between quantifiers and variables is described as *variable binding*. Accordingly, in $\forall x$, the argument x is bound to the universal quantifier, and in $\exists y$ the argument y is bound to the existential quantifier.

Next, a strong analogy can be drawn between co-indexing in s-structure and variable binding in formal logic. Thus, linguists often represent LF in such a way that the traces left by *wh*-movement are marked as x, to indicate their status as variables. Accordingly, the s-structure (omitting the phrasal labels) of *John saw everyone* is

[John [-ed[9] [see everyone]]]

which has the LF representation:

[everyone$_i$ [John [-ed [see x$_i$]]]]

Note that *everyone* has moved – by move-α – to the head of the string (see next paragraph). Similarly the LF of

Which teacher did John see?

would be:

[which$_i$ teacher did [John see x$_i$]]?

(In the s-structure, the x$_i$ would have been the trace t$_i$.)

(10) Everybody likes someone

Let us now consider the motivation for moving the quantifier to the beginning. This LF procedure is called *quantifier raising* or QR (May, 1985). As in predicate calculus, this *renders transparent* the way in which a quantifier ranges over the other items in the representation, known as its *scope* (as mentioned earlier). To illustrate, the sentence in (10) can give rise to two possible thoughts: (1) that every person likes

---

[9] This represents the past tense.

somebody or other or (2) that there is one person who is universally liked. These possibilities can be represented as (11a) or as (11b).

(11) a. For everyone x, there is someone y, such that x likes y.

$\forall x$ (x is a person) $\exists y$ (y is someone) (x likes y)

b. There is someone y, such that everyone x, x likes y.

$\exists y$ (y is someone), $\forall x$ (x is a person) (x likes y)

In (11a) *everyone* has *wide scope* in so far as its scope includes *someone* (which has *narrow scope*); and in (11b) the opposite relation holds, as *someone* has scope over *everyone*. These facts are captured by quantifier raising to produce the two LFs shown in (12), this time using trace notation

(12) a. [everyone$_i$ [someone$_j$ [t$_i$ likes t$_j$]]]

b. [someone$_j$ [everyone$_i$ [t$_i$ likes t$_j$]]]

What has happened here then, is that *raising a quantifier to a higher position in the structure has determined the content of the thought that the sentence encodes.* This change has not exhausted the meaning of the sentence (it is not a complete semantic representation), but it has constructed a representational level – LF – intermediate between the s-structure representation and the full semantic representation.

(13) To whom did John give what?

Wh-phrases can also undergo raising. Here is an example of the process (from Haegeman, 1994, p. 449). In (13) the second *wh*-element *what* has not moved from its d-structure position because it is not possible in English for a sentence to be headed by two *wh*-elements. To construct the LF for this sentence we again perform an operation that is a hybrid of variable binding and co-indexing in order that the two *wh*-elements can be treated in the same way, thus rendering their meaning explicit, as shown in (14).

(14) [what$_i$, to whom$_j$ [John gave x$_i$ x$_j$]]

With this in mind, let us return to one of the earlier examples of a problematic interpretation, given in (5c) – *His mother likes everyone.* In this case the word *his* is of the same kind as in (8), meaning something like 'for any son you care to mention'. Now there is certainly something odd about this sentence, and it is a challenge (for many of us!) to construct a coherent thought from it with the co-indexing given in (5c). But if we put the sentence into the *passive* form the difficulty is mitigated, as in (15)

(15) Everyone$_i$ is liked by his$_i$ mother.

Why? Because the passive form, in which *everyone* is in the subject position, *is closer to the LF*, which is constructed by the quantifier-raising move-α, as in (16)

(16) Everyone$_i$[[his$_i$ mother][likes e$_i$]]]

This has been rather a long excursion into LF; but it can be justified by its adumbrating an idea that is absolutely central to the Minimalist Programme. As Atkinson (1992, pp. 67–68; emphasis added) puts it:

Like PF, LF functions as *an interface between the language system and other cognitive mechanisms.* If 'meaning' in a broad sense is embedded in a general conceptual system, LF can be seen as encoding the contribution of the theory of linguistic structure to the study of meaning. What this contribution is is an empirical question, and it is not to be resolved by stipulation.

Atkinson goes on to point out that the originator of the notion of quantifier raising, May, has more recently denied, from syntactic considerations, that scope ambiguities such as those illustrated in (10) *are* resolved at LF. Rather, he argues (May, 1985) that sentences like (10) have a *single* LF representation, compatible with either of the interpretations, the ambiguity being resolved by 'real semantics'. The nature of the interface and its location was, then, a somewhat open issue in the mid 1980s; it was to this issue that much of the Minimalist Programme is devoted; and we shall return to questions about the division of labour between LF and 'real semantics' in a while, when the minimalist programme is assessed.

The final, but still substantial, task in this exposition of P & P is to describe some of the modular principles – the quasi-autonomous sub-theories – which ensure that projection from the lexical level to the full syntactic representation is adequately achieved and ensure that the operation of move-α is adequately constrained. Recall that some of these are paramaterized; although I will have little to say about this immediately. I will discuss only the following:

- X-bar theory
- Binding theory
- Bounding theory

and much more briefly:

- Control theory
- Theta (θ) theory
- Case theory.

This is not, in fact, the complete list; and some (e.g. Atkinson,1992, p. 69) would treat move-α as one of the 'modules' of the theory.

Turning first to X-bar theory, recall that we discussed in section 2.1 the essentially theory-neutral reasons for postulating a level of representation between XP (e.g., NP) and X. And recall also that, within P & P, X-bar structures contribute to the process whereby lexical representations (LRs) project into d-structures. All I wish to add to that earlier discussion is the mention of one consequence for LRs of treating NPs, VPs etc. as exemplars of the single X-bar module.

As Chomsky (1970) noted before P & P came to be developed, there are a number of reasons for making a structural parallel between clauses and noun phrases. One of his examples is given in (17).

    (17) a. The enemy destroyed the city.

          b. The enemy's destruction of the city.

In this example, the noun *destruction* seems to be structurally related to *the enemy's* and *the city* in much the same way as the verb *destroyed* is related to the subject and the object of that verb. Recall that under X-bar analysis there is indeed a strong cross-categorical similarity captured by the fact that (17a) is most adequately analysed as a VP instantiation of XP and (17b) most adequately analysed as a NP instantiation of

XP, and that, as XPs, they can be analysed in terms of specifiers (*the enemy, the enemy's*) Xs (*destroyed, destruction*) and complements (*the city, of the city*).

The upshot of this for LR is that on X-bar theory we will have an LR for *destruction* which takes a similar form to that for *destroy*, namely:

> *destruction*: N, Agent$_i$, Patient$_j$

The Agent and the Patient will then be projected as NPs for reasons we discussed earlier in the context of Grimshaw's ideas.

The important point to note here is that this parallel between categories is not specific to nouns, like *destruction,* that are obviously derived from verbs. For the power and parsimony of X-bar grammar ensures that any lexical item that can head an XP (prepositions, adjectives, etc., as well as verbs and nouns) will come complete with a LR that can be projected 'upwards', and that the commonalities between kinds of phrases, which is of the essence of X-bar theory, provides a format within which phrases can to slotted recursively inside other phrases.

I now turn to the *binding module*. First, recall that in P & P, unlike in ST, pronouns appear in the d-structure. The upshot of this is that some constraint must be introduced to ensure that in the LF interpretation of the projected s-structure the co-reference (or lack of it) between the pronouns and *referring expressions* (typically NPs) is respected and that the differences in co-referential possibility between definite pronouns like *him* and reflexive ones like *himself* are also respected. Recall sentence (5a) in which something has clearly gone wrong with the LF interpretation: This is reproduced here as (18).

> (18) *He$_i$ likes John$_i$'s mother.

This problematic LF can be explained in terms of its violation of a sub-principle within *binding theory*, which can be defined as dealing with:

> restrictions on the co-reference of anaphoric[10] elements, including definite and reflexive pronouns and the traces left by movement.

Before looking at the sub-principles in binding theory the reader is advised to revisit the concept of c-commanding (see above), which formalises the notion of 'height on the tree'. This is of the essence here.

There are three subprinciples:

1) Principle A: An anaphor (e.g., a reflexive) is *bound* in its *local domain.*

2) Principle B: A definite pronoun must be *free* in its local domain.

3) Principle C: A referring-expression (e.g., a noun or proper name) must be free.

The italicised elements mean the following:

- *bound* = when an element both co-refers with another element and that other element is higher on the tree than that element, or the same height;

---

[10] Anaphora is the process whereby a linguistic unit depends for its interpretation on some previously expressed unit or meaning (its 'antecedent'). It marks the identity between what is being expressed and what has already been expressed.

- *local domain* = the area of the tree within the node immediately above the element; roughly the clause in which the element resides;
- *free* = not bound by a lexical item that precedes it in the local domain and so it can refer to something elsewhere in the tree (or deictically to something not mentioned in the sentence).

See Figure 2.21 and see p 204 for further description.

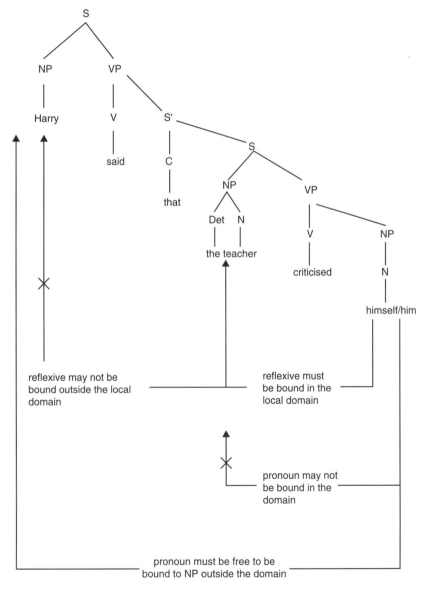

Figure 2.21

Figure 2.21 illustrates Principles A and B, and Figure 2.22 illustrates Principle C. With regard to Principle C, note that it captures the fact that a pronoun and an NP cannot co-refer if the pronoun is in a structurally dominant position – if it c-commands it. In Figure 2.22a, *he* and *Jones* can co-refer because the former does not c-command the latter; but in 2.22b they cannot.

In the light of all this, we can return to sentences like (18). We see here that Principle C has been violated due to the fact that the referring expression *John* is bound, being both c-commanded by *he* and co-referential with it. However in (19), the possessive pronoun *his* still co-refers to *John*, but it does not c-command it:

(19) John₍ᵢ₎ likes his₍ᵢ₎ mother.

I now turn to *bounding* principles. These concern structural restrictions on the operation of movement.

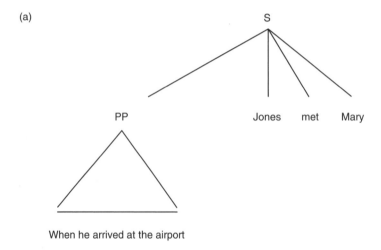

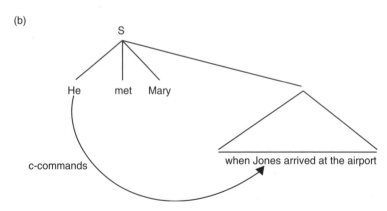

Figure 2.22

They are thus called because they concern constraints on the crossing of *bound-aries* (a term which I will unpack a little later) in movement. The general field of restrictions was first noted by Ross (1967), who dubbed them restrictions on the movement of *wh*-elements from within *islands*, although he did not offer any general account of the kinds of restriction that he collected under that term.

We will consider, then, ways in which these constraints can be violated with regard to movement of *wh*-elements. The constraint is on movement from within clauses (a temporal one in the following example). Imagine a scenario in which John asked Mary whether he should help Jane with the washing up; after which he did indeed help Jane. About this scenario we might ask the question in (20).

(20) Who did John ask before helping?

To this question we would surely give the answer 'Mary'. We do not feel there is any pull of ambiguity towards giving the answer 'Jane' to it. This would make it a question about who was helped, with the phrase about asking being a mere aside. In which case the sentence might be paraphrased as in (21).

(21) Who, about his helping whom John asked somebody, did he help?

To interpret the sentence in this way would be to take it as having been derived from a d-structure whose essential structure is:

John asked somebody before helping who?

But in this case, the *who* at the end of the d-structure would have been extracted from a temporal clause ('island'), and this is violation of a bounding constraint.

This serves as a lead-in to what is the defining principle in bounding theory – a formalisation of the kind of island constraint just considered. In fact, it was described by Chomsky (1973) well before it became a module with P & P theory. It is often taken to be exemplary of the whole P & P approach, and is much discussed.

The subjacency principle: an element can only move over one layer of structure, meaning that it can only move from a layer that is *sub*ordinate and ad*jacent*.

This amounts to saying that *there cannot be movement across more than one boundary*. I will return to the notion of boundary when I have given an example.

Consider a scenario in which the final words of the sentence (22) are inaudible:

(22) John saw a girl who swore at [inaudible].

The way we would frame a clarification in response to this would be by a question like (23) rather than one like (24). (The d-structure of the question would be essentially *John saw a girl who swore at who*.)

(23) Who did John see a girl swear at?
(24) *Who did John see a girl who swore at?

To say (24) would be to have moved the *who* in d-structure across two boundaries. In the problematic sentence, *who* has moved from its d-structure position leaving a trace, and in so moving it has traversed the additional layer of structure *a girl who*.

I will now flesh out the notion of boundary a little; though readers who desire the full technicalities are advised to visit Haegeman (1994, section 6.2). A bounding node can be either a sub-sentence/inflection phrase (IP) or a noun phrase. Thus, with regard to (24), we see the two layers revealed in (25), while the single one of (23) is shown in (26). In these, e = empty category; and they are simplified.

(25) Who$_i$ did John see [$_{NP}$a girl$_j$ [$_{IP}$who$_j$ swore at e_i]]

(26) Who$_i$ did John see [$_{IP}$a girl swear at e_i]

Note that in (26) [$_{IP}$a girl swear at e_i] is not only a *subordinate* element but also *adjacent* to the main verb. In (25) [$_{IP}$who$_j$ swore at e_i] is not similarly adjacent.

In passing, readers who know something of Oriental languages may find this a very parochial principle, given that in Chinese and Japanese interrogative expressions remain *in situ*; they do not move to the head of the sentence. Answering their concerns will afford a way of illustrating the operation of move-α between s-structure and LF. Consider the Chinese for the English question *Who do you like?* shown in (27) along with the literal English translation.

(27) ni xihuan shei
     you like who?

(In an officious style of English, favoured by policemen and old-style school masters, the form *You left your X where?* is acceptable.) Huang (1981) argued that in such languages there is in fact movement between the s-structure of (27) and its LF interpretation – although this is a Chomskyan gloss on what was argued in that paper. That is to say, in the LF interpretation of (27) and of the officious English form there is *covert* movement to the head of the sentence as the interrogative element has 'scope' over the whole utterance.

S-structure traces of movement in questions do not constitute the only case of empty categories (e) co-indexed with other elements. The next module we will consider – *control theory* – concerns another kind, a kind that is *not the result of movement*. In the sentences shown in (28) and (29), an empty element PRO ('big pro') is co-indexed with referring expressions in different ways.

(28) a. John told Mary to leave.
     b. John promised Mary to leave.
     c. John kissed Mary before leaving.
     d. Mary was kissed by John before leaving.

(29) a. John told Mary$_i$ [PRO$_i$ to leave].
     b. John$_i$ promised Mary [PRO$_i$ to leave].
     c. John$_i$ kissed Mary [before PRO$_i$ leaving].
     d. Mary$_i$ was kissed by John [before PRO$_i$ leaving].

Let us consider (28a) because doing so will enable us to encounter another module – *theta* (θ) *theory*. In (28a) what is the argument of the verb *leave*? The LR of the verb says that its argument needs to be an agent and that the d-structure projection will be of the form:

[NP [$_{VP}$leave]].

Is it, then, *Mary?*

The immediate difficulty here is that Mary also has a role to fulfil in relation to the main verb *told* whose LR is:

tell: V; Agent, Goal, Proposition.

Mary is obviously the Goal (the 'tellee'). It is, however a principle of θ-*theory that an expression cannot fill two argument roles at the same time: Mary* cannot be both the Agent of *leave* and the Goal of *told* at the same time. (Agent, Patient, Goal etc. are all θ-roles.) Given this, the position after *Mary* and before *to leave* must be taken up with an empty category – PRO – that is *controlled* by *Mary* in the main clause, as illustrated in (29a). In (29b) it can be seen that the controller of PRO is the subject of the main clause; in contrast to (29a) where it is the object. In the other two examples the controller of PRO is also the subject of the main clause, though in (29c) it is the agent and in (29d) the patient. (Note how the control theory and the θ-theory modules can be stated as independent structures and yet interdepend; so the Chomsky bodily organ analogy springs to mind.)

Atkinson refers to control theory as being 'a poor relation among the modules, in that it is not associated with any independent principles' (1992, p. 82). It would though seem to be related to binding principles, given that it concerns co-reference. But PRO itself has a somewhat ambiguous status, for in cases like those covered in (28) it is anaphoric whereas in cases like *PRO to leave would be a mistake* it is pronominally 'free in its local domain' (see Principle B above).

My final example of a P & P module is that of *Case theory*. This states that all NPs can be assumed to require a *case*[11]-*marking* by some other element (verb, preposition, inflection) which may or may not be represented in morphology. In English pronouns, case is overtly marked (e.g., *he* = nominative; *him* = accusative; *his* = genitive) but it is usually not marked on nouns, with the genitive form being an exception (e.g., *knight's move*). Case theory sets conditions on the assignment of case, with the central constraint being that all (non-empty) NPs are assigned case. I will make just two observations here, the first of which will prepare the ground for a later discussion in the Minimalism section, 2.3.

Not all lexical categories assign case. Thus, in the following N′, the head N is governing the complement but has not succeeded in assigning a case to it; and so it is ill-formed:

*destruction the city.

What is required is the preposition *of* to act as a case assigner and thus produce *destruction of the city*. It is necessary to note here that *of* is playing *a purely syntactic role*, in so far as it does not express the semantic function of denoting possession, as in *the car of John*. This means that we are seeing an example of a syntactic feature that is not *interpretable* at LF, *given that LF can contain only semantically interpretable features*. This apparent anomaly will be tackled in the Minimalist Programme.

---

[11] Case identifies the syntactic relationship between word classes or their associated phases in the sentence – nominative, accusative, genitive etc.

The second observation (which is based on the discussion in Atkinson (1992, pp. 85–6), concerns the intimate relationship between Case theory and constraints on move-α. The so-called *case filter* rule, which states that every phonetically-realised NP must be assigned a case, renders the operation of move-α obligatory in passivisation. To illustrate, (30) shows an s-structure and its d-structure.

(30) a. John was kissed

b. ($_S$e [$_{VP}$ was kissed John]]

So (30a) is the result of applying move-α to (30b). With regard to the d-structure shown in (30b), it can be said that because *kiss* has a passive morphology in d-structure the accusative case that this verb would normally take has been neutralised, with the consequence that *John* is now without a case. As this state of affairs is a violation of the case filter, *John* has to move to the empty slot to take the nominative case. The case filter is operative, then, at the level of s-structure.

I now turn finally to the question of *parametric variation.* Recall that this enables P & P to deal with structural differences between the world's languages. The essential claim is that knowledge of the principles just described is innate in the sense that child's mind–brain represents them (like a switch in a neutral position) as parameters to be fixed by the input. Much can be said on this topic, but I will restrict myself to illustrations of the way in which the fixing of one parameter has 'knock-on' implications for the way in which others are fixed. Not only does this illustrate how Chomsky is able to minimise the contribution of the input but, more important, it shows (1) that the modules are only *quasi*-autonomous and (2) that, whatever the empirical validity of P & P, it is exemplary of the triad 'elegance, simplicity, economy': the pieces slot together so neatly.

Chomsky (1981, p. 6) pointed out that setting a parameter in one direction will cause a cluster of superficially dissimilar parameters also to be set in a certain direction. The most studied case here is that of the so-called *null-subject* or *pro-drop*[12] parameter. In Italian and Spanish, and in Romance languages generally, it is possible to omit the subject in tensed sentences (because the relevant information is marked on the verb). Thus, it is possible in Italian for a speaker to say that she is going to the cinema in either of the two ways shown in (31).

(31) a. Io vado al cinema

b. Vado al cinema

However, (31b) corresponds to the English sentence **Go to the cinema* which is ill-formed when used indicatively. English requires that sentences have subjects: the null-subject parameter is, then, set to 'off' in English. Setting the parameter to 'on' goes along with the following settings (among others).

1) Null-subject languages will not contain so-called 'expletive' elements like the English *it* and *there* in the expressions *it seems that* ... and *there appears to be....* Note that (like the *of* in *destruction of the city*, discussed above) these expletives

----

[12] This is 'little pro' (c.f. 'big pro' or PRO above) meaning an empty category where the subject of a clause should be. Elizabethan English did contain pro (e.g., *Wilt* [you] *come?*), but modern English does not.

have only a syntactic role, and are consequently not interpretable in semantic terms at LF (as we shall later discuss).

2) Null-subject languages will violate the *that-trace filter* (discussed by Chomsky, 1981 p. 240ff), discussed immediately below.

3) Null-subject languages will express a more liberal version of the subjacency principle.

The that-trace filter states that there cannot be traces after the word *that*, thereby rendering sentences like (32a) ungrammatical (the general motivation for this principle need not detain us). (32c) shows the trace archaeology and (32b) the grammatical form.

(32) a. *Who do you think that left?
    b. You think that who left?
    c. Who$_i$ do you think that t$_i$ left?

In null-subject languages, however, the trace subject of *left* can be deleted, with the result that the that-trace filter has not been violated.

With regard to subjacency, sentences in Italian like (33a) appear to be violating this principle (example taken from Atkinson, 1992, pp. 96–7).

(33) a. Tuo fratello, a cui mi domanda che storie abbiano raccontato, era multo preoccupato.
    b. Your brother, to whom I wonder which stories they have told, was very worried.

In moving from the end to the beginning of the clause starting after *fratello, a cui* has traversed three bounding nodes: (i) the S beginning *mi domando*, the S′ beginning *che storie* and the S *abbiano raccondato*. (Note, by the way, that *which stories they have told* is an S′ not an S because it must appear as the complement of a verb: it cannot stand alone as a sentence as can *I wonder which stories they have told* and *they have told*.) To illustrate this by co-indexing d-structure positions we have the analysis shown in (34).

(34) [S′[C a cui$_i$][S mi domando [S′[Cche storie$_j$][S abbiano raccontato e_i e_j]]]]

In order to avoid the conclusion that Italian is violating the subjacency principle (as made by Rizzi, 1982, p. 50) we would need to say that in Italian S is not counted as a bounding node. If this is so, it can be said that *a cui* has only traversed the bounding node S′. This fact is related to Italian's being a null-subject language. Perhaps the claim can be made that in d-structure the Ss *mi domando che storie abbiano raccondato* and *abbiano raccondato* do not have subjects, and that these are only added in s-structure. In this case they would not constitute boundaries, but would be stretches of 'non-structure' like *wonder which … and *have told*.

What I hope to have done in this section is to illustrate how explanatory adequacy is sought within Chomskyan linguistics.

As a theory picks up speed the wind will strip extraneous features from it. But if there is any principled methodological division between the Minimalist Programme and the theories that lead up to it one might say that it lies in the designer's decision to make minimalism an *intrinsic design goal* rather something that is part and parcel of theory development itself.

2.3 The Minimalist Programme

A report in the *Guardian* newspaper in 1997 announced that Chomsky had abandoned his old theory and constructed a new one. This is not so. Neither is John Searle correct when he announced, in *The New York Review of Books* in 2002, that the new theory marks the end of the Chomskyan revolution – as I will discuss in 3.2. The Minimalist Programme (MP) is, in fact, a clear continuation of the P & P approach. For if there is a point of theoretical discontinuity in the evolution of his linguistic theory it came with the transition from ST to P & P, with *Lectures on government and binding* (1981) – an account of seminars Chomsky had given at the University of Pisa in 1979. This is illustrated vividly in an interview Chomsky gave in Siena with Adriana Belletti and Luigi Rizzi to mark the twentieth anniversary of these seminars (published as Chomsky, Belletti and Rizzi, 2002). 'What happened at Pisa' he says (Chomsky *et al.*, 2002, pp 94–95).

> is that somehow all the work came together for the first time in the seminars, and a method arose for sort of cutting the Gordian knot: namely eliminate rules and eliminate constructions altogether because there aren't any rules and constructions. There is no such thing as VP in Japanese or the relative clause in Hungarian. Rather, there are just extremely general principles like 'move anything anywhere' under fixed conditions that were proposed, and then there are options that have to be fixed, parametric choices: so the head of the construction first or last. Within this framework of fixed principles and options to be selected, the rules and the constructions disappear, they become artefacts.
>
> … the grammatical constructions are left as artefacts. In a sense they are real; it is not that there are no relative clauses, but they are a kind of taxonomic artefact. They are like 'terrestrial mammal' or something like that. 'Terrestrial mammal' is a category, but it is not a biological category. It's the interaction of several things and that seems to be what the traditional constructions are like, VPs, relative clauses and so on.

One might say that MP inaugurated a search for the abstract biological principles that underlie these linguistic 'artefacts'. In MP there is, however, some degree of meta-theoretical discontinuity as well as the continuity just sketched. In P & P, the elimination of redundancies in the theory became a primary goal; but in MP Chomsky went one step further and set up the working assumption that the faculty of language itself possesses *an optimal design* in which there are no true redundancies (though many apparent ones). In other words, *one moves from making the elimination of redundancy a methodological desideratum to taking the absence of redundancy to be a property of the system under study.* Of course we cannot know this fact about the system a priori; and so MP really is a research programme, an endeavour guided by a working assumption.

In the Siena interview, Chomsky makes it clear that P & P marked a transition to a more 'bottom-up' style of linguistic theory, in the sense that syntactic rules and constructions came to be regarded as the manifestation of deeper, more biologically-grounded operations, rather than as autonomous templates determining how lexical items come to be placed and interpreted. This progression to a more bottom-up approach gathers speed in MP, to the extent that there are now no X′-style phrase structures existing within a module to determine at the outset the course of lexical insertion (though the intermediate level may be computed in the course of the derivation – as discussed below). The lexicon is now seen as carrying enough structure to, as it were, 'do it for itself'. Similarly – as can be seen from Figure 2.23 – there are no longer the levels of s- and d-structure existing as distinct levels of representation.

It naturally follows from this that the process of deriving syntactic structure must itself take a bottom-up form. In this regard, paradoxically, we see a return to a way of conceptualising derivation that Chomsky employed in his pre-1965 theory (Lasnik, 2002). In this, rather than being inserted en bloc at the outset, the lexicon is inserted bottom-up from the most deeply embedded unit in a stepwise, ascending fashion. For example, in the sentence *the cat will chase the mouse, mouse* is the most deeply embedded element. This will be combined with the determiner *the* to produce the DP *the mouse*, which will in turn be combined with *chase* to produce a V-bar construction. The DP *the cat* is created in the same way as *the mouse* and is combined with the V-bar to create *chase the mouse* as a VP. Next, the VP merges with the inflection *will* to produce an I-bar. The DP *the cat* moves, finally, to the specifier position to yield the full clausal projection IP. This process is called 'merge' (or 'merger'), and it will be discussed at some length. The bottom half of Figure 2.23, which I borrow, modified, from Jackendoff (2002, p. 110) is supposed – I take it – to represent this step-by-step process.

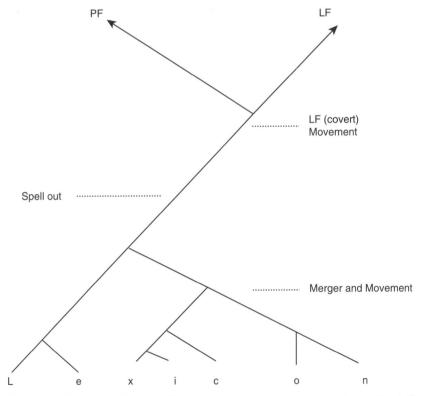

Figure 2.23 The basic architecture of the Minimalist Programme. Adapted from Jackendoff (2002, p. 110).

Well, to all this the developmental psychologist is likely to say 'So *what?*'. This looks as much like more of the same as less of it, while – as ever – the proposals all float in the high ether of the 'competence' realm (are these serial derivation processes real mental operations or are they just formally necessary moves motivated only by a priori assumptions?). And what can it tell us about the course of development? Some generative linguists have likewise been unimpressed. Frederick Newmeyer, the current President of the Linguistic Society of America and an advocate of the P & P approach, has written that

> At the present time, I find the concrete claims of MP so vague and the total set of mechanisms that it requires (where I have been able to understand them) so *unminimalist* that I see no reason to encumber the exposition [in his book] with my interpretation of how the phenomenon in question might be dealt with within that approach.
>
> (Newmeyer, 1998, pp. 12–13)

But in fact there is something about MP that should capture the attention not only of developmental psycholinguists but also of students of cognitive development. The fact is that, for the first time, Chomsky not only tries to cash his previous, disappointingly vague (Russell, 1987b) references to the 'interaction' of the cognitive and the linguistic systems, but he puts this enterprise in the very engine-room of the theory. This is so because the 'optimal design' or 'perfection' of the language system, definitively assumed within MP, is a perfection in how the language faculty mediates between the thought systems and the sensorimotor systems for speech. *It is exactly the interface between these systems that he is concerned with.*

At least in the early phase of MP, the idea was retained that the thought–syntax interface was at LF, though more recently Chomsky (2000b) has suggested, in his notion of 'multiple spell-out', that at stages prior to full syntactic derivation the syntactic structure thus far created is sent off to interface components for phonological and semantic interpretation. But before we become immersed in the details I would like to dramatise Chomsky's view of the 'thought system'/syntactic system relationship by quoting at some length from a radio interview he gave.

In an interview with BBC Radio 3, broadcast in 1999 ('Viewing the Century', interview by Jonathan Steinberg), Chomsky said the following. (The emphasis is mine, as is the transcription.)

> How good a design is language? So – suppose – let's imagine a fairy tale. And suppose we imagine a primate, just like us, wandering around thousands of years ago. It has our sensorimotor apparatus, our articulatory organs, inner ear and so on. It has our thought systems. *So it has the same thoughts as we do,* so far as they can't be expressed by language. And it has the same wishes and aspirations, hopes whatever; but it has no language faculty. So that's this organism. Suppose – you know – a shower of cosmic rays comes by and causes some (maybe very small) mutation which reorganises the brain. That's how complex systems work: some slight change can lead to massive effects. And what it does is insert a language faculty. What does the language faculty have to *do* to be usable – accessible to the external systems? It has to be accessible to the sensorimotor systems, otherwise you won't even know you have it. It has to be able to externalise it somehow. And it has to be accessible to the thought systems – conceptual systems – because it has to express your thoughts. I mean the function of the system and what it's doing is enabling you to *pick the thoughts, beliefs and attitudes and hopes, and so on and put them with some external medium.* And the opposite is true. It has to be able to pick up noises that others are producing and create the thoughts that you could have produced yourself if you'd thought about it – basically a Cartesian point.

So going back to the fairy tale, we can ask about the system we've inserted. It has – what you might consider as – design specifications. It has to connect these external conditions which are given independently. Or you can ask how perfect a design is it. So if you had some engineer who was given a design specification and was asked to construct an optimal system, how close does language come to that? It's an intriguing question because the biological world doesn't work like this. You don't find perfect design in this sense. Everyone who has a spine knows it's really not that well designed. It's the best that Nature could do with whatever was around. It ends up less than optimal… .

If the Minimalist Programme turns out to be true it could show that language is more like a snowflake than a giraffe's neck. It has some specific form because of the laws of Nature, not something that just develops because that's the way the accidents of history were.

(By the way, I think one would be advised to take the reference to 'cosmic rays' as meant in the spirit of *épater les functionalistes*. At the end of Part 4 I will set out Chomsky's more considered, and more recent, views on the evolution of language.)

Reading this, nobody could accuse Chomsky of failing to face up to the uncomfortable consequences of his claim that syntax is an autonomous system. Here indeed, he almost seems to be revelling in them. The central source of discomfort might be expressed like this. On the one hand, syntax has, for Chomsky, a host of *sui generis* principles whose nature is not determined by the need to achieve adequate communication nor by the nature of the human conceptual system; for it is, rather, the product of pressures internal to the system – pressures towards elegance, simplicity, and economy. But at the same time language *does* express our thoughts and enables us to gain access to the thoughts of other people. So how then does it come about that syntactic structure is so well suited to the task? Thought and language would appear to have quite different success conditions and motivations and yet 'miraculously' (in the sense that all snowflakes having six sides is a kind of miracle to somebody who bet on their having six) they interface as neatly as if some cosmic designer had determined it to be so. Could this just be a happy chance? After all, we have had eternity to get it right; and perhaps the universe is littered with the brilliant but inarticulate and with the volubly mindless. Or is this whole way of thinking about the language–thought relationship hopelessly misconceived: that saying language is 'well designed' to express thoughts is like saying that beaches are perfectly designed to interface with the sea or that, luckily, legs are just long enough to interface with the ground.

Indeed, for some readers this passage will serve as a fine illustration of just why pragmatism must be the favoured meta-theory of the language–thought relation. They will think that we can surely escape from this jungle of paradoxes simply by assuming that language gradually evolved from cognition and social life by Darwinian selection. This is not only the voice of 'common sense' but also an echo of the timeless appeal of pragmatism, captured by Menard (1997, p. xi) when he says that taking the pragmatist option can feel as if some 'pressing but vaguely understood obligation' has suddenly been lifted from our shoulders, as if a final examination for which we could never have been properly prepared had just been cancelled (from section 1.3). From this perspective, Chomsky is like the mildly sadistic examiner with a penchant for questions whose function is not to tap knowledge but to 'sort the sheep from the goats'.

But is it really so easy to escape? *Is there really a sense in which language is no more than an articulate cognition simpliciter?* There is, after all, nothing self-evidently absurd in the idea that inarticulate creatures might have thoughts with all the expressive power of those of a language user. What's more, the idea that thought and language are simply identical, with silent thought being inner speech, *is* self-evidently absurd. For how is the self-talker in English (or 'thinker') able to understand what he says to himself – by generating more English? And most important for our purposes, *the way in which language and all its seemingly arbitrary and Heath Robinsonesque features interfaces with thought would indeed seem to stand in need of explanation.* This is an issue indeed that has broadly been ignored in psycho-linguistics, in which we find conceptualisations of thought in terms of 'mental models', 'scenarios', 'semantic networks', and the like, but scant attention to how such non-syntactic entities are supposed to find syntactic realisation.

Rather more contentiously (and folk-psychologically and discursively), while the fittedness of syntax to thought does indeed seem more like a contingent fact of nature than a conceptual necessity, what is remarkable in the experience of the language user is how infrequently syntax lets us down. We often struggle to find the right form of expression for our thoughts, often to the extent of doubting whether there actually is a coherent way to express quite what we think, but our common experience is not that this is because *syntax* is inadequate to our purposes. (Recall the subjacency principle discussed towards the end of the previous section. This does not put any kind of barrier against the kind of questions we can ask but determines rather *how* they can be asked.) And while we sometimes believe that only an *idiom* of another language can express quite what we mean, it seems to make little sense to say that only a *syntactic construction* in another language can quite express how we think that the arguments are related to the verb in the sentence we want to say. In other words, we understand what it means for thought to fall short of adequate expression, but find that this falling short *is not something that happens at the syntactic level.* Conversely, the common experience of speakers is not that their syntax is otiose and ripe for paring back to something similar to formal logic: it seems to be adequate to the job and no more. In any event, it would appear to be an intellectually lazy and quietist option simply to assume that the fittedness of syntax to thought is a conceptual necessity *about which nothing of empirical interest can be said.*

If one does not adopt, then, the pragmatist assumption that every feature of syntax is ultimately to be explicated in terms of cognition (subsuming the social and the neurobiological under this term) then the problem has to be faced of how syntax interfaces with what Chomsky calls the *conceptual-intentional (C–I)* or 'thought' systems. Back to the early primate in the fairy tale. As Chomsky (2000, p. 93) wrote

> Suppose some event reorganises the brain in such a way as, in effect, to insert [the faculty of language]. To be usable, the new organ has to meet certain 'legibility conditions'. Other systems of the mind/brain have to be able to access expressions generated by states of [the language faculty] … to 'read' them and use them as 'instructions' for thought and action.

Later in this passage Chomsky suggests that the imagined primate would, for this reason, have to be credited with something like LOT. But what is of central importance here is the notion of *legibility conditions*. The language faculty must be such as to be legible or *interpretable* by both the C–I systems and by the articulatory–perceptual (A–P) sytems. In fact we have already encountered the notion of interpretability in our discussion of how syntactic features have to be semantically interpretable at LF.

This language organ would be expected to consist of a lexicon and procedures for combining lexical elements such that they are 'readable' at both the C–I and the A–P systems and such that this results in articulated sentences (at A–P) that not only have meaning but are non-deviant. Accordingly, to take Chomsky's own example, the A–P sentence *John is easy to catch* lines up with the 'C–I meaning' IT IS EASY TO CATCH JOHN appropriately enough; whereas, while *John is easy to be caught* might more or less line up with IT IS EASY TO CATCH JOHN it is not a well-formed English sentence. In short, legibility is not only a matter of getting a meaning across by articulating sounds (or gestures) but of getting this meaning across in the right way. Given this, it is by no means inevitable that language will turn out to be a particularly good solution to these legibility conditions. As Chomsky said in the interview, language may, like the human spine, turn out to be somewhat jerry-built. But – I hope so much will have emerged from the review of the theories which led up to MP as well as the discussion of explanatory adequacy in Part 1 – we would surely expect Chomsky to take the view that language is an elegant, simple and economical solution to legibility conditions. For Chomsky does not draw a firm and impermeable line between elegance, simplicity and economy as touchstones of linguistic enquiry ('methodological minimalism' perhaps) and minimalism as a thesis about the object of the enquiry. It might indeed be said, that the difficulty in keeping minimalism as methodology distinct from minimalism as a thesis is inevitable in linguistics in a way in which it is not in the (at least) biological sciences. Thus, the fact that the brain might, in some respects, be said to be jerry-built does not imply that neurobiological theories can be full of redundancies and ad hoceries. But language, unlike the brain, is a *formal* object, at least for all those who adopt a broadly rationalist view of the language faculty. And this being so, one would expect it to exemplify the same rational structure as a good theory, to have an internal coherence and parsimony. In P & P, for example, we saw that the various principles/modules of the theory relate to one another and to operations like move-α under minimalist constraints: they do all they need to do and no more to sustain the coherence of the theory. Similarly, the replacement of re-write phrase structure rules by X-bar theory was determined by, what Chomsky calls in fact, methodological minimalism while at the same time carrying the empirical assumption that the language organ itself is a manifestation of minimalism.

In any event, Chomsky states the Strong Minimalist Thesis (SMT) thus:

> Language is an optimal solution to legibility conditions.

'Language design may really be optimal in some respects … The conclusion would be surprising and interesting if true' (Chomsky, 2000a, p. 98). In other words, good design is something we might *not* find – and this makes SMT an empirical theory, not merely a way of viewing language. On SMT, then, all that motivates/ constrains what goes into a theory of syntax are two things: (1) legibility requirements, (2) the assumption of good design.

It is worth pointing out, in passing, that optimality of design is not an absolute fact: it can only be assessed in relation to how well the design of a certain organ in the body of language enables it to interact successfully with the other organs. Chomsky (Chomsky *et al.*, 2002, p 107–108[13]) illustrates this fact (in the Siena interview) in the following way.

> So instead of asking the standard functionalist question 'Is it well designed for use?, we ask another question: 'Is it well designed for interaction with systems internal to the mind?' It's quite a different question, because maybe the whole architecture of the mind is not well designed for use. Let me see if I can make an analogy: take some other organ of the body, say, the liver. You may discover that the liver is badly designed for life in Italy because people drink too much wine there and they get all sorts of diseases of the liver; therefore the liver wasn't well designed for function. On the other hand, the liver might be beautifully designed for interaction with the circulatory system, the kidney, and so on, and those are just different things. From the point of view of selection, natural selection, things must be well designed, at least moderately well designed for use, well designed enough so that organisms can reproduce and so on. *But a totally separate question is: forgetting the use to which the object is put, is it well designed from the perspective of internal structure? That's a different kind of question, and actually a new one* (emphasis added).

With specific reference to the question of how well designed is the language faculty in relation to the C–I systems, Chomsky goes on to say this.

> The way I would like to think of it now is that the system is *essentially inserted into already existing external systems*: external to the language faculty, internal to the mind. So there's a sensorimotor system which is there, independently of language; maybe it's something modified because of the presence of language, but in essence it is there independently of language. The bones of the middle ear don't change because of language. And there is some kind of system of thought (conception, intention and so on) which is sort of sitting there. That includes what were traditionally called 'common notions' or 'innate ideas'. Perhaps also analysis in terms of what is called 'folk psychology', interpreting people's actions in terms of belief and desire, recognising things in the world and how they move, and so on (emphasis added).

Before tackling the specific proposals of the theory I wish to mention two potential difficulties for STM raised by Atkinson (2000), one a procedural difficulty that may turn out to be a 'crippling handicap', the other an aspect of the theory which Atkinson confesses to finding 'inscrutable'. In the first place, consider the so-called *external systems* of C–I and A–P which impose legibility conditions on the language system at the interface. It is clear that the cogency of claims about good design and legibility made from one side of the interface must be assessed against what we know about C–I and A–P; it depends, for one thing, on our having a rich cognitive psychology. It is certainly a paradox, then, that while Chomsky rejects the pragmatist view that syntactic structures are at bottom cognitively motivated, *SMT is no less dependent upon cognitive psychology*. But instead of regarding cognitive (or socio-cognitive) psychology as the bedrock (as in pragmatism) it regards it as a neighbouring landscape whose contours determine the state's boundaries and internal

---

[13] The exact wording is taken from the pre-publication version revised in March, 2000.

political structures. From the perspective of cognitive *developmental* psychology, in fact, this does not look like a 'crippling handicap', in so far as the researcher can study the relation between the acquisition of certain cognitive abilities and language development – in ways to be discussed in the next section. To do this, one does not need an up-and-running theory of adult cognition.

Atkinson's 'inscrutable' feature of SMT concerns the question of how, according to Chomsky, one should regard the features of the language system that do have the appearance of imperfections. 'They call,' writes Chomsky (2001, p. 1), 'for some independent account: perhaps path-dependent evolutionary history, properties of the brain, or some other source'. This suggests that while we should not seek reductionist accounts of where language is optimally designed we can happily seek them *where it falls short of perfection*. But does Chomsky really mean to say that the study of evolution and of the brain can yield no insights into language *in so far as it is well designed*? Not only is this unjustified, but it seems to be a way of protecting SMT against negative evidence: the language system is optimally designed (except where it isn't by reason of evolutionary accident and contingent features of the brain). One way of defending Chomsky here would be by saying that he is overextending a reasonable proposal about when working from the neurobiological level upwards is appropriate and when it is not. For it might be said that while the bottom-up approach cannot provide us with adequate accounts of those competences that go to make humans rational animals, it is entirely appropriate when we seek accounts of mental pathologies such as schizophrenia and autism. While work on what is wrong with the schizophrenic or the autistic brain may inform us about some of the kinds of information-processing that support rationality, they do not provide us with theories of how we reason – for which top-down theories are necessary (e.g., Johnson-Laird, 1983). Chomsky is carrying over this 'asymmetry of effort' (Atkinson's phrase) to the realm of linguistic enquiry – unwisely perhaps.

2.3.1 Surveying the architecture of MP

As a first step towards understanding the architecture of MP we can consider what Chomsky has written recently about the way in which it differs from P & P. Chomsky (2000a, p. 10, emphasis added) asks whether:

> there are any levels other than interface levels: Are there levels 'internal' to the language, in particular, the levels of deep and surface structure that have been postulated in modern work? *The minimalist programme seeks to show that everything that has been accounted for in terms of these levels has been misdescribed*, and is as well or better understood in terms of legibility conditions at the interface: for those of you who know the technical literature, that means the projection principle, binding theory, Case theory, the chain condition,[14] and so on.

He goes on to say that no structural relations can be posited 'other than those forced by legibility conditions or induced in some natural way by the computation itself' (ibid, p. 11). As an example of the first kind (forced by legibility conditions) at the C–I interface he gives argument structure and quantifier-variable relations in semantics.

---

[14] Chaining refers to the relationship between moved items and their traces.

That is to say, the linguistic system must be designed so as to mesh with facts about our conception of how objects are related to one another and to states and events as well as to our conception of how arguments relate to concepts like *all, some, none*, and so forth. As an example of the second kind ('induced by the computation itself') he gives the c-commanding relationship which, while being 'highly unnatural', plays 'a central role throughout language design'. We will return to these proposals very shortly.

It is now at last time to describe the architecture of the programme, and do so with the following two caveats in mind. In the first place, because MP is a research programme, or at least something between this and a policy statement about what form a theory of the language faculty should take, the proposals are not intended to penetrate through all of the language system; and there are a number of undecided issues. Second, it is perhaps inevitable that the less knowledge a theory ascribes to language users the more work has to be done to justify what *is* ascribed to them; and this is 'work' of a highly abstract kind. In contrast to P & P, which lists modules and stipulates levels (d- and s-) and constraints, MP cannot be described in terms of a body of tacitly-known principles, but must instead be regarded as a system of operations that have to be performed a certain way, given the foundational assumptions of the programme and what follows from these. One intriguing feature of MP is the concrete nature of the proposals about the nature of syntax that are supposed to flow, directly or indirectly, and by a kind of necessity, from these foundational proposals.

So what is this 'kind of necessity' that is supposed to determine proposals made in the programme? Chomsky calls it *virtual conceptual necessity*. This means that the necessity of the language faculty having a certain property is not a matter of philosophical, logical, or *sub specie aeternitatis* necessity. These are conceptually necessary properties *of human* syntax, positing which leaves open the possibility that they will not be present in, let's say, Martian or Venutian. The force of the 'virtual' is to remind us that the proposals are necessary *only within the assumptions we are making*. The main assumption that Chomsky makes (one which is not, of course, shared by empiricist and pragmatist approaches) is that there is indeed a language faculty – which Chomsky now refers to as the 'computational system for human language' (C_{HL}), as distinct from the cognitive systems (C–I systems) and from the articulatory–perceptual (A–P) systems. On the one hand, Chomsky does not take the pragmatist option of grounding syntax in socio-cognitive structures while, on the other, he is not content to construct a grammar with no cognitive commitments at all, as is, for example, Gazdar *et al.* (1985). Given these assumptions, it is 'virtually conceptually necessary' that (1) there will exist interfaces between C_{HL} and the external systems, (2) what is computed in C_{HL} must be legible at these interfaces, and (3) that these 'external' epistemic and sensorimotor systems will impose constraints on the nature of C_{HL}. Furthermore, while it is virtually conceptually necessary for there to be a lexicon of features and for syntactic categories to be sets of features (a radically pragmatist approach would dispute the need for purely syntactic categories) it is *not* conceptually necessary for there to be, say, movement. As Neil Smith (1999, p. 87) puts it 'the reason for the ubiquitous existence of movement, which is clearly not conceptually necessary, may be that it is a response to requirements of communication: putting old information before new, for instance.' As we go along I shall point out when a proposal in MP is supposed to arise out of virtual conceptual necessity and when it is taken to be imposed by such external conditions.

We can now return to Chomsky's imaginary primate to consider how external systems might constrain its newly-gifted C_{HL}. (We will concern ourselves exclusively with the C–I interface, while noting that the need to output phonemes and morphemes serially[15] will constrain C_{HL}.) If the creature is thinking thoughts then we must assume that these thoughts have a combinatorial and recursive structure. And if this is so, and if what is computed in C_{HL} is to be interpretable at the C–I interface, then the objects that are computed must be complex objects made up of simpler ones. Accordingly, we would expect C_{HL} to contain a procedure for combining elements of the lexicon. This, as we have seen, is called the operation of *merge*, (or *merger*). 'Such an operation,' Chomsky (1995, p 243) writes, 'is necessary on conceptual grounds alone, an operation that forms larger units out of those already constructed'. However, it must be cautioned at this point that the distinction between virtual conceptual necessity and externally-imposed legibility conditions is not one that can be drawn cleanly in the context of merge. That is to say, we end up with an argument for the conceptual necessity of merge whether one starts from considerations of conceptual necessity itself or from legibility considerations. In the first place, the virtual conceptual necessity of merge arises from the fact that once we assume that human language is a combinatorial, compositional system (an assumption justifying the 'virtual') it would seem to follow as a matter of conceptual necessity that we require a merging operation. Alternatively, a demand from the interface is that it will need to work with *integrated* linguistic objects if a derivation is be successful (to 'converge' rather than 'crash' – see below); so this too is an argument for merging that can also be regarded as adverting to conceptual necessity, though less directly. That said, the first kind of consideration is, perhaps, more persuasive than the second ('demand from the interface') kind.[16] This would appear to be Chomsky's view. He writes:

> The property 'converges at IL [interface level]' may hold of an expression formed in the course of a derivation that then proceeds on to IL. If, say, particles or adverbs have only LF-interpretable features, then they converge at LF when extracted from the lexicon and at every subsequent stage in the derivation to LF.
>
> (Chomsky, 2000b, p. 94)

What this suggests is that there are some kinds of lexical objects that are interpretable at LF *by their very nature*, and consequently do not need the intervention of merge to render them legible at LF. Given this possibility, the conceptual necessity of *merge* cannot follow from the external requirement that only 'integrated' syntactic objects

---

[15] It is conceivable that there should be a non-human language which is not serial. Its phonemes and morphemes might be like strings on an enormous guitar, with the speaking being similar to the act of strumming, words, and sentences being like chords.

[16] I am grateful to Martin Atkinson for this observation.

can be read; so we should perhaps run with the first ('from the combinatorial and compositional nature of language') consideration in favour of the conceptual necessity of *merge*. In short, compositionality and combinatorial structure in LOT demands the same of language – by 'virtual conceptual necessity'.

As we have just seen, the third source for the features of MP (i.e., after virtual conceptual necessity and external imposition via legibility conditions) are principles 'induced in some natural way by the computation itself'. In the present case, if *merge* results in pairs of lexical items being merged with a further pair of lexical items it is inevitable that relations will hold between some of them of the c-commanding kind described above in the context of P & P.

C_{HL} must be then – the 'must' springs from virtual conceptual necessity – as much a combinatorial system as is thought. Distinct from this is the lexicon from which C_{HL} will be woven. In order for this weaving to be achieved it is necessary to posit an operation (*selection*) that will construct an *array* (A) of lexical items from the lexicon. In fact, selection is a two-stage operation (select$_1$ and select$_2$) within MP: the first for the construction of the array, the second for operating on the array to make linguistic objects available to C_{HL}. The term 'array/A' is being used here in a technical sense to refer to 'array or numeration' because the array of words selected$_1$ from the lexicon will have each item tagged in terms of how often it is used in the sentence. (Thus, Melanie-2 would mean two occurrences of the word in *Melanie knew her name was Melanie*). Given this, A will contain information about both lexical *types* and lexical *tokens*.[17] Select$_2$ then takes items from A to form an object that is accessible to the computational system – which can be understood as making phrases out of lexical items. In by-now-familiar jargon, phrases are *projected* from lexical items. Ultimately, of course, the derivation must find its way to the interfaces with C–I and A–P, or more precisely will have to become manifest in terms of, respectively, LF and PF. If all goes well, the derivation will *converge* at LF and PF; and what determines whether all goes well is whether the external conditions existing at C–I and A–P are met. If they are not, the derivation is said to *crash*. At LF there exists, what Chomsky calls, *the inclusiveness condition*, whereby every object at that level is built from features of the lexical items within an array.

The obvious and persistent question here is: What is the status of the objects existing at C–I with which the derivation will either converge or against which it will crash? In a comprehensive text on MP by Uriagereka (1998), which has Chomsky's blessing and in which he appears in the character of 'the linguist',[18] 'the linguist' says with regard to such questions that while:

> we have no idea about what the possible range [of constraining instances] is ... when (or if) we say that the symbols of LF are things like predicates and arguments, and so on, we're saying that there's something natural about those symbols, in terms of their interpretability in relation to some cognitive component.

(Uriagereka, 1998, p. 102)

---

[17] Type is a lexical kind and token is a single occasion of its use.

[18] In the following I will take Uriagereka's 'linguist' to be equivalent to Chomsky - at least when it comes to direct statements of policy.

I will take this to mean that the interface level of LF is constituted out of arguments and predicates, because these are the 'natural' manifestations of the distinction between an entity and the properties of that entity, between an entity and its current state, and between sets of entities and how they are related.

Perhaps one way to regard the relation between select$_2$ and merge is by saying that the process of selection$_2$ makes lexical items available for use in a particular phrase and *merge* is how they are actually combined.

The output of the merge operation must obviously be an entity that is legible at both interfaces *as* the same entity, but whose concrete characters (sensorimotor in one case and broadly semantic in the other) are quite different. This is the operation of *Spell-out*. Spell-out sends the derivation simultaneously to PF and LF. Figure 2.24 shows the set of derivational steps running from top to bottom. It is a slight elaboration on Figure 2.23.

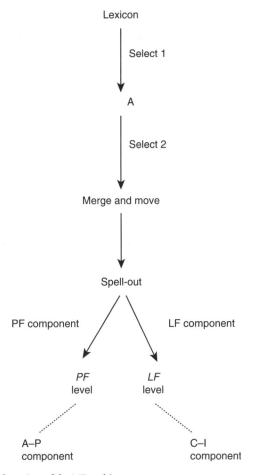

Figure 2.24 An elaboration of the MP architecture.

2.3.2 Merge – general character

As promised, I now turn to the nature of *merge*. Merge consists of a set of principles determined via virtual conceptual necessity from the fact that LF requires sets of phrases for legibility and that lexical items consist of sets of features. (For this reason, Chomsky writes of the computations of *merge* as being 'costless'; i.e., in the sense that no purpose-built phrase structure rules of the X′ kind need to be posited in addition to this.) What native speakers have, then, is *knowledge of lexical items each with a set of abstract features*. And if knowledge of the lexicon is enriched, the positing of computationally costly sets of phrase-structure rules becomes otiose. Inevitably, this also means that, because *merge* allows the combination of any two lexical items, a filtering procedure is required to police this process so as to prevent illegal combinations. This is called *checking*, a process which will shortly be described. But the immediate point is that *merge* is the culmination of the process within Chomskyan theory, begun post-ST (as described at the start of section 2.3), away from the positing of knowledge about rules for the construction of phrases towards *lexical* knowledge. (In a relaxed sense, and in contrast to other kinds of theory, speaker-hearers are still assumed to know rules. Knowledge of rules might be said to result from merge, but knowledge of rules is not what merge reduces to. I discuss rule-following in Chomskyan theory in section 3.2.)

Merge is obviously a much simpler notion than that of phrase-structure rules and X-bar grammar. But – as was warned earlier – the more basic the proposal, the more 'work' has to be done to justify its existence; and indeed the more imagination is required to understand it. One might see this as being due to the fact that simple components in a sparse conceptual landscape have to be *self-justifying* (by virtual conceptual necessity, by imposition from external conditions, by 'falling out' of the C_{HL} computations). In contrast to this situation, less *foundational* work has to be done in the modular system of P & P (modestly baroque components in a populous conceptual landscape) because each element of the architecture was justified in terms of the way in which it meshed with the other elements. Merge has relatively few features, but they need careful justification within the tenets of MP. This will now be done in some detail.

Merge, while not consisting of phrase-structure *rules*, is nonetheless a theory of phrase structure – called by Chomsky *bare phrase structure*. It applies not only to individual lexical items but also to the construction of clauses from phrases (Radford, 1997a , pp. 94–97). One thing we should note about the bare phrase structure is that it dispenses with the intermediate or 'bar' level of X-bar syntax. Recall that on this theory there are taken to be three levels.

> XP (X″)
>
> X′ (of which there can be more than one)
>
> X⁰.

Chomsky (1995, p. 249) writes:

> The bare theory departs from conventional assumptions in several respects: in particular, categories are elementary constructions from lexical items, satisfying the inclusiveness condition, there are no bar levels and no distinction between lexical items and 'heads' projected from them. A consequence is that an item can be both X⁰ and an XP.

This rejection of intermediate levels in bare phrase structure illustrates two aspects of MP, one substantive and the other an illustration of the theory's research-programme status: one the determination of C_{HL} by legibility constraints at the interface, and the other Chomsky's continuing debate with himself about even the fundamentals of MP.

In the first place, the claim is made that intermediate projections are not relevant at the LF interface, and that, given this, they are not 'visible' to C_{HL}. Let us remind ourselves what this intermediate level is. In Figure 2.25, *pledges to re-nationalise railways* is an N′ since it projects into the larger nominal (NP or N″) structure *Government pledges to re-nationalise the railways*.

Chomsky does not deny that intermediate levels exist and that parses like the one in Fig. 2.25 are necessary. What he denies is that *merge* itself operates on any level other than the levels of heads (items from the lexicon) and maximal projections. The intermediate level is something that is computationally present but that does not motivate the computation itself; in the sense that carrying over column totals is something that is computationally present when we add numbers together without it being a basic feature of addition as a mathematical operation. Figure 2.26 illustrates how the intermediate level is represented in MP. It is necessary to understand a little more about merge to make sense of how an intermediate level of representation can emerge from a computation, so I will say a few words about this before turning to formal proofs of properties of merge which are not conceptually necessary.

First, merge is *asymmetrical*. This means that the operation is not a blending of equals into some third kind of entity, but rather the process whereby one lexical item takes another as its *target*, which results in the target becoming the entity that determines the nature of the phrase. That is to say, the target of merge *projects*; just

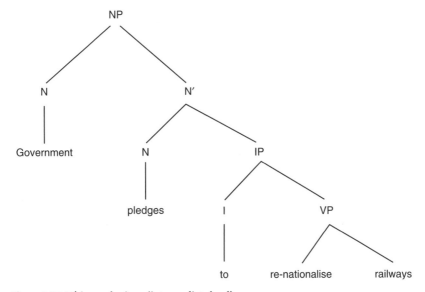

Figure 2.25 N′ (noun-bar): an 'intermediate level'.

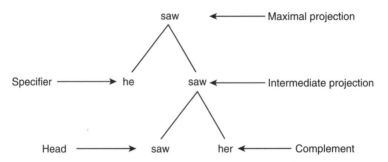

Figure 2.26 The representation of the 'intermediate level' in MP.

as a verb projects to VP, a noun to NP, and so forth. For example, *her* might merge with *saw*, in which case *saw* is the target and the resulting phrase is a verb phrase that is a maximal projection. In merge, then, one 'partner' is the stronger and sought-after partner, and when their marriage has taken place, *it* determines what kind of partnership will result.

With this in mind we can return to the role of intermediate projections in merger computations. Consider what happens when the sentence *He saw her* is constructed. The phrase *saw her* is a product of merge which in turn merges with *he*. In this process, what sense can be given to the idea that intermediate projections are 'computationally present' and are 'terms which result from merger and engage in further merger'? (Uriagereka, 1998, p. 181). See Figure 2.26. In the first place, *her* merges with the maximal projection *saw*. The reason *saw* is a maximal projection is that *at this point* in the computation it is not immediately dominated by anything. Indeed it is, as Chomsky promised, in the passage quoted above, both X^0 and XP. However, after the merger with *he, saw* ceases to be a maximal projection because it comes to be dominated by a higher representation of *saw* that is the maximal projection of the whole phrase. As Uriagereka (p. 181–182, op cit.) puts it:

> At the point of merger, the two terms of the merge operation are maximal projections, although later on one of them gets 'buried' inside its own projection. From that point on, although the 'buried' operation is still a term, it won't lead to a formal object, which in itself determines a convergent derivation as a head or a maximal projection does [...] [N]otions like head or maximal projection are necessary for various subsystems of grammar, that specifically operate on these structures, and intermediate projections aren't.

There are also empirical considerations supporting the idea that C_{HL} does not compute over the intermediate level. For example, only heads and maximal projections can undergo movement.[19] But it is not this kind of consideration that motivates Chomsky's claim made in *The minimalist programme* (1995) that, in addition to heads, 'only maximal projections are relevant to LF interpretation' and that 'bare output

---

[19] Uriagereka (1998, p. 181) gives the following as an example of the illegitimate movement of an X′: *[good to be true_i], though it was [too [———_i] he nonetheless believed it.* Cf. maximal projection movement: *[too good to be true_i] though it was [———_i] he nonetheless believed it.*

conditions make the concepts "minimal and maximal projection" available to C_{HL}' (p. 242). It has to be said, however, that his reasons for making this stipulation are less than transparent. Indeed in the accompanying footnote he says that 'The exact force of the assumption depends upon properties of phrases that are still unclear'.

This brings me briefly to the second aspect of MP that can be illustrated via the treatment of intermediate levels (i.e., the research-programmatic, rather than *marmoreal*, status of the theory). A few years later Chomsky (2001, p. 32) was to write '... the assumption that X′ is not interpreted at LF ... is questionable and in fact rejected in standard approaches'.

Finally in this subsection, I will make some comments about the way in which merge enables the *semantic* properties of lexical items to percolate up through the derivation. Lexical items come complete with selection restrictions, a notion that will be recalled from the standard theory. Accordingly, *eat*, for example, will come with [+agent, + theme]; indeed we might add in Grimshaw's canonical structural realisations (p. 116) and expand this to [+ subject, agent; + object, theme], although the necessity for this to MP is unclear. *Eat* will thereby become the target of a suitable theme (e.g., *cheese*) to produce the product {*eat, cheese*}. Then, because merge creates phrases with heads (i.e., it is asymmetrical) the next merger will still have to satisfy the selection restrictions on *eat*, say {*mice* {*eat, cheese*}}; and this is a kind of *semantic projection*. If these selection restrictions are not met, the derivation will not crash, but will converge as gibberish.[20]

2.3.3 An analysis of merge – some proofs

In this section, I provide detailed support for the claim that the nature of merge (rather than its very existence, which is a matter of virtual conceptual necessity) is determined by minimalist principles such as the 'good design' and the requirement for legibility at the interfaces. So I shall make no apology for spending so much time on the following proofs of some central properties of merge.

We have covered these properties of merge before, but this time we encounter the proofs of why they should be the way they are. There are three properties to be considered, and in describing their proofs I shall be relying heavily on Atkinson (2000).

1) The binary nature of branching

2) The headedness of phrases

3) Projection.

We encountered 2 and 3 a little earlier, while 1 is an assumption made by many students of syntax. It is worth pausing to consider what might underlie 1. According to the authors of a recent book (Weisler and Milekic, 2000, p. 157) restricting branching to a binary nature is a move which is

> theoretical, subject to revision in the face of contravening evidence. But we are motivated to adopt it in order to restrict the range of possible grammars admitted by our theory, aiming to provide an account of grammatical knowledge that helps us to understand how children can, in a limited period of time, acquire systems of great apparent complexity (i.e., grammars)

----

[20] I am grateful to Martin Atkinson for pointing this out.

on the basis of limited exposure to primary linguistic data. By radically restricting the form that grammars can take, and by positing that children are restricted to considering only the 'available' grammars, we hope to begin to illuminate the process of language acquisition – the ultimate goal of linguistic theory.

It would be preferable, however, if there were some more *principled* motivation for restricting the branching operation to being binary, which did more than rely on the assumption that restricting the range of options is a good thing in so far as it restricts our theories of what the child has to learn. Rather, we need a reason for stipulating that merge must be binary which recruits MP-based considerations alone, such as, considerations of 'good design', and facts about C_{CH} which 'fall out in some natural way from the computational process'.

First, Atkinson (2000) suggests a way of proving the binarity of merge, which begins by considering how the notion of c-commanding 'falls out' from merge. First, if K is the label of the merger of α and β, then it would seem to follow from the very idea of merge that α and β will be sisters and both $[K - \alpha]$ and $[K - \beta]$ will be in the relation of 'immediately contains'. From this we can in turn derive the notions of 'containing' as a generally-applicable, transitive[21] principle, and of c-commanding. In the first place,

α contains β iff[22] α immediately contains β or there is a sequence $(\gamma...\gamma_n)$ such that γ_i immediately contains γ_{i+1}, α immediately contains γ_1 and γ_n immediately contains β.

In other words, the very idea of merging gives rise to embeddings of the operation, and thus to the fact of containing 'at a distance'. And given this, the relation of c-commanding 'falls out' in a natural way from the computation itself.

α c-commands β iff there is a γ such that α is a sister of γ and γ contains β.

Armed with these notions, we can return to the question of the binarity of merge whilst bearing in mind that the external systems constrain us to speak, hear, and read words sequentially. Atkinson (2000, p. 17) presents the following proof of binarity based on Kayne (1994).

1) terminal strings are linearly ordered at PF;

2) The syntactic objects produced by C_{HL} do not contain order information;

3) The phonological component must impose linear ordering on the basis of information which is supplied by C_{HL} (i.e., there must be some relation R, accessible to C_{HL}, such that $L(\alpha, \beta)$ iff $R(\alpha, \beta)$, where L is linear ordering;

4) Asymmetric c-command is accessible to C_{HL};

5) Asymmetric c-command requires branching to be binary.

Looking at each step, 1 is simply a legibility condition; 2 is suggested on the basis of 'good design', in so far as it would be unparsimonious for C_{HL} to build in a property that was not necessary for the computations to operate. Given that linear ordering will have to be imposed at the phonological interface if it is not already present, and given 1 and 2, 3 follows. R is the fact of c-commanding and this relation is required

---

[21] Atkinson does not use this term.

[22] Iff = if and only if.

if there is to be linear ordering. C-commanding contains the information on which the ordering will operate. The 'asymmetric' in 4 is important because it captures the fact that c-commanding results in a hierarchy – in which some lexical items are higher that others. The conclusion is essentially that *one cannot have both linear ordering and asymmetric c-commanding without restricting the operation of merge (from which asymmetric c-commanding 'falls out') to binary branching*. If, *per impossibile*, we could produce and understand language without linear ordering, then (say) ternary merge would be possible. One cannot, however, say 'if asymmetric c-commanding did not exist' because this is a function of the very idea of merge itself.

The next proof we will consider establishes that the 'label' of the phrase which results from the merging of α and β will be that of either α or β. In other words, one of the two elements of the phrase resulting from merge will be a *head*. I will not present the proof in detail, but instead describe its basic claim.

If K is the result of merging α and β, then, on set-theoretic assumptions, there are three possibilities:

1) K is the intersection of α and β;

2) K is the union of α and β;

3) K is identical to either α or β.

What is wrong with 1 and 2? First, intersection can only be acceptable if α and β have elements in common; for if they have no elements in common then K will have no properties at all. But the fact is that α and β do *not* have elements in common beyond the fact of both being lexical items. Difficulties of a similar kind crop up when we consider the property of set union (in 2). Imagine that α and β are representing nouns and verbs and bear in mind that lexical items are sets of features. In this case verbs can be thought of as [+V, −N] and nouns can be thought of as [+N, −V]. It goes without saying that in constructing the union of these two elements the pluses and the minuses will lead to straight contradictions. This leaves us with 3 as the only surviving option.

Without going into the details of the proof, which are to be found in Chomsky (1995, p. 244), let us consider the roles of legibility constraints and good design in constructing it.

1) Why can't α and β be equipotential, with K simply being equivalent to $\{\alpha, \beta\}$? The reason is that the LF interface *necessarily interprets different kinds of lexical items in different ways*; and if it did not it is impossible to imagine how the domain of language would ever make contact with the domain of thought. This, then, is a *legibility condition*. As Atkinson (2000, p. 18) expresses it:

> One way to put it is that there is a fundamental distinction between predicates and those of which they are predicated, a distinction which is represented in some way in any system which is designed to make contact with the way we think. Now, some expressions correspond to predicates, and there is every reason to believe that the LF-interface and the interpretive systems beyond require information about this contrast.

2) Considerations of *good design* dictate that objects at LF can only be built from features of lexical items. (This is the *inclusiveness condition* again: 'every object at LF is built from features of the lexical items within an array'.)

3) The three possibilities of set intersection, set union and identity are enumerated.

4) To say that intersection leads to emptiness and that union leads to contradiction is, in fact, to say that they lead to violation of LT *legibility conditions*. Clearly, empty and contradictory objects cannot be interpreted.

The final proof (of the fact that merge projects) builds upon the results of the previous one. We have established that the result of merging α or β will be a phrase bearing the label of either α or β. What we have yet to establish, however, is what determines the label it will take and thus what the resulting phrase will be projected *as*. We have, in fact already enjoyed a brief glimpse of the principle at issue here, which is that the label – *the head of the phrase, e.g., the V in VP* – will be that of the *target* of merge and that this target will project. Here are some features of the proof to consider, which, it will be seen, takes the form of a *reductio ad absurdum*.

1) As we also discussed earlier, intermediate projections (X′) are not legible at the LF interface, and are not, therefore, 'visible' to C_{HL}. This means that the only levels at issue are those of maximal (XP/X″: projections that project no further) or minimal (X⁰/heads: lexical items) projections. This, says Atkinson, is a mixture of 'uncomfortable stipulation' and allusion to both legibility conditions and considerations of good design.

2) The *reductio* premise is the supposition that α targets β and *that α projects*;

3) Given 1, α must either be a maximal or a minimal projection.

4) The proof then takes each case in turn (α as maximal and α as minimal) and shows, in the first case, that it will become intermediate as a result of the derivation and thereby become illegible at the interface with LF, and in the second case the target β will become a complement in the phrase, with the result that *checking* will be unsuccessful. (The notion of checking will be explained very shortly, and the details of these two steps need not detain us.)

5) Given the unacceptable consequences of α projecting, it must be the case that β (the target) projects.

6) Therefore targets project.

I hope that what the discussion of these three proofs has illustrated is the way in which considerations of legibility, optimal design, and 'falling out' from virtual conceptual necessity illustrate the 'optimal' nature of C_{HL} – a central claim of MP. It is difficult to be entirely confident that these proofs actually establish what they aim to establish; and the reader may recall, in this context, Chomsky's uncertainty over whether intermediate projections are relevant at the LF interface (cf. point 1 in the proof immediately above). But for our purposes, what is more important than questions about their success is that the very existence of such proofs illustrates the viability of the MP as a research programme. The issue of whether 'bare phrase structure' is perfectly designed to deal with 'external' pressures and the demands of parsimony seems to be a real one.

This immediately stirs deeper questions about Chomsky's still more radical claim that where imperfections are detected in language these will turn out to be more apparent than real. I will end the discussion of the architecture of MP with that question, but before doing so we need to consider how the operation of merger is 'policed'. A well-formed phrase (one whose derivation converges at the interface) cannot be made up of just any two lexical items. So in accordance with the project originated by P & P, in which constraints on move replaced a host of purpose-built transformational rules, MP does not posit rules to ensure that words are appropriately combined in merge (and move) but rather proposes an operation to ensure that the features of the two lexical items are correctly matched. This is the operation of checking.

2.3.4 Checking, the 'interpretability' of features, and the question of optimal design

The success of the merge operation obviously depends on whether the syntactic features of the merged elements bear the right kinds of relationship to each other. To put it in the language of the *syntactic structures* theory, we require that there should be context-sensitive constraints upon the free combination of any kind of element with any other. And to put it in the language of the MP, lexical items consist of features of various kinds which must be checked against each other. Put this way, the business of checking might seem to be self-evident and familiar to the point of dullness. However, the way in which Chomsky develops *checking theory* takes us to the very heart of MP's most fundamental working assumption: that language is optimally designed.

The first thing to appreciate here is that every feature is either *interpretable* or *uninterpretable* at the interface with LF. Given that LF must necessarily make the right kind of semantic liaisons, this boils down to the claim that features either have a *sui generis* semantic character (interpretable) or they do not (uninterpretable). This immediately raises the question of how a system that is supposed to be optimally designed can be lax enough to allow the very things that constitute syntax (formal features) to be illegible to semantics. The answer is that the process of feature checking is not simply a matter of making sure that features match with each other. It is a matter of *erasing* uninterpretable features once their work is done. To put it metaphorically, words have purely syntactic features like hooks looking for an eye; and once the eye has been located the hook and eye dissolve into one smooth, interpretable surface of fabric. The derivation of a phrase will only converge at LF if it consists only of interpretable features; otherwise it crashes.

A second thing to bear in mind (something on which I will shortly expand) is that uninterpretable features are regarded by Chomsky as being *apparent imperfections* of the linguistic system. Needless to say, the working assumption of MP that language is a 'perfect' solution to legibility conditions imposed by the external systems – that it is 'optimally designed' – will be shown to be faulty unless Chomsky can demonstrate that they are indeed apparent rather than real.

Semantically interpretable features are ones like number, person, gender, and tense.[23] These line up with real-world referents – such as one versus two, me versus you, boy

---

[23] There are conditions in which tense and number, at least, can be *un*interpretable. These will be discussed below (2.4.4.).

versus girl, happened yesterday versus is happening still. Semantically uninterpretable features, on the other hand, are language-internal formal entities. Case marking serves as an example. For example, *She kissed he* violates a case marking rule in English that the objective (or 'accusative') case should be used to refer to a patient/theme. The sentence does not, however, mischaracterise reality. By contrast, *John saw me* when said to refer to the fact that John can presently see you converges at LF but is false.

In passing, it might strike the reader as odd to claim that case is semantically empty, given that the choice of the appropriate case marking can determine what kind of event or relation 'in the real world' is being referred to. Thus a dative or ablative[24] marking (in, say, Latin) will pick out the semantic fact that some object was displaced towards X or that some act was done with a Y. But, does the fact that the ablative and a dative cases have semantic properties not suggest that nominative and accusative have them too? 'But, well, they don't', insists Chomsky (Chomsky *et al.*, 2002, p. 113) …

> There's a split between the ones that have semantic properties, like, say, Dative mostly, and the ones that don't, like Nominative and Accusative. As far as I am aware, this split was not noticed until the P & P approach came along … So the inherent Cases, the ones which are semantically associated, are really not an imperfection: they are marking the semantic relation the interpreter has to know about (like plurality on Nouns). On the other hand, why do we have Nominative and Accusative, what are they doing?

As an example of the uninterpretable nature of the latter two cases, Chomsky gives the following example:

    a. John believes that *he* is a liar
    b. John believes *him* to be a liar

In both cases the property of being a liar is predicated of a third person singular masculine referent; but the nominative (a) and the accusative (b) case markings play no role in the semantic interpretation of the sentences. (Recall our earlier discussion of the *destruction the city* example (p. 127) in which it was pointed out that the requisite *of*, plays a purely syntactic role: it is not the genitive *of* meaning possession.)

Another kind of uninterpretable feature is certain kinds of verb-marking other than tense, such as a verb's being infinitive in form (e.g., go) versus being a participle (e.g., gone). Thus, *She has go* has crashed, whilst being a recognisable attempt to report that somebody has gone. *He has gone*, by contrast, when used to report that a female person has gone, has converged at LF, while being false.

We will now work through an example borrowed from Andrew Radford's excellent introductory text on minimalist syntax (Radford, 1997b, pp. 69–72) of how checking is achieved in an inflection phrase/sentence (see Figure 2.27). We are dealing here both with the distinction between interpretable and uninterpretable features and one between three (what might be called) 'layers' of features. On the top layer (see lower section of the Figure), there are the features (interpretable and uninterpretable) with which all lexical items come complete: *head* features. On the two

---

[24] By, with, or, more rarely, from X.

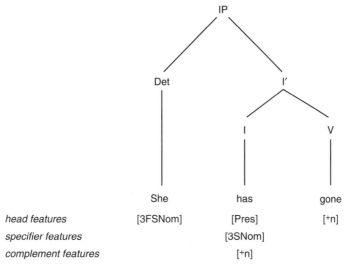

		IP

Det		I′

	I	V

She	has	gone

head features	[3FSNom]	[Pres]	[⁺n]
specifier features		[3SNom]	
complement features		[⁺n]	

Figure 2.27 Feature checking in an inflection phrase. From Radford, *Syntax: a minimalist introduction* (1997), reproduced with permission from Cambridge University Press.

layers beneath we have to consider words as components of XPs. These will be either specifier features or complement features. The important point to note here is that because specifier and complement features have no semantic interpretation they will be uninterpretable. Thus, in the present example (on the next 'layer' down) the inflection-word (*has*) will carry a set of uninterpretable features which will be *looking for the corresponding head features on the specifier* – hooks looking for eyes. As can be seen from the figure, these are third-person, singular, and nominative case – [3SNom]. The word *has* will also carry a complement feature (*n*-participle), which ensures that the complement following on will take the form of a perfective participle. This complement-feature layer is the final layer.

What happens is that the specifier-features of a head (*has* in this case) must be checked against the head features of its specifier, while the complement features of a head must be checked against the head features of its complement. Then, if there is a match between any features, the relevant specifier or complement feature is erased, because these are uninterpretable at LF. But no interpretable features are erased, as these are legible at LF. Referring again to Figure 2.27, we see that this process will result in the removal of [3SNom] and [⁺n] from *has* in addition to the uninterpretable head feature of Nom from the specifier *She* and the uninterpretable head feature [⁺n] from the complement *gone*. All that remains, then (see Figure 2.28) are the semantically interpretable features of third-person, single, feminine and present tense. This is the representation that is delivered up to LF – the thought stripped bare SHE GONE [NOW].

It is, perhaps, evident from this example that being uninterpretable boils down to the fact of being apparently superfluous. It can also be seen from this example that the verb is carrying a set of features that are entirely superfluous, given that these are

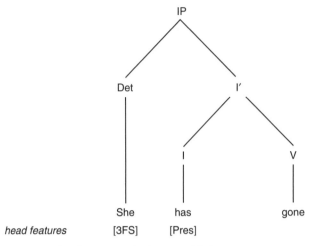

Figure 2.28 Checking, after the erasure of uninterpretable features.

already represented on the head features of the noun with which the verb has to agree. *Morphological markings on verbs, then, seem to constitute at least a prima facie example of an imperfection in the language system.* As Chomsky (Chomsky *et al.* 2002, p. 111) puts it:

> What is an imperfection is plurality on verbs. Why is it there? You already have it on the noun, so why do you have it on the verb, or on the adjective? Inflection for number looks redundant there, and that is an imperfection. To put it differently, that feature, or that occurrence of the feature, say plurality on the verb, is not interpreted. You only interpret it on the noun, and that's why in traditional grammars it was always said that the verbs agree with nouns and that the adjectives agree with nouns, and not conversely.

This leaves us with something of a puzzle. Checking is the process of wiping away uninterpretable features so as to ensure that the resulting derivation is legible at LF. So in this case the pressing question is: *What were the uninterpretable features doing there in the first place?* Perhaps one might, somewhat simplistically, answer that the facts about which word is agreeing with which word (the domain of checking) yields interpretable semantic information. In a highly inflected language, like Latin for example, the specifier features on the verb can tell us who did what to whom. But this does not get us very far, as it still leaves unanswered why some kinds of agreement are *not* interpretable, why we have *structural* (as opposed to *inherent*) case, and so forth. In order to solve the puzzle as to why there are uninterpretable features at all it is necessary to refer to a second apparent imperfection of the language faculty – *displacement/ dislocation*. We will see that Chomsky thereby attempts to reduce two imperfections to one before claiming that the resulting imperfection is not really an imperfection at all.

  In explaining the nature of dislocation, it is useful to reconsider the properties of natural language, which distinctions such as that between deep and surface structure and between d- and s-structure were supposed to be describing. Speaking loosely, at the surface level there are discourse-related properties, arising from how we wish to say something, with this being determined by whether a piece of information is new or old, what is the 'topic' and what is the comment, the focus[25] versus presupposition. At this level, the local ordering and grouping of the elements can be quite different to that which one might regard as the logical, natural or canonical (for that language). With regard to the latter, we expect the grammatical object to follow the verb as closely as possible in English, the grammatical subject to precede the verb as closely as possible, adverbs to be grouped with their verbs, adjectives with their nouns, and so forth. These are the 'semantic liaisons and environments' referred to in Figure 2.11. But it is not in the nature of *natural* language to be as predictable and prescriptive as this: there is never only one way of saying something. Rather, natural language has the property of *allowing the displacement/dislocation of an item out of the local position in any underlying structure (e.g., an object with its verb) that we would expect it to fill into a different position in the surface form*. In the underlying structure containing non-dislocated properties, what is involved are 'local relations to other elements that assign the semantic property [cf. deep structure]; a Noun Phrase related to a verb, a preposition or something like that. That gives the theta relations' (Chomsky *et al.*, 2002, p. 114). While the non-dislocated information is 'local' then, the surface, discourse-related information is what Chomsky calls *edge-related*, referring to the fact that pragmatic exigencies can shift the focus to the edge of a phrase; for example, *John it was who lost* shifts the subject to the left periphery of the phrase in *It was John who lost*. 'Edge' simply means 'non-local'. This is how Chomsky (2000b, pp. 113–114) expresses it – in a technical paper this time (as opposed to an interview):

> [...] we have two 'imperfections' to consider: uninterpretable features and the dislocation property. These properties (in fact morphology altogether) are never built into special purpose symbolic systems [e.g., formal logic, programming languages, JR]. We suspect, then, that they might have to do with externally-imposed legibility conditions. With regard to dislocation, that has been suggested from the earliest days of modern generative grammar, with speculations about facilitations of processing (on the sound side) and the dissociation of 'deep' and 'surface' interpretive principles (on the meaning side). The boundaries [i.e., between deep and surface, JR] are not clear, nor the mechanisms to express them. One approach to the array of problems was to distinguish the role of deep and surface (D- and S-) structure in semantic interpretation: the former enters into determining quasi-logical properties such as entailment and theta structure; the latter such properties as topic-comment, presupposition, focus, specificity,[26] new-old information, agentive force, and others that are often considered more discourse-oriented, and appear to involve the 'edge' of constructions. Theories of LF and other approaches sought to capture the distinctions in other ways. The 'deep' (LF) properties are of the general kind found in language-like systems [formal logic, programming languages, again, JR]; the surface properties appear to be specific to human language. If the distinction is real, we would expect to find that language design marks it in some way – perhaps by the dislocation property, at least in part.

In more informal terms (in the interview) he elaborates (Chomsky *et al.*, 2002, p. 115; emphasis added):

> If that's the way the thought system works, there are two kinds of information it is looking for: one edge related, the other locally related. Then well-designed languages are going to

---

[25] For example, *It was Mary who caught the train* is likely to be an answer to the question *Who caught the train?* rather than *What did Mary do?*

[26] For example, the difference between saying *There is a man in the garden* and *There is the man in the garden*.

have a dislocation property. An expression will somehow have to distinguish these kinds of information and in fact an optimal way of doing it would just be to resort to dislocation; expressions are phonetically interpreted at the edge even though they are semantically (thematically) interpreted at the local position, *the position of merge*. That's a plausible reason, external reason, as to why languages have the dislocation property.

We think a thought then, and in finding its verbal expression, this thought retains its basic semantic character (e.g., including thematic relations) at a certain level, with the semantically local groupings retaining their integrity. One might say that the way this representation is constructed is determined essentially by virtual conceptual necessity; note the reference to the conceptually necessary process of merge in the previous quotation. But in *expressing* the thought we are not hamstrung by some blind and mechanical translation of the thought into the phrase structures of our native tongue. We can, within limits, express the verbally-encoded thought how we choose and how it seems appropriate in the circumstances. However, in doing so, the sentence has not been cut loose from its semantic and canonically-syntactic moorings: the fact of dislocation sees to that. Well, *it is the very existence of uninterpretable features that enables dislocation to be implemented.* How this happens cannot be understood without revisiting the familiar process of move. But it is now time for an example of dislocation.

(36) Clinton seems to have been elected.

(37) It seems they have elected Clinton.

In (36) – this is Chomsky's (2000a, p. 12) own example – we interpret the relation between *Clinton* and *elect* as being the same kind of relation that we find in the sentence (37). In the latter case, the two words inhabit the same syntactic locality, with *Clinton* being the direct object of *elect*. Whereas in the former case *Clinton* has been displaced to be the subject of *seems*. But note that while the subject and the main verb agree in inflectional features (i.e., it's not **Clinton seem ...*) the *semantic* relation is between the subject and verb *elect*.

But merely to point this out is (on Chomsky's analogy: 2000b, p. 120) like a physiologist saying that the function of the eye is to see and leaving it at that. Just as the onus is on the physiologist to lay bare the mechanisms ('a particular protein in the eye reflects light etc.',) that implement seeing, so must the linguist explicate the mechanisms that implement the displacement property. *For the dislocation property to be implemented, uninterpretable features must exist.* How?

For the checking and erasure of uninterpretable features to proceed, the checker and the checkee have to be within the same domain: 'erasure requires a local relation between the offending feature and a matching feature that can erase it' (Chomsky, 2000a, p 14). For them to inhabit the same domain, movement is necessary. In the case of (36), *Clinton* has to move into the locality of *seems* in order to check it. As Chomsky (2000a, p 14) puts it, it is

> as if the sentence were actually 'seems to have been elected Clinton'. The main verb of the sentence 'seems' has inflectional features that are uninterpretable: it is singular/third person/masculine, properties that add nothing independent to the meaning of the sentence since they are already expressed in the noun phrase that agrees with it, and are ineliminable there. These offending features of 'seems' therefore have to be erased in a local relation, an explicit version of the traditional descriptive category of 'agreement'. To achieve this result,

the matching features of the agreeing phrase 'Clinton' are attracted by the offending features of the main verb 'seems,' which are then erased under local matching. But now the phrase 'Clinton' is displaced.

This is, then, an example of overt movement in which not only the features of the agreeing phrase are attracted and move, but also the phrase itself. And there can also be *covert* movement, as in (38).

(38) a. There seems to be a problem.
     b. There seem to be some problems.

(39) John seems to be awake.

What is notable here is that the verb agrees in number with *a problem* in (38a) and *some problems* in (38b). This is because the uninterpretable case feature of *problem/ problems* undergo *covert* movement to be within the checking domain of *seems*; while in doing so other features, such as plurality, move along with it. A little elaboration is necessary here. In (39) we need to regard this final form as the outcome of an earlier stage of the derivation:

T seems [John to be awake]

where T is an infinitival tense marker called a *tense head*[27], and in which *John* is still in its 'natural' location heading a phrase whose adjective predicates something of this head. T is supposed to carry with it a set of uninterpretable features. Chomsky refers to T as the *probe*, which seeks a *goal* item elsewhere in the derivation to enable matching, checking and thus the erasure of its offending uninterpretable features. Probes naturally seek goals.

To look, in turn, a little more closely at this process, it is necessary to introduce another notion – *agree*. The meaning of this term is, as Chomsky says in the last passage quoted an 'explicit version of the traditional descriptive category of 'agreement''. Explicit in what sense? In order to answer this question, let us examine a standard passive sentence. (The example and its treatment are taken from Atkinson, 2000, p 23–24.).

(40) a. several prizes are likely to be awarded
     b. T be awarded [several prizes]

In (40), a. is the manifest sentence and b. an intermediate stage in its derivation. T contains an uninterpretable ϕ (meaning 'feature for checking') set, but comprising only the feature of third person, which functions as a probe seeking its matching goal. Now, as in the *problems/problem* example in (38), the lexical item *prizes* is deemed to contain an uninterpretable case feature that enables the [person] feature of T to identify the uninterpretable [third person] feature of *prizes* as its goal. This then is the first stage of the operation of agree: an *active* probe seeks an active goal – active in the sense of containing uninterpretable features. In the final stage of agree the uninterpretable feature of [person] is deleted from T by virtue of its

---

[27] According to Chomsky and others, finite clauses contain separate tense and agreement heads, each of which projects into its distinct kind of phrase. The operation of the tense phrase (TP) can be seen in the role of adverbs like *probably*. See Radford 1997a, pp. 225–244.

matching [third person] of *prizes*; however the uninterpretable Case feature of *prizes* is not deleted (as it has found no match in T's ɸ set) and so remains active for further operations.

The next operation to play a role in the derivation is the so-called *extended projection principle* (EPP), which simply states that all sentences have subjects, or more formally, that it is obligatory for an IP to have a specifier. [This is entered as one of the stipulations of MP.] In the present context, EPP manifests itself as the demand that tense phrases (TPs) have specifiers: T leaves a subject slot to be filled. That is to say, T has an uninterpretable EPP feature in addition to its set of ɸ features. As there is no suitable candidate to fill the specifier role in T's local domain, *several prizes* moves to yield the intermediate structure. Recall that it still has an uninterpreted case feature, and so it needs to move into a checking domain for this to be erased.

[several prizes][T be awarded t²⁸]

I will not follow the steps of the derivation through to the point at which *likely* has been added, all uninterpretable features have been erased and the derivation converges, but will finish this brief illustration of dislocation by noting, in Atkinson's (2000, p.30) words that

> Move is a more complex operation than Merge. Not only does it include a token of Merge, but it also presupposes a token of Agree and of whatever operation is necessary to determine that *several prizes* (rather than just *prizes*) is the expression undergoing movement. Thus, this 'additive' notion of complexity of Move supplements the purely conceptual considerations from Chomsky (1995), where it is noted that it is characteristic of *any* combinatorial system that it includes an operation akin to Merge [cf. the combinatorial nature of LOT, JR], while this is not the case for Move.

In this sense then, move – the servant of dislocation – is a quintessential property of *human* syntax. Merger-like operations, by contrast, are richly represented in the *formal* languages constructed by human beings.

Back now to the *strong minimalist thesis*, which we are now in a position to reconsider in the context of the dislocation phenomenon. Recall that it states that 'Language is an optimal solution to legibility conditions'.

Given this, if the claim that uninterpretable features exist to implement the dislocation property which itself is not really an imperfection at all because it is imposed upon the language faculty by legibility conditions then, as Atkinson (ibid., p. 28) puts it, the following two questions have be addressed within the minimalist research programme.

(a) what LF-legibility conditions motivate cases of syntactic dislocation?

(b) what PF-legibility conditions motivate cases of 'phonological dislocation'?

With regard to (a), Atkinson goes on to say, the strong minimalist thesis has to assume that *every case of movement must be solving an interpretation problem of some kind* and so 'any token of movement which does *not* have such a consequence will constitute an instance of *phonological* dislocation' (emphasis added).

Here is an example (taken from Atkinson, 2000, p. 34) of how a form of syntactic dislocation does indeed effect a change in interpretation. The phenomenon in question

---

²⁸ This is the trace of *several prizes*.

is that of *object shift*. It occurs in Germanic languages other than English and, as its name suggests, involves the movement of an object-word from its position directly following the main verb; it is also contingent upon so-called 'verb raising'.[29] Consider, in illustration, the difference between the following two sentences of Icelandic shown in (41).

(41) a. Hann les lengstu bókina sjaldan
   He reads longest book.the seldom
   'He seldom reads the longest book'
   b. Hann les sjaldan lengstu bókina
   He reads seldom longest book.the
   'He seldom reads the longest book'

While the two sentences (which differ in the placement of the object-word *bókina* – book) mean the same thing in English, the interpretation differs in Icelandic, with the difference corresponding to the distinction between a *de re* and a *de dicto* reading (see p. 77). In (41a.) the 'longest book' refers *de re* to a particular book that the individual seldom reads, whereas in b. the meaning is that he seldom reads whatever book happens to be the longest one (*de dicto*). Broadly speaking, the shifting of objects fixes one among the various possibilities for reference, specificity and old information (e.g., it is assumed by the speaker that the listener knows what long book is being referred to). Without going into details (Atkinson, 2000, pp. 34–35 for them), Chomsky is able to describe how internally consistent principles handle this movement/interpretation relationship without anomaly. In so doing, in Atkinson's words (ibid., p. x.)

> the interpretive motivation for movement is inextricably linked to the interpretive motivation for the uninterpretable features that drives it, a clear illustration of the principle that uninterpretable features are only 'apparent' imperfections in that they serve to drive tokens of movement which, if they did not occur, would fail to resolve an interpretive anomaly at LF.

Well, it has to be said right now that there are issues surrounding the displacement property pitched at a technical level far beyond the reach of most of us. Perhaps it is sufficient for our (i.e. developmental psychologist's) purposes merely to keep the fact of dislocation in mind, comforted by the following metaphor. There is a line of rowing boats out in the bay, each of them anchored to the sea bed. Even if it is a windless day currents will shift the relative positions of the boats on the surface, and high winds can scramble them; though all the while the relative positions of their anchorages remain undisturbed. It is well not to insult the reader by spelling out the image, except to caution that the sea-surface is *not* the PF interface – or at least not that exclusively – but the interface with the squalls and becalmings of *discourse*. There might, though, be some profit in pressing the distinction between the different ways in which wind and current might tug at the boats. The wind is the entirely external force of pragmatics – of how a thing should be said at the time – while the currents are the internal urgings towards a way of saying. Though Chomsky himself

---

[29] Consider the contrast between the French *Jean aime pas Marie* and the ill-formed English **John loves not Mary*. In French, but not in grammatical English, the verb has raised out of the VP.

would doubtless resist the idea, this allows us to understand why, despite the fact that syntax is a formal and quasi-mechanical system, there is nonetheless always scope for 'singing in our chains like the sea'.[30]

The description of the Minimalist Programme is complete. So it is now time to assess it both as a theory of the language faculty and in terms of the kind of bearing that it might have upon developmental issues.

2.4 Assessment for the time being

This point is obviously not going to be the terminus of Chomskyan theory; and doubtless the next generation of developmental psychologists will be knitting their brows over whatever supersedes MP, and pestering linguist colleagues for elucidation. But the essential trajectory of the journey has not, as I hope this survey of nearly five decades of theory development has shown, changed; and neither has the set of intellectual concerns that fuelled it changed. The question we can now ask is: What does theorising of this kind say to the developmental psychologist about the relation between linguistic and cognitive development? What I say will not, of course, constitute a full assessment of the Chomskyan enterprise, because such a thing is impossible without a survey of empirical work inspired by Chomskyan theory in the 1980s (to come later in Part 2) and without a thorough discussion of the empiricist and pragmatist alternatives (to come in Parts 3 and 4). It will be a broad-brush assessment of the *kind* of enterprise that is represented here. And where critics are cited, these will be linguists or philosophers who are broadly *sympathetic* to the research programme that began in the mid-1950s.

I will begin by standing back some distance from minimalism, to consider the theory in the light of the Chomskyan intellectual context described in Part 1. Developmental issues will not emerge clearly till 2.4.4.

2.4.1 The autonomy of syntax, and the Rationalist stance

Given the rationalist perspective from which Chomsky views mental capacities, the central proposal of MP that human language is a *perfect* system should come as no surprise. Language may indeed be the expression of a faculty or mental organ that 'interacts' with other mental organs, such as the cognitive and the sensorimotor organs, but it is in no sense reducible to the functioning of these other organs. It is an autonomous system with *sui generis* workings, workings which the pre-minimalist theory dubbed 'rules and representations' and which MP takes to be a system of operations ranging from the 'virtually conceptually necessary' like merge to the all-too-human operations like move, agree and checking. The interaction of the language organ with the system of cognitive 'organs' at LF can, therefore, be something that is achieved 'perfectly', in the sense of being achieved correctly (such that every clear and coherent thought can find accurate verbal expression) and without redundancy (the features and operations of the language faculty constitute all that is required to express clear and coherent thoughts – and no more).

....

[30] 'Though I sang in my chains like the sea': final line of *Fern Hill* by Dylan Thomas.

This tells us, at least, why the concept of perfection should gain a foothold in a rationalist linguistic theory. But there is more to the rationalism-perfection linkage than this. Consider the cases of logic and mathematics. Unlike human intelligence, with all its biases, capacity limitations, susceptibility to short cuts and quick fixes, which makes use of these systems, logic and mathematics are perfect systems in the sense that it is simply inconceivable that further reflection or research should reveal flaws in them. Can we conceive of a situation in which it was demonstrated, for example, that $p \rightarrow q$, p, therefore q or that $2 + 2 = 4$ are really nothing more than folk-psychological illusions? The rationalist takes such inviolability as paradigmatic of human thought, and will in his or her more romantic moments add 'of human free-dom'. As Winston Smith wrote in his diary, 'Freedom is the freedom to say that two plus two make four. If that is granted all else follows'.[31]

With regard to logic, empiricist thinkers, by contrast, will embrace some form of *psychologism* in relation to it.[32] This is the view that logical propositions, far from possessing epistemic autonomy, are either concise generalisations about how we think or prescriptions about how thinking should be done. The pragmatist, meanwhile, will ground logic in the constraints on adequate communication and the 'negotiation of meanings' perhaps adding something about the 'logic of action'. Either way, logic can be reduced to human information-processing or to human practices. There is no room within either of these epistemologies for the view that logic is an autonomous system, perfect in itself, with which human intelligence, in the broad sense, interacts.

One might say, then, that it is in the domains of logic and mathematics – within the domain of formalisable systems – that the rationalist 'scores'. After all, there seems to be something wrong-headed about the alternatives: that formal logic text-books contain no more than generalisations about how the brain processes infor-mation or about the communicative ground-rules for hunter-gatherers. But is the rationalist justified in extending the same courtesy to *language*? Prima facie at least, nothing could be less universal and inviolable than the 'rules' of human language. For one thing, syntactic systems vary, to some degree, from language to language. Moreover, there is quite a lot of slack in the criteria for sentences' well-formedness. If we woke up tomorrow to find that Modus Ponens ($p \rightarrow q$, p, $\therefore q$) had been 'revoked' we would be living in a universe beyond our current imagination; but if we woke up tomorrow to find that one of Chomsky's 'shower of cosmic rays' had reor-ganised our brains to obliterate the dislocation property in language and replace the property with a gestural system, things would carry on much as before, though with a very boring literature. Furthermore, there would appear to be no alternative to adopting *some* kind of psychologism about language, given that language is what we

---

[31] This is what George Orwell's protagonist wrote in his diary in chapter seven of *Nineteen Eighty-Four*.

[32] The position (associated with J. S. Mill) that the laws of logic are essentially psychological in nature. Thus modus ponens becomes no more than a generalisation about how we happen to reason.

use to express thoughts. Logic and mathematics might be conceived of as existing in some transcendent Platonic realm; but language is surely something which exists down at the coal-face with cognition and social interaction.

The rationalist believes the exact opposite of course; and that is why he or she will expect a kind of perfection from language. Back to Winston Smith and to the thoughts he was entertaining just before he made his diary entry: 'Truisms are true, hold on to that! The solid world exists, its laws do not change. Stones are hard, water is wet, objects unsupported fall towards the earth's centre.'

Any developmental psychologist will tell you that humans' ability to represent at least the last-mentioned of these truths is something that exists long before the acquisition of language (Spelke *et al.*, 1992). And, in any event, to regard these truths as essentially being truths relative to a system of linguistic representation is a quintessentially pragmatist position, as we discussed in Part 1 in the context of Rorty's ideas. Here is where the Chomskyan rationalist might be said to stand on the matter. The knowledge that (say) water is wet exists in cognitive systems 'external' to the language faculty, but in order for this knowledge to become a judgement (taking Winston Smith here to be talking to himself) the LF interface must achieve *a perfect fit between cognitive representation and verbal expression*. There can be no 'slippage' between cognition and its linguistic manifestation. At least, where there is slippage this will be *recognised* by language users as (Chomsky's term) 'gibberish'. This is true not just of the fundamental elements of our physical knowledge but of *any* thought – thoughts about whether Mary is the object of John's love, thoughts about John arriving at the airport and meeting Mary.

The notion of (virtual) conceptual necessity comes into play at this point. The merging of predicate and subject into a phrase expressive of a cognitive episode must never be just 'good enough'; its adequate operation must possess a form of necessity, a necessity which ensures that when we think in language we recognise our mind – that we can trust our own mind echoed back to us in words. Contrast the case of language with that of perception and memory. We say things like 'Unless my eyes deceive me … ', 'I can't believe my ears … ' and 'If memory serves … '. It is not surprising that there are no equivalents of these expressions in the domain for verbal judgement. A clear and coherent thought finds expression via a certain syntactic structuring, and it is not possible to imagine that our syntactic engines might have slipped a cog. We can, of course, wonder about whether our speech and writing is grammatically well-formed; but this is similar to questioning whether we have miscalculated or fallen prey to a logical fallacy – whether we have produced a performance error. In these cases there is no questioning of the operation of addition or of Modus Ponens itself; and in the parallel case of language, we are not questioning whether (say) the verbs we are producing really do represent the process of predication within our thought.

It is not only the conceptually necessary operation of merge that is immune from thought–language slippage, exhibiting the perfection we are discussing. While the twin 'imperfections' of uninterpretable features and dislocation (supported by the operations of move, agree, and checking) do not reflect conceptual necessities, the dislocation property (to which they reduce) is 'forced by legibility conditions: it

is motivated by interpretive requirements that are externally imposed by our systems of thought, which have special properties (so the study of language use indicates)' (Chomsky, 2000a, p. 130). Accordingly, this forcing by legibility conditions
will insure against thought–language slippage not only in the reflections of heroic
solitaries such as Winston Smith but in our everyday communication. A question,
for example, must be the perfect reflection of an interrogative thought, with the
expression of such thoughts being no less fundamental to human nature as our
beliefs about the hardness of stones and the wetness of water. As we have seen, dislocation occurs in English questions and passives, among many other kinds of
English sentence. We also saw at the end of the previous section that a speaker of
Icelandic will mark the distinction between 'a particular X' and 'whatever item happens to fulfil the description "X"' in terms of the dislocation property of object shift.
This distinction is not marked in English (and English-speaking children struggle
with it until the age of seven or so: Russell, 1987a), so does this mean that some
thought–language slippage exists in English that does not exist in Icelandic – that
Icelandic is a 'more perfect' expression of thought than English. A host of similar
examples exist.[33]

To voice a worry of this kind is to misunderstand what is intended here by 'perfection'. A perfect language is not one that reflects every nuance of every cognitive
episode without the slightest ambiguity and without scope for further interpretation.
A sentence is a representation, and, as Wittgenstein (1953) urged, no representation
exists that is not open to interpretation and has no potential for ambiguity. What is
demanded of a perfect language is that it will express thoughts without redundancy
and without error. For somebody to tell his friend *He seldom reads the longest book*
and to say this with the *de dicto* reading in mind is not for the thought to overflow
its means of expression: the expression fits the thought 'perfectly', but not that
thought *exclusively*. It is no less true to say that my coat is a perfect fit for me if it also
happens to be a perfect fit for you.

Chomsky is a great admirer of Orwell (Barsky, 1997) and refers to him frequently
in his political writings. What I am suggesting here is that the commonalities
between the two go beyond the political, in at least the following respect. Orwell had
Winston Smith treat the verbal expression of mathematical truths and the verbal
expression of basic empirical truths about the physical world as expressing a similar
kind of inviolability, an inviolability acting as a guarantor *against the social imposition of reality*. Chomsky would agree with this equation on the grounds that, while
general physical judgements are open to error, the individual's framing in language
of his own clear and coherent thoughts is not open to error *in so far as the language
faculty is a system that is the perfect expression of these thoughts*.

This, then, is my reading of the rationalist position as manifest in minimalism. It
is not difficult to see how both nativism about the language faculty and scepticism
about explanation of it by classical Darwinian adaptation flow directly from it;

[33] See Schlesinger's (1988) examples of what verbs mark in different languages. For example
John chopped versus *The axe chopped*, is marked on the verb in some languages.

though the latter is the harder nut to crack. In the first place, it is clear that a 'perfect' system, in so far as it is the system that anchors (recall the boat metaphor from the end of the previous section) correct expression to the thought it expresses, cannot be learnable. What – the Chomskyan rationalist will ask – are the chances of all human children converging upon this perfect system, when it seems little short of a miracle (Chomsky's 'shower of cosmic rays') that human kind ever did so. The Chomskyan answer to those who insist that the human child, unlike early man, has adult exemplars to learn from is the familiar one (which sometimes goes under the title of the 'poverty of the stimulus argument') that all the child can ever be exposed to are the surface results of syntactic operations, not the operations themselves. The boat metaphor again: this would be like viewing the arrangement of the rowing boats from a helicopter and having to deduce from that the position of the anchors and the intertwinings of the ropes.

What renders Chomsky's un-Darwinian account of the language faculty so unsympathetic to many people must be its failure to produce arguments as to why a perfect system could not have evolved through natural selection. What Chomsky does instead is to say that nobody has succeeded in spelling out quite what the adaptive function of language is supposed to be (see section 6.6 of Uriagereka, 1998), allied to the fact that when we look for adaptive functions *we inevitably find them* – thereby guaranteeing vacuity. Chomsky also insists that because there can be no such thing as a 'science of communication' (any more than there can be a science of 'being near') – we cannot talk about different languages competing with one another so as to produce the one most 'fit' for our communicative purposes (see sections 1.3 and 1.6 of Uriagereka, 1998). Indeed, it should be said that, viewed from the perspective of communication, language is *not* perfect. For example – as we have just been discussing – languages inevitably afford various kinds of ambiguity, which is an imperfection of *communication*. Language is not, then, a perfect *medium* (whatever that might be) but rather the perfect solution to legibility conditions imposed by the external systems, one of which is that of communication itself. Language-as-communication should be conceptualised as an imperfect external system, with the C_{HL} being a perfect internal system. Given this, concludes Chomsky, the perfection of language cannot be regarded as having emerged from the gradual process of improving the communicative channel through selective pressure; instead the perfection is a purely formal affair, a structural optimality that can be seen sometimes in biological morphology, where a structure might be the perfect mathematical solution to a problem such as how to pack as much structure as possible into a given area.[34]

Perhaps the Chomskyan rationalist might again point up a parallel here between language on the one hand and logic and mathematics on the other. With regard to logic, there is an obvious survival value in 'being logical' and in abiding by the 'rules' of addition and subtraction. But this is not the same as saying that we can explain why these two systems are the way they are by reference to human evolutionary

---

[34] Discussed in Uriagereka (1998, pp. 68–71).

history, in the way in which we can explain (say) how we come to walk upright or to have opposable thumbs. That we use logic and mathematics is surely a fact that holds in virtue of our having evolved through natural selection; but this is not to say that the forms these two systems take is explicable in terms of such processes as group competition between, say, a tribe who believed $p \rightarrow q$, q, therefore p, and our ancestors who believed that $p \rightarrow q$, p, therefore q. This is just the kind of account that Chomsky lampoons with regard to language.

But how far can we press the logic–language parallel? While one might see some parallel with regard to the so-called conceptually necessary aspects of the language faculty (e.g., merge), when it comes to the apparent imperfections, such as the uninterpretable features evident in structural case, the parallel with logic and mathematics seems to be stretched; and the ability to produce utterances whose elements employ (say) the checking operation begins to look not unlike the possession of opposable thumbs. Perhaps it is not, in fact, as quixotic as Chomsky thinks to try to propose plausible scenarios for why having a language with the dislocation property would have conferred a cognitive advantage in early man. Why should these features of language not have emerged through the exigencies of parsing and of framing sentences in a way that requires the least of working memory and self-monitoring? I discuss this possibility at length at the end of section 4.5.

With final regard to evolution, what general considerations are there in favour of the drawing of a clear line between human language as a representational system and human physical and broadly psychological evolution? This is how Fodor supports the Chomskyan position. He asks by what phylogenetic process the 'language module' could have acquired sets of 'contingent truths' about (say) the processes by which negatives are formed. And he cautions (Fodor, 2000b, pp. 95–96):

> However, in the language case, in contrast to the others, the answer does not need to invoke an instructional mechanism by whose operations contingent facts about the world can shape the content of the creature's beliefs. The reason, of course, is that the facts that make a speaker/hearer's innate beliefs about the universe of language true (or false) *aren't* facts about the world; they're facts about the minds of the creature's conspecifics. [...] What makes one's contingent beliefs reliably true is that they are formed by processes that are sensitive to the way the world contingently is. But, in special cases like language, what makes one's innate contingent beliefs true is that they are about the minds of creatures whose innate cognitive capacities are determined by the same genetic endowment that determines one's own. According to the usual Chomskyan story, the conspecificity of speaker and hearer is what guarantees that what they innately believe about another's language is true, and hence that their offspring (who generally are conspecifics) will be able to learn the language that they share. *If that is so, then there is no particular need for what the language organ believes to have been shaped by natural selection.* That's why Chomsky can (and, if I read him right, in fact does) hold both that human language is innate and modular, and that it is not an adaptation. My guess is that all of these claims are true (second emphasis mine).

There are a number of things to be said here. First, (if *I* read Chomsky right, at least with regard to minimalism) the subcompetences which together make up the C_{HL} do not, for him, constitute beliefs, even of the most metaphorical kind, about the minds of conspecifics. They are forced to be the way they are by legibility conditions; and the external cognitive systems which contribute to this pressure will themselves come to be as they are in virtue of contingent facts about the world (e.g., that unsupported objects fall). Given this, the structure of human syntax does not float free from our contingent beliefs about the world. Second, there seems to be something wrong with saying that the kind of innate contingent facts about language that the child knows (e.g., as represented as possible values for parameters) are 'truths' about language – truths with the unique property of not being about the world but about the genetically-similar community of language users. In fact, these would seem to be more like a programme of instructions for parsing the speech input and performing operations on the elements of the target language so as to frame well-formed utterances as an expression of one's thoughts.

Crucially, even if Fodor's reading of Chomsky is entirely accurate, his conclusion in the italicised sentence is less than compelling. This is that, because the elements of the language faculty ('what the language organ believes') are not as they are because of facts about our environment, nothing compels us to explain why these elements are as they are in terms of a long history of species–environment interaction. This only holds true if we think of a language on the model of a *game*. Games are – it is the point of them – insulated from reality (from 'the way the world contingently is') and so the legality ('truth' for Fodor) of their rules is entirely a matter for the minds of the players. Thus, only in a loose and provocative sense can we say that chess, for instance, evolved by natural selection: the ability and disposition to play games of this kind did, but rules of such and such a kind did not come about by selective pressure. But the incontestable difference between chess and language is that while chess requires thought to play, *language is the expression of thought itself,* which, generally speaking, concerns 'facts about the world'. What makes MP such an impressive intellectual achievement is that it finds a way of acknowledging this fact (legibility conditions imposed by the external systems) whilst holding on to rationalism and the autonomy of syntax. (My advice to readers who are beginning to appreciate this achievement and to feel that it presents both constraints on developmental explanation and a source of developmental ideas is not to be deterred by Chomsky's un-Darwinian position and to contain themselves till the final section of the book, when his more considered views on language evolution are presented. In any event, I shall be assuming that the un-Darwinian element in minimalism can be jettisoned without threatening its essentials.)

Finally in this subsection, I consider an alternative view of the perfection of syntax owing to a linguist who is essentially sympathetic to the aims of MP – Michael Brody (1998a). These views are of interest in the present context because they bring into clearer relief the intimate relation between the 'doctrine of imperfections' and the autonomy thesis.

Broadly speaking, Brody's view is that Chomsky does not go far enough: not only are the imperfections in language only apparent, but the appearance of these apparent imperfections is itself apparent. His aim is to 'take the minimalist programme at least in certain respects to its logical conclusion' (ibid., p. 212). Brody begins by drawing a distinction between putting the weight of explanation on linguistic derivation versus linguistic representation, with derivation meaning the assumption that there exists a series of steps between lexical insertion and the interface level of LF. Chomsky has always placed the explanatory weight on derivation (something which we will be examining in its own right in the next subsection), an assumption which Brody says 'is unjustified, and probably wrong' (ibid., p. 207). To illustrate the distinction between derivations and representations we can take the contrast between move and chaining. Chaining (see footnote 14 p. 137) refers to the relation between a moved lexical item and its trace. Move is a derivational operation (originally describing how s-structure is derived from d-structure), whereas chains are the linguistic *representation* that results from it. Given this, says Brody, derivations and representations duplicate each other, and so a truly parsimonious theory would dispense with one or the other. Because the representational option appears to be more 'restrictive' Brody opts for it. For our purposes, the important consequence of doing so is that, because derivational operations like move are supposed to be symptomatic of imperfections on MP, taking the representational rather than the derivational route will alter the conception of 'perfection'. Taking the representational stance will encourage the following alternative to the view that external systems force imperfections on syntax. This 'perfect syntax' view (details in Brody, 1998b) assumes that where we find 'imperfections' these will turn out to 'result from the interplay of perfect systems or simply from our incomplete understanding of these' which means that language will indeed turn out to be perfect *in just the way that formal logic is 'perfect'*;[35] it will be seen to be a system with 'a simple set of primitive axioms'. This would *seem* then to be just the outcome the rationalist would desire: one which tends towards eroding the distinction between logic and language.

Brody argues that the onus is upon Chomsky to demonstrate a conflict between external requirements and what would be an optimal system; for such a conflict must exist if language is to be said to have imperfections. With reference to move, for example, if it is really an imperfection then 'we would like to know why it cannot be avoided by, say, freely deleting features or by checking features always being generated in a position that is accessible without move, etc.' (ibid., p. 211). In fact, there are a number of ways in which one can imagine that the need for move could be avoided (and would be avoided by perfect syntax), and this suggests for Brody that 'in order to demonstrate conflict between external requirements and move-less perfection all [of these possibilities] would need to be excluded on principled grounds. Nothing like this has been established, or looks demonstrable' (Brody, 1998a, p. 211). As move cannot be an imperfection it therefore becomes necessary to find an alterative way of regarding the relation that it instantiates. Given that a representational rather than derivational conception of syntax is being adopted it can be replaced by the 'copy' relation. According to this conception there must exist – it being a necessary feature of language – a copy relation between lexical items and syntactic structure.

The kind of linguistic issues raised by such a proposal exist at a level of abstraction and technically are far beyond the concerns of the present book, and we will not pursue them. What is worth noting, however, is Brody's claim that such an alternative to MP would mean jettisoning the notion of uninterpretable features, which obviously carries with it the assumption that all features in 'perfect syntax' must be

---

[35] In the sense of faithfully representing the form of thought without redundancy.

semantically interpretable. In fact, this is taken to be 'a natural further restriction on syntactic primitives and as such it is desirable independently of the derivational/ representational duplication issue' (ibid, p. 213).

But this kind of perfection must be bought at very high price: the loss of the syntactic autonomy/modularity thesis, meaning the thesis that syntactic features are not a mere *codification* of facts about meaning. For once we give up on the autonomy thesis we open the door to the kind of pragmatist reduction of language to cognition to be discussed in Part 4. There is a paradox here: Chomsky needs there to be 'apparent imperfections' in language *for language to be the perfect resolution of them,* for language to be the perfect solution to legibility conditions imposed at the thought–language interface, and thus for syntax to be distinct from cognition. Chomskyan perfection is therefore a kind of second-order perfection, the additional order being that which is necessary to maintain the autonomy of syntax. In many ways it is an odd thesis, the thesis that – as Higginbotham (1998, p. 223) puts it – 'the very existence of morphology is more like a survivable accident than a necessary feature of language'. But, if we adopt Brody's alternative position, which is the apparently more parsimonious one that perfection really is a first-order affair, that there is no derivation, and that syntax has kind of perfection similar to that of formal logic, then there will ultimately be little to choose between the rationalist and the pragmatist positions. One may say, then, that it is the 'survivable accident' that is apparent imperfection that keeps the autonomy thesis on the road. If language really did act as a perfect *reflection* of the logical form of thought then we would have to explain language cognitively.

Returning then to the rationalist status of MP, as argued above, the reason rationalists can place their faith in the inviolability of human verbal judgement ('stones are hard', 'water is wet', etc.) is not that human thought is incorrigible but that human language can act as a perfect expression of thought – 'perfect' in the sense of being accurate and non-redundant to the speaker (not unambiguous to a listener!). It is this which gives us confidence in own judgements; what we can be confident about is not the contingent *truth* of our judgements but our verbally expressed thoughts as being adequate expressions of these judgements. This is a Cartesian way of thinking, which brings us back to the question of knowing our own minds. If, on the other hand, linguistic judgement reflected cognition Brody-style like a mirror or printout – pick your own metaphor – there would be no real distinction between a thought and its verbal framing and, if so, there would be no linguistic framing to be confident *about*; and we would cease to be creatures who know our own minds in language. There would also be lacking the essential element of choice in how a thing can be said – language as an *expressive* medium.

2.4.2 The syntactocentrism charge 1: Does Chomskyan explanation by 'derivation' lead to a psychologically (and thus developmentally) unrealistic theory?

Here we return to the issue, raised by Brody, about whether Chomsky is justified in placing explanation by derivation at the centre of MP. This is a question going right to the heart of the Chomskyan enterprise, as it reminds us that the concept of derivation inhabits similar territory to that of generation itself. While it is strictly *grammars*, not people, that 'generate' an infinity of well-formed sentences, with derivation being the name given to the series of operations by which an individual sentence is put together, the two notions are based on a similar conception of language, which I will refer to – after Ray Jackendoff (1997, 1999) – as *syntactocentrism*. In fact, the next two subsections will be devoted to Jackendoff's critique of MP in particular and syntactocentrism in general.

First, a few orienting words about the concept of generation. It is ironic that while Chomsky's conception of this process is mathematical/mechanical,[36] in *Cartesian linguistics* (1966, pp. 21–28) he claims common Cartesian cause with Humboldt and his use of the term *erzeugen* (to procreate, produce, breed, generate) to describe how sentences are framed, as we saw in Part 1. The irony lies in the fact that Humboldt has something altogether more romantic in mind, in contrast to Chomsky's stern classicism. For some commentators this has proved to be a source of considerable irritation. Indeed, for Koerner (1995, p. 13), this is

> the best-known example of the distortion by a twentieth-century linguist of ideas about language held by seventeenth, eighteenth, and nineteenth-century scholars. What the excitement of the 1960s and 1970s with Chomsky's interpretation had largely covered up became evident to every serious linguistic historiographer: that Chomsky's distortions were due in no small degree to the improper identification of terms and concepts of previous centuries with present-day definitions and concerns. It can easily be recognised that Chomsky's particular use of '(to) generate', which has its source in mathematical work and translation theory in the 1950s, has little to do with Humboldt's idea of 'erzeugen', which has its source in eighteenth-century psychology and philosophy of language. Unlike Chomsky, Humboldt did not see speech as the mechanical production of sentences by a high-powered machine (Chomsky's frequent disclaimers notwithstanding) but as the truly creative effort of the individual (in fact Humboldt has the artist and thinker in mind not everyday small-talk).

This might be thought to be overstated, and bordering on the unfair. In another guise it is the much debated tension in Chomskyan theory between a competence theory (theoretical linguistics) and performance theory (psychology) of language. But the fact that it was Chomsky himself who named this distinction does not render it any the less problematic for him. That is to say, the danger is ever-present of producing no more than an abstract idealisation of how sentences express thoughts, which turns out to be of no real relevance to questions about how we actually frame our thoughts linguistically or how we develop the capacity to do so. The problem is not that linguistics can never be of relevance to psychology – obviously it can. Rather, it is that linguistics of the Chomskyan kind may be guaranteed to produce an empirically false theory of performance, given its grounding assumption that the uttered sentence is the product of a series of mechanical operations and its assumption that this derivational work (indeed the so-called 'creativity' of language) is fundamentally syntactic in nature. With regard to the latter, recall that while Chomsky's view of the relation between syntax and semantics has changed over the years (with deep structure providing all the information necessary for semantic interpretation in the ST and logical form filling a similar role in P & P and MP) his assumption that semantic processes are secondary to the syntactic has not changed.

---

[36] A parallel is sometimes drawn with the sense in which πr^2 'generates' circles.

Needless to say, it is those working out of the pragmatist tradition who will most vehemently reject the decision to locate the workings of linguistic creativity in syntax; and so we need to wait till Part 4 to debate the issue at its roots. In the present context, it is more useful for us to consider the sceptical reactions of those who are sympathetic to the generative programme, but who have clear problems with the syntactocentrism. Ray Jackendoff is one such. A linguist whose name is at least as strongly associated with the development of X-bar grammar as Chomsky's, his views can hardly be dismissed as the result of mere impatience with syntax formalism! For our purposes, the most important elements of Jackendoff's critique are (a) his claim that the syntactocentrism which still infuses Chomskyan theory results in an abstract formalisation that may be of slight psychological relevance, and (b) that MP continues the error of downgrading the role of structured *semantic* processes in mediating between thought and language. We will discuss (b) in the next subsection.

Jackendoff (1997) lists a number of claims made within MP, with some being accepted and many rejected. In the first place, the following three virtual conceptual necessities are accepted:

- the C_{HL} must interface with the articulatory–perceptual (A–P) system;
- the C_{HL} must interface with the conceptual–intentional (C–I) system;
- the C_{HL} must interface with the lexicon.

The following are among the minimalist claims Jackendoff rejects:

- the C_{HL} performs derivations – 'The computational system takes representations of a given form and modifies them' (Chomsky, 1993, p. 6) – rather than imposing a number of constraints and satisfying them *in parallel*.
- the interface with the lexicon is located at the *initial* point in the derivation (in ST and P & P this was done by lexical insertion projecting lexical entries via phrase-structure/X-bar at d(eep)-structure; in MP it is the done by the merging of items from a lexical array).
- the fundamental generative component of the C_{HL} is the syntactic component, the phonological and semantic components are 'interpretive'. This is an essential claim of 'syntactocentrism'.

In tandem with this, argues Jackendoff, is Chomsky's pessimism about formal semantics as a research programme. Indeed, the picture of semantic knowledge which MP paints is that of something whose existence we only need to acknowledge in so far as it impinges upon C_{HL} at the C–I interface. What this adds up to, then, is the view that semantics somehow 'colours in' the frameworks drawn by syntax, with it having no discoverable forms of its own. Jackendoff argues that this is a position that neglects the real advances in formal semantics which have been made since Chomsky's standard theory was set out – by Jackendoff (1983) and others.

Jackendoff's aim, most explicitly and concisely set out in Jackendoff (1999), is to replace Chomskyan syntactocentrism with an approach in which (see Figure 2.29):

- Phonology, conceptual-semantic structure, and syntax are three relatively independent generative systems which go to work in parallel, rather than the first two

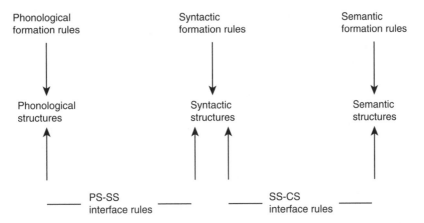

Figure 2.29 Jackendoff's 'parallel' architecture of the speech, language, thought relationship.

being interpretive systems parasitic on the third – after spell-out and move respectively;

• The explanatory effort is transferred from syntax towards the 'correspondence rules' or 'interface systems' which specify how syntactic structure is to interface with the other two systems (more on the syntax–C–I interface a little later).

What implications does this have for the competence-performance distinction? For Jackendoff, Chomsky's competence model provides unhelpful ideas about performance, given that it assumes that sound and meaning are 'read off' from syntactic structure: 'The derivation is therefore inherently directional, going outward from syntax to sound and meaning' (1999, p. 397). A moment's thought, however, tells us that when we hear a sentence our perceptual system is able to deliver up some representation of phonological structure and that when we speak we begin with a meaning to be expressed, not with a syntactic form. Perhaps a parallel architecture might account for such everyday facts, one in which the rules that relate the systems are non-directional, replacing Chomsky's assumption of uni-directionality – syntax 'outwards'. (We will not go into the detailed proposals here about how these tripartite parallel computations take place in speech production.)

What is the evidence for the phonological and the semantic systems possessing the degree of computational autonomy that Jackendoff describes? It has to be said that the phonological evidence is easier to come by. For example, it is well known that the intonational grouping used in speaking a sentence cuts across the syntactic bracketing.[37] Considerations in favour of a semantic component carrying out

[37] The following example is given by Jackendoff (1999);
Syntactic grouping =
[Sesame Street] [is] [a production] [of [the Children's Television Workshop]]]]
Intonational grouping =
[Sesame Street is a production of] [the Children's Television Workshop].

autonomous computations will be offered when we turn to Jackendoff's alternative conception of the C–I interface (see Jackendoff, 1997, section 2.3). We will consider this in the next subsection.

For now, it has to be said that when we turn to the psycholinguistics of speech production, the Chomskyan serialist model in which there is assumed to be early lexical insertion seems to have rather more going for it than Jackendoff's parallelist alternative. For empirical work in this area is dominated by a theory owing to Willem Levelt (Levelt, 1989; Levelt 1999) which proposes three non-interacting strata in the process of production: the conceptual stratum, the *lemma* stratum, and the lexeme stratum. The lemma of a word is not semantic information, because this is already present at the conceptual stratum, but syntactic information about the formal linguistic liaisons into which the word can enter. This point is made very clearly in the following developmental illustration from Levelt, who conjectures that around the age of two-and-a-half semantics ceases to dominate the process of word production. Instead lexical concepts acquire

> syntactic category and subcategorisation features, verbs acquire specifications of how their semantic arguments (such as agent or recipient) are to be mapped onto syntactic relations (such as subject or object), nouns may acquire properties for the regulation of syntactic agreement, such as gender etc. More technically speaking, the child acquires *a system of lemmas, packages of syntactic information, one for each concept.* At the same time the child quickly acquires a closed-class vocabulary, a relatively small set of frequently used function words. These words mostly fulfil syntactic functions: they have elaborate lemmas but lean lexical concepts. This system of lemmas is largely up and running by the age of four. From them on, producing a word always involves the selection of the appropriate lemma.
>
> (Levelt 1999, emphasis added)

There is a wide range of evidence for the existence of an autonomous lemma (or syntactic structure) stratum in the process of speech production from analyses of speech errors – word exchanges are constrained by grammatical properties (Garrett, 1981) – to the cognitive neuropsychological literature on the effect of lesions of the left hemisphere on speech production (Damasio *et al.*, 1996), to picture-naming experiments on normal adults (Levelt *et al.*, 1991). It would be entirely wrong to say that there is a simple consensus around Levelt's serial model. There is not, for there is evidence that phonological encoding can begin before lemma access is complete (Cutting and Ferriera, 1999; Peterson and Savoy, 1998). But the notion of the lemma has very substantial support.

It seems to me that the conceptual stratum can be thought of as Chomsky's conceptual – intentional system and that the lemma level is equivalent to Chomsky's notion of lexical representation, with perhaps Grimshaw's notion of the canonical structural realisation (GSR, p. 77) playing a crucial role in the developmental process which Levelt describe in the quotation. This is pretty good going for a competence model!

At this point, indeed, we need to ask whether the competence–performance distinction really has a major bearing upon *developmental* explanation. That is to say, even if Jackendoff *is* correct that Chomsky's derivationally-based competence model, with its assumptions about early lexical insertion and the like, actually inspires unrealistic hypotheses about real-time production and comprehension, this fact may not weigh heavily with those of us whose main concerns are with (1) what, if anything, the child innately knows about syntactic structure and with (2) how this knowledge interacts with the process of cognitive development. The developmentalist – it might be said – need have little concern with how and why children say what they say – with, that is, the 'romantic' reading of *erzeugen*; and this is in contrast to the pragmatist. The developmental question – the deep question rather than the descriptive enterprise – is about how it is possible *at all* that children are able to articulate their thoughts in language and read off the articulated thoughts of others. For this we need a competence model and some conception of how mental development relates to this. It is clear that this is provided by MP.

Indeed it might be said that MP is far *less* syntactocentric than the earlier Chomskyan theories described here, in so far as it acknowledges the role of the C–I systems in determining the functioning of C_{HL} – as contrasted with Chomsky's earlier remarks about LAD and cognition 'interacting'. What it achieves is an articulation of how conceptual development can become manifest in language development, whilst giving the pragmatist position that language development is achieved via the general problem-solving capacities of the child a wide berth. Indeed, because it makes C_{HL} responsive to what is happening in the 'external systems' (via the semi-permeable membrane at the C–I interface) it suggests a *less* modular position than that inspired by earlier versions of the theory. Consider, in illustration, Cromer's (1991) recanting on his earlier 'cognition hypothesis' about language development and his replacement of it with a modularist position. The cognition hypothesis is, more or less, the view of the cognitive development/grammar development relationship that MP inspires: syntactic advances must wait upon a corresponding cognitive advance (to be discussed in detail in section 2.4.4). The modularist position, by contrast, is that grammar and cognition have essentially *independent* developmental trajectories; which leaves open the possibility that syntactic development might run ahead of cognitive development. Cromer (1991) presented clinical data which can be taken as evidence for this running ahead (though that is not the *only* way to take them[38]). In this light, MP can be said to achieve *a competence model of the cognition hypothesis*. As presented by Cromer, the hypothesis was a conjecture based on production and other data. But as presented by Chomsky it is a competence theory derived from an analysis of language itself. That is how rationalist developmental psychology is done.

To sum up this subsection, despite being a competence model, MP accords quite well with current psycholinguistic ideas about speech production. Indeed, even if Jackendoff's parallelist model is to be preferred to Chomsky's derivational model in

---

[38] While the IQ was very low, it is far from clear that, in the case Cromer discusses, the individual's syntactic abilities outstripped her *mental age*. For the discussion of the young woman whose syntactic abilities seemed to outstrip her cognitive abilities see Cromer (1991, pp. 132–135).

adult psycholinguistics, this fact is of doubtful relevance to the developmental enter-prise, in so far as this cannot be launched without an adequate theory of how lin-guistic competence relates to cognitive competence. To ignore this desideratum would be to proceed happily unencumbered by a theory of what the empirical work is supposed to be explaining.

2.4.3 The syntactocentrism charge 2: Does Chomsky give a too syntactically-based account of the C–I interface?

The best way to view the issues to be discussed in this subsection is in terms of the following choice about how to spread the explanatory load. The first (non-Chomskyan) option is to say that we cannot offer plausible theories of how concep-tual structure interacts with linguistic structure unless we are prepared to offer some account of the nature of conceptual structure; and this will take the form of a semantic theory with a richness at least the equal of our syntactic theory. From this perspective, the conception of the syntax–semantics interface is incomplete because it is fatally vague about the contribution of semantics. There is also the following related claim. It is possible that, 'minimalist' as it is, MP is still packed with too much complexity because a lot of the work that Chomsky gives to the syntactic com-ponent should in fact be given to the *rules that mediate between the syntax and semantics modules*. This is the position of Ray Jackendoff, a discussion of whose work will again dominate the subsection.

A second position is one that can be naturally associated with Jerry Fodor, partic-ularly in his very recent writings. On this view, talk of 'semantics' or 'conceptual structure' is misleading, because what is actually being referred to by the 'C–I' sys-tems is *thinking itself*. Next, the 'global' nature (Fodor, 1983; 2000b and see p. 28) of 'the central systems' – where thinking takes place – guarantees that, for the foresee-able future at least, we will not understand them well enough to say meaningful things about how 'cognitive structures' impact upon syntactic structures. All we can say with any certainty is that thought has a compositional structure (see 1.1.5). Given this, the best we can do is to focus upon the role of syntax, of whose struc-tured nature we at least have *some* understanding, rather than working towards it from the side of the interface on which we find semantics/meaning/conceptualisa-tion/cognition, about whose structuring we can actually say very little. (In fact, one might view this as the 'classical' versus 'romantic' reading of *erzeugen* in a different guise, with the Fodorian being sceptical about taking the romantic route; as this really is romantically cloudy as far as our present knowledge is concerned.)

Turning first, then, to Jackendoff's position, he replaces Chomsky's term 'C–I sys-tems' with the term *conceptual structure* (CS), presumably in order to make the point that this non-linguistic system *is* indeed structured. To be more precise, this is a system of mental representation

> in terms of which reasoning, planning, and the formation of intentions takes place. Most everyone assumes that there is such a system of the mind, and that it is also responsible for the understanding of sentences in context, incorporating pragmatic considerations and 'encyclopaedic' or 'world' knowledge.

> (Jackendoff, 1997, p. 31)

The elements of CS can be listed as objects, events, times, properties and intentions. Jackendoff insists these entities are not only structured, but that they interact in a

> formal system which mirrors in certain respects the hierarchical structure of (narrow) syntax. For example, where (narrow) syntax has structural relations such as head-to-complement, head-to-specifier, head-to-adjunct, conceptual structure has structural relations such as predicate-to-argument, category-to-modifier, quantifier-to-bound variable. Thus, although conceptual structure undoubtedly constitutes a syntax in a generic sense, its units are not NPs, VPs etc., and its principles of combination are not those used to combine NPs, VPs, etc.; hence it is not syntax in the narrow sense. In particular, unlike syntactic and phonological structures, conceptual structures are (assumed to be) purely relational, in the sense that linear order plays no role.

Given this, it becomes a conceptual necessity (of a Chomskyan kind) that there be *correspondence rules* to mediate between syntactic structure (SS) and CS. Thus:

> *General form of SS-CS correspondence rules:*
>
> Syntactic structure X
>
> {must/may/preferably does} correspond to
>
> conceptual structure Y.

While language is not necessary for conceptual structure to exist – 'it is possible to imagine non-linguistic organisms such as primates and babies using conceptual structures as part of their encoding of and understanding of the world' (ibid, p. 33) these SS-CS correspondence rules *are part of language* because if there were no language there would be no point to the rules. It would be like, in Jackendoff's metaphor, ending a bridge in mid-air over a chasm.

There are relatively few things that can be said definitively about these correspondence rules, but one of them is that the relation between conceptual and syntactic units is not one-to-one but many-to-many. Thus, while all physical objects are represented in syntax by nouns, many nouns do not refer to physical concepts (e.g., *game*); while all verbs express events or states, some events and states are expressed by nouns (e.g., *game* again). Jackendoff schematises the 'sloppiness' of the SS-CS relationship as in (42).

> (42) Noun: Object (*dog*), Situation (*concert*), Place (*region*), Time (*Tuesday*), etc.,
> Verb: Situation (events and states)
> Adjective: Property
> Preposition: Place (*in the house*), Time (*on Tuesday*), Property (*in luck*)
> Adverb: Manner (*quickly*), Attitude (*fortunately*), Modality (*probably*).

Other familiar examples include the fact that in some languages (e.g., German and French) grammatical gender bears only the loosest relation to the conceptual properties of the nouns. Also, it is clear that syntactical properties such as *being the direct object of a verb* can hold while the conceptual structure of the referent can vary widely – see (43).

> (43) Theme/Patient (... *threw the ball*), Goal (... *entered the room*),
> Source/Patient (... *emptied the sink*), Beneficiary (... *helped the boys*),
> Experiencer (... *annoyed Harry*).

Less familiarly, there can be a number of ways in which a conceptual distinction is manifested syntactically. Take the distinction between so-called *telic* events (whose duration is delimited) and *atelic* events (whose duration is not). This differentiation can be achieved by choice of verb, of preposition, of adverb, of determiner in the subject, or of prepositional object. Given this, the ill-formedness of the sentences of (44) is *not a purely syntactic matter*, but is a result of the *wrong kind of mapping* between conceptual structure and syntactic form:

(44) a. *John pushed the cart in an hour
     b. *The light flashed once for an hour
     c. *John ate peanuts in an hour
     d. *John crashed into three walls for an hour
     e. *John crashed into walls in an hour.

But while the relation between conceptual and syntactic structure is nothing like a direct one, some properties of conceptual-syntactic mapping must be preserved. While it is the case that the conceptual representation may have a finer grain than the syntactic, and while the type of syntactic expression of a conceptual representation can vary over certain parameters, it would seem to be something like a conceptual necessity that relations between (say) predicates and arguments or categories and modifiers at the conceptual level are preserved at the syntactic level. (If they were not then Winston Smith would be quite unjustified in thinking that his expression of certain simple truths just had to be accurate, no matter what anybody else tried to make him believe). The principle Jackendoff uses to illustrate this kind of necessity is one which holds that if certain elements in SS and CS correspond to each other and if there is an embedding relation between two of them at one of the levels then the same embedding relationship must hold at the other. This is expressed formally in (45).

(45) If syntactic maximal phrase X_1 corresponds to conceptual constituent Z_1 and syntactic maximal phrase X_2 corresponds to conceptual constituent Z_2 then iff X_1 contains X_2, preferably Z_1 contains Z_2.

Jackendoff points out that within 'traditional generative grammar' the word 'preferably' in the above would be omitted, because there is no room in that approach for an acknowledgement of the relative sloppiness and complexity of the SS-CS interface. Given this, when a case appears in which the above generalisation does not seem to hold, the problem is dealt with *by adding complexity to the syntactic component.* Indeed, one might say that doing so is the essence of Chomsky's 'dislocation property'. Indeed, viewed from Jackendoff's perspective, the dislocation property is not really a property of syntax at all, *but rather a window onto the complexity of the SS-CS interface.* Here is a standard example of this – one of a kind we have already discussed above. In (46) the syntactic arrangement of parts does not reflect the conceptual arrangement of parts, given that *Bill* is what might be called the logical object of the fact of seeming, when syntactically *Bill* is the subject. (Cf. Chomsky's famous *John is easy/eager to please* example in which surface structure fails to mirror distinctions present in deep structure.) In Chomskyan theory (46) is taken to be derived from a string of the kind shown in (47).

(46) Bill seems to be a nice fellow
(47) e seems [Bill to be a nice fellow]

Recall the earlier discussion (in 2.3.4) of how such a sentence illustrates the operation of agreement, checking, and movement – of the dislocation property more generally. An alternative proposal, Jackendoff points out (1997, p. 37), would be that we simplify the syntax (abandoning the derivational form of explanation) and to 'base generate' the first sentence; and this would be at the cost of introducing additional correspondence rules. As an illustration of why we might prefer the latter option, Jackendoff provides the example of (48), after Perlmutter and Ross (1970).

> (48) A man and a woman walked in who happened to look sort of alike.

The problem for a derivational account raised by sentences of this kind is that neither of the noun phrases can be said to be the 'host' of the relative clause (*who happened to look sort of alike*) in underlying syntactic structure, because this clause contains a predicate (*look alike*) that cannot apply to one argument alone, but must apply to two jointly. Jackendoff concludes (ibid., p. 38, original emphasis):

> The point … is that some mismatch between meaning and surface syntax exists, and that the content of the mismatch must be encoded *somewhere* in grammar, either in the syntactic movement or in the SS-CS correspondence.

According to Jackendoff, what the distinction between these two positions boils down to is their differing over the kind of work that is done at the SS-CS interface. For Chomsky, this is essentially syntactic work, in so far as LF deals only with those semantic properties that 'are strictly determined by linguistic rules' (1979, p. 145). On this view, LF is blind to semantic properties of the lexical items; LF does not encode meaning per se; and indeed it does not encode those features of meaning *internal to lexical items*. Accordingly, to take Jackendoff's example, while LF will encode the scope of a quantifier it does not encode the lexical meaning of the different quantifiers (e.g., the difference between *all* and *some* or *three* and *four*), with this being the responsibility of conceptual structure. Thus, we have a contrast between two positions, whose essences are the following:

1) The internal structure of lexical conceptual structures (LCSs) plays no role in determining how LCSs are combined.

2) The way LCSs are combined into conceptual structure is determined in part by the syntactic arrangement of the lexical items and *in part by the internal structure of the LCSs themselves.*

Perhaps the following metaphor might be helpful. We can think of the interface as a membrane against which various kinds of objects impress themselves. On the first account (Chomskyan) this membrane is very thick, so that all that can be judged from the language side of the membrane are the external contours of the objects – their rough size and shape. On the second view, the membrane is so thin that the internal contours of the objects, and even their colours, are visible. On the first view the information about rough size and shape is *sufficient* to make the right kind of causal liaisons with the objects on the language side of the membrane – sufficient to drive the syntactic machinery (classical reading of *erzeugen*). On the second view, the syntactic operations are less those of an engine than of a bespoke tailoring factory, whose operatives will reach for the right kind of patterns and the matching swatches; and while, like any good tailor, there will be fixed ways of proceeding and firm implicit assumptions about the kind of body for whom the tailoring is being done, the customer is King.

How is communication achieved on this metaphor? On the first view, the end result of the syntactic machinery's being put into operation is that it will impinge upon *another thick membrane*; but the thickness matters not because the imprints are sufficiently clear to make the right kind of causal liaisons with the conceptual structure behind this (*the mind of the listener*, on the metaphor). Readers familiar with the Chinese Room argument might like to imagine a John Searle figure between the two thick membranes picking up little or nothing about what is being said. On the second view, by contrast, the John Searleish mannequin knows just what is being put across; and the very thin membrane on the other side of the communicative channel receives a photo-realistic imprint without ambiguity, but with a good deal of redundancy. It has the 'clarity' of a fashion shot, while doing too much for the mere browser (a hint that flares are back or tummies can be revealed would have been enough). The first position, but not the second, is minimalist in a fairly obvious sense.

Metaphors aside, we can now consider the kind of empirical (in the sense used in linguistics) considerations that Jackendoff uses in support of the second position. His main contention is that the binding and quantification phenomena that LF is supposed to deal with cannot be described 'in their full generality' by reference to the syntactic level alone; rather 'they can only be most generally encoded at conceptual structure, a non-syntactic level' (1999, p. 50). I will reproduce two of Jackendoff's examples, concentrating on binding.

On the Chomskyan view that binding between lexical items is a purely syntactic affair, one NP is simply co-indexed to another in the following manner:

NP_i binds [NP anaphor]$_i$

However, on the view that it is co-determined by syntax and the 'internal structure of LCS' the contribution of conceptual structure might be represented as below (adapted from Jackendoff (1997, p. 69)).

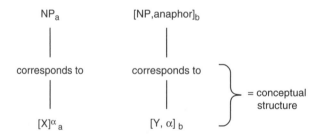

In this, the antecedent NP expresses a conceptual structure X while its anaphor expresses conceptual structure Y, with the superscripted Greek letter indicating a binder and the same Greek letter within a bracket indicating a bindee. The idea here is that the *actual binding relation obtains between X and Y, at the level of conceptual structure.*

In order to show that we should prefer the latter way of conceptualising binding, it is necessary to find examples in which a purely syntactic account cannot characterise the relation between anaphors and their antecedents. Here is one such example.

According to LF there is no significant lexical difference between the verb *obtain* and the verb *buy*. However the LCS of *buy* is twice as complex as that of *obtain*, in the following sense. When we talk of X buying Y from Z we do not only mean that X obtained Y from Z but also that Z reciprocally obtained money from X. In other words the LCS of *buy* has to assign two semantic roles to the subject and to the object of *from*:

    a. Y changes possession from Z to X

    b. money changes possession from X to Z

But this constitutes a violation of θ–theory (see page 126) which states, recall, that an expression cannot fill two argument roles at the same time. The reason that this syntactic principle is violated, argues Jackendoff, is that a binding relation is implicitly at work here, and it is one that has a conceptual basis of the kind just sketched:

    a. Y changes possession from Z^a to X^b

    b. money changes possession from β to α

The Greek letters in b. function as variables, bound to the superscripts in a; and the upshot is that whoever it is gives Y to somebody receives money and whoever turns over the money receives the Y.

The importance of this kind of example is taken to lie in the fact that there is no way to represent this kind of complexity in LF alone. For example, in *Bill bought a book from each of the students*, whose reading is that 'For each student x, a book changed possession from x to Bill and money changed possession from Bill to x', the problem arises that while two occurrences of the variable x are 'inside' *buy* these never appear as separate syntactic constituents. Therefore there is no way to express this complexity at LF, whose only materials are syntactic.

Here is another of Jackendoff's examples of how a complexity of binding cannot be represented syntactically, and must therefore be represented conceptually. In (49), there is an ambiguity of the binding relationship – a so-called 'strict versus sloppy identity' ambiguity.

    (49) John took his kids to dinner, but Bill didn't.

Does this mean that Bill didn't take John's kids to dinner or his own kids? What is at issue here is not the fact of ambiguity itself, because of course syntax can afford to give rise to ambiguities in reference. Rather, the problem is that the implicit VP ('take his kids to dinner') must contain some variable – take kids of x – that can be bound to *either* John or Bill. Moreover, this variable must behave like a variable in the predicate calculus bound to a quantifier, because the same problem of ambiguity arises when a quantifier is used in this kind of sentence instead of a proper name, as in (50).

    (50) John took his kids to dinner, but *nobody else* did.

At what level of representation (syntax or conceptual structure) is this binding achieved? Examples like that in (51), which, like the *buy* example, show that a further layer of complexity is lurking, suggest that the binding cannot be achieved without a contribution from conceptual structure. (The capitalisation indicates semantic focus manifested in speech by stress: see Jackendoff, 1997, p. 77).

> (51) JOHN is ruining his books by smearing PAINT on them, but BILL wants to do it with GLUE.

In (51) the ambiguity hovers over the question of whether Bill has John's books in mind or his own. Well, in order for the ambiguity to be *afforded* there must be a level of representation containing a variable *y* (which we can read as 'some substance') of the following kind: *ruin his books by smearing y on them*, where *y* is a presupposed empty slot that is filled by *glue* in the second clause. But can we represent *ruin his books by smearing y on them* in the LF of the first clause? This can be shown not to be possible, argues Jackendoff, because when we remove from that clause the lexical item that fills the variable slot (namely *PAINT*) an ill-formed sentence is produced, as in (52).

> (52) *It is PAINT$_i$ that John is ruining his books by smearing t$_i$ on them.

The failure of the trace to bind to *PAINT* in such a way as to produce a meaningful sentence *marks out the lack of the requisite kind of LF*, according to Jackendoff, and shows that LF cannot represent strict/sloppy ambiguity.

As before, the same kind of difficulty emerges when we replace the second proper name with a quantifying expression, as in (53).

> (53) JOHN is ruining his books by smearing PAINT on them, but everybody else is doing it with GLUE.

In all such cases, the binding relations are achieved via a conceptual, rather than syntactic, representation whose complexity cannot be captured by syntactic facts alone – the argument runs. For Jackendoff, examples like this show that there are certain 'hidden' elements in binding that LF must necessarily miss, because they are really conceptual.

These are highly technical issues and my exposition has abstracted away from much of this technicality. But perhaps enough has been said to show what is at stake. To re-employ the membrane analogy, Jackendoff thinks these examples show (just two from a host of them) that the kind of causal liaisons made through the thick membrane are sometimes inadequate to set the syntactic machinery into the right kind of motion in the mind of the listener. The lingering question is whether these kinds of examples are devastating for the thick-membrane, minimalist approach.

At this point, we face two kinds of issue. There is, first of all, a difference of opinion between linguists about what can and should be computed by LF, on which a non-linguist is not in a position to adjudicate, and which has no obvious developmental cash value. (Though noting it does colour in the controversial status of LF, even among those sympathetic to generative linguistics.) And second, there are some wide but deep issues of concern to us all, about legibility between mental modules. I think the Chomskyan would say here that if you make the membrane between the C–I systems and C$_{HL}$ as thin as Jackendoff desires then (a) you will have to abandon the whole idea that the language system is modular and end up doing a kind of pragmatism, though in a formalist style, or (b) you will have to defend a view of the central systems as being *entirely modular* – which, for some, is not a defensible view at all. I will spend more time on (b), though with the following brief regard to (a): if we make all semantic liaisons of, to return to the above example, *buy* legible to LF rather than having them dealt with under what Chomsky calls 'full semantic interpretation' then where are we going to stop if the semantics is not to be pulling the syntactic cart? It we fail to draw the line at the point at which we have sufficient syntactic structure for the derivation to converge, then the question of whether we call something a 'semantic' or a 'syntactic' fact will lack any principled motivation.

Be that as it may, let us examine the cogency of (b), which is Jackendoff's view that the semantic and the syntactic systems are each modules of a similar status within the massively modular mind. (We should keep at the back of the mind, of course, the absolute contrast between this and Fodor's view that what we have rather is a modular syntactic system interfacing with the global central systems.) On Jackendoff's view then, one asserts that the mind is modular in its entirety, but that these modules are not of the Fodorian kind in so far as they *communicate* with one another (Fodor's 'informational encapsulation' criterion is dropped). We know they must communicate – the argument runs – given our cross-modal abilities, given the fact that we can talk about what we can see – and so forth. Jackendoff calls this *Representational Modularity* (1997, section 2.6). Moreover (ibid., p. 41):

> Representational modules differ from Fodorian modules in that they are individuated by the representations they process rather than by their function as faculties for input or output;[39] that is, they are at the scale of individual levels of representation, rather than being an entire faculty such as language or perception. The generative grammar for each 'language of the mind', then, is a formal description of a repertoire of structures available to the corresponding representational module.

The pressing question then becomes: How are these modules supposed to communicate with one another if they each speak their own language? The answer is that they do so via *interface modules*. Such an entity 'communicates between two levels of encoding, say L_1 and L_2, by carrying out a partial translation of information in L_1 form into information in L_2 form (or, better, imposing a partial homomorphism between L_1 and L_2 information)' (ibid., p. 42). To which the still more pressing question becomes: Is this kind of thing possible *at all*? There are good reasons for thinking that it is not. And these are reasons which, I will argue, after Fodor (2000b), need to be understood in the light of impediments that lie before *any* purely modular theory of mental architecture.

Fodor presents the following a priori argument against what he calls 'massive modularity', by which he intends theories such as Jackendoff's in which the mind is inhabited by modules and nothing else. For simplicity of exposition, imagine a mind consisting only of two modules, call them M1 and M2. These obviously have to be responsive to – have to turn on only when they encounter – perceptual representations of a given kind, call them P1 and P2. Now, for this to work within the constraints of massive modularity the procedure by which the assignment of P1 to M1 and P2 to M2 *must itself be a modular process.* The question is how perceptual

---

[39] But note that Fodor does not entertain 'output modules'.

information comes to be packaged as grist for the P1 or the P2 mill? How is this assignment done? There are essentially two options.

1) There is a mechanism which takes 'representations in general' and assigns them to either P1 or PS.

2) There are distinct mechanisms with distinct input domains (call them in this case BOX1 and BOX2) which package information for either P1 or P2.

There are clear difficulties with each of these solutions. With regard to 1, to claim that a mechanism might take as its input 'representations in general' is to violate the core assumption of massive modularity which is that there is no level of mental representation less modular than the modules into which it directs data. Meanwhile, a moment's thought tells us that 2 threatens an infinite regress. If we propose that BOX1 and BOX2 are only sensitive to inputs of a certain kind we *then* have to ask ourselves how the inputs were themselves represented so as to be thus selected. They might be represented as (in Fodor's example) GOTO-BOX1 and GOTO-BOX2, with these being features which get attached to some representations and not to others. But this in turn raises '*the question of how the representations in their domains got assigned the properties to which they are selectively sensitive*' (my italics). 'What we've got so far', writes Fodor, 'is, in effect, an argument that each modular mechanism presupposes computational mechanisms less modular than itself, so there's a sense in which the idea of a *massively* modular architecture is self-defeating' (ibid., p. 73).

(Note, by the way, that this is not a case of Fodor recanting on the idea of input systems; because there is nothing here to suggest that the idea of an input module is incoherent. The incoherence in the present case is supposed to derive from the assumption made within massive modularity that the modular input systems *serve only modules* and that these input systems cannot be less modular than the modules which they serve. In Fodor's *The modularity of mind*, by contrast, the modular input systems served the non-modular 'central systems', so the problem did not arise.)

Fodor points out that the only way for the massive modularity theorist to escape from this dilemma is by being prepared to become an empiricist. That is to say, the above difficulty is only present when we take that which is delivered up to modules (i.e., construed as that which is responsible for central cognition, as opposed to a Fodorian input system) to be *the world as represented as being such and such*. To take perception in this light is to be a non-empiricist: it is to assume that the organism picks up information on the basis of its prior capacities for parsing input; it does not resonate to objective 'structure' (*à la* J. J. Gibson) nor siphon up data into a network (*à la* connectionism). But if we think we can afford to be empiricist about perception – at least about at the kind of perception that gives rise to thought – then there is no regress, because P1 is caused to go into the right kind of state to feed into M1 because of the *structure of the sensorium* – not because of the representations delivered up to it; indeed perception is not a matter of representing at all, and so there is no infinite regress of kinds of representations. Can one, therefore, be an empiricist about perception while being a massive modularist about central cognition? No, because once we are happy to accept that experiential data get into the mind unmediated by any processes of representation then we are faced by a dilemma not unlike that with which we began. One either goes the whole hog and says that the mind is representationally unstructured prior to experience, this being the empiricist principle that 'nothing is in the mind that is not first in the senses'. Or one is forced to re-confront the issue of how a module employing a *sui generis* representational format ('speaking its own language') is supposed to glean information from something (the sensorium) with no representational format *at all*.

Perhaps it can be said that what lies behind Fodor's 'argument from perception' against massive modularity is the following intuition: *if the mechanism that ensures engagement of the correct module is central then you have central globality; if the mechanism is peripheral you have empiricism.*

This leads us to consider the difficulties that confront Jackendoff's notion of 'interface modules'. A few words of orientation first. The difficulty we are tracking is not with massive modularity itself, which, if Fodor is correct, is self-defeating in any event; nor is it with the fact that cognition just *is* a global rather than a modular process (for reasons given in Fodor, 1983 and 2000b; and to be discussed later). Rather, the difficulty is with the postulation of interface modules as an answer to the question of how modules that speak only in their own tongues are supposed to communicate.

The very idea of interface modules, able to communicate between modules by 'carrying out a partial translation of information in L_1 form into information in L_2 form (or, better, imposing a partial homomorphism between L_1 and L_2 information)', must confront a familiar dilemma. On the one hand, the translation between modules is effected in virtue of the fact that the representational format used by the interface module is less modular than that of the two communicating modules; and this is to say that the format has a degree of module generality. But if so, then the reasons for insisting that each mental module should have its own representational format begin to melt inexorably away. For we are admitting that mediation between modules is conducted in a format that has access to both languages; and if the mind conducts its operations in a language of such general application then the mind would seem *not* to be massively modular after all. On the other hand, we might explain the work of the interface modules in terms of proposals similar to Fodor's P1 descending to BOX1, descending to GOTO-BOX1, descending … ? In other words, if the interface modules do not have a format that is more general than that possessed by the modules between which they are communicating then the interface with L_1 must necessarily fail to enter into fruitful liaison with L_2, because there will be a regress. This is because, more generally, what makes L_n what it is is that *all of its descendants* – no matter how fine the cut – must be senstive to L_n-like features *and to no other kind*. In the present case, L_1 will have within its domain a range of representations 'within' the interface module, but, to reformulate Fodor's original question: How can the representations in the L_1 interface domains get assigned the properties to which they are selectively sensitive if all the representations within this interface module are descendants of L_2?

I have been painting with a broad brush in this subsection; and an accusation of insensitivity to technical issues within linguistics (the contribution of semantics to syntactic interpretation most notably) might have some justification. But given that our main concern is with whether the Chomskyan conception of the C–I interface is indeed *massively misconceived*, it is perhaps forgivable to have one's sights focused upon issues of broad principle. In fact, I think it is fair to conclude, within this focus, that no compelling reason has emerged for rejecting the Chomskyan 'thick-membrane' conception of the interface, coupled with a hybrid approach to mental architecture in which the language faculty is modular while the C–I systems that interface with it are not. There has also been some echoing of Fodor's almost nihilistic attitude towards our present state of knowledge about the C–I systems and towards the prospects for enriching it. (My seeming to be happy with the picture of the central systems as a dark, unexplorable continent peopled with creatures we only know through their bumping up against the C_{HL}'s thick membrane is likely to impress few!) But one might say that if there is some truth in Chomsky's minimalist approach then the study of language development offers us, if not a 'royal road' to an account of cognitive development, then at least a handy rat-run (with numerous speed bumps) towards such an account. We come then to view mental development from the vantage of language development through a membrane dimly and densely. But before we overdose on metaphors we should consider the kind of detailed suggestions about language development that can be derived from MP – as well as being more specific about how the MP–conception of syntactic development relates to the main alternatives.

2.4.4 Miminalism's more specific empirical implications: minimalism as a developmental theory

Immediately to renege on my decision to shun metaphors, I need to begin this subsection by reprising a powerful and popular metaphor owing to Leila Gleitman (Gleitman and Wanner, 1982). Gleitman characterised the distinction between 'discontinuity' and 'continuity' theories of syntactic development in the following terms:- *tadpole-frog theories* versus theories which assume there to be *frogs all the way down*. In the first (discontinuity) case the principles on which the younger child categorises and arranges the words in utterances are entirely semantic (such as 'object or person' rather than 'noun', 'action' rather than 'verb', 'event' rather than 'verb phrase'); the child is a semantic tadpole. But later, by some process or other, the child is transformed into a syntactic frog. Syntactic nativists tend to react to such theories by saying that they violate developmental common sense in claiming that a child has to undergo a period of doing the wrong thing before doing the right thing: why take the wrong road first and then backtrack? Nativists can admit that semantic information is indispensable if one is to discover what *are* the nouns, verbs, and so forth, in the target language (see the discussion of Grimshaw's CSRs above, and Pinker's Semantic bootstrapping hypothesis in 4.4) but for the child to do this she must be in possession of an innate tacit knowledge that nouns etc. *exist in the input*. Tadpole-frog theories are favoured by pragmatists, who take the children's knowledge of human intentionality, their capacities for analogy-making, and their inferential and general conceptual capacities to be so rich that they can penetrate deeply into the language using these alone, with the specifically syntactic knowledge being acquired through learning.

To say, by contrast, that there are 'frogs all the way down' is to take there to be continuity between the linguistic categories of the child and of the adult. Thus, when the young child says *bring truck* she is not doing this because she has acquired the pragmatic generalisation that in order to get what you want you must say 'bring + X'. Rather, the child is using a proto verb phrase, because she has been employing specifically syntactic knowledge to comprehend and produce language from the beginning. On such a theory, if children make grammatical errors this is because of their cognitive immaturity. Accordingly, the continuity theorist Kenneth Wexler (1994) explains the fact that children appear to undergo a period of development (the so-called 'optional infinitive stage') in which they use the infinitive form of a verb in the main clause when they should be using the finite form (e.g., saying *Daddy come* instead of *Daddy comes*) in terms of their inability to represent tense in the adult way: it is due to difficulties external to syntax.

Minimalism is obviously a nativist theory, but it is one that does not fit comfortably with the continuity assumption. (There will also be a discussion of this question in section 4.3.3.) MP's foundational claim is, of course, that the language system is an optimal solution to legibility problems posed at the interfaces. On this view then, complete continuity with adult grammar can only be possible *if there is no cognitive development*, if, that is, the child's 'system of thought' (Chomsky's phrase) is essentially the same as that of the adult! This is a position taken by almost *nobody* within developmental psychology; for even the most radical nativist accepts that there is cognitive change – *maturation*. What nativists reject is the idea that the basic cognitive architecture in childhood is fundamentally different from that present in adulthood. On the safe assumption, then, that there is indeed cognitive advance during childhood we can propose that, if one is a minimalist, one will think that the nature of the 'legibility problems' posed at the interface between language and the 'system of thought' will change over time. This is what Martin Atkinson calls the 'thesis of dynamic minimalism' (TDM), which he states thus (Atkinson, 2000, p. 38)

'At any point in development, the child's language system is an optimal solution to legibility problems posed at the interfaces'.

On Atkinson's view then, we should adopt a position that is a third way between the tadpole-frog and the frogs all the way down approach; though not in the sense of being something bland and ecumenical. Like the first, it can assert that the child's syntax is profoundly influenced by the process of cognitive change. That is to say, cognitive change is not introduced as an explanatory principle merely to explain away awkward evidence of syntactic inadequacies, but is taken to be responsible (by virtue of its exertion of 'external' pressure) for processes as fundamental – as 'conceptually necessary' – as the construction of phrases. But like the second, it can assert that the child is no less of a linguistic creature than is the adult. On this view the child's language is 'perfect'; it's just that it represents an optimal solution to a different, simpler, set of legibility problems. Dynamic minimalism certainly has some attractive features, for, while clearly requiring syntactic nativism and the modularity of the language faculty, it is able to explain both why children's early syntax, while being surprisingly free of errors, is not like adult syntax and how cognitive development becomes manifested in linguistic development. While this is not Atkinson's way of putting it, one might say that on dynamic minimalism one regards the innate character of syntax in the following light: the language faculty has the capacity to realise in linguistic structure developments that occur in the 'system of thought'; while its operations are autonomous, in the sense that they are in no sense reducible to cognitive operations – they are formal, not cognitive – they do not develop unless they are 'pressured' to do so by cognitive advances.

Before I describe minimalist developmental proposals emanating from linguists (Andrew Radford and Martin Atkinson in particular) I would like to give an example of how one might work from the cognitive-developmental end towards the linguistic.

According to dynamic minimalism, what determines whether and when a child will distinguish between arguments and predicates is not the autonomous development of these innate representations, but the 'external' pressures at the interface so to do. One might say, in fact, that the distinction is innately represented, but that its coming to fruition depends upon 'external' cognitive pressure. In this language-external, pressure-imposing system the child will come to know which properties of an object are mutable and which are not. Accordingly, the spatiotemporal features of the kind of small-to-medium-sized objects that people the child's world (persons, pets, toys, vehicles etc.) can change, but what might be called their inherent properties – the ones that make them what they are – cannot. These (e.g., '– is a cat', '– is a chair') fix their nature, while the mutable ones cover where they are at any one time. Well, to know this is to know something about what, viewing things linguistically, we would call the 'predicate-argument' relation. So it might be said that, unless a child can conceptualise inherent properties, then that child will be unable to engage in *naming*. Similarly – though less to the present point – unless the child can conceptualise these kinds of mutable properties then he or she would be unable to control locatives, indeed control prepositions in general.

With this in mind, let us consider the following looking-time study carried out on infants towards the end of the first year of life – the time when the first words appear – by Xu and Carey (1996). Infants, watching a screen, saw a toy (say) truck emerge from one side and then go back behind it. Shortly after, a (say) teddy emerged from the other side of the screen, which also returned behind it. What would one naturally expect to see when the screen is removed (Figure 2.30)? If one has the object/inherent property distinction in place one will expect to see two objects, because inherent properties, unlike spatiotemporal features, are not mutable; trucks don't change into teddies. In considering the results we must bear in mind that infants of this age have a natural tendency to look longer at two objects than at one and that the longer the looking-time the more 'surprised' at an outcome we can assume the infant to be. Well, when the 10-month-olds experienced the 'impossible' revelation of a single object they did not overcome this natural tendency and looked for *less* time at this than at the 'possible' outcome of two objects – truck and teddy. The 12-month-old infants, by contrast, *did* overcome their natural tendency to look longer at two objects, looking longer at the single toy. One may say they did so because their understanding of the relation between an object and its properties was

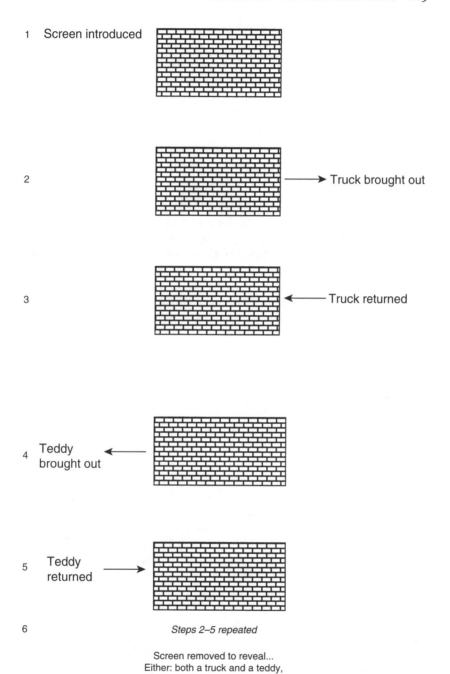

1   Screen introduced

2   Truck brought out

3   Truck returned

4   Teddy brought out

5   Teddy returned

6   *Steps 2–5 repeated*

Screen removed to reveal...
Either: both a truck and a teddy,
or only one of them

Figure 2.30 Schematic illustration of one experimental condition of the study by Xu and Carey (1996).

essentially adult-like. What's more, (a) the mothers reported that many of the 12-month-olds knew the names of the objects in the final two experiments (*ball, bottle, cup, book*) and that few of the 10-month-olds did, and (b) the authors found there to be a significant association between showing the correct pattern of looking and word comprehension in the 10-month-olds.

Turning to the linguistics-to-cognition approach, Atkinson (2000, p. 39) points out that dynamic minimalism raises the following three kinds of questions about:

1) the emergence of interpretable features;

2) the developmental relationship between interpretable and uninterpretable features;

3) the question of *why* uninterpretable features enter the language system at all.

The first question might appear to be the most tractable, given that semantic features would naturally be expected to have clear correlates in 'the system of thought'. (Recall that examples of interpretable features are tense, aspect, number, person and natural gender.) One interesting issue here concerns the extent to which it is possible to predict the order in which interpretable features emerge in the language *on the basis of assumptions about the cognitive complexity of the abilities they represent.* Andrew Radford (2000) has discussed the issue of how interpretable features emerge in these terms.

Consider first the relative cognitive complexity of number, aspect, tense and person. Radford argues that number and aspect are less 'relational' than tense and person, in the sense that the first two do not require the speaker to mark a relation between him/herself and another entity in space or time. Thus, while numbers (one versus more-than-one, say) are obviously related to one another, a number is not the number it is relative to the speaker's location in space and time; similarly, with regard to aspect, an action's being either discrete (e.g., *cut*) versus continuous (e.g., *lived*) has a similar non-relational character. Person (*you, me, my, I, he* etc.), on the other hand, marks distinctions between the speaker and addressees – between different bodies in space. And so by definition, to understand tense is to understand relations between the present time of the utterance and past and future events in relation to a reference time and speech time. Relational knowledge is the more complex form of knowledge in the sense that an extra step is necessary, namely the coding of not only the character of the referent (one or more, discrete or continuous) but the character of the referent in relation to the speaker's location in space and time (e.g., not just the referent 'my mother' but the person in front of me who can hear me, making the form *you* appropriate; not just the fact of Daddy coming in the door but that the event happened before I started this utterance.

Radford notes that Lois Bloom's daughter Allison (from her CHILDES[40] files at 1y 8m and 1y 10m) had acquired the ability to mark plurals, saying things like *cookies, toys* and the irregular *children*, but at the same time failed to mark person, using nouns

---

[40] CHILDES = The Child Language Data Exchange (MacWhinney and Snow 1990).

and proper names instead of personal pronouns. She would say *Wiping baby chin* instead of 'I'm wiping *my* chin', and she would say *Eating Mommy cookie* instead of '*I'm* eating *your* cookie'. Furthermore, although Allison added modifiers to her nouns (e.g., *green cup, tiny cow*) at this time she never used determiners (e.g., *a/the, this/that*) with nouns, thereby producing utterances like *Man drive truck* instead of *The man drives the truck*. This fact is notable given that some linguists (e.g., Abney, 1987) take determiners like *the* to be marking the person properties of the nominal. (Certainly, an expression like *the man* can function like the personal pronoun *he*, used deictically.)

It has been reported that children mark aspect on the verb before they mark tense (Antinucci and Miller, 1975; discussed in Part 4), and Allison Bloom was no exception. Before she was able to mark tense on the verbs describing discrete actions she marked continuing actions with progressive participles such as *Walking around* and *Peeking Mommy*. Here too, then, the child is marking a non-relational interpretable feature before she marks a relational interpretable feature.

Turning to question (2) (developmental relation between interpretable and uninterpretable features), both Radford and Atkinson argue that we should expect interpretable features to appear in speech before uninterpretable ones. The basic reason for this might be expressed by saying that while uninterpretable features 'need' interpretable features if a phrase is to converge at LF the converse is not true: interpretable features do not need uninterpretable features to achieve convergence. Recall the examples given earlier of the way in which the tense head T functions in the derivation of sentences like *John seems to be awake* and *Several prizes are likely to be awarded*. In these derivations T has uninterpretable features that are checked by the interpretable features of nominals ('goals') after their movement; and if they are not checked the derivation will not converge. However, as Atkinson cautions, (1) such considerations are also logically consistent with the *simultaneous* emergence of interpretable and uninterpretable features and (2) that they do not imply that there is an interpretable feature *stage* followed by an uninterpretable feature *stage,* because the different subspecies within the two general types could be appearing at different times (cf. the strong verb over-regularisation literature, in which children over-regularise on a verb-by-verb basis, not in a stage-wise manner).

The relatively late arrival of uninterpretable features implies that structural case (see p. 150) will not be marked in early speech. This is indeed the case – as noted by Radford (ibid., p. 7). Martin Braine's child Jonathan at 1y 11m, 2y and 2y 1m did not mark the possessor with the genitive case marking (-'s), producing utterances such as *Daddy shoe*, and *Elliot cookie*; and he invariably omitted the dummy case mark *of* in obligatory contexts: *drink water* instead of 'drink *of* water', *out car* instead of 'out *of* the car', and so forth.

One might also expect children to go through a period of *treating uninterpretable features as if they were interpretable*. Radford discusses the evidence for their doing this with regard to tense-marking and the number-marking of nouns. With regard to tense, there is an important complication to be considered here, which is that in adult language tense-marking has both an interpretable and an uninterpretable face. (The uninterpretable face of tense has already been encountered in our discussion of the role of the abstract tense head T as a probe, which attracts nominals partly in virtue of its possessing a set of uninterpretable features.) In illustration of the way in which tense-marking can utilise uninterpretable features, consider the following contrast between the child's and the adult's use of progressive and perfect partici- ples. As we have already discussed, Allison Bloom produced utterances such as *Peeking Mommy* and *Eating Mommy cookie*, utterances in which the continuous aspect is marked but no progressive auxiliary *be* is used (as in 'Mommy is peeking' and 'Mommy is eating a cookie'). Can this be counted as failure to mark an unin- terpretable tense feature? In support of the claim that it can indeed be counted this way, Radford illustrates the operation of an uninterpretable tense marker in English with reference to elliptical structures of the following kind: *He hasn't yet gone home but probably will ~~go home~~ soon* and *John went swimming yesterday, but I don't think he will ~~go swimming~~ tomorrow.* For there to be ellipsis, the phrases obviously do not have to be PF-identical (i.e., gone/go; went/go are different *words*), so the identity must be at *LF* in terms of an identity of features. In the first example, however, the LF-identity requirement cannot be met if *gone* carries an interpretable perfect aspect feature which is absent in *go*. But if we assume instead that *gone* carries an *un*inter- pretable aspect feature, there will be *LF identity* between the two lexical items, both carrying uninterpretable features; and *recall that two checked uninterpretable features cancel each other out.*

By a similar logic Radford argues that in the second ellipted sentence, *went* [swim- ming] carries an uninterpretable past tense feature. Radford continues (op.cit., p. 11):

> However, as already noted, it seems likely that in child structures like *Eating Mommy cookie* which contains an aspect-inflected verb but no superordinate auxiliary, aspect is an inter- pretable feature.

The essential idea here is that, while the adult speaker uses auxiliaries as uninter- pretable features to check the uninterpretable features on the participle and thus achieve convergence, *the child does not feel the need to do this as her use of the partici- ple comes with an aspect feature that is semantically interpretable for the child as if it were an adjective.*

Radford gives a similar kind of account (i.e., children taking uninterpretable fea- tures to be interpretable) of why children who can otherwise use plural markings sometimes fail to do so when the noun is paired with the word *two* and why children who can pluralise do not use the indefinite article *a* to indicate a singleton. Taking the second example first, while Allison Bloom could use plural markings she would say things like *Build tower* instead of 'Build *a* tower', inspiring the question of why she did, as it were, bother to mark plurality but not singularity. Using a similar line of argument to that employed in the tense-marking example, Radford suggests that number is an uninterpretable formal feature of count nouns but an interpretable feature of the article *a*. Given this,

> the noun *tower* enters the derivation carrying an unvalued, uninterpretable number feature [u-Num]; once *a* has merged with *tower* to form *a tower*, the interpretable [Sg-Num] feature of *a* can value the uninterpretable feature of *tower* as [Sg-Num] and erase it.

As before, the empirical evidence for such an analysis comes from the behaviour of elliptical sentences. In a sentence such as *She tried on both dresses but the blue ~~dress~~ was too big*, the LF-identity of *dresses/dress* must be an outcome of the fact that the number feature they both carry is uninterpretable. For this reason, *Build tower* crashes. So why did the child produce it? Because, just as Allison treated participles like *eating* as possessing an interpretable aspect feature, so she is regarding *tower as possessing an interpretable singular feature*. Given this, *Build tower* for her *already carries* a singular marker.

Radford's suggestion is, then, that at a certain period children take lexical items to carry more semantic 'weight' than do adults; which is because they are taking uninterpretable features to be interpretable.

At this point Atkinson's third question becomes pressing: why do uninterpretable features enter the child's grammar at all? In other words, what particular kinds of 'external' cognitive pressures lead to the development of which uninterpretable-feature-fuelled syntactic operations? Note that from the perspective of the continuity theorist this is not even a meaningful question, because it is assumed on this view that syntactic development is autonomous, rather than being something that takes place in response to 'external' developments in the system of thought. Also, from a pragmatist perspective children are *getting by* without uninterpretable features; they are obviously making themselves understood without (say) marking genitives. From the minimalist perspective however, the question is obviously pertinent because it assumes that advances in how and what the child is able to think will, with causal inevitability, manifest themselves linguistically. Thus, if a form of cognitive distinction, category or ability becomes available at certain age (e.g., the ability to understand aspects of quantification or to recall particular events) it will force its way into the language system.

I will cover two of the questions that Atkinson raises in this context – doing so sometimes more in the spirit than in the letter of Atkinson (2000):

1) What kind of 'external' cognitive acquisitions cause the child's language system to move operators[41] like *what* into presentential positions (e.g., when asking questions) and to carry out the kind of movement operations involved in passivising sentences?

2) What kind of 'external' cognitive acquisitions cause the child's language system to introduce the uninterpretable features involved in case-agreement?

Turning to 1, it would help the understanding of what is at stake here to consider the different kinds of uninterpretable features possessed by operators like *what* and by nominals. A nominal like *man* comes complete with a set of interpretable (semantic) features like third-person, singular, and masculine, together with an unvalued and therefore uninterpretable case feature which may gain the value of (say) 'nominative' if it needs to be assigned that in the derivation. By contrast, a word like *what*

---

[41] 'Operator' is likely to refer to an interrogative or negative expression, expressions that trigger auxiliary inversion (e.g. *What have you eaten?*; *Nothing would I do to annoy you.*) The movement of operators is a non-argument or *A′ (A-bar)* movement.

has very little in the way of interpretable features (beyond the fact that it generally refers, unlike *who,* to things rather than persons) and it has, not an uninterpretable case feature, but an open, and thus uninterpretable *scope* feature. That is to say, the lexicon cannot determine the variables that are covered by the term, this being determined during the course of the derivation. Briefly to illustrate what is intended by 'scope' here, a sentence such as *What was stolen and sold?* has ambiguous scope in so far as it can either mean *What thing was stolen and (then) sold?* or *What thing(s) were stolen and what things were sold?*.

One, coarse-grained way of setting up the present issue would be by asking whether children frame questions when they begin to have 'interrogative thoughts'. In a similar spirit we could ask if they begin to say things like *Nobody came or played* (with *nobody* being the operator in this case) when they begin to have 'negating thoughts'. From the point of view of dynamic minimalism, on the other hand, this syntactic advance *is a function of the cognitive ability to represent the scope of a symbol.* Unless scope is represented as an uninterpretable feature of operators like *what* and *nobody* there can be no possibility of such words moving to a pre-sentential position to check the set of φ [uninterpretable]-features occupying that structural position. In the case of *what* in particular there cannot be movement to enter into agreement with an interrogative complementiser unless *what* is 'active', i.e., unless it has an uninterpretable scope feature. Again, compare the situation of nouns which, as we have seen, move to be checked at T (p. 155 and p. 156) in virtue of their uninterpretable case features. (One more piece of jargon: in footnote 41 (p. 189) operator movement is dubbed *non-argument (A')-movement* because the operator is moving into a position not filled by arguments, while the movement of nominals is *argument(A)-movement* as the item is being moved into an argument-filling slot.) This account makes the following plausible assumptions: children will be able to question by other means before this time (Halliday, 1975, on early non-sentential questioning) and they will use the word *what* other than as an operator before this time (e.g., *wha'dat?*) Now it is far from obvious how one would devise tests of the ability to cognise scope pre-linguistically! But the empirical question looks far more tractable than do ones about when children have 'interrogative thoughts' or 'negating thoughts' which somehow become manifested as sentences.

Next, it is generally observed that children engage in operator movement before they produce passives (Borer and Wexler, 1987). Atkinson speculates that this is because they can appreciate the scope of symbol before they can engage in whatever cognitive advances put pressure on the linguistic system to operate with the EPP principle, which, recall, states that sentences need subjects/XPs phrases need specifiers. Putting it very loosely, the suggestion here is that (a) passivisation will not proceed unless there is the ability to represent subjecthood (given that subjecthood is exactly what passivation manipulates), (b) the EPP principle (on which subjecthood is based) will not be utilised unless the cognitive system can *specify,* which in this instance means distinguishing between 'a particular X' and 'any item that fulfils the characterisation of X-hood'. *Chomsky dubs this distinction INT (specific) versus INT' (any item filling description).*

I would like to float the conjecture that we see the arrival of INT' in the cognitive system when the child engages in pretend play. That is to say, when, to use a popular example, the child pretends that a banana is a telephone she is recruiting banana-features to stand for, not a particular telephone, but for telephone-hood, for whatever happens to be able to play the telephone role; and if we can assume, as we surely can, that the child can think about particular telephones (and the child surely knows the banana is not a particular telephone but a particular banana) then one can say that INT versus INT′ is in place. In passing, it is important to note in support of this conjecture the interesting correspondence between the possible analysis of INT/INT′ in terms of the *de re/de dicto* distinction discussed above and Alan Leslie's (1987) analysis of pretend play in terms of referential opacity.

Turning to point 2 and the question of what 'external' pressures operate on the language system to cause the acquisition of structural case, the guiding question might take the following form: What kinds of interpretive anomalies result from cognitive development that are resolved by the marking of case either by inflection (in a language like Latin) or by the use of prepositions and word order (in a language such as English)? The first thing to note is that the importance of case to the derivation is that it makes nouns 'visible' for θ-marking (pp. 126–127): they need case so that the role of their referents in the situation represented in the sentence can be determined. Second, there might be cases where this step in the derivation is not necessary because the predicate with which the noun is merged renders the case immediately interpretable; in 'X ran', for example, the language system has the agenthood of X visible to it. Third, let us imagine a child who is only able to attach a single predicate to a single argument, who is able, that is, to think only in terms of one-place predicates. Such a child might be able to think thoughts like WALK (DADDY), FALL (DADDY) and ON (DADDY), thoughts which represent the θ-roles of agent, theme, and location, respectively. In which case, then, the θ-role is a more or less direct function of the 'role' played in reality: walking is what one does, falling happens to one, objects can be located on one, and so forth. Given this, *the cognitive system does not present the linguistic system at the interface with the task of making the θ-roles of nouns visible, and so uninterpretable case features will not be present.* But the situation changes dramatically when the child becomes able to think thoughts in which a single predicate co-occurs with two arguments, when, for example, the child is able to think about the act of *kissing* (a two-place predicate) in which an agent does something to a patient. Now the interface is presented with the problem of how to ensure, for example, that, the thought KISSING (POSTMAN→ MUMMY) is not articulated as *Mummy kiss postman*. If the child were speaking Latin then the nouns would have nominative and accusative inflections (structural cases), whereas in English the job is done by word order. Note that, as Baker (1988) has argued, it is possible to regard word order as an uninterpretable feature on a par with case inflections; it is an uninterpretable feature that enables interpretation to be achieved (via checking).

Well, the reader is surely entitled to feel some discomfort with my Micawberish confidence that some means or other will turn up for assessing young children's ability to (say) cognise scope, while it is very unclear what this will look like. That is to say, while the empirical substantiveness of dynamic minimalism depends upon our being able to identify developments in the external system, the best we can do in the context of uninterpretable feature acquisition is the floating of somewhat vague analogies with pretend play. And recall, in this context, Martin Atkinson's warning that the dependence of the strong minimalist thesis on cognitive psychology may prove to be a 'crippling handicap' given that we know so little about (not Atkinson's choice of phrase) central-system cognition. As I said in response to this, the study of the order of acquisition of fundamental cognitive abilities is far more tractable than is the study of the process of thinking itself. But there is scope for a more radical answer. Here is Chomsky's (2000b, p. 123; emphasis added):

> Suppose we understood external systems well enough to have clear ideas about the legibility conditions they impose. Then the task at hand would be fairly straightforward at least to formulate: construct an optimal device to satisfy these conditions. If all such efforts fail then add 'imperfections' as required. But life is never that simple. *The external systems are not well understood. Progress in understanding them goes hand-in-hand with progress in discovering the language systems that interact with them.* So the task is simultaneously to set the conditions of the problem and to try to satisfy them, with the conditions changing as we learn more about how to do so. This is not surprising. It is much what we would expect in trying to understand some complex system. We proceed with tentative proposals that seem reasonably firm, expecting the ground to shift as more is learned.

From the point of view of developmental psychology, this implies that a good theory of the language faculty will be a *source of information and hypotheses about cognitive development itself.* Despite occasional spasms of gung ho, developmentalists know that mental development is not well understood; and, on the present view, we would be well advised to give the discipline a 'linguistic turn'.

Finally, it will probably have not gone unnoticed that my reading of Atkinson's proposal of dynamic minimalism is a very relaxed one–in the following respect. Tacitly, and with an eye to the tractability of experimental child psychology, I have been taking it to mean what is shown in (54).

(54) At any point in development, the child's language system is an optimal solution to legibility problems posed at the interfaces.

This conjecture is substantive as it is. The 'optimal' modifier can guide the linguistic enterprise; but I frankly have no idea how it might guide the developmental one. In any event, it is to empirical matters that we now turn.

2.5 The question of evidence: experiments with young children

2.5.1 Experimental studies – general considerations

In a book reviewing the experimental evidence for young children's early acknowledgement of Chomskyan principles, Crain and Thornton write that '[t]he most compelling evidence of innateness comes from the observation that children sometimes make *nonadult* grammatical hypotheses' (1998, p. 37, emphasis added). That is to say, while one may (as do the authors) subscribe to the continuity assumption, which assumes that children's grammars can only differ from the adult grammar in ways in which adult grammars can differ from one another, the children's grammar might differ from that of the adult because their language acquisition device is still in operation. That is to say, the child is still in the process of settling upon the precise nature of the parametric option that is present in the target language; and the kind of errors that are made will be a dipstick indicator of her no-more-than-partial acknowledgement of its presence in the language.

The fact of major importance here is that if language acquisition were merely a process of mimicking surface forms (called by the authors 'input matching') then acquisition errors would tend to be sketchy versions of sentences they hear, rather than sentences that differ *systematically* from the sentences they hear.

A good example of the process just described comes from children's production (either spontaneous or as the result of laboratory elicitation) of so-called *Medial-Wh* (Thornton, 1990) sentences such as:

>   *What do you think what pigs eat?

Such questions would seem to exemplify a failure to delete, at its original location, the *what* that has undergone movement but which began life as the object of the verb *think* in the underlying structure, and are therefore symptomatic of *doing the right kind of thing but not well enough*, from the point of view of universal grammar. Medial-wh forms do, however, appear in some dialects of German, as I will discuss in 4.3.3. (iv). In minimalist terms, the wh-trace is 'spelt out' in German. For example, *Wen glaubst du wen sie getroffen hat?* = 'who think you who she met has?'.

While such growth errors can be informative, however, they would fall very far short of the compelling if they did not exist before a background of syntactic precocity. Indeed, one might equally well say that the facts that make the nativist stance so compelling are facts about the *adult-like* nature of young children's syntax; and it will be this which will concern us in the first part of this subsection.

How then do the various forms of nativism deal with data showing (a) that children are not 'doing the right kind of thing though well enough' but *the wrong kind of thing;* (b) that while children's behaviour in experiments might be better than chance overall many children are failing? These outcomes can be viewed in the context of the following two kinds of nativism, mooted by Crain and Thornton.

1)   *The modularity matching model:* Not only are all of the linguistic *abilities* of the child the same as those of the adult but, additionally, the child's linguistic processing capacities are similar to adults'; which is to say that children and adults parse sentences in much the same way. Moreover, extra-linguistic factors (such as real-world knowledge, pragmatics, attentional and memorial biases) have only a minor role to play, because the autonomous operation of the language faculty ensures that these factors will be *pre-empted.* According to this view, if an experiment shows children to be performing in a non-adult way this must be due to either (a) the fact that the children cannot perform the computational operations necessary for the underlying syntactic knowledge to become manifest or (b) the experimental procedure is simply insensitive.

2)   *The competing factors model:* On this view, it is accepted that children do innately know the relevant principles, but additionally it is anticipated that children will frequently not perform in an adult-like way because they are more likely to experience processing limitations and to be sidetracked by

extra-linguistic influences. For example (see Clark, 1971), their bias towards acting out instructions on the basis of order-of-mention ensures that they will frequently fail to perform the instruction 'Before you touch your nose, touch your ears'. The main difference between this approach and the previous one lies in its rejection of the view that children's sentence framing and inter-pretation of linguistic operations pre-empt the operations of non-linguistic mental processes.

To these, we can now add the following third alternative.

3) *Dynamic minimalism:* At any point in development, the child's language system is an optimal solution to legibility problems posed at the interfaces: On this view, what is innate is the capacity of the language faculty to respond to cogni-tive challenges presented to it at the cognition–language interface, resulting in the proposal that as mental development proceeds so will syntactic abilities advance. The principal contrast between this view and that of the modularity matching model is as follows: dynamic minimalism is happy to accept that, to the extent that the child's cognitive capacities are not as advanced as those of the adult the child's syntax will not be advanced as that of the adult. Accordingly, if children's syntax is found not to be adult-like in some regard this is not neces-sarily due to the fact that the experiment has required the performance of a cog-nitive operation, the failure to perform which *masks* the presence of a syntactic knowledge. Instead, what may be the case is that, because the relevant cognitive ability has yet to mature, the language faculty has not been called upon to develop the 'solution' (at which it is innately configured to arrive) to the set of 'problems' which this development presents to the interface. Where Dynamic minimalism differs from the competing factors model is in its rejection of the view that non-adult-like syntax must be symptomatic of a performance difficulty. Rather, it may be due to the fact that the development of cognitive competence has not yet provided the necessary pressures at the interface.

With these theoretical alternatives in mind, we can consider some experimental studies of the following forms of linguistic knowledge:

- X-bar grammar;

- Parameters and binding principles;

- Trace theory;

- Bounding principles.

Two caveats. First, I shall be making no attempt to *review* the literature, but will instead present a sample of exemplary studies. Second, the topics to be considered emerge from P & P theory; so what relevance do they have to the minimalist pro-gramme? I think it is fair to say that evidence for the early acknowledgement of the principles of P & P will tend also to be evidence for minimalism, given the overlap in apparatus between the two theories (e.g., with regard to the roles of c-commanding and movement) and given the fact that the theories differ mainly around how to explain the presence of certain kinds of syntactic knowledge rather than over what knowledge is present. With regard to the latter, while MP does not place X-bar gram-mar at the centre of the picture – denying, for example, that intermediate (X′) levels are legible at the C–I interface – the early acknowledgement of X-bar principles by children learning languages like English can be taken as evidence for their fluency with operations such as merge. In any event, it is to X-bar principles that we turn next.

2.5.2 The X′ level: is it late-developing?

In a landmark study, Roeper (1972) presented 4- to 5-year-old children with the array shown in Figure 2.31 and asked them to point to 'The second striped ball'. Surprisingly, many of them chose the ball shown in the figure, rather than the one that is second *among* the striped balls. Their error was, however, not illogical, because if one interprets the instructions to mean 'the ball that is *both second and striped*' then the position they chose is correct. Given this possibility for interpretation the instruction to pick the 'second white ball' would make no sense (because there is no ball that is both second and white); and indeed Roeper's subjects often refused to make a selection in this case. I will refer to the erroneous interpretation, after Matthei (1982), as *intersective*, as this takes the referent to be the intersect of the classes striped and second.

The question then becomes: Why is our natural interpretation of this question one that can be paraphrased as 'Of the striped balls only, pick the one that is second from the left'? An answer is that we give a syntactic analysis of the question in terms of X-bar grammar (see Figure, 2.32 (1)) in which *second* is the modifier of the N′ *striped ball*: *second* is not the modifier of *ball* on a par with *striped*, and if it were (Figure, 2.32 (2)) then we would be able to paraphrase the NP as meaning 'both second and striped'. Prima facie, this result suggests that children are not operating with the intermediate level N′ at an age at which a nativist would expect them to be doing so. (See Radford [1990] for interpretations of very early speech production in X′ terms, discussed also in 4.2.3.)

Roeper's study has been replicated and extended by Matthei (1982). Two of the more interesting extensions of the original finding were the following. First, children's difficulty was only clearly in evidence when two prenominal modifiers were employed. When the array consisted of a set of toy animals (hippos and bears) there were relatively few errors in picking out *the second bear*, which, according to Matthei (though see below), suggests that the challenge presented by the task is indeed a linguistic one, rather than a 'conceptual' one – given that they were required to perform

"Point to the second striped ball"

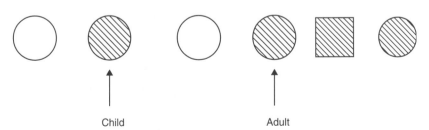

Child   Adult

Figure 2.31 The array used in Roeper (1972), plus child and adult selections.

(1) adult analysis

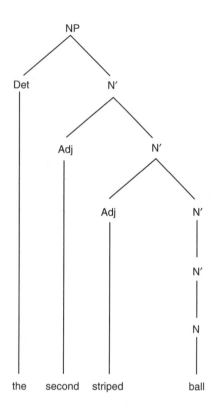

(2) child analysis

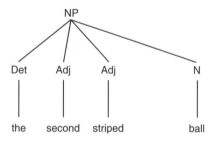

Figure 2.32 Child and adult analyses of the instruction in Figure 2.31.

'the same conceptual operations' as in the second-striped-ball task. (In fact, the difference between the two conditions was not dramatic: 36 per cent error rate in the animals condition, versus 52 per cent error rate for two modifiers, which difference falls far short of the difference between child and adult performance.) Second, the intersective error was not one specific to right-branching trees, because it was also found in left-branching (Matthei, 1982, pp 120–22) forms like *the red bird's hat,* when the display consisted of two birds – one red bird wearing a blue hat plus a bird of another colour wearing a red hat. The latter is the intersective choice, a reading equivalent to 'the red bird's-hat'.

The children were, therefore, producing the non-adult interpretation, which, under the taxonomy sketched above, was a case 'doing the wrong kind of thing' (as opposed to 'doing the right kind of thing not well enough'). Potentially, this presents a clear challenge to the modularity matching model, one that that Crain tries to meet in the following way. The idea is that children of this age are challenged by the requirement to execute the kind of complex plan necessary for carrying out the instructions; their difficulty is not a conceptual one but one caused by inadequate computational resources. In other words, they are taken to have basic knowledge of X' structures of this level of complexity which is *masked* by non-linguistic computational limitations.

In contrast to more familiar proposals made in a similar spirit (e.g., Fodor, 1987, on theory of mind) Hamburger and Crain (1984) are able to spell out exactly what is intended by 'computational complexity' in this context. They explicate the planning steps in counting objects, in selecting one kind of object from a series, and of ordinal counting of a subgroup by reference to Lisp-like lines of programming. The details of this need not detain us, except to note that the analysis is in terms of the fact that the presence of two predicates (*second striped X* instead of, say, *second X*) adds extra lines of program. The following gives the *flavour*:

> An extra level is present in the exit test of the inner loop, where the simple predicate in line 8 of the Fig. 10 plan for *second ball* is replaced by the logical conjunction *and*. This change arises from the need to check two predicates, in lines 9 and 10, instead of one.
>
> (Hamburger and Crain, 1984, p. 106)

Then, in order to find out whether, indeed, planning complexity rather than syntactic complexity was responsible for the children's difficulties, Hamburger and Crain made the following two modifications to the procedure – intended to smooth the path for planning.

1) The test display was withheld until after the experimenter had uttered the instruction, which was expected to oblige 'the child to operate in compile mode' (p. 113).

2) The children underwent a handling procedure in which the child was required to hand over to the experimenter the various groups of identical objects to be used in the display.[42] 'In our view,' the authors write, 'this active experience with the objects provides an opportunity for the child to work on a sub-plan that can then be incorporated into the plan for the main experimental task' (ibid., p. 113).

---

[42] Each subject was informed that during the session s/he would provide the objects that the experimenter would use to make the displays. In requesting the objects for each display, the experimenter refrained from using linguistic material from the experimental phases, instead simply pointing to the piles of objects and saying, 'Give me four of these … and three of those …' and so on. The children then carried out the instructions (Hamburger and Crain, 1994, p. 118).

The facilitation achieved by this means was quite impressive. In these children, whose ages ranged between 4y 4m and 6y 2m, the average error-rate in the experimental groups (with the handling procedure either in a second session or in a single session) was around 15 per cent, which is less than half of the error rate in the control group – 32 per cent.

Crain and Thornton take this result to be generally supportive of the modularity matching model in so far as the handling procedure can be thought to have enabled the children to perform the cognitive operations that underlie the parsing of sentences in terms of intermediate levels of syntactic representation. They add a further piece of evidence. Recall from 2.1 that one of the acid tests for whether a sequence of words forms an N' is whether the string can serve as the antecedent of a proform, such as *one*. Given this, the prediction can be made that children who make the erroneous intersective interpretation of *second striped ball* by virtue of their difficulties with 'compiling' the requisite plan may nonetheless be able to interpret instructions of the kind 'Point to the first striped ball; *point to the second one*' because they have the underlying ability to take the N' *striped ball* as a syntactic unit. (If they did not, then they would take *one* to refer to the bottom (N^0) level – *ball* – pointing to the second ball whether or not it was striped). Of 10 children who had made the intersective error on at least three out of four trials, nine of them made the correct interpretation of *second one* on at least one of the two opportunities (five of them did it on both). For Crain (1991, p. 609), this confirms that a syntactic capacity was being masked by computational complexity in the Roeper task.

But does the outcome of the Hamburger and Crain study necessarily support the modularity matching model? A supporter of the competing factors model might be tempted to claim these data on her own behalf, saying that what the handling procedure actually achieved was a reduction of the working memory load (by virtue of making the holding-in-mind of the relevant subgroups something that was 'practised' at the time of giving the instruction). Perhaps one would be unwise to attempt to adjudicate on this issue. For when is an explanation in terms of extra Lisp-like programming steps (analogous to the language of thought?) to be preferred to explanations in terms of pre-loading in working memory making performance more fluent!

A more tractable and interesting challenge comes from dynamic minimalism. Recall that, on this view, cognitive factors may do more than *mask* an existing syntactic competence. Rather, cognitive change will itself become *realised* syntactically during development. In the present case this amounts to the claim that there may indeed be a period in development during which X-bar syntax is not fully developed because the 'external' pressures have not been present at the C–I/C_{HL} interface sufficient to bring it into complete fruition: children rarely if ever operate with intermediate phrasal levels during this period because they simply cannot think the relevant thoughts. What is being alluded to here is the controversial distinction between performance (modularity matching, competing factors) and competence (dynamic minimalism) failures on developmental tasks: between failure to do the right kind of thing well enough and lacking the conceptual grasp.

A complicating thought here is that the psychologist whose name is most closely associated with the idea that children acquire qualitatively novel competences – Jean

Piaget – took the acquisition of concepts (e.g., of number, space, time, length, area) to be grounded in the executive process of 'autoregulation' (see Russell, 1999, for discussion), which is itself a kind of performance. That said, a supporter of dynamic minimalism can make the following proposal. Children within the age range under discussion are in the process of developing what Piaget (1952) called *class inclusion* abilities. That is to say, when presented with a class of objects made up of two sub-classes one of which is clearly larger than the other, they are essentially unable to think about – this is not a 'planning' deficit – the class and the larger of the subclasses at the same time. For example when a 5-year-old is shown a bunch of 12 roses, 10 of which are red and two of which are white, and is asked whether there are more red flowers or flowers altogether she is likely to say 'More red flowers'. The explanation for this error given by Piaget was in terms of younger children's thought lacking the kind of flexibility necessary for their cognitive spotlight (not Piaget's term) to move between the larger of the two subclasses (red flowers) and the total class (flowers) and back again. Thought of this kind is, according to Piaget, prey to capture by local, perceptuo-cognitive saliences (that the red set is bigger than the white) and that once captured it remains 'centrated' (Piaget's term) on that salient fact. (Readers familiar with Piaget's conservation experiments will recognise a similar inadequacy there, in terms of the child's witnessing the perceptual transformation of the materials, such as one stick being pushed up higher than another stick of equal length, and the child's stubbornly continuing to frame her answer in terms of the fact that because one of the sticks is higher up it is therefore longer.)

Let us now consider what a Piagetian account of the younger child's failure would look like, as contrasted with the kind of account offered by Hamburger and Crain in terms of planning complexity. For Piaget, the development of 'autoregulation' – surely an endogenous development (in the prefrontal cortex predominantly), making Piaget a kind of maturationist – renders a kind of thought possible for a child that was impossible before. The claim is not that younger children are incapable of thinking about subclasses in relation to classes, but rather that when a question ensures that they must think about both a class and its larger subclass *at the same time* the larger subclass pulls them towards error. This is not due to the fact that class inclusion tasks are more 'complex' in the sense of requiring additional computational steps: it is because these *kinds* of tasks – tasks in which the cognitive spotlight must be prised free of a local saliences – challenge the executively immature brain. For Piaget, children's cognition does not only differ from that of adults in respect of its being less well adapted to complexity.

In what sense, then, does the Roeper task tap class-inclusion abilities? It is clear that the two tasks do not make exactly parallel demands, but both do require the ability to model the embedding of two subclasses within a class one of which is smaller than the other (though this is a subset of the subclass in the Roeper task). See Figure 2.33 for the adult (a) and the child models.

But here is a second possible kind of external demand that the Roeper task could be making – for spotting referential ambiguity. Construed in this way, the task does not so much tap the *conceptual* ability of class inclusion as a more *pragmatic* sensitivity. It is known that the following kind of 'referential ambiguity' task challenges children

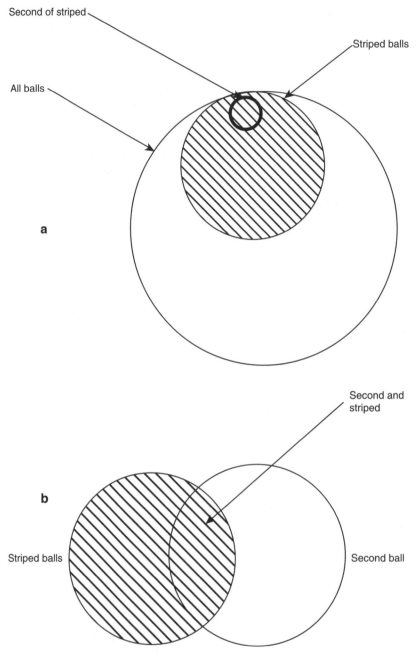

Figure 2.33 The correct, class-inclusive (a) and the incorrect, intersective (b) cognitive models of the instruction in Figure 2.31.

of about the same age as those who fail the Roeper task. In one version of it (see Robinson, 1983, for a review) child and experimenter sit either side of a large screen, with each of them having a mutually duplicating set of picture cards. The child is told that she must pick out from her cards the one that the experimenter is currently holding, when she hears a description of it. She must say when she has received enough information to make her choice. What makes the task difficult for younger children is the fact that two modifiers can sometimes be needed to uniquely identify a given card. There are, for example, two cards showing a red balloon – one with a big balloon and one with a small one. The younger ones will say they have found a card as soon as they see one that is correctly described by the experimenter (e.g., 'showing a red balloon'). Applied to the Roeper task, the child scans the display from left to right, stopping when she sees a card of which the description 'second and striped' is true.

My graduate student Emily Jones (Jones, 2003) looked at the developmental relationship between these three tasks. In her first study she found the standard class inclusion task to be more difficult than the Roeper task, which counters the possibility that the former tested abilities required for the latter. However the Piagetian form of the question has often been criticised for its artificiality, so in a second study she posed the class-inclusion question by means of a sharing procedure borrowed from Sophian and McCorgray (1994) which had previously been found to attract more correct responses than Piaget's original question. She also presented the referential ambiguity task. Broadly speaking, Jones's data were consistent with class-inclusion abilities, as measured by Sophian and McCorgray's simplified procedure, being necessary for success on the Roeper task; while the referential ambiguity task did not seem to be tapping a necessary ability because it was somewhat harder than the linguistic task. When chronological ages and verbal ability were partialled out, the class inclusion ability still correlated significantly with success on the Roeper task; but performance on the referential ambiguity task did not correlate significantly with performance on the Roeper task. Thus, the 'external' challenge might be seen to be more conceptual than pragmatic.

What I hope this discussion of the Roeper task has demonstrated is that taking a dynamic minimalist position – at least the 'relaxed' reading of it in (54) – enables one to explain what appear to be late-developing syntactic abilities without saying that the ability is present but *masked*. One can do this whilst being a nativist.

2.5.3 Children's acknowledgement of a parameter – branching direction

Recall the claim made within P & P theory that one of the parameters children innately know is that between right-branching versus left-branching languages. Given this, evidence that very young children 'acknowledge' that the *principal branching direction* (PBD) of the language they are learning is one or the other can plausibly be taken to support syntactic nativism. This acknowledgement can be gauged by *elicited imitation* tasks, in which children simply have to repeat sentences spoken to them, with the incidence of errors being recorded. What renders this technique informative is the fact that, while each language has a principal branching direction, individual sentences can vary in the degree to which they build up syntactic material on the left- or on the right-hand side. Bearing in mind that English is a right-branching language, consider the following two sentences in (55).

(55) a. The cat eats and walks

b. The cats and dogs run

In (55a) syntactic material (two verbs) bunches on the right-hand side while in (55b) syntactic material (two nouns) bunches on the left-hand side. Barbara Lust (1977), the author of the key studies in this area, was able to demonstrate that English-learning children of two and three years of age were more successful at repeating the first, right-branching kind of sentence than the second, left-branching kind. By contrast, children learning Japanese, the principal branching direction of which language is left (see Figure 2.17b), show the opposite order of difficulty (Lust and Wakayama, 1979). Nativists conclude from this that such early attunement to surface features of the target language suggests that the children's LADs were 'expecting' the language to have one character or the other.

Put like this, however, it would seem to be an easy matter to explain such data in an empiricist style by simply saying that children find one kind of sentence easier to repeat than the other because of their frequency in the input. But even if it could be shown that children are indeed exposed to more sentences of type (55a) than of type (55b) it still remains to be explained why children find them easier to *process*. We need, it might be said, a linguistic theory to explain what such processing amounts to – beyond mere reference to there being two nouns on the left and two verbs on the right.

What the sentences like the ones in (55) can be used to exemplify is the way in which recursive structures[43] can be built up either on the left or on the right of sentences. What's more, however, they can be used to illustrate the role of *anaphora* in such recursion. To explain, readers will be aware that pronouns can be used anaphorically as well as deictically (and recall the earlier discussion of binding principles). Thus, in *John came, and he danced* the pronoun *he* is functioning as an anaphor. However, null sites can function as anaphors too, as in *John came and danced*. Given this, we can have the situation shown in (56), showing how (55) was a product of anaphoric reduction.

(56) a. The cat eats and ~~the cat~~ walks

b. The cats ~~run~~ and the dogs run

The generalisation being suggested here is that having a principal branching direction of right makes a *forward* direction of anaphor more natural, while left-branching favours a *backward* direction. Indeed, Lust (Lust and Wakayama, 1979) found the predicted differences between the English-speaking and the Japanese-speaking children: the former were more likely to reduce in a forward direction when repeating sentences while the latter were more likely to reduce in a backward direction.

....

[43] There will be a discussion of recursion in 3.1.3; but for now this can simply be taken to mean structures that replicate themselves without limit – by conjunction in this case. Recursion is a mark of hierarchical structures.

In fact, the authors found that the 2- to 3-year-old Japanese children did not spontaneously reduce redundancy in the forward forms at all. Given this, what the children could be said to have been demonstrating is a sensitivity not to trivial surface features of the language but to how the principal direction of recursion fosters direction of anaphoric reduction, which is, in the words of Lust and Chien (1984, p. 53) 'a principle of syntactic organisation which goes beyond obvious surface evidence'.

There is, however, a simpler explanation for the difference between the behaviour of the English and the Japanese children. It refers to the fact that, in addition to differing in terms of principal branching direction, English and Japanese also differ in terms of canonical word order: SVO in English and SOV in Japanese. We know that children are sensitive to word-order regularities from a very early age; and some have argued that this sensitivity might underlie children's early generalisations about surface features (Slobin and Bever, 1982). This fact was one of the motivations behind an elicited imitation study that Lust and Chien (1984) conducted with Chinese children. For Mandarin Chinese, like Japanese, has a left principal branching direction while being, like English, an SVO language. Accordingly, if Chinese children were to find sentences with backwards-anaphora easier to repeat, and as more naturally affording anaphoric reduction, than those with forwards-anaphora it would suggest that their sensitivity is to the language's direction of recursion rather than to its canonical word order.

To give the flavour, Chinese, despite being an SVO language, places relative clauses *before* head nouns. For example:

> [[Zhànzài ménbian-de] nà=ge rén] shi wo jiùjui
> standing door by that man is my uncle
> The man who is standing by the door is my uncle.

In their study, the sentences which the children (mean age 3y 3m) had to repeat varied in the direction of anaphora, in whether the sentences were subject-verb (SV) or verb-object (VO) and with regard to whether or not the redundancy was in fact reduced to produce null anaphora. Here are some examples.

> *Unreduced, forward, SV*
> Bàba gongzuo bàba ye xiuxi.
> Father works and father rests.
> *Reduced, forward, VO*
> Xiao péngyou ye chàngge ye tiàowu.
> Children sing and dance.
> *Unreduced, backward, SV*
> Gege paishou jiejie ye paishou.
> Elder brother claps and elder sister claps.
> *Reduced, backward, VO*
> Xi-yi-xi ye ca-yi-ca wawa.
> Wash and dry the doll.

Not only did these Chinese children find backward anaphora easier to repeat but their spontaneous elaborations of reduced sentences and reductions of unreduced sentences respected a preference for the backward anaphora. At an early age they reduced redundancy backward but rarely forward, while they frequently elaborated forward VO forms.

As it is not possible to explain the difference between the behaviour of the English-learning children and the Chinese-learning children in terms of sensitivity to canonical word order we are free to explain it in terms of sensitivity to recursive direction – an abstract structural principle. To be sensitive to recursive direction is obviously to be sensitive to formal properties of the target language; and when sensitivity to what is formal, as opposed to what is a transparent statistical regularity in the data or a regularity that manifests a pragmatic principle, is evident in young children then nativism of the Chomskyan kind is supported. In fact, for Lust and Chien, what is notable about the Japanese and Chinese data is that finding backward anaphora to be more natural than forward anaphora is something that cuts against 'discourse principles', cuts against what we might call 'common sense pragmatics'. That is to say, one would 'naturally' expect discourse anaphora to work in a forward direction, and therefore that if discourse principles alone determined direction that all languages would favour the forward direction. To take their example, there seems to be something far more 'natural' about 'I like Tom. He's a fine fellow' as compared to the 'extraordinary' 'I like him. Tom's a fine fellow'. 'This is,' they write, 'presumably a fact about human cognition which is independent of sentence grammar' (op. cit., p. 57).

2.5.4 Children's acknowledgement of some 'principles'

We now turn to two of the principles of P & P – Principles B and C. The reader is advised to consult Figures 2.21 and 2.22 (pp. 123–124) to refresh the memory, at this point.

It should be noted that these principles depend for their definition, not merely on the semantic notion of co-reference but also on formal syntactic notions such as c-commanding (still present, recall, in MP) and 'local domain' (roughly, 'clause'). Principle B states that a definite pronoun (i.e., a term like *him* or *her*, as contrasted with a reflexive anaphoric expression such as *himself* or *herself*) must be *free*, rather than *bound* within its local domain. That is to say the word *him* in (57) must refer to a male person *other than* Balloo bear:

(57) Balloo Bear washed him.

If the speaker means the term to co-refer with Balloo Bear then the reflexive *himself* must be used (this is Principle A).

In this area, one can ask the questions not only about whether young children acknowledge these principles but about whether the level of success that they achieve supports the modularity matching model or the competing factors model. Consider the modularity matching model. Supporters of this view insist that it is the one to be preferred by the convinced nativist, in so far as it is based on the null hypothesis of there being no difference between children's and adults' linguistic and cognitive mechanisms. If, however, one allows the possibility that children, despite their 'knowing' Principle B, sometimes process sentences in a non-adult way (the claim made within the competing factors model) then we have thereby added

> Unwanted degrees of freedom, by tolerating a wide range of processing explanations for differences between children and adults. Moreover, it leaves a new question to be addressed for each such account: how does the processing system of children change, so as to converge on the adult system?
>
> (Crain and Thornton, 1998)

In the context of these two kinds of nativist stance we will consider the tension between the position of Grimshaw and Rosen (1990) (henceforth, G&R), on the one hand, and Crain and Thornton (1998) and Thornton and Wexler (1999, pp. 52–66), on the other (henceforth C&T and T&W). The former position is more consistent with the competing factors model, while the latter group of workers champion the modularity matching model.

In common with certain other workers (e.g., Chien and Wexler, 1990) G&R report that, while a substantial majority of 4- to 5-year-old children (83 per cent) judge the adult interpretation of sentences to be correct, only 48 per cent of them judge the non-adult interpretation to be *in*correct. This latter result would seem to pose a problem for the modularity matching model. In fact, G&R's data are very similar to those of Chien and Wexler (1990), who found only 49 per cent rejection rate, and to those of Kaufman (1988) who argues, in a competing-factors style, that the difficulty of rejecting the ungrammatical form is due to the additional processing load associated with spotting violations of the Principle.

The experimental procedure G&R employed was the Truth–Value Judgement task, devised by Crain and McKee (1985), in which the child is encouraged to reward a puppet for saying something true and punish it for saying something false. As in the original study, children watched videotapes of scenes acted out by characters from Sesame Street. After a frog puppet had named all the characters, he uttered a target sentence. When this was done, the child either rewarded 'Froggie' by feeding him a biscuit, if his report of the event was accurate, or punished him by feeding him a rag, if the report was inaccurate. For example:

Grammatical

Scenario: Big Bird pats Ernie.

Froggie: 'I saw Big Bird doing something with Ernie. Big Bird patted him.'

Ungrammatical

Scenario: Big Bird pats himself.

Froggie: 'Big bird was standing with Ernie. *Big Bird patted him.'

The issue is, then, why children are not as good at rejecting ungrammatical sentences as they are at accepting grammatical ones.

What G&R argue is that if children were not obeying principle B then they would accept the grammatical and the ungrammatical forms *equally often*: the difference between 83 per cent and 48 per cent represents the contribution of their syntactic abilities. For the modularity-matching enthusiasts C&T, however, this is a case of being too easily satisfied – of giving hostages to fortune. What one should expect to find, T&W (1999, p. 55) argue, is a level of appropriate rejection of about 90 per cent; for in their view – note the rationalist style of thought – it is formal knowledge that determines how processing will be done: it pre-empts information processing. Syntactic knowledge is not a mere *contribution* to output, interacting with processing and pragmatic factors. They attempt to demonstrate the weakness of the G&R position by illustrating how somebody who wished to deny innate knowledge of Principle B could try to explain the data. If somebody's working assumption is that children do *not* know Principle B then they are free to assume that the sentence *Big Bird patted him,* which is not remotely ambiguous for the adult (because *him* cannot co-refer with *Big Bird*), *is* ambiguous for children; that they have access to both possible interpretations; but they *prefer* one interpretation over another. Furthermore, this preference might take the form of interpreting pronouns in a *disjoint* and *deictic* manner rather than anaphorically. When coupled with the fact that children witness a disjoint scenario (A pats B) this will ensure a high level of performance when Froggie should be rewarded. However when the scenario shows a self-directed action, performance is likely to be around chance level, as a deictic bias (i.e., against an anaphoric reading) is matched to a self-directed context, with the two variables tending to cancel each other out.

It has to be said at this point that, while the distinction between the modularity matching model and the competing factors model is clear enough in the abstract, the relation between the data cited by G&R and by C&T and T&W and the different positions they espouse is really quite ambiguous. With regard to G&R in the first place, they argue that the reason less than half of the 4- and 5-year-old children correctly rejected the co-referential reading of sentences like *Big Bird patted him* in previously published studies is not to be found in the children's misunderstanding of pragmatics or in their processing limitations but in experimental artefacts (e.g., in some of the studies there was no linguistic material presented before the target sentence). However, the data they themselves report in a study designed to overcome such biases is clearly in line with the earlier literature: the number of successes stubbornly refuses to rise. Second, when discussing the data of Chien and Wexler (1990) and Grodzinsky and Reinhart (1993) showing that young children are much more successful at correctly rejecting sentences with *quantificational* NPs (e.g., *every*) they take a sceptical line, despite their nativist assumptions, and argue that the children were doing the right thing for the wrong reason. To explain, in the Chien and Wexler study the children were presented with a picture showing three girl bears washing themselves while Goldilocks is standing by. The sentence they had to evaluate was:

Every bear is washing her.

The children rejected this sentence as being true of the picture 86 per cent of the time; while they rejected *Mama bear is washing her* against a picture of the bear washing herself only 46 per cent of the time. This result does indeed seem anomalous, as one would expect the presence of a quantifier to increase the difficulty. In any event, G&R argue that the children's success was illegitimate, for the following reason. The children were unable, they argue, even to consider the possibility of interpreting *her* as a variable bound to a quantifier, which left the disjoint reading of *her* as the only other option; and so, as Goldilocks was not being washed, they rejected the sentence. This account depends, however, on the assumption that young children are indeed unable to process the relation between quantifiers and bound variable, an assumption which T&W call into question in their review of the data (ibid, pp. 59–66). That said, the position of C&T and T&W inspires still more puzzlement. First, why is 'no cognitive development' taken as the null hypothesis? True enough, the competing factors model, when liberally interpreted, can allow nativists to explain away some embarrassing failures by children, but the modularity matching model saddles one not only with an assumption of wild implausibility (no cognitive development) but with the insistence that success rates of under '90 per cent' should be discounted. In the present case, T&W are forced to make some fairly desperate attempts at explaining why the incidence of successful rejection of sentences like *Mama bear washed her* (i.e., when the bear washed herself) is well below 90 per cent.

> There is also empirical support for the observation that children attempt to understand sentences in a way that *makes them true*. Experience with the truth–value judgement task has shown that children attempt to access an interpretation of the sentence that makes it true, if this is at all possible. In the kinds of experiments in which children were found to produce non-adult responses, over-accepting local co-reference, the target sentences were true on a local co-reference interpretation and false on the adult interpretation.
>
> (Thornton and Wexler, 1999, p. 99; emphasis added)

But, setting aside the fact that explaining failures by children's interpretive biases looks awfully like the competing factors model, this leaves unanswered the awkward question of why children were so good at rejecting *Every bear is washing her* in the Chien and Wexler study; because in this case the fact of three bears washing themselves would 'make it true' – as did the presence of a single bear washing herself make *Mama bear is washing her* true.

What T&W do in order to defend modularity matching is to argue that children's strong assumption that uttered sentences will generally be true of their referents is a manifestation of more innate knowledge – of *pragmatics* in this case. Specifically, they argue that knowledge of the Gricean (Grice, 1975) conversational implicatures is innately specified. Thus, in the present case children's adherence to the principle of 'quality' (say only what you believe to be true and adequately supported) leads them to look for confirmation of what Froggie has to say, and to be correspondingly lax in their criteria for confirmation. On this view, what happens in development is a tuning down of a natural tendency.

It has to be said that this way of arguing can encourage impatience with nativism. For if any instance of early non-adult-like performance can be explained away in terms of the lack of fine-tuning in another innate module then it looks as if nativism is always going to be irrefutable. Because we simply do not know what *are* the innate modules or how their development comes to be calibrated against that of the other modules, we are 'free' to posit modules (a pragmatics module in this case) whose exuberant progress masks the effect of the one in which we are presently interested. The competing factors approach and dynamic minimalism both seem preferable to this position. These two suggest that we should expect behaviour that is only an intimation of that of the adult because (1) we only see the operation of innate knowledge through a glass darkly and (2) there *is* cognitive development.

Finally in this subsection, we consider principle C. This states that a referring expression, such as a noun or proper name, cannot be bound by a pronoun that precedes it and c-commands it – that is 'higher on the tree' than the referring expression. Thus, to revisit our earlier example, *he* and *Jones* cannot co-refer in the sentence *He met Mary when Jones arrived at the airport,* whereas the two words can co-refer in *When he arrived at the airport Jones met Mary.* Principle C is somewhat less straightforward than principles A and B and its exact definition is a matter of some controversy. Chomsky (1982, p. 78), indeed, has speculated that A and B may be the only principles, while some linguists have argued that principle C really states a pragmatic rather than syntactic regularity. Be that as it may, if we wish to find out whether young children appreciate basic facts about c-commanding (an element of Chomskyan theory, recall, which is retained in MP) then studying their knowledge of principle C is one of the best ways of doing it.

There are three main techniques that researchers have used to assess knowledge of principle C: elicited imitation, comprehension by acting out with dolls, and the truth–value judgement task. The first two are primarily associated with the work of Barbara Lust and her colleague and the third, as we have seen, with the work of Crain and McKee (1985). Grimshaw and Rosen (1990) also assessed acknowledgement of principle C by the truth–value judgement task in the study described above, finding the children to be more successful than they were on the principle B task.

Lust, Loveland and Kornet (1980) presented children between 3y 5m and 7y 5m with relevant contrasts of the following kind shown in (58).

> (58) a. He turned round when Snuffles found the penny.
>
>   b. When he closed the box, Cookie Monster lay down.

Consider a task in which the child has to act out each of these sentences with dolls. In the first sentence, *he* and *Snuffles* must be interpreted in a disjoint manner on pain of violating principle C, so the child must not have the doll Snuffles both turning around and finding the penny. In the second sentence, however, either a disjoint or an anaphoric reading is possible: *he* can either refer to the Cookie Monster or to another doll on the table. Given this, we can ask whether children were more likely to produce a co-referential interpretation in the second kind of sentence than in the first kind of sentence. The data were somewhat difficult to interpret because the youngest group (mean age 3y 10m) had a general bias against co-referential interpretations of either kind of sentence; however a preference for co-referential interpretation of (58b) versus (58a) did emerge. Taking a more relaxed line than that of the modularity-matching ultras on what can be concluded from such a trend it is possible to argue that *something* must be determining the beginning of this preference and 'acknowledgement of principle C' looks like a not-implausible candidate.

But might, instead, the onset of a pragmatic sensitivity be responsible for the preference? In the absence of a theory of pragmatic development as elaborated as the Chomskyan theory of syntactic development it is difficult to extract a competing pragmatic principle. What one can do, however, as a way of examining the potency of pragmatic assumptions in this task, is to manipulate the pragmatic context in such a way that it can encourage an illegitimately co-referential reading of a sentence like (58a) in order to see whether the relative preference for a co-referential reading of the second kind of sentence survives. This is what Lust *et al.* (1980) did. They introduced the sentences with the 'pragmatic lead' 'Now I am going to tell you a story about X … ' (where X might be Snuffles). In fact this increased the proportion of co-referential interpretations for both kinds of sentence. However the increase was greater in the second kind of sentence (59 per cent) than in the first kind of sentence (35 per cent) in nearly all of the age groups, including the 3-year-olds. Presumably acknowledgement of principle C still continued to block the co-referential interpretation in the first kind of sentence.

That said, it is necessary to be vigilant against pragmatic influences upon children's successful performance, as cautioned by Lust, Eisele and Mazuka (1992) with reference to a truth–value judgement experiment by Crain and McKee (1985). Recall that in this technique children have to judge whether a sentence offers a true account of a situation represented by an acting-out, by a video, or by a picture, and that the Crain and McKee study procedure for eliciting such judgements from children required them to reward a frog puppet with a biscuit for saying something true and feeding him a rag if he said something false. The sentences in question were of the kind shown in (59).

> (59) a. He ate the hamburger when the Smurf was in the fence.
>
>   b. When he ate the hamburger, the Smurf was in the fence.

In one context they saw the Smurf eat the hamburger while it was inside the fence and in the other they saw a character called Gargamel eat the hamburger while the Smurf was in the fence. The most interesting result to emerge was that 87 per cent of the children fed the frog a rag when he said the first sentence in the context of the Smurf being inside the fence and Gargamel was outside eating nothing. Indeed children as young as 2 years responded appropriately. Two years of age is impressively young sure enough; but there are reasons to question whether all of the children rejected this sentences on syntactic grounds. I will briefly review Lust *et al.*'s (1992) reasons for scepticism. Essentially, the children may have judged the sentence to be untrue because the context biased them to take Gargamel as the referent of *he*, thus making it an inaccurate report. The authors say that the first sentence was presented in a context in which the Smurf was eating a hamburger in the fence, but another character, Gargamel, 'was NOT because he hates them' (ibid., p. 107; original emphasis). It would be sufficient for the children's attention to have been drawn to Gargamel (e.g., via the reference to his strong dislike of hamburgers) for them to take the first clause to be about him. Indeed, some of the children's comments reflected just such a bias: 'No, Gargamel didn't'; 'He said 'yuk, yuk''; 'No he didn't like it'; 'He kicked it'; as if they were really assessing the sentence *Gargamel ate the hamburger*. Such an interpretation may have been encouraged by principle C's blocking of the *he-Smurf* anaphora, but caution is surely to be advised.

Caution is also to be advised for another reason. It is possible that something much simpler and less formal than principle C is responsible for children's behaviour in these experiments: their recognition of the fact that, unless the context is explicitly deictic, reference is generally secured via a noun-phrase *before* an anaphoric pronoun is used. Recall Lust and Chien's remarks about forward anaphora that it is 'presumably a fact about human cognition which is independent of sentence grammar'. Lust *et al.* refer to this as a *directionality effect* (NP→PN), and report earlier studies in which there was an attempt to tease apart the influence of directionality and principle C. Consider the following two sentences of (60) presented, in a truth–value judgement task, by Eisele and Lust (1989)

> (60) a. *Forward anaphora*: Big Bird touched the pillow when he ate the apple.
>
> b. *Backward anaphora*: When he ate the apple Big Bird touched the pillow.

Both of these sentences afford a co-referential interpretation (it is not blocked by principle C); but directionality assumptions make it more natural in (60a). Lust and Eisele found that the children in their study both rejected a co-referential picture and accepted a disjoint-reference picture significantly more in the backward sentence type (60b) than for the forward sentence type (60a). This confirms, then, that the directionality effect is in operation independently of the blocking effect of principle C. Given this, it becomes necessary to compare the degree to which children reject the co-referential reading of 'backward' sentences like the one in (60b) with the degree to which they reject similar sentences that *do* block a co-referential reading via principle C – such as (61). This is the comparison that Lust and Eisele made. They found that children accepted a co-referential picture significantly less often for sentences like (61) than for ones like (60b). Indeed this difference was observed as young as age 3.

> (60) He ate the apple when Big Bird touched the pillow.

Next, if principle C is indeed a universal constraint on language acquisition then we would also expect to find it in languages that differ in certain fundamental respects from English. As we have seen, Japanese is one such language, being left-branching and having a canonical SOV word order. Using the elicited imitation technique, Lust and her colleagues (see review by Lust *et al.*, 1992, pp. 351–352) were able to show that Japanese children of between 3y 1m and 5y 11m are acknowledging this constraint. When added to the converging evidence for the operation of principles B and C in the early language of English-speaking children, it is possible to conclude that, despite the fact that we only seem to be seeing the acknowledgement of the principles through a glass darkly, and despite the necessity for vigilance against success by virtue of the pragmatic structure of the tasks, acknowledgement is what we appear to be seeing.

Finally in this section, I wish to insert a long corrective against this summation being too upbeat. The fact is that it is not only theoretical linguists working within the pragmatist framework who argue that the binding principles we have been considering are pragmatic rather than syntactic in nature. Some linguists, who are fundamentally sympathetic to the Chomskyan programme, do not deny that some principles of anaphora reveal deep facts about syntactic competence; but they do deny that principles like principle C is one of them. Such a linguist is Tanya Reinhart. The following discussion of Reinhart's position will also serve as bridge to the final subsection, in which we do confront full-blooded pragmatist attacks on syntactic nativism.

A distinction to bear in mind in what follows is that between (1) intended co-reference of pronouns and definite NPs and (2) the role of LF in fixing an interpretation of bound variables in relation to quantifiers and operators. There are, then, two kinds of anaphora.

Reinhart (1986) pointed out that the assumption (one she herself once shared in fact) had gone unchallenged that binding conditions essentially concern problems of definite NP co-reference raised when language legislates about how a speaker's intended co-reference can and cannot be expressed. For example, (61b) should be used rather than (61a).

(61) a. He$_i$ likes Fred's$_i$ car.
      b. Fred$_i$ likes his$_i$ car.

This assumption has tended to go hand-in-hand with the view that when co-reference exists between operators (like *what X*) or quantifiers (like *each X*), on the one hand, and pronouns regarded as logical variables (like *his*) then what we are dealing with is not binding principles *but interpretive phenomena to be dealt with at the level of Logical Form*, captured independently of binding conditions: (62) shows examples of such *bound-variable anaphora*.

(62) a. Each of the men$_i$ brought his$_i$ car.
      b. Which man$_i$ brought his$_i$ car?

But it is Reinhart's alternative contention that the core issues in the syntax of anaphora *belong to bound-variable anaphora* of the kind shown in (62), while the binding phenomena covered by P & P theory belong not to the grammar at all but to *pragmatics*.

These pragmatic currents define, for Reinhart, 'a relation between linguistic structures and their potential uses for the purpose of *expressing referential intentions*, rather than defining referential or semantic relations *between expressions in the sentence*' (Reinhart, 1986, p. 124, emphasis added). An important point to note here is that one cannot talk about quantified NPs in (62) as having an intended reference or co-reference as they have *no* reference at all, unlike *Fred* in (61).

I will touch only briefly on Reinhart's reasons for putting bound variable anaphora at the centre of the picture, concentrating instead on the reasons given for regarding principle C in a pragmatic light. Let us merely note two things about bound-variable anaphora versus (Reinhart's term) *pragmatic co-reference* (aka principle C) before passing to the nub of the matter.

First, there is a stronger condition on bound variable anaphora than on pragmatic co-reference because, while *bound variable anaphora requires the antecedent to c-command the pronoun*, pragmatic co-reference requires only that the pronoun does not c-command the antecedent. Thus, in (63a), exemplifying an attempt at bound-variable anaphora, the sentence is ill-formed because *no boy* does not c-command *his*.

(63) a. *His$_i$ bear accompanied no boy$_i$ to the party.
      b. No boy$_i$ brought his$_i$ teddy bear to the party.

In (64) however, in which a proper name rather than a quantifying expression is the co-referent of the pronoun, and in which therefore pragmatic co-reference is evoked, the sentence is well-formed because the pronoun does not c-command the proper name.

(64) His$_i$ bear accompanied Christopher$_i$ everywhere.

Second, the bound-variable interpretation of anaphora is not restricted to quantified antecedents. This can be seen in cases of so-called *sloppy identity* . If we say, for example, *Fred polished his car and so did John* there is an ambiguity, in so far as it can mean either that John polished Fred's car or his own car. (See discussion of Jackendoff's analysis of such sentences in 2.4.3.) The first reading is the pragmatic co-reference one, in which a specific co-reference is fixed for *his*, which is then copied to the second conjunct (= they both polished Fred's car). In the latter and more pragmatically plausible case, the first conjunction contains, what Reinhart calls 'an open formula' of *x polishes x's car*, satisfied by Fred in the first case and John in the second: the identity is not so much 'sloppy' as belonging to *variables* rather than referents: (65) reproduces one of Reinhart's examples of this phenomenon.

(65) Even Linda is fed up with her husband.

(66) Most women are fed up with their husbands, and Linda is one of them. (For most women x, x is fed up with x's husband.)

On the pragmatic co-reference reading this means that most people are fed up with Linda's husband. On the more plausible bound variable anaphora reading it means what is shown in (66).

Reinhart argues that, rather than being something requiring separate treatment at LF, bound variable anaphora is the basic binding case, and that intended co-reference does not belong to grammar at all but follows pragmatically from the conditions on bound anaphora. Let us now consider the reasons for her claim. In the first place, the claim is that:

> When syntactically permitted, bound anaphora is the most explicit way in language to express co-reference, as it involves direct dependency of the pronoun upon its antecedent for interpretation. So *if this option is avoided* we may conclude that the speaker did not intend co-reference.
>
> (ibid., p. 143, original emphasis)

The pragmatic strategy, derived from the Gricean principle of 'manner' (be as explicit as the conditions permit) is as follows:

> *Speaker's strategy*. When a syntactic structure you are using allows bound-anaphora interpretation [i.e., it can require the antecedent to c-command the pronoun, JR] then use it if you intend your expressions to co-refer, unless you have some reasons to avoid bound-anaphor.
>
> *Hearer's strategy*. If the speaker avoids the bound anaphora options provided by the structure he is using, then, unless he has reasons to avoid bound-anaphora, he didn't intend his expressions to co-refer.
>
> (ibid., p. 143)

(67) Winnie$_i$ ate his$_i$ honey.

(68) *He$_i$ ate Winnie's$_i$ honey.

For example in (67) the bound anaphora interpretation is allowed because one NP c-commands the other and the second is a pronoun; so co-reference is possible on the pragmatic strategy just described. But if the speaker avoids the bound anaphora options by choosing a different placement of NPs as in (68) the hearer will assume that co-reference was not intended.

Note too that the pragmatic analysis of principle C predicts that there can be pragmatic contexts in which it is appropriately violated: (69), an example of this, comes from Gareth Evans (1980, p. 49).

> (69) I know what Ann and Bill have in common. She thinks that Bill is terrific and *he thinks that Bill is terrific.*

The clause in italics constitutes a clear violation of principle C. And note that here *bound variable anaphora is not intended*: the intended reading is not that of 'x's finding xs terrific'; because Ann may *not* find herself to be terrific. Such cases are important because, as Reinhart (1986, p. 145) points out, the pragmatic analysis of principle C predicts that violation of it should be possible if there are good pragmatic reasons to avoid bound anaphora while still intending co-reference. That is to say, *when there is no bound anaphor there can be a violation of principle C* – evidence that the latter depends upon the former.

Finally, how does Reinhart square this analysis with the data from acquisition experiments, in particular with Lust's cross-linguistic data suggesting children's treatment of anaphora can *cut across* pragmatic 'common sense'? Reinhart's reading of the literature is that the evidence for children's early acknowledgement of (what she calls) 'the c-command restriction on pragmatic co-reference' is 'not too conclusive' (ibid., p. 140). The argument is that what is captured by principle C is no more than a tendency towards forward anaphora rather than backwards anaphora, i.e., mentioning the definite NP (e.g., proper name) before the pronoun. It is not surprising that children do this, she argues, because 'backward anaphora requires holding the pronoun in memory and going back to it' (ibid., p. 140).

This seems, in fact, rather a rash dismissal, given that principle C requires only, as Reinhart herself points out in contrasting it with bound variable anaphora (above), that the pronoun should not c-command the antecedent. This allows the pronoun to precede the co-referent NP so long as it does not c-command it. Recall that young children accept sentences of this kind as in (59b) reproduced here, from Crain and McKee (1985):

> When he_i ate the hamburger, the $Smurf_i$ was in the fence.

Be that as it may, Reinhart is mainly concerned with the data of Lust and her colleagues on the acquisition of Japanese and Chinese, which we have already discussed at length. Recall that Lust demonstrates that directionality effects (forward versus backward anaphora) are determined by the 'principal branching direction' (PBD) of the language – by whether this is left- or right-branching. Lust's claim is the Japanese and Chinese children allow backward anaphora because these languages are left-branching, whereas English-speaking children do so less often because English is right-branching. Reinhart's reaction to this is that when 'pragmatic co-reference' is at issue the fact of PBD is not relevant to binding conditions. But the evidence which she adduces for the claim is, ironically enough, the very evidence I have just mentioned in favour of the idea that backward anaphora can be found in English: that when the pronoun does not c-command its co-referent NP it can precede it. See the Smurf sentence above, and recall Reinhart's (64), reproduced here:

His$_i$ bear accompanied Christopher$_i$ everwhere.

For Reinhart, the moral to be derived from all this is that right-branching languages allow backwards anaphora and so Lust's generalisation about the link between forward anaphora and right-branching is false. But, as we have seen, this fact also undermines Reinhart's own assertion that English-speaking children favour forwards anaphora because of 'pragmatic or processing reasons' (ibid., p. 140): children allow it *under certain structural conditions,* the very conditions captured by principle C.

Moreover, Reinhart is happy to accept that children's processing of anaphora is determined by *bound variable anaphora,* as opposed to the 'c-command restriction on pragmatic co-reference'. In discussing another of Lust's studies of Chinese (Lust, Chien and Mangione, 1984) she points out that it demonstrated backwards anaphora not to be uniformly easier than forwards anaphora. That is, it was not uniformly easier with pragmatic co-reference, but it *was* clearly easier with bound variable anaphora. With regard to acquisition then, Reinhart's conclusion is that it is crucial to draw a firm distinction between the grammar (binding theory) and pragmatics. It is possible, she concludes

> that the child has, at the relevant stage, some knowledge of the major issues of the binding theory, *i.e., the rules for bound anaphora,* so when bound anaphora is involved there are fewer mistakes and less 'directionality' effects: the Chinese child correctly interprets it 'backwards' and the English child 'forwards'. However, when pragmatic co-reference is at issue, the pragmatic factor of linear order plays a crucial role, regardless of the branching direction of the language; it might take longer for the child to learn the pragmatic subtleties of the use of backward anaphora.
>
> (Reinhart, 1986, p. 142, emphasis added)

The reason I have taken Reinhart's work as exemplary is that it illustrates that it is possible to do careful justice to the role of pragmatic and processing factors in acquisition while stopping well short of the claim that children's early acknowledgment of syntactic principles is in fact illusory (i.e., because these principles actually 'reduce to' pragmatics). We now consider two attempts to do precisely the latter.

If readers have been feeling that thus far in 2.5 the disputes have had too subtle a flavour, being more about emphasis than essence, then they can be assured that this will end in 2.5.5.

2.5.5 Syntactic or pragmatic knowledge? Non-Chomskyan accounts of early competence

In this subsection we consider more principled questions arising from the tension between young children's acknowledgement of structural principles in their early grammar and their ability to tune in to pragmatic regularities. Accordingly, instead of treating pragmatic factors as Clever Hans variables or 'noise' we will be assessing the way in which authors of pragmatics-based accounts of linguistic knowledge offer alternative accounts of early competence.

Two topics will be discussed, one bearing upon the psychological reality of the trace and on children's abiding by trace-governed constraints and another which has to do with bounding constraints.

First, turning to questions about traces, it is necessary to consider the phenomenon of *reduction*, in which, for example, *is not* is reduced to *isn't*, *I am* is reduced to *I'm* – the same going for *shall, would and should*. There are somewhat subtle constraints operating here that centre round the fact that if there is no following word reduction does not occur. It sounds odd, for example, to reduce *Mary is cleverer than John* is to *Mary is cleverer than John's,* while it is perfectly natural to reduce *John is clever* to *John's clever.* Note that the orthography is misleading here because the *'s*, or *'m* etc. form is attached to the preceding word in writing, whereas syntactically it is attached to the succeeding word, a phenomenon called *rightward attachment.* While we write *I'm going* [syntactically *I m'going*] *to resign*, we don't add things like *because that's the kind of guy I'm.*

Next, if a trace happens to intervene between (say) the verb *is* and further items, this counts syntactically as an empty slot – equivalent to no word at all, and thus the reduction is blocked. Consider the sentences in (70):

(70) a. He told me the meeting's in college.
    b. *I wonder where the meeting's on Wednesday.
    c. I wonder where$_i$ the meeting is t$_i$ on Wednesday.

To the ears of most people (70b) sounds wrong. The reason is that in moving towards the head of the clause *where* has left a trace between *meeting is* and *on*, as shown in (70c). Given this, the *is* has only empty space to which to attach itself; and so reduction is not possible.

Let us now turn to the *wanna*, from *want to*, a reduced expression which children, at least US children, often produce. This is of course a slang construction, unlike *is* reduction, and it is more usually referred to as *wanna contraction* – an example of the general principle that there cannot be contraction across a trace. For this reason, (71b) sounds wrong; whereas (71c) sounds fine, as no trace is intervening between *want* and *to* in this case.

(71) a. Who$_i$ do you want t$_i$ to help you?
    b. *Who do you wanna help you?
    c. Who do you wanna help?

The demonstration that young children appreciate the constraints on *wanna* contraction is an important result for syntactic nativism. Given that the contraction *is* permissible in so many contexts, we can be fairly confident that children do not receive corrective feedback for the incorrect usage (Brown and Hanlon, 1970; Hirsh-Pasek *et al.*, 1984), and that it is a simple piece of slang whose use is nonetheless limited by an entirely formal syntactic principle. Here is one such demonstration from a study by Crain and Thornton (1991; see Crain, 1991).

This was an elicitation study with children between 2y 10m and 5y 5m. They were introduced to a toy rat who was too timid to speak up for himself, and of whom they were encouraged to ask questions. In one case there was a context in which the *wanna* question contraction would involve extracting from the *object* position of the infinitival clause (legal, as no subject has been moved from the subordinate clause) and in another the extraction was from the *subject* position (illegal, as a subject has been moved from the subject position in the subordinate clause, *leaving a trace*). Here are examples of the two kinds of protocol:

1) Encouraging object extraction questions

    Experimenter:

    The rat looks hungry. I bet he wants to eat something. Ask Ratty what he wants to eat.

    An appropriate question that might be elicited from the child:

    What do you wanna eat?

    Rat: Some cheese would be good.

2) Encouraging subject extraction questions

    Experimenter:

    There are three guys in this story: Cookie Monster, a dog, and this baby. One of them gets to take a walk, one gets to take a nap and one gets to eat a cookie. And the rat gets to choose who does each thing. So, one gets to take a walk right? Ask Ratty who he wants to walk.

    An appropriate question that might be elicited from the child:

    Who do you want to take a walk?

    [Who do you want t$_i$ to take a walk?]

    Rat: I want the dog to take a walk.

The children's questions in the object-extraction case contained the wanna contraction 59 per cent of the time whereas they contained uncontracted forms only 18 per cent of the time; so they were clearly happy to produce the contracted form in this case. By contrast, contraction was much less common in the subject-extraction case, where it is illegal: contracted forms 4 per cent of the time and uncontracted forms 67 per cent of the time. Crain (1991) also points out that of the 75 opportunities children had for contraction in the subject-extraction cases one child aged 3y 9m accounted for all three violations of the constraint.

'These results,' concludes Crain (1991, p. 604), 'were clearly in accord with the theory of universal grammar'. They clearly were; but there may well be other, radically non-Chomskyan theories with which they might be in accordance. The one we will consider is owing to John Haiman (1985).

Rather than moving straight to the specific claims which Haiman makes about the *wanna* contraction, we need first to step back to consider his general views on language in order to appreciate their non-Chomskyan, pragmatist flavour. We will shortly return to wanna contraction, after this rather long detour.

As Haiman points out in the very first pages of his book *Natural syntax: iconicity and erosion*, the essence of rationalist linguistics is the idea, owing to the first rationalist Plato, that reality is not as it seems. We see phenomena as shadows on the cave wall, the surface perception a flickering reflection of a reality beyond our direct acquaintance. Applied to the study of language, we have the position that the structure of sentences as immediately perceived, and understood by the versatile instruments of common sense, (their surface structure) does not inform us about their abstract, underlying (deep) structure. (Recall that an echo of the deep-surface distinction lingers in the minimalist programme; see the discussion of the dislocation property, pp. 153–156). This is in clear opposition to the work of linguists like Jacobson (1965) for whom linguistic universals are not formal properties of the mind but are fairly direct reflections of how we commonly perceive and interact with the world. Here are three examples of this. First, the order of clauses in a sentence generally follows the order of events described (e.g., *veni, vidi, vici*). Second, the fact that many languages mark the first and second persons by a personal affix while leaving the third person with a null marking reflects a *conceptual* contrast of the following kind – one obscured within the Western linguistic tradition. For the Arab grammarians, the distinction between non-third and third persons was indicated by non-null and null forms, respectively, as a means of reflecting that only the speaker and the hearer were present in the exchange, with the third person who did not participate in the speech act being 'the absent one'. Third, there is Greenberg's universal that 'there is no language in which the plural does not have some non-zero allomorphs, whereas there are languages where the singular is expressed only by zero'. This is taken to be '*an icon* of a conceptual contrast between less and more' (Haiman, 1985, p. 5, my italics). Such regularities are nowadays held in 'consistent disdain', says Haiman, due to the 'almost charismatic stature of one man: Noam Chomky' (ibid., p. 6). For Chomsky's first thought is the Platonic one that linguistic regularities represent not the world of speakers and hearers, but the operations of their minds (Chomsky 1981, p. 3): 'Our interpretation of the world is based in part on representational systems that derive from the structure of the mind itself and does not mirror in any direct way the form of things in the external world'.

Trace theory carries a clear echo of this view, expressing as it does the idea that sentences contain elements whose existence can only be inferred and never perceived.

Haiman is also right to insist that nativism is a direct consequence of the hidden-reality assumption. For if the child's perceptual apparatus is not able to deliver knowledge about syntactic rules and representations, and if the culture does not teach them formally, then they are going to have to be innate. For Haiman, by contrast, the regularities of language represent in a more or less iconic manner distinctions that need to be drawn and the categories that need to be established if communication is to be effective: if we are to capture those features of reality that concern us. He cautions that iconicity is certainly far from perfect, because the pressures on language to be economical will naturally erode it. As he says, if this is true it does not establish that there are no innate universals. But it does help to dissolve the conceptual linkage between deep structures and innateness; because what we require is on the surface: things are exactly as they appear to be. It hardly needs to be added that this thesis is thoroughly Pragmatist in nature. Indeed the basic thesis of the book that languages are like diagrams, derives from the notion of 'diagrammatic' which originated with C.S. Peirce (1932; and see Newmeyer, 1998, pp. 114–115). There will be an extensive discussion of iconicity and of Newmeyer's sceptical view of it in 4.2.

Haiman places the matter of the *wanna* contraction within a long discussion of the way in which languages mark the distinction between so called 'conceptual distance' and 'conceptual closeness'. For example, my mouth is conceptually closer to me than is my son, and my entrails are conceptually closer to me than is my dinner – the distinction between inalienable and alienable possession. He illustrates how a number of languages, most usually Australasian and Native American, formally mark such distinctions, and also discusses the way in which a conjunction is used to mark a conceptual distance between elements and to mark when two verbs might have different objects. Such processes bring out clearly the fundamental difference between Haiman's iconicity approach and transformational grammar: on the former view, linguistic distance marks conceptual distance, while on the latter view transformations can reduce the linguistic distance between elements whilst preserving the meaning. We can see this in operation in (72) in which the first phrase has had applied to it the *coordination reduction* transformation to produce the second:

> (72) a. the ability to read and to write books
>
>   b. the ability to read and write books

But these two phrases do not mean the same thing because (72a) leaves open the possibility that *books* is not the object of the *read*. Similarly, a pre-reduced sentence is often used to mark a contrast – conceptual distance – as in (73), which Haiman takes from Luke Rhinehart's novel *The Diceman*. The comic effect is due to the reader being set up for a contrast between *build* and *mentality* by their formal separation.

> (73) Frank Osterhood had the build of a professional wrestler and the mentality of a professional wrestler.

It is on the marking of *change of subject* that we need to focus to appreciate how Haiman accounts for the constraints on *wanna* contraction. Many languages mark change of subject by the use of a 'consecutive marker'. For example, in one of the Bantu languages (Anderson, 1979, p. 114) we have what is shown in (74). Anderson glosses this marker by &.

> (74) O nam kibe gha? ?uiaaa zi
>
>   she cook fufu we = exc & eat
>
>   'She cooked fufu and we ate it.'

Otherwise, the *identity* of subjects, as can be marked by the use of the suffix, as in the -*ip* in Turkish shown in (75).

> (75) gel-en-lere ve gid-en-ler
>
>   come-part. 3pl and go-part.3pl
>
>   'those who come and those who go'
>
>   *versus*
>
>   gel-*ip* ve gidenler
>
>   'those who (both) come and go'

Well, as originally argued by Frantz (1977), in English the *wanna* contraction plays much the same role: *the contraction is legitimate when there is no change of subject and illicit when there is change of subject.* This then is the reason why *Who do you want to help?* can be contracted (*you* is the subject of both *want* and *help*) and *Who do you want to help you?* cannot (*you* is the subject of *want*, but another person is the subject of help – of which *you* is the object). From which Haiman (ibid., p. 126, original emphasis) concludes that

> English, like a host of other languages in exotic parts of the world, *grammaticalizes* switch reference: thus *want to* is ambiguous between same-subject and different-subject readings: *wanna* is unambiguously same subject.

Why should we prefer this account over the one offered by trace theory? For Haiman, his iconicity theory has the advantage that it can explain an apparently unrelated fact about the behaviour of English which trace theory cannot – the constraint on the contraction of *let us* into *let's*. In his example, an English-speaking Moses might well have said to the Pharaoh *Let us go*, but he surely would not have contracted this to *Let's go*. This is because we contract *let us* when it is the 'us' doing something (e.g., the children of Israel) but we do not contract it when beseeching a third person to allow the 'us' to do something. Where does the switching of reference come in? If we assume that imperatives, of which both forms are a variety, always have *you* as an implied presence before the verb (*You! let us go*) then, in the contractible case, the *you* and the *us* refer to the same people (except that the *us* also includes the speaker). In the non-contractible case, however, the *you* and the *us* form two mutually exclusive sets of people, with the speaker only being included in the latter set. For Haiman, the formal unity of the two phenomena (*wanna* and *let's*) 'is so neat, that one might wish for a unified analysis' (ibid., p. 127). I leave it to the reader to decide upon the neatness. In any event, Haiman's (ibid., pp. 127–128, original emphasis) conclusion is upbeat:

> Once again, harking back to the promise on p. 3, an analysis of linguistic data is possible here: according to this analysis, things are *exactly what they appear to be.* A contraposed generative analysis [i.e., trace theory, JR] posits two null elements with different properties and explains less data. Unless one has a predilection for mystery, the choice between contending explanations, in this case at least, seems reasonably clear.

But is it *really* so clear? For one thing it is simply wrong that trace theory explains fewer data. The trace theory accounts for the constraints on wanna contraction by locating it within the principle of rightward attachment, a principle that explains the constraints on reduced *'s 've, 're* and the reduced forms of *am, will, should, shall, and should.* (And where, by the way, is the iconicity account of why we do not say things like **That's the kind of guy I'm?*) While trace theory may struggle with *let's*[44], it is able to account for a host of reduction phenomena within a single principle, which is itself located within an overarching theory of human language and its relation to human thought.

Moreover, what kind of knowledge of language are the successful children in Crain and Thornton's (1991) study supposed to be evincing, on Haiman's account? The knowledge that reference switching is not possible with *wanna* is surely a piece

----

[44] For a discussion of *let's* see 4.5.2 (p. 495).

of abstract knowledge about the mapping between structure and meaning. And it is difficult to appreciate how the *wanna*s and *want to*s that the children had heard up the point at which they participated in the study were functioning as *clear windows* onto two kinds of semantic reality.

But crucially, this longish excursion into an anti-rationalitist view of language, while motivated by a seemingly trivial constraint on a single idiom, serves to illustrate why enthusiasts for the Chomskyan approach find it so satisfying. The Platonic assumption that things are *not,* in fact, just as they seem is no more than an early manifestation of a commonplace of modern science: that phenomena in the biological and physical worlds are as they are because of universal mechanisms whose nature can only be understood via the imaginative construction of abstract theories. These phenomena are not local and ad hoc, like legal systems or customs. Studying the language faculty as a biological phenomenon requires just the same kind of imaginative projection – not to 'mysteries' as Haiman calls them – but to unperceivable mechanisms. Haiman's book illustrates that while rejecting the Platonic assumption can result in something that is provocative and richly informed about the world's languages, the proffered alternative tends to be rather thin stuff. In this case it is based on metaphor (the Peircean metaphor of the diagram) rather than a theory of mechanism; and the case for it is advanced by a somewhat bottom-up, stamp-collecting process of finding examples consistent with the metaphor.

These kind of criticisms cannot, however, be launched against the pragmatist approach of Robert Van Valin. Van Valin, while casting his cross-linguistic net as wide as Haiman, bases his theory on a far from commonsensical redrafting of the syntactic vocabulary. This will be fully described and assessed in section 4.1, but for now we will discuss the alternative he offers to explaining children's early abilities in terms of their knowledge of bounding phenomena. I will present some data before reprising the bounding principle in question.

Helen Goodluck (Goodluck, Foley and Sedivy, 1992) carried out the following study (based on a technique pioneered by Otsu [1981]) with children between three and four years of age. The children heard simple stories which were four or five sentences long and which were illustrated with simple pictures. Here are two of them.

Story one
The fox ran down to the river.
He ate an icecream cone.
Then he whistled a tune he heard on the radio.
The fox felt pretty happy.
Question:
What did the fox eat before whistling?
Story two
The elephant liked to work.
She asked the tiger 'Shall I help the horse carry those boxes?'
The tiger said 'Yes!'; so the elephant helped the horse.
The elephant was tired at the end of it all.
Question: Who did the elephant ask before helping?

To a child who does not appreciate a certain constraint on the nature of movement from a d-structure position to the head of a sentence these questions would carry an ambiguity. In the first story the child might think that 'a tune' would be an answer to the question and in the second story 'the horse'. However, to think this would be to, assume, on P & P theory, that the movement had been from a d-structure position (corresponding to *something* or *someone*) following *whistling* or *helping* to form the S-structure *wh*-question. This violates the so-called *island* constraint that movement cannot take place from within an 'island' of syntactic material such as relative clauses, indirect questions and, as in this case, temporal clauses (see p. 125).

As a check against the possibility that the children were simply incapable of entertaining the possibility of long-distance movement, a further kind of the question was asked: e.g., *Who did the elephant ask to help?* In this case 'the horse' is the *correct* answer because the wh-movement has not taken place from within an island but rather from within the complement of the verb to *ask*. The children were happy to say 'the horse' in this case.

Recall that the island constraint exemplifies the more general principle: the *subjacency* principle, which states that an element can move only over one layer of structure (i.e., it can move only from a layer that is *sub*ordinate and ad*jac*ent). To illustrate, from the sentence (76a) we can frame the question (76b) but from (77a) we cannot form a question like (77b).

(76) a. Mary saw a cat eat a Cornish pastie.

     b. What did Mary see a cat eat?

(77) a. Mary saw a cat that ate a Cornish pastie.

     b. *What did Mary see a cat that ate?

As I said before, there is less than general agreement on what is to count as a 'layer of structure', but students of P & P theory normally focus upon the barrier-like status of bounding nodes such as NP, S, and S' (see discussion on pp. 128–129). In any event, the notion that a stretch of structure such as 'a cat that' adds a further level to be crossed during movement is easy enough to appreciate on an intuitive level.

Before passing on to a discussion of Van Valin's views on subjacency, however, it is necessary, in the interests of completeness, to mention a wrinkle that emerges when we look more closely at data of the kind collected by Goodluck *et al.* Goodluck and her colleagues have also been studying the Akan language, a language spoken by the Kwa people of Ghana, which freely violates island constraints (Saah and Goodluck, 1995). In spite of that, however, Akan adults give very similar answers to English-speaking adults when they are presented with the kind of stories described above: they avoided linking the question word to a position inside a temporal clause. This raises, of course, the distinct possibility that the English-speaking children's and adults' avoidance was not really due to their recognition of a constraint in their native tongue, but due to some kind of processing strategy, as Goodluck (1997) herself argues. One does not have to look very far for such a strategy. Note that in order to give the correct answers in the above stories one merely has to stop processing the question as soon as the terminus of a sentence has been reached: *What did the fox eat?* and *Who did the elephant ask?* are complete sentences. The same conclusion can be made about similar work in this area (de Villiers and Roeper, 1995). In her discussion of this possibility, Goodluck (1997) points out that such a parsing-for-completeness strategy is certainly in evidence in adult parsing research; though this is more frequently treated as adults' online sensitivity to islands! (Stowe, 1986).

Given this, Goodluck (1997, p. 16) concludes that '[t]he strongest results in support of knowledge of islands in children are confounded with a processing preference'. This confounding *may* of course prove fatal. But, as Goodluck goes on to say, one can also argue that the processing bias just noted is there to aid language acquisition. She argues that children do indeed sometimes produce violations of the island constraint in their spontaneous speech, while research on adult responses to children's ungrammatical sentences (Brown and Hanlon, 1970; Hirsh-Pasek *et al.*, 1984) tells us that these would not be corrected. Three examples from spontaneous speech she gives in the paper are: *What else are there signs that say?* Smith (1981); *What are you cooking on a hot?* (Wilson and Peters, 1988); *What do dogs sweat through their?* (Partee, 1977, personal communication to Goodluck). Given this possibility, a parsing preference for not linking wh-elements to positions outside islands will serve as a corrective mechanism: 'the parser's predilection for non-island positions for fillers may act as a quantitative mechanism for the correction of a qualitative error' (ibid., p. 17). The existence of parsing strategies has to be explained; and this one's existence is explained in terms of its role as a corrective mechanism.

In passing, the existence of these parsing strategies does not undermine the reality of island constraints within the speaker-hearer's competence. In support of this, Saah and Goodluck (1995) report that, although Akan-speaking adults respond to the Goodluck stories like English-speakers, they *judge* extraction from a temporal clause in their language to be acceptable, whereas native speakers of English do not. And recall that, on the Chomskyan view, a theory of competence must encompass intuitions about grammaticality, as well as use.

We now consider how Van Valin (1991) regards the status of such island phenomena, and the developmental evidence for children's early acknowledgement of them, from within his *Role and Reference Grammar* (RRG). In accordance with his strategy of putting pressure on Chomskyan analyses by reference to constraints present in, or missing from, more exotic languages, he points out that in Lakhota (a Sioux language) there are what can be regarded as island constraints *in the absence of wh-movement*. This would seem to undermine the Chomskyan analysis of island constraints in terms of movement. For example, in Lakhota, (78) can be turned into a question about what the dog bit by adding an interrogative marker *he* and by replacing the relevant argument by the equivalent of an English *wh*-word *taku*, to give (79).

> (78) su ka ki igmu wa yaxtake.
>   'The dog bit the cat'.
>   dog the cat a bit.

> (79) su ka ki taku yaxtake he?
>   'What did the dog bite?'
>   dog the what bit. Q

But if a relative clause is involved, this substitution of a *wh*-element for the argument is illicit, as we see from (80):

(80) *wichasa ki [[sy ka wa taku yaxtake] ke le waya ka he?
man the [[dog a what bite] the this] saw. Q
'*What did the man see the dog which bit?'

Chomsky (Chomsky, 1986) attempts to deal with awkward cases of this kind by arguing that in a language like this subjacency is a restriction at the level of LF, not at the level of syntax, adding that there is no way in which children could *learn* to abide by a restriction as abstract as this. But, as we have just seen in the discussion of Reinhart's analysis of the binding principle C, the question of what is computed in the syntax and what is an interpretative operation performed between the s-structure and LF is a controversial issue. Certainly, otherwise-neutral readers might feel some unease with this seemingly obscurantist move and think that a more pragmatist account of island phenomena might be given a run for its money.

Van Valin's (1991) analysis begins with the assumption that island phenomena manifest speaker-hearers' knowledge of which parts of a *yes-no* question can form the focus of the answer and which can not. Broadly speaking, it is only material within the main clause of a *yes-no* question that can be questioned – not material in adjunct relative clauses, temporal clauses, and so forth. To give one of Van Valin's examples, in (81) the listener might give the answer 'no' for a number of appropriate reasons (e.g., *No, Max didn't* or *No, Bill returned them*) but some kinds of negative answer are profoundly inappropriate: *No, Bill photocopied the papers* or *No, it was the IRS agent she photocopied them to.*

(81) Did Max return the papers which the secretary photocopied to the lawyer?

So what is the relation between phenomena of this kind and subjacency phenomena of the kind shown in (77)?

From a functionalist perspective the [two kinds of phenomena] are closely related, since they involve the same communicative function, namely the formation of interrogative speech acts … In the RRG [his] analysis, the restrictions on the potential focus of *yes/no* questions and those on *Wh*-questions are stated in the same terms: the focus of the *yes/no* question and the site of the *Wh*-word must be in what is called the *potential focus domain* of the IF [illocutionary force] operator over the sentence.

(Van Valin, 1991, pp. 30–31, original emphasis)

He (ibid, p. 31) goes on to illustrate how potential focus domain operates in Lakhota in much the same way that it operates in English.

Van Valin's argument is based, then, on an analogy between a pragmatic and a syntactic restriction. For our purposes, questions about the legitimacy of this analogy are less immediately pressing than Van Valin's developmental claim inspired by it: that children's experience of the way in which *yes/no* questions are restricted in terms of potential focus domain are extended to other types of question, in particular to *Wh*-questions. Evidence of such a process is not, of course, easy to come by. However the following case provides an example of something cognate. As just mentioned, violations of island constraints are sometimes encountered in children's speech. Here again is one owing to Wilson and Peters (1988) *What are you cookin' on a hot____?*, which was from the spontaneous speech of a 3-year-old. This was not the only one he produced (e.g., *What are we gonna look for some ____ with Johnnie?*) According to Wilson and Peters, these constructions had their source in questioning routines of the following kind engaged in with his primary caretaker:

> Adult: What did you eat? Eggs and ...?
> Child: bacon.

This routine led the child to assume that when *Wh*-questions are formed by movement – Van Valin does not deny that they can be – the moved *Wh*-term can legitimately refer to an empty slot; and when this is done a violation of an island constraint will result. This example does not of course establish the existence of generalisations from pragmatic restrictions on *yes/no* questions to island constraints in *Wh*-questions; but it does at least illustrate how strategies for asking *Wh*-questions can be determined by exposure to kinds of question formation – as Van Valin suggests.

   Van Valin's analogy is a provocative one, but one needs, it might be said, some prior sympathy to the pragmatist position to find it convincing. In other words, one has to believe that when we travel from the domain of communicative appropriateness to the domain of linguistic structure no line has been crossed: that the distinction between the inappropriate and the ill-formed is one foisted on us through the structuralist tradition. The proper assessment of such a view must wait until Part 4.

   In any event, our immediate concern is with Van Valin's proposed developmental mechanism. What might be the nature of the 'abundant evidence available to the child regarding the range of possible interpretations of *yes/no* questions from his/her own interactions with caretakers and peers and from observing the verbal interactions of others' (ibid., p. 32)? The problem is that it is only too easy to imagine situations in the child's life – a life measured out by conditional commandings and permittings – in which the focus of the *yes/no* question is *not* the main clause. For example.

> Child: When I've finished this broccoli, can I watch TV?
> Adult: No, when you've finished the carrots.

And one would have thought that if a child is going to learn how island constraints operate in English then the following kind of positive evidence would be more informative:

> What was on the plate that I gave you?
> [Cf. *What did I give you a plate that had on it?]

But of course to make use of this positive evidence the child would need to know a lot about syntax.

2.6 Evidence for syntactic modularity from atypical development: children with specific language impairment

Taking their cue from two of Fodor's (1983) nine criteria for modularity ('characteristic and specific breakdown pattern'; 'characteristic developmental pace and sequencing') researchers with a Swiss-army-knife[45]-nativist cast of mind have tended to argue that if X is a mental module then it must be possible for there to be a population lacking X and X alone, or in which X and X alone develops deviantly, and in which all other cognitive delays and deviancies are caused by the absence/deviant nature of X. Can such a research programme further the empirical assessment of the developmental claims made by Chomsky since the 1980s? For Fodor himself, as might have been evident in the discussion in Part 1.1.4, caveats need to be inserted about the difference between the Chomskyan module and the Fodorian module. For Fodor (2000b) has recently been at pains to stress the differ-ence, taking the Chomskyan variety to refer to an innate data base – 'a body of 'innately cognised propositional contents' (Fodor, 2000b p. 57) – in contrast to the Fodorian variety which refers to mechanisms of informationally encapsulated cog-nitive processing. (See discussion in 2.4.3.)

> Much of the terminological confusion about modules in the cognitive science literature derives from an unhelpful policy adopted by Fodor (1983) where Chomsky's term for innate data bases is borrowed to refer to mechanisms of informationally encapsulated cognitive processing.
>
> (Fodor, 2000b, p. 57)

Maybe. But it has to be said that this Fodor-fuelled assumption has paid some heuristic dividends in the past 20 or so years. Leslie's (1987) attempt to explain the core cognitive impairments of autism in terms of a lack, delay or deviance of a 'theory of mind mechanism' (ToMM) roused many from dogmatic slumbers and revitalised autism research. Although the problem with the ToMM-hypothesis of autism turned out to be that many features of the syndrome resisted attempts to explain them as outcomes of an impaired ToMM (Russell, 1997), the strategy of arguing back from a cognitive-developmental disorder to the existence of a mental module does generally inspire new ideas, positively or reactively.

One finds the same working assumption in research into Specific Language Impairment (SLI), taking this to mean the phenomenon of children with normal intellectual development but below-normal syntactic abilities. This research strategy was initially inspired by P & P theory, and so it is worth pausing to consider how the advent of minimalism and of dynamic minimalism might affect it, some-thing on which I will elaborate in 2.6.3. There are two possibilities offered by minimalism:

1) C–I systems intact but language faculty innately faulty.

2) C–I systems impaired and language faculty also faulty.

This is in contrast to the more radically modularist position which some (e.g., Cromer, 1991, see p. 171) have derived from the pre-minimalist Chomsky, which is that syntax and cognition have distinct (though somehow 'interacting') develop-mental trajectories. On this view one might have:

3) Cognitive development delayed or deviant but syntactic development normal.

----

[45] That is, a toolkit of modules: Cosmedes and Tooby (1992).

A few years ago, in the first blush of research into the disorder (e.g., Bellugi, Wang and Jernigan, 1994), it would have been said that children with Williams Syndrome (WS) exemplify possibility 3. However, more recent work by Annette Karmiloff-Smith and others (e.g., Grant, *et al.*, 1997; Karmiloff-Smith, *et al.*, 1997) has shown such a claim to be questionable, and that it might be based on a somewhat over-simple, missing-part conception of the brain development of atypical populations (Karmiloff-Smith, 1998). For it turns out that intact morphosyntax is extremely unusual in individuals with WS, that across a range of languages such individuals display an impaired grasp of grammatical gender (note, an uninterpretable feature on minimalism) and embedded relative clauses, and that what appears on the surface to be intact syntax is more likely to be supra-normal auditory memory. Accordingly, my aim in this final section is to assess the possibility of 1 (C–I intact, but language faculty faulty).

Loosely defined, SLI is any form of language delay and deviance in which general intelligence is within the normal range. It takes such a bewildering array of forms that the term 'specific' would seem to be something of a misnomer (see Bishop, 1997). Distinctions are commonly drawn between 'semantic-pragmatic', 'familial' and 'grammatical' forms of SLI; and we will be concerned exclusively with the last of these – grammatical.

To begin with inflection, one of the most striking features of grammatical SLI is difficulty with *inflectional morphology,* particularly of verbs. Accordingly, SLI children might say:

    *My dad make breakfast. (e.g. past tense intended)

    *He jump. (e.g. present tense intended)

    *Yesterday I swimmed a mile.

    *Jane falled over.

This problem emerges not only in production but also when the children are asked to judge whether certain sentences are well-formed.

With this in mind, let us reconsider the importance of verbal inflection in X-bar grammar. Recall that introducing the notion of the INFL (or I-) phrase makes it possible to treat a whole sentence as an XP (see Figure 2.10), in such a way that the 'specifier' is the subject NP and the 'complement' is the verb phrase. The 'head' is then an abstract element called 'inflection' – INFL.

As we also saw earlier, INFL determines such things as tense, number, agreement, modality (e.g., *could, might, ought,* etc.) and aspect. (Different languages represent different verbal features on INFL). If the sentence contains a modal verb, INFL will be represented by a word (e.g., *might*), but, if not, it will be represented by an inflexion such as '-ed' for regular past tenses, '-s' for present tense verbs with singular subjects. This is because the tense and agreement properties of the V heading the VP will 'percolate up' to INFL.

Recall that INFL exemplifies what are called *functional categories*, which, in distinction from *lexical* categories such as noun and verb, determine the formal structure of the sentence. The ones we are most concerned with are tense (TNS) and agreement (AGR). To put it loosely, if we know what the tense is and what the verb agrees with we already know a lot about the structure of the sentence.

The modular approach to grammar would seem to predict that children might be born with this knowledge of functional categories represented too weakly, or not represented at all. The most radically modular theory of SLI, owing mainly to Mabel Rice (1996) and Kenneth Wexler (1996), states that the essence of grammatical SLI is difficulty with an aspect of INFL, to be discussed in the next subsection.

2.6.1 The 'extended optional infinitive' theory of SLI

If a verb is marked for tense and agreement it is +finite; if it is not it is –finite (infinitive). I will keep my examples close to Wexler's (1996). In (82) the verbs are plus-finite and in (83) they are minus-finite.

> (82) a. The man *walks.*
>
>   b. The man *walked.*
>
> (83) a. The man likes to *walk.*
>
>   b. The woman made the man *walk.*

Wexler (1996) claims that there is a period in normal development during which children, while knowing how to inflect verbs, sometimes use the infinitive form in a matrix (main) clause of a sentence when a finite form is required, saying such things as *'Daddy walk' rather than 'Daddy walks'. This is the *optional infinitive* stage or *OI* stage.

There are also a set of morphemes that mark finiteness – the *do* and *be* forms, shown in (84).

> (84) a. Do/did you want something?
>
>   b. Is/was he happy?

One would expect children to omit these, on Wexler's analysis; and they do. Note the claim is not that these young children lack adequate concepts of time, but rather that they behave as if tense need not be marked when it should be.

The claim then is that children with SLI undergo an *extended optional infinitive* (*EOI*) period. If this is so then we might expect to find the following:

1) A lower-than-expected use of finite forms where adult grammar requires these.

2) A longer-than-expected OI stage – perhaps into adulthood.

3) Auxiliary and main verb use of *be* and *do* will tend to be omitted. (E.g. *'you hungry?'; *'you want to eat?').

4) But they will use the target form correctly if they do use it. Thus, they *will not* say things like *She are hungry.

Remember there is no prediction being made here that such children will have *general* problems with agreement and produce forms such as *they walks* and *I goes.*[46]

Rice, Wexler and Cleave (1995) tested these predictions with a group of 18 SLI children (mean age five years). There were two control groups: one matched for

---

[46] Unless of course they hear this form spoken by adults, as would some working class Bristolian children for example.

chronological age, the other matched for language age (mean CA about three years). They recorded spontaneous speech and also gave verbal probes for the relevant verb forms. The outcome was that the SLI used even less of the forms than did children two years younger than them. Moreover the prediction about lack of *'She are hungry'-type errors was borne out. In short, the SLIs showed *consistent marking of agreement but not consistent marking of tense.*

Challenges to the EOI hypothesis have come mainly from cross-linguistic research, challenges which are usefully reviewed by Fletcher (1999). If a crucial part of universal grammar is only weakly represented in children with SLI then one would expect to find that other countries contain populations of SLI children whose problems parallel those of English-speaking SLI children in this specific regard. If, however, SLI in different languages were found to be *sui generis,* then this would be a challenge of the EOI theory.

We turn first to Greek. A study by Dalakakis (1994) showed that Greek SLI children were more likely to make errors in verb selection than age-matched counterparts. In elicitation tests for tense marking, the SLI children scored around 20 per cent as against 87 per cent for controls. This is consistent with EOI theory. However, the Greek SLI children *did*, unlike the English-speaking children, make errors of subject-verb agreement. Moreover, it is not possible in Greek to use a bare verb stem (the infinitive form has an inflection), and so the error of using the bare stem for finite could not be made by the Greek children, as it could by English-speaking children.

With regard to Japanese, a study of 8 SLI children was carried out by Fukuda and Fukuda (1994). In Japanese, verbs are not only marked for tense but also for addressee status, while number is not marked on the verb. Adjectives are tense-marked. As in Greek, the adult forms do not contain bare verb stems as the infinitive is inflected, and so over-using this form is not possible. Again, the SLI children performed poorly on an elicitation task: 40 per cent as against 90 per cent correct.

Both of these studies, however, suffered from the shortcoming of not including verbal-mental-age matched controls: they only included CA matches. This means that we cannot say how much these children were *delayed* (a crucial question for the EOI theory) relative to children functioning at similar level of verbal ability. More usually, researchers in SLI include, as we shall see, both CA- and language-matched controls. Moreover some of the Japanese data suggested that it is aspect, not tense, that caused the problems. For example, when they had to say the equivalent of 'John is walking' (continuous aspect) they produced a simple present tense 'John walks'. English children produce continuous verb forms very early, so there is absence of a parallel here. As Fletcher (1999, p. 359) concludes from these and a number of similar studies, 'It seems that interaction between an impaired language learning mechanism and a particular language is going to have consequences specific to the structure of that language.' This of course inevitably makes the EOI hypothesis very difficult to test.

The point is illustrated most clearly in experiments with Italian SLI children. What is remarkable from the work of Leonard and his colleagues is just how well Italian SLI children perform on verbs compared to English-speaking SLI children.

In a study by Leonard *et al.* (1987), Italian SLI children were matched in general language ability (e.g., mean length of utterance) with English SLI, and when this was done it was notable how difficult the English children were finding the marking of tense compared to the ease with which the Italian children achieved it. This suggested to Leonard that the relative ease/difficulty may be a function of how *salient* the relevant inflections were in the surface forms of the two languages. This view has become known as *the surface hypothesis*. To explain, in English the final -s and -ed of regular verbs are not stressed: they are non-salient. In Italian, however, the verb inflection is not only stressed but it is a *full syllable*. It is as if in English we did not pronounce 'walked' as 'walkt' but as 'walk-èd'.[47] Leonard (1994, p. 100) writes: 'Limited processing capacity makes inflections with difficult surface characteristics more vulnerable to loss when combined with the operations of paradigm building'. (By the 'paradigm building' he means working out rules like stem + ed or stem + s.)

The surface hypothesis is one of number of *input-processing deficit* accounts of SLI, which form the principal challenges to a modularist view of the disorder. We will return to the debate between these two general views when more evidence is in. But for now, what should we make of the EOI hypothesis? It would seem to be a too specific, and essentially Anglophone, account of SLI. It also ignores other kinds of problems that SLI children have, problems which can be explicated in terms of P & P theory. If there is to be a Chomskyan theory of SLI then it might need to be a more general one – such as the next.

2.6.2 van der Lely's Representational Deficit for Dependent Relationships (RDDR) hypothesis about grammatical SLI children

A general problem with X-bar grammar should manifest itself as difficulty with understanding the relation between constituents of a sentence and between a sentence and its constituents. Given this, one would expect SLI children to have problems understanding and generating a number of different kinds of syntactically complex sentences – beyond tense marking. If they happen instead to succeed on such tasks then the theory must assume that this is because of the presence of rich semantic and pragmatic cues. We now consider the work of Heather van der Lely, which is directly addressed to such issues. She takes care to study the subset of SLI children whose problems are indeed syntactic – the so-called Grammatical SLI children (G-SLI). These G-SLI children form a homogenous subgroup from a generally heterogeneous population. For inclusion in this group the children must be over 6 years[48] of age and have an IQ of above 85, and not be exhibiting a pragmatic disorder. Van der Lely's general hypothesis about the core SLI impairment is dubbed '*Representational Deficit for Dependent Relationships*' (RDDR).

....

[47] It would support the surface hypothesis if it were found that, while English-speaking SLI children experience difficulty marking the plurals of words like 'cars' (pron. 'carz'), they have no difficulty with pluralising words like 'horses' in which the plural marker is a full syllable. This is not, however, the case (Oetting and Rice, 1993).

[48] In later studies, the children are over 9 years.

First, van der Lely and her colleagues have demonstrated that G-SLI children have difficulty with *thematic role assignment*, which means, recall, working out the relations between arguments and predicates; e.g., what is the agent and what is the patient in a passive sentence. Van der Lely and Harris (1990) showed that 6-year-old G-SLI children have difficulty assigning thematic roles to semantically *reversible* passives (e.g., 'The girl was kissed by the boy' – as opposed to the irreversible 'The flower was watered by the girl'). They had problems with datives ('to the X') and locatives ('on the X'), but these were particularly marked when the forms were non-canonical, e.g., the locative 'on the table is a cup' or the dative 'The boy gave the girl the book'.

Note that the EOI theory, focusing as it does exclusively on inflectional morphology, would not necessarily predict such a difficulty.

In a further study, van der Lely (1994) assessed thematic role assignment by the use of so-called *semantic bootstrapping* and *syntactic bootstrapping* tasks. In this case she compared the G-SLI children's ability to act out the meanings of novel verbs, as used in a novel sentence frame, whose meaning had been demonstrated to them with their ability to infer a meaning for a novel word heard in a sentence and act it out. The first was the *semantic bootstrapping* task and the second a *syntactic boot-strapping* task. These terms were used because, in the first case, the child had to use what she already knew about meaning (it was demonstrated) and syntax to act out a new construction (e.g., the passive form); while in the second case the child has to *work from the syntax* to the meaning – figuring out that the action must be (say) a transitive one. For example:

> *Semantic bootstrapping task* (moving from meaning to a novel syntactic structure):
>
> The child is shown a toy horse jumping up and down on a toy lion and is told that this is '*voozing*'. The child then has to act out (among other things) 'The pig is voozed by the cat'.

> *Syntactic bootstrapping task* (constructing a plausible meaning from a syntactic frame):
>
> The child hears, for example, 'The lorry yols the car' – a transitive argument structure. He or she then has to invent an action that will fit the bill. Will she invent a transitive one?

Rather surprisingly given the van der Lely and Harris result, the children did quite well on the semantic boostrapping task; but they were clearly challenged by the syntactic bootstrapping task.[49] This shows that SLI children can generally work out the argument structure of a verb when given semantic information (even generalising to passives) while their grasp of syntactic principles is too weak to enable them to move in the other direction: working out how meaning is constrained by a certain syntactic frame. These results were replicated by O'Hara and Johnson (1997).

We now turn to a question that gains pertinence from the P & P-inspired research on typically-developing children we have recently been discussing: *Do G-SLI children have specific problems with binding phenomena?* Here again are the three binding principles (see Figures 2.21 and 2.22).

---

[49] Note that in the semantic bootstrapping task the child does not have to analyse the whole sentence and work out possible/plausible thematic roles for NPs.

> Principle A: An anaphor (e.g., a reflexive) is bound in its local domain.
>
> Principle B: A definite pronoun must be free in its local domain.
>
> Principle C: A referring-expression (e.g., a noun or proper name) must be free.

In everyday life, G-SLIs children would not be expected to have much trouble working out what pronouns refer to because the context will tell them: 'John is washing himself' (principle A) for example. So van der Lely and Stollwerck (1997) took pains to remove such clues. The children (a G-SLI group between 9 and 12 years plus three language-matched control groups) saw a series of pictures and heard a sentence with each. They had to say Yes or No depending on whether the picture matched the sentence. In some cases a simple rule such as '*himself* in a single-clause sentence means reflexive on the agent' will ensure that they will be correct but in crucial cases it did not. For example if they see a picture in which *Baloo Bear is shown tickling Mowgli* and are told:

> 'Mowgli says that Baloo Bear is tickling himself.'

To which the answer is No. But for

> 'Baloo Bear says that Mowgli is tickling him.'

The correct answer is Yes. The 11-year-old SLI children performed at the level of normally-developing 6 year olds.

2.6.3 G-SLI and minimalism – is movement optional for some children?

The emergence of minimalism has inevitably led to modifications of RDDR. Now, rather than arguing, individually , that G-SLI children fail to acknowledge the P & P principles, struggle with θ-role assignment and so forth, van der Lely has attempted to unify the variety of difficulties under the umbrella of *optional movement*. She does not argue that move is absent, but rather that these children fail to appreciate that it is obligatory.

Let us remind ourselves, first of all, of what it means for move to be obligatory. (This might be done by revisiting the account of the role on move in feature checking in 2.3.4. pp 155–156) Recall that uninterpretable head features, such as T (infinitival tense marker), serve as *probes* (sometimes called 'attractors') seeking *goal* items elsewhere in the derivation to enable matching, checking and thus the erasure of their offending uninterpretable features. Goal items move to check probe items. It is also useful to insert here Chomsky's view that move is a 'last resort' phenomenon. It comes into operation when neither merge nor agree are able to achieve uninterpretable feature deletion. It is 'the last resort chosen when nothing else is possible' (Chomsky, 2000b, p. 102).

For van der Lely, following Manzini (1995), this last resort principle can be seen to comprise two 'economy' principles: (1) that move will only occur if there are unchecked features; (2) that move is 'forced' under the circumstance of (1) – the so-called 'must-move' principle. If G-SLI children lack this must-move principle then one would expect that move will not be absent in their speech, but that they should employ it less often than control children.

Given this, and looking back to the kind of deficits described in 2.6.1, van der Lely (van der Lely, 1998; van der Lely and Battell, 2003) argues that G-SLI children's difficulty with marking tense and agreement is caused by a tendency to neglect head-to-head movement (moving V to I in this case[50]). Similarly, the difficulties in assigning thematic roles to noun phrases, particularly in passives, (described in 2.6.2.) are claimed to be caused by difficulties with argument movement.[51] Van der Lely (1998, pp. 183–184) also claims that the binding difficulties, described above, can be explained in terms of failure to utilise move properly. To explain, as Reinhart and Reuland (1993) have argued, in a sentence like *Mowgli says that Baloo Bear is tickling himself, self* has to move to the closest predicate in order to mark it as a reflexive, resulting in the abstract form *Baloo Bear is self-tickling him,* thus forcing co-reference between *Baloo Bear* and *him.* If this is not achieved, there will be a violation of principle A. I will leave these three claims unexplored and turn to a more directly testable prediction that this hypothesis inspires.

One clear prediction made by this account is that G-SLI children should be unsuccessful at asking wh-questions. This might seem a rather unexciting prediction given the rich variety of grammatical problems already in evidence. But this optional-move account predicts not global errors with wh-questions, but quite specific ones. It predicts that asking object wh-questions (e.g., *Who did George see?*) will result in more errors than asking subject wh-questions (e.g., *Who saw George?*).

(85) a. $[_{CP}$ Who$_i[_{C'}$ did$_j$ $[_{IP}$ George$[_{I'}$ e$_j$ $[_{VP}$ $[_{V'}$ see$[_{NP}$t$_i$?$]]]]]]]$

b. *$[_{CP}$ Who$_i[_{C'}$ did$_j$ $[_{IP}$ George$[_{I'}$ e$_j$ $[_{VP}$ $[_{V'}$ see$[_{NP}$Fred?$]]]]]]]$

In cases such as (85a), two kinds of movement are involved. First, obviously, there is movement of the wh-operator to the specifier position of the CP, leaving a trace behind bound by the operator. This precludes the filling of this gap with a determiner phrase as in (85b). The second form of movement involves adding 'do' and the infinitive form. With regard to the latter, suffice it to say that 'do' is assumed to bear a Q(question)-feature (uninterpretable), and that its movement is from the I-phrase to the complement – as can be seen. This will be referred to as T/Q feature movement (also called '*do support*').

With regard to *subject* wh-movement, by contrast, there is no need for do-support and therefore no need for inflection-to-complement movement. There is also, of course, no long-distance operator movement leaving a trace at the end of the sentence which should not be filled with a DP. There are two views of the kind of operations involved in subject wh-questions (Rizzi, 1991). Either the wh-operator moves from

---

[50] What is at stake here is the child's having the features of verb heading the VP 'percolate up' to the I′ node; see Figure 2.10 and associated text. Without this, there can be no checking of features with the subject/specifier and therefore no 'agreement' between verb and subject. It is as if the verb is quarantined from the rest of the sentence.

[51] A(argument)-movement is involved in passivisation. For example, in the sentence *He was seen to kiss her, he* has moved from an argument position before *kiss,* to that before *to,* to that before *seen* to the subject position, at each stage of the journey being directly beneath the I′ node. This is also a case of 'argument raising'. See Radford (1997a, pp. 187–88). Recall (see footnote 41) that operator movement (the wh-term) is non-argument (A′) movement.

an original position in the IP to the complement phrase – (86a) – or it remains inside the IP functioning primarily as an interrogative pronoun (86b). (In the latter case the situation can be paraphrased as 'Somebody [who] saw George?')

(86) a. [$_{CP}$ Who$_i$ [$_{C'}$ [$_{IP}$ t$_i$ [$_{I'}$ [$_{VP}$ [$_{V'}$ saw George?]]]]]]

      b. [$_{CP'}$ [$_{C'}$ [$_{IP}$ Who [$_{I'}$ [$_{VP}$ [$_{V'}$ saw George?]]]]]]

Despite their differing in complexity, these two kinds of wh-question seem to be in evidence at much the same period of development (Stromswold, 1995), while we know from Goodluck's work (Goodluck *et al.*, 1992), discussed above, that children of five years of age can control complex long distance wh-movement. So, on the present analysis, one would expect G-SLI children to produce more errors when encouraged to ask object wh-questions than when encouraged to ask subject wh-questions because the former make more demands on the movement operation, while language-ability-matched control children should not show such a difference.

Van der Lely and Battell considered the following three possible kinds of error in object wh-questions.

> A Wh-operator movement correct, but T/Q movement errors (e.g., infinitive only, 'do' omission or 'do' plus finite.)
>   a. *What cat Mrs White stroked?
>   b. *What did they drank?
>
> B T/Q movement/features correct, but with wh-operator movement errors [e.g., DP (determiner phrase) inserted into the gap left by the operator (a) or lack of movement of the referential noun ('what *X*' in (b)]
>   a. *Who did Reverend Green see someone?
>   b. *What did Mrs. Peacock like jewellery?
>
> C With neither Wh-word movement (lexical DP in the position of the gap, or no movement of the referential noun) nor T/Q feature movement (e.g., 'do' omission, 'do' plus finite verb form)
>   a. *Who Mrs. Scarlett saw somebody?
>   b. *Which Reverend Green open a door?

The authors used a 'Who-done-it?' game based on Cluedo, in which the children had to question a police sergeant who was currently investigating a crime.

As expected, the G-SLI children did struggle more with object questions than with subject questions. The latter trend was absent in the two groups of control children, one of which has been matched on standard tests of grammatical ability and one of which has been matched on vocabulary tests. The groups did not, however, differ in frequency of semantic and pragmatic errors.

This result spurs the question of what the G-SLI children did when they did not abide by must-move. The answer forthcoming from MP is that they would be making merge work harder than it should be working. The simplest case to consider here is when, in the absence of move, there is a direct merger between the wh-element and the complement phrase. This is in evidence in errors such as the *Which one did he wear the coat?* Category C errors also exemplify this.

Let us also consider errors of commission. (For reasons to be discussed in the next subsection, commission errors provide a stronger test of the RDDR position.)

One kind of commission error involved the addition of an auxiliary to a finite verb in either object or subject questions. Some examples of these are given in (87).

(87) Object-wh commission errors:
   a. *What did they drank?
   b. *What did she spotted in the library?

Subject-wh commission error:
   *Which telephone did rang?

The explanation of these errors takes a rather complex course, but I will present it here as a further illustration of how minimalist ideas can be applied in this area. In the case of the object errors the argument runs as follows. First, the assumption is made that covert movement is 'cheaper' than overt movement (certainly, less is required in the way of spell out). Given this, one can suppose that the inflected verb moves covertly to T to check its uninterpretable features. The result will be that no features will remain at T needing to be checked by an auxiliary (see Figure 2.27 p. 151). This in turn means that the auxiliary in the head of the complement phrase ('did' in all the current cases) will have been directly merged in the complement phrase without carrying the T/Q features. If it does not carry these features then no infinitive form will be necessitated, and an error will result. Putting this in more informal, cartoonish terms in order – I hope – to make the proposal more vivid, one might say that, for the SLI child a past-tense form like *drank* carries scope over the whole question (*in virtue of is covert movement*) as if the form were *Drank: what did she?* Because of this, any link between *did* and the verb would have been severed, so that the usual requirement for the auxiliary to be coupled with an infinitive can be dropped.

2.6.4 Is G-SLI an input-processing deficit or a grammar-specific deficit?

We have already discussed, within the context of Leonard's surface hypothesis, the possibility that SLI may be caused, not by the malfunctioning of an innate module for syntax but by the faulty auditory perception of rapid, brief sounds. In this subsection, I will discuss recent evidence that these difficulties may be specific to speech stimuli, then discuss the kind of commission errors that would appear to be more explicable in terms of a syntactic deficit, then suggest how an input-deficit theory may, paradoxically, bolster the psychological reality of the Chomskyan model of competence, before finally raising a significant problem for 'surface-style' views.

In support of the surface hypothesis, Wright *et al.* (1997) report that there is a massively enhanced backward masking effect in SLIs, while Tallal *et al.* (1993) have presented evidence for difficulties with rapid auditory processing in the population. The fact that a substantial proportion of adolescents and adults with SLI do not display any acoustic processing deficits (van der Lely, Rosen and McClelland, 1998, for a case study) is not fatal to this view because Tallal's hypothesis is the developmental one that the input-processing deficit early in life will have knock-on effects on syntactic development and that the perceptual deficit might fade with development.

Turning to the first issue, some controversy exists around the question of whether the auditory–perceptual difficulty in SLI is domain-specific or domain-general. In other words, is the difficulty with any kind of brief, rapid auditory signal or only with those that make up the speech stream? Tallal argues that it is the former, while recent data collected by van der Lely and her colleagues (van der Lely, Rosen and Adlard, in press) suggest that the problem is essentially language-specific. The task used by the latter authors required subjects to make same/different judgments about pairs of stimuli: (1) speech sounds distinguished by rapid acoustic transitions (e.g.,/ba/da/); (2) isolated second-formants that are not distinguished as speech sounds but which contain the same acoustic feature; (3) non-speech, short, complex tones differing both in fundamental frequency and inter-stimulus interval. As the authors say, any group differences revealed by using speech sounds 'could arise from the phonological component of the grammatical system'.

Van der Lely *et al*.'s study demonstrated that the G-SLI children were relatively worse, compared to age-matched controls, at processing speech sounds than non-speech sounds. However, there was an absence of a relationship between purely auditory ability and grammatical ability, plus the presence of a relationship between *speech* sound perception and grammatical ability. With specific regard to the latter result, the one control group from which the G-SLI children did not differ was that matched for grammatical ability, suggesting that there is a linkage between phonological development and the ability to process speech-relevant, contrastive formant transitions. In other words, as the child's linguistic abilities develop there is progressively more fine tuning in the skill of identifying acoustic elements in speech, so it becomes easier to selectively attend to brief, rapid sounds. Broadly speaking, indeed, van der Lely *et al*. (in press) found that the majority of G-SLI children showed normal auditory processing of non-speech sounds. When added to the facts that van der Lely *et al*. found no relations between auditory performance and language abilities and that what auditory/grammatical relations existed were ones between phonological and grammatical skill (i.e., both within the linguistic domain) we see a threat to the auditory-deficit theories. (I will discuss further threats to the surface hypothesis right at the end of this section.)

Moving on to our second topic, one clear impediment to deciding between the domain-general, perceptual account of the disorder and the modular, Chomskyan account is that the omission of inflectional morphemes (as focussed on by EOI theory in particular) and failure to process the more complex grammatical forms (see 2.6.2) can be accounted for by either theory: both seek to explain errors of *omission* and the *absence* of syntactic forms. For this reason, it is necessary to find procedures for evoking errors of *commission* – errors that involve the generation of inflectional morphemes which should not be there and syntactic structures which are paradoxically richer than the correct forms, but erroneous. If G-SLI children were found to be impaired on these tasks, the failure would be more convincingly explained by the grammatical deficit theory – explained in terms of faulty syntactic machinery generating superfluous forms. They would less plausibly be explained by a theory that is designed to explain what information SLIs fail to pick up & process online.

Van der Lely and Christian (2000) employed a technique for evoking errors of commission in children – for producing inflectional morphemes that should not be there, derived from the work of Gordan (1985). Gordan made use of a phenomenon noted by the linguist Paul Kiparsky (1982). Why is it that it seems acceptable to refer to a *mice-eater* but not to a **rats-eater*, why (in Pinker's, 1994, p. 146 example, does it seem legitimate to sing about a *Purple-People-Eater* but not about a **Purple-Babies-Eater*, why, in short, do we construct compound-nouns out of irregular plurals but not out of *regular* plurals? Kiparsky explained this within his 'level-ordering' framework for word formation. The details of this need not detain us. All we need to note is that compound nouns are made up of the root, or stem, forms of words or *irregular* forms – 'level 1' on Kiparsky's theory. This means, in the present case, that either the bare singular stem *rat* or *baby* contributes to the compounding process or an irregular plural like *mice* or *people*. To fail to acknowledge this regularity is, on the Kiparsky model, not merely to have failed to notice a regularity in the data but to be failing to build up lexical forms in the correct rule-bound manner. For example, children who produce forms like **rats-eater* might be assumed to be storing regular plurals like irregular plurals in memory rather than generating them by the morphosyntactic rule 'stem + s'. They will, in short, be generating plurals via associative memory rather than computing the regular plural form via a rule. Gordon (1985) found that by the age of five years children appear to be doing the latter, being happy to call a monster who eats mice a *mice-eater* and one that eats rats a *rat-eater*, but not a **rats-eater*.

Using a similar elicitation technique to Gordon's, van der Lely and Christian (2000) found that G-SLI children were far more likely to add this illicit inflectional morpheme than were control children and teenagers. And it is relevant to add that these same G-SLI children were no less fast and accurate on a lexical decision task with nouns in regular and irregular forms than were controls; indeed they were faster than the language-ability control group (Jones and van der Lely, 1998). This counterindicates the possibility that this group of children simply had inadequate access to words due to their less accurate phonological representations.

In 3.2 we will encounter a connectionist model of these constraints on compound noun formation, owing to Haskell, MacDonald and Seidenberg (2003), one that explains it in term of statistical learning from the input rather than in terms of 'level ordering'. Essentially, these authors argue that what people have to do to abide by the constraint is not to engage in level ordering, but rather to pick up the *phonological* information that determines whether words are acceptable as modifiers. Generally, a word's having an /-s/ ending blocks its use as a modifier. In the light of this kind of model, SLI children's difficulties with these formations may be difficult to explain in terms of their failing to perform formal syntactic operations. In any event, psycholinguists are likely to continue to think they have found reasons to be sceptical about the grammar-specific account of SLI (Tomblin and Pandrich, 1999; reply by van der Lely, 1999).

I will round off this section by considering what the consequences might be for Chomskyan theory if it *did* turn out to be the case that difficulties with auditory perception are at the root of SLI, and then end with some final empirical reasons why the auditory-impairment theory may not, in fact, triumph in the end. In the first place let us consider the possibility that the following two propositions could *both* be true. The first is derived from the work of Tallal and others and the second from that of Chomsky and of Atkinson.

1) SLI is caused by a domain-general deficit in perceiving brief, rapid auditory signals.

2) The C_{HL} depends for its development upon there being adequate development of the two external systems, C–I and A–P.

We have already discussed the dependency on the C–I system in the light of Atkinson's proposal of a dynamic minimalism. Well, something of a similar nature might be said about the C_{HL}/A–P interface. In this regard, if children are impaired in their ability to perceive speech-relevant sounds this will necessarily impact upon their syntactic development. Consider the Chomskyan analysis of sentence structure, which has survived into MP. In this, recall, the whole sentence is regarded as an inflection phrase (IP). Recall also that if the sentence does not contain an auxiliary verb, the I′ branch will not contain a leaf, but the tense marker of the matrix verb will 'percolate up' to the I′ node. (See Figure 2.10 and associated text.) The upshot of this is likely to be that, in an individual who finds it difficult to perceive verb affixes, the control of I′ will be impaired. In broad-brush style then, fixing the inflection of the verb high in the tree, especially fixing it as finite or infinitive, determines the phrasal analysis of the whole sentence. If this is not achieved therefore, whatever abilities the child has for movement and so forth will not adequately come to fruition. It is, then, perhaps possible to be both an advocate of SLI as a perceptual impairment and also a Chomskyan about syntactic competence and its innate foundations.

So, returning to our original parallel with autism research, it is possible to believe that some particular form of early executive dysfunction might impede the development of the innate apparatus for computing a theory of mind while also believing that the relative specificity of the theory of mind impairment in this population of children is evidence for the modular nature of theory of mind.

That all seems neat and ecumenical enough then. But in fact the same kind of data threaten both the auditory deficit theory of SLI and the executive-deficit theory of autism. These are data showing the presence of the putatively-determining, sensorimotor deficit along with absence of the higher-level impairment. With regard to SLI then, we find children *with* the auditory deficits but *without* G-SLI. In the van der Lely (2003) study just discussed, for example, six children *without* SLI were found to be impaired in their auditory processing. This theme is one on which Dorothy Bishop's research group has elaborated extensively (Bishop, Carlyon, Deeks and Bishop, 1999; Briscoe, Bishop and Norbury, 2001; Norbury, Bishop and Briscoe, 2001, 2002). For example, Norbury *et al.* (2002) compared children with SLI against children with mild-moderate hearing loss. While both groups were poor at phoneme perception, the SLI children did especially poorly on tests assessing the binding principles and in assigning thematic roles in passive sentences. (With regard to the presence of executive deficits together with the absence of theory-of-mind deficits, plus an attempt to salvage something from the executive-deficit theory of autism, see Russell, 2002.)

2.7 Taking stock

As soon as we accept that having a language means *knowing* a language (albeit non-consciously for the most part), as soon as we abandon any ideas about having a language being a matter of being caused to produce correct outputs in virtue of possessing an associative network mediating message and form, or of possessing a repertoire of conventional schemes for communication, it becomes clear that any theory of language acquisition must contain a theory of what is known – a competence, or I-language, theory. One might conceive of this as a recipe book for moving between thoughts and sentences. This is really all one needs to do to establish that developmental psychology needs a theory of the kind that Chomsky offers.

However *nativism* does not necessarily follow from this assumption. For one can accept the need for a competence theory whilst taking the view that this competence is learned no less than the 'competence' required to play chess. Conversely, one can be a nativist of sorts and yet repudiate Chomsky's theory of language, as does Gopnik, for example, in her 'starting state nativism' (see 1.3.4). Moreover, it is surprising how little in the way of explicit defence of nativism is on offer in Chomsky – at least these days. It is possible, indeed, for a linguist as sympathetic to the general Chomskyan programme as Frederick Newmeyer to say, in comparing the generative with the functionalist approaches (Newmeyer, 1998, p. 364, original emphasis) that

> [i]t is important to conclude ... by stressing that there is no *logical* necessity for a set of parameters of variation to be innate; one can imagine the possibility of a theory in every aspect like the recent principles and parameters models, but in which the parameters are arrived at inductively by the child ... [I]t does seem clear that one has to reject the idea that all principles, and their range of possible parametric variation, are innate.

Learnability theory – recall the brief account of Gold's work in Part 1 – is an enterprise quite distinct from Chomskyan linguistics.

It might be said, however, that the onus lies with those who believe that, say, merge and move and the basic lexical knowledge on which these depend, not to mention computing logical form, are learned by the child to show how this learning is possible in principle. If however, you reject Chomsky's competence theory then learning-based theories of development become easier to construct – obviously enough.

But when we turn to the competence theory itself other, long familiar, issues come into view, issues about the *status* of the claims, about, one might say, the explanatory realm they inhabit. Where do we locate, for example, Chomsky's debate with himself over whether the intermediate (X′) level of phrase structure is legible at the C–I interface, or whether it is only computed during the course of the derivation? And when it is proposed that movement is necessitated by the existence of abstract tense elements (T) containing uninterpretable features serving as probes for goal elements to move to cancel these features this looks like a realm in which the theorist gives himself *carte blanche* to postulate any entity. A sceptic is likely to say that what directs the course of one's views on this kind of matter are currents that swirl within the hermeneutical circle of Chomsky's own thought.

One can perhaps understand such a reaction. But if this kind of scepticism is allowed to grow unchecked one ends up being sceptical about theoretical linguistics itself, berating it for both escaping the empirical discipline of psychology while merely helping itself to one kind of philosophical programme or another. Moreover, it is likely to be the case that whatever turns out to be the most adequate account of how language and thought are related is going to tax our imaginative resources to the limit: it may no more accord with everyday forms of understanding than does particle physics. Thus, Chomsky's proposal that thought and language liase in virtue of the process of checking uninterpretable features so that only those (interpretable) features with a determinate semantic content remain as legible to the thought systems does indeed look like a metaphor in search of a content. It is, one might say, a novel kind of entity – a formal metaphor, not a model but not a mere figurative sweep either. That right now it is well-nigh impossible to imagine how this content could be explicated in terms of the kind of processes that a psycholinguist would recognise is surely not sufficient to damn the very attempt. After all, it is an account of why human language has all the features it seemingly does not need for the expression of thoughts. To return to the example given in 2.3.4, the sentence *She has gone* expresses a bare thought which might be represented as SHE,GONE[NOW]. It might be said that Chomsky has the (predictably) Cartesian idea that, for the thinker, the meaning and structure of this bare thought has a kind of private integrity and accuracy: we know our own minds. That is to say, my knowing that the content of my thought is SHE,GONE[NOW] does not depend upon any intersubjective system of symbolic schemata (*pace* pragmatism). And it does not, *pace* Rorty, gain its incorrigibility 'externally' because this is how human culture happens to regard self-reports (see Part 1, pp. 62): it is I-knowledge. And when the thought comes to be expressed, when it is necessary to ensure that this thought will have the same status in the mind of the hearer, there needs to be some mechanical process to encode its structure in such a way that only what is essential to it and no more is transmitted – the optimal system. This process, too, had better be a deterministic one, one that is not dependent upon any Davidsonian processes of interpretation relative to a context. For the fact is that when you read or hear *She has gone* you know the thought expressed by the sentence without any contextual support. These mechanisms, these micro-ladders that can be thrown away when climbed, are conceived on a mathematical model, analogous to the multiplication of plus and minus signs … Well, if this formal metaphor really does capture a real content then the anti-Rationalist is likely to be hard pressed to say the mechanism is 'learned'.

But none of this implies that the process of language development involves no substantive learning. Perhaps one of the more unfortunate utterances Noam Chomsky ever made was that the term 'learning', as employed in human psychology, is on a par with the terms 'rising' and 'setting' when applied to the sun. For children do learn *a* language, and there is very little in Chomskyan theory to tell us about the mechanisms through which particular languages are learned. How, to anticipate a discussion in 3.2, do German children learn to assign the correct form of the definite article, given the six possible forms?

Perhaps one might regard parameter-setting as a theory of learning, but it is really couched as a theory of how substantive learning is *not* needed. And perhaps the dynamic minimalism which Atkinson derives from MP is a theory of what drives syntactic development (challenges for expression set at the C–I interface). Indeed it is, but when cashed as an empirical developmental theory it resolves itself, as I argued above, into the view that the language faculty offers not the optimal solution to conceptual challenges, but *a* solution. And that theory will be, as I said, familiar to older developmentalists as Richard Cromer's (1974) 'cognition hypothesis'.

Finally, we have seen that, relative to the earlier theories, the minimalist programme is bottom-up in nature. In Part 3 we encounter an approach that is bottom-up through and through.

Empiricist connectionism as a theory of language development

Connectionist simulations of language learning can be viewed as empirical tests of learnability claims, based on very different assumptions about the nature of grammatical knowledge and the nature of the learning device. Some of these simulations have already shown that the impossible is in principle possible ...

(Elman *et al.*, 1996, p. 385)

The productivity of this network is of course a feeble subset of the vast capacity that a normal English speaker commands. But productivity is productivity, and evidently a recurrent network can possess it. Elman's striking demonstration hardly settles the issue between the rule-centred approach to grammar and the network approach. That will be some time in working itself out. But the conflict is now an even one. I've made no secret of where my own bets will be placed.

(Churchland quoted in Marcus, 2001, p. 25)

In the case of language, the evidence for connectionist models is, for the moment, about zero.

(Chomsky quoted in Smith, 1999, p. 135)

The standard current alternative to Turing architectures, namely, connectionist networks is simply hopeless. Here, as often elsewhere, networks contrive to make the worst of both worlds. They notoriously can't do what Turing architectures can, namely, provide a plausible account of the causal consequences of logical form. But they can't do what Turing architectures can't, namely provide a plausible account of abductive inference. It must be the sheer magnitude of their incompetence that makes them so popular.

(Fodor, 2000, p. 47)

The 'Empiricist' in the title is supposed to carry weight. For some – and, despite their protestations that 'we are not empiricists', Elman *et al.* (1996) are among them (see 1.2.4) – connectionist models are demonstration proofs of the viability, if not the absolute truth, of the empiricist view of linguistic and mental development. Part and parcel of this belief, and keeping one eye on Fodor's arguments for nativism in *The language of thought*, is the claim that a full computational model of human language and cognition can be achieved without recourse to symbolic representation: error-based learning algorithms that extract structural regularities from the training environment without pre-existing representations of any domain will prove to be sufficient.

But this is only one side of the connectionist coin. There is another, less ideologically fuelled, connectionist enterprise, some of which will make its appearance in Part 3. Here are some illustrations of this second kind. In a critical review of the Elman *et al.* book, Marcus (1998) points out that a number of connectionist workers concede, exactly as Elman *et al.* do *not*, the existence of and need for symbol-manipulating machinery, with Smolensky (1995), for one, saying that his general aim is to 'explain how symbolic computation is built upon neural computation'. (Even the staunchest rationalist must accept that it, somehow, is.) Meanwhile, Berent, Everett and Shimron (2001) draw a distinction between 'pattern associator' models that seek to eliminate the role of variables (in the sense of putatively symbolic 'slots' fillable by instances – more of this later) and those that do not. In the latter case, '[t]he ability of some connectionist networks to implement symbolic functions is well known' (Hornik, Stinchcombe, and White, 1989; Siegelman and Sontag, 1995). Existing connectionist models that implement variables include the analogical reasoning model by Hummel and Holyoak (1997), and Prince and Smolensky's (1997) optimality theory, an account of linguistic competence based on the principles of Harmony theory (Smolensky, 1995). (See Berent *et al.*, 2001, pp. 2–3). While Chang (2002) contrasts the eliminativist (i.e., of variables/symbols) with the 'structuralist' approach, which 'takes a pragmatic approach to building networks, focusing on particular operations like variable binding (Shastri and Ajjanagadde, 1993) or task decomposition (Jacobs, Jordan and Barto, 1991)'. In 3.4 we will be discussing one of the papers in a book entitled *Connectionist symbol processing* (ed. G. Hinton).

It will perhaps come as no surprise to the reader, however – this is something to be discussed in 3.5 – that the more relaxed and ecumenical approach of Smolensky and others, in which symbol-like processes are added where needed, falls far short of satisfying Fodor (1997).

In what follows I will be essentially concerned, then, with the first, more radical kind of connectionism, because *it is this which expresses the empiricist world view*. I discuss a model that leans towards the second school right at the end, in section 3.6.

Here then, is the road map to Part 3.

3.1: I return to questions raised in 1.2.4 about the status of connectionist representations. As I suggested there, a sceptic is likely to regard hidden-unit representations (e.g., of 'the nouns' or 'the verbs') as no more than statistically structured *records* of how a network has achieved the mapping of input to output units. For the worry here is that only if a representation is *used* as such by the system, only if it affects the system in virtue of its content, is it any more than a record of past processing. In this sense, the rings on a tree trunk are records of the years, not representations of them. To this, the connectionist will most likely reply that a trained-up network can achieve some degree of generalisation to new data sets, so it is not simply a creature of its past. The record is not historical, but productive. That, as we shall see in 3.3.3, is a very moot point in many cases. But a more radical rejection of the connectionist-representations-as-records idea would be the demonstration that these acquired representations can be recruited in the service of language *production*. Imagine, for example, that a network constructed representations of noun-hood and verb-hood, of subject-hood and object-hood, and that it then went on to utilise these in the construction of sentences when fed with 'messages' in which there was represented the facts of (say) agent, transitive action, and patient together, perhaps with CSR (after Grimshaw; see 2.2.3) rules that both agents and patients can be nouns and that transitive actions can be verbs. If the network could produce sentences from messages with a novel vocabulary then something substantial would have been demonstrated about the representational status of what the hidden units are encoding. I will consider two approaches to sentence production. One of these involves a deliberate blurring of the distinction between next word prediction and next word production and the other sets up complex associations between units coding meaning and units coding form. This will, in fact, be one bread-slice of the sandwich of Part 3; for I shall return to production, discussing a more recent model of it at the very end in the light of issues raised both in the 'filling' and in 2.3. 1 will mainly be concerned with how the models fall short, but will leave the door open for future successes.

3.2: In this section, having just considered what is perhaps the most ambitious task a connectionist language modeller can undertake, I turn back to more foundational issues, issues that predate the rise of connectionist modelling by a few years. These are raised by Brian MacWhinney's 'competition model'. The central issue here is whether it is possible or advisable to reject Chomsky's famous distinction between competence and performance, replacing it with the functionalist idea that syntactic processing is performance *tout court*, along with the added assumption that performance should be explained in terms of computing statistical regularities. The section begins with the back-to-basics question of whether the rationalist assumption that linguistic performance should be explained in terms of speaker-hearers' following of known *rules* rests, as the sceptical functionalist would say it does, on quicksand. What I suggest here is that Wittgenstein's remarks about the problematic nature of rule-following explanations of behaviour do not justify any abandonment of the idea that language users, though tacitly for the most part, follow rules. Wittgenstein is frequently taken to be the functionalists' equal-and-opposite force to Chomsky's structuralism. Nonetheless, the Wittgensteinian view of rule-following as a kind of *bedrock* is an entirely sympathetic one to the Chomskyan project. I suggest that functionalist theories may suffer from the lack of such a bedrock.

Later in 3.2, I consider the strengths and weaknesses of the competition model, construed as a proto-connectionist and, later, connectionist, theory. In the first place, when it restricts itself to performance matters it clearly scores. Here I describe the MacWhinney, Leinbach, Taraban and McDonald (1989) model of learning to output the correct forms of the German definite article on the basis of information about noun number, gender and case. Next, I look at the basic proposals of the model itself in order to note, among other things, that, while eschewing generativist-style tree diagrams, movement and so forth, the competition model places great weight on the linkage between lexical cues and 'roles' (e.g., subject and object). These roles, MacWhinney insists, are learned by children before they are able to produce multiword utterances, on the basis of extra-linguistic knowledge (e.g., of figure and ground), rejecting nativist views by saying that while 'there is some prima facie evidence for such a nativist possibility, the untestability of this position makes it one that we should only accept as a last resort'. However the competition model differs from 'pure' connectionist theories in so far as the latter typically (though see the model of sentence production discussed in 3.6) do not bind cues to roles but to lexical items. These roles are variables (e.g., subject slot, fillable by any noun). For example, a transitive verb 'opens up' both subject and object roles whatever the actual transitive verb happens to be, and given any potential subject and object. And this 'opens up' my discussion of the place of variables in connectionist modelling – to be treated at length in the next section.

3.3: The guiding assumption here is the unexceptional one that modelling thought and language will necessitate computing over variables of the kind 'whatever the verb happens to be', 'whatever the noun happens to be' and binding items to these variables. I begin with a general discussion of variable binding in thoughts about individuals, and then give a rather sceptical analysis of how this might be achieved in networks, with much reference to the recent writing of Gary Marcus. With this issue in mind, I turn to what has become known as 'the algebraic infant' debate, this being the debate about whether infants, as evinced by their performance in violation-of-expectation experiments, are computing over variables at an age before they are using language. There is, predictably, linked to this the question of whether their performance can be modelled in a connectionist style. The conclusions are that 'they are' and 'it can', but that the 'algebraic' tasks on which the infants succeed are of dubious relevance to the acquisition of syntax. Indeed, the debate has needlessly polarised the field because, unsurprisingly, infants are both algebraic and statistical creatures.

3.4: Here I discuss something that must surely be *right* about the stochastic approach to syntactic development: the *utility* of stochastic processes of categorisation in the assignment of words to form classes. The work of Nick Chater and his colleagues will be discussed. I balance this discussion, however, with another connectionist research area in which Chater's name also features: modelling recursion (e.g., centre embedding). I argue that these models do not demonstrate that neural networks can model recursion in any interesting sense, by which I mean the sense in which merge is recursive. The discussion is carried forward in the context of Chomsky's (1957) original denial that recursion can be modelled in 'steady state', Markov models. Next in this section, I consider Mark Steedman's assessment of associative models of phrase structure, such as Pollack's RAAM, and his view that, while such models do not model syntactic structure itself, they might be seen as describing what must interface with universal grammar to achieve an explanatorily adequate account. I end with Steedman's proposal that we should equate *conceptual structure* with universal grammar. In other words, the non-associative structures must come from somewhere and this 'somewhere' may well be conceptual rather than Chomskyan-syntactic in nature. I then turn to the prospects for modelling conceptual structure in a connectionist style.

3.5: I begin by reprising my discussion of the rationalist view of mental structure from Part 1.1, taking 'structured' as the synecdoche for 'systematic, compositional and productive'. I discuss whether systematicity can be modelled in neural networks, with particular attention to the work of Smolensky, van Gelder, and Hadley. My conclusion will be that there may be a sense in which a kind of systematicity can be modelled, but this possibility needs to be set beside the hard fact that classical, symbol-processing models have this property *inherently*.

Finally in this section (3.5.3), I discuss a more radical, 'externalist' stance on the issue of cognitive structure owing to philosophers such as Andy Clark and Daniel Dennett. I argue that the externalist stance on conceptual structure is unconvincing in itself, and that it cannot, accordingly, be recruited by connectionists to obviate the need for *inherent* conceptual structure.

3.6: This is the second 'bread slice': the promised reprise of connectionist models of sentence production. This will enable us to reflect on some of the themes that have emerged in the main body of Part 3. This is another, more recent sentence production model owing to Franklin Chang (2002). Like the Chang *et al.* model considered in 3.1.1, it exploits what might be seen as commonalities between word prediction and word production. This complex and challenging work, however, provides the message with a qualitatively greater degree of conceptual structure than did the previous model. The basis of this structure is a distinction analogous the well-known division between the 'what' and the 'where' neural coding of objects. The 'what' is the semantic representation of the kind of entity being referred to and the 'where' is the location of the role of the word in the sentence. I briefly discuss the scope for (modest) optimism about the future which this kind of model can be seen to afford.

3.1 Do connectionist representations have 'causal roles'? Two connectionist models of production

One of the many benefits of studying connectionist models is that it forces one to examine what Chomskyan theory might be committed to with regard to innate representation. (As I said when 'taking stock' in Part 2, these days one has to *infer* the exact claims about innateness.)

Reading Elman *et al.*'s (1996) discussion of Elman's model of sentential processing by next word prediction and its implications for syntax acquisition, one would suppose that the essential nativist claim is that the form classes (noun, verb, and so forth) are innately known. (The Elman model was touched on briefly in 1.2.4, and it will shortly be described in more detail.) Two points here. In the first place, we have seen that what is emphasised in minimalism are *operations* rather than representations. What the MP makes clearer than any of the earlier Chomskyan theories is that an innate language acquisition device (LAD) is not merely an innate set of abstract categories, but rather an innate capacity for operating on lexical items – in a bottom-up style in the present case. There certainly are representational elements in LAD, but they are there to enable the operational capacities of merger, move, agree, checking, etc., to do their work. Recall, in this context, the discussion in 2.4.1. of Brody's views on MP and his view that Chomsky is mistaken in putting the explanatory weight on derivation (what I am calling operational capacities) instead of on the representational element, with move being an example of a derivation/operation and chaining (the relation between a moved item and its trace) as an example of representation. But whatever the rights and wrongs of the matter, chaining is not something independent of the operation of move, and it certainly makes no sense to say that the chains themselves are innately represented. Rather, the relation between a moved element and its trace *emerges from an operation.* Similarly, one may say that the categories of NP and VP, and so forth, do not exist as representational elements independent from the operation of merge. Recall also the proofs outlined in 2.3.3 that the outcome of merge will be a phrase whose nature is given by the target and that target projects. Thus if the target of merge is a verb what will result is a VP, which projects upwards into the sentence. It is fair, though, to say that the lexical categories are innately known at least in the sense one observes in Grimshaw's CSR model, to which Chomsky (1986) gave his blessing and which is now better known as 'semantic bootstrapping'. But this process is no more than a necessary condition for the derivation's getting under way. In short, what minimalism takes to be innate is the capacity of the LAD to perform operations on lexical items that it recognises as falling into certain categories; and *this recognition without the operational/derivational capacity is empty.* The real challenge, then, for empiricist connectionism is the modelling of an operation such as merge. (As noted earlier, we will encounter a taking-up of this challenge – modelling recursion – in 3.4.)

The second, and related, point is that if it were demonstrated that networks can correctly categorise nouns, verbs etc. on the basis of the statistical properties of the input and that a network, thus trained, could then continue its work with a new data set, we would still have to ask questions about whether it had categorised these data *as* nouns and verbs. What would our criteria be for this? Two clear candidates are: (1) making grammatically judgements on this basis and, more ambitiously, (2) producing sentences from semantic messages on this basis.

It seems to me that outputting sentences in a novel vocabulary, by utilising hidden-unit representations gleaned from stochastic regularities in a training set from messages with only a semantic structure is *the* major task for connectionist models of language acquisition. Efforts to achieve this will bookend Part 3, while the main body of Part 3 will contain discussions of both foundational and modelling issues broadly relevant the task.

The agenda here is one based on the venerable belief that a system can only be said to be achieving a form of representation significantly similar to mental representation if these putative representations have causal roles *as* representations within the system: if they affect the states of the system in virtue of their being representations of such-and-such. Accordingly, the rings in a tree trunk do not represent the years in this sense: they are records or traces of past processes, and that alone.

In 1.2.4, I outlined the sceptical view that hidden unit representations could equally well be construed as being no more than records of the network's having achieved its (input/output) correlational task. But if it could be shown that these so-called records supported grammaticality judgements and the (un-Chomskyan) 'generation' of sentences from messages then it would indeed look as if they were affecting the states of the system in virtue of their being representations of such-and-such.

I will discuss two models of sentence production, only the second of which will touch on grammaticality judgements.

3.1.1 An SRN model of production analogised to prediction

'Psycholinguistic research into language production', begins a paper by Gary Dell and his colleagues (Dell, Chang and Griffin, 1999) '– the process of translating thoughts into speech – has long been associated with connectionist models'. Connectionist models of *lexical access* have indeed been very influential. But what are the prospects for connectionist models of framing syntactic structures on the basis of lexical and semantic information alone? If connectionist networks are well placed to model production, in contrast to perceiving regularities in the data, then, as I have just argued, it is a realistic demand to make that networks which appear to have made certain crucial syntactic categorisations should be able to *utilise* this knowledge in production – as do children. So we ask what modelling in this area has achieved.

We will first consider Chang, Griffin, Dell, and Bock's (1997) model (as reported in Dell *et al.*, 1999) of sentence production. This builds upon Elman's hugely influential model of sentence comprehension, a model that is one of the undoubted success-stories of connectionist research on language acquisition (see the quote from Churchland at the beginning of Part 3). It employed a simple recurrent network (SRN) in which the activation-levels of the hidden units are copied into a bank of context units, 'frozen', and then fed into the hidden units along with the activations travelling up from the input units as the next item of data is introduced – and so on through a series of items (see Figure 3.1). Such networks enable information about previous items of data to influence the processing of subsequent items, and so any task in which predictions have to be made on the basis of a *history* of inputs can be

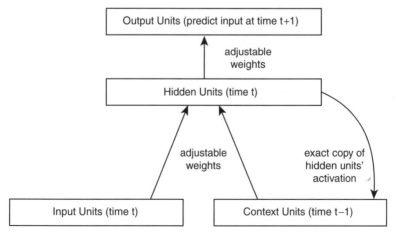

Figure 3.1 The simple recurrent network (SRN). From Dell *et al.* (1999), permission sought.

modelled. Next-word prediction can be thought of as being just this task. In the most well-known demonstration of sentence processing, Elman (1993) provided the network with a vocabulary of 23 words that could appear in sets of simple sentences (see Figure 3.2). The input and output were encoded in a *localist* fashion, meaning that a single node corresponded to a single word. The task of Elman's network was to predict a syntactically acceptable continuation of the sentence, word by word, and to maintain noun-verb number agreement. Semantic plausibility was not at issue here, only syntactic correctness. Thus, given the fragment *boys who chase dog ...* the network should predict a verb and might indeed predict one marked for a plural subject like *see* rather than *sees*. What was particularly impressive, then, about this model was that verb-noun number agreement was achieved across clausal boundaries, so that, in the previous example, agreement in number was not with the nearest noun (*dog-sees*) but appropriately with the subject of the sentence (*boys-see*). This result, seeming to demonstrate that acknowledgement of syntactic regularities can be achieved without 'wired in' syntactic categories and rules, empiricist connectionists carry before them like a banner.

The basic assumption behind Chang *et al.*'s (1997) production model was this. If an SRN is indeed capable of extracting something of the syntactic structure of sentences, as represented on its hidden/context units, in virtue of learning to predict the next word, then it might be possible to train a network with a similar architecture to *produce* 'next words'. In this case, the model's output of the previous word informs it about what the next word should be. In addition to this it will require: (a) the

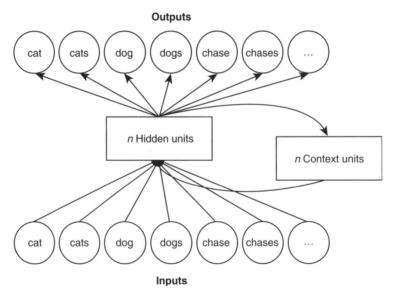

Figure 3.2 A schematic version of Elman's (1990, 1993) model of next-word prediction after Marcus (2001, p. 25, permission sought).

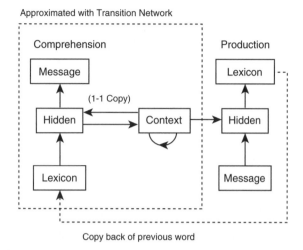

Figure 3.3 Chang *et al.*'s (1997) model of how comprehension can provide the dynamic context for production. From Dell *et al.* (1999), permission sought.

input from a prediction network's context units (the learned structure) and (b) a static semantic message. On this view, production is construed as something one learns to do in the process of comprehending, with the SRN's context units bearing the fruits of what is learned by predicting/comprehending. In its pure form then, this could become a test of whether learned syntactic representations have causal roles – as discussed above.

Figure 3.3 represents an idealised version of such an architecture. The first thing to note, however, is that there is more to sentence comprehension than the hidden-unit clusterings acquired via next-word prediction. As we shall see, Chang fully appreciated this, and accordingly idealised the work of the comprehension part of the model in terms of a so-called 'transition network' (see labelling in the Figure),[1] to which we will turn when the other features of the model have been sketched. I should also add that one of the motivations for the model was an attempt to simulate the so-called *structural priming effect*, meaning our tendency to use similar syntactic structures in successive sentences. (For example, subjects are likely to describe a picture using the syntactic frame with which they have been primed. They will describe it in the passive voice if they have been primed with passive sentences, for example.) Chang and his colleagues assumed, however, that one may regard this

---

[1] Chang *et al.* (2000) later employed a model in which the input from the comprehension sub-network was learned rather than crafted like the transition network. This model has certain shortcomings.

effect as exemplifying the kind of implicit learning involved in moving between learning to comprehend sentences and learning to produce them.

This is how the model worked. First, with the context units set to null values, and at the instigation of the message, the production side of the model would output the first word, which would then be fed into the input of the comprehension side (see Figure 3.3). This event would, in turn, update the context units' activations, which would then serve as contextual input to the production side, via the production system's hidden units, serving as the signal to produce the second word; and so on until the end of the sentence.

How was the message structured? Like the Elman prediction model, coding was localist, with one semantic atom per unit. The message itself, which remained active throughout the production of the sentence, contained a number of event roles (*agent, patient, recipient, location*) which could be associated with sets of features representing concepts such as 'girl' and 'walking'. For example, in the agent 'block' there were 18 units representing elements such as CHILD, FEMALE and UNITARY. The patient, recipient and location blocks also had 18 features coding for the *same* features. (Thus, 'dog', for example, would be represented four times each in different event role block.) The action block had 15 features, including units for WALK-ING, GIVING, and CHASING, together with the number of the arguments they were taking. For example, the message CHASE(GIRLS, DOG) would be associated with the activated agent units CHILD, FEMALE, MULTIPLE, with the activated patient nodes BARKS, ANIMAL, UNITARY, and with the action units CHASING and 2-ARGUMENT.

What determined the order in which the argument and action units fed information to the production network's hidden units? Differences in 'conceptual accessibility' were implemented in terms of one event role being more activated than others. For example, if both the agent and the patient roles had been filled in the message, an active sentence would be produced if the agent role was more highly activated than the patient role; and vice versa if the sentence was passive. Similarly, a double-object dative (e.g., 'give A B') was discriminated from a prepositional dative ('give B to A') in terms of whether the patient or the recipient role was more highly activated.

The connections between the message units and the hidden units were modifiable in virtue of the fact that the model's output layer (a single word from a vocabulary of 59) received a teaching signal and that the hidden units received inputs from the comprehension side of the model. This output layer contained single and plural nouns, verbs that had to agree in number with them, and a *PERIOD* marker at the end of the sentence.

The transition network was that which 'digested' the output of the production part and triggered next word production on that basis: it 'reflected the current state of the sentence from the perspective of the comprehension system' (ibid., p. 534). This too was coded in a localist style with a set of 10 nodes each standing for a syntactic or 'event role' category (PERIOD [boundary node], VERB, AUX, Past participle, Present participle, PREP, AGENT, PATIENT, RECIPIENT, and LOCATION). Each node had connections with modifiable weights to each hidden unit. The activations of the transition network nodes changed throughout sentence production in the following way. If the target sentence was the double-object dative 'girls give man robot' then the sentence boundary node PERIOD would initially turn on, and would remain partly on throughout sentence production. Meanwhile the message would be presented to the hidden units of the production sub-network's hidden units. If the production output then produced 'girls' the transition network had to determine that this word is either functioning as an agent (if an active sentence) or a patient (if a passive sentence). To implement this ambiguity both the AGENT and the PATIENT nodes of the transition network were turned on, while all nodes otherwise stayed half on during the production of the sentence. (Note that there was no ambiguity at all in the agent/patient assignment as far as the production system was concerned.) The AGENT and PATIENT nodes being on then signalled the production of the next word 'give'. The arrival of 'give' at the transition network subsequently turns on the VERB node. This node being on triggered the next word 'man'. This would give rise to further ambiguity in the transition network, this time with regard to whether this is a patient or a recipient; accordingly, both the PATIENT and the RECIPIENT nodes turned on. The ambiguities produced in the comprehension system (between NP event roles) contributes to error in the production system, which in turn lead to learning, by weight changes, on the production side. The authors say that this contributed to the model's success at simulating the structural priming effect.

The model was trained on 36,000 of the 175,152 sentences that could be produced with the vocabulary and range of sentence frames available. After training, the model was tested on 400 sentences, representing the proportion of sentence types in the corpus, 74 per cent of which were novel sentences. The model was correct in the next word produced 94 per cent of the time.

This model presents the following general picture of what happens in sentence production. First, a message prompts the outputting of the first word on the basis of the relative degree of activation of its elements. Next, this word re-enters the production system, feeding into the hidden units, along with syntactic information to construct the syntactic basis of the lemma for the outputted word. After this, the process continues, word by word, to the end of the sentence. To remind the reader of what 'lemma' means: this is the term coined by Levelt (1989) to refer to a lexical item plus the syntactic information about the formal linguistic liaisons into which a word can enter (see 2.4.2). In my previous discussion of this notion, in the context of Jackendoff's ideas about production, I said that the weight of evidence favours the view that lemma selection is complete before any phonological information is activated. Some studies, however, have suggested that phonological encoding begins before lemma selection is complete (e.g., Cutting and Ferreira, 1999). This latter possibility is what the Chang (1997) model seems tacitly to assume.

I will postpone the full discussion of the model till 3.1.3, when the second approach to modelling production has been described.

3.1.2 Richly associating form and meaning: Allen and Seidenberg's model

Allen and Seidenberg (1999) took up the challenge from generative grammar of simulating judgements of grammaticality. What was assumed to be involved in such judgements was the three-stage process of computing a meaning for a sentence, then passing this representation through a production system before detecting a mismatch – or not – between the sentence presented as input and the sentence that the production system produced on the basis of the computed meaning. As if we hear *The paper was full mistakes*, compute the meaning [the paper had a large number of mistakes in it], generate *The paper was full of mistakes* and note the mismatch. Our concern, however, is with the production phase.

The architecture of the network is shown in Figure 3.4. The purpose of the two layers of 15 'clean-up' units was to enable the units within each set of form (sentence) and meaning layers to interact with one another, thus allowing a more complex set of relations among the units to be encoded. The technical aspects of this process need not, however, detain us (Hinton and Shallice, 1991, for discussion). Note that there was full interconnectivity in the network, such that all 297 of the semantic units connected to all 50 units in the hidden layer which in turn were connected to all 97 words in the form layer.

The network broadly took the form of an SRN, but it differed from the one used by Elman (1990, 1993) in two principle respects. (I mention these for the sake of completeness; neither is strictly germane to our concerns.) First, the state of the units changed continuously over time in response to input from other units, rather than discretely at each timestep after an error signal as in a standard SRN. The use of this so-called 'continuous activation function' boosts the network's short-term memory of its learning history and thus enables it to utilise information about longer sequences. This continuous change was achieved by dividing the discrete steps of back propagation through time into so-called 'ticks' of a very short duration. Second, rather than having a layer of context units that store the hidden unit activations for one timestep and then feed them back to the hidden units on the next timestep, all sets of connections were continuously trainable (note from Figure 3.4 that all connections were bi-directional). This affords the following advantage. Rather than having a distinct set of units and connections for each element (e.g., each letter or word) so that the set of weights encoding knowledge about that element in one position is completely independent from the weights encoding knowledge about that same element in a different position, in this case information derived

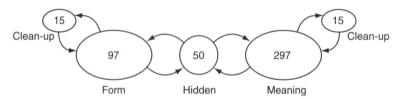

Figure 3.4 The architecture of Allen and Seidenberg's grammaticality judgement model. The arrows represent full connectivity between layers and the numbers the number of hidden units in each bank of units. Reproduced from Allen, J. and Seidenberg, M. (1999) The emergence of grammaticality in connectionist networks. In B. MacWhinney (ed.) *The Emergence of Language*, pp. 115–151. Lawrence Erlbaum, Mahwah, NJ., with permission.

from an element occurring at time t is available to the network when the element occurs at $t \pm n$.

In the simulation, the authors defined an 'exemplar' as a sequence of states, each representing either a word or the word's semantics.

> Under the version of back propagation utilised here, the network does a forward pass on the entire string (all of the words), integrating activity up, and remembering its state for the whole utterance a every tick [see previous paragraph JR]. On the backward pass, error is injected for each tick ... based on the error associated with each unit for each tick, and on what flowed backward from the following tick.

(Allen and Seidenberg, 1999, p. 128)

How was meaning represented on the 297 units? The semantics of each word was represented as a space within the total 297-dimensional space, with each unit representing a semantic feature (e.g., *house*: lodging, structure, construction, arte-fact, physical object, etc.; *he*: singular, male, animate) and with the semantic struc-ture of the utterance being represented by a series of these states. It is important to bear in mind, however, that the semantic *relations* between the elements within the utterance were not represented. That is to say the semantic roles of the arguments of a verb (e.g., agent, recipient), the linking of adjectives to nouns, the co-reference of pronouns and nouns and other relations were not represented. The 297-dimensional space did not then represent, in any sense, structured propositions, but rather a set of, albeit complex, associations between semantic features.

The form of representation was localist, so that each word was encoded by a separate unit, as in the Elman word-prediction task. The vector[2] representing each word was, then, the simple matter of a single unit being on and all other form units being off for the appropriate time steps. Each word of an utterance was activated in sequence, the 97 units representing 97 words.

Now to consider the way in which the network was trained and tested. (I will ignore the role of non-grammatical sentences in training.) The corpus consisted of ten types of sentence with 20 exemplars of each type, making 200 sentences in all. The following are some of the sentence types: reflexive agreement (e.g., *I helped myself to the birthday cake*); tag questions with pronoun agreement (e.g., *The little boy fell down, didn't he?*); 'strict subcategorisation' (e.g., *He came to my house at noon*). The exemplars were what the authors called *partial paradigms* of each basic type. For example, if the type was reflexive then there would be, in addition to the basic reflexives such as *The little boy cut himself while playing* and *An old man cut himself while shaving* there were not only further reflexives but also sentences that had been created by replacing words with other words 'that might be used gram-matically in these positions' (Allen and Seidenberg, 1999, p. 131), such as *The little boy fell while running*. The training set consisted of half of the total set of exemplars (100) and the testing set the other half.

---

[2] In mathematics, a vector is an ordered array of numbers, as is a 'representation' on an array of units in connectionist modelling.

On comprehension trials, the network's task was to compute the correct semantic representation of each word in sequence when the unit representing each word in the string was activated in sequence. The reverse had to be achieved in the production trials, computing the formal trajectory of the utterance by activating the correct units in the right sequence at the right time. In the production trials, the correctness of the word sequences for the 100 novel semantic representations was assessed in the following way. As in the comprehension task, the form vector for each word was computed at a fixed interval (11 ticks) after the semantics of a word was presented and compared against the formal target vector for that word. If the computed vector was closer to the target vector than to any other formal vector, and the activation was within 0.2 of its target, the network was considered to have produced the correct word. Correct performance for production ranged between 86 per cent and 99 per cent.

3.1.3 Assessment and prospects

These models obviously fall far short of achieving the idealised situation sketched earlier in which putatively syntactic representations, acquired by extracting statistical regularities from a data set, are employed in a sentence production model, thereby demonstrating their 'causal roles' *as* representations of that kind. In the case of the Chang model, it is the transition network, not learned representations, that provides the syntactic input, while in the case of the Allen and Seidenberg model there is, in fact, nowhere that syntactic operations mediate between lexical items and semantics. Nonetheless, these models do spur some central thoughts about what one would need to add to them to satisfy an observer who is mildly sceptical but open-minded.

I will organise this assessment around these 'thoughts', which also happen to make up the major topics in the sections in Part 3. We can ask about the models' shortcomings in terms of the assumed necessity to compute over variables (3.3), about the limited prospects for modelling recursive operations (3.4), and about the lack of structure displayed on the message/meaning side (3.5). I will end the subsection with a 'bridge' to 3.2 that is also a question: Is insisting that these *are* shortcomings merely symptomatic of being in thrall to the competence-performance distinction? Perhaps the functionalist meta-theory should be preferred, one that dissolves competence into performance.

What is it, first of all, to insist that a model of syntactic processing should contain variables? A variable, in this context, is the syntactic or semantic role that a lexical item can play in a sentence – as a noun, a subject, argument, and so forth. A role is like an empty slot fillable by any lexical item or semantic atom of the right kind. Indeed, one might say that a syntax processor should manifest the possession (not prejudging the issue of whether this possession is explicitly symbolic) of a 'recipe book' for framing sentences from thoughts made up of variables – such as $S \rightarrow NP + VP$.

Well, on the surface at least, it would appear that the Chang model does contain such roles. After all, in the message component there are event roles (agent patient, recipient, location) as well as the category of actions. Moreover, the model's transition network tagged the outputted words as being verbs, present participles, and so forth. Where then is the falling short? With regard to the message component first of all, there is scope for scepticism about whether variables were indeed being represented. Consider, for example, the semantic representation DOG. As pointed out earlier, DOG was represented four times. Recall that sets of features (e.g., BARKS, ANIMAL, UNITARY) were re-represented on each of the four event role 'blocks' – dog as agent, as patient, as recipient, as location. So one may say that there was no representation of dog *tout court*. Because the argument DOG was exhausted by its event roles there could be no unit or set of units representing DOG as distinct from any event role into which it might enter; and for this reason there was no question of binding DOG to what Chomsky calls a theta role. Conversely, there was no (say) agent role *tout court* and therefore no question of binding arguments to this, as each of the four roles came *ready-bound* to a set of 18 features, just as the actions came ready-bound to a set of 15 features. Accordingly, one would expect the model to fail a kind of generalisation task I will be discussing in 3.3. In this, the network is trained to produce sentences like 'a dog is a dog', a 'girl is a girl', and so forth, after which a new argument-word is introduced to the network (e.g., 'blicket'). Because argument words are not represented as being such the rule 'argument X is argument X' cannot be followed and so the model should fail to continue 'a blicket is a …'.

With regard to the lemma-like representation on the comprehension/transition sub-network, rather different concerns can be raised this time – about the causal significance of the labelling. Consider the case in which the word 'give' receives VERB as a marker of comprehension. As far as the model is concerned, the only causal implication of this is in enabling the production of the next word – in the sense of its timing not of its construction ('man' has already been made ready in the message). So the 'comprehension' of the word has no implications for any causal liaisons into which that type of word can enter (e.g., heading VPs, taking arguments). In fact, the main contribution of this sub-network seems to have been in feeding error (in relation to the ambiguity of representing the event role – e.g., agent/patient; patient/recipient) to the production side, leading to greater weight changes and thereby to success in modelling the structural priming effect. For the VERB to have engaged argument structures it would have been necessary to compute over variables representing verbs and arguments.

Allen and Seidenberg, meanwhile, are quite upfront about the fact that the representation of meaning in their model does not capture the propositional level because, as they say themselves:

> It is difficult, if not impossible, to represent the semantics of propositions without a system for binding arguments to roles … As a consequence, many relations like co-reference, binding, predication, and a host of others relevant to the semantics of propositions (whether semantically or syntactically represented) are not captured by this approach.
>
> (Allen and Seidenberg, 1999, p. 129)

After stressing that the 'technical' challenge of modelling variable binding presents itself in a number of other domains in addition to language (i.e., not accepting that the challenge might be a principled one), they deny that these limitations are relevant, saying that 'many grammatical and ungrammatical utterances can be

distinguished using much simpler and more local types of knowledge representations than are required for complete syntactic analysis or semantic interpretation'
(ibid., p. 129). This seems to suggest that the kind of production that is, on their
position, a sub-process of assessing whether a sentence is or is not grammatical
requires less in the way of analysis by propositional structure that does the process
of production itself.

   We now turn to recursion. This is a term that can appear to be both protean
(Johnson-Laird, 1983, for discussion of its varieties) and ineluctable. Partly for this
reason, I had little to say about it in Part 2; for it comes into clearer relief when we
consider the consequences of *denying* its relevance to comprehension and production. The fact that syntactic structures are recursive is assumed by all but the most
radically functionalist/cognitivist linguists, because the very idea of analysing sentences in terms of hierarchical structures, indeed of embedded levels intermediate
between word and sentence, whether expressed as trees or as bracketing, involves the
recursive property.

   In mathematics, hierarchies are bottom-up symbolic systems that classify entities, in which higher-level classifications are defined in terms of lower-level
classifications – a noun phrase, in terms of the lower-level presence of a noun, and
so forth. A recursive procedure, meanwhile, is one that replaces a symbol by a string
of symbols that can include that symbol (e.g., $S \rightarrow NP + V + S$; $N' \rightarrow Adj + N'$),
while this new symbol can be replaced via further applications of the recursive rule.
To say that a rule applies recursively, then, is to say that one application of it creates
the conditions necessary for its re-application. Given this, the term will also cover
the addition of lexical items without limit. This will not be mere iteration, but the
addition of items on the tree, such as adjectives, that modify items lower down. See
Figure 2.32 (p. 196) for an example of this: the recursive addition of N's. Within current Chomskyan theory, merge is a self-evidently recursive operations: A is the target of B, and the resulting A-phrase can itself become the target … and so on.
Similarly, movement, while having constraints on its operation, can be performed
without limit, e.g., in argument raising (see footnote 51, Part 2).

   As applied to production models, we would naturally expect recursion to enter in
the following way. From the message/meaning side of the model a semantic atom is
generated, say GIVE. The tagging of this atom as 'verb' should, however, require it to
be a lower-level manifestation of a higher layer of structure, VP or V', which latter
construction should in turn itself require liaisons with items on the same level (e.g.,
NP) or lower (NP if the verb is transitive). More generally, the syntactic realisation of
a semantic atom will not merely iteratively produce another syntactic atom, but will
open up a phrase that will itself be part or partner or dominator of other phrases. As
we shall discuss in 3.4, Chomsky spent some time in *Syntactic structures* (1957)
explaining why, what might be called, 'one-syntactic-atom-after-another' models of
sentence generation must necessarily fail to capture the recursive nature of English.

   From the perspective of empiricist connectionist models of production however,
it might be said that recursion is no more than a property of the descriptions
favoured by generative linguists, and that it need have no relevance to modelling of

the move from message to form. This attitude will receive some discussion, but for now: it is in virtue of syntax being recursive that one can force a strong distinction between syntactic production and prediction, one which boils down to saying that the producer always *knows* what the next stretch of structure is going to be. For the predictor, by contrast, there can only be a 'good chance' of a word's being an acceptable continuation. To illustrate, imagine that both a human predictor and a human producer were stopped in her tracks at 'The boys who … '. The producer will know at this point whether *who* is the subject ('… chase dogs') or object ('… I saw') of the relative clause; whereas the predictor will only be in a position to make a guess based on past experience with the data set. (Evincing the structural priming effect effectively equates to being a good guesser in the latter case – rather as Chang argues in fact.) Now the producer will not only know more about what is coming next because an agent will, all things being equal, know more about her next act than will an observer. Rather, it is in virtue of the producer's constructing sentences in accordance with recursive rules for forming relative clauses, and for producing wh-subject and wh-object varieties in particular, that *there is something to know*. The predictor, if it is a human predictor, may also know this, but it is only past experience with the data set that fuels the prediction of, say, a wh-subject continuation rather than an wh-object one. By the same token, an Elman SRN, lacking as it does a competence model with recursive procedures, does not 'know' at the time at which it predicts the word 'dogs' after the word 'two' that one of the words in its vocabulary will have to be marked for plural.

It would appear to be the case that having the recursive capacity requires computing over variables. It is surely impossible to implement a recursive rule without being able to represent something like 'another of the type X'.

I now consider the way in which the message/meaning component of these models is regarded. Both models share the assumption that the molecular level is constituted in terms of atoms being simultaneously active. They 'come on' together; although in the Chang model the relative amount of activation will determine the actual order in which they arrive at the production sub-network. As we have seen, in the latter model there are 'agent blocks', 'patient blocks', and so forth. The pressing question is, however, whether one can accept that in a message such as CHASE (GIRLS, DOG), what might be called the structure of the proposition is being represented, or whether all we really have are three meaning atoms being above threshold in such a way that they will be outputted in the order appropriate to the language. What does 'structure' mean here? It means whatever guarantees that in a message like the one above it is indeed A that is the chaser and B the chasee. (In a classical, Turing-like system this is simply guaranteed by the way the symbols are written down, with Fodor's LOT being the mental analogue of this.) This must be something 'prior to the arrival' of the thought *in English*, so it must do more than simply guarantee that A is outputted before B. As we shall see in 3.5, Fodor and Pylyshyn (1988) employed the expression 'being in construction with' to capture the fact that the semantic atoms must liase with one another in the right kind of way. Consider, in illustration, a way of *not* being in construction. The system represents independently:

GIRLS – in the agent block, high activation
CHASE – in the action block, moderate activation
DOG – in the patient block, low activation

What can here guarantee that it is indeed the girls doing the chasing? Who is to say that this is more similar to somebody thinking about the dishes of her favourite meal, with some being more favoured than others, than to framing a proposition? The modeller might say that this guarantee comes directly from GIRLS being in the relevant block. But labelling a block as 'agent' does not of itself make the features thereby grouped behave as agents, so long as 'agent' lacks the causal powers of an agent within the system. Its only relevant causal role here is of having a changeable activation which can determine when it is outputted. As long as agent is not a variable – as discussed – little more could be done.

This idea of being 'in construction with' comes into somewhat clearer focus when we consider how semantic atoms can be related to each other by logical operators such as &, v, and →. In 'A & B', 'A v B', and 'A → B', both A and B are in play, but each is in construction with the other in a quite different way. It might be said, in answer, that one of the early success stories of connectionism was the modelling of the non-linear rule of 'exclusive or' (XOR[3]), so the sceptical point misfires. But what is at stake here is not performing disjunction on a data set, but representing two elements of a proposition as being disjunctively, or conjunctively etc., related to each other. For Fodor and for many others, this not only requires the constituents to be entities represented by their *sui generis* forms ('shapes' for Fodor), but also that the system should contain an operation that computes disjunction for any fillers of the twin roles.

While Chang's model of semantic representation makes some gestures, at least, towards structuring the message input, Allen and Seidenberg, as we have seen, frankly admit the barriers to

> representing phrasal- and propositional-level relations among words such as *subject of predicate* or *object of verb*. Although we assume that a good deal of knowledge concerning the formal expression of these higher level structures is also *emergent from form-meaning pairings available in the listener's environment*, the technical challenges involved in modelling such knowledge are considerable.
>
> (Allen and Seidenberg, 1999, p. 129; emphasis added)

Finally, I flag the issues to be discussed in the very next section: whether the kind of sceptical points raised so far about the two production models reflect no more than an inappropriately reverential attitude to the Chomskyan notion of competence in particular and to traditional linguistic analyses of sentential structure in general. Why not jettison the assumption that linguistic theory, as a theory of speaker-hearer knowledge, will tunnel forward from one direction and meet the performance tunnel of empirical psycholinguistics and connectionist modelling

---

[3] Respond to A, respond to B, but don't respond to A and B together.

coming from the other. The two tunnels will miss each other because they are not advancing along the same trajectory; and a tunnel built from performance machinery alone can work through into the light. As the passage italicised in the previous quotation from Allen and Seidenberg implies, forging the basic linkages between meaning and form may depend upon no more than our ability to pick up information about how two kinds of cues are related – an assumption at the heart of the preconnectionist 'competition model', as we shall see.

One thing that justifiably fuels this view is Chomsky's own attitude to the relevance of his theory to adult and child psycholinguistics. The attitude is at once ambiguous and lofty. As Allen and Seidenberg remind us, in *The minimalist program*, Chomsky stresses, as he has always stressed, that his theories may have little bearing on psycholinguistic accounts of performance: 'The ordering of operations [as described in MP] *is abstract*, expressing postulated properties of the language faculty of the brain, *with no temporal interpretation implied*' (1995, p. 380; emphasis added). In which case, Allen and Seidenberg argue, there need be no objection to a performance-led approach to language acquisition that treats competence theories as *idealised descriptions* of performance rather than theories of what underlies it.

Elsewhere, Seidenberg is still more explicit in his rejection of competence models. In Seidenberg and MacDonald (1999, pp. 571–573) he states that knowing a language should not be equated with knowing a grammar but that, rather, the *functionalist* assumption should be adopted that knowledge of a language is something that is acquired as an emergent property of learning to perform 'the primary communicative tasks of comprehension and production' as suggested by proto-connectionist models of language development like the competition model of Bates and MacWhinney (1982). In learning to do this, the child exploits statistical regularities in the input of the kind that simply cannot be countenanced in competence models, adding that 'the appropriate way to assess our models is in terms of terms of people's performance, not the idealised characterisation of linguistic knowledge that is competence grammar' (ibid., p. 573).

3.2 Trying to replace competence with statistical regularity: the limits and the uses of cue learning

We can, if we so wish, describe the performance of a connectionist model in terms of the following 'rules' (e.g., 'copy activations from this timestep'; 'reduce discrepancy between target and output'), because *any* process can be made to fall within this descriptive ambit. The rule-following to be found in competence models is, however, a different matter. In this case, the speaker-hearer's behaviour is not only described in terms of certain rules but is taken to be tacitly *guided* by them: rules are being *followed*. That we have linguistic intuitions about grammaticality is one of the considerations that differentiates rule-following from producing behaviour merely describable by rules. Another is the internal coherence and step-by-step rationales of each rule (e.g., the reasons to be given why violations of subjacency sound wrong). While a central question here is whether any other rule-bound account could capture the behaviour. If the aim is explanatory adequacy then the answer is assumed to be No.

But is this still the case in MP? Is Chomskyan explanation still in terms of rule following? John Searle (2002) thinks not. This is with some justification, for recall the following quotations from Chomsky *et al.* (2002), apropos P & P, given at the beginning of 2.3:

> ... cutting the Gordian knot: namely *eliminate rules* and eliminate constructions altogether because there aren't any rules and constructions. There is no such thing as VP in Japanese or the relative clause in Hungarian. Rather, there are just extremely general principles like 'move anything anywhere' under fixed conditions that were proposed ... (emphasis added).

But what is being rejected here is not the very idea that competence is constituted in part by rule following – performing operations guided by certain principles. The notion of rule following being rejected here involves the reification of 'idiolect'-specific regularities ('VP in Japanese or the relative clause in Hungarian') as if they were explanatory principles. As Chomsky goes on to say: 'they are a kind of taxonomic artefact. They are like "terrestrial mammal" or something like that. "Terrestrial mammal" is a category, but it is not a biological category'.

Well, Chomsky is not arguing against the very idea of rule any more than he thinks that a biologist should reject the notion of category. It's a matter of choosing the right explanatory level.

In objecting to Searle's position, the MIT philosopher Sylvain Bromberger (2002) says that the term 'rule' can indeed be used to characterise the operations of both pre-MP and post-MP competence theories. He suggests, though, that because the term is freighted with meanings (some of which fuel Searle's interpretations of Chomsky) it should be replaced by the term *mapping*. He writes that one of Chomsky's main assumptions has always been that 'each hierarchical structure [in a derivational sequence] is related to its predecessor by a mapping which satisfies specifiable (though by no means obvious) universal conditions'. So the operations of merge and move play the role of mappings.

In any event, one man's mapping is, in this context, another man's rule following. I will use the term 'rule' in what follows because its application extends beyond linguistics, and so it can focus a discussion of foundational questions about competence theories in general – in relation to the connectionist enterprise. I take rule following to mean an agent's performing (tacitly or otherwise) operations guided by a principle with a rationale.

Opponents of competence models deny that explanation can take the form of unearthing the rules being followed – as one reveals a bedrock. Is this justified?

3.2.1 Competence and rule following

We have, at this point, reached an arena of such fundamental divergence that it is necessary to step back for a little, before returning to the discussion of connectionist developmental theories and models, and consider two questions:

1) Why do rationalists care so passionately about the competence-performance distinction?

2) What, if any, is the philosophical justification for rejecting explanation by competence theories – understood as theories of the rules being followed by individuals?

With regard to 1, it might be said that, for the rationalist, we do not look only at what people do, at their performance, to assess whether they are 'rational animals'. On this criterion the answer would probably be that we are blank underachievers. Around 80 per cent to 90 per cent of university students, for example, fail the Wason Selection Task,[4] suggesting that even people of above average intelligence do not know the first thing about hypothesis-testing: that one should test the validity of a rule by seeking disconfirming instances of it rather than confirming instances. But from the rationalist perspective, what is a more central question than whether or not participants choose the right card is how they respond to correction of their erroneous choices. As anyone who has run undergraduate practical classes on this topic will attest, while there are always a handful of stubborn characters who refuse to accept correction, for whatever reason, most people realise that they have made a mistake and appreciate where they went wrong. When they clap their hands to their heads and or give an embarrassed grimace they are not 'performing' but coming to a realisation – a mental process that may lead to improved performance *but does not reduce to it.* To undergo this, individuals need to possess a set of interdependent concepts (of a rule, of logical truth and error, of evidence) which we might think of as their 'competence'. To approach the task as a logical task at all, this competence needs to be in place. And part and parcel of this correction process is the notion of *doing the right kind of thing but not doing it well enough.* On this conception, human rationality consists in the possession of a set of *intuitions and goals* that together constitute rationality itself, part of which consists in knowing the inevitability of falling short in performance.

The parallel with syntax is not exact; but it is real. To know a language involves having linguistic intuitions, and to be a speaker of the language is to guide one's productions in accordance with rules that are either only thinly present in consciousness or not present at all. A supporter of rationalist linguistics does not have to subscribe to any particular theory of competence, but she does have to subscribe to the view that comprehension and production are not performances *tout court* but manifestations of formal competence complexly and indirectly glimpsed in behaviour. This is of course a dogma. The price of ignoring it however, as I argued in 2.4.1, may be its becoming impossible to explain how we operate with the idea of sentences as being an accurate (or inaccurate) expressions of our thoughts.

---

[4] Subjects are shown four cards marked (say) A, K, 4, and 7. The are told that each card has a digit on one side and a letter on the other and that they must turn over the fewest number of cards to test the truth of 'If there is a vowel on one side then there is an even number on the other side'. The most common response is that A and 4 should be turned over. 'A and 7' is thought to be (but see Stenning, 2002) the correct answer.

If the framing of sentences did not involve rule following, and if instead sound streams were mapped to thoughts (structured or otherwise) in virtue of implicit associations between their elements, there would – so runs the dogma – be no sense in which speakers could be said to be, or could think themselves to be, succeeding or failing to say what they meant – in the sense of framing the right armature for the thought.

We now come to the second issue – 2: the philosophical grounds for rejecting competence explanations of the Chomskyan kind, explanations that depend upon the idea of language use as rule following. This rejection certainly seems to have a good pedigree – a Wittgensteinian one. I will argue, however, that Wittgenstein's position on rule following is compatible – *pace* Chomsky himself – with competence-based explanations.

In his discussions of rule following, Wittgenstein's target was the pervasive assumption that understanding (of a rule or of the meaning of a word) should be identified with a representation coming before the mind's eye together, perhaps, with an ineffable feeling – a mental event with a duration – that was the process of understanding the rule or word in terms of that representation. Indeed he said that 'understanding is not a mental process' (Wittgenstein, 1953, §, 154). This was by way of denying that it was a timeable event that we have to undergo in order to achieve the state of having understood. He denied, indeed, that we should identify mental process with ineluctably private, subjective states; and this because meaning and the correct application of rules were taken by him to be fixed intersubjectively not subjectively. This is nothing if not a pragmatist position and one would need a very capacious mind indeed to be both a Chomskyan and a Wittgensteinian about language. But it does not, I shall argue, provide comfort for those who look for reasons to regard language understanding as being something other than rule understanding.

Wittgenstein gave the example of a pupil who has appeared to understand a rule as 'add 2 to the previous number' and so continues 10, 12 ... 96, 98, and so forth. We are tempted to think, then, that his understanding consists in his having before the mind's eye something like 'n + 2' and that understanding the rule is constituted by following this representation. However, it so happens that after 1,000 the pupil continues '1004, 1008, 1012 ... ' explaining that he interpreted the rule to mean 'add 2 up to 1,000 and then 4'. The essential difficulty being identified here is that if all there was to understanding a rule were entertaining the correct representation of that rule then it is open to the individual to interpret it idiosyncratically: representations cannot fix their interpretation as such and such and that alone. The solution to this dilemma might appear to be to adopt an entirely mechanistic conception of rules, in which the formula is regarded as *causing* the correct mathematical response without the need for any interpretive intermediary. What is wrong with this solution, says Wittgenstein (*ibid*, § 193), is that it requires us to regard the machine as if it were providing a kind of necessity to the interpretation, whereas what machines provide is high probability. (The analogy with connectionist 'associative engines' is real enough here.) Real machines, as opposed to the ones that inhabit our metaphors, can malfunction because there is always the possibility of parts 'bending, breaking off, melting, and so on'. The machine analogy fails in two ways: as applied to real machines, it puts successful rule following at the mercy of the merely physical (confusing 'the hardness of a rule' with 'the hardness of a material'[5]) thus robbing it of its psychological character; whereas if we idealise the machine as an impossibly perfect one (the machine as abstract program: *die Maschine als Symbol*[6]) we fail to leave open the possibility that rule following can indeed go wrong; just as if 2 + 2 can never be given the answer '5'. (One may consider the analogy with the idealised Turing machine here.)

Wittgenstein seemed, then, to be placing us upon the horns of a dilemma (either up-for-grabs interpretable representations or the representation as strict causal determiner), but without his having any positive thesis about the individual psychology of following a rule. Be that as it may, it is clear what he thought it was psychologically *not*: enjoying some, perhaps introspectable, mental content that constituted the following of a rule as being one way or another.

It might be objected that the apparent emphasis on introspection here robs Wittgenstein's point of any relevance to Chomskyan rules – which are supposed to be followed *tacitly*. But the conscious status of the represented rule is really something of a red herring. What is more central is the division being here assumed between the agent as a kind of rational homunculus and the represented rule, with the latter being that by which the rational homunculus guides its behaviour. The same kind of point would apply – I shall at least argue – to the subjacency principle. The next issues to be covered will tend to reinforce this point.

I now turn to a highly influential, though certainly controversial, interpretation of Wittgenstein's position owning to Saul Kripke. Kripke (1982) argued that Wittgenstein was denying the existence of *any psychological fact of the matter* about how a rule is being interpreted by an individual. It is not merely that an individual's beliefs about the rule he is following can be wrong, but they are not even in the running for truth. Indeed, Kripke takes Wittgenstein's remarks to express a kind of scepticism similar to that expressed by Hume when he famously denied that causal connections possess a 'necessity' beyond a history of prior connections; so that in Kripke's Wittgenstein there is the denial that an individual episode of rule-following has *any* meaning outside of a history of past rule-following behaviour. Accordingly, in Kripke's own example, a subject, who has been using the '+' sign correctly thus far, one day gives the answer '5' to the sum '68 + 57?' because up till now he has been interpreting what we call 'plus' as 'quus' which means giving the answer 5 to all additions beyond 57. Indeed, he interprets Wittgenstein as denying that there is anything is our past arithmetical intentions that fixes 'plus' rather than a 'quus': 'First [the sceptic] questions whether there is *any* fact that I mean plus not quus, that will be his sceptical challenge. Second he questions whether I should be so confident that I should answer "125" rather than "5"' (Kripke, 1982, p. 11; original emphasis).

---

[5] Wittgenstein (1956) § 87.

[6] Wittgenstein (1953) § 193.

It certainly *seems*, then, that Kripke-Wittgenstein would thereby have reasons for denying the very possibility of explaining linguistic performance in terms of following sets of rules whose existence we deduce from analysis of human grammar itself and from facts about linguistic creativity and the way in which language is acquired (e.g., not by teaching). Although Kripke insists that neither he himself nor the Wittgenstein of his reading has any objection to the competence-performance distinction itself but only to the *dispositional* (as opposed to *normative*) conception of 'competence'[7] (ibid., pp. 30–31; original emphasis) he does go on to say that if Wittgenstein's standpoint is accepted:

> the notion of 'competence' will be seen in a light radically different from the way it implicitly is seen in much of the literature in linguistics. For *if* statements attributing rule following are neither to be regarded as stating facts, nor to be thought of as *explaining* our behaviour, it would seem that the *use* of the ideas of rules and competence in linguistics needs serious reconsideration, even if these notions are not rendered *meaningless.*

Chomsky quotes this passage himself and spends the best part of a chapter (in *Knowledge of Language*, 1986) on an attempted refutation of Kripke. But (a) Kripke's reading of Wittgenstein may well be open to question, and (b) Kripke himself does not follow through on this combative stance (taken up early in his book).

With regard to (a), a number of philosophers have questioned Kripke's reading (e.g., Blackburn, 1984; McDowell, 1984). Just a few words about McDowell's un-Kripkean Wittgenstein in particular. McDowell shows that in some places (1953, § 201 in particular) Wittgenstein actually argues explicitly against the Kripke reading of his position (see Russell, 1987c). But what then do we say about the horns of the interpretation-versus-mechanism dilemma on which Wittgenstein impales us? For McDowell, these horns are pointing to *a conception in which rule following is 'unthinking' while not being mechanical.* When we follow a rule there is no possibility of our justifying our practice, because the following of a rule is a kind of psychological *bedrock*: 'If I have exhausted the justifications I have reached bedrock, and my spade has turned' (Wittgenstein, 1953, § 217), while a little later he says 'When I obey a rule I do not choose. I obey the rule blindly' (§ 219). McDowell takes Wittgenstein to be making a strongly anti-reductionist point about rule following: anti reduction to the neural and to the social (Russell, 1987c, p. 30). This position has become known as quietism (Smith, 1998) because it suggests that we can expect no explanations of rule following in terms of something beneath that bedrock. For McDowell's Wittgenstein then, explanations in terms of competence theory promise a kind of explanatory terminus and autonomy.

I now turn to (b) and to the issue of whether even Kripke-Wittgenstein is really placed in such firm opposition to Chomskyan ideas. We find the following passage in Kripke (1982, p. 97; emphasis added) in which he says that generative linguistics

---

[7] That is to say, competence encompasses the rules we should be following, not our dispositions to behave in a certain way when framing or comprehending sentences.

inasmuch as it explains all my utterances by my 'grasp' of syntactic and semantic rules generating infinitely many sentences and interpretations, seems to give an explanation of the
type Wittgenstein would not permit. For the explanation is not in terms of actual 'performance' as a finite (and fallible) device. It is not a purely causal (neuropsychological) explanation [see above on the mechanistic view of rule following JR] … *On the other hand, some
aspects of Chomsky's views are very congenial to Wittgenstein's conception.* In particular,
according to Chomsky, highly species-specific constraints – a form of life – lead the child to
project, on the basis of exposure to a limited corpus of sentences, a variety of new sentences
for new situations. There is no a priori inevitability in the child going on the way he does,
other than this is what the species does.

These last two sentences are all-important. Kripke is interpreting – as one is free
to do – Wittgenstein's famous phrase about 'forms of life' (*Lebensformen*) as referring
not to social life only, but to biological endowment. Like Wittgenstein, Chomsky
does not explain our ability to follow linguistic rules in terms of past learning causing us to have before the mind's eye a representation whose content exhausts what it
means to continue following the rule correctly; *and this looks like empiricism in any
event.* Neither does Chomsky reduce rule-following to a necessity-infused mechanism; and note that 'virtual conceptual necessity' does not refer to the stages or
'mappings' in the derivation, but to the existence and nature of the C_{HL}/C-I interface. Indeed he leaves elbow-room, as we have seen (end of 2.3.4), for the mysterious process of choice in how we express our thoughts. Rather, he insists that the
ability to 'go beyond the information given', must be grounded in the human nature
that we bring to the learning process. On a relaxed conception of 'form of life' this,
as Kripke points out, is not at odds with the Wittgensteinian position.

Thus, while the differences between Wittgenstein and Chomsky are real and deep,
in ways illustrated in Part 1, those opposed to competence-based theories of human
language will not find Wittgensteinian arguments waiting on the shelf. What's more,
one might regard the notion of competence as Chomsky's 'bedrock' – that against
which our spade turns.

I now turn to a functionalist theory of syntactic development that places performance above competence. It is one that predates the rise of connectionism and that
eventually came close to merging with it.

3.2.2 Syntactic development as cue learning: the 'competition model'

In their *competition model*, Brian MacWhinney and Elizabeth Bates (1982, 1987,
1989; MacWhinney, 1987) concern themselves exclusively with mappings between
forms and functions. By functions they intend the elements that make up an act
of communication – picking out a topic, referring to the feminine gender, pluralising etc – and by forms they intend surface elements such as a pre-verbal slot, being
preceded by an definite article, having the suffix '-*e*'. One central insight of
the model is that there is a many-to-many mapping between these two levels (many
forms mapping to one function, many functions mapping to a single form) and
that there is competition between the sets of mappings both in the evolution of
a particular language and in the development in the child. (Details of this process
will follow shortly.) Different languages will, of course, resolve this competition in
different ways.

In the pre-connectionist manifestation of the model (Bates and MacWhinney, 1982), the central concern was with how different languages realise the outcomes of competition between surface forms and semantic/communicative functions. They outline the six 'basic tenets' motivating their approach; and we shall consider four of these. Tenet three states that there will tend to be two kinds of linguistic outcome from the pressures described in tenet 1 (resulting from the 'limitations' of the channel) and those described in tenet 2, resulting from 'informational' pressures on the channel (semantic-cognitive, pragmatic-attentional, social-motivational). They name these two outcomes 'dividing the spoils' and 'peaceful coexistence'. In the first place (spoils-dividing), each 'sector' of the surface form will receive its own set of mappings, with there being one informational function for one signal. For example, case role relations may be marked by word order exclusively, while pragmatic information about agents and patients will be marked by stress. Conversely, in a highly inflected language, case role will be assigned by morphological marking and pragmatic information will be conveyed via word order. Alternatively, ('peaceful coexistence') the language will reflect 'certain statistical regularities in the discourse in which two roles are shared by the same element a very large proportion of the time' (Bates and MacWhinney p. 193). For example, a language may mark *both* agent and topic by a surface device that is conventionally called subjectivation. Meanwhile, passivisation will evolve to deal with the exceptional cases where the agent is not the topic. They mention Japanese and Tagalog as examples of the divide-the-spoils solution. In Japanese, the topic is more clearly marked than the agent, whereas in Tagalog[8] the opposite is true. English is an example of a peaceful-coexistence kind of solution (another is Lisu[9]) in the sense that agent and topic are typically merged, though when the two fail to overlap it is agency that tends to dominate in the assignment of subjecthood. Lisu, on the other hand, expresses the opposite tendency of having topic determine subjecthood when the agency and topic are not correlated.

Tenet 6 ('vestigial solutions') covers those cases where conventional surface forms have lost sight of their original 'motivational base', meaning those aspects of syntax to which the term 'arbitrary' can be applied. Consider, by way of illustration, the contrast between inherent case (e.g. the dative; see p 150) and gender marking in languages like French and German. The marking of case clearly has a functional motivation, telling us – say – who was the recipient; whereas the fact of 'knife', 'fork' and 'spoon' each having different genders in German has no discernable functional relevance. The gender marking is, then, 'vestigial'.

I mention these foundational assumptions of the model at this point because they illustrate quite plainly the contrast between what it means to be a performance-based account and what it means to be a competence-based account. The contrast is, in fact, quite a symmetrical one in the following sense. It is fair to say that tenet 1

---

[8] Spoken in the Phillipines.

[9] Spoken in Thailand.

(limits on the channel) can be regarded as doing the same kind of work as the minimalist programme's A–P external system, while tenet 2 (informational pressure) corresponds (if we can ignore the pragmatic emphasis) to the external system of C–I. Meanwhile, Tenet 6 (vestigial solutions) covers, more or less, what Chomsky intended by 'uninterpretable features'.

The divergence, though, is glaring. The performance-based theory has, *for the rationalist*, a vacuum at its very heart: an A–P component is wired *straight* to a C–I component with no language faculty playing a role 'between' these two, nor in their framing and motivation. (It is not so much *Hamlet* without the Prince as *Hamlet* in which the characters do nothing more than exchange Pokémon cards with one another.) That is to say, the rationalist would continue, the competition model attempts something *other* than an explanation of how an individual frames sentences from thoughts and of what children need to know about language in general to learn a particular language. Rather, it describes how languages differ in terms of six tenets and describes those features of learning a particular language that yield to such a description, doing so in the language of metaphorical associationism. Furthermore, it simply declines to consider the possibility of universal forms of syntactic knowledge. 'Any model,' Bates and MacWhinney (1987, p. 158) write, 'that rests exclusively on universalist principles will fail to provide veridical accounts of language acquisition' – an assertion that seems beside the point in the light of Chomsky's concern with parameter-setting.

But in fact, the competition model cannot be dismissed in this way. In a little while I will discuss some more recent proposals from MacWhinney (1987) which complicate the distinction between generative and performance-based accounts and explicitly acknowledge the senses in which the competition model is more than a kind of metaphorical connectionism. Before doing so, however, I shall describe a connectionist model published by MacWhinney and his colleagues (MacWhinney *et al.*, 1989) that illustrates just what *can* be explained on this approach.

The rationalist is forced to acknowledge that some of the achievements of the language learning child take the form of cue learning rather than rule learning. Take the 'vestigial' system of German gender. Those of us who were obliged to learn this at school did so 'explicitly' (i.e., by staring at a printed sheet, panicking, then testing one another before the lesson began). German children, by contrast, must be utilising subtle and probabalistic cues to a noun's gender. These cues are phonological (e.g., masculine nouns tend to begin with umlauts) morphological (e.g., words ending with -*ion* tend to be feminine) and semantic (e.g., superordinates like *Tier* – 'animal' – are neuter). Similar considerations apply to pluralisation. There are eight different forms of pluralisation in German and which one is applied depends probabalistically upon morphology, gender and animacy. With regard to case, there are both suffix cues and prepositional cues (e.g. all words preceded by *mit* – 'with' – are dative). Armed with these facts, we can consider how a German child might learn to use the appropriate form of the definite article. There are, in German, six different forms for 'the' – *der, die, das, den, dem, des*, with noun gender, number and case determining the form.

From the perspective of the competition model, the child is learning to relate semantic functions (natural gender, number and inherent case) to surface forms (markings on the noun for grammatical gender, form of definite article, markings for case). It is more fruitful in the present context, however, to think in terms, not of competition between forms and semantic functions, but rather competition between surface *cues* (such as *-ion*) and linguistic *categories* (word classes and syntactic classes). Given this, let us consider the two kinds of competition – between categories for a cue and between cues for a category. In the first place, the cue *-e* can be a marker for the categories of (non-semantic) feminine gender, plurality and for the first-person singular present on verbs. Conversely, many cues can map to the same category: *-ie*, *-ung*, *-ie* and natural gender all map to the category of feminine gender. This means, among other things, that the informational value of a cue will depend not only on how reliably it predicts that category but also upon its strength of association to *other* categories.

In the competition model, cue acquisition and cue strength depend upon the following four properties of cues: detectablility (e.g. spotting the difference between *den* and *dem*), frequency, availability, and reliability. With regard to the final two, *-e* is a more available cue for feminine gender than is *-nis* – and therefore likely to be acquired earlier. Finally, a cue may be salient, frequently encountered and highly available without necessarily being reliable. Thus, while *-e* is highly likely to indicate a feminine noun, this ending can also be found on the masculine noun *der Junge* (boy) and the neuter noun *das Ende* (end).

The first network's architecture is illustrated in Figure 3.5. From this it can be seen that its task was to output one of the six possible definite articles when German nouns were presented to the input units together with cues of the relevant type. There were 102 nouns in the training set, with 305 tokens representing their relative frequencies in the real world. Each node on the input layer represented a single cue. The 'lexical disambiguation cues' in the Figure refer to the codings used to discriminate individual nouns from one another, with 4 from a possible 11 input nodes being turned on. Each of the 102 nouns was thereby given a unique feature code. Needless to say, the network could learn the training set, because connectionist nets can learn *any* mapping; and it did so with 100 per cent accuracy. The proof of the pudding, however, was whether the weights thus trained could successfully generate definite articles for novel inputs. It was able to do this with a high degree of accuracy both for the familiar words in novel case contexts (92 per cent accuracy) and for novel words (62 per cent accuracy). What's more, the model mimicked some of the characteristics of flesh-and-blood German children's learning, showing, for example, early acquisition of nominatives, delayed acquisition of genitives, early omission of the article (i.e., none of the six possible outputs reaching activation threshold at test), and early use of the *-e* cue. A later network (see Figure 3.6) that received less 'hand-crafting' of the inputs (gender and number being coded only by raw phonological form) actually outperformed the first one in generalisation.

Does such a result really lend credence to performance-based, as opposed to competence-based models? At first blush it would indeed appear to be showing the competition model in action. On more mature reflection however, it might be

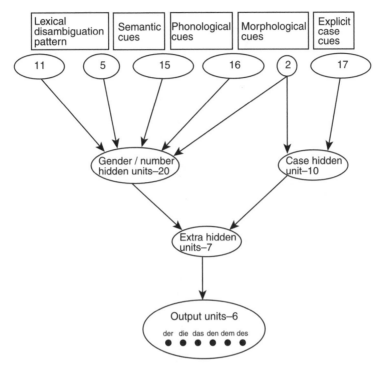

Figure 3.5 McWhinney *et al.*'s (1989) first model of the German definite article learning; redrawn from p. 264 of the paper (permission sought).

thought that the model was not mapping functions to forms or cues to categories, so much as mapping perceptual forms to perceptual forms: the input forms of phonological features, plus case cues, to the output forms of *der, die, das,* etc. That is to say, from the point of view of the network – from the point of view of *any* network (see section 3.4) – the inputs and the outputs were perceptual features. Accordingly, while the networks can be described in such a way that they appear to be expressing a substantive distinction between perceptual elements (phonological) and functional ones ('semantic' and 'case' units) and a distinction between input cues and output forms, the network was in fact mapping combinations of many input forms to only six output forms. The fact that the later network was more successful than the first one serves to reinforce this point: the more perceptual information available on the input units the better, because perception-based learning is what is really being done.

To say this is not to disparage the relevance of this model to language development, in the sense of those aspects of linguistic development that can be explained in broadly associative terms. Indeed, just about the only way we can conceive of

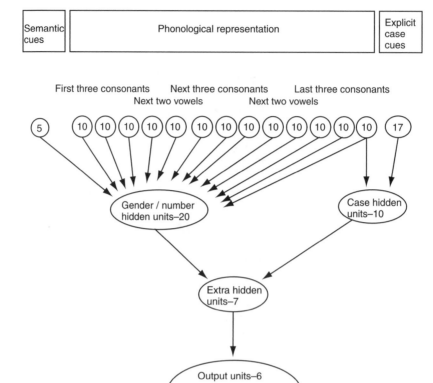

Figure 3.6 McWhinney *et al.*'s (1989) second model of the German definite article learning (simplified). The top bank of squares represents the broad nature of the input unit representations. (Redrawn from p. 271 of the paper, permission sought.)

learning the correct forms of the German definite article is as an associative process, because what is being learned is associations between sounds and sounds (*Spiegel* will suggest *der* and Reingold will suggest *das* even to non-speakers of German) and sounds and sentential contexts (*dem* will come to mind as the correct form between *mit* and *Spiegel*). But this is not 'learning language': it is learning *German*. For the rationalist, just as my classmates and I were able to learn German because we already knew a language, so German children are in a position to learn the different sounds of the definite article because they already know what a noun phrase is, what case is, and so forth. Coding case, for example, on notional input units of the German child's mind is to assume that the child's mind is already a syntactic, symbol-using, and rule-following device. In short, the associative performance rests upon a bedrock of competence. That is what the rationalist would say.

And the empiricist would say 'not so fast'. To argue in this way is to *take it for granted* that rule learning as the competence theorist regards it is what syntax acquisition essentially is, with the associative, rote-learning aspect being placed beyond that pale. It is to assume that the child needs innate knowledge of rules qua 'mappings' (see comments by Bromberger above), such as merge and move, in order to learn local idiolect-style 'rules' such as, in Chomsky's example, how to form relative clauses in Hungarian. The rote-cum-associative learning of the kind just described is hived off to another system. But who is to say that this rule-versus-rote/associative distinction holds in reality? Where are the foundational arguments and the evidence against the possibility that it is associations 'all the way down'?

And so we approach territory that will be familiar to many readers: the dispute over whether the rule-rote distinction applies to learning the English past tense, with 'stem + ed' being the putative rule and strong verb forms being those whose learning yields naturally to an associative account (Pinker, 1999a, for a full review). Because this issue has already been well, if not hyper-, ventilated in recent years, I will not dwell on it. I will though mention in passing another domain in which it arises, because it is one that has a bearing on the discussion of specific language impairment in 2.6. Recall the demonstration by van der Lely and Christian (2000) that G-SLI children are more prone than are control children to produce erroneous compound nouns such as **rats-eater*. The explanation for this difficulty favoured by van der Lely is one in terms of the children's failing to execute the rules expressed in the 'level ordering' theory of Kiparsky (1982). Recall that the assumption behind level ordering theory is that singular nouns like *rat* and *mouse* are stored in the lexicon, as are irregular plurals like *mice*. It is only further 'downstream', at Kiparsky's 'Level 3', that regular plurals like *rats* are formed. Crucially, Kiparsky claims that the rule governing the formation of compound nouns is applied at Level 2 – *before* the pluralisation of regulars, which takes place at level 3.

Recently however, Haskell, MacDonald and Seidenberg (2003) have called this idea into question, motivated by the thought that the constraints against compounds such as **rats-eater* may be probabilistic and applying to surface forms rather than rule-bound and applying within hidden principles of generation. The probabilistic claim certainly has some plausibility given that there are exceptions to Kiparsky's generalisations (*awards ceremony, weapons inspectors*, and many others). (Kiparsky explains such anomalies in semantic terms.)

To examine this possibility, Haskell *et al.* ran both behavioural studies of modifier acceptability and corpus analyses. On the basis of these they came to the view that it was *phonological* information that tends to determine whether words are judged to be acceptable as modifiers: the /s/ ending was blocking it. For example, (1) semantically singular but phonologically plural nouns like *scissors, pants*, and *pliers* were dispreferred as modifiers, while (2) nonce words with plural phonology (like *fants*) were also dispreferred as modifiers. The authors employed a neural network to test this idea. First, the network, (whose architecture is shown in Figure 3.7), was trained to derive a measure of how adjective-like a word was by using phonological information alone. The resulting model was then tested on the kinds of words given to the human subjects, for them to judge acceptability as modifiers – with similar results.

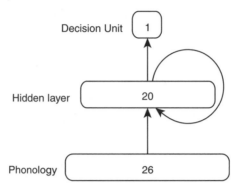

Figure 3.7 The architecture of Haskell *et al*'s. 'adjective acceptability' network.

For example, the model gave broadly similar 'adjective' ratings to nonce words and fillers as did the human subjects.

For the empiricist connectionist, the moral of stories of this kind is that, before assuming that linguistic behaviour is rule-bound, look at the surfaces and give probabilistic explanations a good run for their money. This would also be counselled by the competition model, to which we now return after this 'orienting hiatus'.

So back now to the main menu: the competition model as a performance-based alternative to the generative approach. I will now discuss the way in which MacWhinney (1987) has complicated the distinction between generative models and the competition model and then reprise and elaborate on earlier ruminations about 'competence' that the model rejects, before describing the mild misgivings about the full-blooded connectionist approach which MacWhinney voices in that paper – as a bridge to discussing the binding problem and other conceptual difficulties with connectionist modelling in section 3.3.

The competition model does not posit the kind of direct (albeit mediated by hidden units) wiring between semantic functions and auditory systems of the kind that we observed in the Allen and Seidenberg simulation of sentence production. MacWhinney (1987) is clear that the model does not only concern itself with 'the auditory and the semantic systems'. While these two systems, he points out, provide the 'basic skeleton for language', lexical items that emerge from the many-to-many competitive process cannot convey 'complex meanings' because there must be a 'way of showing how [lexical] meanings relate to one another', without which 'our verbalisations would be an unstructured set of verbalisations'. To solve this problem, he says, language has evolved a system of *grammatical roles* that uses cues to place lexical items in relation to one another. In accordance with the assumptions behind the competition model, these grammatical roles are taken to be directly traceable to form-function relations no less than is performance at the lexical level. He writes (ibid., p. 260) that

> the forms are the surface word order patterns and morphological patterns that cue particular relations; the functions are the underlying meaningful relations without which semantic

interpretation could not proceed. If we were just to utter lexical items one after the other, we would only have a vague notion of how to fit the words together into ideas. Grammatical roles provide us with a way of knowing what goes with what.

No supporter of the Chomskyan approach would disagree with any of this. Indeed the distinction being drawn here is not a million miles from that between surface and deep structure. So what *is* the essential difference between Chomskyan theory and the competition model? It is that in the 'work of the transformational school, syntax is a purely formal object. In the Competition Model, as in other work in the functionalist school, role relational-structure (i.e., syntax) is viewed as a way of expressing relational functions'. (ibid, p 261).

What does this mean in practice? Roles are taken to be 'opened up' by predicates (by verbs for example) and they are 'filled' with arguments (such as nominals). For example from

> predicate – role – argument

we move to

> *goes* – Subject – argument

to

> *goes* – Subject – *John*

At this point the reader might wonder how this kind of proposal is supposed to differ from those made in from within the generative-nativist camp, such as Grimshaw's notion of the canonical structural relations (CSRs, see p. 116) and of course the Chomskyan notion of a lexical representation (LRs, pp. 115). This question becomes still more pressing when we consider how this kind of analysis is applied at the level of the sentence. In this case, the task is to show how roles build up dependency structures. The relational structure of *The cute puppy always likes bones* is shown on page 274.

In this case, because *like* is a transitive verb, it opens up an object role in addition to the subject role. The directions of opening up are represented by the arrows. I will not describe in detail the work that 'head' is doing in this example except to say that MacWhinney takes heads (of which he describes three kinds[10]) to be opened up by a wide range of 'operators': markers, logical operators, articles, and adjectives, adverbs. Accordingly, *like* is itself a head opened up by the present tense marker /s/ (cf. Chomsky's 'percolation' of verb inflections up to IP) and the adverb, while *the*, *cute* and the plural marker open up heads as shown.

What is notable here is that while, as we have seen, the model expresses a distinction doing similar work to deep/surface, and while it enlists a conception similar to the notion of lexical representation found in P & P theory and the minimalist programme, and while indeed it uses the traditional syntactic categories of subject and object

----

[10] These are: heads that stand outside of prepositional phrases ('exoheads'), heads that function as the heads of relative clauses, and heads in the more traditional sense (e.g., 'the man' in 'the man I saw chased Bill'), called 'relheads'.

```
      <----- H ----- / s /
      |


      |

      like ----- S ----> the ----- H ---->(cute ----- H ----> puppy)
      |


      |

                O ----> (plural ----- H ----> bones)
      |

      <-----  H ----- always
```

S = subject
O = object
H = head

(albeit as conceptualised from the functionalist perspective of MacWhinney's earlier work: MacWhinney, 1978), it eschews the tree diagram. And that is what its deeper eschewing of competence models boils down to. For the generative linguist, this ensures that the model must necessarily fail to attain even descriptive adequacy. There are no phrase structures in the model, no attempt to derive an ordered string, no real attack on the problem of how agreement is marked by inflexional morphology, and no attempt to show how underlying representations (canonical word orders or the more traditionally conceived deep-structure necessary for semantic interpretation) are mapped to surface forms. Now if the process of competition were being demonstrated to be sufficiently pervasive to render these levels of explanation redundant then the performance model would *indeed* be seen to be preferable to the competence model on the grounds of parsimony alone. However the notion of competition only makes guest appearances in the account in MacWhinney (1987). For example (ibid, pp. 265–266), when explaining why the transitive form of the verb *sink* might happen to be selected over the intransitive form, or vice versa, MacWhinney says that 'competitive processing' will decide which one receives 'lexical activation' on the basis of whether there are two nominals present (transitive) or one (intransitive). On page 275 is the 'lexical role representation' for *sink* in the transitive and intransitive forms, with C meaning a 'connection to competing case role assignments' and R meaning 'the set of connections to major grammatical roles (subject and object)'.

But in this case the notion of competition is doing only *psycholinguistic* work, being posited as a process in real-time sentence parsing. The notion of competition is ubiquitous in the empirical literature on parsing (Altmann, 1998); but in this work it is not being used to explain how the speaker-hearer *comes to be able to understand any sentences at all* but to explain why some sentences happen to be parsed as transitive:

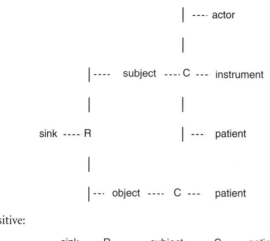

intransitive:

sink ---- R ----- subject ---- C ---- patient

they are. That is to say, competence-based models and performance-based models are in symmetrical conflict over how humans come to be able to understand and frame any sentences *at all*; but when it comes to accounts of their real-time performance then of course performance-based notions like competition are the ones to reach for.

This is how MacWhinney deals with true, symmetrical conflict over the place of phrase structure analysis in the how-can-we-do-it-at-all question. His claim is simply that adults do not utilise phrase-structure rules.[11] Both we and children utilise only lexical knowledge, roles and connections: 'In the Competition Model, the connections between lexical items and roles learned by the child are the same connections used by the adult' (ibid., p. 267). From this point on the style of argument is similar to that used by supporters of the pragmatist approach, to be discussed in Part 4. The impediment to the phrase-structure analysis – the argument runs – is the existence of languages (such as Welsh) whose canonical word order is VSO rather than SVO and the existence of so-called non-configural languages such as Hungarian and Walpiri in which word-order is essentially unconstrained because the morphological cues are sufficiently informative that the listener will know 'what goes with what'. In the first (Welsh) place, the language does not, it is claimed

----

[11] MacWhinney does, in fact, make many references to phrases in his account of the competition model, so to some degree one is left wondering about his rejection of phrase-*structures*. Perhaps there is acceptance of phrases as epiphenomena of roles, competition etc., but rejection of phrase structure as playing 'a role as the central organiser of all syntactic development' (MacWhinney, 1987, 267).

by some, have verb phrases, and so the competition model is supposed to have an advantage over models which assume that verbs and grammatical objects are grouped into a separate phrase. In the second case, the cue-based processor of the competition model 'is ideally suited for dealing with non-configural cue processing, since it allows affixes on stems directly to cue the roles of those stems' (ibid, p. 268).

When we read further however, we come across some statements that would not be out of place in the mouth of the Chomsky of MP cheek by jowl with dismissals of the linguistic reality of phrase structure. MacWhinney writes:

> In the Competition Model phrase structures are epiphenomena, with the core of the grammar being composed of the arguments entered on particular predicates. By relating arguments to predicates, *the listener* builds up something like a parse tree, but the construction is from the bottom up and is promoted by competition between alternative attachments.

(ibid., p. 268, emphasis added)

Note the reference to 'the listener', by the way. Are phrases epiphenomena for the *speaker*? But more centrally, it is surely possible to have a thoroughly bottom-up theory of how phrase structure is derived – one is found, of course, in MP – without this implying that the result is no more than an *epiphenomenon* of binding arguments to predicates. Something results from this building process on which further processes – movement, for one – operate. So one wonders whether it is possible for the competition model to explain the variety of syntactic phenomena that MP can explain, having jettisoned phrase structures as a computational reality. But perhaps what MacWhinney is expressing here is a similar kind of generalised animus against a certain conception of 'rule' to which Chomsky gave vent in the Siena interview when he said, 'There is no such thing as VP in Japanese or the relative clause in Hungarian. Rather, there are just extremely general principles like "move anything anywhere" under fixed conditions'. But as I noted very recently, this is not to derogate the whole idea of rule-bound operations. Indeed, a moment's thought tells us that were there not deep rule-governed commonalities between languages whose phrase structures are quite dissimilar it would not be so easy to translate languages like Latin and Welsh into languages like English; which returns us to the old Chomskyan theme of there being a single language, Human, of which there are idiolects. It also recalls Donald Davidson's opposition to 'the very idea of a conceptual system'; for if they were really different we would be entirely unable to move from one to another. (MacWhinney is friendly to the 'very idea' of different syntactic systems.)

In any event, the competition model's replacing tree-diagram analyses with ones based on lexical items, roles, and connections alone assumes that the successes gained to date in giving principled explanations for why certain English sentences are judged to be grammatical and others are not by the use of tree-based analyses (i.e., the stuff of much modern theoretical linguistics) can be emulated by using only the resources of the competition model. One is not saying that tree-drawing is the only game in town – indeed in Part 4 we will look at Van Valin's pragmatist theory and at the 'cognitive grammar' of Langacker and others – but more work needs to be done here to convince us to adopt the items/roles/connections taxonomy of the competition model.

Another reason given by MacWhinney for preferring the machinery of his performance-based model over that of the generative approach is, predictably, that, because it makes fewer assumptions about innate knowledge, it is to be preferred on the grounds of parsimony. But – and again in parallel to the pragmatist approach – this parsimonious outcome is bought at the price of profligacy of metaphor. MacWhinney speculates that 'roles are learned' by children before they are able to produce multi-word utterances on the basis of 'exposure to perceptual regularities'. For example (ibid, p. 267; emphasis added):

> it is reasonable to imagine that the relation of coordination [e.g., in *Mary and John*, *Mary* is the head and *John* the 'coordinate' JR] is learned early on when the infant scans his visual environment and discovers pairings of similar objects that move in a common trajectory or which share a common fate. There are *probably* also early antecedents of the topic and head relations in the figure-ground organisation of infant perception. Perception may not be the only basis for the development of these relations in infancy. In action, the infant also works with recurrence, focussing and modification. Thus, both perception and action may provide precursors to grammatical relational structure.

Well, one is entitled to respond to this kind of argument that if you look for precursors with such a wide-angle lens then you will always find them. And is such a view remotely testable? Ironically, MacWhinney's response to the main alternative to it is that although 'there is some prima facie evidence for such a nativist possibility, the untestability of this position makes it one that we should only accept as a last resort' (p. 267).

Moving on now to the rumination about competence promised earlier, a more central issue than that of testability (which might be said to exist in the eye of the beholder in this case) is that of whether a model eschewing the notion of competence, as a system of tacit knowledge of syntactic structures and operations of the kind described in Part 2, is even in the running for being a plausible account of linguistic *performance*. Let us return to two notions, one discussed in Part 2 and the other in this section: that of generation (*erzeugen*, p. 167), and the Wittgensteinian idea of a bedrock to rule-following that consists of formal machinery but which is not an impossibly perfect machine (*die Maschine als Symbol*) that can never go wrong. First, *erzeugen* is, as we discussed, a Janus-faced concept, which, on the classical reading, captures the formal nature of syntactic knowledge and which, on the romantic reading, captures the fact that framing a sentence from a thought is a creative act. *Their intersect is the idea that we act freely in virtue of what we know.* While there are, needless to say, causal aspects to sentential parsing (with Fodor famously quoting Merrill Garrett's statement that parsing is 'basically a reflex', to illustrate the concept of an input system) there is no parallel sense in which framing a sentence from a thought is something that happens to us rather that something that we do. *We say 'Why did you say that?' but not 'Why did you understand that?'* This returns us to the Wittgensteinian notion of a rule-following bedrock that is at once a system of knowledge grounding performance and knowledge that can be misapplied: there can be performance errors. Now while MacWhinney's development of the competition model in terms of role-theory does, as I said, 'complicate the distinction' between generative and connectionist models to some degree, there is still no place in that model for the idea of a speaker acting from (tacit) knowledge. What the model does is to construe speaking as a matter of 'opening up' the right kind of roles from cognised predicates through a process that, while involving symbols (a role is surely a symbol, see below), is essentially causal, in a similar way to that in which parsing (any kind of parsing, not just sentential) is a causal process.

This is why, then, one might say that that a purely performance model such as the competition model must provide an unsatisfying account of speech performance. On that model we successfully articulate our thoughts just in case mechanisms with a fundamentally associative nature come into play, with performance errors being explained in terms the failure of the competitive processing dynamics. By contrast, on the generative theory, speaking our thoughts is a rational process, in which a reason can typically be given in answer to questions like 'What makes you say that?', in which we act on the basis of what we tacitly know about the language and choose between an explicitly known range of alternatives in framing the expression. Sticking with the latter conception may seem like a romantic and quietist move, but the alterative does feel to many like the kind of cul-de-sac radicalism trumpeted by the behaviourists (on connectionism and behaviourism see Smith, 1999, pp. 131–135).

That said, the competition model is really one couched in a connectionist *style* rather than a species of connectionist model. What prevents it from being a full-blown connectionist model is the central place of the 'role' within it, as clearly articulated by MacWhinney (ibid., pp. 268–269). In the competition model, each predicate is connected to roles, which are in turn connected to cues that ensure the correct assignment of lexical items to these roles. Thus, the predicate *kissed* will, because it is a transitive verb, 'open up' both subject and object roles, after which the word-order cue of *John* preceding *kissed* and *Mary* succeeding it will ensure that these two arguments are assigned, respectively, to subject and object roles. In a connectionist model, as MacWhinney points out, the cues are not connected to roles but rather to the *lexical items* that fill these roles. I will illustrate what is intended here by reference to Elman's (1993) next-word-prediction model. In this case, after presentation, say, of the words *boys chase* to the input units the network will be likely to predict a word like *girls* or *dogs* as a continuation, and it will do so because it had learned that there is a set of words among which is *chases* that precede a set of words including *dogs*, *girls* and others. In this case, the cues utilised by the network are sequences of items on the input units and the material that is predicted takes the form of individual lexical items rather than grammatical types. That is to say, the network predicts words that *happen to be* nouns, but it does not in any sense known about the form class 'noun' as being the kind of class that follows words like *chase;* and neither, of course, does it need to code items like *chase* as transitive verbs. The situation is quite different in the competition model because here a word like *chases* would be treated as a predicate that 'opens up' not one of a set of lexical items (picked up by learning or hard-wired in, as in the Chang *et al.*, 1997, production model) but the object argument role. As, MacWhinney puts it, 'in the Competition Model the connection between the role and the candidate argument is not hard-wired in the lexicon but built up dynamically during processing' (p. 269). To put no finer point on it, the competition model is a kind of symbol-processor, given that 'role', 'object', and so forth, are symbols whose nature is not exhausted by their perceptual features.

Connectionist models do not represent syntactic categories such as 'role', 'subject', and the like, so how might the competition model be instantiated in a network?

One solution might be to hard-wire every item in the lexicon to every possible role. Recall that this was the Chang *et al.* (1997) solution. However, as MacWhinney points out, this solution (earlier proposed by Cottrell, 1985) struggles to deal with cases where the sentence has two subjects: *The big dog and the little dog both ate the ham*, for example. In this case the item *dog* must be bound twice to the subject role, which would require connections not only from *dog* to the subject role but from the second *dog* to a copy of the subject role. Classical, symbol-processing architectures have no problem with such multiple representings (they have a 'copy' function); but networks do. What networks need to be able to compute here is the distinction between *tokens* and *types*, that is to say, the distinction between particular coinings of a lexical item in a sentence and that very lexical item. Without having such a distinction in place, it would not be possible to distinguish between cases like the 'dog' one just mentioned, in which two subjects are of the same type (each entity being mentioned once) and cases in which a single entity is mentioned twice, as in *Jane is taller than Mary and Mary is taller than Sally*. This challenge for connectionist networks is variously called 'the type-token problem' (e.g., Norman, 1986) or 'the problem of multiple instantiation' (e.g., Mani & Shastri, 1993). For a network to solve this problem it must first solve a more fundamental one, which is that of how a system that does not compute over symbols can bind predicates to the appropriate arguments – the 'binding problem' – as discussed in 3.1. In the next section we will examine this issue by first standing back from it in order to appreciate the fundamental importance of the binding of variables in language and cognition, by noting how binding is achieved and not achieved in networks and by looking at how infancy dishabituation data have been brought to bear upon the question of whether networks have inherent limitations when it comes to learning 'grammars' that are defined in terms of the way in which their types are repeated.

3.3 Variables: in thought, language, and in connectionist modelling

The issues raised at the end of the previous section about computing over roles rather than over lexical items, about binding predicates to arguments, and about multiple instantiation, centre upon the question of whether empiricist-connectionist networks could ever compute over *variables* in anything more than a thin and metaphoric sense – in anything like the sense, that is, in which the human thinker and speaker computes over them.

Let us reflect, first, upon what the term 'variable' means? Variable is a notion that originated from the mathematics of ancient Greece and which was later incarnated in formal logic independently by Frege, Peano and Peirce in the nineteenth century. Many readers' sole acquaintance with the notion will have been in school algebra lessons in which they had to solve the value of x in an equation. In this case, x meant *something-or-other whose value can vary* (and your job is to find out what it is in this case). The variables of the formal logical system of *predicate calculus* can also be said to take values – though not usually numerical ones. In this case a variable such as x can be quantified – with the term 'quantifier' having been coined by C.S. Peirce, by the way – either universally ($\forall$) or existentially (E) (also see pp. 119–120). $\forall x$ means 'for all x' and ∃x means for some *x*. Variables can also take predicates, such as F and G. The following expression, for example, represents the logical form of the sentence *All men are mortal* in predicate calculus with F meaning 'is a man' and G meaning 'is mortal':

∀x (Fx & Gx)

If we wished to do the same for the sentence *Socrates is mortal* then we might introduce the predicate H meaning 'is Socrates' and therefore have:

∃x (Hx & Gx)

In these cases, *x* is said to be a *bound* variable – bound to quantifiers.

In symbolic computation a variable is a piece of program as contrasted with an item of data. In Lisp programming, for example, data are indicated with a single mark ('). Thus, if one types in

'MEMBERS

the program treats it as data. If, however, one types in

MEMBERS

it will be treated as a variable, and Lisp will attempt to print out its value. If it has no value – if it is unbound – the system will reply UNDEFINED. By the operation SETQ a variable can have values bound to it. Thus:

(SETQ MEMBERS '(BRIAN KEVIN PAULA))

There are a 'local' variables associated with particular functions (e.g., EVAL, which evaluates Lisp expressions) and there are 'global' variables which are not associated with any particular function. The latter are bound to values all the time and the former are only bound when that particular function is in use.

What is to be noted, then, is that symbolic computing systems (a) always distinguish between variables and data and (b) can bind values to variables at a stroke (by operations such as SETQ). In connectionist modelling, by contrast, there is no distinction between program and data because *everything is data*. With regard to variable binding however, the enthusiast for connectionism will say that one can describe certain linguistic and cognitive processes in terms of variable binding, but that positing a human-cognitive operation that does a similar job to SETQ is merely a piece of high-level shorthand for an operation that is in fact sub-symbolic and associative.

We now turn to variable binding in language. We have already discussed, in Part 2, an explicit form of variable binding to universal and existential quantifiers in our discussion of Chomsky's notion of logical form (LF). At this point, however, we will be regarding variable binding as a much more pervasive – though more subtle – phenomenon.

One must regard variables as the players of syntactic or semantic roles such as [*whatever happens to be the subject*] or [*whatever happens to be the shorter entity*]. It is the universally-quantified variable that plays a central role here because the following of linguistic rules involves the ability to apply the rule to any case. By way of illustration, let us consider the ability to produce the regular form of the English past tense. We have here a universally-quantified injunction: for all stems of English verbs add the suffix *-ed* to form the past tense. The fact that we encode this quantification as universal enables us to inflect nonce verbs and to coin new meaningful ones, as in 'Blair outthatchered Thatcher'. Famously (and see the discussion of Haskell *et al.*'s work in the previous section) empiricist connectionists such as McClelland (1989) and Plunkett (Plunkett and Marchman, 1991) have denied that rule-following is indeed taking place, insisting that the same processes of 'associative' learning occurs here as when we learn that the past tenses irregular forms such as *go-went*. No more than it did before, the debate around this issue will not detain us, partly because it is an issue in morphology (strictly, morphosyntax) rather than syntax. In any event, in the case of unambiguously syntactic rules (e.g., for forming a sentence from a NP and a VP) a Chomskyan would say that it is the universally quantified nature of these rules, among other things, that makes language use creative. (Recall from the discussion of rationalism in Part 1 that it is the existence of universal truths, such as the whole is greater than the sum of the parts, to which rationalism naturally accommodates and with which empiricism struggles. And recall the discussion in 3.2 of Wittgenstein on rule following. It might be said that the notion, attacked by Wittgenstein, of a representation before the mind's eye exhaustively instantiating a rule is a dogma of empiricism.)

Needless to say, most of our everyday sentences are existentially quantified (and in the next subsection I will spell out what it means for *thoughts* about individuals to be existentially quantified). But the armature of rules that turns thoughts into sentences takes a universal form. I will illustrate this in terms of the binding of variables (e.g., 'whatever is the subject') to values (e.g., 'dog'). Note that in binding a lexical item to a syntactic role, one is following a universal injunction of the following form: 'for all English nouns that do X, Y, and Z in a sentence (e.g., agree in number with the verb) that noun is the subject of the sentence). In *The big dog chased the little cat*, we have at least two variables: x [*whatever is the subject of the sentence*] and y [*whatever is the object of the sentence*] with x taking the values 'big and a dog' and y taking the value 'small and a cat'. Comparably, in the sentence quoted by MacWhinney above *The big dog and the little dog both ate the ham* the speaker expresses and the hearer understands that there are two agents in question not one agent that is both little and big. What's more, he or she knows this not through the semantics (that dogs cannot be both big and little) but by virtue of the syntax (two noun phrases). In this case, we have one variable [*whatever is in the subject role*] with two different values being tokened (though of the same kind – dog]. Conversely, in the following examples we have two variables with a single value, meaning one entity playing two syntactic roles: *John loves Mary and Mary loves John back*. In other words, the value of the variable x [*whatever is the subject of the sentence*] and the value of the variable y [*whatever is the object of the sentence*] is the same, namely, John. We see a similar phenomenon in transitive relations such as *Peter is taller than Paul and Paul is taller than David*. In this case the variables of [*whatever is the taller*] and [*whatever is the shorter*] are taking the same value – Paul.

Later in this section we will discuss how variable binding and multiple instantiation are tackled by networks. But first, we will consider how these processes are manifested in our thoughts about individuals, whose existential quantification must become manifest in sentences.

3.3.1 Variables in thoughts about individuals

I shall be arguing here that variable binding underlies our thinking about individuals.

With regard to the role of variables in the modelling of thought, it is useful to regard the successful binding of values to variables in terms of the fulfilment of Evans' generality constraint. Recall the previous discussion of this in Part 1.1.4. The generality constraint formalises ideas about the kind of capacity that must be being exercised if an individual can be said to be attaching a predicate to an argument. The ability to attach predicate F to argument a and predicate G to argument b is intrinsically related to the further ability to think Ga and Fb. That is to say, predicates can be 'detached' from one argument and 'moved' to another; and *mutatis mutandis* for arguments from predicates. He writes (Evans, 1982, p. 100):

> The thought that John is happy has something in common with the thought that Harry is happy, and the thought that John is happy has something in common with the thought that John is sad.

But Evans goes on to caution – recall – that this is not to be taken as an argument for the language of thought because there is nothing in this to suggest that having such thoughts involves the manipulation of symbols with non-semantic properties or 'shapes'.[12] He also cautions that this is not a constraint on the structuring of *language*, because it is possible for a structured system of thought to be expressed by an unstructured language. The latter claim is not that linguistic capacities do not fulfil this constraint, but rather that their doing so is a contingent matter; while it is a necessary matter in the case of thought. (In passing, Chomsky's deployment of the notion of *virtual conceptual necessity* in the minimalist programme would seem to point to a different view, unless we interpret the 'virtual' as being there in order to make a similar point to Evans's.)

If we accept the necessary application of Evans' constraint in thought (while bearing in mind that the 'virtual conceptual necessity' that the ability to understand one sentence entails the ability to understand a whole complex of other sentences) then one might wish to think of the role of variables and their binding in the following way. Taking $F = $ *is happy* and $G = $ *is sad*, $J = $ *is John* and $H = $ *is Harry*, then the ability to think

$$\exists x \, (Fx \,\&\, Jx)$$

entails the further ability to think

$$\exists x \, (Fx \,\&\, Hx)$$

and to think that

$$\exists x \, (Gx \,\&\, Jx).$$

If that kind of variable binding can be achieved in the first case then there is every reason to believe it can also be achieved in the other two. This is, by no stretch of the imagination, an *argument* for the conclusion that human thought involves variable binding. But putting things this way does lend some transparency to the notion of

---

[12] This means their formal properties. Contrast the symbol 'cat' with an iconic representation of a cat. Turing symbols interact in virtue of their inherent shapes.

thinking as a structured capacity – as illustrated by the generality constraint. Now it is quite uncontroversial – among those with a rationalistic cast of mind at least – that language use is also a structured capacity. As Evans cautioned, the structured nature of language use may be a contingent fact, and as Chomsky cautioned by his qualifier 'virtual' in 'virtual conceptual necessity', the perfection of the language system is a matter of good design, not of strict logical necessity. But it would seem to be a good bet that thinking in natural language does indeed utilise binding operations similar to those utilised in thought; that at least is the rationalist assumption.

As we saw in Part 2, such assumptions form the warp and weft of Chomskyan theory from P & P to the minimalist programme. And partly from considerations similar to those just sketched, Chomsky calls the highest level of sentential computation 'logical form' (LF). The role of variable binding in trace theory was discussed there in some detail (see pp. 118–121 on co-indexing). So in the short and general view, rationalist theories simply *help themselves* to such symbolic operations.

Empiricist connectionism, however, cannot help itself to any kind of symbolic operation, because its computations are not over symbols. It has, however, to explicate both (1) how variable binding is possible at all and (2) how operations can be performed over variables. This will be discussed shortly.

Something further that minimalism helps itself to is the type/token distinction. Recall (pp. 140–141) that the operation called selection (or *select*) makes lexical items available for merge to operate on. This is achieved by constructing an array (*A*) of items from the lexicon. This is however an array that includes a numeration, given that the array of words selected from the lexicon will have each item tagged in terms of how often it is used in the sentence. Accordingly, to reprise the example used before, *Melanie-2* means two occurrences of that word in *Melanie knew her name was Melanie*. And so *A* will contain information about both lexical types and lexical tokens. That is to say, the type/token distinction has to made at the very earliest stage of the derivation, and if it were not then merge would frequently result in derivations that crash.

Backing off from linguistic issues for now and returning to cognition, let us, as we did for binding, consider the crucial role of the type/token distinction in thought. It is not difficult to appreciate that (what Piaget called) 'the object concept' cannot be exercised in creatures who do not make the type/token distinction will now elaborate on this claim. In knowing that the ball that has gone behind a screen is still there we are able to do more than maintain a representation of a stimulus in thought ('*representation persistence*' – Meltzoff and Moore, 1998; 'representation permanence' – Russell, 1996). This is a question of 'out of sight, in the mind'. Object permanence, by contrast, means 'out of sight, still in the world'. That is to say, one might have object-representation *persistence* without any belief that the mental representation we entertain refers to something in the mind-external world ('externality' – Russell, 1996). In Meltzoff's example, toddlers and even older infants seem to be able to remember for a matter of weeks the actions on an object that an experimenter modelled. But this does not imply that they represent *these actions* as continuing to exist in the world. Additionally, the object concept cannot be reduced to the ability to predict that the identical object – not something that looks exactly the same as the stimulus that vanished but the self-same one ('identity' – Meltzoff and Moore, 1998) – will reappear when an occluder is removed; because the conception must be present of one-and-the-same object existing unperceived *in the interim*. Object permanence implies conceptualising a unique, enduring, perduring, mind-independent '∃x'.

As we discussed in 1.2.4, multi-layered perceptrons are able appropriately to predict the reappearance of the same kind of stimulus after its temporary occlusion, with this being due to certain of the hidden units having learned to maintain activation during the period of the occlusion. This is, in present terms, a form of representation persistence. What needs to focused on in the present context, however, is not the issue of whether a multilayed perceptron could ever model externality (on which Russell, 1996, 2.8) but that of whether identity ('one and the same') knowledge could ever be modelled on such systems (notably, those of Mareschal *et al.*, 1999; and of Munakata *et al.*, 1997). *What is a stake here is knowledge of the type/token distinction: exemplars versus kinds.* Consider, in illustration, that I lose a cricket ball. I can identify it easily from its perceptual features – by its patterns of scratches and by places where its seam is coming away. I find a ball two months later, but it looks in even a worse state than the one I lost. Given this, I might wonder whether it is the same ball despite the perceptual differences, but still come to the conclusion that it is. Conversely, I might have a number of identical felt-tip pens, and of two pens that look and function exactly alike I can wonder if this pen I'm writing with now is the same one that I used to write a cheque this morning. If I happen to see the two pens together on my desk it would be a case of two tokenings/instantiations of the same type, whereas in the cricket ball case we have a single tokening of one type, a single instantiation of a type despite the perceptual differences.

It seems to be evident from these examples, then, that identity-thoughts are not grounded in perceptual experience alone: one and the same thing can look different at different times, while two perceptually-identical objects are not thought of as sharing identity. What identity thoughts do, rather, is to represent something-or-other as existing at a certain point in space at a certain time. And this is what the existential quantifier (∃x) captures. I think it is fruitful, then, to treat a thought about a unique object along the following lines:

$$\exists x \, (Fx)$$

where F = the object's permanent, inalienable character (e.g., 'is a cat').

Furthermore, adequate thought about objects involves exercising the dual capacity for (1) positing a something uniquely defined by spatiotemporal coordinates and (2) positing a value bound to it. It appears to be the case that human infants cannot exercise both of these capacities before the end of their first year of life. Infants of around four months of age can use spatiotemporal information to maintain representations of objects in their immediate environment, as indexed by their surprise reactions to anomalous outcomes. For example, in the procedure used by Spelke and Kestenbaum (1986), infants of four months saw the same kind of object (e.g., a teddy) emerge sequentially behind each of two screens separated in space. They looked longer ('surprise') when the screens were removed to show a single object than when two objects were revealed. In this case, however, the nature of the variable (i.e., 'teddy bear') had no role to play. Contrast this situation with that obtaining in a study by Xu and Carey (1996), previously discussed in 2.4.4 (see Figure 2.30).

In this case, there was only one screen present. First, one object (a toy truck) emerged from one side and then returned; then a different object (a teddy) emerged from behind the screen and returned. The screen was removed to show either two different objects (possible) or only one of the two objects (impossible). Infants of 10 months generally failed to show the appropriate surprise reactions to these two outcomes. But infants of 12 months did show them.

In the present terms we might say that infants of 12 months appropriately bind variables to values, while infants of 10 months do not. My point is not, however, just a developmental one. It is that object identification is not only a matter of tracking perceptual features through time (representation persistence) but of relating those features (of binding those values) to a particular spatiotemporal coordinate. Without this ability, no distinction can be drawn between types and tokens, given that a token, in this instance, is a particular object of a certain type. On the view that I am pressing then, the object as the spatiotemporal coordinate is the 'variable' and the type is the 'value'. It is in this sense, then, that one can say that variable binding underlies the distinction between types and tokens.

There is a further parallel that can be fruitfully drawn, in this context, between variable binding and the type/token distinction. I suggested earlier that a capacity for variable binding is what enables our thoughts to fulfil the generality constraint. As Evans (1982) goes on to argue, the thoughts about objects that are exemplary of this constraint are of the following kind: they involve 'Ideas'[13] of objects, that make it possible for 'a subject to think of an object in a series of indefinitely many thoughts, in each of which he will be thinking of the object in the same way (ibid., p. 104). One might say that an Idea of an object is the abstract kernel to which a *range* of predicates can become attached – a variable, as the term was used in the previous discussion of object permanence. In this case, F might be ' is a cat' , G, 'is my pet', H 'a thing in my way', and so forth, all attached to a single x.

The pressing question at this point then is whether multilayer perceptrons are capable of instantiating the binding of values to variables and thus of computing operations over them. That is to say, can a system of this kind express the binding of perceptual features to an abstract 'kernel' that is irreducible to perceptual experience? This is the issue to which I now turn, also returning to language processing. The foregoing discussion will owe much to the treatment of this issue by Gary Marcus (1998, 2001, chapter 3).

3.3.2 Variable binding in networks

While the sense in which syntactic rules involve the universal quantification of variables is fairly transparent, what can and cannot count as a variable in a connectionist network is a cloud-obscured question, as is the distinction between binding variables and performing operations over variables. Accordingly, if we return once again to Elman's (1993) next-word prediction network we see that while the network does not bind values to variables in the sense of binding particular lexical items to syntactic roles (e.g. *boys* to 'noun + plural' or 'subject') one can nevertheless think

---

[13] This notion is derived from Geach (1957).

of *current word* as a variable and of whatever happens to be the current word as its bound value. This is not, however, the kind of variable binding that gives us the creativity distinctive of language, in which universal quantification guarantees that we can generate and understand an infinity of sentences. This is so because syntactic units are not being quantified over (e.g., for all x such that x is an NP and for all y such that y is a VP, a sentence can be formed by conjoining them for any value of x and y). As we have already seen, the reason why Elman's model was able to predict a plausible (i.e., of the right syntactic category) next word was that the corpus was such that each (say) noun had appeared in roughly the same set of contexts. To illustrate this fact, Marcus (1998) tested the model using a novel noun that appeared just once. It did not elicit the same pattern of activation as the other nouns in the set but 'appears in roughly the middle of n-dimensional[14] space, relatively far from all other nouns, which tend to occupy a corner of n-dimensional space' (p. 164). This is so, he goes on to say, because these nouns were clustering together in state space by virtue of having all appeared together in the training set in similar circumstances, not because they were from the same syntactic category. He takes this to be a 'devastating' difficulty for what I am calling the empiricist connectionist position. The problem is that while *current word* is, in a sense, a variable, such a variable does no syntactic work for the network.

Marcus goes on to argue that the kind of network architecture that Elman used is incapable of generalising beyond its training set. The model used localist rather than distributed encoding on the input and output units, which means, in this case, that one particular node represented a particular word rather than a word being represented by a set of simultaneously active nodes each of which could also contribute to the encoding of other words. It is important to note, however (for reasons that will shortly emerge) that this localist model allocated multiple nodes to a single input variable. That is to say, the variable *current word* necessarily took different nodal values depending on what the current word happened to be.

Marcus provided a further demonstration that variable binding of this kind limits the network to generalising only to data familiar from the training set. All that such a network knows is what it has 'seen', because binding was of particular pieces of perceptual data to *current word*. Given this, the network cannot compute the *identity function*, something that a symbolic network can do simply by calling up the function 'copy'. The identity function is a one-to-one mapping between inputs and outputs, such that whenever (say) A is inputted A is outputted, whenever C is inputted C is outputted, and so forth. Marcus (1998, pp. 165–166) reports that networks of the Elman variety (localist and where multiple nodes are allocated to a single variable) cannot learn the following task. On the input layer there is a 'right bank' and a 'left bank' of units. The model is trained to respond 'same' when the input from the two banks is identical (/ba/ + /ba/; /da/ + /da/), otherwise 'different'. After training, the model is tested for generalisation to a new pair, such as /ga/ + /ga/. No generalisation to the new pair was found, something that was inevitable given the local nature of the learning in the training phase. To explain, the /ga/ input unit during training would have been

---

[14] The n corresponds to the number of input units.

activated at the level of zero; and, given the way in which the back-propagation algorithm works (no contribution made to error, no change), the weights leading from that input unit to the hidden units remain completely unchanged *regardless of the activity levels of the other hidden units*. The upshot is that nothing is learned about that node during training. The major point to note here is that it is because the variable that the model computes over is *current word*, rather than a higher-level variable instantiating the identity function, that it is so dependent upon learning about particular inputs – about what might be called perceptual features. Computing over higher level variables would free networks from the tyranny of perceptual features.

A brief aside about the importance of the identity function in modelling recursive structures of language might be useful at this point. As discussed in 3.1, a recursive procedure is one that replaces a symbol by a string of symbols that includes that symbol (e.g., S → NP + V + S; N′ → Adj + N′), while this new symbol can be replaced via further applications of the recursive rule; and so to say a rule applies recursively is to say that one application of it creates the conditions necessary for its reapplication. It is difficult to see how such reapplication could be achieved without the copy function. In any event, the notions of recursion, hierarchy and the copying/identity function can be said to be intimately related.

Moreover, it is a necessary feature of the identity function that it is applicable *universally*: for all inputs *x* output a copy of *x*. Marcus (2001, p. 36) calls this a *universally quantified one-to-one mapping* (UQOTOM).

What Marcus – at least in his book (2001) rather than the critical review (1998) of Elman *et al.*'s *Rethinking innateness* – is at pains to point out, however, is that connectionist networks do not *necessarily* fail to compute UQOTOM. This failure is linked to the fact of allocating more than one node to each input variable (such as *current word*). Networks that allocate a single node to a variable *can*, in fact, represent UQOTOM. In the simplest case, these will consist of a single input unit and a single output unit with a connection weight of 1.0. Similarly, if the connection weight were 2.0 the function of doubling could be instantiated for any given input. Indeed Marcus (2001) also argues that multilayer perceptrons can indeed be said to be computing operations over variables in cases where one input node is allocated to a single variable. This is, in fact, the case in the two published simulations of the balance beam problem (Shultz, Mareschal and Schmidt, 1994; McClelland, 1989), in which there are four variables: number of weights on left side, number of weights on the right side; distance of weights from the fulcrum on the left, distance of weights from the fulcrum on the right. In the Shultz *et al.* model, one input node coded weight and one input node coded distance, with each of these varying in an analogue style to code the value. In McClelland's model, by contrast, there was a bank of four input units for encoding weight and a bank of four units for encoding distance, with each of these taking the values of 1, 2, 3, or 4. We shall discuss further features of these one-variable-to-one-node architectures in the next subsection. But for now, the point needs to be made that the inadequacies of the Elman architecture in generalising to data beyond the training set is not a principled limitation of connectionist networks, but a limitation specific to networks that code a single variable (current word in this case) with mulitiple units. This is what Marcus argues.

To strike another upbeat note, the point needs to be made that there is a sense in which networks can be crafted so as to achieve the appropriate binding of arguments and predicates and of variables (roles) and values (instances). One of the most discussed of these is binding by *temporal synchrony*, or *dynamic binding* (Shastri and Ajjanagadde, 1993; and see Sougné, 1998, for a review of this solution and others). In these architectures, variables and their values are represented by nodes which oscillate on and off. Given this, there is taken to be binding between these (and also between arguments and predicates) when they are in phase. Thus, if we wish to capture who is doing what to whom in the sentence *John kissed Mary* we make the John node (the value) oscillate in phase with the 'agent-of-kissing node'(the variable) and the Mary node oscillate in phase with the 'patient-of-kissing' node. Using a similar technique, Sougné (1996; discussed in 1998) offers a solution to the multiple instantiation problem. In this case one models the processing of a sentence like *John loves Mary and Mary loves John back* by ensuring that the 'John' node oscillates in phase with both the 'lover' and the 'lovee' nodes, and similarly for the 'Mary' node.

To continue the theme of connectionist models that bind values to variables, here is another, though less well known, connectionist solution to a problem that strongly parallels that of multiple instantiation: the problem of learning serially-ordered material, not in speaking but in a laboratory memory task. Barnes and Underwood (1959) initially asked subjects to learn a list (list 1) of pairings between nonsense syllabus (e.g., *dax*) and adjectives (e.g., *regal*) till performance was 100 per cent (i.e. they provided the correct adjective for a nonsense word every time). Next, in list 2, they learned a set of new adjectives paired with the *same* nonsense words, until performance was 90 per cent correct. When they were asked to recall the list 1 pairings, there was a predictably large effect of retroactive interference (a reduction to 50 per cent correct). However, when this task is modelled on a multilayer perceptron there is *catastrophic* forgetting: list 1 memory is simply wiped out. This raises the issue of whether networks could ever model transitive sentences (e.g., A > B, B > C), where value B is taken by the variable 'smaller thing' in the first clause and by the variable 'bigger thing' in the second clause. In the Barnes and Underwood task, a non-sense word variable has to take different values in different contexts. Compare this to a linguistic case in which the variable 'subject' will take on the value 'John' in the context of his being the agent of kissing and the value 'Mary' when he is the patient of Mary's kiss, just as *dax* is associated with both *regal* and another adjective in the above.

Here is the solution to the catastrophic forgetting problem[15] offered by McLaren's (1993) adaptively parametrised error correcting systems (APECS) model.

Refer to Figure 3.8, which schematises the three phases of the solution. In phase A, two input units are activated, one (a) encoding the nonsense syllable and the other (b) encoding the context 'list 1'. During this phase, one of the hidden units comes to be 'selected'[16] (shown as the fuzzy-outlined icon), by a competitive process, to carry

---

[15] For another kind of solution to the problem see McClelland, McNaughton and O'Reilly (1995).

[16] Its learning rate parameters become non-zero.

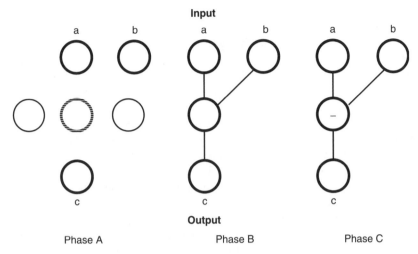

Figure 3.8 McLaren's APECS model.

the mapping between these two units and the correct adjective. In the second phase B, the weights for the connections from input to the selected hidden unit and from that to the output unit(s) is increased, with the result that the hidden unit grows in activation. In phase C, a new mapping is being learned in list 2, with the result that neither input unit b nor output unit c are activated. Consequently, a negative bias develops on the selected hidden unit. This means that, because the learning rate of the selected hidden unit has returned to zero, the other weights do not change and so the complete unlearning of list 1 does not occur.

I will postpone the assessment of such solutions to the problems of how to model variable binding and multiple instantiation in a sub-symbolic systems until we have considered the modelling of some infant learning data. These data are taken by Marcus (2001) to indicate that human infants are binding values to variables rather than performing statistical analysis of perceptual features of the input: infants are 'algebraic' rather than stochastic. We will be better placed to consider the sense in which networks can – and cannot – be said to be binding variables when this has been done.

3.3.3 The algebraic infant debate
In this section I will describe some recent studies of infants' ability to learn simple 'grammars'. We shall see, predictably enough, that enthusiasts for empiricist connectionism argue that some of this work shows an early manifestation of statistical learning (of transition probabilities between verbal units), while enthusiasts for syntactic nativism argue that some data (different data) demonstrate that infants are able to utilise algebraic rules in which variables can take on different values – rules that go beyond the extraction of the statistical regularities within the data. We will begin with the latter work as it is directly relevant to the issues discussed in the

previous subsection. The data were collected by Marcus, Vijayan, Bandi Rao and Vishton (1999).

For Marcus *et al.* (1999), establishing that infants can generalise from a training set of verbal stimuli to a test set in such a way as to demonstrate the extraction of 'algebraic' regularities in which one substitutes 'any value x into the equation $y = x + 2$' (ibid, p. 77) is tantamount to the demonstration that they possess the right kind of representational format for learning syntactic rules in their native language. These are UQOTOM rules (see above) of course. In this sense then, if infants can be said to be, for example, following the rule 'all first and third words [whatever they are] are the same' (giving any values to these variables) they are doing a much simpler version of following the rule that 'all plural noun phrases will serve as subjects for all verb phrases with plural agreement'. Such a view receives enthusiastic endorsement from Steven Pinker (1999b).

In the Marcus *et al.* study, infants of seven months of age were exposed to one of two grammars, either an ABA grammar (e.g., *ga na ga, li ti li*) or an ABB grammar (*ga na na, li ti ti*). After a period of familiarisation there followed a test phase in which the children were exposed to both grammars in order to see whether they would attend longer to the novel grammar – dishabituation. Their attention was measured by how long they looked at banks of flashing lights above loudspeakers playing the three-'word' sequences. The crucial point to note is that *the stimuli used in the test phase were different to the ones used in familiarisation.* The infants did indeed attend more to sequences from the unfamiliar 'grammar'. In order to do this they might be said to have been utilising the abstract character (ABA or ABB) of the word sequences, a character in which the position of the word in the sequence is a variable, and which two values are identical – whatever they are. (There were also control conditions, which I will not mention.)

Two issues immediately arise: (1) Can connectionist models simulate this kind of generalisation? (Because if they can, something substantial will have to be conceded to empiricist connectionism); (2) Do the Marcus *et al.* three-word sequences actually instantiate simple grammars in any interesting sense? (Because if they do not the relevance of these data to syntactic nativism may only be tenuous.)

Turning to (1), Marcus has demonstrated (2001) that an architecture of the kind used by Elman in the next-word-prediction model fails to reproduce the generalisation that infants can make. As discussed in the previous subsection, this is because models that code a single variable (current word in this case) with multiple nodes can only generalise to data sets that share features with the training set.[17] Such models cannot instantiate a UQOTOM, which, in this case, means the rule that 'all third words are the same as the first/second word'. Recall, however, Marcus's insistence that this does not highlight a shortcoming of network models themselves because models that code one variable on a single node can represent UQOTOM, thereby

---

[17] To some extent (see Marcus, 2001, pp. 60–61), using distributed encoding can enable one to avoid these consequences.

performing something analogous to the copy function of a digital computer. Given this, it comes as no surprise that a model that uses each node (input and output) as a variable can model the Marcus *et al.* data. This model is owing to Thomas Shultz (1999). In it, rather than each node being used to encode particular words (as in Elman's next-word-prediction model) each node codes the variable *position of word in sentence* (i.e., first, second, third). This coding must be done in an analogue style, so that, for example, if the first word is *ga* the first node is activated to (say) 2; if the first is *ni* it is activated to a value of (say) 7; if it is *li* it is activated to a value of (say) 6.

Next, as discussed earlier, a one-variable-one-node model can instantiate the copy function by having an input and an output node connected with weight of 1. This enabled Shultz to construct an auto-associating[18] network in which the activation structure of the output units had to match that of the input units. For example, imagine that the network was learning an ABA grammar. In this case it would, in training, auto-associate an input sequence of the activations (say) 5–2–5 with an output sequence of 5–2–5. However, this would be done in such a way that the third input unit was not wired to be the same as the third output unit, but rather the first input unit activation was wired to be the same as the third output unit's activation. Consult Figure 3.9, which is a reproduction of Marcus's simplified version of the Shultz model. During training, of course, the value of the first input unit (5) would always be the same as that of the third output unit. Next, at test, the input sequence might be 2–8–2. In this case input and output would match and there would no error signal. If, however the input was 2–8–8 (i.e., an ABB grammar) the first word's input activation would not map to the third word's first activation output, and so the model would 'dishabituate'. So the answer to the first question (of whether the Marcus *et al.* data can be modelled on a connectionist network) is, therefore, Yes.

For Shultz (1999, p. 665) these 'results demonstrate that a symbolic rule-based account is not required by the infant data'. But this spurs the question of whether encoding a syllable in an analogue style as, say, activation '7' is not itself a form of symbolic encoding. Could an activation level count as a Fodorian 'shape'? I will leave this question as rhetorical, to illustrate just how slippery is the concept of a symbol, and pass on.

We now begin to approach the second question – about whether ABB versus ABA are two different 'grammars' in any interesting sense.

For Marcus, this one-variable-one-unit model can implement 'operations over variables' where the one-variable-multiple-nodes models cannot. These are operations 'defined for all instances of some variable (or what I have called *algebraic rules*)' (Marcus, 2001, p. 66; original emphasis). It is not, however, transparently clear why 'current word' in the one-variable-multiple-nodes models is a variable in

---

[18] Auto-association = when feedforward networks are trained to reproduce their input; a pattern is passed through itself until it is reproduced on the output layer. Also called *identity mapping*.

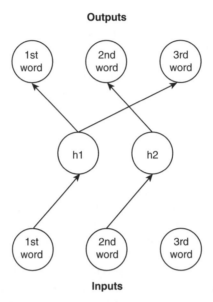

Figure 3.9 Shultz's model of infant 'algebraic' performance, based on Marcus' (2001) simplified diagram of it (permission sought). This models the ABA grammar, auto-associating ABA sequences rather than ABB sequences.

a fundamentally weaker sense than that in which 'first/second/third-word' are variables. Perhaps deciding what does and does not count as 'computing operations over variables' is not in fact a very useful criterion on which to distinguish these two kinds of model. The more obvious difference between them resides in the fact that the Shultz model is designed to code for repetitions relative to place of occurrence and the Elman model is not. Which naturally invites the question of whether item repetition relative to place of occurrence is ever employed as a syntactic feature in human language. That is to say, is the repetition of perceptually identical phonological or lexical items ever used to mark a syntactic category or operation? Or is, instead, one of the things that is special about syntactic categories and operations that they have *no* common perceptual features?

Marcus (2000, footnote 2) states that the ABB/ABA/AAB kind of discrimination is indeed of 'real linguistic relevance' despite the 'simplicity' of the structures that were used. But one might say that it is not the simplicity of the triads that can inspire scepticism about their linguistic relevance but the fact that the participants have to mark the repetition of a perceptually identical stimulus. As illustration of this linguistic relevance Marcus (2000) cites a study of Hebrew speakers by Berent, Everitt and Shimron (2001). The way in which these authors set up and discuss their study – not to mention that it concerns triads of stimuli in which two are identical! – does indeed suggest a parallel; but one can afford to be sceptical.

Let us briefly consider Berent *et al.*'s study, which was of morphology. Hebrew words contain a 'root' and a word pattern. The latter contains the vowels and the affixes; and the root, which is our concern, consists of a triad of consonants. (This is also, by the way, true of Arabic.) For instance KaTaB (= 'he wrote') is formed by inserting the root KTB into the word pattern -a-a-. Next, there is a constraint (called the obligatory contour principle or OCP) that bans identical and adjacent consonants from the representation of the root in the mental lexicon. But Hebrew does nonetheless exhibit forms in which consonants of the root repeat (so-called 'geminates'), roots like SMM for example. To explain this apparent anomaly, McCarthy (1986) has argued that in cases like this the root is stored in the lexicon as a *biconsonantal* root (i.e., SM) with the geminates emerging in the process of word formation. Furthermore, according to McCarthy, this biconsonantal root must be aligned with a word pattern containing three slots for the root consonants, a process which proceeds *from right to left*, thereby leaving the rightmost slot for the root consonant unoccupied. To fill this empty slot the second consonant becomes duplicated *rightwards* – to form SMM. This avoids violation of OCP. Given this, a root exhibiting geminates on the left (i.e., SSM) must have been stored in the lexicon, and thus be a violation of OCP.

If Hebrew speakers have OCP within their competence then they should rate nonce-words generated from nonce-roots with forms like SSM (with the initial item duplicated) as broadly unacceptable, which they do (Berent and Shimron, 1997). What Berent *et al.* (2001) further demonstrated was that when Hebrew speakers are asked to form words from novel biconsonantal roots they prefer to duplicate the final two consonants rather than the initial two. Their data also counterindicated an explanation of this preference in terms of the statistical frequency of the root tokens, which, for the authors, in turn counterindicates an explanation for this preference by a connectionist 'pattern associator' models (equivalent to the models that Marcus says do not utilise variables).

These data are surely relevant to the question of whether speakers' possess a morphological competence of a broadly Chomskyan kind, understood as the ability to manipulate mental variables in the service of productivity. But it is far from clear that they support the linguistic relevance of the Marcus *et al.* data. Recall the discussion of artificial grammar learning by adults in 1.2.2. It was suggested there, following the discussion of Mackintosh (2001), that what appears to be the transfer of abstract rules between training and testing with a novel set of stimuli may be nothing more than the subjects' noting the repetitions of stimuli. In support of this I mentioned a study by Whittlesea and Dorken (1993) who showed than when subjects were told to count item repetitions during training they performed as well on the set with novel stimuli as on the set with familiar stimuli (as compared with a substantial decrement from familiar to novel in a standard memorising condition). Humans are not the only animals highly sensitive to stimulus repetitions. Corvids (birds of the crow family), though not pigeons, are able to solve and transfer two-stimulus, same-different discriminations of the kind: AA or BB versus AB or BA (Wilson, Mackintosh and Boakes, 1985). Adults in artificial grammar learning studies are obviously doing something more sophisticated than this, but again one might call it sensitivity to number and place of repetitions rather than the picking up of an abstract regularity; which would enable them to spot, say, the parallel between TYKKKKSD and POMMMMGH. A similarity of *pattern* was being detected. The performance of Marcus's infants seems to lie somewhere between these two extremes, consisting of a sensitivity to differences between patterns of identical elements.

The fact that cotton-top tamarins show abilities similar to Marcus *et al.*'s human infants (Hauser, Weiss and Marcus, 2000) is entirely consistent with the present position. There is no reason to believe that there is anything especially linguistic about the task.

This rather sceptical take on the Marcus data would be further justified if it turned out to be the case that infant transfer between familiar and novel grammars did not take place when the cue of item repetition could not be utilised. This appears to be the case. Gómez and Gerken (1999) report a study with a similar message to that of Marcus *et al.* In this case the infants were 12 months old and the grammars were more complex. The infants were able to transfer their knowledge between grammars with the same 'word order' rules: they dishabituated to unfamiliar grammars. However Gómez and her colleagues (Gómez *et al.*, 2000) went on to show that such transfer did not take place when the grammatical and ungrammatical strings *were not distinguishable by differences in patterns of identical elements*. It was only in the case of grammars with repeating elements that abstraction beyond specific word order occurred. As Gómez and Gerken (2000) point out themselves, such data highlight strongly the area in which there is no significant analogy between patterns like ABA and (their term) 'category-based repetition' of the kind Noun-Verb-Noun. In the first case (e.g., *ba-po-ba; li-ti-li*) there is a perceptually bound physical identity and in the second case there is not (*John loves Mary; Boys play football*).

Not only can the 'algebraic' status and linguistic relevance of the kind of data reported by Marcus be brought into question but so too can its trailing implication that human infants are *essentially* algebraic rather than 'statistical' creatures. For we know that infants as young as eight months of age are hugely skilled at picking up stochastic regularities in sound sequences. Saffran and her colleagues (Saffran, Aslin and Newport, 1996) exposed them to two minutes of continuous speech consisting four three-syllable nonsense words presented in a random order (e.g., *bidakupadotigolabudidakutkupiropadoti*). In these, sounds were either invariably followed by other sounds (e.g., *pa-doti*) or only some of the time (e.g., one third of the time *pi* occurred it was followed by *gola*) or with a transition probability of zero. In the test phase – as in Marcus *et al.* – the amount of attention to kinds of sequences was measured. The infants attended longer to those in which the transition probabilities had been lower – less to *pabiku* than to *pigola*, for example. This suggested that they had picked up the different transition probabilities. A further experiment demonstrated that the infants' discriminative success was based on their computing the conditional probabilities between successive syllables rather than the simpler computation of the frequencies of syllable co-occurrences. In a subsequent study

Saffran and her colleagues (Saffran *et al.*, 1999) reported that similar results were forthcoming when the stimuli were tone sequences rather than speech-like stimuli.

Infants are, then, good at statistics as well as good at algebra. Predictably, empiricists and rationalists argued their corner armoured with one set of data or the other. In a vociferous attack on the Chomskyan view of language development entitled 'Learning rediscovered' Bates and Elman (1996) cite the Saffran *et al.* data as refuting *their characterisation* of the Chomskyan view that no human language is learned and that the concept of learning is just a folk-psychological myth. But this is not, of course, the Chomskyan view. Chomsky does not deny that English, French, Swahili, are learned by exposure to them! What he denies is that language in its fundamentals is learned. He has made this point often, and the following quotation illustrates it. Ironically this is one cited by Bates and Elman (1996) in a later round of the same controversy:

> The evidence seems compelling , indeed overwhelming, that *fundamental aspects* of our mental and social life, including language, are determined as part of our biological endowment, not acquired by learning.

> (Chomsky, 1988, p. 161, emphasis added)

And with regard to the use of the term 'learning', Chomsky's concern is with its explanatory application in science ('... we would gain in clarity if the scientific use of the term were simply discontinued'[19]). He does not deny that we learn facts. Does Noam Chomsky never ask directions when he arrives in a new town because he believes he knows the way innately?

On the other side of the divide, Steven Pinker (1999b, p. 41) takes Marcus's data to be a 'reminder that humans also think in abstractions, rules, and variables'. But, as we have seen, it is not at all clear that the data do show this; as simpler mechanisms may be in play.

Where have we reached at this point? The strategy we have been considering is that of taking one aspect of natural language processing – variables and their binding – and then asking whether connectionist networks can implement this. The answer is that, to a somewhat limited extent, they can – doing so in addition to processing transition probabilities between elements. Next, one gathers evidence for variable processing in pre-linguistic infants and finds that some kinds of network can model these data; but that, in any event, infants are also skilled at utilising transition probabilities as well. One might feel some dissatisfaction with this state of play. Why?

The kind of research strategy being exemplified here is that of collecting circumscribed linguistic or language-relevant (c.f. the APECS model) challenges for connectionism, constructing network-based solutions to them and assuming that when it comes to explaining language development itself the solutions will scale up. We have, for example, considered (1) the dynamic binding of variables (roles) and

---

[19] Cited in Piattelli-Parlmarini (1989).

values (instances) by Shastri, (2) the modelling of multiple instantiation in McLaren's APECS model, and (3) the representation of absolute word position in a string in Shultz's model of Marcus's ABB/ABA data. But while the models converge upon similar issues (i.e., they are all concerned with the problem of multiple instantiation) they are quite different. They are local solutions to problems locally construed; and they are so because the research strategy is bottom-up. And this is because the associative view of learning that empiricism espouses is itself bottom-up.

The obvious drawback to this approach is that nothing seems to justify any confidence that the models will scale up. A pressing question is whether connectionist models that bind values to variables in various ways can implement the kind of recursive operation that Chomsky called merge. It is transparently clear to many that speakers do weave phrases from lexical items and clauses from phrases; and the question whether sub-symbolic associative engines can model such a process remains unanswered by the approaches considered in this section.

In the next section we move away from the bottom-up approach to consider the way in which some kind of connectionist approach seems to be highly nutritious to our understanding of syntactic development, and then, in the second half of the section examine a case of the more familiar kind of connectionist overreaching. To do this we will be contrasting the kind of connectionist approach that is not radically empiricist with the kind that certainly is – a distinction sketched at the head of Part 3. In the first case the modeller seeks to demonstrate the role of distributional learning in the assignment of lexical items to syntactic categories, with there being no overarching assumption that this is a process of category learning *tout court*; for there is elbow-room for the view that the abstract character of these categories is 'known' prior to the task of assigning items to them. In the latter case, however, the assumption is that a process as fundamental to language processing as recursive embedding can by learned by a network – from scratch.

3.4 The clear utility of associative models – and more on their overreaching

The following logical problem for syntactic nativism will be thoroughly aired in section 4.4, when we look at the necessity for some kind initial semantic-level analysis of syntactic categories by the child. The problem is this. It is all very well ascribing to the child innate knowledge of syntactic categories such as noun, verb, and so forth; but without some learning mechanism to tell the child what *are* the nouns, verbs, etc. in the sentences she is hearing this innate knowledge can never be used. At some level then, the nativist must propose (as does Grimshaw in fact, see 2.2.3) that the child must be employing *non-syntactic* cues to form a bridge between abstract innate knowledge and (say) English words. Some of these cues are likely to be semantic (e.g., 'things are represented by nouns, actions by verbs', and so forth). Putatively innate assumptions of this kind can help to bootstrap the child into the recognition of what are the nouns, verbs, adverbs etc. in the target language. However, the first thing to note about this solution to the problem of bridging from innate category knowledge to sets of words in a target language is that the semantic generalisations will not hold in many cases. *Party*, for example, is not a 'thing word', any more than *own* is an action word; indeed the list of exceptions is endless. So the learner will need some further source of information to supplement these rules of thumb, and this will almost certainly be distributional in nature: i.e., information about the sentential context in which the word appears. Accordingly, while *party* and *ball* are not both 'thing words' they do appear in similar contexts within the sentence – preceded by *a, the, my* ..., preceding words like *is, was* ... and maybe even preceded by words like *throw*. It was Michael Maratsos (Maratsos and Chalkley, 1980) who famously argued that distributional learning may infact be sufficient to account for acquisition of the form classes; but it is *utility* not sufficiency which is the issue right now. And distributional – stochastic, probabilistic – learning is of course what connectionist models do supremely well.

Moreover, the point may well be pressed that just about all the learning about the local contours and character of the target language is distributional in nature. It so happens, for example, that the learner of English will have to notice that nouns (or if you like 'thing words and their cohorts') are pluralised by *–s* but that verbs (or 'action words and their cohorts') have their present tense marked by *–s*. For even if it is a rule that has to be noticed, we still have to posit mechanisms for the 'noticing', for sifting constants from the flux. And, moreover, does anybody seriously believe that it is by *one trial learning* that children fix parameters? Imagine the mass of converging information that they need to tell them that the language is right-branching or relatively relaxed about subjacency. (On the process of rule strengthening see Braine, 1988.)

Now the empiricist connectionist will insist, of course that there is no *more* to learning the form classes than this process of distributional learning. I will tackle that point later.

We need then to distinguish as clearly as possible between the claim that children perform statistical analyses on the distribution of word and phrasal types to help them find out what are the members of the syntactic categories in the target language, on the one hand, and the claim that there is sufficient information in the input for children to discover these categories for themselves – the empiricist connectionist position.

As we have seen, Elman *et al.* (1996) claim that the latter is what next-word prediction networks using SRNs are doing: stochastic learning is sufficient. We have spent some time detailing the shortcomings (relative of course to the claims made for it) of this kind of network; and to these we can add two further ones, as pointed out by Chater and his colleagues.

1) These SRN models do not 'scale up' from the small domains of no more than 30 or so words to more realistic vocabulary sizes of around a 1,000 words. This is mainly because making the language more complex ensures that the next word will become less predictable – with the result that the error score is less amenable to reduction by learning (Chater and Conkey, 1994, p. 293).

2) The only sense in which linguistic categories are present in the Elman next-word-prediction models is an *implicit* one. That is to say, it is the cluster analyses

performed on the hidden units' state space that reveals these categories, not the output of the network itself (Finch and Chater, 1994). This is a rather similar point to that raised above regarding the representations' lacking 'causal roles'.

The more modest and direct approach to the issue of stochastic learning of form classes, adopted by Chater and his colleagues, is to apply familiar statistical algorithms – as familiar to psychologists as Spearman correlation – to natural language corpora in order to allow a network to classify the words and phrases into categories which at least approximate those of English. This was done both for a very large sample of English downloaded from web sites (Finch and Chater, 1994) and for samples of the speech addressed to children gleaned from the CHILDES database (Reddington, Chater and Finch, 1998).

The working assumption here, recall, is that language development involves the solving of complex statistical problems, that these need to be solved if the acquisition system is to make use of crucial distributional information, and that the possession of an innate syntactic database does not make the statistical problems any less formidable. This claim, write Finch and Chater (1994, p. 314), 'is easily confused with two very different and much more contentious claims: the empiricist claim that no language-specific innate information is used in child language acquisition, and the view that language should be modelled statistically'. Moreover, under this approach, the central assumption is that the statistical problem must be solved *somehow or other*, not that the particular methods utilised by the net-like model are actually those used by the child's brain. (The child is not assumed to be a prodigiously skilled Spearman correlator.) This amounts, then, to an acceptance of a methodological distinction familiar from the work of those who design symbolic computer systems and from the work of David Marr (1982) – rejected by empiricist connectionism (Elman *et al.*, 1996) – between *what* computation must be performed to solve the problem (a notion close to that of Chomskyan competence) and *how* the solution to the problem is actually implemented.

But enough has been said about the status of the research programme, so I will now sketch the main features of the methods. In the first place, there was the assumption, shared with theoretical linguistics, that the question of whether two words or phrases belong to the same type can be settled by asking whether one can *replace* the other (see 2.1.1). Of course, in the case of the purely linguistic test we can rely upon linguistic intuitions to decide whether this has resulted in a well-formed sentence. In the present case, by contrast, one has to be content with finding out whether the two words or phases appear in the same kind of 'context'.

There were three stages towards achieving the syntactic categorisation of single words (much the same can be said about phrases, though I will not dwell on these).

1) The distribution of each word was measured. This was done by fixing a word's context of appearance as being the two words preceding it and the two words following it, while also restricting attention to the contextual words that were among the 150 most common words in the corpus (thereby picking up on the closed class of morphemes without ever defining them a such, and thereby

avoiding a problem with distributional analysis raised by Pinker, 1984). Given this, the context of a focal word had, in connectionist terms, the status of a vector of 4 (2 preceding, 2 following) sets of 150 values, each of which corresponded to the frequency with which one of the 150 most common words appears in a given context position.

2) The distributions between pairs of words were compared. Given the procedure outlined in 1, what this involved was measuring vector similarity. As previously mentioned, the Spearman rank correlation coefficient was employed to this end.

3) Words that had similar distribution were clustered. Sokal and Sneath's (1963) hierarchical clustering method was used here. This begins by combining items that are closest together according to a similarity metric. Then, once a cluster is formed, this can itself be clustered with 'nearby' items or clusters. The resulting hierarchical structure can be drawn as a so-called *dendrogram* – a familiar form of tree structure but conventionally declining horizontally from left to right rather than from top to bottom.

Attempts have been made by Chater and Finch to implement this procedure as a neural network (see Figure 3.10). This network collects the distributional statistics, computes the similarity metric, and performs the cluster analysis. The first (distributional statistics) is achieved by simple associative learning and a completely localist representation of words (2000 words each with its own input node). Each of the four banks of hidden units represents the context words, having, for reasons given in 1. above, 150 nodes each. In the final stage, cluster analysis is carried out by a competitive, unsupervised algorithm owing to Kohonen (1982) in which a given number – k – of output units correspond to the k-means which compete to account for portions of the data coming up from the four banks of hidden units.

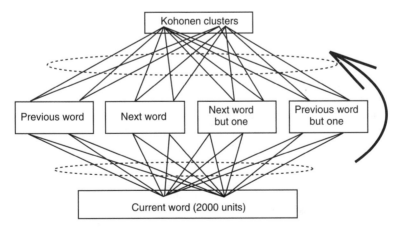

Figure 3.10 Finch and Chater's (1994) network architecture to implement the statistical algorithm for assigning words to syntactic categories. Reprinted (simplified) from "Learning syntactic categories" (Finch and Chater), in *Neurodynamics and psychology*, Oaksford and Brown (eds), pp. 296–322. Copyright (1994), with permission from Elsevier.

Now to return to the crucial, postponed issue of what is supposed to be wrong with the connectionist claim that this is not merely a correlational process which aids the learner's discovery of what are the nouns and verbs in English and how they happen to behave but rather the process of 'constructing' these categories *de novo* and from the data alone. To argue in this way is, according to Fodor (1998a), to confuse the experiential correlates of an entity with the entity itself. More broadly, it is supposed to be the old empiricist error of 'forever trying to reduce the concept of a cause of experience to the concept of the experience that it causes' (Fodor, 1998a, p. 149) – as if a noun were not something that causes us to have certain linguistic experiences, but something no more than those very experiences. (Compare – Fodor's example – being a chair and causing certain kinds of experiences.) With specific regard to Elman *et al.*'s treatment of the next word prediction SRN Fodor writes in response to their claim that 'because both grammatical category and meaning are *highly correlated* with distributional properties the network ended up learning internal representations which *reflected* the lexical category of the structure of the words' (Fodor's emphasis):

> However the problem of language acquisition is how a child learns grammatical structure, not how he learns *correlates* of grammatical structure. [Elman *et al.*'s book] does remember this distinction for almost three pages. But then it quite forgets, and Elman's network is described as having learned 'distinctions between grammatical categories; conditions under which agreement obtained; differences between verb argument structure; and how to represented embedded information'. These are not distributional correlates of structure, notice; they're the very thing itself. The equivocation is striking; what explains it? I suppose [they] are assuming, tacitly, that grammatical structures *are* just distributional patterns. To be a noun is just to be (or to be distributionally similar to) a kind of word that appears to the left of a word like 'runs' (or to the left of words that are distributionally similar to 'runs') and so on. The trouble with that sort of reductive proposal, however, is that the reductions aren't ever forthcoming. In linguistics and elsewhere, it invariably turns out that there's more to the content of our concepts than there is in the experiences that prompt us to form them. (For example: There are, I suppose, nouns in Russian. If so, *being a noun* couldn't be a property that words have in virtue of their distribution in *English*.)

(ibid, p. 150; original emphasis)

But is it that *simple*? The necessity for acknowledging the distinction between the experiences that prompt us to form concepts and the mind-independent entities (e.g., chairs) that cause the experiences and that are the extensions of the concepts, together with the view that the experiences radically underdetermine the conceptual content, is, of course, a central dogma of rationalism. But even to one who is sympathetic to the dogma, it is less than clear that the point about the form classes goes through from that basis alone. For one thing, it is open to the empiricist to reply that it is precisely the mind-independent (chair-like) status of the form classes that she wishes to undermine. A noun, on this view, is no more than a role player in the linguist's competence story: its only reality lies there. Linguists have posited the concepts 'noun', 'verb' and so forth partly in order make cross-linguistic judgements about sentential structure; but this does not, for the empiricist, have any implications for their psychological reality. They are merely descriptively convenient abstractions away from performance, a performance which is actually grounded in correlational learning, and that alone.

But this reply only has force in so far as linguistics can be regarded as being no more than a descriptive enterprise; however, central to the so-called 'Chomskyan revolution' is the view that linguistics must be construed as a form of theoretical psychology, providing models of how we move between thoughts and sentences. For such a theoretical psychology to work, certain entities, operations and levels have to be proposed. Now I'm unsure about the sense in which 'noun' and 'verb' still have a central role to play in Chomskyan theory, but one thing is certain: a model of moving between thoughts and sentences will have to posit entities at a level of abstraction similar to that of noun and verb (e.g., the αs and βs of merge). Such entities are taken to be no less real than are genes for the biologist, and they are needed in sentence generation no less than are genes in transgeneration. (It might be asked, in passing, whether an empiricist connectionist has, in fact, to be troubled by the question of whether networks succeed in virtue of constructing abstract representations. For a radical connectionist might be a Berkeleyan who, echoing Berkeley's rejection of abstract ideas, will similarly reject the psychological reality of abstract linguistic categories.)

In this light, the surface manifestation of categories like noun and verb is a trivial affair. Yes, a network can learn what correlates with them, but unless it can compute over the entities themselves it could never model the thought-sentence transitions. Accordingly, learning these correlations *tells the child about English, but it does not tell her about the operations involved in getting from thoughts and the lexicon to sentences.* In fact, this distinction between modelling the surface manifestation and modelling the process responsible for them will loom large in the remainder of this section.

What empiricist connectionism has to do, then, if it is to make its alternative conception palatable, let alone preferable, is to convince us that we can do away with the whole idea of a syntactic level of representation that is anything more substantial than the linguists' descriptive convenience. Well, in this case, why do Elman *et al.* claim to have shown that a network can acquire this chimera!

But such combative gestures are out of place here, for the central lesson is about the utility – maybe necessity – of correlational processes in syntactic development. So much, then, for what – to the rationalist – is the acceptable face of connectionist modelling of syntactic development: it gives a procedure for grouping the exemplars of form classes in the target language. This kind of modelling can leave the essential rationalist assumptions intact. In the next case, by contrast, one sees a further attempt to undermine one of the very foundations of rationalist linguistics, namely, the notion of linguistic competence as distinct from linguistic performance, with particular regard to the claim that, while performance limitations set bounds upon our ability to process recursive sentence structures, the brute fact of syntactic competence being governed by recursively applicable rules rather than by statistical tendencies cannot be undermined by any form of computational modelling.

At this point we need to visit an issue omitted from my treatment of Chomsky's 1957 theory, namely, Chomsky's analysis of why languages cannot be described by a so-called 'finite state' grammar. Such a system – a 'Markov' grammar – processes one word (or one state of the sentence production process) at a time, being concerned entirely with the nature of the transition from one word/state to the next. It is called a finite state grammar because it imagines the language faculty as a machine that can only be in one of a finite number of different internal states at any one time. Chomsky's own example is shown in Figure 3.11.

While 3.11a only produces two grammatical sentences, the assumption is that it can be scaled up to a descriptively adequate model of English by adding loops of the kind shown in 3.11.

Such a model is probabilistic in so far as it assigns a probability to each state-to-state transition, allowing calculation of the 'uncertainty' associated with each state. Chomsky's dismissal of this was swift (1957, p. 20, my italics): '*Since we are studying grammatical, not statistical structure of language here, this generalisation does not concern us*'.

This sentence of Chomsky's can be made to yield two points: (1) there *is* a real distinction between word-to-word statistical regularity and grammaticality; (2) actually, it doesn't matter what the model's attempt at explanatory adequacy is (statistical) because it completely fails the test of descriptive adequacy. And (2) is the case because *English is not a finite state language*.

The proof which Chomsky offers for the latter claim is based upon two related features of language – recursion and long-term dependency. The face of recursion we are concerned with here – I did warn it was a protean notion – is not the one we have previously encountered, which, recall, was an essential feature of phrase-structure grammar and of tree structures is general. In this sense, a system is recursive just in case it contains symbols that can be replaced by a string of symbols

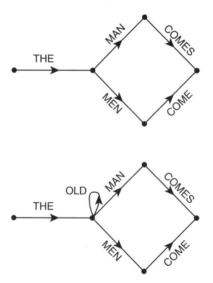

Figure 3.11 Chomsky's (1957) illustrations of a finite state (Markov) model. Reproduced from Chomsky, *Syntactic structures* (1957), with permission from Mouton, The Hague.

including itself (A → BA). In fact, a finite state grammar can output many of the sentences generated by a phrase-structure grammar, with *The old men come* being one of them.

A more decisive challenge to finite state grammars is presented by structures that are recursive in the sense that they afford the embedding of strings within other strings without limit – or rather within limits emanating only from the performance systems. (Note that, in contrast, 3.11 affords only the addition of words, not the embedding of strings.) I now describe a central feature of Chomsky's case against finite state models.

As an abstract characterisation of languages that could not be generated by a context-free (see pp. 99) finite state automaton, Chomsky imagined three general forms of grammar, of which I will mention just two. The first exemplifies what has since come to be known as *counting recursion*, with forms such as *ab, aabb, aaabbb*, and so forth. In order to parse strings of this kind it is necessary not only to process element-to-element transitions but also to count the *as* and *bs* so as to ensure they match. The second kind of recursive grammar Chomsky called *mirror-image*, with forms such as *abba, baab, aabbaa*, in which, after the mid point, the sequence is expressed in reverse order. Here too of course, it is not sufficient merely to process element-to-element transitions: the pattern of each subsequence must be recorded and coordinated. In both cases then, the 'gestalt' must be parsed as well as the parts.

Chomsky then went on to note that certain constructions in English correspond to counting and to mirror-image recursion.[20] In the first place, counting recursion is evident in sentences of the form *if S₁, then S₂* and *either S₁, or S₂*. Not only must the number of *S*s match before and after the comma but, as Chomsky (1957, p. 22) writes, 'in each case there is dependency between words on opposite sides of the comma (i.e., 'if' – 'then', 'either' – 'or')', a dependency which is across phrases not between words. However, he also noted that these constructions can be nested arbitrarily deep. Thus:

If [if S₁ then S₂] then S₃.

If [if [if S₁ then S₂] then S₃] then S₄.

(Note how one application of the procedure creates the conditions necessary for its re-application – in classic recursive style.) But sentences of this kind can also be seen to exemplify mirror-image – now more usually called *centre-embedded* – recursion. In these, the dependencies between the subject nouns and their verbs are such that the first noun is matched with the last verb, the second noun to the second to last verb, and so on (e.g., $a_1 a_2 b_1 b_2 b_2 b_1 a_2 a_1$). For example: *The mouse that the cat that the dog that the man frightened chased bit ran away.*

How then might empiricist connectionism view counting and mirror-image recursive structures? First, it would reject the idea that humans possess a competence

---

[20] The third form ('identity', e.g., *abab*) is not found in English, but it is found, at least, in Swiss-German and Dutch.

grammar that generates, say, centre-embedded sentences in virtue of its recursively applicable rules, and it would also deny the other side of the rationalist coin: that our difficulty with processing sentences like *The mouse that the cat that the dog that the man frightened chased bit ran away* is due to 'performance' limitations alone. It would also deny the need for psycholinguistic models – such as the 'CC reader' of Just and Carpenter (1992) – to enshrine this competence-performance distinction. Instead, the perspective is shifted radically towards performance *tout court* and to the question of what a computational system needs to do to simulate human performance on, say, centre-embedded sentences as it is in reality, not in terms of how it might be in some 'frictionless' ideal domain of competence. On this view, there is no need to assume that the syntactic processor really instantiates recursion or that structures of arbitrarily large complexity are 'possible sentences of the language', in any significant sense.

This at least was the starting assumption of a modelling project by Christiansen and Chater (1999). It employed what was essentially an Elman SRN network in an attempt to simulate human performance on counting recursion, mirror image recursion and a third kind of recursion not found in English but mooted by Chomsky (1957) – see footnote 20. Indeed, thinking back to Elman's next-word-prediction model, it might be said that this had *already* succeeded in modelling the long-distance dependency which is part and parcel of such forms of recursion, given that the net was able, by and large, to predict subject-verb number agreements across clausal boundaries as in *the girls the boys chase love ice cream* or *the boy the girls chase loves ice cream*. In any event, Christiansen and Chater claim that 'SRNs can capture the *quasi-recursive* structure of actual spoken language' (1999, p. 165, italics added).

As in the Elman model, this 'connectionist model of recursion' initially involved training the network to predict the next word in a sequence, given the previous context. Would it, for example, be able to make a plausible prediction given *The man the snake bit ...?*

In the model, each of the three recursion corpora had a vocabulary of 16 words (four single nouns, four single verbs, four plural nouns, four plural verbs). Again, the architecture was localist, with there being a single input and output unit to represent each word, plus one as an end-of-sentence marker – making 17 units in all. An important variable was the number of hidden units, which ranged between 2 and 100. The training corpus consisted of 5000 sentences of differing lengths, while the testing corpus consisted of 500 sentences. The three kinds of complex recursive structures were interleaved with right-branching recursive sentences (e.g., *the girl likes the boy that runs*).

Unsurprisingly given the original Elman (1993) result, the network was able to learn to make plausible next-word predictions for all three kinds of language; although the number of hidden units had little influence, with 15 hidden units being no less effective than 100. After 40 or so epochs of training the network attained a very low mean square error that did not change with additional experience. The authors also found that the network was significantly challenged by deeply-embedded recursive structures, something that was not mitigated by increasing the number of hidden units or by training exclusively on doubly-embedded constructions. However, they took this fact as evidence for the psychological reality of their model, given that human performance too degrades as the embedding gets deeper.

Christiansen and Chater also modelled the *production* of sentences using a proce- dure comparable to those discussed in 3.1. The basic procedure here involved treat- ing the output of the SRNs not as predictions about the next word to be spoken but as set of possible continuations of the sentence – as if the predictor were also the speaker. One of these predictions could then be selected by a statistical algorithm *and then fed back as the next input* (see Figure 3.12). As can be seen from the figure, they called this algorithm the stochastic selection process (SSP). The process works in the following way: given a randomly chosen noun as input to the network, this produces a *distribution* of possible successors, which the SSP treats as a set of prob- abilities (they sum to 1) and then chooses one of them according to the probabili- ties. This item then becomes the next input to the network – and so on. In this case, performance fell well short of human levels. On the centre-embedded languages, for example, 31 per cent of sentences were ungrammatical. The errors varied widely in nature. Around a quarter were errors of number agreement, while some of the remainder were quite gross, such as inserting verbs into the initial string of nouns and nouns into the subsequent string of verbs, or having unequal numbers of nouns and verbs.

What is to be made of this? In the first place, Marcus-style scepticism about what such a network had succeeded in doing can be taken as read. The network did not need to construct 'abstract representations of nouns and verbs' (of the kind probed by the authors in the state space – p. 193, ibid.) to succeed in its purely statistical task

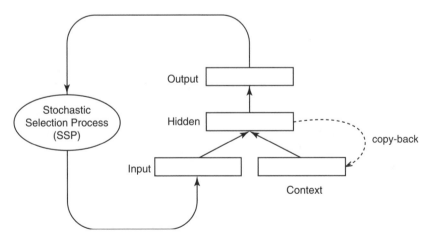

Figure 3.12 Christiansen and Chater's (1999) network model for generating centre- embedded and other sentences. See text for exposition (permission sought).

of next-word prediction, because the local context in which each word appeared in the training set was sufficient for this. Consider, in illustration, the way in which the Xs and Ys overlap statistically in the following examples: *the X the dog bit ran; the Y the dog chased ran*; or: *the man the dog X-ed died; the dog the man Y-ed sneezed.* Second, it is important to lay to rest any lingering thought that the hidden units of SRNs are doing their work in virtue of constructing representations of the kind that 'purely' statistical engines like Markov models cannot. This is because a modified form of Markov model, called a hidden Markov model (HMM), can perform just as well as – or, in some situations, better than – SRNs on tasks in which the next item in a sequence has to be predicted. (To date, HMMs have mainly been used in speech recognition systems, exploiting the fact that they can capture temporal dependencies in a series of utterances in the service of identifying phonemes.) The essential difference between a standard Markov model and an HMM is that, whereas in the Markov model predicting the next node is done entirely on the basis of the state of the current node, in the HMM it is done on the basis of *all the observations* of states that led up to the current state. (See Bengio 1996, section 4.8, for the mathematics of HMMs.) In fact, Visser, Raijmakers and Molenaar (2000) showed that human performance on implicit sequence learning tasks, in which subjects have to guess the next item in a sequence generated by a finite state automaton, is approximated more accurately by HMMs than by SRNs. Indeed, it would seem to be tasks of this kind, rather than our linguistic abilities, that provide the human analogue to next-word-predicting networks.

I now turn to the parallel between SRN and human performance drawn by Christiansen and Chater; which boils down to the claim that because the performance of both degraded with deeper embeddings they might well be computing recursion in the same way. But, quite apart from the fact that it would have been surprising indeed if the network's performance had not degenerated as the statistical task became more difficult, it is worth noting what this increase in difficulty amounts to in the case of human performance. The problem we have with parsing sentences like *The mouse that the cat that the dog that the man frightened chased bit ran away* does not take the form of our simply producing an erroneous parse – the comprehension analogue of gibberish. It takes the form of non-comprehension and then, if we have the patience, of dedicating more processing resources to working out the correct parse – something with which readers of late Henry James will be familiar. To say that there is no analogue to this in the case of the network is not just to make the obvious point that neural networks do not enjoy any analogue of conscious states. Rather, the point is that humans deploy – setting aside the conscious status of this – a body of knowledge, whose formal nature is clearly non-conscious but *of* which we know consciously, in the service of an explicit linguistic goal. In other words, we know what it means for nouns to be the grammatical subjects of verbs and we know how recursive English sentences determine which noun is the subject of which verb. We step up our performance towards a goal that we have erected for ourselves in terms of a competence that makes both the goal and its solution possible. This might of course be nothing more than a bit of unexamined rationalist dogma; but little in the model's performance argues for its abandonment. Recall, in particular, that when the network was made to 'devote more processing resources' to the task by increasing the number of hidden units, its performance did not improve. And one might imagine that this was because it was hamstrung by having only statistical regularities in the training set to go on, rather than a competence model.[21]

Next, we need to focus upon what 'modelling recursion' amounts to here. One easily dogmatic line is that this simply cannot be a simulation of linguistic recursion, because only symbol-processing systems can be recursive. As defined above, a system is recursive in so far as it contains symbols which can be replaced by a string of symbols including itself (A $\rightarrow$ BA). Given this, some would insist that sentential recursion can only be a property of an hierarchical symbolic system. Certainly, it is recursion in this strong sense that is supposed to explain what Chomsky and Fodor call the *productivity* of our linguistic and cognitive capacities (see 1.1.5), given that possession of recursive rules enables us to produce (/understand) an infinite number of sentences. Perhaps such a system might be implemented sub-symbolically; indeed in one sense we *know* it can be, given that brain's wet-ware contains no symbols! But there is still room for dispute between empiricist connectionists and rationalists over whether symbol processing supervenes on[22] the sub-symbolic in something like the way in which a computer program supervenes on silicon chips.

But it is not necessary to take this dogmatic line in order question the authors' claim that recursion has been modelled on a connectionist network. At this point, I return to the distinction, mooted earlier in this section, between the surface manifestation of syntactic processing and the set of operations over abstract elements, mediating between the thought systems and speech, which enable the surface form to be expressed at all. (Earlier, I mentioned the difference between the surface distributional contexts of English nouns and verbs and computations over the elements of merge.) In the present case, most evidently, what we witness is modelling the statistical structure of certain kinds of sentence which, had they been generated from thoughts, would have required recursive rules to come to fruition. Obviously, all sentences *have* statistical structure, and so, up to a point, all kinds can be modelled by prediction/production algorithms. But equally obviously, what is being modelled the result of a process not the process itself.

To put it another way, when we view recursion in this light it is clear that Christiansen and Chater are not modelling recursion, which is a feature of the sentence generating system, but rather the surface forms of certain English (and Dutch,

---

[21] I am grateful to Rainer Spiegel for suggesting this point.

[22] Phenomena of one kind 'supervenes on' phenomena of another kind when differences with respect to the first kind require differences with respect to the second kind. For example, if one painting is more beautiful than another there must be some *non-aesthetic* difference between the two of them. Thus, one set of properties depends on another set of properties, *without being explicable in terms of them*. Philosophers of mind have used the notion of supervenence to capture the relation that appears to obtain between mental and physical properties.

see footnote 20) sentences, doing this not in terms of how they were generated but in terms of what the exemplar sentences have statistically in common. To achieve this, the network had to note how, in the training set, certain verbal contexts predicted the appearance of certain words. What might be called the 'grammatical motivation' behind this predictability was of no relevance. To take an analogy, it is like copying an inverted drawing while having no idea that the drawing happens to represent, say, a kettle. The drawing may turn out very well; indeed copies of inverted drawings are often better than of drawings set the right way up. But in so far as the copyist proceeds blindly she is unable to draw a kettle at will – when told to draw one. Framing a sentence to express a thought is, however doing something at will on the basis of knowledge.

Note too, in passing, that in treating the challenging cases like that of centre embedding as representing the core of recursion and thereby concluding from the putative success of their model that recursion has been modelled, Christiansen and Chater are taking a traditional connectionist tack. For, in a similar spirit, Rumelhart and McClelland (1986, p. 119) denied that the fact of the productivity of linguistic capacities are 'of the essence of human computation' on the grounds that complex centre-embedded sentences are hard to understand, as if – as Fodor and Pylyshyn (1988, p. 35) point out – the fact of centre-embedding was an *embarrassment* for those who take linguistic capacities to be productive. But the difficulty of parsing centre-embedded sentences is not a direct consequence of their recursive nature, for many recursive structures are easy to understand – right-branching ones most notably. See Wanner and Maratsos (1978) for a symbol-processing account of why centre embedding challenges our performance capacities.

Finally, to reprise some remarks made in 2.4.1 in the context of a speaker framing a thought linguistically, it can be said that the notion of competence – abstract knowledge possessed by the speaker that serves as a recipe for constructing sentences from thoughts – enables one to capture the *certainty* that speakers have about whether they have succeeded in constructing the *right* sentence. (Here, of course, some Cartesian roots are showing.) When, however, we abandon the notion of competence we are left with a conception of sentence framing on the model of phrase book use. On this model, the speaker's brain is able to induce what would be an adequate sentential expression of this thought on the basis of past experience – being doomed, thereby, to mere hopefulness. She can never know for herself whether or not she has succeeded. Now, to the radical or 'Berkeleyan' connectionist – mentioned above – whether or not SRNs construct abstract representations of linguistic categories cannot be an urgent issue because there are no such entities. To this, the rationalist will shrug his shoulders and say 'Well, if the phrase-book model of linguistic abilities is what you want, you are welcome to it'. Much more about the phrase-book conception in Part 4.

At this point, before we become smothered by metaphor and dogma, there clearly needs to be some balanced assessment of the utility, as against the pretensions, of connectionist models of acquisition, and indeed of parsing, from *another* source. As we saw earlier in this subsection, stochastic associative processes would seem to be a necessity for the learner at some level, while more recently we have been discussing how they fall short of capturing fundamental syntactic operations. For such an assessment I turn to a discussion by Mark Steedman, somebody whose work in *symbolic* computational linguistics and in psycholinguistics is well known, but somebody whose work displays an open mind about computational architectures.

First, Steedman (1999) draws an equation, one which emerged, in fact, from my discussion of the Christiansen and Chater model, between SRN next-word-prediction models and HMMs, understood as a species of symbolic yet stochastic models. In addition, he says that another kind of finite-state symbolic model called a part-of-speech (POS) tagger (e.g., Brill, 1992) also performs next-word prediction very accurately (better than 95 per cent precision) without there being any implication from this that POSs embody a *grammar*. And he points out that such symbolic models are more often than not ignored within the connectionist literature.

He goes on to say that the claim made by Elman (1995) and others that SRN's hidden-unit state space representations capture sentence meaning is too strong. This is because of the familiar and fundamental linguistic fact (illustrated in 2.1.1 of this book) that a mere sequence of words, even if that sequence has its elements unambiguously tagged by syntactic category and by sense (which a stochastic tagger might achieve), is not in itself a sentence meaning. This fact is most vividly illustrated by cases of ambiguity (cf. Chomsky on deep structure). To give Steedman's example, a sentence such as

Put the block in the box on the table

would remain structurally and semantically ambiguous when the lexical categories have been unambiguously identified. The point is that a substantial component of grammar induction and parsing remains to be dealt with once POS-taggers/HMMs/SRNs have done their work. These can therefore serve as input to 'parsing proper' but no more.

Steedman does not, however, end on this pessimistic note. Rather, he tells us that the recent trend in 'symbolic stochastic language processing is away from grammar-independent POS tagging' and towards 'a greater integration of probabilistic information with the grammar and recursive parsing algorithms' (ibid, p. 623). In other words, the boundary between the stochastic input to the parser and the symbolic processes in parsing itself is showing signs of melting. Indeed the fact that the 1990 issue of the journal *Artificial Intelligence* was later published as a book (ed. G. Hinton) under the title of *Connectionist symbol processing* carries just this implication. I will very shortly discuss a paper in that volume – by Pollack.

Steedman expresses enthusiasm for a form of connectionist processor that uses an associative memory to build up recursive syntactic structures. This is the recursive auto-associative memory (RAAM) architecture of Pollack (1990). And note that if such a model really is doing what it advertises itself as doing then the rationalist's a priori denial mentioned a little earlier – that no sub-symbolic system can model 'true' recursion – would be radically undermined. In any event, it is worth looking at RAAM with some care, while bearing in mind that its network does not extract knowledge from natural sentences but from strings that have been pre-structured in Lisp-like nested lists.

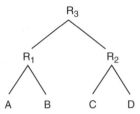

Figure 3.13 A tree structure that Pollack's (1990) RAAM might model. Reprinted from *Artificial Intelligence*, Pollack, J., "Recursive distributed representations", pp. 77–105. Copyright (1990), with permission from Elsevier.

Consider the tree structure shown in Figure 3.13. The computational task of representing this structure could be seen as that of translating in two directions between the labelled terminals and the tree. That is, the model would both induce the tree structure from the terminals and reproduce the terminals from the tree. This would involve three steps for a 'compressor': A and B would be compressed into pattern R_1, C and D compressed into R_2, and then R_1 and R_2 would be compressed into R_3. After this a 'reconstructor' would decode these patterns into facsimiles of their parts – R_3 into R_1' and R_2' down to A', and so forth. In connectionist terms this is training a net to reproduce a set of input patterns while making the input pattern also the target – hence *auto-association*. In learning to do this, the network develops a compressed code on the hidden units for each of the input patterns. As can be seen from Figure 3.14, there needs to be twice the number of input/output units than hidden units to achieve this. In this way, the hidden-unit encodings can be used themselves to develop a database of encodings of various tree structures and can then be used as inputs for either branch of a new tree. In this sense then, the model is recursive, being able in principle to represent any binary branching tree. The network develops representations of the sub-components of structured inputs, which then become input for processing the components.

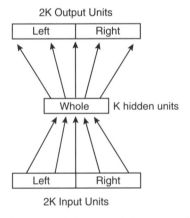

Figure 3.14 Pollack's (1990) auto associative network for representing binary free structures. Reprinted from *Artificial Intelligence*, Pollack, J., "Recursive distributed representations", pp. 77–105. Copyright (1990), with permission from Elsevier.

This system can represent on its hidden units the syntactic parse tree for a sentence such as *The little boy ran up the street* – having the structure ((Det (Adj Noun)) (Verb (Prep (Det Noun)))) – encoding each of the elements on 20 input/output units feeding into 10 'compressed' hidden units. Different patterns of hidden-unit activation emerge with each structure. Thus, in this case, the network is trained to auto-associate on the simple constituents (Adj Noun) and (Det Noun) first, before being trained on (Det (Adj Noun)), (Prep (Det Noun) and (Verb (Prep (Det Noun))); then finally on the whole string.

Pollack insists that RAAM is doing more than simply *memorizing* the training set, because it represents sequences and trees beyond that set. Indeed he claims that the network's competence is *systematic*, as defined by Fodor (see 1.1.4, and 3.5). (For example, being able to think *John loves Mary* entails the further capacity to think *Mary loves John.*) Thus, in all 16 cases of the form (loves X Y), with the Xs and Ys being John, Mary, Pat or Man, all 16 could be reproduced despite the fact that the network had been trained on only four of them. (In the next section we will discuss whether demonstrations of this kind do *indeed* reveal sub-symbolic systematicity.)

What form do the representations underlying RAAM take, if they are not symbolic in the traditional sense? Because the primitives of the model are represented on the input/output units in binary form, this representation can be captured geometrically with a 'hypercube' in which the primitives begin at the bottom corners of the cube and $R_1 \ldots R_3$ are the vortices of triangles leading up from these located on faces or corners of the cube. See Figure 3.15, taken from Pollack.

Setting aside concerns about whether RAAM can scale up beyond the very small vocabularies to which it has been exposed so far (on which, Marcus, 2001, p. 105) and about whether the sense of 'recursion' employed here is the same one as that used in symbolic computation, we return to the Steedman paper. 'This device should not,' writes Steedman, 'be confused with a parser: it is trained with fully articulated structures which it merely efficiently stores' (ibid, p. 625). In other words, *RAAM does not induce a grammar from quasi-natural strings but learns to represent structured representations as such* – representing trees *as* trees – achieving, in doing so, some degree of generalisation (discussed in the next section). So what needs to supplement devices like RAAM if an underlying grammar is to be induced from strings? Steedman's answer is 'conceptual structure'. Thinking developmentally, let us imagine that the child has the kind of associative capacity of the kind exemplified in RAAM as part of her innate endowment. According to Steedman (ibid., p. 626, emphasis added), the child needs, in addition to this, not pre-minimalist-programme-style linguistic universals, but a structured semantic system:

> the only plausible source of pre-grammatical knowledge has always been semantics, under the assumption that the child comes to language learning equipped with universal conceptual structures on which language-specific grammar is *rather directly* hung by pairing words and sentences with conceptual structures describing the situation of utterance ... although Chomsky has always insisted that our access to the detailed nature of conceptual structure, other than via syntax itself, is so inadequate as to make the observation empirically useless ... *conceptual structure represents universal grammar.*

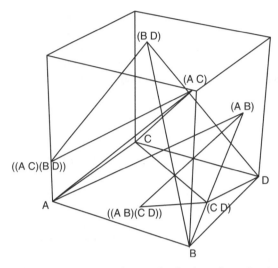

Figure 3.15 Pollack's (1990) perspective diagram for the three-dimensional codes developed for trees ((AB)(CD)) and ((AC)(BD)).

While we are now bordering territory that will be fully explored in Part 4, it is worth briefly reflecting now on Steedman's position *vis-à-vis* Chomsky's minimalism. While Steedman takes his combinatory categorical grammar (CCG) (Steedman, 2000) to be a species of minimalism, it would seem to be *more* minimalist than Chomsky's in the following sense. In this theory, as in Chomskyan minimalism, much of the work that used to be done by phrase structure rules is now assigned to lexical representations on which combinatory rules (cf. Chomsky's merge) operate to produce sentences. But the divergence lies in the fact that in CCG *surface syntax maps directly onto compositional semantic representations* of predicate-argument structures, quantification, and the like, eschewing intermediate syntactic levels. There is no need, on this view, to posit any Chomskyan interface between the conceptual-intentional systems and the language faculty, as all we see are direct pathways. And yet Steedman does not belong in the pragmatist camp along with linguists such as Ronald Langacker (see 4.1.1), because he is not proposing that syntactic processing reduces to the utilisation of cognitive schemas. Needless to say, all this just serves to illustrate how difficult it can be to draw a clear line between what might be called 'minimal minimalism' and cognitive-functional ('pragmatist' in the present taxonomy) conceptions of the language–thought relationship.

 With regard to the present issue, what Steedman is saying in effect is that linguistic structures, within the parser or the acquisition device, have got to come from somewhere. They will not emerge from purely associative devices such as RAAM, so they had better be seen as coming from conceptual structure, with the implication being that this is innate. The challenge to the empiricist is then to face this claim head on and show how conceptual structure *can* emerge from associative learning. To put it another way, can we offer a connectionist account of the cognitive-intentional systems? This is the topic of the penultimate section of this Part.

3.5 Connectionism and the conceptual-intentional systems

In this section we will be centrally concerned with what it means to say that the cognitive capacity of the language learner is 'structured' and with the possibility that this structuring might be modelled in a connectionist style – whatever connectionism's successes and failures in modelling syntax and its acquisition turn out to be. To put the issue this way, and to assume that this cognitive structure must make contact with syntax, is implicitly to deny that the structure of adult cognition is inherited from syntax itself. One might, in fact, take up the latter view in either an 'internalist' (see 1.1.4) or an 'externalist' style. In the former case, the development of a syntax module would be seen as impacting upon the cognitive systems with maturation, while, in the latter case, language as a sociocultural artefact would be seen as moulding thought in a Whorfian style. Needless to say, both of these views are anathema to holders of the language of thought doctrine (1.1.5) and to the minimalist Chomskyan; but it should be noted that they would also be rejected by supporters of Piagetian-style pragmatism (to be discussed in Part 4). As mentioned in Part I, it is possible for empiricists, and therefore empiricist connectionists, to adopt the nominalism of the externalist alternative, while pragmatists of a Rortyan stamp, recall, espouse something similar though more ideological in style ('Being that can be understood is language'). But a discussion of this kind has got to start somewhere, and mine will begin from the premise that the thought of language-learning children possesses a kind of 'structure' that is the cognitive bedrock for syntax acquisition. (Later I will discuss the connectionist challenge from *externalism* made by the philosopher Andy Clark.)

To a large extent I shall be bracketing off the question of whether connectionism can model conceptual content (i.e., of concepts like DOG, ANIMAL and WALK), which might be regarded as the cognitive atoms, in order to focus on the *molecular* level. But I think it would be well to say something about this at the outset in order to head off any quick dismissal of the very possibility that the human conceptual atoms could be modelled in a connectionist style. Consider the following from Fodor (1998a).

> In linguistics and elsewhere it invariably turns out that there's more in the content of our concepts than there is in the experiences that prompt us to form them … The empiricist programme was in place for several hundred years, not just in psychology but also – indeed especially – in epistemology and the philosophy of science, where a lot of clever people wasted a lot of time trying to reduce 'theoretical' concepts (like TABLE) to 'observation' concepts (like RED and SQUARE). There were in the course of those centuries *no successes at all*; literally *none*; which is to say *not one*. […] So it looked, until just recently, that the argument between empiricism and rationalism had been put to rest. The connectionists have revived it.

If this is taken as gospel – I am not denying its truth – then one will pronounce that, in so far as empiricist connectionism deals only with perceptually-delivered-up features and in so far as concepts are more than aggregations of such features, connectionism is doomed to fail to model concepts. And from a developmental perspective the sceptic would remind us of empirical work showing that young children will often ignore an object's superficial appearance in determining its category membership, as well as revealing themselves to be 'essentialists' or 'theorists' who take a thing's nature to be some imperceptible core and source of causal power about which experts can inform us (Gelman, *et al.* 1994). To take an example of the former kind of work, Gelman and Markman (1986; see also Gelman and Coley, 1990) gave pre-school children a task in which category membership was placed in conflict with visual appearance. The children were asked to make a series of inductions. For instance, in one case they saw a brontosaurus, a rhinoceros, and a triceratops, which were labelled 'dinosaur', 'rhinoceros' and 'dinosaur' respectively. The category labels and the appearance conflicted in the following sense: the brontosaurus and the triceratops are members of the same category, while the rhinoceros and triceratops looked more alike. Children then learned a new property of the brontosaurus and the rhinoceros, which was that they had cold and warm blood respectively; and after this they were asked if the triceratops had cold or warm blood. They said it had cold blood like the brontosaurus, seemingly generalising on the basis of some biological essence that the term 'dinosaur' named.

Well, it turns out that this result can be modelled in a connectionist style (Rogers and McClelland, in press). Indeed, the book in which the simulation is reported takes a number of well-known results in the child-as-theorist (as opposed to perceptual-category-learner) research tradition and models them on a neural network. As one would expect, however, there is plenty of scope for scepticism. In particular, it pays to look closely, if this work is to be taken as a series of empiricist thought experiments, at what is being encoded on the input units. If one is putting non-perceptual 'theoretical' features like 'has warm blood' and 'is alive' then, in a sense, it is not surprising that the network behaves like a 'theorist' rather than like an empiricist engine. But perhaps it would be well to give connectionism the benefit of the doubt on this question and let it remain as a possibility that there are no deep impediments to modelling the cognitive 'atoms' of the language learning child in a connectionist style. In any event, few would dispute that the real challenge lies at the *molecular* level.

3.5.1 Systematicity and her sisters

In 1988 Fodor and Pylyshyn published a paper called *Connectionism and cognitive architecture: A critical analysis* in which they tried to demonstrate that connectionist representations do not, in fact, *possess* a molecular level in any serious sense. Symbol-processing, or 'classical', architectures combine cognitive atoms in such a way as to capture the productivity of thought and its *systematicity* (the fact the ability to think one thought implies the ability to think other thoughts with semantically related contents, and recall the discussions of Fodor and of Evans' generality constraint from Part 1). Connectionist representations lack this property, they argue. They lack it, argued Fodor and Pylyshyn, not because modellers had yet to come up with a way of making neural networks behave in a systematic fashion, but because the eschewal of symbols necessarily entails that systematicity (taking this as

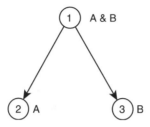

Figure 3.16 Fodor and Pylyshyn's (1988) caricature of a network's 'inferring' from A & B to A.

the synecdoche for a group of related attributes of structured cognition) must fail to be a feature of connectionist representations. Accordingly, if modellers did ever produce outcomes for a task consistent with representational systematicity these could not have been achieved in virtue of such systematicity, but by some other means. Classical architectures, on the other hand, have this property *inherently*; and as human thought also has the property inherently it looks like classical architectures are the ones to be favoured.

Before tackling the issue of systematicity itself, we need first to think about the different ways in which connectionist and classical architectures represent. Fodor and Pylyshyn give the example of the molecular thought 'A&B', from which the inference 'A' can be drawn. In a neural network (see Figure 3.16) the excitation of node 1 (labelled by the modeller A&B) results in the activation of node 2 (labelled by the modeller A). In a classical architecture, by contrast, the program contains the symbols 'A', 'B', 'A&B', 'C', 'D', and so forth; while, as Fodor and Pylyshyn put it, 'the machine's causal constitution' ensures that when a token of the *form P&Q* is presented to the program a token of the form *P* is outputted. In this way, a token is caused to be produced not by spreading excitation but by the *shape*[23] of the token being processed. Given this, Fodor and Pylyshyn stress that the labels attached to the nodes in 3.16 are profoundly misleading, for these are not symbols with causal powers. That is to say, node 1 has, in reality, no semantically interpreted parts, *and so the label plays no role in determining how the network functions*. The three nodes might equally well have been labelled 'Camden Town', 'Tufnell Park' and 'Finchley Central'. In contrast, the transitions between the classical machine's states are determined by the structure of the symbol arrays, including that of its constituent parts. In short, the network's putatively molecular thought 'A&B' is not really a conjunction of parts at all. To be a conjunction of parts there have to be symbols somewhere to represent these parts.

What if the connectionist replies to this: 'Well, combinatorial complexity can be attained at the more global level by virtue of the state of the network rather than of

---

[23] See footnote 12 (p. 282) and associated text.

a single node. Thus, to represent the conjunction of A and B one simply ensures that A and B nodes are simultaneously active. Similarly, if one wishes to model the molecular thought [JOHN LOVES MARY] one ensures that the node or node sets representing JOHN, LOVES, and MARY are simultaneously active'. (Recall the 'messages' in the Chang *et al.* (1997) production model discussed in 3.1.)

To this, Fodor and Pylyshyn's classicist would reply that there is all the difference in the world between nodes being simultaneously active/mental representations being concurrent and a complex *thought* being entertained. This is because, when representations express concepts which belong to the same population, these are not merely 'coming on together' but they are – in Fodor and Pylyshyn's phrase – *in construction with one another*. (Recall the discussion of the Allen and Seidenberg model in 3.1.) In a sense, the rest of their paper is given up to unpacking what this phrase means, but for now we might think of the fact of elements being in construction with one another as being something that is captured by the linguist's, the logician's, and the programmer's system of bracketing and by the logician's armoury of operators (v, &, → etc). In the first place, the very point of adding the fact of the deduction of A from A&B to the example was to reinforce the fact that the *conjunction* of A and B had to be represented. The deduction is possible in virtue of the conjunction; whereas when A and B are merely simultaneously active the further logical step of deducing A is not afforded: no further logical moves are potentiated and so one thought cannot lead to another. If this is too quick and metaphorical, the [JOHN LOVES MARY] examples makes the point more elegantly; and it is how Fodor and Pylyshyn make it. For example – I am simplifying their own example somewhat – imagine a person thinking [JOHN LOVES MARY] while looking up at the blue sky and registering this blueness – JOHN, MARY, LOVES and BLUE are all active. Well, how do you ensure that the thought you have modelled is not 'John loves blue Mary' or 'Mary loves John' or 'Mary loves blue John'? To get round this problem, the modeller might try to introduce the necessary degree of structuring by having a node labelled SUBJECT-OF to link JOHN with LOVES. (Recall that something like this is done in McWhinney's competition model; see 3.2.) But this is no good, because some kind of bracketing arrangement has to ensure that [JOHN, SUBJECT-OF, LOVES, MARY] does not in fact model the thought Mary loves John. This is of course our old friend the binding problem. And recall that one well-known putative solution to the binding problem – Shastri and Ajjanagadde's (1993) synchronised oscillators – is essentially a way of *narrowing down* the notion of 'simultaneously active'. Binding variables to values (e.g., 'agent' to 'John') by simultaneous oscillation might be said to be a '*practical solution*' to the binding problem; but it certainly fails to capture what it means in human thought to attach a predicate to an argument. This is because capturing which concepts are active and which are in construction with one another are quite different kinds of achievement.

Now, it is natural , as we saw in 1.2.1, to think of 'being active' along the Humean lines of having 'force' and 'vivacity', suggesting that a theory of molecular thought in a Humean spirit would be one on terms of a co-occurring elements of vivacity. The critique of this way of thinking has been around since the eighteenth century. Its foremost critic was Immanuel Kant. In a passage quoted in full by Fodor and

Pylyshyn (ibid, p. 27) Kant distinguishes between a judgement 'as belonging to the understanding' and one construed in terms of 'the laws of reproductive imagination' (i.e., according to associationism) – 'which has only subjective validity'. He gives the example of judging that something is heavy when supporting it. In the judgement 'The body is heavy' there is 'a relation which is *objectively valid*' (original italics) as distinct from the 'subjective' validity of two ideas linked through laws of association. In the latter case

> All I could say would be 'If I support a body, I feel an impression of weight'. I could not say [developmentally, would not have the cognitive resources to learn to say, JR] 'It, the body, is heavy.' Thus to say 'The body is heavy' is not merely to state that two representations have always been conjoined in my perception, … what we are asserting is that they are combined *in the object.*

(original italics)

The notational device which Kant uses to differentiate the objective from the subjective case is the possible presence of, as he puts it, 'the copula "is"' in the former case. Nowadays we are more likely to do so, say Fodor and Pylyshsyn, by employing the bracketing structures of linguists' constituency trees.

To pull us back briefly to developmental concerns, imagine, as a thought experiment, a child of, say, 20 months who is only capable of the subjective combination of impressions. She enters a playroom and tries to play with one of the toys, but finds it to be too heavy to lift. All she can represent is the co-occurrence of lifting and heaviness. Well, how could – and why should – this child ever come to tell her mother that the toy is heavy? What objective fact is there to report if she has not succeeded, in virtue of making 'is heavy' a constituent of her thought about the object, in taking something to be true of something? In other words, a creature who is going to learn to attach verb phrases to NP subjects in her native language is going to have to be a creature who can first do the mental version of this in a mental format.

Next, before moving on to systematicity, we need to note a tension – one I touched upon in 1.1.5 and to which I will return – between this mental format, understood as a language of thought (LOT), and natural language. The authors mention this in a footnote (ibid, p. 29). In the case of what they understand as LOT there is an intimate relationship between semantic and syntactic structure which guarantees the smoothness of inference based on constituency. This fact gives us a window on the constituent structure of LOT. Here is their example.

(1) John went to the shops and Mary went to the shops.

(2) Mary went to the shops.

(2) is semantically entailed by (1) (the inference is truth-preserving), while syntactically (2) is a constituent of (1). If, (1) were *syntactically atomic,* this would not be the case. However in English, and surely in many other natural languages, it is not uniformly the case that syntactic constituents can be so cleanly extracted (*John and Mary are friends → John are friends*) nor that inferences based on the extraction are truth preserving (*The flag is red, white and blue → The flag is blue*). All this probably goes to show, they say, is that English is not a LOT. At this point I think it would be

well to refer the reader back to the discussion of Evans in 1.1.5 and his claim that while sentences need not be 'structured', thoughts are 'structured' in their essence, and that any meaning expressed by a structured sentence can be expressed by an unstructured one. Perhaps one might say that the level on which the structure of thought is manifested more or less directly in language exemplifies Chomskyan 'virtual conceptual necessity'. Now back to the main thrust of the paper.

After a discussion of the productivity of thought, in which the role of recursive rules is emphasised in a way that should by now be familiar and in which the authors sound the caveat that 'the status of productivity arguments for classical architectures is moot' pp. 315–317, they discuss systematicity. Whether or not, they argue, our cognitive capacities are truly productive, they surely are systematic; and the fact of systematicity demonstrates what up till now has only been assumed: that thought has a combinatorial structure. They write (ibid., p. 37, original emphasis).

> What we mean when we say that linguistic structures are *systematic* is that the ability to produce/understand some sentences is *intrinsically* connected to the ability to produce/understand certain others.

The reference to sentences should not blind us to the fact that Fodor and Pylyshyn also assume systematicity to be a 'thoroughly pervasive feature of human and *infrahuman* mentation' (emphasis added).

In fact we are on territory that will have become familiar not only from my previous discussion of systematicity in Part 1, but also from my disparaging references to 'phrase book' models of linguistic capacities. The point about phrase book use in this context is this. The linguistic ability of a phrase book user is (the authors' term) *punctate*, in the sense that it consists of unrelated islets of capacity. The phrase book user may be able to ask for two beers and say he likes the sausages, but be unable to say/understand 'two sausages' and 'I like the beer'; and this because his grasp of the language need only be atomic, as is a native speaker's grasp of the *lexicon*. Accordingly, if understanding/saying 'John loves the girl' is to manifest a grasp of the formula for English 'NP-Verbtrans-NP' this understanding/saying will also apply to sentences like 'The girl loves John', 'John loves John' and 'The girl loves the girl'. In the atomic case, however, there is no structural parallel between 'John loves the girl' and 'The girl loves John' and no more reason to expect that understanding one goes along with understanding the other than understanding 'train' goes along with understanding 'grass'.

At this point there is every reason to wonder whether language-learning children pass through a kind of 'phrase book' or 'punctate' stage of syntactic development – failing to note the structural properties of utterances. (We will see in 4.4 that theorists such as Tomasello and Pine base their accounts of syntactic development on the claim that they *do*.) Fodor and Pylyshyn say in a footnote, however, that there is no good evidence that they do so – in any serious sense. While very young children (roughly before 18 months) do sometimes use fixed verbal formulae like 'clever girl' – never using 'clever' to modify any other noun and never modifying 'girl' with any other modifier – once they are using NP-verb-NP forms they do appear to possess rules with 'identical symbols' in the subject and the object positions.

$$\left\{ \begin{array}{c} \text{Pro} \\ \text{N}+\text{N} \\ \text{M}+\text{N} \end{array} \right\} \quad \left\{ \begin{array}{c} \text{V}+\text{V} \\ \text{V} \end{array} \right\} \quad \left\{ \begin{array}{c} \text{Pro} \\ \text{N}+\text{N} \\ \text{M}+\text{N} \\ \text{N} \end{array} \right\}$$

Table 3.1 The range of S-V-O constructions used by Roger Brown's children (M = modifier).

Pinker (1984, pp. 131–138) provides an interesting discussion of the evidence. At first blush, it does look as if children do not behave systematically because the subject NPs in early speech tend to be bare nouns or pronouns with the object NPs often expanding as possessor-possessed (e.g., *John bed*), modifier-object (e.g., *little girl*), and so forth. But Pinker argues that this pattern is 'a statistical tendency not an absolute generalisation'. In the first place, the rarity of subjects with the full internal structure of objects may well be caused by performance factors independent of grammar. Broadly speaking, it is assumed to be easier to leave the elaborated combinations to later in the sentence because to do the reverse would mean having to load more information into working memory. In the second place, while elaborated subjects are not common they are far from being completely absent. That is to say, we do find utterances like *Dale shoe right there*, *Dale Panda march*, and *big doggie boot bit me shame*. In fact, in the table Pinker constructs from Roger Brown's data from 'Adam', 'Eve' and 'Sarah'[24] it can be seen that a little under one-fifth of subjects were modified, and also that the absolute rarity of modified subjects is attributable to the rarity of subjects relative to objects. Third, Pinker reminds us of Brown's finding that the children produced almost the full range of constructions that would be predicted on the assumption that pre- and post-verbal elements are selected from the same set of structural possibilities (see Table 3.1, taken from Pinker). He concludes that these children were utilising 'maximally general grammatical rules': they were behaving systematically.

Data of this kind seem to legitimise the following line of reasoning. If language-learning children broadly express the same kind of linguistic structure in the NP subject as in the NP object slots, and if they understand what they say, and if 'understanding X' in this context means much the same kind of thing as 'thinking X', and if the acquired linguistic ability did not bring these thoughts into being by itself, then we can say that the systematic linguistic ability expresses a systematic *cognitive* ability.

Digging a little deeper, we need to consider what it is about the representations that support systematic cognition that makes the capacity possible. The question

---

[24] These are children from Roger Brown's classic study, whose speech is recorded in the CHILDES data base.

almost answers itself: it is their *compositional* nature – an essential feature of classical models, as we have seen. For Fodor and Pylyshyn, compositionality and systematicity are part of 'a single phenomenon'. But in what way does the addition of the compositionality notion further our grasp of this 'phenomenon'? Going back to our example of John loving the girl, it is obviously not an arbitrary fact, from a semantic point of view, that sentences like 'John loves the girl' and 'The girl loves the John' are systematically related, while a sentence like 'The cat is on the mat' is not systematically related to either of them. This may seem a trivial truth deriving from nothing more than the fact that the two sentences contain the same words. But not so, because it is perfectly possible for there to be a creature who understands what 'John loves the girl' means, who knows that 'The girl loves John' contains the same words as that sentence but who does not know what 'The girl loves John' means. So what does such a creature lack in relation to the language? It lacks the knowledge that 'in so far as language is systematic, *a lexical item must make the same semantic contribution to each expression in which it occurs*' (ibid., p. 42, emphasis added). That is to say, 'John', 'the girl' and 'loves' make the same semantic contribution to the two sentences. This is the *principle of compositionality*; and it goes without saying that it is a principle of semantic *context-independence*.

But a moment's thought tells us that English lexical items' semantic contribution to the meaning of a phrase or sentence can often fail to be semantically context-independent. So we have another case, then, in which English shows itself up as not being an LOT. To take some of Fodor and Pylyshyn's examples, 'chicken' means a kind of animal in the context of feeding it, but it means a cooked dish in the context of its feeding us. Similarly, a modifier like 'good' means something quite different in the context of 'a good fight' than in the context of 'a good book'.

Generally speaking though, compositionality holds. It certainly holds when we look at entailment relationships between the modifiers and nouns that can make up predicates. Thus '… is a brown cow' strictly entails '… is brown' and 'is a cow'; and the same goes for any predicate of a similar form.

Fodor and Pylyshyn conclude that we must assume (at least some degree of) compositionality in English sentences if we are to explain the phenomenon of systematicity and also to explain the parallelisms, of the kind we have just seen, between sentences' syntactic structures and their entailments. But if English sentences are compositional then so too must be the mental representations that they express. Evidence for the compositionality of English is, then, evidence for the compositional mental states of its speaker-hearers. And so, in so far as connectionist models do not have compositional structure they must fail to model human (they would add 'and a good deal of infra-human too') cognition.

This will leave many with a queasy feeling. For the brain consists of real neural networks and *this* supports systematic thought. Surely we need a bridging theory from wet-ware networks to competence; and connectionism is the only one we have. To this Fodor and Pylyshyn reply that the fact remains that connectionist models cannot compete against classical models because they lack compositionality; and so they must be regarded as, at best, attempting to explain 'how the brain (or perhaps some idealised brain-like network) might realise the types of process that conventional cognitive science has hypothesised' (ibid, p. 65). They can only, therefore, be models of *implementation*. The argument is that such models cannot replace truly cognitive, classical models in psychology any more than the physicist's models of the interactions of molecules can replace the 'autonomously-stateable principles of geology' (dispensing with 'old fashioned "folk geological" talk about rocks, rivers and mountains!').

This denial cries out for critical assessment. And this will be provided after we have looked at what happened when the connectionists picked up the gauntlet and tried to model systematicity.

3.5.2 Can systematically be modelled on neural networks?

The year 1990 was an *annus mirabilis* for sceptics about Fodor and Pylyshyn's argument. In that year, six papers appeared which claimed to have undermined the authors' denial that networks can compute systematicity and compositionality: St John and McClelland (1990), Elman (1990), Chalmers (1990), Pollack (1990), Smolensky (1990) and Van Gelder (1990). We have already discussed the substance of the Elman and the Pollack pieces – and we will shortly look again at the latter. In this subsection I shall examine the Smolensky and the Van Gelder solutions, before making some general remarks about the relevance of the debate to our developmental concerns. I have chosen these two in particular, because, in the case of Smolensky, Fodor has published two papers claiming to show why the solution is inadequate and, in the case of van Gelder, because Elman *et al.* (1996) cite his paper as demonstrating the kind of compositionality that networks can indeed achieve.

3.5.2(i) Smolensky's solution

Recall Fodor and Pylyshyn's argument that systematicity is ensured by a compositional fact, namely, that each lexical item (or each atom of thought) makes a determinate semantic contribution to a sentence/thought. It is partly in virtue of this that somebody who can say/understand 'John loves the girl' is guaranteed to be able to say/understand 'The girl loves John'. We should understand Smolensky's (1990) modelling of systematicity in this context. The basic assumption is that variable binding holds the key to compositionality, and thus to systematicity. In the 'John loves the girl' example, 'the girl' must be understood as an agent and thus as something that can be *both* the subject and the object of love (unlike a table, for example). Given this, the first move to make is to bind the variable *agent* to the value *girl*. Smolensky achieves this in a distributed manner by the matrix-like process of computing the so-called *tensor product* between the variable and the value. In this, both are expressed as vectors, in the usual sense in which a row of n input units, some of which are on (1) and some of which are off (0) expresses a vector in n-dimensional space. The tensor product can be understood as the result of multiplying the two vectors together. For example, one might put the value *girl* as a vector, expressed as a series of zeros and units, on the Y axis and the vector for *agent*, expressed in the same way on the X axis – resulting in a two-dimensional vector. Note, by the way, that this mode of representation is distributed, in so far as every node can partake in any binding despite the fact that there is a unique vector for each value and for each variable.

Armed with this procedure for binding variables to values we can proceed to bind elements of complex structures of the 'John loves the girl' kind. If we have bound *girl* to *agent* as tensor-one (T_1) and we have also bound the variable *transitive action* to the value *loves* (T_2) then we can bind these together to represent the verb phrase $(T_2 T_1)$. This can, in turn, be bound to a tensor representing the binding of the value *John* and the variable *agent* – as T_3. Thus, we have the following tensor product that can represent what a symbolic computation would write as $(T_3 (T_2 T_1))$ – 'John loves the girl'. This could be further bound as a sub-tree to 'Fred thinks' – expressed in a symbolic, recursively embedded style as $(T_5 (T_4 (T_3 (T_2 T_1))))$ – 'Fred thinks John loves the girl'.

Fodor and McLaughlin's (1990) response to this idea (first presented in Smolensky, 1988) was to say that it can be accepted that tensor products are able to *represent* constituent structure, but that what is at issue is whether multiplied vectors of this kind *have* constituent structure. What the difference turns on here is whether tensor products have 'the kind of constituent structure to which causal processes can be sensitive, hence the kind of constituent structure to which an explanation of systematicity can appeal' (Fodor and McLaughlin, 1990, p. 200). That is to say, 'John-as-agent' in $(T_3 (T_2 T_1))$ is not really *there* as an element and so it cannot – to sink into metaphor – be disengaged from one thought and re-engaged in a different thought in a different syntactic role (NP_{OBJ} rather than NP_{SUBJ}) but the same semantic role (AGENT). For if there is no element tokened *as such* there can be no systematically causal linkages between thoughts. In the classical case, by contrast, when a complex symbol is tokened, its elements are also tokened; just as surely as when we say 'John loves the girl' we have to articulate 'John'. In the tensor product case the elements are no more 'there' to play a causal role in further mental representations than the 3 and the 2 of (3×2) are 'there' in the number 6 to play a causal role in further computations.

Smolensky's (1995) reply that while the constituents of tensor products 'do not have a *causal* role in the sense of being the objects of operations in algorithms actually at work in the system [t]hese constituents are *acausally explanatory*' (p. 249) is, predictably, mocked in Fodor (1997). In this later paper Fodor also makes much of the fact that, because it is not possible to derive a *unique* tensor product corresponding to each tree then it must be the case that tensor products do not preserve the structural distinctions present in trees. If, that is to say, trees map to tensor products in a many-to-one manner then the latter must be failing to preserve something of the former. And given this failure, their 'success' in deriving a constituent from a complex symbol (such as 'John' from 'John loves the girl') cannot really be a derivation at all. To expand the latter point, Smolenky's equation between something's being a (classical) constituent of complex symbol and something's being a *derived* constituent is a false one. For while such derivation is possible (as compared with *nomologically necessary* in the classical case – see below) in the connectionist case this does not show that what has been derived is real a constituent – only that *if* some procedure *were* applied to the complex representation a certain element would result. But nothing in the tensor product architecture, argues Fodor, 'requires that such subjunctives ever get cashed ... all the tokens of [the complex representation] are *counterfactual*' (1997, p. 114; emphasis added).

Back now to Fodor and Pylyshyn's geological metaphor. Just as you cannot use 'rock talk' to explain what holds up Manhattan and yet 'endorse a rock-free ontology' in saying what the world is made of, so you cannot use the notion of constituent structure to explain the compositionality of thought and yet deny, as Fodor thinks Smolensky does, that mental representations have classical constituent structure. 'It's the special convenience of acausal explanations', says Fodor (1997, p. 119) 'that they carry no ontological burden'.

Is this fair? As we shall discuss later, those with a more radical stance than Smolensky would have it that it is the Fodorian symbols that are not really there. Recall Clark (1993, p. 227, emphasis added) from Part 1: '... the language of thought is, at best, the symbolic problem-solving tip of a large and developmentally extended iceberg. Beneath the symbolic waters ... lie the larger, less well-defined shapes of our *basic cognitive processes*'. Perhaps we presently stand in need of some ecumenical holding position before we pass on.

Certainly, Fodor is right that any explanation of how one thought leads to another (e.g., 'A' from 'A and B') is going to require that each symbolic element be present in complex representations in a far stronger sense than that in which an individual tomato is present in the red liquid being poured from the blender – 'present' but in no fit state to enter any causal liaisons as an individual vegetable. And of course linguistic theories of the Chomskyan kind require the same thing: merge is not the same operation as blend! But everything hinges on how serious one is about the modern project for a neuroscience of human language. (Chomsky himself seems fairly serious about this at times; see Chomsky, 2000a, pp. 116–18.) In any event, nobody wants to construe symbol manipulation as something that happens in an immaterial element. Of course one can always take the quietist option, with Fodor (1998a), and say that, because we have no idea how cognition is realised in the brain, the sensible course is for the neuroscientists and the cognitivists to stick to their own lasts. But surely some computational models are more brain-friendly than others; and computational neural networks, in a 'virtual machine', and real ones, in the wetware, share the property of being non-symbolic. So we return to the notion floated earlier of connectionism as a bridging theory, and also to the question of how symbolic operations supervene on the sub-symbolic.

A painting of a kettle supervenes on a certain distribution of pigment, and symbolic operations supervene on neural mechanisms. If the pigment were not distributed thus and thus, there would be no painting of a *kettle*. So in some sense, the way the pigment is distributed does 'explain' why this is a representation of a kettle, and not, say, of a saucepan. But it 'explains' it only in a very weak sense, in which no causal story is implied about how *that* painting came to be made (by the planful behaviour of a human agent or by a series of historical accidents – a pattern that emerged on Francis Bacon's paint-spattered studio floor). Analogising then to the brain–cognition relationship and analogising also to the tensor product–parse tree relationship, Smolensky's notion of 'acausal explanation' may not be the hopeless bit of handwaving that Fodor takes it to be. To this, perhaps, a Fodorian would say that this just goes to show that network models can only attain the status of implementations. But most psychologists with an open mind would find the 'only' here to be monstrous. What motivates the Fodorian dismissal is philosophical functionalism (not to be confused with functionalism in linguistics), which understands mental states as causally individuated entities whose mode of implementation is essentially irrelevant to this individuation; it might be neurons or silicon chips or it might be John Searle's (1984) beer cans. But philosophical irrelevance is not psychological irrelevance. All theories of implementation are not equal, and to find one that seems to be in the running for plausibility is to find something like a bridging theory between neuroscientific explanation and cognitive explanation. The tensor product solution is almost certainly not the right bridging theory between neuronal computation and parse trees by reason of its computational implausibility (Marcus, 2001, p. 106).[25] But a bridging theory is almost certainly going to be *mathematical* in nature; and Smolensky's account is certainly in that ball park. I'll deal with the relevance of all this to empiricism at the end of this section.

3.5.2(ii) Van Gelder's kind of compositionality

Elman *et al.* (1996, p. 103, emphasis added) write:

> The criticisms that connectionist models cannot implement strict recursion nor support syntactically composed representations (Fodor and Pylyshyn, 1998) are well grounded, but the conclusion – that therefore connectionist networks are insufficient to capture the essence of human cognition – *seems to reflect a profound misunderstanding about what human cognition is like.* We believe that human cognition is characterised by interactive compositionality (or in van Gelder's terms 'functional compositionality', van Gelder, 1990) and that it requires exactly the kind of interactive and graded representations, and non-linear operations which are the natural currency of connectionist models.

The question is, of course, whether this 'functional compositionality' is worth having. Or, from our perspective, whether a mind whose only form of compositionality is 'functional' has the right kind of representational format to acquire the syntax of a natural language.

This is how van Gelder argues then. First, he focuses entirely on constructing complex representations by combination, taking this to be a 'paradigm of compositionally structured representations'. In propositional logic (and in the classicist's representational format) we can express this in the following way:

P

(P&Q)

((P&Q) & R)

Compositionally speaking, *P* is ineluctably 'there' in *(P&Q)* and systematically speaking, anybody who can derive *P* from *(P&Q)* must also be able to derive *Q* from it. Van Gelder calls this kind of combination *concatenative*. Functional

---

[25] Marcus argues that it must result in a combinatorial explosion.

compositionality is something we have already considered in Pollack and Smolensky's models, in which the complex object *(P & Q)* is represented in such a way that *P* or *Q* might – note the subjunctive, emphasised by Fodor – be derived from it, while neither the *P* nor the *Q* nor the conjoining function is represented as such. For van Gelder, this is not to *fail* to represent compositionality: it is to represent it in a way that is merely *different* from the classical way. To represent – or should it be implement? – compositionality, for van Gelder:

> All that is required of a mode of combination is to have systematic methods for generating tokens of compound expressions, given their constituents, and for decomposing them back into these constituents again ... *there is no inherent necessity that these methods preserve tokens of constituents in the expressions themselves.*

(1990, p. 361, emphasis added)

Van Gelder invites us to consider the following analogy. There is, in mathematics, something called 'Gödel numbering', a scheme for a formal logic which assigns a unique natural number to every expression of a given compositional scheme. Thus, in propositional logic, P might be 32 and (P&Q) 51342984000. Now this system is entirely reversible in so far as, for any compound Gödel number, there is an algorithm (apparently 'by virtue of the prime decomposition theorem') for decomposing it into its elements. And so we can retrieve 32 from 51342984000 in a comparable way to that in which we can extract 'John' from the tensor product representation of 'John loves the girl'. Van Gelder insists that there is a sense in which the decomposition works in virtue of the physical structure of the compound number – for 32 could not be extracted from, say, 51342811111. Indeed van Gelder imagines an 'eccentric logician' who prefers to do his propositional calculus in Gödel numbers; and, if so, we would have no warrant for denying that logic was what he was doing. It just so happens that he is working with *functional* compositionality rather than the concatenative variety.

Whatever functional compositionality is, it is not, unlike the classical kind, *syntactic*, in so far as the constituency relations among the expressions do not find 'direct, concrete' instantiations in the corresponding token. It is in virtue of this direct and concrete instantiation that *(P & Q)* has something in common with *((P & Q) & R)* and with *(PvQ)*. So what is it that makes a functionally compositional representation one of *(P & Q)* if not some syntactic fact? In what sense is *(P & Q)* *structurally similar* to *((P & Q) & R)*? There can, argues van Gelder, be 'non-syntactic structural similarities among representations' of the following kind. The compound representations are vectors in high-dimensional space and these stand in similarity relations to others

> in virtue of their internal configuration, relations that can be measured using standard vector comparison methods ... usefully understood as similarities (or indeed dissimilarities) of *location* in the space, and they are of *direct causal significance* in Connectionist networks, since the behaviour of these networks, which are complex dynamic systems, depends crucially on the particular current activity values of the units themselves (i.e., on the precise location of the current representation).

(van Gelder, 1990, p. 380, second emphasis added)

Putting to one side for a short while the question of whether the phrase 'direct causal significance' can be cashed in anything like the way in which Fodor intends 'causal' in his critique of Smolensky, let us consider finally what van Gelder has to say about the achievements and prospects for functional compositionality. The real challenge, he says, is to devise models in which structure-sensitive, causal processes 'operate on the compound representation themselves *without* first stopping to extract the basic constituents' (ibid., p. 381, original italics). That is to say, such a model would be able to map the nonconcatenative vectoral representation of a conjunction directly to the vectoral representation of its conjuncts without first extracting the constituents.

As it turns out, van Gelder denies that the Smolensky and the Pollack methods (and indeed Hinton's (1988) method of representing hierarchies by 'reduced description') fulfil this desideratum. While these models learn to generate functionally compositional representations they do not interact with other representations of the same kind to yield a systematic result. Pollack's RAAM, for example, is no more than a method for storing structured symbol sequences and then retrieving them – rather as Steedman argued. It just so happens that 'Connectionists have simply not yet gotten round to taking up the challenge' (van Gelder, 1990, p. 382).

In fact, this does not worry van Gelder because he takes the onus to be on the sceptics like Fodor and Pylyshyn to show that such a thing *cannot* be achieved by networks. Why? He notes that the form of the classicist's argument is – as we saw in Part 1 – that of 'inference to the best explanation'. To remind the reader, the form of the argument is:

- having compositionality, classically understood, makes systematic cognitive capacities possible;
- we have these systematic behavioural capacities;
- therefore our minds possess compositionality of the classical kind.

In its bare form this does indeed look like the fallacy of affirming the consequent: $P \rightarrow Q$, Q, therefore P. Recall Fodor's reaction: 'So be it: one man's affirmation of the consequent is another man's inference to the best explanation'. But for van Gelder this insouciance is only warranted when alternative explanations for Q (for syntactic cognitive capacities) have been rejected. At which point, one wonders whether van Gelder has managed to come up with an 'explanation' at least as 'good' as the classicists'. As hinted above, everything hinges on whether he has managed to cash the phrase from the long quotation above – 'direct causal significance' – as something with the equivalent explanatory power to that of a constituent symbol within a complex representation with the integrity to enter into further causal liaisons on the kind observed in linguistic theory, and thus, *ex hypothesi*, in thought. But what the 'direct causal significance' of a representational element means for van Gelder is something more like

> Some location in vector space which, if it were not *this* location, would not ensure that a complex but functional and nonconcatenative representation would interact with another of a similar kind so as to produce a systematic result – in a way yet to be specified.

It is unlikely that a confirmed classicist would lose any sleep over van Gelder's attempted refutation of Fodor and Pylyshyn, simply because of the way he sets up the debate. That is to say, there is surely something misguided in the setting up of syntactic and functional modes of representation as if they were alternative means to the same compositional end. For if the representation has syntax, as van Gelder defines it, the end has been reached; whereas the functional route looks like doing the opposite of what you need to do – it eschews symbols – while hopefully predicting that a systematic result will be achieved. Let us return to our kettle. Painting a spout, a handle, and a chamber for water spatially connected to one another thus and thus is not something one does as a *means* of painting a kettle: it is the act of painting the little itself. And with final regard to the issue of inference to the best explanation, it would indeed seem that the method of the 'eccentric logician', with his Gödel numbers, is clearly one which makes life difficult for no good reason, like travelling from A to B by going A-B-C then back to B; which looks like an inference to the *worst* explanation.

Developmentally, a supporter of van Gelder's position would feel justified in saying that the mind of the language-learning child need have no syntactic structure. But are the reasons for thinking this strong enough?

I next ask whether there is a determinate and more tractable goal for connectionists interested in modelling compositionality/systematicity than the rather broad and promissory one suggested by van Gelder? One seems to have been provided in a useful paper by Hadley (1994).

3.5.2(iii) Hadley's criterion for 'strong systematicity'

Quasi-systematicity means, for Hadley (1994), a network's ability to infer from the training corpus to the test corpus the correct syntactic role of a word that appears in the *same* syntactic role in both. For example, the network will be able to process 'Tom' as appearing in the object position in 'Bob knows that Mary saw Tom' but only if 'Tom' appeared in the object position in a simple sentence in the training corpus (e.g., 'Jane saw Tom'). In *strong systematicity*, by contrast, the network is able to process a range of novel simple and novel embedded sentences containing previously learned words in positions in which they did *not* appear in the training corpus. The word in the novel sentences must not have appeared in the same syntactic position in any of the simple or embedded sentences in the training corpus. That is to say, 'Tom' would have only appeared in the subject position in the training corpus in the previous example. Hadley cautions, however, that 'training corpora that are used to induce strong systematicity must not present the entire training vocabulary in all legal syntactic positions, but should refrain from doing so for a *significant fraction* of that vocabulary' (ibid., p. 251, original emphasis).

What Hadley obviously has in mind here with his 'strong' systematicity is Fodor and Pylyshyn's famous desideratum that an agent who might never have thought of John as the patient of any loving relationship, thinking only 'John loves the girl', is nonetheless capable of entertaining this thought. (It may well not, of course, be his or her own belief, but s/he can embed it within the belief of somebody else: 'Jane thinks that the girl loves John'.)

In a review of six putative modellings of systematicity (see papers cited at the start of 3.5.2) Hadley denies that any of them achieves strong systematicity. While dissenting from Fodor's a priori dismissal of the Smolensky (1990) solution, Hadley takes the view that the 'static' and 'hard-wired' nature of the tensor product representations cannot be put to the kind of generalisation test required for strong systematicity, but concludes that there may indeed be hard-wired implementations of classical symbol processing. With regard to Elman's (1990) attempt do demonstrate the generalising power of his network by introducing a novel word 'zog' to the net, playing the same syntactic role as 'man', Hadley points out that 'man' had appeared in all legal noun positions in the training set, making this a case of quasi-systematicity. Pollack's model evinces only quasi-systematicity for the following reason, Recall (p. 311) Pollack's statement – his only argument for systematicity in fact – that 'All 16 cases of (LOVE XY), with X and Y chosen from the set JOHN, MARY, PAT, MAN were able to be reliably represented, even though only four of them were in the training set'. But Hadley points out that although 'man' never appeared as an argument to 'loves' in the training set, each of the nouns occurred as subject and direct object somewhere in the training set; so strong systematicity had not been achieved. He also, like Steedman (p. 312), points out that RAAM networks are trained on 'pre-parsed, explicitly parenthesised structures whose syntactic structure had already been analysed' (p. 266).

But rather than take any comfort from the fact that these models fall short of achieving strong systematicity, a Fodorian would surely question Hadley's criterion. As he himself admits, Hadley's way of conceptualising systematicity, unlike that of Fodor and Pylyshyn, is centred entirely on *syntax learning*. And while systematicity obviously requires a syntactic grasp (see the remarks at the end of the previous sub-section), it does not boil down to syntax alone. Recall Fodor and Pylyshyn's insistence that an agent's ability to think 'The girl loves John' if s/he can think 'John loves the girl' requires the knowledge that 'John' etc. make the same *semantic* contribution to the two thoughts (despite the fact, one may add, that the syntactic roles of 'John' and 'the girl' are different in each). The agent does indeed 'generalise' John-as-subject to John-as object, but this is not all she does: she entertains two *different* thoughts with two different meanings, and does so in virtue of understanding the semantically compositional structure of the two sentences, not just their surface syntax. As Fodor himself points out in a different context – in outlining his theory of concepts (Fodor, 1998, p. 26 footnote) – what systematicity is all about is the symmetry of *cognitive capacities*, not of *mental states*. That is to say, it is clearly not the case that anyone who thinks 'John loves the girl' also thinks 'The girl loves John'; for the two sentences do not mean the same thing (and – he adds – 'where would the Western Canon be if this were otherwise?').

Now it is worth bearing this point about semantics in mind when turning finally to an intriguing paper by Niklasson and van Gelder (1994). These authors take up the challenge of Hadley's 'strong systematicity' as well as adding a still tougher challenge of their own, in which the test sentences contain entirely novel constituents. The basis of the model is a RAAM which has clamped on to it what they call a 'transformation network' receiving inputs from the hidden units of the RAAM. But note that the task this network was given required it to recognise *the identity of meaning* of two formulae in propositional logic (one of 'de Morgan's laws' in fact): p → q ⇔ ~p ∨ q. This was chosen because the task of transforming one to the other 'obviously requires sensitivity to syntactic structure'. Niklasson and van Gelder introduced a novel symbol 's', which was not allowed to appear on the left of '→' or '∨' in either simple or embedded formulae in training – in order to fulfil the requirements of Hadley's strong systematicity – and was not allowed to appear anywhere in the training set in order to fulfil the requirements of their own tougher criterion. The method used for testing the network is too complex to describe here. Suffice it to say that Niklasson and van Gelder claim that the network succeeded, on both criteria, in correctly placing 's' in the transformed formulae. It must be said, however, that while the successful syntactic generalisation is certainly impressive, what is being modelled here is – for reasons just given – *not* systematicity as Fodor and Pylyshyn define it. For Fodor and Pylyshyn, it is the ability to think two structurally related thoughts with a *different* meaning, not the ability to recognise two sentences as having the same meaning. And one may add that, in so far as the network depended upon a RAAM, these formulae were receiving some degree of syntactic pre-digestion.

3.5.2(iv) What to conclude?

I want just to insert a rather bland judicial conclusion, to keep the debate afloat, before we consider a more radically connectionist take on the way in which cognition is 'structured'. On the one hand, the Fodorian conception of systematicity as a *capacity*, in the sense of a potential that the agent possesses – something she is in a position to exercise but might not exercise in fact – does leave one wondering how it could ever be computationally modelled, in either a connectionist *or* classical style. Moreover, the Fodorian would surely be ill advised to treat work of the kind I have just reviewed as somehow irrelevant to the cognitive sciences, as a case of grossly missing the point; and better advised to be rather warmly disposed to the fuzzily ecumenical and upbeat notion of a 'bridging theory' between neurons and mind. But in any event, I hope this exercise has illustrated the pith and kernel of Fodor and Pylyshyn's position, which is that computing over (1) symbols gives (2) compositionality and (3) systematicity *for free*, in virtue of the fact there is a conceptual linkage between the three. And where there is a conceptual linkage there is likely also to be a psychological interdependency.

3.5.3 The externalist stance on structured cognition, 'representational re-description', and language acquisition itself as the vehicle of structuring thought

> The root cause of this is a failure [i.e., by Fodor and Pylyshyn] to understand the nature and goals of thought talk.
>
> (Andy Clark, 1989, p. 152)

> A fair number of people simply failed to understand the problem. The most recent proposal I've heard for a Connectionist treatment of systematicity is owing to the philosopher Andy Clark.
>
> (Jerry Fodor, 1989, p. 98)

Now when philosophers begin to accuse one other of failing even to *understand* an issue then you know that their differences are deep and symmetrical. Clark, among other philosophers such as Daniel Dennett (see below), and what might be called their progenitor, Gilbert Ryle (1949), are as *externalist* about thought as Chomsky and Fodor are *internalist*; and their differences are as fundamental as – and invite serious comparison with – those between cognitivism and behaviourism.

The internalist is also, as we have seen (1.1.2) an *individualist* who believes that our structured cognitive capacities are as real, as productive and as ineluctably our own as are our structured inner organs. The externalist believes the opposite: whatever can be truly said about an individual's structured mentality is true in virtue of a network of ascriptive practices performed by people 'external' to the individual. Given this, human thought can only be said to be compositional and systematic *because of how we take our thought to be* – in virtue of the conditions for being judged to be a thinker which we have erected for ourselves.

In his first monograph on the subject (*Microcognition*, 1989) Clark argued that the deepest of Fodor and Pylyshyn's many misunderstandings is their taking facts about systematicity to be *contingent, empirical* facts. For it is not – Clark insists – an empirical fact that you don't find thinkers who can only entertain 74 unrelated thoughts, any more than (my analogy) it is an empirical fact that you don't find married bachelors. Rather, engrained within the concept 'thinker' we have evolved are a set of stipulative conditions, such as systematicity, that we operate with when we ascribe thoughts to agents. Systematicity does not describe an empirical fact about the mental machinery of the objects of the ascription. For this reason then, thought ascription is really a 'means of making sense of a *whole body* of behaviour (actual and counterfactual). We ascribe a *network* of thoughts to account for and describe a rich variety of behavioural responses' (1989, p. 147, original emphasis). This echoes Dennett's (1981, p. 48) view that 'thought ascription might best be viewed as a rationalistic calculus of interpretation and prediction – an idealising, abstract, instrumentalistic interpretation method that has evolved because it works'. Fodor's (1998b, p. 97, footnote) reaction to the conceptual necessity point is to say that if it is conceptually necessary that thoughts are systematic then it is *nomologically* necessary that creatures like us have thoughts, and this is a necessity in need of an explanation. And recall, in this context my point above that 'where there is a conceptual linkage there is likely also to be a psychological interdependency'.

In any event, on this view the fact that connectionists do not posit representations with the syntactic and semantic structure of sentences in a natural language does nothing to undermine networks' explanatory power, because the role of *sentences* in all this lies within the process of thought ascription, not within the process of thought and behaviour generation itself. Clark adds that Fodor and Pylyshyn actually offer no 'independent argument for the conceptual-level compositionality of internal representations', and without this the fact of systematicity does not count against connectionism.

But surely, not just any old thing can count as an object of ascription. There must be something about the behaviour of the objects of ascription to provide a foothold for ascribing concepts like systematicity. To modify a later example of Clark's (1993) we might explain the behaviour of a lectern by ascribing to it the desire to stay put, the belief that it is succeeding in fulfilling that desire and the systematically related desire to keep on succeeding! Clark's way out of this dilemma is by saying that the systematicity of 'the *behaviour* that holistically *warrants* ascriptions of thoughts' is indeed an empirical not a conceptual matter.

> But there is no obvious pressure for a system of internal representations that *themselves* have conceptual-level systematicity. All we need is to be shown an internal organisation that explains why a being able interestingly to respond to a blue square inside a yellow triangle, for example [invoking here Fodor and Pylyshyn's example], should also be able interestingly to respond to a yellow square in a blue triangle.

(1989, p. 149, original emphasis)

One natural response to all this is that it would seem much more convincing if connectionist models could *indeed* model systematic behaviour; for taking a radically externalist stance does nothing to relax the demands we must make on networks. In fact, Clark turns his attention to this matter in his second monograph on connectionism and cognitive science (*Associative engines*, 1993). One of the things he aimed to demonstrate here is that 'systematicity – if such models are to show it at all – must emerge as a *product* of the *knowledge* acquired by the system as a result of its training' (1993, pp. 37–38, original emphasis). The principle example he gives of such a developmental progression to systematicity in networks' 'behaviour' is that of Elman's next-word-prediction model. He cashes the phrase about 'training' in terms of the fact that successful networks had, as Elman put it, to 'start small' (Elman, 1993), meaning that the net had initially to be presented with a short sub-string of the complete sentence (by selectively eliminating feedback from the context units) which was then gradually increased word-by-word. (Though recall Hadley's [1994] conclusion that the Elman model only achieves his 'weak systematicity' and the views of Fodor and of Marcus that the network was simply learning the local correlates of individual works – e.g., that being a noun is just to be distributionally similar to words that precede 'chase' or to words with a similar distribution to 'chase'.)

When he revisits Fodor and Pylyshyn's sceptical argument, Clark mentions the by-now-familiar, and ruefully admitted (Fodor, 1987), charge of 'inference to the best explanation'/'affirming the consequent'. But he adds to this what he calls a 'gestalt flip' on the issue of systematicity in which he treats it as 'intrinsic to the knowledge we want a system to acquire', referring to it as something that will be *learned* 'as a feature of the meaning of the concepts involved. It will flow not from the shallow closure of a logical system under recombinative rules, but from hard-won knowledge of the nature of the domain' (1993, p. 149). This might be seen, in fact, as a backtracking from ascriptivism, though it is still externalism; and he makes some well-taken sceptical remarks about Dennett's from of ascriptivism later in that passage (1993, pp. 214–215).

Indeed Clark backs away so far from his charge that Fodor and Pylyshyn, as internalists, simply fail to understand systematicity as to admit, towards the end of the monograph, that his treatment has failed to exorcise its ghost (1993, p. 224). He faces the fact that very little has been delivered on the programme of showing how systematicity might be the product of acquired knowledge: 'a "might" is not a proof, and the full puzzle remains unchanged' (p. 224). This 'blow' can be cushioned (p. 224), however, by the following three thoughts: (1) cracking the nut of systematicity requires cracking the bigger nut of consciousness, and so the failure is hardly unexpected; (2) the option remains of explicating the notion of systematicity via the acquisition of language itself while still avoiding nativism; (3) the classical solution to systematicity gives rise to intractable problems about the real-time deployment of the knowledge base (e.g., nets do better than classical architectures at some kinds of categorisation).

Meanwhile, what do we do? 'I believe,' he says, 'that the best way forward is simply to bracket the problem of full systematicity' (1993, p. 225). This was the statement which gave rise to Fodor's charge of failing to understand what's at stake. '"Bracket", Fodor reminds us, 'is a technical term in philosophy meaning *try not to think about*.'

What Clark did in fact was to proceed on two fronts. On one – which was, as it happens, the second (historically) of the advances – he has been exploring the prospects for a radical form of externalism that moves beyond the attributive stance and shifts the metaphysical perspective on the mind-world relationship away from our being 'at two with nature' (Russell, 1995). On this view, the thinker is not regarded as a detached represener but as some*body* actively engaged in the world around her. Indeed the title of his third monograph in the trilogy (*Being there*, 1997) is also a literal rendering of Heidegger's *Dasein* (sometimes glossed as 'being in the world') – not to mention a phrase of Woody Allen's[26] ('Ninety per cent of life is just being there'). He sees this as a new paradigm for cognitive science of which robotics is the computational wing (Clark, 1999). This is definitively a pragmatist position.

The other advance followed immediately from the second monograph. It was, as one would have expected, a withdrawal from Dennett's ascriptivism in the opposite direction (inwards) – towards a serious engagement with the question of what the thinker's 'innards' have to be like if systematicity is to develop. In this case, far from 'bracketing' systematicity Clark even moves some way to an acceptance of symbolic competence, albeit one that develops from a connectionist base. This brings me to a second theme of the subsection – the 'representational redescription' (RR) approach of Annette Karmiloff-Smith, with which Clark came to align himself.

In their co-authored paper called 'The cognizer's innards' (1993) Clark and Karmiloff-Smith express both Clark's connectionist stand on the starting state of the child's mind and Karmiloff-Smith's ideas about how what Clark (1993, pp. 33–38) calls 'strong representational change' might come about – change, that is, which, increases the 'representational power' of the system. Recall that this is something that the more traditional kind of a connectionist learning theory did not seem to deliver.

What then is the RR approach? Since the late 1970s Karmiloff-Smith has been arguing that the post-Piagetian view of a developmental theory in which across-the-board processes of cognitive reorganisation and maturation are measured out by in age-wise stages can blind us to forms of U-shaped, domain specific developmental

---

[26] Allen it was who also made the quip about being 'at two' with Nature.

change which can be seen at almost any age, and indeed micro-developmentally within adulthood (see, for example, Karmiloff-Smith, 1986, 1984).[27] (Just to flag a paradox in passing: if such micro-genetic, task-specific patterns are common to childhood and adulthood then the nativist might say 'There – just like I told you – children think like we do!' But this is hardly devastating.) Within a domain, the child begins with a period of 'data-driven' success, which then gives way to a temporary 'theory-driven' failure (due to the over-application of a rule) before a final competence is achieved in which the bottom-up and the top-down are in harmony. One should note that, in symmetrical conflict with the Piagetian concept of 'accommodation', the progression from one phase to a higher one is success-driven rather than failure-driven. For example (Karmiloff-Smith, 1984), younger children might successfully balance a stick containing a concealed lead bar at one end, somewhat older children however will over-apply the theory that things balance at their middle point and perform more poorly, after which still older children will regard the middle-balancing theory as containing an 'unless weight is unevenly distributed' rider – as being defeasible. In another task, a progression to compositionality in graphic skill (not Karmiloff-Smith's way of putting it) is nicely illustrated. In this task, the child is told to draw a man (or a house, etc.) 'that does not exist'. Younger children simply changed the size or shape of the bodily elements while essentially generating a prototypical man. The older children (around 9 years) were, by contrast, able to conceptualise each bodily element as making the same, as it were, 'semantic contribution' to any figure in which it occurs, and could therefore treat them as capable of being uncoupled and transported to new and anomalous contexts – drawing a man with a human head and a bird's body, for example.

In the paper, Clark and Karmiloff-Smith argue that connectionist models account well for the initial phase of data-driven success, but what they cannot do is explain how the information stored within a domain 'becomes a data structure available to other parts of the system' by being *redescribed*. Somehow or other the data *implicit* in the networks must be rendered *explicit* so that they can be operated on by other systems. Here is an example specifically of this implicit–explicit transition. A child must be able to represent word boundaries at some level if she is to become a speaker-comprehender of her native tongue. However, the fact that younger children do not treat the function words (such as articles and prepositions) as 'words' when asked to count the words in a string or to report on-line the words immediately preceding a signal suggests to Karmiloff-Smith that this representation has yet to become 'explicit'.

Two pressing questions at this point.

1) Do we have any inkling of how this redescriptive process might work – from a connectionist base?

2) Is RR supposed to result in an internalist but non-nativist solution to the problem of systematicity?

----

[27] For example, when trying to complete Rubik's cube.

The answers to the questions are 'Not really' and 'Yes'. Turning first to 1, Clark and Karmiloff-Smith give the example of Mozer and Smolensky's (1989) 'skeletonisation' procedure. In this, a network that has achieved success on a task computes a 'measure of relevance' in order to identify which input and hidden units are contributing most strongly to success, and deleting others, resulting in a leaner and fitter net. This is indeed an instance of 'going beyond behavioural mastery', but it surely falls miles short of explicating Karmiloff-Smith's rich ensemble of metaphors. For what is it that takes the skeletal network as the object of its second-order procedures; and how does it do it? They also discuss in this context Finch and Chater's work, which we looked at early in 3.4, on networks that represent, by virtue of distributional analysis, syntactic categories in a dendrogram style. But the only reason for doing so is that in a paper earlier than the one we discussed (Finch and Chater, 1991) the authors essentially pay (what is no more than) lip service to the idea that the output of the dendogram analysis can serve as the 'interface between a vector space representation in the network and a structured symbolic representation of the data' (Finch and Chater, 1991, p. 18). Again, how is this to be done unless the symbolic structures are *already there* in the system?

With regard to 2, Clark and Karmiloff-Smith present no less than the thesis that RR explains how it is that 'real thinkers' are governed by the Generality Constraint (on which see 1.1.4 and 3.3.1). Now the generality constraint *is* systematicity, despite the fact that, as we have seen Evans himself was unconvinced that it leads immediately to the LOT doctrine. What they argue is that if thinkers move, in many domains, beyond connectionist success to redescribe the fruits of this success (symbolically? yes – pp. 514 of their paper) then they possess the kind of mental flexibility that the generality constraint describes.

> Real thinkers, we argue, meet the Generality Constraint by courtesy of the endogenous drive towards redescriptions which increase the general availability of the information they are privy to.
>
> (Clark and Karmiloff-Smith, 1993, p. 512)

But, to put it bluntly, this is less of a theory than an expression of what one would like to be true. Now this may seem rich coming from somebody who not so long ago (Russell, 1996, pp. 40–48) was arguing that the connectionist metatheory offers a better account of the generality constraint than the LOT doctrine because connectionism naturally encompasses 'the holism of the mental'. But the problem is that connectionism is *too* holistic, throwing the baby of context-invariant cognitive atoms out with the bathwater. (This point is pithily made in Fodor's *The mind doesn't work that way* [2000b, pp. 38–52] a book that squares up to the difficulty that a thoroughly syntactic theory of mind has with holism; but that's another story.) In other words, it is only possible to argue in the way Clark and Karmiloff-Smith do by ignoring the grounding of systematicity in compositionality. Clark and Karmiloff-Smith simply ignore the issue of how compositionality can emerge from a thoroughly sub-symbolic system – the issue discussed at length in 3.5.2.

It might be said that at least RR theory is founded upon empirical findings which demand an explanation, and that the notion of success-driven 'redescription' does find a toe-hold here. Three points can be made in reply. First, I think a developmentalist is fully justified in saying: 'If the theory doesn't try to account for age-wise development then I'm not interested. Cognitive development *is* an age-relative phenomenon, if anything is. Can RR theory help us explain, for example, why young infants' knowledge about object permanence does not become available to the executive/intentional systems till many months after their original 'reactive' success (Meltzoff and Moore, 1998)? It offers only metaphors.' Second, there is no reason to believe that the same kind of developmental change is taking place across the various tasks described by Karmiloff-Smith, and some may yield to far more mundane explanations. For example it is likely that children do not count function words because they tend not to think of them as good examples of words. Children are famous for doing this kind of thing. Very many years ago my 6- and 7-year-old peers and I used to believe that the only muscles are biceps, because biceps are the prototypical muscle. Third, the main motivator for the view that the encapsulated, data-driven starting state is connectionist in nature rather than symbolic seems to be an empiricist instinct stemming from an aversion to the dread hypothesis of 'representational nativism' (Elman *et al.*, 1996). The data cited by Karmiloff-Smith do not of themselves suggest a connectionist reading of phase one.

My modern history lesson ends here by noting that both Clark and Karmiloff-Smith have moved away from RR theory in their more recent writings. Karmiloff-Smith (e.g., 1992) has been concentrating on the converse process of developing modularization (in so far as RR theory is about 'de-modularisation'; see Fodor, 1998c, on RR). And we have already seen that Clark has taken a *Dasein*-stance on cognitive science. In fact he has also written in favour of the third approach to be considered in this subsection – the view that it is language acquisition itself that structures cognition. We now turn to this, in fact.

If we contrast Clark's and Dennett's versions of the thesis that public language (and, by extension, language development) structures cognition we find, as is to be expected, that Clark is the more externalist – by a short way. For him (Clark, 1998, p. 169, emphasis added), language is an 'external artefact', that is 'designed to *complement* rather than recapitulate or transform the basic processing profile [a connectionist one] we share with other animals'. This view 'does not depict experience with language as a source of profound inner re-programming (*pace* Dennett)' (1998, p. 169). Thus, the connectionist mind has it in it to use public language without itself partaking of its structured nature. As to Fodorian worries about such a view (that use requires understanding, that this is compositional and systematic, and that it requires some form of determining representational format), Clark simply calls it the 'Fodorian image' (p. 180) – one possible picture among many, rather than a serious argument about how things may well *have* to be.

Dennett, then, accepts that something inner stands in need of explanation. First, he (Dennett, 1991) reminds us that connectionist systems are 'virtual machines' that can be simulated on digital, serial, symbol-processing computers. In fact, is it well to bear in mind that *all* of the models considered in Part 3 will have been constructed in just this way – probably in Lisp or (less likely) in the wonderfully useful connectionist packages t-learn or l-learn (available within the covers of Plunkett and

Elman, 1997) which run on Macs or PCs. After all, what these models do in essence is a lot of linear algebra (Jordan, 1986), and digital computers are ideal for running this. The only 'true', non-virtual connectionist machines – connectionist in their innards – are the electronic brains of certain kinds of robot (e.g., Brooks, 1991). Well, Dennett (1991, pp. 217–221) asks, why can it not also be the other way round? Why can we not say the connectionist machines, that our brains really are, are simulating a serial, symbolic processor, and why can it not be the case that it is *public language* that enables this virtual machine to run? In Dennett (1993) he suggests how this might work taking the Peircean (p. 68) example of a child learning about hot stoves. In the life of a young child the following might happen. 'Hot!' says mother. 'Don't touch the stove.' The child keeps this word string refreshed on her articulatory loop, although she does not know what 'touch' or 'stove' mean beyond their association with a certain kind of situation. What happens is that

> As the child lays down more associations between auditory and articulatory processes, on the one hand, and patterns of concurrent activity, on the other, this would create 'nodes' of saliency in memory; a word becomes *familiar* without being understood. And it is these anchors of familiarity that could give a label an independent identity within the system. Without such independence, labels are 'invisible'.

> (Dennett, 1993, p. 544, original italics)

A process of this kind will 'soon be turned into the *habit* of redescription' (p. 544, emphasis added) and will eventually 'wrest concepts from their interwoven connectionist nets' (p. 547).

Rightly, Clark and Karmiloff-Smith reject this kind of approach as getting 'the cart before the horse. It is more plausible to see our abilities with language as one *effect or product*' (1993, p. 505, original emphasis) of the kind of cognitive achievement whose development RR tries to explain. Absolutely. (See Russell 1999, p. 265, for a brief critique of this just-so story.)

I want to leave this Dennett passage without further comment; but use it as a signpost to Part 4 – and pragmatist perspectives on language acquisition. While it is instinct with a kind of empiricism, it is fundamentally pragmatist in the sense that it regards the developing child as somebody who is going to have to *do* something – something set in train by a social experience – if linguistic development is going to happen. Moreover there is a tacit 'bracketing' of issues about the kind of representations the child is in a position to manipulate, about how in fact she bootstraps herself from being an associationist engine to being a true thinker. As we shall see, issues of representation do not loom large for pragmatism; whereas – we have seen – they are the be-all and the end-all for rationalists and empiricists. The pragmatist concern is about the kind of things that have to be done.

3.6 Some new moves in modelling production

In this final section, I will present and discuss a new model of sentence production, owing once again to Franklin Chang (2002) – the second promised 'bread slice'. There are a number of reasons for doing this. Most generally, it shows the dynamically evolving nature of connectionist modelling and why the sceptic must keep on her toes if she wishes to pronounce on the 'principled limitations' of such models. But what the model more substantively illustrates is how some of the central issues tackled in Part 3 might be addressed. There are three in particular.

1) Sentence production modelling addresses big questions about the status of con-nectionist representations – questions about their causal powers. A network will 'learn internal representations' of a data set, the fruits of this learning will be visible within the hidden units, and they will support some degree, at least, of generalisation to new data. But, as argued in 3.1, if these are to be regarded as being any more than records of the history of solving the input–output mapping – records which may or may not reach some way 'beyond the infor-mation given' – and if they are truly representations of syntactic categories and rules then they should support the production of novel sentences, given a lexi-con and a message. But the most successful production model we considered (Chang *et al.*'s model, reported in Dell *et al.*, 1999) utilised a kind of compre-hension hack called the 'transition network' (Figure 3.3). Not only did this sub-network have minimal bearing on the success, but it could be said to have contained innate structure. So is there an approach to this challenge that allows the modeller to retain the empiricist purity of the original thought-experiment?

2) It is generally accepted that language acquisition networks must bind instances to variables. Section 3.3 showed that there have been some suc-cesses here, but they seemed more tailored to particular tasks than princi-pled. One way of viewing successful variable binding is in the light of fulfilling the desideratum of Hadley's (1994) 'strong systematicity'. This is that a network should be able to process a novel sentence at test in which words appear in different syntactic roles than they appeared in the training set (e.g. as a subject in one and direct object in the other). In this case, the role is the variable and the word the instance. Setting to one side the qualms I expressed about whether this actually captures what Fodor and Pylyshyn intended by systematicity, this is clearly a challenge that must be met.

3) As argued by Steedman (at the end of section 3.4), even highly sophisti-cated associative models such as Pollack's RAAM require some 'source of pre-grammatical structure – a universal semantics'. What would be the result of adding extra-linguistic knowledge to a model that started out as no more than a statistical learner?

3.6.1 The model
Chang's model approaches these issues in the following way.

- *Point 1*: Rather than providing the production model with a comprehension hack, Chang construes comprehension input to the model as being – develop-mentally speaking – no more than the processed target input from a heard version of the sentence one is learning to produce. Although Chang does not put it this way, the picture here is of a child, as she listens to sentences which she understands, practicing, no doubt tacitly, her own production of them. This is something like how we learn new dance steps. We have no good reason to dismiss such a view on the grounds of developmental implausibility; and it's worth bearing in mind, as Chang puts it (personal communication, May, 2003) that 'children learn language from hearing others speak it (not from having someone shape their mouths)'.

- *Points 2 and 3*: Chang defines 'generalising symbolically' in terms of 'placing words in novel sentence positions'. If you learn a new word you can use it in a variety of frames' (Chang, 2002, p. 614). This seems close to Hadley's strong systematicity, and it certainly captures the process of binding instances to variables. But what is original and intriguing about Chang's approach is that, in order to meet this challenge, he analogies from the problem of embedding meaningful lexical items in syntactic roles to the sphere of spatial processing. (This is the 'pre-grammatical structure' I mentioned in 3.) In processing visual input, we have at once to categorise an object as being of a certain kind and record its position in a scene, in such a way that one is independent of the other and yet coordinated with it (if we are to see where things are). In categorising an object, its location is irrelevant, just as is its nature to coding its location. These two distinct functions have famously been identified with two brain regions, the *what* (object type) and the *where* (location) pathways by Mishkin and Ungerleider (1981). These areas must be distinguished but coordinated so that familiar objects can be recognised in new locations and unfamiliar objects can be located in known places.

As Chang writes (ibid, p. 615; emphasis added):

> Just as the spatial system can generalise in different ways because it has separate *what* and *where* representations, a model of sentence production should be able to generalise well if it represented its message in several representations that were linked together. That idea was the basis of the *Dual-path* model. This architecture had two pathways, *one for representing the mapping of object semantics to word forms*, and *another for representing objects (and the words that describe them) into appropriate sentence positions.*

However, in addition to using this DUAL-path model, Chang also did 1 alone – the *Prod-SRN* model. That is to say, he designed a network in which 'comprehension' was no more than the target input from the previous word, and the task was to produce the next word based on a message (of a similar kind to that in his 1999 model discussed in 3.1, Figure 3.3) but in which no what/where distinction was drawn in the message. Imagine, in illustration, that the target sentence is 'girls chase dogs', with the message being CHASE(GIRLS, DOGS). In this case, 75 per cent of the time the model would be in 'comprehension mode', meaning that simultaneously with producing an attempt to output the first word, the input to the hidden units was the target input 'girls' as well as the produced word (which would of course be inadequate early in training). In the remaining 25 per cent of the training period (in 'production mode') this input would be the previously produced word *alone*. The model was tested in production mode (see Figure 3.17). In this, *cword* signifies the fact that the input is fed back through the 'comprehension system'. This model does, then, truly learn production during comprehension, in which the *cword* units were a combination of the previous produced word and the previous target word. 'The analogue to this,' he writes, 'in human behaviour is that people sometimes mishear what people say (the *cword* units), because they have filled in their own predicted continuations' (ibid, p. 10). The model was tested in production mode.

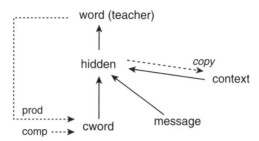

Figure 3.17 Chang's (2002) Prod-SRN model. The lines marked prod and comp represent, respectively, the feedback from the previously produced word and the target input of the previous word (Permission sought).

I now turn to the dual-path model itself (see Figure 3.18). As can be seen from the figure, the model consisted of two sub-networks. First, in the *message-lexical* one, the message fed forward to the label. As discussed, the message was made up of a layer of *where* links (thematic roles of agent, patient, goal; and action information) and a layer of *what* units (word semantics). This means that, unlike all other message representations we have considered, the same *what* units could code the meaning of a word *irrespective of its role in the sentence*. Also, as was the case for the Prod-SRN, localist representation was used – one unit per semantic or role-related 'atom'. Accordingly, to construct a message, a semantic value could be linked to a role-related one by setting the weight between certain *what* and *where* units to 'on'.

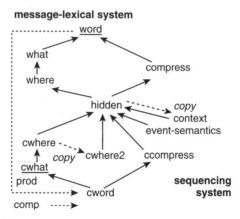

Figure 3.18 Chang's 'dual-path' model of production. Layers underlined receive teaching signals. The order of activation is from bottom to top, with back propagation of error being in the reverse order. Lines marked prod and comp represent the feedback from the previous word and external input respectively (Permission sought).

With regard to the message-lexical linkage itself (learning labels for message atoms), it should be noted that, because there was only one set of *what* units (unlike Prod-SRN and the model shown in 3.3 in which these were duplicated for each role), a meaning atom (e.g., DOG) mapped to only one word 'dog', *enabling the network to generalise this word to different roles.* Adjectives were encoded in the *what* layer as separate units. So, for example, *happy boy* would have the meaning BOY and HAPPY connected up to a single *where* unit.

The second sub-network, the *sequencing system*, was a simple SRN which mapped a *cword* (à la the Prod-SRN) to the hidden layer. The hidden layer, as can be seen, interfaced with message-lexical system, mapping to *where, what,* and *word.* (In passing, the terms in the figure *compress* and *ccompress* refer to compression layers, as used by Elman [1990] which helped the sequencing network to generalise over words rather than developing representations specific to individual words.) As for all other SRNs, this hidden layer received inputs from the input units as well as from the context units. These context units are a copy of the previous hidden unit activities and thus enable the network to represent a history of the previous states. From this point on, things become still more complicated. The sequencing sub-network also had to receive information about the role of the last word the model produced. Without this, the model would not, given (say) 'dog' as the *cword,* be able to distinguish between a continuation as 'dog chased cat' or 'dog chased by cat'. So the correct *cwhere* to *cwhat* links had to be learned. For the network to learn this, it was of course necessary to learn the correct *cword–cwhat* mapping, i.e., learn the meaning of each word *in the comprehension direction.* (For this reason – note from the figure – *cwhat* was lower in the net than *cwhere;* whereas the opposite was the case for *where* and *what* in the message-lexical system.) Next, because the error signal on the *word* unit had been weakened as it passed back down through the network, this signal was not sufficient to learn the *cword* to *cwhat* mapping. Therefore, to aid this learning, the cwhat units were given the previous *what* word's unit activations as targets. (Note from the figure that only *word* and *cwhat* units received teaching signals.) Doing this was complicated, however, by the fact that the *what* units depended on the *where* units for activation. Because the *where* units gave only low-grade information early in learning (they depended on input from the hidden layer), *what* targets did themselves provide relatively poor input to the *cwhat* units early on. Essentially, *where* depended on hidden, and hidden depended on *cwhere,* so learning of *cwhat* information was necessarily incrementally directed by role-based information. Chang makes the point that this also seems to be true for children, according to the work of Tomasello (1999) and others, in so far as they can use information about a word's status as action, agent or patient to work out its meaning.

The event semantics layer has so far gone without mention. To achieve this, and to give the reader some idea of how a trained model would produce a sentence, I will reproduce Chang's account of the timesteps in production. Here they are for the sentence *A man bake a cake for the café.*[28]

---

[28] The sentences did not have tense agreement.

- Before the first timestep, the message is set in the *what-where* and the *cwhat-cwhere* links. The agent *where* unit would be linked to MAN semantics, the patient *where* linked to CAKE, and the *where* goal to CAFÉ as well as to the feature DEFINITE. The corresponding links in reverse order were set up for *c-what-cwhere*.

- The *event semantics* would be set up at the same time. These were introduced in order to code *similarities* between kinds of sentence, and thereby to aid generalisation. In this case, the event semantics was CAUSE, CREATE, TRANS-FER. (Another might have been CAUSE MOTION TRANSFER for *The man gave the girl the book*.) The relative activation of the features was CAUSE > CREATE > TRANSFER. This weighted information helps also to create the target word order. (Recall something similar in the Chang *et al.* 1997 model discussed in 3.1.)

- The first timestep begins. Because the model is in production mode it must output the first word without *cword* input, so *cword* activation is set to 0 and context activation to 0.5. The outputted word is then compared to the target and any error back-propagated.

- The second timestep. The word *a* is copied back to the *cword* units. As described earlier, the activation values of the *what* units at the previous timestep would be used as target values for the *cwhat* units. In this case, the model needs to associate the *a cword* activation with the agent lexical semantics for MAN. The activation of the *cwhere* units is copied to *cwhere2* units and summed with the previous activation of the units. The context units receive a copy of previous hidden units states. Activation spreads up to the word units. As the model has been trained, it should then say 'man' at this point. This output will be compared to the target 'man' and back-propagation will take place.

The process will continue to the end of the sentence. In comprehension mode, by contrast, the 'external' comprehended word and the previous produced word would be summed to set the *cword* activation values.

The performances of the Prod-SRN and the dual-path models were compared with each other and also with those of models in which (a) *no event semantics* was included and (b) in which the *what* and the *where* paths were *linked* rather than separate. (In the latter, the sequencing system had access to the lexical semantic content of the message by links from the *what* layer to the hidden layer.)

The four models were trained on 501 sentences (after 2400 epochs performance did not differ between the four) and tested on 2000 sentences generated from a grammar. In terms of overall performance, Prod-SRN did not rise above 13 per cent accuracy after 4000 epochs, whereas the dual-path model achieved a plateau of 80 per cent accuracy after 1600 epochs. The plateaus reached by the *no-event semantics* and the *linked-path* models were 50 per cent and 70 per cent respectively, suggesting that event semantics was more important for generalisation success than the *what-where* separation.

More interesting than overall success, however, was model performance on the following set of tasks: (1) binding words to novel event roles; (2) the 'identity construction task', which we previously encountered in the context of Marcus's (1998) test of the Elman next-word model, in which the challenge is to output according to the identity principle 'an X is an X'; (3) novel adjective-noun pairing, which we have previously touched on in the discussion of the generality constraint: being able to think, say, 'black shirt' and 'white car' entailing the ability to think 'black car' and 'white shirt'.

In (1) the word *dog* never appeared in the goal role in training, but it did appear in that role in some of the test sentences. The dual-path model was 82 per cent correct and the Prod-SRN 6 per cent correct. In (2) the model has heard a few identity sentences in the training set and was presented with new ones at test. Here the dual-path model is 80 per cent correct and the Prod-SRN is 3 per cent correct, with the no-event-semantics and the linked-path models being 14 per cent and 43 per cent correct. (3) Here the models were trained on sentences including, say, the phrase *nice dog* but not the phrase *nice cake*. Success on the novel adjective-noun pairs was 73 per cent for the dual-path model and 2 per cent for the Prod-SRN.

But was the model so given to generalisation that it made errors, for doing which, if it were a child, it would not be corrected? Or was it, like children, something which did generalise but not promiscuously – so as not to run this risk? (Here I anticipate the discussion of Berwick's 'subset principle' in Part 4.) Chang asked this question in the context of double object dative (or ditransitive) constructions such as *The boy throw the girl a cup* (on which it was trained). The model was happy to generalise to *pour*, though much less so to generalise to *load* after 2000 epochs. It was far less happy to generalise for *surprise, chase*, and *hit*; and it *never* generalised with *dance*. So it was an appropriately conservative generaliser.

One thing about which we can all agree is that this model is mind-boggling, in the sense that it is difficult to hold its global operation in working memory. With more circumspection, we can also agree that it does seem to answer some of the challenges set by Marcus – as discussed in 3.3. And with no hesitation at all we can say that it complicates the sub-symbolic-symbolic distinction in ways that will keep the cognoscenti busy for a long time. But perhaps the best way of proceeding would be to imagine how a convinced Chomskyan would react to it. Here are some of the sceptical points that might be made.

3.6.2 A sceptic writes...

First, the reference to spatial processing and the 'what' and 'where' routes is *gratuitous*. That is to say, the motivation for, in Chang's words (ibid, p. 615), 'allow[ing] the model to ignore the content of the variables' (e.g., to represent DOG in no particular role, and to represent AGENT with no particular role-player) is simply to fulfil a core requirement of being a variable. Binding semantic atoms to roles only in the instant of sentence production is simply what human speakers have to do. All that has happened is that the author has withdrawn from the misguided technique (seen in Chang *et al.*, 1997 and in the Prod-SRN model) of hard-wiring roles and semantic atoms. The reason why this was done in the first place may have had something to do with making the training set easier to learn or with making the structural priming effect easier to simulate. In any event, the efficacy of the *what-where* layer does not tell us that some extra-linguistic form of cognitive organisation has provided a scaffolding which inherently linguistic pressures failed to provide. Furthermore, we should view the introduction of the *what-where* layers as providing the model with innate structure, thus making the model a kind of demonstration proof of its necessity.

Second, the model is more *mimetic* than productive. In the first place, there is no real distinction between next-word prediction and next-word production, and little real distinction between comprehension and production. As Chang himself puts it, in fact, 'comprehension and production modes both attempt to predict the next word in the sequence with a message, but they differ in terms of whether they use an external sequence to help them to do this' (ibid., p. 616). In fact, we get a clearer picture of what is going on if we eschew the terms production and comprehension and think only in terms of predictions made on the basis of the training sentences. The model reproduces with modifications the kinds of sequences encountered in training for the 63 words in its vocabulary. For example, having encountered in training *The man bake a cake for the woman*, it is able, with practice, to predict the correct final word in *The man bake a cake for the café* so long as the *what* unit CAFÉ comes on at the right time, the CAFÉ-'café' link is well learned, and the event semantics of CAUSE, CREATE, TRANSFER is there to support the word-to-word transition. In training, it learns to associate word sequences with certain internal states of the model. So everything it learns concerns local facts about the vocabulary and sets of sentence types.

Consider, for example, the role played by the event semantics layer in determining verb selection. If the event semantics is, for example, CAUSE AFFECTED then the model knows that the following verbs, and these verbs only, will be utilised: *hit, chase, eat, drink*. This is in addition to the HIT-*hit* etc., links it will be learning. Given this, the model is *really learning associations between particular possible sentences*. In so far as there is anything of a general nature being learned about the training set, this is only in the service of next word prediction. The dual-path model is indeed doing better than that Elman's model of next-word prediction model but it is doing so because it is being provided with sets of *aides memoires* at each timestep, both about the subset of words that might come next (20 verbs, 22 nouns, 11 adjectives, etc.) and about sentence types.

Third, the model has *no recursive capacity*. It is not surprising that Chang equivocates when discussing recursion. He turns to Chomsky's famous observation that we are able to recognise a kind of well-formedness in meaningless sentences like *Colourless green ideas sleep furiously* because we have an abstract grammatical competence that is not reducible to memory of past statistical and semantic regularities. This too is a feature of the dual-path model, says Chang.

> The model's ability to produce novel adjective-noun pairings (as in *green ideas*) and violations of the lexical experience of verbs (as in *ideas sleep*) is a reflection of its ability to use finite means to generate a greater set of possibilities.

(ibid., p. 639)

344 PART 3: EMPIRICIST CONNECTIONISM

And later he says that while the model is

> constrained in a finite way, its approach to creating language strings *would allow it to handle languages with recursive properties.* In the model, sentences are produced incrementally, making use of the representations that are activated at any one moment. This approach does not place finite constraints on how long a sentence can be. But at this point, *it is not clear whether messages can be controlled in a way that allows for recursive structures.*

(ibid., p. 641, italics added)

(This is another example of the protean nature of the term 'recursion'.)

As was evident from the discussion of the Christiansen and Chater model in 3.4, it is one thing to do well at next-word prediction when trained with some, say, centre-embedded sentences and tested with others and another to possess a recursive capacity – a recursive generative capacity. The dual-path model is indeed able to predict the continuation *cake* after the adjective *nice* when in training only animate nouns like *dog* and *man* were paired with *nice*. It was able to do this, of course, because of the association it had built up between the *what*-atom CAKE and *cake*. Doubtless it could do the same with *colourless* and *ideas*. But (putting to one side the fact that Chomsky's point is about linguistic intuitions of grammaticality, not about productivity) this capacity is irrelevant to the recursive capacity to generate adjective-noun pairs with a merge-like operation.

To explain, the language faculty for syntax 'knows' that it can legitimately pair any adjective with any noun and no adjective with any verb; and this knowledge gives it the 'recursive capacity' to pair them ad infinitum. The dual-path model, by contrast, does not represent either adjectives or nouns as a class, and so the question of possessing this recursive capacity does not arise.

This point comes into clearer relief when we consider what production and comprehension amount to in the human case. Three things are required:

1) A thought in the mind of the speaker and the capacity for having the same thought in the listener.

2) Lexical representations (LRs) which include information about bare syntactic character (e.g., the LR for a transitive verb will include slots for agent and patient), and which project upwards unmodified (the 'projection principle') to the sentence: 'Syntactic representations must be projected from the lexicon, in that they observe the lexical properties of the items they contain'.

3) Knowledge of how to project the LRs from lexicon to sentence. Since minimalism, recall, Chomsky has eschewed the idea that this knowledge contains any kind of template of phrase structure rules – like X-bar. Rather, merge, move, checking, agreement and so forth ensure a kind of bottom-up system of derivation. But this, *pace* Searle (2002, see section 3.2 above), is abstract rule-bound knowledge nevertheless.

Now it might be said that the dual-path model has something like LRs in the sense that it knows the kind of syntactic frames in which certain verbs will appear. (Note the example of *hit, chase, eat,* and *drink* given above.) But where there should be syntactic knowledge, it has memories of semantic atom-label associations, of the members of the subset of word types that can succeed others, and of the general event structure expressed in the set of training sentences as a way of further scaffolding word order. The model has lots of interrelated concrete knowledge about the data set; but, like all essentially empiricist models, it struggles with abstract knowledge.

Whether or not these sceptical responses are entirely fair, they do remind us yet again of how central the question of competence is to the connectionist-generativist debate. Questions about whether 'symbols' are being computed over are minor ones by comparison.

A combative connectionist reply might be that the explanatory goal of the field of psycholinguistics, within which the field of language development is located, is not that of elegant, economical *characterisation* of our linguistic abilities. It is that of providing a theory of the computations the brain undergoes in producing linguistic behaviour. Linguistic theory may be a poor guide to the nature of this competence just as folk psychology is a poor guide to neuroscience. The dual-path model may indeed be highly dependent on the body of training sentences, but so too are very young speakers (this question will be debated in section 4.4). There are two questions here: (1) Will models of the dual-path kind scale up/grow up?; (2) Is the model going in the right direction, though maybe not very far? From our perspective, the answers are 'Let's find out' and 'Probably'. To give a blanket 'No' to both is to imitate the action of an ostrich.

The generativist reply, in turn, would focus on this 'going in the right direction'. To borrow a metaphor from John Searle (1984; about 'strong AI'), the man who climbs a tree can be said to be going in the direction of the moon. Competence theories set out the conditions for arriving.

3.7 Taking stock

It is fair to conclude from all this that while the prospects for empiricist ('eliminativist', if you will) connectionist modelling of language development seem to be poor, it may well turn out that models that are connectionist in style but eclectic in approach have the potential to explain not only the rote/associative aspects of development (e.g., German gender and definite article morphology) but also some of the rudimentary features of syntax itself. But something seems to be the wrong way round …

The approach we have witnessed has been one of taking a basic connectionist architecture, such as an SRN, and then applying it to some language-learning task while bracketing off any possible concerns about whether something that is nothing if not rule-governed and symbolic can be modelled by something that is nothing more than stochastic. One hopes for the best and fiercely defends what successes are gained, while other, less ideologically committed, workers add symbol-like features to the model to improve its power. The upshot is that connectionist modellers and generative linguists live on opposite sides of an unbridgeable ravine.

But there are, of course, alternative courses of action. The modeller might withdraw from the kinds of debates reviewed in 3.5 about whether associative models can capture the systematicity of cognition and withdraw from making claims about capturing the recursive etc. power of human syntax with such models, and look first at the inherent powers of the stochastic models themselves. Rather than trying to scale Mount Syntax armed only with an SRN, one looks at SRNs' ability to solve initially simple and later more complex language-*like* problems, adding 'cognitive', supra-associative capacities to them where necessary. This way, there is a building up to a non-generativist computational theory of language acquisition that gives stochastic processes their due without being hamstrung by them.

One such 'language-like' task is *sequence learning*. Although some human languages make little or no use of word order rules, all configural languages are learnable, and it is unlikely that speakers of non-configural languages make no syntactic use of word order at all. So one might ask how far into sequential complexity SRNs can progress and with what they have to be supplemented to go farther. There is, in fact, already a substantial literature on this question, but I wish to focus on a single very recent development.

First, what is a good candidate for being 'cognitive' modelling? The modelling of analogy-drawing could hardly be a better one. As Fodor (1983) famously argued, the mark of 'central system' processing is that it travels 'horizontally' across encapsulated perceptual domains, which is exactly what is involved in analogy drawing and not involved in stochastic generalisation from a data set. Second, the generalisation phenomena that Marcus and others (see 3.3) display as evidence for the algebraic, rather than stochastic, mind of the human infant are also pure cases of analogy drawing: the similarity of *ga-ti-ga* to *wo-fe-wo* is analogical as well as variable-involving. And there is, in passing, still stronger evidence for analogy-making in infants in Wagner, Winner, Cicchetti and Gardner's (1981) work on so called 'metaphorical matching'; 'stronger' because cross-modal. They showed that babies as young as nine months have a visual preference for an arrow pointing 'up' rather than down in the presence of an ascending tone and for the 'down' rather than the 'up' arrow when the tone was descending. They also preferred a broken line when the tone was pulsing and a continuous line when it was continuous.

At this point, though, one is forced to be mindful of Fodor's caution that 'the more global (e.g., the more isotropic[29]) a cognitive process is, the less anybody understands it. '*Very* global processes like analogical reasoning aren't understood at all' (Fodor, 1983, p. 107; original emphasis). It is certainly true that the kind of analogical reasoning involved in scientific discovery is a closed book to cognitive psychology (a point made by Chomsky, recall, in his commentary on the child-as-scientist approach; see 1.3.4). But we can surely say something about the kind of analogical processes involved in solving problems of the kind encountered in Raven's matrices (on which: Carpenter, Just and Schell, 1990). And what's more to the present point, computational models exist of IQ-test-like analogy-finding performance. These emanate both from ideas put forward by Marvin Minsky in his

---

[29] It is sometimes claimed that data from any domain are potentially relevant to the testing of scientific hypotheses.

book *The society of Mind* (1986) and from a set of modellers calling themselves the Fluid Analogies Research Group (FARG); see Hofstadter (1995), Mitchell, (1993), and Marshall (1999). Both groups take the view that analogy problems can be solved by utilising sets of independent but interacting sub-processes operating in parallel. Minsky called these *agents* and defined them as 'any process of the mind that by itself is simple to understand, even though the interactions among groups of such agents may produce phenomena that are much harder to understand (Minsky, 1986, p. 326). The FARG group calls a similar entity *codelets*.

Next, we need some sequence-learning task that shares some features with human syntax. The Serial Reaction Time task, first used by Lewicky, Czyewska and Hoffman (1987) and by Nissen and Bullemer (1987), fits this bill. In such tasks, subjects have to press buttons in series to light stimuli whose sequence has either been generated by a very simple 'grammar' or it has not (the control group). By comparing RT between the experimental and control groups on both learning and generalisation we gain a measure of how much subjects are benefiting from having extracted the grammar. Subjects might, for example, sit before a computer screen showing three white, unfilled circles on a black background arranged in a triangular pattern. We can think of each of these as A, B, and C. Each of the circles is assigned a particular key on the keyboard, with the subject's task being to press each key as quickly as possible as each of the circles fills with white in a particular sequence. Here are two 'grammars':

AB[a variable number of Cs]BA

ABB[a variable number of Cs] BBA

These are *consistent* sequences. Inconsistent ones might be as follows: – AB[a variable number of Cs]BB and ABB[a variable number of Cs]BAA. Learning can be measured, as I said, in terms of gains in speed and accuracy over inconsistent sequences and in terms of generalising the same rule to novel sequences in which the number of Cs was different to those in training. Note that such tasks are solvable by noting the analogy between sequences such as ABCBA and ABCCCBA, as well as by recording transition probabilities between the elements. Maskara and Noetzel (1993) showed that grammars of this kind were not learnable by SRNs.

It would not be stretching a point to say that grammars of this kind have recursive properties. For not only do they have a centre-embedded structure but they allow for the potentially infinite, but structurally constrained, introduction of elements.

What all this is leading up to, in fact, is notice of some recent work by Rainer Spiegel (2003; Spiegel and McLaren, 2003), which I take to be exemplary of the kind of bottom-up, pragmatic approach to the modelling of language learning I am trying to illustrate. Spiegel not only compared human and SRN performance on these grammars but looked at how machine performance could be improved by introducing analogy-solving elements of the codelet variety. This was his SARAH model (an acronym for Sequential Adaptive Recurrent Analogy Hacker); and note that this was an associationist-cognitive *hybrid* model which also contained an SRN. In comparing SRN and human performance Spiegel found that SRN's performance was similar to that of human subjects both in terms of training and generalisation to novel sequences. This was only the case, however, when the sequences were relatively long and numerous. When they were shorter and less numerous human subjects outperformed the SRNs. Furthermore, interviews with the subjects revealed that those who noticed the grammar were the more successful ones.

The SARAH model was then applied to the problems, with the kind of analogy tasks given to its codelets being informed by successful subjects' reports on the kinds of features they tended to notice. Accordingly, some codelets searched for symmetries, some for repetition and some for order – e.g., whether the current element was the same as the previous one. (As in more standard connectionist models, the sequences were presented as vectors rather than as symbolic letters.) Other codelets assigned probabilities to whether certain of these regularities would be activated, again informed by the subjects' interviews. (Order regularities of ABCBA were noticed by 50 per cent of the subjects who did spot any regularities.)

Broadly, Spiegel found that human subjects could successfully generalise when trained with sequences containing a small number of different C-sequences (2 or 3) of a small size (range: 1–4) and tested on ones of a similar kind even when the training set contained odd numbers of Cs and the testing set had even numbers, and vice versa. The SRN failed to generalise when one was odd and the other even, and the hybrid SARAH model succeeded, like the human subjects, on both odd→even and even→odd. However, when the C-sequences were longer and more varied, all three sets of subjects, human and mechanical, tended to perform poorly. The threshold for engaging SARAH's cognitive component had not been reached in these cases. Interestingly, when those subjects who could correctly articulate the rule were removed from the analysis, the remaining (majority) of subjects were seen to behave rather similarly to the SRN. Broadly, SARAH did well at modelling the human data on this kind of grammar learning.

It might be objected here that, in so far as SARAH is modelling *conscious* processes it must necessarily be dis-analogous to human syntactic abilities which are, on all theories, tacit. But, turning the coin over, in so far as SARAH employed processes that were definitively non-conscious in the service of *successfully* matching human performance, it could equally well be said that it was modelling those tacit processes which, at a certain threshold, led to verbal report. And do we really want to say that conscious awareness is the *cause* of success, with no regard to the non-conscious processes that lead up to it? To dismiss the model for this reason would be like saying that Chomsky's agree mechanism cannot be viable because we are consciously aware that subjects and verbs must agree in (say) number.

I hope it goes without saying that this brief excursion into some recent 'grammar' modelling is not supposed to imply that ever merge and move will ever be modelled by codelets. It is merely an illustration of how pragmatic, gradualist, and eclectic modelling may remove the force from Searle's tree-climbing-to-the-moon metaphor. All in all, Spiegel's work is exemplary of the kind of open-minded connectionist project that is likely to impact upon our ideas about language development; and it is surely likely to be highly productive within cognitive science more generally.

But a major caveat is in order. Is Chomsky not correct that a grammar is far more than a rule-bound sequence of elements. A grammar is an abstract characterisation of the mechanisms – by means of which we get from thought to speech and back again. It seems to me that the modern exponents of associationist psychology, of the Elman *et al.* (1996) variety, should produce an alternative account of these mechanisms that is associationist in character, rather than trying to provide hopeful 'demonstration proofs' that SRNs or some other associative engine can 'learn grammar'.

In any event, learning by analogy will be re-encountered in Part 4, as it is a mechanism favoured by the principle researcher within the pragmatist camp – Michael Tomasello.

The pragmatist approach to language acquisition

As we begin the final Part of the book the reader may be feeling some sympathy for Goldilocks in the bears' house. For Goldilocks, the first bed was much too hard – too formal, and over-concerned with classical elegance, at the expense of common – sense – indeed of experimental – psychology. Its rigour bore comparison with the rigour of symbolic systems such as formal logic. (Moreover, it was a Procrustean bed on which any extended semantic, pragmatic, or information-processing limb would be swiftly lopped off.) The second bed was too soft for her. Its constraints were, by its own admission, 'soft constraints'; it dealt best with fuzzy categories, with pattern completion, and hardly at all with rules; it dealt with statistical tendencies. Vector algebra is 'hard' on anybody's criteria; but what results is as shadowy and implicit as the innards of hidden units.

Now the next bed, she thinks, will be 'just right'. It will get its hardness from its intellectual basis in Darwinian theory and from its being empirically constrained by rigorous studies of when children's syntax is productive and when it is piecemeal and bound by special cases. But at the same time this approach is nothing if not comfortably psychological. Its practitioners treat syntactic categories as cognitive categories grounded in knowledge of the physical and social world, while they regard syntactic operations as no different from non-linguistic mental operations. And I intend here not the developmental psychologists who research within the framework but the work of the 'cognitive–functional' linguists which, as Michael Tomasello (certainly the main developmental protagonist here) dubs the 'new psychology of language' in the title of his first edited volume of their work (Tomasello, 1998).

Goldilocks is, in my judgement, mistaken. There is surely intellectual and empirical richness in this approach, but it is an entity quite different from modern rationalism and modern empiricism. Indeed it is so different that its successes do not bear upon, and certainly fail to undermine, the successes of these two approaches. One should, in fact, draw the clearest line between the body of language development work I gather under the label 'pragmatism' and the Chomskyan and connectionist approaches; for the deepest gulf lies here, not between the more usually contrasted 'nativist' and 'learning based' approaches. This is for two reasons. First, and less important, the approaches described in Parts 2 and 3 express vertebral theses, in the sense that every empirical study (e.g., of binding) and every model (e.g., of learning syntactic categories) grows from an epistemological backbone and an hypothesis about language development that can be expressed in a couple of careful sentences. This is not true of pragmatism. Nothing could be less vertebral, for one thing, than the view that language, far from having a set of centrally organising principles or processing substrates, consists of an *inventory* of symbols, constructions and idioms – a set of tools for communicating. Indeed, it is its very unbuttoned (no: not spineless!) nature that many people find attractive. Recall the images used by writers on pragmatism: 'open air and nature' (James), feeling like an examination for which we could never be properly prepared has been cancelled (Menard), taking off the dinner jacket to change the tyres (Wendell-Holmes). And perhaps present-day philosophical pragmatists like Rorty would find the backbone metaphor – like that of 'depth' – to be phallocentric.

Second but centrally, rationalists and empiricists are *representationalists* whose deepest debates concern the form of representation with which the mind operates. The whole *raison d'être* of pragmatism, by contrast, as we discussed at length in Part 1, inspires, if not always anti-representationism, then at least the programme of stockpiling reasons for why we should be agnostic about representational questions. This is ineluctably bound up with functionalism – not the functionalism about mental state properties we find in Fodor and others but the externalist variety that explains something's nature by telling us what it is for, which is the mode of explanation that reaches it apotheosis in evolutionary psychology. Consider the following from Tomasello (1998, p. xii):

> The claim is simply that both cultural artefacts and biological structures are understood primarily in terms of their functions, and so to leave them out is to miss their point entirely. Thus, we could physically break open an artefact such as a traffic light and dissect its internal structure so as to determine the electrical wiring circuits that turn the lights on and off, the timing mechanism that determines when the lights change, and how the lights get their colours. But we can only understand a traffic light fully when we understand what it is meant to do. How else could we understand the fact that when red is lit on one side, it is also lit on the opposite side, and the green is lit on the other two sides? We can only understand this pattern by relating it to the desired endstate of a particular pattern of automobile traffic flow in the world outside the traffic light itself.

What would a representationalist have to say to this? She would probably say that knowledge of the function of language is part of our folk psychology. We know it already; although there may be scope for undermining some of its postulates (as the Churchlands and others have argued). She would also say that taking this view certainly does not have to result in anti-nativism ('the categories and schemas of a language are not given to children innately' ibid., p. xix); for is not evolutionary psychology replete with innate modules? Next, working out how a young child is trying to do things with words does not tell us how she does it and certainly not tell us how she goes on to develop adult competence. But crucially, if we take the analogy between the traffic light and the language-using mind seriously then it is the traffic light as a 'virtual machine'[1] we wish to explain, not its wiring – at least for now.

---

[1] Not the machine in its physical existence, but a computational model of it – a model of its inner functioning.

This, then, is the functional–methodological face of the pragmatist's anti-representationism. But, as we saw in Part 1, anti-representationalism – or at least representational agnosticism – is also instinct in its philosophical view of truth. There are two aspects to this. On the one hand, what is true is what is adapted to reality, adapted, that is, to the needs of the agent; it passes the tests that experience sets it and that we set it through the continuous process of enquiry. On the other hand, it is something sustained intersubjectively through what Wittgenstein called 'forms of life' (*Lebensformen*), meaning a set of practices grounded in socially (though see p. 265) corrigible criteria. What is being rejected is the notion of truth as necessarily involving a representation of a determinate kind within the contemplating mind of the solitary thinker. Applied to language, we gain from this the idea of the well-formedness of a verbally expressed thought as being, at once, a form of words adapted to the circumstances of action and to the circumstances of social life. Moreover, human language is seen as providing for us a repository of schemas, not for getting our (solitary) meaning across, but for expressing our cognitive adaptation to reality in a symbolic form and for establishing the intersubjectivity that is constitutive of human consciousness.

This is capacious. Indeed it is capacious enough to house two developmental thinkers traditionally treated as opposites – Jean Piaget and Lev Vygotsky. In the first place, Piaget's developmental theory was nothing if not adaptationalist, and one which emphatically rejected the represesentationism of rationalism and of empiricism. It was the child's active adaptation to the contours of reality that resulted in a conception of the external world and the 'logico-mathematical' thought that was grounded in sensorimotor adaptations of infancy. For Piaget, language was one of the 'symbolic functions' expressing the child's capacity for 'mental representation'. (Needless to say, representational agnosticism does not deny that language has a representing function; it denies that the explanation of our mental capacities should necessarily involve an account of the nature of the representations that makes language use possible – in the sense of the computations of a competence theory or, more literally, of a symbolic or sub-symbolic model.) The representing function of language was, for Piaget, not essentially different from that of pretend play, deferred imitation, drawing and dreaming; though it did achieve a higher level of adaptation than these, in the sense of an equilibrium between the assimilation of experience to schemes and their accommodation to it. Meanwhile, the syntactic structure of language is seen as not essentially different from that of structured actions (e.g., the embedding of subroutines within means–end actions is the sensorimotor grounding of embedding clauses within sentences). Here, then, we have language as a scheme for 'expressing our cognitive adaptation to reality in a symbolic form'. It is not a set of *sui generis* 'rules and representations' that interfaces with the thought systems, as in Chomskyan theory.

Turning to the Vygotskyan view – I say Vygotskyan, as the substance of L. S. Vygotsky's actual claims is the topic of some debate (Lloyd and Fernyhough, 1999) – one sees the thought of the individual regarded as the product of verbal exchanges in early life which, through a transitional phase of 'private speech', become internalised as the 'dialogic mind'. Perhaps the notion of thought as internal dialogue is one owing more to the literary theorist Mikhail Bakhtin, but it is certainly Vygotskyan. In any event, the term 'Vygotskyan' can be used to refer to any theory of the thought–language relationship that takes the roots of structured cognition to be found in the interpersonal structuring of social exchanges.

The representational agnosticism of Piaget and Vygotsky took rather different forms. In Piaget it was a methodological fact, in the sense that he took constructing a theory of development to mean arriving at the correct account of the current state of the 'structuring' of the child's intellect as expressed formally in terms of the mathematical theory of 'groups'. And it is fair to say that these logico-mathematical abstractions were supposed to represent the stage which the child's adaptation to reality had reached, not the state of the child's developing mind, conceived of in an internalist manner. This lead to a regrettable lack of interest in cognitive mechanisms, which Philip Johnson-Laird (1983, p. 250) highlights by saying that Piaget never 'described the developmental process in a form that constitutes an effective procedure. The relation between his theory and his observations is consequently problematical. This flaw runs through all of his work like a geological fault.' In the Vygotskyan case, representational agnosticism is the direct outcome of the view that the individual mind does not entertain representations of reality as set apart from a social nexus. So here we have both anti-individualism and anti-internalism, which add up pretty comprehensively to anti-representationism, or at least to representational agnosticism.

Pragmatism is presently making something of a comeback within cognitive–developmental psychology. One of the most successful books on cognitive-linguistic development in recent years – I mean real books with a thesis, theme and a (Bakhtin's term) 'voice', rare enough in this field – is Michael Tomasello's *The cultural origins of human cognition* (1999). A survey of the orienting quotations printed at the head of each chapter gives not only the flavour but the essence. Apart from one quotation from Aristotle, there is Peirce (2), Mead (2), Wittgenstein (1) and Bakhtin (1). Note the absence of Piaget from this list. This is not surprising as the individualist element in Piaget's thought looms large, while his concern with 'structure' reminds one of the Chomsky of the 1960s (Russell, 1978). But in so far as Piaget is a thinker who takes the emergence of language to be a fundamentally cognitive phenomenon he clearly belongs in Part 4. It emerges, then, that the term 'socio-cognitive' is not a bad alternative to 'pragmatist'. And in fact I shall often be using this term when discussing pragmatism within an entirely developmental context.

This is the order of business:

4.1: I begin with a description of two *functionalist* theories of grammar. These epitomise the kind of grammars that researchers within the pragmatist acquisition camp think provide the right conceptual framework for their work – an equal and opposite force to the generative grammars. The first discussed will be the *Cognitive grammar* of Ronald Langacker, and the second the *Role and reference grammar* of Robert van Valin.

4.2: An assessment of the relative strengths and weaknesses of functional and generative grammars follows next. Some attempt will be made to spell out the implications for development.

4.3: Here I survey the kind of developmental theories and research that pragmatism has inspired. There are two distinct phases here, covering the 1970s and the 1990s. In the 1970s the hills were alive with the sound of socio-cognitive theories of language acquisition, theories which, deservedly, came to nothing. The later phase was altogether more modest and successful. The success was due, in part, to the modesty. For this time the broad theorising was left to linguists like Langacker and van Valin and the empirical aims were pared back to showing that syntactic development is slow and characterised by errors (and is thus, the argument runs, symptomatic of learning), that its bases are punctate areas of local, case-law learning, and that syntactic knowledge is the analogy-grounded outcome of learning, not its starting state.

4.4: Next, I present a debate in which the proposals of pragmatist and rationalist developmental theories are thrown into such clear relief as to reveal how they differ about specific developmental mechanisms. This is the *semantic assimilation* (Braine, after Schlesinger) versus *semantic bootstrapping* (Pinker, after Grimshaw) debate. In passing, both Braine and Pinker are somewhat ambiguous members of their respective camps. In the case of Braine – as previously mentioned – his theory of syntactic development has its foundations in the LOT doctrine, while Pinker now works within the framework of evolutionary psychology, which is, as a meta-theory, about as pragmatist as you could wish.

4.5: Finally, I discuss theories of the evolution of language with the following question in mind: Does a Darwinian perspective on syntax undermine the rationalist's autonomy thesis and thereby bolster the pragmatist's view? Moreover, if the process of 'grammaticalisation' is known to be far more recent than the evolution of the brain of modern humans, does this undermine the conception of an innately specified syntactic system and bolster the pragmatist view that syntax is learned?

4.1 Two functionalist grammars

4.1.1 The cognitive grammar of Ronald Langacker

Langacker began his linguistic career, as did the other major cognitive linguist, George Lakoff, as a practitioner of 'generative semantics', which, as the name suggests, developed out of Chomsky's generative syntax. In fact it was Langacker (1969) who first stated the fundamental pronominalisation constraint of c-commanding (on which a pronoun cannot both precede and command its co-referential NP) which readers will recall from Chomsky's P & P theory.

In the mid 1970s, however, Langacker came to the view that the 'conceptual foundations of linguistic theory were built on quicksand and that the only remedy was to start over on firmer ground' (1987, p. v). Consequently he began to develop his theory of cognitive grammar in the spring of 1976. On this 'firm ground' one stands foursquare by the claim that acts of meaning lie at the heart of syntax, that there is no unique language faculty, no membranes (cf. pp. 181–182) and only continua, between syntax and semantics, semantic structure and cognitive structure. Moreover, a grammar is a system of symbolisation (see below), and syntactic systems are no more than the conventional symbolisation of semantic structure.

Note that this kind of position is not to be confused with that of Jackendoff, for while Jackendoff argues that much of the structure that Chomsky took to be syntactic is in fact semantic, he also assumes there to be an autonomous syntactic component – as Langacker (1987, p. 5) himself points out.

In a nutshell, cognitive grammar posits that grammatical structure is fully describable by means of three kinds of units: *semantic, phonological* and *symbolic.* A symbolic unit consists of a semantic unit paired with a phonological unit, and it may be of any size – from a single morpheme to an entire sentence. Syntax is characterised in terms of a system of *conventional symbolisation,* which speakers master by exposure to expressions. Furthermore, these conventional patterns are captured by *schemas* – templates extracted from expressions and used to construct new expressions. The phase structures of a language are described entirely in terms of these schematic patterns, and not in terms of syntactic rules.

I will base my exposition of cognitive grammar mainly, though not exclusively, on Langacker's very substantial two-volume work *The foundations of cognitive grammar: Theoretical prerequisites* (volume 1, 1987) and *Descriptive application* (volume 2, 1991). In the first volume, the aim is to carve out a new conception of grammatical structure from cognitive marble alone. I will set out some of the main proposals in roughly narrative order.

First, on this view, a grammar is not a device that generates a potential infinity of well-formed sentences. Indeed to say that it is such means to be in the grip of what Langacker calls the *process metaphor.* Replacing this, we have the conception of a grammar as an *inventory* of *conventional linguistic units,* with a unit being a 'symbolic association' between a semantic and a phonological structure.

Langacker often represents these symbolic units by putting the semantic associate in upper case and the phonological in lower; thus – 'GARAGE/garage'. Morphemes are the basic symbolic units, and these combine to form progressively larger symbolic structures which are themselves 'mastered' as units; and so a grammar consists of *large inventory of conventional expressions.* (Given this starting point, it comes as no surprise that Langacker downplays the distinction between the lexicon and the grammar.) Within this 'inventory' conception, a grammar is seen as *nonconstructive.* This should not be taken to mean that the inventory is unstructured, for indeed it is structured, of course, in the sense that units function as the components of other units. But this componential process is more *encyclopedic* (Langacker's term) than creative (Chomsky's). One might think of it as trying to have compositionality (on which see 1.1.5 and 3.5 and the discussion to follow shortly below) without productivity – and possibly even without systematicity. Encyclopedic knowledge, like that of the phrase book user, need not be systematic.

Turning to the kind of cognitive ability that is taken to constitute/underpin grammar, the one that Langacker is mainly concerned with is that of *imagery.* This means the speaker/hearer's ability to construe a situation in alternative ways in the service of thought or expression. It is more or less equivalent to what he (Langacker, 1998) later came simply to call 'construal'. For example 'A is above B' and 'B is below A' are alternative instances of imagery, while syntactically being a matter of A being the subject in the first sentence and B being the subject in the second. To leave matters at the syntactic level is to omit the core of their linguistic difference, for Langacker. In fact, speaking of imagery, a reader of Langacker will immediately see that the author typically represents the cognitive processes underlying grammar in terms of diagrams in which the focal elements are drawn in bold, the representation of temporal sequence is in terms of a line of boxes above an arrow, corresponding elements are linked with dashed lines, and so on. This is of course a far cry from the kind of symbolisation that is assumed to lie at the heart of LOT; and it echoes the *iconicity* and *diagrammatic* impulse originating in Peirce (discussed in Part 2 in the context of Haiman's work). Langacker cautions that

> A diagram like this makes no commitment to visual imagery. It is analogous to the drawing a biologist might make of a cell to show the relative positions of the cell wall, the nucleus, the mitochondria etc.: it is not a formal representation but a sketch (or crude graph) of the relations among entities in a domain. Although such diagrams have considerable heuristic value, the structures they represent should ultimately be characterised in terms of their constituent cognitive events (just as cell bodies are analysed for their molecular composition).

(ibid., p. 184, footnote)

The diagrams seem, in fact, to exist somewhere between icons and Johnson-Laird's (1983) mental models.

I now consider the way in which Langacker 'cognitivises' syntactic categories like noun, verb, subject and object. The starting point is that there are two kinds of predicates: *nominal predicates* that designate *things* and *relational predicates* that designate *temporal relations* or *processes* – realised in syntax as nouns and verbs respectively. A *thing* is intended in an abstract, technical sense to mean, not a physical object, but a *cognitive event* – a 'region in some domain of conceptual space'. To those who balk at this as a piece of hopeful hand-waving, Langacker would no doubt remind us that the pro-form *something* can cover the total semantic domain of nouns – events, abstract concepts, mental states, and all non-physical points further. He also points out that the syntactic category of noun is essentially undefinable beyond the banal observations that nouns can be preceded by articles and can take pluralising suffixes, which is just what one would expect of a 'thing' – in this relaxed sense.

Along the way, Langacker introduces us to the notion of *profiling*, which means bringing the focal semantic element or elements of a sentence into cognitive bas-relief, and whose result is represented by bold outlines in his diagrams. It is profiling, rather than 'the structure of constituent events', which makes the difference between a nominal and a relational predicate. To introduce an example of my own, the difference between *there was an explosion* and *something exploded* lies not in the speaker's bare cognitive grasp of a situation – the two sentences express the same knowledge – but in the way in which elements of the iconically-structured graph are 'profiled'. In a nominal predicate what is profiled (by bold encircling – all else is *base*) are the linked elements (be they physical objects or events); whereas in a relational predicate it is the linkage between (probably) two elements. And so in the case of *explosion* there will be a bounded network of things and happenings, and in *explode* there will be – between the before and after states – a line profiled in bold.

There are long discussions of the two cognitive faces of relational predication (of which being a verb is one instantiation) – atemporal relations and processes.

First, a moment's thought tells us that the atemporal relations expressed in sentences are not symmetrical, in the sense that one of the elements tends to be the cognitive focus. Syntactically, one of things that this asymmetry manifests is the distinction between subject and object while cognitively it is, for Langacker, the distinction between the *trajector* (subject) and the *landmark* (object). Indeed at a higher level of generality this can be regarded as the distinction between figure and ground.

The term 'trajector' is intended to capture the fact that the entities that typically appear as subjects are often in motion of one kind or another – literally or figuratively. The landmark, on the other hand, provides a point of reference from which to locate the trajector. 'The notions of a subject and object', he writes, '*prove to be special cases* of trajector and landmark respectively, but separate terms are needed for the general case if confusion is to be avoided' (ibid., p. 217, emphasis added).

I show Langacker's diagrams for 'with' (e.g., *There is a car with a driver*) and 'across' (e.g., *There is a mailbox across the street*) sentences in Figure 4.1 in order to illustrate both the notion of profiling and the way in which multiple landmarks are dealt with. In 4.1(a) the landmarked reference point is the smallish bounded area of space there needs to be for the preposition 'with' to be meaningful. (We would not say the driver was 'with' the car if they were in different neighbourhoods.) In 4.1(b) the landmark reference point is, however, the assumed location in space of the speaker or of the addressee. And note that in both cases all elements bar these landmark reference points are profiled.

Let us pause briefly to consider the difference between this conception and the syntactic conception of subject/object. Syntactically, it is a good generalisation across languages that subjects control verb agreement, are the antecedents for reflexives and pronominalisation, control adverbs and subjectless adverbial clauses, and so forth. That this generalisation is much less than perfect, however, has encouraged some (e.g., Foley and van Valin, 1977) to deny that there is such a category as subject (and see the next subsection on this question). But to become exercised over this matter is, for Langacker, to miss the point. The point is that the subject/object distinction is essentially semantic and so the grammatical correlates of subjecthood

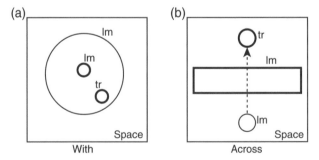

Figure 4.1 Langacker's (1987) diagram for 'with' and 'across' (tr = trajector, lm = landmark). Figures from Ronald W. Langacker, *Foundations of cognitive grammar, volume 1.* Copyright © 1987 by the Board of Trustees of the Leland Stanford Jr. University.

are not criterial but *symptomatic* of the 'special salience' that trajectors (of which subjects are an instance) have by virtue of being the principle participant in a relation.

> Because salience is a matter of degree and since factors other than figure/ground alignment enter into it, a certain amount of language-specific variation is to be expected; the grammatical properties in question should be associated with subjects only *preferentially* instead of *exclusively*.

(ibid., p. 235, original emphasis)

Recall that *process* is the second face of the relational predicate … 'a verb is a symbolic expression whose semantic pole designates a *process*' (ibid., p. 245). As the name suggests, a process is the evolution of a 'situation' over time, consisting of a continuous series of states, which Langacker wants us to understand in terms of *sequential scanning*, meaning processing component states in series rather than in parallel, transforming one configuration into another – something that is supposed to apply even to stative verbs like *resemble* and *have*. In Langacker's terminology this series has a *temporal profile*. In Figure 4.2 , I reproduce Langacker's schematic diagram for the verb 'enter'.

'A hard-nosed linguist,' Langacker writes, 'will doubtless ask for evidence to support these claims. How can one prove that the concept of a process (hence the meaning of every verb) requires sequential scanning and has the schematic form indicated?' In answer he says that he can no more substantiate this claim than the proponent of a 'more fashionable model can prove that movement rules leave traces without explicating the function of these constructs as part of a larger theoretical and descriptive framework' (ibid., p. 253).

Is this – in passing – reasonable? In some ways it is not, given that (1) Langacker's conception of the semantic 'pole' of verbhood looks rather like a metaphor standing free of theoretical apparatus, and (2) there is a clear area of empirical engagement over trace theory, in which evidence can be cited for and against – as we saw in Part 2 in the discussion of verb reduction (Chomskyan structuralism versus Haiman's iconicity). In fact, a structuralist might say that the present conception of verbhood is a generalisation looking for empirical (to borrow William James's term) *cash value*.

Now back to Langacker's conceptual foundation-laying. Perhaps the greatest challenge for cognitive grammar is to give a well-motivated account of how 'symbolic

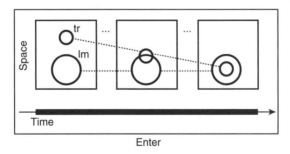

Figure 4.2 Langacker's schematic for the verb ENTER. Figures from Ronald W. Langacker, *Foundations of cognitive grammar, volume 1*. Copyright © 1987 by the Board of Trustees of the Leland Stanford Jr. University.

structures' combine into clauses and clauses into complex sentences. Taking an analogy from chemistry (one which appears to be absent from his later work), Langacker writes of there being *valence relations* between symbolic elements. There are four aspects to this: correspondence, profile determinacy, conceptual (and phonological) autonomy and dependency (A/D), and constituency. I will restrict myself to a brief discussion of A/D, as this will be useful when we come on to Langacker's account of case in his second volume.

Langacker regards relational notions as being essentially dependent ('one cannot conceptualise the process of chasing without conceiving to some extent of the thing doing the chasing and the thing being chased') and things as being essentially autonomous – 'we can conceptualise a cat without activating to any significant degree the notion of its participation in a relationship with other objects (e.g., we simply visualise a cat)' (ibid., p. 300). More interestingly, he describes the distinction between autonomous and dependent structures as being the cognitive underpinning of such syntactic relations as that between verbs and complements, heads and modifiers, and central versus peripheral elements of a sentence (a distinction discussed by Chomsky, 1965, in generative terms). An autonomous bit of structure is one that can stand alone. At the phonological 'pole', vowels can stand alone while consonants cannot. At the semantic 'pole', heads can stand alone and modifiers cannot, complements can stand alone and verbs cannot, central structure can stand alone and peripheral cannot. Thus, in the sentence *The verdict rendered him speechless*, the verb is the dependent element in the sentence in so far as reference to *rendering* is meaningless unless we know the thing being rendered and the state into which it is being rendered. The complement *speechless*, by contrast, can stand alone as a meaningful predicate. In the sentence *We chased squirrels in the park*, however, we see a relationship between what, for Langacker, is the clausal 'head' of a sentence (*we chased squirrels*) and an adverbial modifier (*in the park*). In this case, the head is autonomous and the modifier is dependent. Additionally, *in the park* also functions as a piece of peripheral structure which is similarly dependent.

For Langacker, what this account achieves is a 'going beyond' a mere acknowledgement of the existence of constructs like head, modifier and complement to provide a reasonably explicit characterisation of their conceptual basis (ibid., p. 310).

It is worth attending, at this point, to the way in which Langacker describes the background motivation for the notion of valence relations; because this takes us straight to the heart of the pragmatist conception of the thought–language relationship. To give his example (ibid., p. 279), supposing I wish to tell somebody where he can find his football. Because there happens to be *no single morpheme or other fixed expression* to convey the information I have to construct the novel sentence *Your football is under the table*. It so happens that this can only be done by 'isolating and separately symbolising various facets of my unified conception'. What this suggests is the following logical order:

- a felt need to communicate some information,
- search for an off-the-peg symbolic structure to express this,

- failure, followed by a search for symbolic structures that express the informational elements,

- combining these in the hope that the information will be conveyed.

Consider now the way in which this echoes the use of a phrase book. A tourist in her hotel room needs to phone down to Reception for a hairdryer. She knows (1) the word for 'soap', (2) the expression 'Can I please have some soap' and (3) the word for 'hairdryer'. She subtracts (1) from (2) and adds (3) to it in the same slot and makes the call. Setting this into a broader perspective we have the following:

1) There is no *organic* relation between a structured thought and a structured sentence, in the sense that the role of language is to provide an inventory of off-the-peg symbolisations of cognitive atoms and cognitive molecules, which something other than *structured* cognition (one might analogise it to Norman and Shallice's (1986) supervisory attentional system or SAS) brings into alignment. This contrasts strongly with the minimalist conception in which structured language is nomologically related to – is a 'perfect' expression of – structured cognition.

2) Given this, the role of cognition is, as analogised to an SAS-like system, to find a solution to an ad hoc communicative need.

3) To the extent that language is compositional, compositionality is *externally* motivated, in so far as the contingent resources of the language to hand determines where pressure for composition will fall. (Imagine a language forced to evolve, through the exigencies of its tourism-based economy, to have a single morpheme meaning *Please send up a hairdryer*.)

4) The speaker's conception of the intrinsic well-formedness of a sentence plays no *essential* role in this process. Not only this but there *can* be no certainty (see 2.4.1) from one's own case that a sentence expresses one's thought; and to think that there can is to be guilty of the crime of being a Cartesian!

This brings me to Langacker's account of the determinants of well-formedness. In his view, the question 'How does cognitive grammar ensure that the right output is produced?' betrays a misconception. It is *generative* grammar that results in an output. Cognitive grammar, he says, does not. Speakers 'output' sentences, but these are not the result of a derivational process which can converge or crash – to use minimalist terminology – but are, instead, the result of their employing an *open-ended* range of conventional symbolic expressions for communicative purposes. Well-formedness, then, is not something *intrinsic* to the grammatical mechanism in the way in which it is within generative grammar.

How then does cognitive grammar deal with the fact that languages sanction some forms and forbid others? Do speaker/hearers not need some high-level schema or operation determining their 'compliance'? First, within cognitive grammar, there is assumed to be no 'reductive' account of grammatical construction, in the sense of there being no single, underlying rule or operation that explains (generates?) any one grammatical construction. Indeed, the grammatical knowledge a speaker has is supposed to take the form of a *network* – a 'full schematic network where specific structures co-occur with categorising schemas extracted to describe their commonality at various levels of abstraction' (ibid., p. 411).

Let us consider Langacker's discussion of prepositional phrase construction, within this context. In English, this is quite a simple matter involving the combination of a preposition and a nominal [P + NML], in that order. Within a broadly generative approach, [P + NML] is a *maximally parsimonious* description of the rule being followed. But cognitive grammar has no interest in what is maximally parsimonious, only in giving 'an accurate account of a speaker's mental representation of linguistic organisation' (ibid., p. 411). This account will tell us about which 'cognitive routines' the speaker has 'mastered'. But what about those she should *not* have mastered? How are they avoided?

With this in mind, we can examine what a generative linguist would call a 'constraint' on prepositional phrase construction and see how Langacker's 'network' model deals with it. In the Southern Californian Native American language Luiseño, there is a restriction on how prepositional phases are formed of a kind that does not exist in English – discussed by Langacker. In this language, there is a set of prepositional suffixes – 'postpositions'. But these *can only combine with inanimate nouns and personal pronouns*. So, in the first case we have:

ki-yk	*palvun-ŋay*
house-to	valley from
'to (the) house'	'from (the) valley'

and in the second

ʔ0-yk	*caamo-ŋay*
you to	us from
'to you'	'from us'

If speakers wish to attach prepositions to *animate* nouns, what they have to do is add the suffix to the noun's pronoun as a separate word. Thus:

yaʔas po-yk	*hunwutum poomo-ŋay.*
man him-to	bears them-from.
'to (the) man'	'from (the) bears'

Within cognitive grammar there is no constraint operating here in the sense of there being any procedure to prevent the application of the suffix in accordance with the schema $[N_{anim} -P]$ (where P = postposition). Viewed developmentally (though Langacker does not mention acquisition in the book), children would simply not learn that animates receive postpositional suffixes as this is not in the input and so they build the schema $[N_{inanim} -P]$ bottom-up; while they do the same for personal pronouns, inducing $[PRON -P]$, and, ultimately, for animate nouns, inducing $[N_{anim} [PRON -P]]$. They do not have to *avoid* the incorrect schema $[N_{anim} -P]$, which is not in the input.

One cannot argue with Langacker when he says that 'the solution is straightforward and commonsensical'. Speakers simply learn what they are exposed to and shun the unfamiliar.

In passing, on such a developmental hypothesis, is not a further assumption required to the effect that children tend conservatively to stick to the forms that they encounter in the input and not promiscuously draw analogies along the lines of 'if *mat* can take a postposition then why not *cat*?' To say that they do is, in fact, entirely in accordance with generativist-inspired developmental accounts. To explain this, I need briefly to refer to Berwick's (1985) *subset principle*, something which will receive fuller elucidation when I discuss van Valin's '*Role and reference grammar*' in the next subsection. In a nutshell, this principle states that children are innately designed to assume rules ('schemas' for Langacker) are restrictive (i.e., that the input contains all legal constructions), and so they can rely on positive evidence only to expand their initially over-conservative grammars rather than needing negative evidence (instructions about illegitimate forms) to shrink the initially over-liberal grammars. This is just as well as research shows (Brown and Hanlon, 1970; Hirsh-Pasek *et al.*, 1984) that they do not receive such negative evidence.

Returning to Langacker's discussion of Luiseño, he sketches out how a generative account of the constraint on postpositional placement might work. This, he says, would begin by positing a uniform, common-denominator style representation of postpositions in prepositional phrases at the deep-structure level, with the motivation of *simplifying* the rules of semantic interpretation. A deep-structure sequence of N + P would thus be generated without regard to the animacy of N or to whether or not it is N or PN. Then a transformation might copy an animate noun to a pronominal form, followed by the attachment of P to the noun or pronoun that immediately precedes it. In this way, the requirement to produce a strong generative, formal mechanism leads the linguist to postulate a *non-occurring* sequence which is 'prevented from surfacing only by the intervention of an obligatory copying rule. Moreover *the patterns that actually occur [e.g., N_{inanim} –P] are not specifically listed anywhere in the grammar*' (ibid., p. 413; emphasis added). This would indeed seem to capture the broad difference between the procedures of the cognitive and the generative grammarian; although it is far less clear that Langacker's characterisation fits MP.

With final reference to the first volume of *Foundations of cognitive grammar*, we consider the way in which Langacker deals with compositionality. In the final chapter called 'Composition' he says

> Compositionality [...] pertains to the regularity of compositional relationships, i.e., the degree to which the value of the whole is predictable from the values of its parts. It therefore concerns the relationship between a constructional schema and its instantiations.

> (ibid., p. 448)

How regular is the integration of component structure with compositional structure? Is it possible to formulate a schema for a particular construction 'that will enable one to predict, for every choice of component structure, precisely what the composite structure will be?' (p. 448). In terms of Fodor and Pylyshyn's discussion of compositionality, which this treatment predates by a year, one would say that indeed the composite *is* highly predictable from the components; and if it were not, competence would not demonstrate systematicity. To know the nature of the semantic contribution made by the elements (John – the-girl – loves) and to know the syntactic rules of combination (word-order rules in this case) is to be in a position to predict the meaning of the composite. And it is also predictable from what has already been said (about symbolic schemas as 'inventories', about the non-existence of high-level formal schemas, and so forth) that Langacker will wish to emphasise the areas where compositionality does *not* clearly hold, and to complicate our conception of it when it does – indeed to deconstruct it into a conception more sympathetic to cognitive grammar.

So Langacker makes two moves of interest here. In one, he re-conceptualises the notion of compositionality into different terms and in the other he explains how a *partial* compositionality, far from being the embarrassment to his view that it is to the generative view, complements his position.

First, the re-conception. In describing this I need to introduce the notion of *categorisation*. Essentially (though Langacker does not put it quite this way), to categorise A as C is to take A to be a real instance of C. Thus, 'banana' bears a categorising relation to 'fruit'. Similarly, given the symbolic unit TRIANGLE/triangle this particular triangle is a categorisation of TRIANGLE/triangle. Langacker calls a particular token of such a symbolic unit a *target*, and distinguishes it with a prime thus: triangle'.

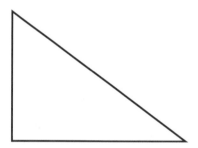

Now take the prepositional phrase *above the tree*. This exhibits 'full compositionality' in the sense that the complete phrase [C] is made up of two components *above* [A] and *the-tree* [B]. But to say this is also to say that [A] and [B] categorise certain facets of [C] – as A' and B'. Or in ordinary language, we might say that being above a tree is an instantiation of (it 'categorises') something being above something. See Figure 4.3, which is a somewhat simplified version of Langacker's own (on his page 467). The semantic schema has a profile consisting of a trajectory (whatever is above the tree) and the landmark for whatever is the thing below. The categorising relationships are shown by the arrows.

How close does this come to the standard structuralist conception of compositionality? The essential differences are twofold. First, for reasons given earlier in my discussion of the 'network' model, prepositional phrases are not schematised by the speaker as such, and they certainly are not generated by abstract symbolic operations. Rather, speakers represent a cognitive schema (something being above something), with *above a tree* being a concrete instantiation of this, whose elements 'categorise' elements of the schema. Second, the general motivation for defining composition in

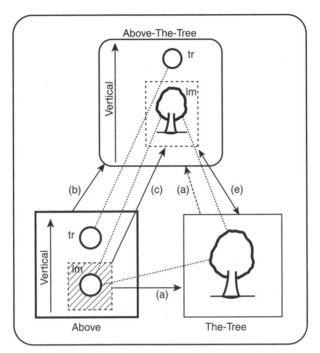

Figure 4.3 Langacker's illustration of compositionality in "above the tree". Figures from Ronald W. Langacker, *Foundations of cognitive grammar, volume 1*. Copyright © 1987 by the Board of Trustees of the Leland Stanford Jr. University.

terms of 'categorisation' appears to be that of *evading commitment* to the view that expressions like *above* and *the-tree* behave in a systematic way ('above the bed'; 'below the tree'. etc.,) in virtue of the fact that they have the kind of *sui generis* grammatical potential that generative linguists ascribe to them. This is the so-called 'building block' conception that Langacker wishes to replace.

Langacker's other way of eroding the building-block metaphor for compositionality is by showing how it is that many expressions which seem to have full compositionality do not actually gain their meaning by virtue of computing the semantic contribution of each of the elements via compositional principles: full compositionality can fall short of full meaning. Here is one of the ways he illustrates this. The commissioner who runs the American football league might issue a decree that every Sunday before the game a beautiful woman dressed as a Dallas cowgirl shinnies up the flagpole to kiss passionately the American flag, then waves as she slides back down the pole, to the sound of fireworks. Over the public address system the announcer says *Let's hear it for the patriotic pole climber!* Having taken us through the way in which his theory would analyse the phrase *patriotic pole climber* Langacker points out that of course the meaning of the phase is far richer than the strictly compositional *patriotic person who climbs poles*. And he goes on to suggest that 'virtually all linguistic expressions, when first constructed are interpreted with reference to a richly specified situational context' after which they coalesce to form 'established units'; and this explains why 'most composite expressions have a conventionalised meaning more specific than their compositional value' (ibid., p. 455). In the imagined scenario, *patriotic pole climber* does not mean 'patriotic person who climbs poles', and neither does *computer* mean 'something that computes'.

Before we come to Volume Two, let us wonder whether considerations of this kind really do subtract anything of importance from the compositional nature of language, and, if so, whether it threatens the integrity of the generative position. Three points might be made, the second being borrowed from Fodor and Pylyshyn (1988). First, the fact that one can produce a fully compositional version of the context-ingrained word-package which fails to do justice to the latter's meaning does not demonstrate the essential tendency of compositionality to fall semantically short. This is because compositionality need play *no* role in the kind of naming ceremony described. The compositional nature of the name is a contingent fact, and the name would have succeeded just as well without it. (Perhaps the commissioner was a fan of the New York avant-garde who decided to call the climber 'Lydia Lunch'.) Now for an example – a real one this time – of the independence of compositionality and the naming of a complex scenario, the point of which is to illustrate how, because it need have *no* role to play in the naming, a compositional reading need not be in competition with a non-compositional one. In the mid 1960s, a group of Bristolian school-boys invented the term *three pastie over four*. (How these words come to be chosen is lost in the cider-mists of time.) What this expression referred to was the act of rocking rhythmically forward in unison to speed the descent of a clapped-out car down the hill towards Weston-super-Mare – from the Star Inn. It is just a fact about language, a fact richly exploited by modern poets, that non-compositional strings (and strings, as in Langacker's example, in which compositionality played no essential role) can be used to evoke or denote situations. Indeed one might even add that if cognition really were as tightly meshed to language as cognitive grammar suggests, rather than being an autonomous system, it would be hard to explain how thinkers could break its rules so freely.

This brings me to the second point. As Fodor and Pylyshyn (1988) point out, idioms prove the compositional rule; and that is why we have a special name for them – *idioms*. The expression 'kick the bucket' is not compositional when taken to mean 'die'; but it can still be used literally, and compositionally, when we are talking about kicking and buckets. Third, as I discussed earlier (pp. 320–321), we must surely accept that it is an empirical question how compositional non-idiomatic language actually is, given that the meaning of the components can depend heavily on context. But this need not threaten generative assumptions. Recall the examples of 'chicken' meaning a kind of animal in the context of our feeding it, but its meaning a cooked dish in the context of its feeding us, and 'good' meaning something quite different in the context of 'a good fight' than in the context of 'a good book'.

But what one cannot be relaxed about – even if one is not a rationalist – is the compositional nature of *thought*; and this fact reveals a potential dilemma for cognitive grammar. If Langacker wishes to argue that syntactic rules are directly traceable to cognitive schemas then there would need to be a *tighter* mesh between cognitive compositionality and linguistic compositionality than on the broadly Chomskyan view; and, in this case, lack of linguistic compositionality would seem to raise difficulties for the theory. On the other hand, cognitive grammar may not wish to commit itself to the compositionality of thought; and in this case it will be faced with the challenge of giving any coherent account of our mental capacities – *if* Fodor and Pylyshyn are correct.

In discussing Langacker's second volume called *Foundations of cognitive grammar: Descriptive applications* (1991) I will tend to stick to those topics that reveal the difference between the cognitive and the generative approaches most clearly.

I will first discuss the distinction between noun and noun phrase so fundamental to generative grammar – with the notion of an X-bar level (N′) intermediate between these still having a role to play. Langacker argues, however, that we should replace the assumption of noun being a constituent of a noun phrase (for which he reserves the term *nominal*) by a distinction based on their different *semantic* functions.

Syntactically, the difference between a nominal and a noun lies in the fact that a nominal can stand alone as a subject or object of a clause, while a bare noun cannot. Thus we have

(1) a. *Those three black cats* ate all the tuna (nominal).

b. *Cat ate all the tuna (noun).

Conversely, a bare noun can be incorporated as the first element of a compound, whereas a full nominal cannot:

(2) Geraldine is a dedicated *cat* lover.

*Geraldine is a dedicated *those three black cats* lover.

Predictably, Langacker seeks 'an underlying conceptual distinction for which their differing grammatical behaviour can be regarded as symptomatic' (1991, p. 52). Thus far (in volume 1), we have only been concerned with nouns as 'things'; and now we need to think about the ways in which things can be thought about and referred to. The fundamental distinction here is between a *type* and an *instance*: *every nominal profiles a thing construed as an instance of some type*. Bare nouns profile types: an instance, but not a type, has a particular location in the domain of instantiation. See Figure 4.4, which is a simplified version of Langacker's original.

What Figure 4.4 says, essentially, is 'of all the instances of this type there could be, this is the one I'm talking about'. Langacker also illustrates this by reference to a device used in American sign language. In this, to establish a referent, the signer points to an arbitrary location in signing space to which he or she can simply point again to re-refer, a procedure that makes it possible to maintain multiple referents.

This account receives a good deal of elaboration in the book – which will not detain us. In any event, the basic proposal is plausible and clear.

Here is another syntactic constraint whose cognitive grammatical explanation grows out of the concept of a nominal. It concerns quantification: (3a) is acceptable, but (3b) is not.

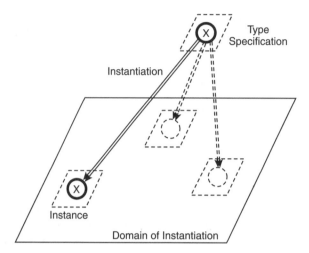

Figure 4.4 Langacker's illustration of the type 1 instance relationship. Figures from Ronald W. Langacker, *Foundations of cognitive grammar, volume 2.* Copyright © 1991 by the Board of Trustees of the Leland Stanford Jr. University.

(3) a. The problems we have to deal with are {three/few/many/several numerous}.

b. *The problems we have to deal with are {all/most/some/any/every}.

Backing off from the particular example temporarily, we can attend to the fact that while quantifiers are frequently applied to nominals, there are two ways in which quantification is achieved: nominals specify quantities either in absolute terms (*two X, many X*) or proportionally (*most X, all X*). And it is also the mark of nominals to effect the *grounding* of designated instances. This grounding is the process of determining whether, within some frame of reference, an instance or set of instances of a type is uniquely apparent to both speaker and hearer. Grounding expressions are words like *those* and *these*. Thus, 'every nominal profiles a thing construed as an instance of some type and further incorporates some specification of quantity or grounding' (Langacker, 1991, p. 54).

Now moving back to the example, Langacker calls the size-specifying kind of predication *absolute*, while the kind in which proportions are quantified is called *relative*. The relative quantifier specifies a quantity in relation to a *reference mass* and it does so through what Langacker calls *grounding predication* – in the sense of picking out something from a ground. The reference mass may be *dogs*, and the relative quantifier (grounding predicate) of this might be *all, some, most, any*, or *every*. On the other hand, an absolute quantification specifies the size of a set without reference to some grounding reference set. Accordingly, *many dogs, several dogs* and, of course, *seven dogs* is not understood in relation to a set of dogs, but absolutely in terms of how substantial is the amount *tout court*. Imagine, in illustration, that we wish to find out how many of a threatened species of animals is still in existence. To give the answer *most* or *some* is quite uninformative; because this might mean a million or ten. To say *several* or *a few* or, of course *200* is, however, to tell us the kind of thing we want to know – how substantial is the amount *tout court*.

We are now in a position to return to (3). Only one of these kinds of quantification – the absolute kind – can behave as the complement of *be* – as in (3a). Having a relative quantifier as the complement of *be* results in a sentence that is ill-formed – (3b). Why? (I will put the reason in my own terms.) A relative quantifier is more deeply nominal than the absolute kind. These cry out for a noun to complete them, with this noun being, in cognitive grammar terms, the grounding reference mass. Absolute quantifiers, however, fill the same kind of complement slots as adjectives, prepositional phrases and participles – all words that, like absolute quantifiers, can convey information without reference to some standard or context (e.g., *is green, is on the table, is walking*). Sentences such as *We are many* tell us something; but ones like **We are all* do not. From the perspective of cognitive grammar, *this shows how a kind of ungrammaticality that appears to be a purely syntactic fact is really rooted in the way in which we think about different kinds of quantity.*

I shall mention three further cognitive grammatical analyses – of passivisation, of case marking, and of raising (to be defined), before describing the account given by a cognitive grammarian other than Langacker of the pronominal anaphora. This will convey more than the flavour.

Passivisation

As we have seen, since 1957 Chomsky has treated passivisation as resulting from a transformation. Thus, the passive *Mary was kissed by John* is derived by a formal procedure, taken to have no semantic content, from *John kissed Mary*. The two sentences share the same underlying structure. For the cognitive grammarian, by contrast, the grammatical morphemes involved in passivisation (namely, *be, -ed*, and *by*), far from making no semantic contribution to the sentence, are all meaningful, so that 'the organisation of the passive clause is a straightforward consequence of their meaning', a proposal which 'has apparently been considered too preposterous for widespread acknowledgment and acceptance' (ibid., p. 201).

On Langacker's analysis, every grammatical morpheme takes on a special sense in the passive construction and each of these senses is a 'straightforward extension from the meanings it has in other uses'. First, what makes the subject (or trajector) come to be identified with the direct object (or primary landmark) is the meaning of the passive participle (-ed). This is called PERF by Langacker. To explain, there are several semantic variants of PERF – $PERF_1$, $PERF_2$, $PERF_3$. $PERF_1$ is the closest to an adjective: the *The windscreen is cracked, The jaw is swollen*. These are called stative participles. $PERF_2$, however, applies only to verbs understood as transitive, that foreground a change of state – that 'cause a shift in trajector' in the sense of taking focal 'energy' from the trajector and transmitting it to the landmark. Consider, in illustration, the sentence *A tornado left the town devastated* ($PERF_2$), and contrast it with *The windscreen is cracked* ($PERF_1$). In the second case the trajector is understood as an entity continuing through time in a changed state; but in the first case the trajector is thought of as affecting the landmark (*town*) through time.

$PERF_2$ is, however, atemporal, something which, of course, a passive verb form is not. To attain the status of the passive participle $PERF_3$ the 'support' of a certain kind of *be* is required, one that has the kind of semantic content that fits the passivisation bill. This is what Langacker dubs be_2, as contrasted with the be_1 that supports $PERF_1$

and $PERF_2$. The semantic content of be_1 is sufficient to merely qualify a trajector (e.g., ... *is a teacher*). By contrast, be_2 implies a series of sequential states ('re-imposes sequential scanning') and thus expresses a process being undergone. Langacker illustrates this by comparing it with the auxiliary and content verb *do*. Indeed be_2 bears more similarity to *do* than to be_1. For one thing, both *do* and be_2 can be used with verbs of both perfective and imperfective aspect[2] (*Do you like him; Is he liked by anybody?; Do you kiss anyone? Was she kissed by anyone?*), while the verbs used with be_1 are understood only under an imperfective aspect (e.g., *is swollen, is devastated*). Another similarity between be_2 and *do* lies in the fact that each has an active variant in which the trajector 'exercises voluntary control' over some activity. Here, for example is the contrast between *do* as auxiliary and as an active form: *What did he do?* The active form of be_2 can be seen in sentences like *John is being mean again.* Well, this kind of *be* fits the bill *when we wish to suggest a progression of states rather than a continuing state.* One might ask here what evidence we have for the passive form implying some kind of dynamic change. In support of Langacker one might mention the case of verbs that do not passivise, such as *resemble*, which are clearly not dynamic. On the present analysis one reason why we cannot say **John was resembled by Larry* is that the verb is stative, and so there is no possibility of reading *be* dynamically – as be_2.

I have abstracted away from many technicalities, but the outlines of the claim are clear enough. First, passivisation is *not* a formal move. It changes the sentence's meaning because if a participant in the relationship has changed from trajector to landmark or vice versa then the meaning has changed. Second, the passive form is woven from separate, *meaningful* strands that complement one another, rather than being derived from the active form. Developmentally, *this implies that children who use the passive form, far from having acquired a transformational rule, have learned how to combine meaningful morphemes in a conventional pattern.* Indeed, one might regard the process of development on the pattern of the 'semantic assimilation' theory we shall be discussing in 4.4. According to this theory, children expand the, say, noun category from physical objects like *ball* to words like *party* and *happiness* by an assimilatory process similar to Piagetian assimilation. Perhaps the 'cognitive linguistic child' might be regarded as expanding a $be_1 + PERF_1$ frame like *was cracked* to a passive $be_2 + PERF_3$ frame like *[X] was kissed [by Y]* by a similar developmental process. In the noun case, the progression is from noun-as-physical-object word to noun-as-generalised-entity word, and in the passivisation case it is from pseudo-adjectival-stative frame to dynamic-temporal-progression-towards-affected-trajector frame.

Case marking

Langacker's views on case marking naturally form a strong, symmetrical contrast to those of Chomsky, especially the Chomsky of minimalism. Recall the discussion of case marking in Part 2 and the view that case is an example of an 'imperfection' of language, containing uninterpretable features. I mentioned there that Chomsky (2000a) draws a distinction between so-called *inherent case* and *structural* case, with the

---

[2] See footnote 2, Part 2 (p. 96), and associated text.

former having semantic content (and therefore having interpretable features) and the latter having no semantic content, and accordingly being uninterpretable. The dative case is in the former category, meaning, as it does, that some object was displaced towards X. Nominative and accusative, however, do not possess inherent case. 'What are they doing?' Chomsky asks, and gives as an example the distinction between sentences like *John believes that he is a liar* and *John believes him to be a liar*.

In both of these, being a liar is predicated of a third person singular masculine referent; but the nominative and the accusative case markings (*he* and *him* respectively) play no role in the semantic interpretation of the sentences.

Just a note, in passing, about the dative as a form of inherent case. Prototypically, the dative marks 'to X', but many dative forms do not have this character. Readers who were taught Latin at school may have been encouraged to learn that verbs took dative complements with rhymes of the following kind.

> A dative put, you always may,
> For pardon, envy, spare, obey,
> Believe; persuade, command; to these
> Add marry, succour, please, displease.
> Indulge, heal, favour, hurt, resist
> Are also on the dative list.

In no clear sense, do these verbs share a 'to X' character. Similarly, although the meaning of the genitive case (of X) would seem to be possession, *Das Lied von der Erde* is not saying that the song belongs to the earth.

With regard to nominative and accusative, the standard position is that they mark the *syntactic* distinction between subject and object. In English, the subject is the argument that precedes and agrees in number with the main verb; and that is not a semantic fact. In languages that do not have a nominative/accusative system – such a Samoan – we find instead a distinction between *ergative* and *absolutive*, and this would seem to have a comparable purchase on the subject/object distinction to that of nominative/accusative. The ergative case covers the subjects of transitive verbs (e.g., *John[ERG] kissed the girl*) while the absolutive case covers both the objects of transitive verbs (e.g., *John kissed the girl[ABS]*) and the subject of intransitive verbs (e.g., *The girl[ABS] slept soundly*). It is the ergative that receives a suffix, while the absolutive receives zero marking.

Langacker rejects the standard reasons for believing that the nominative/accusative and the ergative/absolutive distinctions are semantically empty and replaces them with four considerations:

1) We can interpret subject-object status as having 'conceptual import'.

2) We make an error in assuming that the obligatory governing of morphemes (principally adjectives) by a noun's case is meaningless because being obligatory is not equivalent to being meaningless.

3) It is usual in languages for both lexical *and grammatical* morphemes to carry multiple meanings (polysemy[3]), and the absence of a single semantic value does not entail the absence of meaning.

---

[3] = a lexical item having more than one meaning, e.g., *bank*.

4) Failing to contribute independent semantic content does not imply semantic emptiness, only semantic redundancy.

With regard to datives, ablatives, genitives, locatives etc. Langacker's view is that the semantic contribution they make is entirely evident and that only by 'theoretical gymnastics could one analyse them as being consistently meaningless'. But, as even Chomsky failed to engage in these 'gymnastics' we will confine ourselves to nominative/accusative and ergative/absolutive.

Where, then, might one look for clues to the cognitive basis of these distinctions? We can look towards the presence or absence of marking itself. It is very common for only one member of the pair to be marked, with Latin (in which both nominative and accusative are marked) being a well-known exception. Nominative and absolutive are the members that typically receive zero marking. For this reason Langacker takes them to be cognitively more basic than their respective partners. He writes: 'That the more basic member of each opposite should typically be marked by zero is both natural and predictable' (1991, p. 383).

What nominative and absolutive have in common is analysed in terms of the distinction between autonomy and dependence (A/D) described above (p. 360). The essential claim is that, in so far as sentences represent complex events (broadly construed), there is a *path* running from the autonomous to the dependent elements. For example, in *Floyd broke the glass with a hammer* the essential and essentially autonomous element is the glass's breaking, followed by the hammer and then by Floyd. The glass would be dubbed in more traditional taxonomies the *theme* or patient, and in cognitive grammar it is the initial participant encountered along the A/D path. In the ergative language Samoan the glass would be the (unmarked) absolutive. Viewed cognitively, ergative languages are marking the periphery (ergative) and not the centre. 'Nominative and Absolutive cases are thus alike', Langacker writes, 'in that each marks a participant serving as the origin of a natural path along a parameter known to be both cognitively and linguistically significant (figure/ground; A/D alignment)' (1991, p. 383). But is there not a contradiction lurking here? How do we account for the fact that in the nominative/accusative language English it is the theme/patient that receives marking – as an accusative? In *She hit me with a baguette* 'me' is 'central' in Langacker's terms – yet marked. The argument appears to be that because it is the nominative and not the accusative that covers the subjects of intransitive verbs, as in *John died*, it is, like the absolutive, coding the 'origin of a natural path' – figure rather than ground. Or with regard to A/D structure, intransitive clauses have A alone whereas transitive clauses have a (D (A)) structure. The nominative case is used for A-alone clauses and this is sufficient for them to be given an unmarked status. One might say, in fact, that prototypical nominatives and absolutives are those in clauses in which there is a single argument; and such an argument is sufficiently central as to need no picking out from the ground by marking. That would seem to be Langacker's claim.

Raising

Nowadays this term (cf. 'quantifier raising' p. 119) is used in two ways: (1) to denote any movement operation which involves raising a word or phrase from a lower to a higher ~~position~~ in the sentence; (2) in terms of *subject-to-subject* raising, where an expression is moved from one subject position to a higher one (e.g., from being the subject of a VP to being subject of the IP). As an example of the latter, consider (4).

> (4) That Harry will leave is likely.
>
> ⇒
>
> Harry is likely to leave.

Langacker does discuss raising in his Volume two (1991), but I will describe some of the main features of his more recent exposition presented in a more recent paper (Langacker, 1995).

Shown in (5) is a sketch of how Chomskyan theory first explained this phenomenon in terms of movement from an underlying structure.

> (5) (i) 'Logically' the subject of *likely* cannot be a person. Thus, we do not say **Harry is likely*, but rather that an event is likely: *Rain is likely, That Harry will leave [event] is likely.*
>
> (ii) To explain the fact that we do naturally say *Harry is likely to leave* we must posit an abstract, underlying structure of the form: *[Harry leave] is likely.*
>
> (iii) The raising rule converts the underlying form into the surface form.

According to Langacker (1995, pp. 21–22), the tacit reasoning behind 5 (i) is as given in (6).

> (6) (i) In the construction *X is likely* the subject cannot be a person – only an event.
>
> (ii) This construction 'establishes the meaning (and hence the logical relationships) of *likely* in all its uses'.
>
> (iii) *Likely,* as in *X is likely,* must exhibit the same meaning and logical relations as in *Harry is likely to leave.*
>
> (iv) In the latter the surface structure of *likely* is really an event.
>
> (v) There is, therefore, a discrepancy between the surface and the logical grammar.

What Langacker takes issue with here is step 6 (ii) – the denial of a possible polysemy (see footnote 3 on p. 371). Recall that in cognitive grammar polysemy is supposed to represent *the usual state of affairs*. Next, Langacker illustrates how the polysemy of a verb that clearly does *not* come within the 'raising' ambit (unlike *seems, expect, is likely* etc.,) can, on the generativist reasoning, be said to provide an evidence for derivation from an underlying structure when such an analysis is clearly absurd. This argument is, then, a *reductio.* Consider these sentences:

> (7) a. I washed the car.
>
> b. *I washed the mud.
>
> c. I washed the mud off the car.

On the generativist reading of (7) Langacker argues, *wash* is behaving like a raising verb. *Mud* cannot be the object of *wash*; only things like cars can be. Given this, (7c) must be derived from an underlying structure in which the bracketed portion describes the result of the main clause action, rather than being the logical object of *wash,* as in (8).

> (8) I washed D [the mud ({be/go}) off the car].

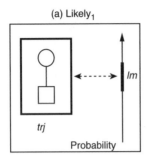
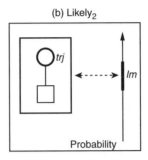

Figure 4.5 Langacker's illustration of the polysemous nature of 'likely'. Reproduced from Figure 7 (p. 24) in Langacker, R. W. (1995), Raising and transparency. *Language*, 71, 1–62. With permission from The Linguistic Society.

Langacker then presents a diagram to illustrate the different meanings of *wash* at issue: (1) in which the landmark is the object undergoing the change of state, (2) in which the landmark is the dirt-like substance.

Likely – Langacker argues – is polysemous in a comparable way; and so again *we can escape the necessity for derivation from a single underlying form and a raising transformation.* See Figure 4.5 in which the two meanings for *likely* are diagrammed. The difference between 4.5(a) and 4.5(b) resides in the choice of trajector. In (b) we see the sense of *likely* operating in the raised construction *Harry is likely to leave.* While (b) has the same 'conceptual content' as (a), it highlights the participant's role in the event so as to make Harry's volition a crucial element. In (a), by contrast – the schematic for *That Harry will leave is likely* – there is neutrality on the question of whether Harry will go or leave *willingly.*

But surely, one might think, there is quite a difference between the merely silly *I washed the mud* and the ungrammatical and meaningless **Harry is likely.* There is no sense in which *Harry* can be the logical subject of the bare *likely*, but I can wash mud – if I so choose. (Julian Barnes, in his days as a TV critic, used to call BBC costume dramas 'washed-gravel drama'; so a 1970s BBC drama set in the First World War trenches might have been dubbed a 'washed-mud drama'.) Langacker replies to this possible objection: 'the argument has no force in the absence of any explicit characterisation of "logical" relations and the independent demonstration that they are criterial for GRAMMATICAL relations, at least at the level of underlying structure' (1995, p. 24; original emphasis).

The reader is probably reminded here of Langacker's treatment of passivisation. In both cases, two forms assumed by the generative approach to be formally derived from a single underlying structure by a transformation are taken to be woven from separately meaningful strands.

Here, briefly, is another of Langacker's cognitivist solutions to an issue within raising theory – one that also concerns the conditions under which passivation can change meaning. I give it because it brings into clear focus the difference between explaining differences and similarities in meaning between sentences in terms of grammatical relations and logical roles, on the one hand, and in terms of the cognitive schemata exemplified by predicates, on the other. A caveat is that the first Chomskyan account given here derives from the Standard (1965) theory. I will describe more recent developments a little later. Consider the following four sentences:

> (9) a. She expected a specialist to examine her mother.
>
> =
>
> b. She expected her mother to be examined by a specialist.
>
> (10) a. She persuaded a specialist to examine her mother.
>
> ≠
>
> b. She persuaded her mother to be examined by a specialist.

In (9a) and (9b) neither *a specialist* nor *her mother* bears any logical relation to *expect*, with the former functioning as the logical subject of *examine* and the latter as the logical object. In (10a), however, *a specialist* is both the logical object of *persuade* and the logical subject of *examine*, while in (10b) *her mother* is the logical object of both verbs. This justified the claim that (9a) and (9b) are derived from the same underlying structure:

> she expected [a specialist examine her mother].

but that the sentences in (10) are derived from *different* underlying structures. (10a) from

> she persuaded a specialist [a specialist examine her mother].

And (10b) from:

> she persuaded her mother [a specialist examine her mother].

We do not have to go to these lengths, argues Langacker, if we provide the correct *semantic* characterisation of the governing predicates. See Figure 4.6 adapted from Langacker (1995, p. 40).

In the case of *expect* we can see that the trajector does not directly interact with the landmark itself, but that their mediation is by what Langacker calls the *active zone* – the area within the box. The trajector 'entertains an expectation' about the occurrence of a process, while the landmark plays the role of a reference point by virtue of

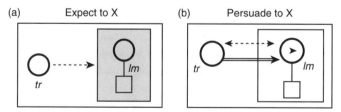

Figure 4.6 Langacker's diagram of the different semantic schemes for 'expect to' and 'persuade to'. Reproduced from Figure 7 (p. 24) in Langacker, R. W. (1995), Raising and transparency. *Language*, **71**, 1–62. With permission from The Linguistic Society.

being the trajector of that process. In short, the inherent constraints imposed by *expect* are limited to

> there being some process (of an unspecified nature) that the trajector can envisage and anticipate. That process will itself have a trajector, which *expect* puts in focus as landmark, but this predicate is quite neutral concerning its possible character.

(ibid., p. 41)

In turning to *persuade* we see a complex *direct* interaction between trajector and landmark. The double-headed, dashed arrow is supposed to represent some verbal, or at least communicative, exchange between trajector and landmark, while the double arrow below stands for the socio-psychological force being exerted on the landmark by the trajector. The resulting 'attitude of intention or volitioanality toward this envisioned process' is shown as the wedge shape within the landmark. These 'specifications' impose a number of 'constraints' on the landmark for *persuade*, which are supposed to account for its lack of what Langacker calls *transparency*. I will say what Langacker means by this term, before contrasting his account with a recent Chomskyan one.

Raising verbs are 'transparent' in so far as any element that can occur as the subject of the complement clause can also function as the raising verb's object in the main clause. Verbs like *persuade*, however, impose restrictions such that the object of persuade *must be sentient and potentially volitional*. For similar reasons, we cannot make dummy words like *there* and *it* their objects, but we can in the case of transparent verbs like *expect*: *She expected/*persuaded there to be problems; She expected/*persuaded it to be a challenge.*

Here now is the post-standard-theory, P & P account of the difference in behaviour between these two kinds of verb. Verbs like *persuade* are said to be *control* verbs. Other examples are *try* and *decide*. In order to explain what control predicates are it will be necessarily to reprise briefly the account given in Part 2 of the P & P modules *control theory* and *theta* (θ) *theory* (pp. 126–128). Recall, first of all, that s-structure traces of movement do not constitute the only examples of empty categories co-indexed by other elements. Indeed, the control principle was introduced to cover another kind of empty category co-indexing *that was not the result of movement*. Consider the following sentences:

(11) a. John told Mary to leave.

     b. John promised Mary to leave.

In the case of (11a), *Mary* seems to be both the object of *told* and the subject of *leave*. But surely a single token cannot play more than one role at the same time. Blocking this possibility is the θ-*criterion*, which states that

> Each argument has one and only one θ-role, and each θ-role is assigned to only one argument.

This blocks *Mary* from playing both the role of GOAL in relation to *told* and AGENT in relation to *leave*. Then, in order to ensure that both verbs have a single argument role assigned to them, the empty category PRO is introduced to serve as the subject (in AGENT role) of *leave*. This is controlled by *Mary* in the main clause.

Similar considerations motivate the PRO in (11b) in which the controller is a subject rather than an object in the main clause. Thus:

(12) a. John told Mary$_i$ [PRO$_i$ to leave].

   b. John$_i$ promised Mary [PRO$_i$ to leave].

Similarly, for the control predicates *try* and *decide* we have: *John$_i$ [tried/decided to PRO$_i$ leave].* *John* is the controller of PRO but it has not moved from the slot before *leave* in d-structure to become this; and to say that it had would be to confuse PRO$_i$ and trace (t$_i$). Where verbs like *try* take an infinitival complement containing a PRO controlled by a main clause subject, control verbs like *persuade* take an infinitival complement whose PRO is controlled by the main-clause object: *I persuaded [him$_i$ to PRO$_i$ leave].* It is an *object-controlled* predicate. (In the previous examples, *told* was object-controlled and *promised* was subject-controlled.)

To ease the exposition, I will now take *seem* (paralleling *expect*) as my paradigmatic raising predicate and *try* (paralleling *persuade*) as my paradigmatic control predicate. First, one obvious difference between these two verbs is that *try* entails agency and *seem* does not. This is dealt with in P & P theory by claiming that it is a thematic property of the verb *try* that it assigns the θ-role AGENT to its subject, and it is a thematic property of *seem* that its subjects are not θ-marked. (This explains why dummy terms like *there* and *it* can be subjects in the latter case.) This fundamental thematic difference between the two captures why *seem* can only function as a raising predicate and why *try* can only function as a control predicate. The following illustration, taken from Radford (1997a, 8.7), should explain why.

Consider the two sentences in (13), whose syntactic structures superficially appear to be similar.

(13) a. He does seem to enjoy syntax.

   b. He does try to enjoy syntax.

With regard to (13a), the claim is that the subject *he* has moved from a d-structure position – [$_{VP}$ he enjoy syntax]. Because *seem* does not θ-mark its subjects *he* cannot be the subject of *seem*; while the only θ-role to be filled is that of the EXPERIENCER of *enjoy*. (The reason *he* had to raise was to check the nominative case of *does* – called *greed* in MP – see discussion on pp. 154–156.) This fulfils the θ criterion in so far as *he* (via two steps of raising) only has a single θ-role – that of EXPERIENCER in this case. If, however, we interpreted *seem* as a control predicate the θ criterion would be violated. This is because *he* would have been raised from a slot before *seem* to be the subject of *does,* and PRO would have filled the role of EXPERIENCER, thereby leaving *he* without a θ-role.

Turning to (13b), PRO will be taken to fill the θ-role (EXPERIENCER) of *enjoy* and *he* will be taken to be the AGENT θ-role of *try*, raised one step to check the nominative subject of *does*. Since both PRO and *he* each have a different θ-role assigned to them the θ criterion is satisfied. On the other hand, had *try* been interpreted as a raising predicate in which a moved *he* is derived by two trace steps from [$_{VP}$ he enjoy syntax] then we would end up with two different θ-roles for *he* – both as EXPERIENCER of *enjoy* and AGENT of *try*.

To put the matter informally, when we say *He does seem to enjoy syntax* we are, in fact, asserting that he is enjoying syntax – though hedging a bit with *seem*. There is a single θ-role in operation. But when we say *He does try to enjoy syntax* we are *not* asserting that he is enjoying something but rather (i) that he is trying to do something and (ii) what that something is. There are two θ-roles in operation. To the generativist, this difference *cannot* be captured by analysis of the cognitive schemata of the two main-clause verbs, but only by reference to such abstract syntactic notions as controlling, θ-roles, checking, and so forth.

It might be said that Langacker's account is 'simpler' and that it is more friendly to our intuitions about meaning. We will discuss in the next section *how much of an advantage this really is and whether it makes development any easier to explain.*

Prononimal anaphora

The treatment of pronominal anaphora has loomed large in Chomskyan theory – and note my reference to Langacker's (1969) pioneering role in this. Recall that a central difference between the deep structure notion and that of d-structure was that in the latter pronouns were present, rather than being constructed by transformations. Recall that this enabled Chomsky to deal with sentences like *Everyone hoped that he would win.* And the reader will not need reminding that binding, c-commanding and logical form all have issues about pronominal anaphora at their heart. In fact, we saw that one motivation behind the positing of logical form was the need to explain why the sentences in (14) are unacceptable (taking the underlined words as co-referring).

> (14) a. *He likes John's mother.
>
>   b. *Who does his mother like?
>
>   c. *His mother likes everyone.

Within the framework of cognitive grammar, Karen van Hoek (1995) presents an account of why sentences like (14a), and those in (15), are unacceptable. (Underlined means co-referring, recall.)

> (15) a. *I spoke to him about finances in Ben's office.
>
>   b. *John gave a book to her for Sally's birthday.
>
>   c. *She detests the people who live next door to Sally.

Needless to say, her analysis focuses upon pragmatic, or 'discourse', principles and carries the assumption that there is no principled way to distinguish these from syntactic analyses in terms of 'height on the tree', 'branching nodes' and the like. Perhaps some *prima facie* evidence in favour of these phenomena being pragmatic rather than sentence-internally syntactic in nature is that many readers will see violations of a similar kind in examples like (16) – marked by # (meaning problematic, rather than ill-formed).

> (16) a. He went into his study. #John picked up the phone.
>
>   b. He checked the mailbox. #There was a letter for John.

The central Langackerian concept van Hoek utilises is that of the *reference point* (see Figure 4.1 and subsequent discussion); though of course she is more concerned here with *conceptual* than with spatial reference points. These are, she writes (1995, p. 313):

> the elements which the conceptualiser (the speaker or addressee) uses to contextualise other elements. The analysis rests on the notion that the conceptualiser makes MENTAL CONTACT with an entity [mental contact is defined as 'singling an entity out for individual conscious awareness'; Langacker 1991, p. 97. JR] against a background provided by other elements in the conception. Reference points are elements which are prominent within the discourse and serve to set up the contexts within which the conceptualiser makes mental contact with other entities. The DOMINION of a reference point consists of the elements that are conceptually located relative to the reference point, whose construal is shaped by their association with the reference point.

Allied to this conception is that of *accessibility theory*, a notion more closely associated with other linguists within the cognitive camp, such as Ariel (1988). This holds that distinct nominal categories (full noun phrases, pronouns, reflexives, etc.) are used to signal differences in the accessibility or retrievability of their referents within the immediate context. What is crucial to van Hoek's analysis is that *full noun phrases (names and descriptive phrases) are used when a referent is not easily retrievable from the immediate context*. By contrast, *pronouns are used when reference is easily retrievable from the immediate context* – either because the referent is currently under discussion or because the person or thing is physically present and perceptible to both speaker and hearer. Combining these ideas we have the following 'constraint on co-reference':

> A full noun phrase (i.e., a name or descriptive phrase) cannot appear in the dominion of a corresponding (i.e., co-referential) reference point, as this would conflict with the specification of a full noun phrase as a low accessibility marker.

Thus, in (14a) (<u>He</u> *likes* <u>John's</u> *mother*) *he* is the reference point, while all the other arguments of the verb are within its 'dominion'. *John's mother* contains a low accessibility marker (*John's*) when the prior reference to *he* has already entailed the high accessibility of this referent.

Note, by the way, that the reference point need not be the trajector. In (17) it is the primary landmark; and also see (15a and b).

(17) a. John put <u>it</u> in <u>the kitten's</u> box.

     b. I told <u>him</u> about <u>Sam's</u> mother.

One assumes that *it* and *him* would be regarded as autonomous (versus dependent; see p. 373) elements by Langacker – and thus as reference points.

How, then, does one explain non-violations of Principle C within this approach? That is to say, why are the sentences in (18) *well*-formed despite the fact that the pronoun precedes ('but does not c-command', adds the generativist) the co-referential full nomimal?

(18) a. After <u>it</u> fell off the table, <u>the ball</u> rolled across the floor.

     b. After <u>he</u> got back, <u>Ralph</u> made a few phone calls.

The answer van Hoek gives is that the pronouns within the temporal clauses of (18) should be regarded as being embedded within a *modifying expression* and accordingly are not 'profiled at the higher level or organisation, and need not be construed as a reference point in relation to the elements in the main clause' (van Hoek, 1995, p. 324). In strictly Langackerian terms, what is profiled is the process coded by the main verb, the other (temporal clause) process being an un-profiled part of the base.

This leads van Hoek to wonder how one can explain the apparent success of c-commanding in explaining anaphor phenomena. This, she says, comes about because 'the tree structures on which c-commanding is defined incorporate *highly schematic representations of some facets of conceptual organisation.*' (van Hoek, 1995, p 324; emphasis added). In other words, what generativists are doing is only *formalising* processes that are, in fact, socio-cognitive. Cognitive grammarians are explaining the *mental operations* that underpin syntactic competence, while generativists are describing them in terms they find congenial; and so any 'success' gained by a generativist account is entirely parasitic on a cognitive-grammatical account.

Before moving on to the next subsection we might pause to imagine what generativists' reactions might be to van Hoek's position. Doubtless they would say that van Hoek has things exactly the wrong way round. For it is our capacity to generate (formally specifiable) representations that makes it possible for us to entertain the various intuitions about semantics on which cognitive grammar trades. More specifically, they would be likely to focus on the cloudiness and ductility of notions such as 'reference point' and 'dominion'. For everything depends upon the account's having the resources for fixing which is which *within* a sentence. Of the two notions, that of 'dominion' would appear to be in the worse shape, having, as it does, less intuitive appeal. In the glossary of Langacker's second volume, dominion is defined as 'the set of entities (or the regions comprising them) that a particular reference point allows one to establish mental contact with'. In the body of the text, things are little clearer: we are told than in a sentence 'the object lies within the subject's dominion, which defines the object's scope of predication in the domain of instantiation' (Langacker, 1991, p. 179). Moreover, when we examine the cognitive grammatical account of a problem that taxes Chomskyan theory it is difficult to be convinced of the notion's utility. This is the problem of 'sloppy identity' that was discussed in Part 2 in the context of Jackendoff's position. (19) is Langacker's example of sloppy identity.

> (19) Ted scratched his nose, and so did Jimmy.

In (19) there is a room for ambiguity around the question of whether each man is scratching his own nose (the likely interpretation) or whether they are both scratching Ted's. Jackendoff argued that the complexity of the binding relation cannot be represented syntactically and must therefore be represented conceptually. But it would appear that concepts like reference point and dominion do rather little to explain this conceptual representation. The natural assumption is that the two agents ('reference points', says Langacker) scratched the noses within their own 'dominion'. But we need an account of how the listener is able to construct a possible interpretation when *Ted's* nose seems to be the antecedent for the implied anaphoric object of *did* in the second clause. Langacker writes that

> There is no presumption that the speaker and hearer have established mental contact with each nose independently of the relation it bears to the reference point. The two clauses thus

instantiate the same process type, which specifies, roughly, that some individual scratched the nose located within the domain of that individual.

(Langacker, 1991, pp. 179–180)

This account is obviously predicated on the assumption that *his nose* (a *prononimal* phrase, note) is within the domain of two reference points *Ted* and *Jimmy*. But is it not possible to take *his nose* as the variable-style reference point and the two agents as sharing its/their domain? Indeed, in terms of Langacker's distinction between autonomous and dependent elements, *his nose* would be judged as autonomous; and it is also easy to construe it as a primary landmark.

In a similar spirit, we might look for stronger reasons for fixing reference points and domains in sentences like those in (20).

(20) a. *Sue sent <u>him</u> a picture of <u>Sam</u>.

    b. *I gave <u>him</u> <u>Sam's</u> book.

Given that Langacker says that 'the object lies within the subject's dominion' why cannot *Sue* and *I* be the reference points, and *him* their dominion? And would this not indeed be likely to be the case if the sentences had been spoken in answer to questions about who sent Sam's picture to him or who gave Sam his book back?

I will postpone summarising and evaluative remarks till the next section.

4.1.2 The role and reference grammar (RRG) of Robert Van Valin

In some senses, Van Valin's *Role and reference grammar* (RRG) is quite a different animal from Langacker's cognitive grammar. Where Langacker proceeds in an a priori style working outwards from the base of English, where Langacker tunnels into the depths of sentences to uncover cognitive foundations with the complexity of (supposedly exhaustive of) syntactic complexities, where he eschews tree-style formalisms in favour of iconic diagrams, and where he practically ignores acquisition issues, Van Valin works bottom-up from cross-linguistic evidence, has relatively little concern with the cognitive nuances beneath syntactic form, seems to produce new formalisms instead of rejecting the whole idea of them (a 'structuralist-functionalist theory of grammar', Van Valin, 1993a, p. 1), and makes explicit developmental hypotheses which he pits against the published evidence.

But the commonalities between the theories are just as we would expect them to be – and just as strong. They both reject the view that syntax constitutes a system autonomous from semantics, as well as the view that language itself is a cognitive system interfacing with other cognitive systems rather than a conventionalised expression of cognitive and pragmatic ability. Moreover Van Valin, no less than Langacker, roots his categories semantically. As we shall be seeing, 'nucleus', 'core', (his conception of) 'clause', 'periphery' are all construed as socio-cognitive notions which happen to have been conventionalised. Inevitably, this leads to Van Valin's sharing with cognitive grammarians the aim of explaining phenomena, which generativists regard as being entirely syntactic, in terms of pragmatic or semantic forces. Recall my discussion in 2.5.5 of Van Valin's attempt to explain subjacency phenomena in terms of sentential pragmatics. This can be seen to parallel Langacker's work on raising and Van Hoek's work on pronoun-antecedent relationships discussed at the end of the previous subsection.

But one area of difference remains substantial, despite its existing within the walls of the socio-cognitive linguistic church. Where Langacker is almost profligate – or 'generous', according to taste – in his invention of concepts and technical terms Van Valin is kind of minimalist. He tries, that is, to get along with the minimum number of constructs, fixing them – in strong contrast to Chomsky – by reference to cross-linguistic evidence. This is essentially because Langacker's linguistics is more 'psychological' than Van Valin's. It exists near where Chomsky would draw the language faculty/cognitive-intentional systems interface. Van Valin, though, is working on the syntax side, wearing socio-cognitive goggles.

Just a word now – taking the form of a caveat – about Van Valin's reasons for rejecting the Chomskyan notion of universal grammar on empirical (i.e., cross-linguistic) grounds. His view is that if a characteristic is not universally evident then it cannot be part of universal grammar. We shall see later how Van Valin draws our attention to languages very different from English (often Native North American and Austroasian) and argues that because we can describe their rules, in some cases at least, in terms of semantic categories (like 'agent' and 'undergoer') alone, rather than syntactic ones like subject and object, then there is no independent justification for saying that children require innate syntactic knowledge, universal to human kind, to acquire them.

In any event, this is Van Valin (1993a, p. 2) in his own words:

> RRG takes language to be a system of communicative social action, and accordingly, analysing the communicative functions of grammatical structures plays a vital role in grammatical description and theory from this perspective ... Language is a system, and grammar is a system in the traditional structuralist sense; what distinguishes the RRG conception ... is the conviction that grammatical structure can only be understood with reference to its semantic and communicative functions. Syntax is not autonomous.

From this perspective, as we have discussed, the linguist does not proceed in an a priori fashion in order to map out the aspects of syntax that are universal. Rather, the question of what is universally present in human languages is to be decided *empirically* by analysing as wide an array of languages as possible, some of which diverge radically from English. In Van Valin and LaPolla's (1997) book on syntax, for example, 101 languages are discussed, the majority of which are not Indo-European.

Van Valin's view is that structuralist approaches have made false generalisations about human language because these have been made on the basis of a small number of languages that share basic features with English. For example, it might be said that the concept of the verb phrase (VP) is fundamental to Chomskyan linguistics. But if there exist languages that cannot be analysed in terms of VP then we should look to a different kind of candidate for universality – perhaps ones that are semantic in nature.

Here are two further examples of how cross-linguistic research puts pressure on Chomskyan ideas about syntactic universals. In the kind of analysis favoured by Chomsky, the goal is to represent sentences in terms of immediate constituent (IC) analysis, in which branches from the tree represent what is an immediate constituent of what.

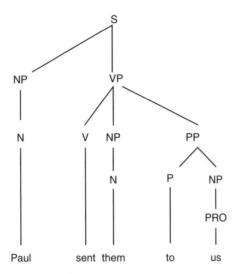

Figure 4.7 Immediate constituent (IC) structures.

Within these, attention is given to the way in which the head of the phrase determines the form of its constituents. Thus (Figure 4.7), in the VP *sent them to us* the
transitive verb *sent* (the head) determines that its object will be in the accusative case
(*them* rather than *they*) while in the prepositional phrase contained therein headed
by *to* the form *us* rather than *we* must be used because the pronoun is in the dative
case. Many traditional structuralist analyses assume, argues Van Valin, that
languages essentially have dependent-marking. However so-called head-marking
languages violate this principle because in these *the relations between the head and its
dependents is coded morphologically on the head rather than on the dependents.* One
such language is the Native American (Sioux) language Lakhota, in which there is
no case marking of noun phrases (NP) because the arguments of the verb are
marked on the verb itself, as shown in (21).

(21) a. Mathó ki hena wichá-wa-kte.

          bear the those them-I-kill.

      b. wichá-wa-kte.

          them-I-kill.

This means in effect that a verb can do the work of a whole English sentence, with
both the subject and the object being coded thereon. While one can draw an IC tree
for the full sentence (Figure 4.8a) a tree of the one-verb sentence (Figure 4.8b) is
entirely unrevealing about the kind of structure that English and Lakhota have in
common. (And they must have some linguistic features in common, otherwise we
would not be able to translate one language into the other; see the discussion of the
competition model, pp. 276–279.) The only way to preserve the IC analysis for
them-I-kill would be to assume that there are indeed separate proforms in the

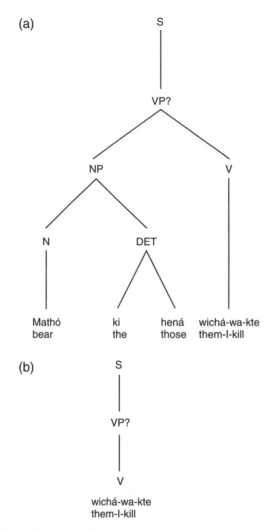

Figure 4.8 (21) a. and b. expressed as IC structures.

sentence but that they do not appear in its phonological representation – a familiar move in Chomskyan theory, as we have seen. Van Valin (1987) argues that there are, in fact, serious difficulties with this analysis. But whether or not this is so, the general point for Van Valin is that 'it would appear that there are serious problems with assuming an IC analysis as the basis for a universally valid representation of … syntactic structure' (Van Valin and LaPolla, 1997, p. 25).

For a further example of how cross-linguistic research is supposed to put pressure on some dogmas of linguistic structuralism we turn to the fundamental distinction between syntactic relations and semantic roles. It will be useful to spend some time on this, as it goes right to the heart of the question of whether a semantic account of grammatical regularities could be sufficient.

Chomsky's assumption of the autonomy of syntax, in the sense of its irreducibility to semantics, would seem to depend upon the syntax–semantics distinction holding universally. Here Van Valin concentrates on the distinction between grammatical subjects and objects (grammatical *relations* in is terminology) and the actor versus the undergoer (*semantic roles*). In English, the subject of a sentence is the argument that precedes the verb and determines the number of the verb. The subject can, of course, be either the actor or the undergoer. Thus, the subject in *John kissed Mary* is an actor, and in *Mary was kissed by John* it is an undergoer; in *The window broke* it is the undergoer.

One of the motivations for positing purely syntactic relations in a language is the existence of phenomena of this kind in which the distinction between (in this case two) semantic roles *is neutralised for syntactic purposes*. This kind of neutralisation is found in most languages, usually in a restricted form, in the sense that the neutralisation is restricted to actor and undergoer, rather than applying to *any* argument bearing a thematic relation to the verb.

But in some human languages, restricted neutralisation is not found. One of these is Acehnese, a language spoken in Sumatra. In Acehnese the agreement[4] of the verb with its argument is determined entirely by semantic role: actor and undergoer are not neutralised. The fact of whether the argument is an actor or an undergoer is coded by a clitic[5] on the verb, whether or not the verb is transitive. The clitics can either be pre-verbal (*proclitics*) or post-verbal (*enclitics*). An example is given in (22).

(22) a. (Gopnyan)   geu-mat-lôn.

　　　(optional 3rd sing.)   3rd-hold 1st person sing.

　　　(S)he   holds me.

　　b. (Lôn)   lôn-mat-geuh.

　　　(optional 1st sing.)   1st sing. 3rd person.

　　　I   hold him/her.

If Acehnese were a language that operated with syntactic rules of the kind found in English then we would say that *lôn* in (a) is the object pronoun and *gue* the subject pronoun; while *lôn* in (b) is the subject pronoun and *geuh* is the object pronoun; indeed we would generalise from this and say that the proclitics code subjects and the enclitics code objects. What is in fact being coded may in reality be the distinction between actor and undergoer. The predictions of the syntactic and the semantic accounts can be tested against each other by examining how *intransitive* verbs are represented. (The two accounts cannot be tested against each other by examining passives, because Acehnese does not have the passive form.) Intransitive constructions are crucial because the subject of an intransitive verb will be an actor in some

---

[4] Strictly the term 'agreement' is not applicable here, as Acehnese is head-marking language – see immediately above.

[5] Recall that this is an element which must be attached to another word to make a word; for example the contracted negative in English *n't*.

verbs (e.g., 'go') but it will be the undergoer in the case of verbs like 'fall'. In (23) is shown the Achehnese for '(S)he goes' – in which the 'subject' is actor:

(23) Geu-jak (gopnyan).

   3rd-go (optional 3rd sing.).

   '(S)he goes.'

Here a proclitic is used, which is what would be predicted by both the syntactic and the syntactic accounts. The deciding case is 'fall', as here the 'subject' is an undergoer. See (24)

(24) a. Lôn   rhët (-lôn).

      1 sing fall   (-1st sing).

      'I fall.'

      b. *Lôn   lôn-rhët.

      1 sing.   1st sing fall.

      'I fall.'

The sentence (24b) is ill-formed because the clitic has been placed before the verb, which is where it should be if it were coding for subjecthood; (24a) is the correct form because the clitic is placed in the post-verbal slot, as this is where the fact of being an undergoer is coded.

But is a *syntactic* reading of such facts possible? Van Valin and LaPolla defend their account on the basis of parsimony:

> In order to interpret these facts in terms of grammatical [i.e., syntactic] relations, it would be necessary to say that verbs like *rhët* ('fall') have only an object without a subject, or that there is a subject, but it is really an object. This is possible, but complicates the theory unnecessarily. The most straightforward account is to say simply that there is one kind of cross-reference [i.e., what would be called 'agreement' in dependent-marking languages JR] for actors and another for undergoers.
>
> (1997, p. 257)

Acehnese does however exemplify *general neutralisation*, meaning that the verb can agree with any or all of its arguments irrespective of their semantic role. A moment's thought tells us that this precludes there being the syntactic distinction between subject and object; for in this case we can no longer say that subjects 'are actors *or* undergoers' – only that 'some argument or other' agrees with the verb while others do not. Furthermore, if the subject/object distinction cannot hold then it should not be surprising that the language has no passive form. This lack of restriction can be revealed in how (what in English would be a) passive complement clauses embedded in a matrix clauses is represented. Schematically, instead of saying

(25) 'The epic is certain to be recited by him.'

Acehnese has the equivalent of:

(26) 'The epic is certain he recites.'

Also, instead of

(27) 'I believe him to have been given money by you yesterday.'

it has (the dash plays the role of PRO):

(28) 'I believe him$_i$ [you gave money [to] ____$_i$ yesterday].

It can be noted here that, where English has a restriction, Acehnese has none, in virtue of the fact that Acehnese lacks the category of subject. Thus, in English, (29a) is well formed and (b) is not.

(29) a. Jane$_i$ does not want____$_i$ to be arrested.

b. *Jane$_i$ does not want the police to arrest____$_i$.

The reason is that in English an undergoer can only appear in a complement clause in an empty slot if it is the *subject* of the clause; not if it is the object – as it is in (29b). In Acehnese, however, the undergoer can appear tacitly in the empty object slot in a complement clause – as in (28) – as well as in the empty subject slot of such a clause. I am glossing a number of technicalities here (see pp. 258–259 of Van Valin and Lapolla, 1997), but perhaps the simplest take-home message is that the very fact of Acehnese lacking a passive form is a good reason to wonder whether there is any motivation for ascribing to it the syntactic distinction between subject and object.

On Van Valin's research programme then, one looks at the various human linguistic practices *before* making claims about universality. Needless to say, Van Valin's avoidance of a priori claims in this regard is entirely pragmatist in spirit. So too is his so-called 'communication-and-cognition' perspective. Combining these two credos the following claims about the putatively universal features of human language are made.

First, the only syntactic categories that can be said to appear universally are verb and noun. (Adjectives, for example, are lacking in Lakhota.) Why are these two form classes universal? For linguists working from the communication-and-cognition perspective this is because the distinction between nouns and verbs is the syntactic realisation of the semantic distinction between arguments and predicates. No language can lack arguments and predicates because all languages must, in some way or another, enable its users to pick out some item in the world (an argument) and say that something is true of it (predicate something of it). This does not mean that making true statements is the only thing we do with words, but it must surely be one of the things that we are able to do with them.

Van Valin also takes the clause to be universal, conceived here as the unit containing the predicate and its arguments. Given this, we have a further universal distinction between:

1) Predicating and non-predicating elements, and

2) Those NPs and *adpositional*[6] phrases that are arguments of the predicate and those that are not.

For example, in a sentence like *John kissed Mary in the library*, the predicate is *kissed*, *John* and *Mary* are the arguments of the predicate, and the phrase *in the library* is an adpositional phrase acting as an *adjunct* to the main clause. However, in the sentence *He looked towards the hills*, *towards the hills* is an adpositional phrase that is *not* an adjunct, as it is a complement of the main clause.

---

[6] A term used to denote prepositions (e.g., in English) and postpositions (e.g., in Japanese).

Van Valin's universal schema for sentence structure is shown in Figure 4.9. Within this basic framework, however, there are taken to be further layers of structure. What is traditionally referred to as the main clause is now the *core*; what we have been calling the predicate is now the *nucleus*, with the adjunct phrase now being referred to as the *periphery*. Van Valin calls this theory of *the layered structure of the clause* (or LSC) (see Figure 4.10). These distinctions are found in all languages, argues Van Valin, even in those with 'free word order'.

This is not to deny that that tree diagrams *can* be drawn to represent layered structure; see Figure 4.11. But note that this kind of tree structure differs dramatically from that used by Chomsky, not least because there is no representation of the verb phrase. (The empirical motivation for this omission is that languages exist which

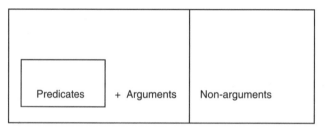

Figure 4.9 Universal oppositions underlying clause structure, according to Van Valin. From Van Valin *et al.*, *Syntax structure, meaning, and function* (1997). Copyright © Cambridge University Press, reproduced with permission of the publisher and authors.

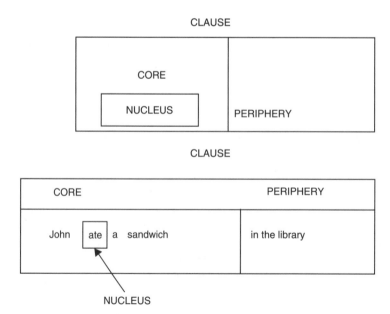

Figure 4.10 Components of the layered structure of the clause.

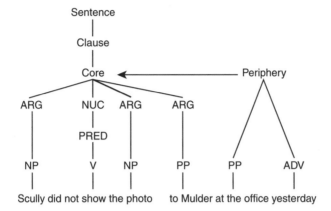

Figure 4.11 English Layered Clause Structure (LCS).

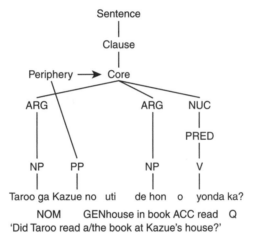

Figure 4.12 Japanese LSC. From Van Valin *et al.*, *Syntax structure, meaning, and function* (1997). Copyright © Cambridge University Press, reproduced with permission of the publisher and authors.

can – controversially – be said to lack verb phrases.) Note also that the drawing of distinctions between nucleus and core arguments etc. does not depend upon the linear order of morphemes in the sentence. In illustration of this I reproduce Van Valin and LaPolla's LSC structure diagram of a sentence in Japanese – Figure 4.12.

There is one further feature of LSC we need to consider – *operators*. Notice in Figures 4.11 and 4.12 that certain elements in the sentence were unattached; for example the phrase *did not* in the English sentence and the Japanese question marker *ka*. These represent operators that modify the clause and its parts. They are represented in LSC as projecting down from the nucleus. Tense, aspect and negation are the most easily recognised examples of operators because in English and in other Indo-European languages these are marked on the verbs (as clitics such as -*n't* in the

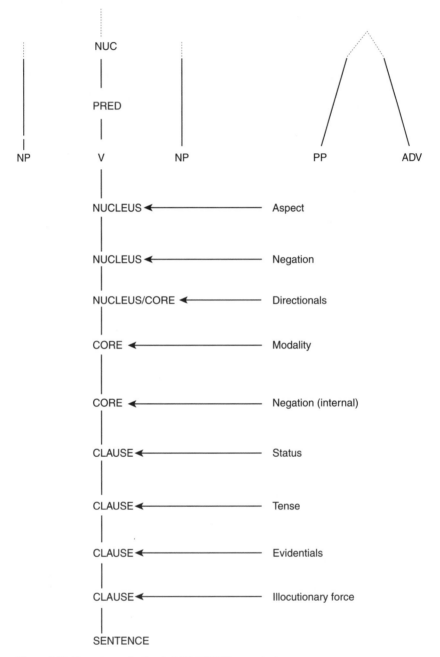

Figure 4.13 Operator projection in LSC (SCOPE, operator).

case of negation) or adjacent to the verb. The deeper we go, the wider the scope of operator. Thus, aspect and tense represent facts about the nucleus – about whether the process is complete and when it happened – whereas illocutionary force determines whether the sentence is an assertion, a statement, a question, etc. (see Figure 4.13).

Note that some of these operators are not found in English. The status of the addressee is not marked in English, for example, while it is in German and French. Similarly, 'evidentials' are not marked in English. That is to say, we have no syntactic means of distinguishing between different kinds of epistemic commitment to the claims we make; so we have to say things like 'I saw it happen with my own eyes' or 'A little bird told me that...'. A language spoken in Brazil called Tuyuca has five forms of evidential. 'Directionals' will also be unfamiliar. These indicate the direction of an action. This is not specifically marked in English, though we can make direction explicit as in 'He shouted up'. German has particles that specifically mark direction of action, with *hin* meaning away from the speaker and *her* meaning towards the speaker. The Tibeto-Burman language Qiang has a system of eight directionals.

Van Valin also proposed that speakers of a language learn a set of, what he calls, either *constructional templates* or *syntactic inventories,* by which he means canonical LSC forms (e.g., the form for a question or an imperative), which can be combined to create complex sentences. (A comparison can naturally be made with Langacker's cognitive grammar schemas here.)

It must be born in mind that LSC is, for Van Valin, a syntactic structure. Recall that he does not deny the necessity for the syntactic level of analysis, only that it cannot be derived directly from the semantics. The two levels are taken to be related by a set of 'linking algorithms' as shown in Figure 4.14.

What is, then, the semantic level of analysis? One main distinction has to be drawn here: between semantic macro-roles and logical structure. The first represents semantic features of nouns and the second of verbs. We have, in fact, already encountered the first, which is the distinction between actor and undergoer. The second is derived from the taxonomy of verb types devised by the functional linguist Vendler in terms of the *Actionsart* (form of action) that a verb expresses. Thus, a verb may encode a 'state' (e.g., ... is shattered), an 'activity' (e.g., ... cried), an 'achievement' (e.g., ... shattered) or an 'accomplishment' (e.g., ... melted).

The technicalities need not detain us here. I will simply reproduce one of Van Valin and LaPolla's figures in which the relation between a syntactic inventory and a semantic representation are represented (Figure 4.15).

It is fair to say that, while Van Valin gives equal weight to semantics and pragmatics, when contrasting his position with that of the structuralists, pragmatics plays something of a secondary role in the theory itself, in the sense that pragmatic distinctions do not underlie syntactic taxonomies in the way in which semantic distinctions such as predicate/non-predicate are taken to do. He refers to pragmatics as 'information structure' and follows a number of other functionally-minded linguists in analysing the different ways in which the communicative focus of a sentence can vary. We have, in fact, already encountered Van Valin's work in this area.

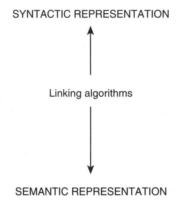

Figure 4.14 The relation between syntactic on semantic structure on RRG

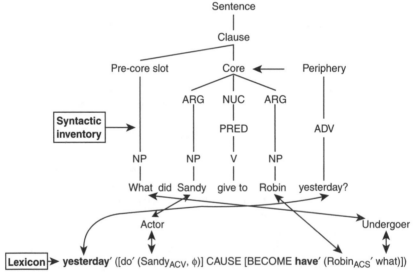

Figure 4.15 Van Valin's account of how syntax and semantics are linked in an English sentence. From Van Valin *et al.*, *Syntax structure, meaning, and function* (1997). Copyright © Cambridge University Press, reproduced with permission of the publisher and authors.

Recall my description in 2.5.5 of his pragmatist account of the subjacency principle in terms on notions such as 'communicative focus'.

What does all this imply about language acquisition? First, it clearly implies, for Van Valin, a non-nativist position on syntactic development. It implies that some innate ability for constructing semantic representations is in place, but that the particular LSCs – the syntactic inventories – are learned on the basis of input from adults. Though Van Valin does not put it quite as explicitly as this, what the child learns essentially are the linking algorithms between semantic representations and syntactic inventories.

He makes common causes with developmentalists such as Bruner (see section 4.3), Braine (see 4.3) and Karmiloff-Smith (see 3.5.5) who argue, in Van Valin's terms, for language being 'learned on the basis of a rich cognitive endowment'.[7] In Van Valin (1991) he described those areas in which his account is in accordance with the developmental facts, claiming that the order in which sentence operators are acquired will be in the direction of narrow to wide scope (down the operator hierarchy Figure 4.13), which implies that children will acquire aspect before tense as it is 'less complex'. It is 'simpler' because it involves only the 'internal temporal structure of the event itself', as opposed to tense, which expresses a deictic relation between an entire event and reference time (initially always the time of the speech event), something that requires the child to 'abstract away from the immediate situation' (Van Valin, 1991, p. 17). There is some cross-linguistic evidence for this order of acquisition: in Italian (Antinucci and Miller, 1976), Walpiri (Bavin, 1989), Hebrew (Berman, 1985) and Turkish (Aksu, 1978). (Contrast Van Valin's account with Radford's minimalist account of why children mark aspect before tense, given in 2.4.4.)

I will now pause to consider the Antinucci and Miller (1976) data in some detail pp. 187–188, by way of illustration. These workers showed that 'tense' marking by Italian children was initially more responsive to the aspectual value of verbs than to their temporal value. This was because it reflected the distinction between two kinds of verbal semantics: (1) verbs that code *states* ('stative' verbs) such as *love, want*, and *know* and also verbs that code *activities* such as *fly, jump* and *dance*, versus (2) verbs that code *changes of state with a clear result* such as *find, throw*, and *give*. There were two symptoms of this in the younger children: (a) they began by making an agreement error on the past participle of the change of state verbs only; (b) they tended to produce past tense forms for the change of state verbs well before they did so for the stative/activity kind.

With regard to the agreement error (a), in Italian there must be agreement between a *pronomimal* object of a transitive verb and the past participle of the verb, as in (30). (Underlining represents agreement.)

   (30) Giovanni la ha aperta. (Feminine agreement)

       'John opened it.'

What the children began by doing however (up to the ages of 2y 0m or 2y 5m), was to enforce agreement between the past participle and the object even if this was a *full nominal*, as in (31)

---

[7] This is taken from a handout for a talk by Van Valin in Darwin College, Cambridge in July, 2001.

(31)   (1;10) *La signora ha chiusa la porta.

cf. La signora ha chiuso la porta.

'The woman has closed the door.'

Antinucci and Miller's explanation for this (their term) 'invention' was that the children were 'focussing on the result of the event described by the verb ... treat[ing] the past participle as an adjective' (1976, p. 172). The past participle was being used to describe the altered state of the object, was therefore functioning like an adjective, and so was being made to agree with the noun with which it was in construction. On this view, then, what they were doing was marking something about the verb's aspect rather than something temporal.

In the second place (b), they tended to neglect to mark stative and activity verbs for past tense while appropriately marking change-of-state verbs. For example, they did not mark the verb *girare* (spin around) for tense but they did mark *rompere* (break). Moreover, this was a tendency which also emerged in the speech of an American child ('Eve' from Brown's [1973] classic Harvard study). From 1y 9m to 2y 2m she tended to mark past tense in change-of-state verbs such as *open, wash*, and *close*, but did not mark it for verbs coding activities (e.g., *ask, wait*) or states (e.g., *have, like*).

In passing, a question mark does linger over the claim that aspect-marking actually *preceded* tense marking. It might be more accurate to say that the younger children did not differentiate between the two. Singling out verbs of a certain aspect for tense marking does not entail that it was not really tense that was being marked. Moreover, one might equally well construe the past participle agreement-marking error as a case of overgeneralisation from pronominalised objects to non-pronominalised ones. The authors reply to this claim is that it leaves unanswered both why the over-generalisation was not from *non*-agreement with the pronominalised objects and why there was not a single instance of a pronominalised object in the relevant children. In fact, constructions like (30) did not appear until children had acquired the adult form. Nevertheless, one could insist that marking the past participle as if it were an adjective is a case of aspect/tense undifferentiation rather than the absence of syntactic acknowledgment of a temporal feature.

More recently, Van Valin has also been able to make predictions about the acquisition of *complex* sentences. In order to describe these, however, it will be necessary first to describe his theory of complex sentence construction (to be found in chapter 8 of Van Valin and La Polla, 1997, and in Van Valin, 2001). In essence, what van Valin does is to predict the order in which sentential constructions will be acquired, based upon an entirely a priori analysis of structure.

Van Valin divides his analysis of complex sentences into three sub-theories: of *juncture*, of *nexus*, and of *interclausal semantic relations*. His theory of juncture is, in fact, what we have already been covering under the title of the 'layered structure of the clause' (LSC). However, he also concerns himself with the different ways in which the three elements of LSC can be brought into correspondence. The three ways in which juncture can be achieved are shown in Figure 4.16.

When, for example, we have two verbs together within a core there is nuclear juncture. These formations are particularly common in French, so I will reproduce

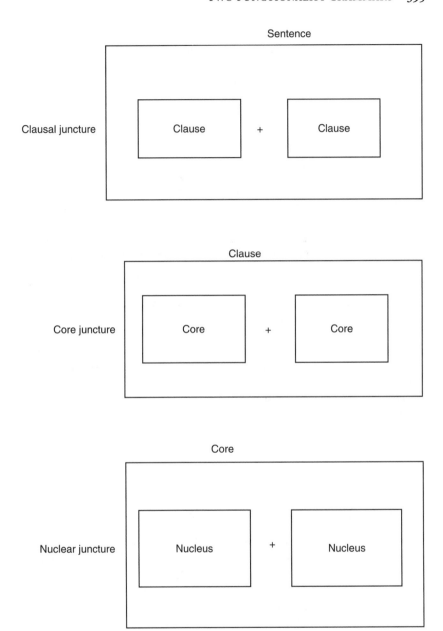

Figure 4.16 Types of juncture.

Van Valin's example from that language in (32a). This has the form $[_{CORE} NP[_{NUC} V]$ $+ [_{NUC} V] NP]$. By contrast, the core juncture in (32b) has the structure $[_{CORE} NP$ $[_{NUC} V] NP] + [_{CORE} [NUC V] NP]$. The situation in which a NP appears between the verbs (core juncture) as in (b) is obviously typical of English.

(32) a. Je ferai manger les gâteaux à Jean.

　　　　 'I will make John eat the cakes.'

　　 b. Je laisserai Jean manger les gâteaux.

　　　　 'I will make John eat the cakes.'

A sentence such as *John talked to Mary this morning, and they will go shopping later this afternoon,* is an example of clausal juncture – two clauses conjoined in a sentence.

Moving on to the theory of nexus, this taxonomises the possible syntactic relations between units in a juncture. Again, there are three possibilities – shown in Figure 4.17.

It is worth dwelling a little on this taxonomy, because it illustrates just how close to traditional grammatical analyses RRG can approach. A *coordinate* structure is simply one in which neither of two clauses is dependent upon the other, as in *John talked to Mary and then they went bowling.* When, however, we have a situation in which one of the clauses (the matrix clause) is modified by one that is grammatically dependent on it and that is generally introduced by a subordinating conjunction such as *after* or *that* we have a *subordinate* construction. This corresponds to the traditional concept of *embedding.* Subordinate clauses can be divided in terms of function: nominal, adjectival, adverbial, temporal, conditional, relative. Sometimes the subordinate clause (underlined) can fill the role of subject (e.g., *That he failed the examination came as no surprise*) and sometimes as object (e.g., *George regretted that he had been rude to Sarah.*) [Note that this is how Van Valin describes subordination himself (Van Valin and La Polla, 1997, chapter 8) despite the fact that 'subject' and 'object' strictly do not appear as categories in RRG.] They can also function as sentential modifiers, as in *Peter met Naomi after he had finished at the gym.*

In traditional analyses, this subordination would be represented, as it were, 'literally' in terms of the clause in question being lower in the tree. Well, something similar happens in the case of RRG. In the figural representation (of the kind shown in Figure 4.11 above) of adverbial and *that* clauses in Van Valin and La Polla (1997, pp. 465–467) – of *Peter met Naomi after he had finished at the gym* – the subordinate clauses are indeed lower in the VanValin-style tree than the matrix clause, in virtue of the fact that it is located at the periphery and that it consists of a core which consists in turn of a predicate (*after* in the above example) and a further core consisting of an predicate (*had finished*) an argument (*he*) and an adjunct argument (*the gym*).

The third element of the nexus taxonomy is one that is not typically found in traditional grammatical analyses – *cosubordination*. Based on evidence from a wide range of languages, Van Valin posits a kind of nexus that, like coordination, does not involve embedding, but which, like subordination, involves a non-matrix clause being in some degree dependent upon the matrix clause.

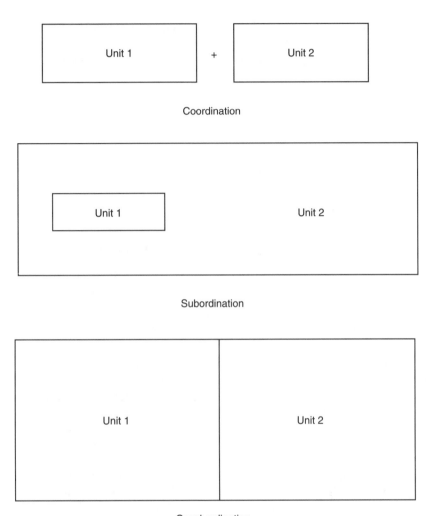

Figure 4.17 Types of nexus.

(33) The delivery man having left the package on the porch, Mary opened the door and picked it up.

In (33), for example, the first clause is not an argument of the matrix verbs and it does not modify the matrix clause as does, say, an adverbial clause; but it is depen-dent upon the matrix clause for the expression of tense and illocutionary force. (For some writers of course, (33) would be produced as two separate sentences.)

Each of these nexus types can in principle occur at each of the three levels of juncture, thereby generating nine possible juncture–nexus types. Korean has all nine, English has seven (34), and Cree (Algonquin) has only two. Van Valin ranks these in terms of the tightness of the linkage between the elements, with nuclear coordination being the tightest and clausal coordination being the loosest, as can be seen in (34 taken from Van Valin, 2001, p. 516).

(34) a. Mary made the woman leave.   Nuclear coordination

       Vince wiped the table clean.

    b. Ted tried to open the door.   Core cosubordination

       Sam sat playing the guitar.

    c. David regretted Amy's losing the race.   Core subordination

       That Amy lost the race shocked everyone.

    d. Louisa told Bob to close the window.   Core coordination

       Fred saw Harry leave the room.

    e. Henry ran down the hill laughing.   Clausal cosubordination

       Paul drove to the store and bought some beer.

    f. John persuaded Leon that Amy had lost.   Clausal subordination

       Bill went to the part after he talked to Mary.

    g. Anna read for a few minutes, and then she   Clausal coordination
       went out.

We come finally to the inter-clausal semantic relations. What we have here is another hierarchy ranging from close to loose relations, top to bottom. The more distinct the content of the two units, the looser is the relation. Causative semantic relations are the closest, in so far as this involves the merging of the content of two units into a single unit coding a single situation. We saw an example of such a relation in the French causative of (32a).

Armed with these two hierarchies, Van Valin points up their intimate, though not one-to-one, relationship, on the basis of which he is able to generate developmental predictions. This is called the interclausal relations hierarchy (IRH) – see Figure 4.18. There is supposed to be an 'iconic' – there's that Peircean term again – relationship between the two hierarchies which, in this case, means that there is taken to be a direct correlation between the strength of the syntactic link between two units in a juncture and the closeness of the semantic relation between these units.

Given all this, children's coming to express their meanings in language resolves itself, for Van Valin, into the acquisition of IRH. How is this acquisition possible? First, Van Valin adopts the view of Braine (to be discussed in 4.4) that the units of the layered structure of the clause (aka the levels of juncture) can be acquired purely on the basis of the child's 'rich cognitive endowment' (Van Valin, 2001, p. 519). (To anticipate, a core argument corresponds to the child's concept of an object and a nucleus corresponds to a predicate, which in turn corresponds to the child's conception of objects' properties or to his/her concept of action; the core corresponds to the child's conception of an event or situation.) Next, nexus relations are based upon the conceptions of juxtaposition and embedding, and these, says Van Valin, are 'important cognitive concepts which are relevant to language and other cognitive

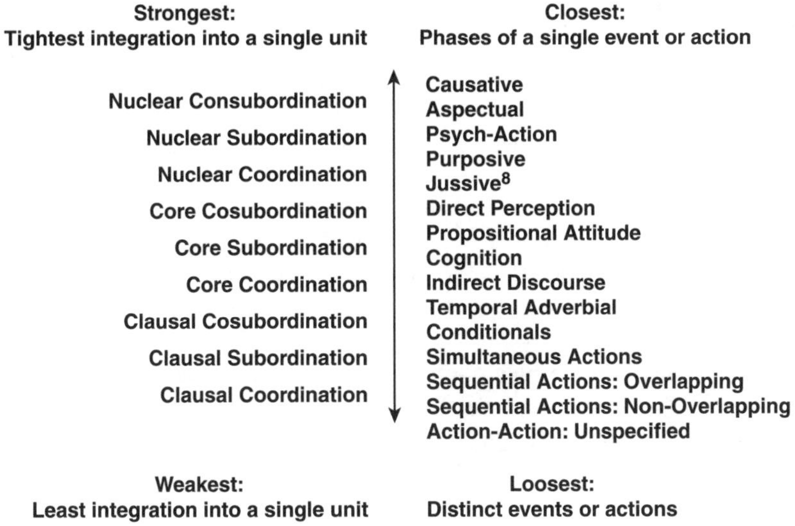

Strongest: Tightest integration into a single unit	Closest: Phases of a single event or action
Nuclear Consubordination	Causative
Nuclear Subordination	Aspectual
Nuclear Coordination	Psych-Action
Core Cosubordination	Purposive
Core Subordination	Jussive[8]
Core Coordination	Direct Perception
Clausal Cosubordination	Propositional Attitude
Clausal Subordination	Cognition
Clausal Coordination	Indirect Discourse
	Temporal Adverbial
	Conditionals
	Simultaneous Actions
	Sequential Actions: Overlapping
	Sequential Actions: Non-Overlapping
	Action-Action: Unspecified
Weakest: Least integration into a single unit	Loosest: Distinct events or actions

Figure 4.18 The interclausal relations hierarchy.

domains: here they are part of the child's cognitive endowment, they are not strictly linguistic concepts at all' (Van Valin, 2001, p. 519). Finally, with regard to inter-clausal semantic relations, we are obviously dealing with the varieties of developing psychological insight that have received a great deal of attention from psychologists in recent years – causation, intention, purpose, belief and so forth. The idea is that development within this domain will line up – given iconicity – with developments in the syntax of complex sentences. Presumably, the cognitive-semantic side of the IRH is the leading developmental edge.

'Once having learned the IRH, a number of important grammatical properties of complex sentences can be deduced by the child' (ibid., p. 519). The order in which these are 'deduced' is then made the basis for some developmental predictions, supplementing those made on the basis of the RRG theory of operators. I will present the first four of these predictions, for illustrative purposes. They are broadly based on the assumption that development proceeds from the top of the IRH.

1) Children will use juncture with sub-clausal units before those involving clauses.

2) With regard to nexus relations, because coordination and cosubordination are 'arguably conceptually simpler' (ibid., p. 519) than the embedding relation of subordination, we should see non-subordinate nexus types emerging before the subordinate type.

3) Cosubordinate structures should be the first non-subordinate nexus type to appear, given that same-subject constructions at the core level are 'simpler

---

8 This means 'expressing a command'.

syntactically' than different-subject ones. To take Van Valin's examples, forms like *Fred remembered to close the gate* exemplify cosubordination, and forms like *Fred reminded Bill to close the gate* exemplify coordination.)

4) Core junctures with transitive infinitival verbs will appear before nuclear junctures with transitive infinitival verbs. This is because core junctures 'present arguments in their *canonical positions* with respect to their verbs while nuclear disjunctions do not' (ibid., p. 520, emphasis added). The French sentences in (32) present a clear example of this contrast. In (b) *Jean* is in the canonical position for interpretation as a direct object ('undergoer' in RRG) of *laisser* and subject of *manger*, whereas in (a) *Jean* is coded as the indirect object of one complex nucleus *faire manger*.

These predictions are highly testable, and Van Valin (2001) presents diary evidence in support of them across seven languages. However, it is surely fair to say that where these predictions would not be made from considerations of the brute principle 'simple-before-complex' alone (1–3), they would be made by the generativist (4). With regard to (4), the nuclear juncture would be said to have greater transformational complexity, being farther from the d-structure, which encodes elements in their canonical order.[9] Additionally, the predictive waters become somewhat muddied when the right-hand side of the IRH is factored in. This is because there can be a tension between syntactic simplicity and semantic closeness. For example, the theory predicts that children's first complex sentences will code the semantic relation at the top of the hierarchy, namely causality. But on the other (left) hand, because causal relations involve a causer and a causee we require the actors of each nuclear juncture to be different. (This is also true in the jussive case, in which A commands B to do something.) Well, this is in conflict here with prediction (3) that same-subject constructions should precede different-subject ones. But the expression of causality obviously requires a syntactic form in which there is a different subject. For example in *You made the gate close* (causation) *the gate* is, for Van Valin, the 'subject' of *close*. In *I'm trying to close the gate* (purposive, and lower in the hierarchy) the sentence is same-subject and therefore 'simpler'.

Finally in this section, I move to the kind of considerations Van Valin fields against the Chomskyan view that children have innate syntactic capacities, rather than a rich cognitive endowment that allows syntax to be 'learned' given the 'iconic' relationship between varieties of meaning and levels of syntactic structure. To explain his position Van Valin (1991, p. 10–11), takes an analogy from a principle that is often adopted by those working in the *structuralist* tradition. This was discussed above in the context of Langacker's proposals about learning constraints on prepositional phrase construction and in the context of Chang's recent model of production in 3.6. The subset principle (see Figure 4.19) of Berwick (1985) was devised to take account of the fact that children do not receive negative evidence

---

[9]   That said, there is a difference between canonical semantic order (in RRG) and canonical order in the language (in P & P theory); but the essential point remains the same.

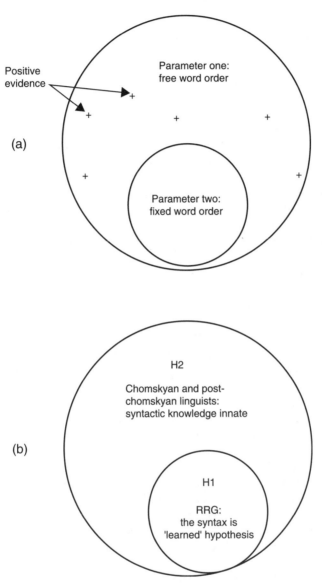

Figure 4.19 Van Valin's analogy between the subset principle (a) and the relation between RRG and syntactic nativism (b). From Van Valin (1991), permission sought.

when acquiring syntax. That is, they are not presented with sets of sentences that are ill-formed while being told that they *are* ill-formed. They must, therefore, acquire language on the basis of positive evidence alone. Next, we have the nativist (P & P) assumption that children are born with the ability to learn all human languages because they innately know the sets of parameters along which all languages vary. These parameters vary in how strict they are. English, for example has very strict word-order, whereas Walpiri (an Australian aboriginal language) allows an almost total scrambling of order. Given this, we can view different language parameters as nested within one another in terms of how many restrictions they impose. See Figure 4.19a, with English-style strictness being the subset of Walpiri-like freedom.

The subset principle, then, proposes that the child's default parameter will be the *stricter* subset (a), because if it were the superset (b) then negative evidence would have to be available to children to enable them to pull back from their relaxed assumptions about word order. If, however, the strict subset is the default then only positive evidence will be needed to tell them that they are learning a language with few restrictions on word order: they are shown what they are allowed to do, not shown what they must not do. There is evidence for the subset principle in so far as children learning languages like Korean, Russian and Swedish (ones with relatively few restrictions on word order) begin by being *conservative* about the word orders they use.

Now for Van Valin's analogy. Take two hypothesis: H1 and H2. H1 is taken to parallel the subset parameter (the one that is conservative and prescriptive) while H2 parallels the relaxed and unprescriptive parameter. H1 is – for Van Valin – the non-nativist theory that syntax is learned and H2 is the syntactic nativist view. Why this way round? Because H1 is 'weaker' in so far as 'it is possible that detailed studies of the acquisition process and the input to it could show that some element of grammar could not in principle be learned' (Van Valin, 1991, pp 10–11). However if H2 (nativist) hypothesis were taken as the subset there could be no positive evidence that could lead us to abandon it because there is nothing that could prove that some aspect of grammar is not part of an innate autonomous grammatical system. Even if one could give a motivated account of how some aspect of grammar could be learned on the basis of evidence available to the child, an advocate of H2 could always maintain that without the antecedently-given linguistic knowledge in the child no learning would be possible, even with plenty of evidence (Van Valin, 1991, p. 11).

Van Valin then follows up this analogy with three further reasons why language development researchers should adopt RRG as their working linguistic theory rather than any of the generative approaches, of which Chomsky's is obviously the prime example.

1) Generative theories are constantly changing, which ensures that it will be nigh impossible for the researcher to keep abreast of advances. The reason they change so frequently is that 'they are built around particular formalisms, and formalisms, being empty formal representations, can change rather rapidly' (ibid., p. 11). RRG, on the other hand, is first and foremost a substantive theory built around well-established semantic and pragmatic notions like Vendler's

Actionsart system of verb classification (described above). Such a taxonomy cannot become outmoded because of changes in 'fashion' and cannot be abandoned without destroying the very fabric of the theory.

2) Unlike the generative grammars, which were originally designed to give descriptively adequate accounts of English, RRG developed out of attempts to write grammars for languages far removed from Indo-European patterns: Lakhota (Sioux, discussed above), Tagalog (Philippines), and Dyirbal (Australian Aboriginal). It is, therefore, better placed to capture those aspects of language that are universal.

3) Where much of child language research is 'irrelevant' to formalist approaches, the RRG grammar necessarily gives empirical work a central place, because it takes children to be 'constructing' their grammars on the basis of evidence. This invites the question of how they do it, where the formalist-nativist view forecloses such questions, reducing empirical work to the task of describing a trajectory that has already been plotted a priori.

In the interests of balance, let us imagine a generativist reaction to these points.

First, the analogy with the subset principle is unconvincing, for a number of reasons. For one thing, if there is to be any such analogy it would need to be other way about: the subset theory should be the nativist one, given that this is the theory that is *conservative and prescriptive*. The nativist approach sees the child as being constrained to interpret the speech input on the basis of tacitly-known rules and representations, just as subset-children are constrained conservatively to assume that the language they are learning has word order rules. It is correct to say that the nativist theory is the 'stronger' in so far as it makes more explicit claims about how development takes place, rather than being content with saying that it takes place by a process called 'learning' or 'construction'. But why should the stronger theory be the superset? Next, is there really 'no conceivable fact' that could falsify a nativist theory? Developmentalists can surely deploy the principle of parsimony (see the empirical work of Tomasello and of Pine discussed in 4.3) as well as connectionist models (see all of Part 3). Moreover, the only thing that might be said to make it hard to imagine evidence against syntactic nativism is our very familiarity with how children develop language – particularly those of us who have observed the process at close quarters. We all know, for example, that when children put two or three words together they do so in a rulebound way (whether these rules are syntactic or semantic). But imagine that word order were completely random until the age of, say, 2y 6m in children learning English. If this were the case, it is unlikely that syntactic nativism would last ten minutes. And, conversely, is it really so easy to falsify claims about syntax being 'learned'? Because no attempt has been made to define 'learning' the RRG enthusiast is free to explain any development post hoc with no constraints on his imaginative construction of how the 'learning' took place.

Next, what of Van Valin's objection to the fact that generative linguistics evolves at a rapid rate, and his assumption that language development researchers would be expected to prefer something with a less protean character? Once again the objection might be said to have things the wrong way round. Perhaps the reason why the generative approach rapidly spawns many novel sub-theories is not because it consists of 'empty' formalisms that can be twisted any way you please, but because there are many linguists working within that framework. And the reason this is so is that Chomsky's work is found to be intellectually *nutritious* by so many people. In other words, advances in generative linguistics come rapidly for much the same reason why they come rapidly in (say) visual neuroscience and do not come rapidly in (say) the social psychology of group decision-making. Indeed it might be something to be held against RRG that controversy and change is not its hallmark (see papers in Van Valin, 1993b). Scientists generally prefer the mercurial and provocative to the stolid and consensus-seeking.

Van Valin's claim that RRG's determinedly cross-linguistic character is a virtue in itself goes to the heart of the debate between rationalist and pragmatist linguists. For the latter, the search for linguistic universals is just that – a search; and the wider this search the better. What results from such a process is the positing of linguistic universals qua lowest common denominators. Compare this with the Chomskyan way of proceeding. Here, the linguist begins by developing a descriptively adequate account of his or her own native language, which means an account of the rules that generate well-formed sentences of the language without generating ill-formed ones. Such a theory must 'compute' the correct inflections and (in a language such as English) the correct word order. It is a description of the competence possessed by the skilled speaker – a description of the end state of acquisition. Next, descriptively adequate theories will compete with one another and will do so on the criteria of 'elegance, simplicity and economy' in order to produce an explanatorily adequate theory – a theory of the child's starting state. Finally, it is a plausible assumption that the simpler the proposed rules are the more likely they are to be the rules that are innately and universally represented. But none of this means that the study of a single language is sufficient to produce an adequate theory of 'human'; indeed we saw in Part 2 how the evolution of Chomskyan theory was influenced by cross-linguistic work. But this cross-linguistic evidence is there to mould a purportedly explanatory theory *that is already in place*. The Chomskyan would say that RRG has no explanatorily adequate theory in place simply because it *has never attempted even a descriptively adequate theory*. RRG has never devised a descriptively adequate account of how speakers are able to produce and understand well-formed sentences in a single language. For example, while the theory looks at the different kinds of agreement across different languages it presents no account of how (say) agreement is actually derived in any one of them. And how, for example, does one explain how passivation is achieved in English, on RRG? In contrast to Langacker's cognitive grammar, none is forthcoming; although there is much said about how passivation is achieved, and whether it is present, in some of the world's languages.

A related question here concerns the way in which Van Valin draws conclusions about which elements of language are universal on the basis of cross linguistic evidence. Does, for example, the fact that the argument structure of verbs in Acehnese need not be analysed in terms of the distinction between subject and object (with the relevant distinction being between actor and undergoer) suggest that 'grammatical relations' are not a universal feature of human languages? Once again, one can turn Van Valin's proposals on their head here. What is perhaps more relevant to the question of what is universal is the fact that many – perhaps most – languages *do* express such relations. (Dyribal, for example, has a system for neutralising semantic roles, although it is not the same as that used in English [Van Valin & LaPolla, 1997, 6.2.2.].) And if they do then we have to be in a position to explain how these relations are learned, which in turn raises the question of whether they can be learned on the basis of semantic representations and evidence from the input *alone*. The answer that nativism gives to this question is 'no'. And perhaps it is better to retain syntactic nativism as an empirical hypothesis, rather than foreclosing options on it on the basis of a few languages.

In fact, we return to questions about the heuristic richness of RRG versus nativism with Van Valin's final point: that RRG opens the door to empirical research by virtue of the fact that it assumes the child is learning syntactic structures. But it is fair to say that this is like opening a door onto an empty room – in strong contrast to the connectionist research programme. To say that something is 'learned' without positing any kind of learning mechanisms is likely to be less than inspirational to the psychologist. Connectionism, by contrast, *does* propose learning mechanisms.

Whether these kinds of response are fair is one of the things to be discussed in the next section.

4.2 Are functionalist theories better placed to explain acquisition than generativist ones?

I have presented two of the major – if not *the* two major – functionalist theories of syntax, rather than characterising the full range of them in a survey. This has the advantage of providing the developmentally-minded reader with the opportunity to see 'what's in it for me'. He or she can imagine how such proposals can be given developmental – to re-coin a pragmatist phrase – cash value. I also think it is fair, within the context of the book, to give individual theorists the floor in something like a comparable extent to that in which Chomsky held it in Part 2.

It should not pass without comment, however, that Langacker's and Van Valin's are two of the less radical kinds of functionalist theory. In order to contextualise them I will borrow the typology to be found in Frederick Newmeyer's rich and judicious *Language form and language function* (1998). (Indeed I shall be drawing quite heavily from this book throughout this section.) Newmeyer distinguishes between three kinds of functionalist theory.

1) *External functionalism (including cognitive linguistics)* As we have seen, such theories reject the idea that one can characterise the formal relations between grammatical elements independently of the characterisation of their semantic and pragmatic (i.e., *external*) properties. There are no purely syntactic rules, but rather semiotic systems in which formal elements are linked to semantic and pragmatic ones. (Recall Langacker's 'symbolic units' and Van Valin's IRH.) For Newmeyer, cognitive linguistics is the kind of external functionalist theory that 'seems to have the greatest support worldwide'. Added to which, 'with the possible exception of Van Valin's *Role and reference grammar*, no functionalist school is as deeply rooted historically in the generativist tradition' (Newmeyer, 1998, p. 14).

He also locates Bates and MacWhinney's competition model in this camp; although I found it more convenient – recall – to treat it as a proto-connectionist theory (section 3.2).

2) *Integrative functionalism.* In contrast to Langacker's view that 'though functional considerations are undoubtedly crucial in the shaping of linguistic structure, it does not follow that they should be incorporated directly into the grammar as descriptive statements' (1987, p. 413) functional linguists of this stripe refuse to draw a principled division between the functional role that a linguistic element might play in relation to other linguistic elements and the external motivation for that element and that role. In Hopper's '*Emergent grammar*', for example, the idea is rejected of there being a grammar in the sense of 'an object apart from the speaker and separated from the use that the speaker might make of it' (Hopper, 1987, p. 141). Rather, grammar is 'provisional and emergent, not isolable in principle from general strategies for constructing discourse' (ibid., p. 132). Indeed, 'there is no room – no need – for mediation by mental structures' (ibid., p. 145).

There is a position more extreme than this …

3) *Extreme functionalism.* Within the 'Columbia School' (e.g., Diver, 1995) we see the claim that all grammar can be derived from semantic and discourse factors, with the only arbitrariness in the linguistic system being within the lexicon.

What I will do now is take a set of claims that are constitutive of external functionalism and that have clear developmental resonance and assess them against the generativist alternatives. The developmental implications are in parenthesis. I will take 'semantic' in the general sense of encompassing *speaker's* meaning – pragmatics – as well as sentence meaning.

> A. Contrary to what generativists claim, syntax is not a system autonomous from semantics. (For this reason, language-acquiring children can 'crack the syntactic code' by utilising semantic-representational abilities derived from their 'rich cognitive endowment'.)
>
> B. The relation between syntax and semantic structure is frequently 'iconic'. (The more iconic the relationship, the less reason there is to argue for innate syntactic knowledge.)
>
> C. The nature of the syntactic system is fully determined externally by semantic and pragmatic forces; and so it can be fully explained in these terms. (Given this, we can make a move analogous to that made by Atkinson in relation to the minimalist programme – to produce dynamic minimalism – and say that we can explain syntactic *development* externally. The difference between this position and dynamic minimalism is, of course, that the latter assumes that cognitive development only becomes manifest linguistically by virtue of the existence of innately specified linguistic capacities which rely, for their coming to fruition, on conceptual development.)

I will discuss each of these in a separate subsection.

4.2.1 The autonomy of syntax

At its broadest, the question is, in the words of James Higginbotham, 'whether the human linguistic system constitutes a realm of knowledge having its own characteristic laws and principles' (Higginbotham, 1987, p. 119).

So when functionalist linguists deny the autonomy of syntax, what is, in fact being denied? It is that our cognitive system contains a sub-system whose primitives are not semantic and not derived from discourse but are syntactic elements whose principles of combination make no reference to system-external factors. This has been Chomsky's position all along. The position does not, however, entail that the points of contact between syntactic elements and operations and the semantic systems are not worthy of study. Not only does the minimalist programme deal foundationally with the necessity for and the nature of such contact but such concerns were acknowledged by Chomsky right at the beginning. Here are some of the closing words of *Syntactic structures* (1957, p. 108; emphasis added)

> ... one result of the formal study of grammatical structure is that a syntactic framework is brought to light which can support semantic analysis. Description of meaning can profitably refer to this underlying syntactic framework, although systematic *semantic considerations are apparently not helpful in determining it in the first place* ... Nevertheless, we do find many correlations, quite naturally, between syntactic structure and meaning, or, to put it differently, we find that the grammatical devices are used quite systematically. These correlations could form part of the subject matter for a more general theory of language concerned with syntax and semantics and their points of connection.

Moving on to more recent years, one area of the theory in which the syntax–semantics relation is clearly an intimate one is that of thematic (θ)-role. Recall that this is defined as the semantic role played by an argument in relation to a predicate (agent, theme, recipient, etc.). And note that syntax has to represent which items are θ-marked and which are not. But as we saw in the discussion of Langacker's work on raising, this still leaves room for a substantial divergence between the way in which generativists and cognitive grammarians explain certain raising phenomena – the former making reference to verbs like *try* being θ-marked and verbs like *seem* not being θ-marked (4.1.1).

Within the generativist camp there is, as one would expect, room for a good deal of debate over what should be placed in the syntactic component and what in the semantic component. Recall the discussion in 2.4.2 of the claims of Jackendoff – who is certainly a generativist – regarding the need for a semantic analysis of binding and for some relaxation of the θ-criterion (each argument has one and only one θ-role, and each θ-role is assigned to only one argument). About ten years previously (Jackendoff, 1990, chapter 2) he argued that that θ-role should form part of the *semantic* component – which entails that control-theory also should be regarded in that light, given the intimate relation between θ-role and control. Recall also my characterisation of Jackendoff's general approach as a 'thin-membrane' (i.e., between semantics and syntax) theory, as opposed to Chomsky's 'thick-membrane' theory; but it is still very much opposed to the functionalist's '*no*-membrane' theory.

On the other side of the coin, external functionalists accept that there are numerous examples of syntactic arbitrariness. They do not think that every syntactic construct can be replaced by a semantic or discourse-based one. (To deny that there is a membrane does not mean denying the distinction. There is no border marking the transition between the Middle East and the Far East, but there is certainly a distinction to be made between these two regions.) Even Haiman (see p. 217), a major theorist of iconicity, writes that 'some arbitrariness is possible' (1983, p. 815). Consider some of the following examples of syntactic arbitrariness in English (taken from Hudson *et al.* (1996) via Newmeyer (1998, p. 28). The meanings of the words *likely* and *probable* are very similar and yet the former can appear in a raising construction and the latter cannot (35a–b); the meanings of *allow* and *let* are very similar and yet the former can occur with an infinitive marker and the latter cannot (36a–b); *enough*, unlike *sufficiently* and other degree modifiers, does not occur premominally (37a–b):

> (35) a. He is likely to be late.
>
>   b. *He is probable to be late.
>
> (36) a. He allowed the rope to go slack.
>
>   b. *He let the rope to go slack.
>
> (37) a. He isn't sufficiently tall.
>
>   b. *He isn't enough tall/He isn't tall enough.

So where then does the essential difference lie between functionalists and generativists with regard to syntactic autonomy? This needs to be understood with regard to two notions that have received a thorough airing in this book – *systematicity* (see 1.1.6 and 3.5) and the *inventory* conception of syntactic constructs (*passim* in Langacker's and Van Valin's work). First, the functionalist does not have to deny – and typically will not deny – that linguistic competence is systematic. (Recall Langacker's, albeit grudging, acceptance of this.) But at the same time, he or she will speak of admittedly arbitrary linguistic rules taking the form of an 'inventory'. Is there not a contradiction at work here? No: the use of the term 'inventory' tells us that, while accepting the systematicity of linguistic competence *as something directly inherited from semantic competence*, they deny that the syntactically arbitrary elements of language bear a systematic relation to one another. Newmeyer (1998, p. 31, original emphasis) makes this point very clearly:

> … the question is whether the relationship between formally defined elements is so systematic that a grammar should accord a central place to formalising the relationship among these elements without reference to their meanings or functions. *Here* we have the key difference between mainstream generative linguistics on the one hand and mainstream functional linguistics on the other. The former accept systematicity in this sense and the latter reject it … I will adopt the following litmus test for whether a particular model of language adopts or rejects AUTOSYN [the autonomy of syntax thesis]. *If it posits rules and principles capable of generating the set of grammatically well-formed sentences of a language (and their associated structural descriptions) independently of their meaning and functions, then it is a model adopting AUTOSYN.* If it posits no such rules and principles, then it is a model rejecting AUTOSYN.

One might put it this way. Functional linguists accept that our grasp of how things and agents liase with properties and processes is a systematic grasp, but they insist that our grasp of how nouns and subjects liase with adjectives and verbs is the *same grasp*. Generative linguists deny this.

However, the generative linguist has to do more in support of the autonomy-of-syntax thesis than simply show that the relation of form to meaning is one:many. External functionalists do not deny this. Recall, indeed, that one *raison d'être* of MacWhinney and Bates' competition model was that the form–functional relationship is not only one:many but also many:one. Rather, the project has to be that of demonstrating that there exists in syntax a set of structural systems consisting of formally defined elements entering into *systematic* interrelationships 'governed', in Newmeyer's phrase (1998, p. 46), 'by *internal algebra*'.

The first necessary step here is to reconsider systematicity in the Fodor and Pylyshyn sense. Recall that this depends upon the 'principle of compositionality' which states that, in so far as language and thought are systematic, a lexical item must make approximately the same semantic contribution to each expression in which it occurs. In so far as 'the', 'girl', 'loves' and 'John' make the same semantic contribution to 'John loves the girl' that they make to 'The girl loves John' the capacity to understand one sentence (or entertain one thought) entails the capacity to understand the other sentence (entertain the other thought).

Now, one would be forgiven for allowing the phrase 'semantic contribution' to conjure up certain of Langacker's proposals. (One could be forgiven; but in error nonetheless, as we shall see.) Recall, for example, Langacker's claims about passivisation. In this case, as I put it earlier: for the cognitive grammarian, in contrast to the generativist, the grammatical morphemes involved in passivisation (namely, *be*, *-ed*, and *by*), far from making no semantic contribution to the sentence, are all meaningful, so that 'the organisation of the passive clause is a straightforward consequence of their meaning'.

But we do not have to look very far into the model of passivisation to see that it is not *similarities* of semantic contribution that interests Langacker, but *differences* between the semantic contributions made by *-ed* and *be* (three kinds of *PERF* and two kinds of *be*). More important, we need to look hard at the significance of the term 'contribution' in Fodor and Pylyshyn. 'Girl', for example, does not just field the inherent meaning of young female, but it contributes to the meaning of the whole sentence in virtue of its being a term that is currently functioning as an object, but which might equally well have functioned as a subject – though not as an article or verb etc. In Langacker's notion of be_2, by contrast, a certain inherent meaning is brought along to the passive form like a dish to a pot-luck supper.

The simple fact is that the term 'semantic contribution' has to be used to describe Fodor and Pylyshyn-style systematicity because they were concerned with the systematicity of thought and sentence meaning. But what if our concern is – as it is now – with sentence form and its contribution to the form of thought? In this case, we drop the term 'semantic' and consider the content of Newmeyer's expression 'governed by internal algebra', while all the time bearing in mind issues aired in 3.3 about the way in which linguistic elements should be thought of as variables. When syntactic systematicity is our concern then, we note *how linguistic elements make the same algebraic contribution to sentences that may have different meanings and functions.* This will help us to explain not only why the use of language is a structured capacity but why this capacity can be thought of as being autonomous from semantics and pragmatics.

With regard to passivation first of all, systematicity is in evidence in the following kind of capacity. Somebody hears *[inaudible] complemented Mary* to which his reply might well be *Mary was complemented by who?* The chances are something like 100 per cent that somebody who can do this – setting aside the issue of whether he happens to be inclined to express himself quite like this – will also have the ability to reply *The vase was broken by who?* to *[inaudible] broke the vase*. The generative linguist will argue that this capacity to passivise is systematic because the speaker has control over a formal operation that guarantees a passivised result from any active sentence. The linguist will back up this claim by saying that this kind of explanation for the capacity should be preferred over a Langackerian one because it is more *elegant, simple and economical.*

But this is a rather vulnerable position in so far as the functionalist is quite entitled to protest that these three properties surely exist in the eye of the beholder, not to mention the fact that there needs to be some strong case for the three actually *being* crucial in the assessment of linguistic competence theories. The functionalist will say that language evolved and that evolutionary solutions are often 'kludges' (Clark, 1987) – neither elegant, nor simple, nor economical. (I once heard a champion of the competition model protest to a generative linguist 'I get my constraints from evolution!') Given this, what the supporter of the autonomy-of-syntax thesis needs is evidence for syntactic systematicity that reveals ways in which mastery of an algebraic operation provides the speaker-hearer with the following:

> (A) the ability to control sentences exemplifying a given syntactic operation *across quite different semantic/pragmatic functions;*

plus

> (B) the ability to control the way in which *other* algebraic operations/constraints interact with this operation.

Here are two examples of this, taken from Newmeyer (1998). In the first, the variables in evidence are 'subject' and 'auxiliary' and the operation is that of inverting their position. Turning to (A), here are some of the semantic/pragmatic functions that the operation can produce, together with the relevant constraints on the operation.

The inversion can be used in framing questions (38a), though with the constraint that it must not happen when the question is embedded (38b) nor when a *wh*-phrase is the subject (38c).

> (38) a. Was she happy?
>
> b. *I wondered whether was she happy.
>
> c. *Has what been worrying her?

Subject-auxiliary inversion also occurs when there is a presupposed negative adverb (39a–b), but not when then presupposed adverb is positive (40a–b).

> (39) a. Under no circumstances, will I go shopping.
>
> b. *Under no circumstances, I will go shopping.
>
> (40) a. *Given half the chance, will I go shopping.
>
> b. Given half the chance, I will go shopping.

The inversion can also be used to signal a conditional, though not one introduced by *if* (41a–b), as well as in a *so*-clause (42a–b).

> (41) a. Had she been early, we would have gone shopping.
>
> b. *If had she been early, we would have gone shopping.

(42) a. So happy is Iris, she is going shopping.

     b *So happy Iris is, she is going shopping.

It goes without saying that this formal operation resists being tied down to a single semantic–pragmatic function.

Turning to (B), it can additionally be seen that the inversion is subject to a purely formal constraint – one that applies across the board. It is that *only a single auxiliary element can occur in the inverted position* (see (43)).

(43) a. *Had been she happy?

     b. *What had been she buying?

     c. *Under no circumstances, will be I taking a shopping trip.

     d. *Had been I aware of her mood-swings, I would never have gone shopping with Iris.

     e. *So keen on shopping has been Iris, she is now bankrupt.

If the operation of subject-auxiliary inversion were not autonomously syntactic, then it could not be subject to a constraining interaction with a purely syntactic rule (operating over the syntactic category of auxiliary).

In the second example, one variable is a *wh*-phrase (*who, what*, etc.,) and the other is a sentential location, namely, the left margin of the phrase immediately dominating the rest of the sentence. (In P & P terminology, this would be called 'the specifier of the complement phrase'.) *Wh*-phrases occupy that position in a number of constructions. Here are some of them.

(44) *Questions*

     a. What did you hear?

       Relative clauses

     b. The man who I met.

       Free relatives

     c. I'll read what(ever) she sends me.

       Wh (pseudo) clefts

     d. What they read was the Will.

With regard to (A), it is clear that each of these constructions has a different function. First, functional linguists have tended to argue that the fronting of *wh*-phrases in questions serves the purpose of 'focusing' the request for information. This will not, however, explain fronting in relative clauses, which Haiman (1985), for one, explains functionally in terms of the iconic principle that 'Ideas that are closely connected tend to be placed together'. In this case, the relative pronoun is placed near the head noun with which it is co-referential. Next, given that they *have* no head noun, such an account will not work for free relatives. Finally, in the case of pseudo clefts the fronting of the *wh*-phrase is clearly not being done to elicit information (in contrast to questions), but to set the scene for some new information coming towards the end of the sentence.

Turning to (B), we also see that not only do *wh*-constructions have a formal consistency whose nature does not yield to any straightforward functional analysis, but the constructions all behave in the same predictable way when there is interaction with another purely structural principle. That the constructions constitute a single formal object is evidenced by facts about how they behave *vis-à-vis* others. To give one example of this, the principle known as *subjacency* applies to all of the *wh*-constructions in the same way. Recall (p. 125) that this principle states that when an element is moving from one position in d-structure to a fronted position in s-structure it cannot pass over more than one 'layer of structure'. More precisely, *movement cannot cross more than one bounding node, where bounding nodes are inflection phrases and noun phrases.* It is not, by the way, fair to object that, because this principle derives from P & P theory one has, more or less, to adopt this theory to accept it as a legitimate example. For recall that the generalisation was first described by Ross (1967), with it being Chomsky who sought to *explain* it in terms of broader, theory-relative notions. Right now we are only concerned with the generalisation at the descriptive level.

Furthermore, note that the definition of subjacency does not mention *wh*-phrases. If it did, then of course the argument that *wh*-constructions interact with subjacency in a systematic way would be circular. Consider – in illustration – the following sentences, which do not contain any *wh*-elements.

> (45) a. *Sally is prettier than I believe the claim that Petra is.
>
> b. *Sally seems that it is likely that Petra likes.

In (45a), for example, *the claim* is a noun phrase that creates a second bounding node.

Returning to the *wh*-constructions, one can see that it is not merely *distance* over which the *wh*-movement takes place that is at issue, as can be seen in (46a-d). In these cases, recursive extensions of the 'to *verb* X to *verb* Y' construction do not constitute barriers.

> (46) a. What$_i$ did you ask Jane to tell Paul to hear ____i?
>
> b. The man who$_i$ I asked Jane to tell Paul to meet ____i.
>
> c. I'll read what(ever)$_i$ you ask Jane to tell Paul to send ___i.
>
> d. What$_i$ Paul is afraid to tell Jane that he read ___i is the Will.

When, however, something intervenes between the d-structure position of the *wh*-element and its s-structure fronting that constitutes a second layer of structure (like the NP complement of the verb *believe*) then the subjacency principle is violated.

> (47) a. *What$_i$ did you believe the claim that he heard ___i?
>
> b. *the man who$_i$ I believe the claim that Jane met ___i.
>
> c. *I'll read what(ever)$_i$ Jane believes the claim that Paul is willing to send ____i.
>
> d. *What$_i$ Paul believes the claim that Jane read ___i is the Will.

These are only two of Newmeyer's (1998) examples. Other generatively-minded linguists would give others. Doubtless, the functionalist sceptic would respond that it's all very well assembling one's favourite 'killer facts' in support of the autonomous systematicity of syntax, but what is required here is something general and principled. Well, as a non-linguist, I am not about to provide this. It is fair to say, however, that the very existence of 'syntax' as a discipline entails what is covered in (B) above: the interaction of syntactic principles. Opening any textbook on syntax – even the recent one written by Van Valin (2001, chapter 4[10]) – shows us that syntactic concepts are understood in terms of one another (e.g., dependency and head). One does not have to subscribe to the principles and parameters approach to accept this. Indeed, one might go as far as saying that knowledge of the form classes is holistic in nature. That is to say, it would seem to be impossible for somebody to understand/control only *one* form class (e.g., verb). How, more modestly, could someone grasp what a preposition is but not what a phrase is?

I want to bring this thought into focus – albeit an unsatisfactorily metaphorical one – by making reference to structural ambiguity in sentences. Backing off a bit, there is typically no ambiguity about what animal, from the 'inventory' of animals, we are seeing before us. While a clever piece of drawing can evoke the 'duck-rabbit' illusion, we do not typically mistake rabbits for ducks. Contrast this with the case of the Necker cube, in which the potential ambiguity resides in the question of which face of the transparent cube is facing the viewer. One might say that it is in the nature of a cube drawn with edges only that if one percept is afforded then so too is the other. This contrasts with the duck-rabbit case where affording a rabbit percept does not *guarantee* affording a duck percept, unless the drawing is done in a special way. The Necker cube effect is not, by contrast, dependent upon drawing tricks; indeed it works just as well with a real 3D cube. Wherein does the difference lie? It would seem to lie in the fact that geometric figures are 'structured' in a way in which natural kinds such as animals are not: their parts relate to their whole in a mathematically lawful fashion. Well, for the generative linguist, the parts of *sentences* relate to the whole in an algebraically lawful fashion. One should not press the analogy too hard because there is a dependency on 'external' meaning systems in the case of syntax which there is not in the geometric case. For example it does not matter whether the cube is a child's brick or a beef-stock cube. In any event, just as the perceptual ambiguity is an emergent property of the geometrical structure so is the syntactic ambiguity an emergent property of the algebraic structure.

For example, the formal inter-relation between prepositional verbs and prepositions heading phrases (48) and between verbs and participles (49), (Chomsky's example) results in structural ambiguity.

(48) John decided on the boat.

(49) They are visiting relatives.

The flipping between the two possible interpretations is not analogous to the flipping between the duck and the rabbit percepts, because they are not caused by any cartoonishly sketchy quality of the sentences. *It is afforded by syntax itself.*

---

[10] '...This is not to say that there may not be semantic properties associated with constituents, which there surely are. Rather it means that the determination of constituents is based on tests which refer to co-occurrence and substitution properties of elements and groups of elements and which make no reference to meaning.' (p. 110).

4.2.2 Iconicity

As noted before in the context of Langacker's theory and in 1.3, Peirce had a diagrammatic conception of iconicity. He wrote 'those [icons] which represent the
relations ... of the parts of one thing by an analogous relation to their own parts are
diagrams' (Peirce, 1902/1932; p. 157). Some extreme forms of functionalism can of
course propose that syntactic structure is really no more than conceptual structure
adapted to a linguistic purpose, but the diagrammatic conception of iconicity also
affords the quite modest view that syntax simply carries over structural features
from one domain to another, with these domains being, perhaps, as different as the
sketch pad and the petri dish. Recall the statement of Langacker quoted earlier in his
characterisation of his diagrams: 'It is analogous to the drawing a biologist might
make of a cell to show the relative positions of the cell wall, the nucleus, etc.,...'.

The theme of the first part of this subsection is that, far from being a selling point
of functionalism *vis-à-vis* generativism, iconicity is something that generative
linguistics naturally *accommodates*.

In a paper on iconicity within generative linguistics Newmeyer (1992) distinguishes between five kinds on iconicity: 'distance', 'independence', 'order', 'complexity'
and 'categorisation'. Categorisation will be the topic of the second part of the
subsection.

Distance. What is conceptually distant/near will be syntactically distant/near. For
example, the modifier of a head will tend to form a constituent with it. Foley and
Van Valin (1984) mention, as an illustration of it, that, in West Greenlandic Eskimo,
the order in which suffixes are inserted correlates with their scope.

Independence. In this case, the degree of linguistic separateness of an expression
correlates with the conceptual independence of the object or event that it represents.
This is reflected in the fact that when nouns are incorporated as subparts of words
they behave differently from non-incorporated ones. We saw an example of this in
the discussion of empirical work on SLI in 2.6.4. When the word *rat* is used to refer
to many rats in a composite word it does not pluralise. While it is acceptable to refer
to a *mice-eater*, *rats-eater* is not acceptable. In this case *rat* is only being used to
qualify *eater*; it is dependent on it.

Order. The order of morphemes reflects the order of logical relations. With regard
to scope, this can be seen in the Eskimo example mentioned under 'distance'. A further example is that typically the order in which conditional statements are
expressed is for the conditional clause to precede the conclusion. More generally,
Greenberg (1963, p. 103) claims that 'the order of elements in language parallels that
in physical experience or the order of knowledge'.

Complexity. Linguistic complexity reflects conceptual complexity. Any linguistic
modification of an element (e.g., by relativisation or subordination) also adds to
conceptual complexity.

Categorisation. There is generally a correlation between syntactic and semantic
types: nouns and things, verbs and actions, subjects and agents, patients and grammatical objects.

It is obviously the case, then, that syntax is not arbitrarily related to conceptual
structure in anything like the way in which the lexicon is arbitrarily related to the

concepts it symbolises. But this does not make functionalist grammars more psycho-logically realistic than generative ones, for the simple fact that d-structure (and the lexical insertion and derivation processes that replace d-structure in minimalism – see below) is designed to represent elements in iconic accordance with their concep-tual relations. For example, in the d-structure of the sentence *Mark seems to have got the job*, *Mark* and *got the job* form a constituent (cf. iconicity of distance), whereas in the s-structure they do not, by virtue of move-α.

This might look like nothing more than a capitulation to functionalist principles, but the fact is that the notion of d-structure was set up – talking only about pre-minimalist Chomskyan theory now – from considerations of syntactic simplicity. For example, 'd-structure plus movement' enables one to capture parallels between the traces of NP movement and reflexive anaphors like *himself* by gathering both under the same principle – Principle A – and explains thereby the ungrammatical-ity of certain sentences with these features in the same way.[11] Traces and anaphors have nothing in common semantically.

Moreover, being responsive to iconic principles via the d-structure conception enables one to account both for the fact that some isomorphism between conceptual and syntactic structure must surely aid thought and communication and the fact that, this notwithstanding, we do have many degrees of freedom in how we say a thing. We can, for example, and without the syntax/conceptualisation mapping coming to grief, front a *wh*-phrase or an NP for emphasis or we can insert adverbs well away from the verbs they modify, and so forth.

Given this, what is required is a set of what Jackendoff (1990, chapter 11), calls *linking rules* to relate conceptual structures to syntactic structures of the kind shown in (50) – taken from Jackendoff (1990, p. 45).

(50) a. *Syntactic structure*

$[_S[_{NP}[John] [_{vp} ran[_{PP}[into[_{NP}the room]]]]]$

b. *Conceptual structure*

$[_{Event}GO([_{Thing}JOHN], [_{Path}TO([_{Place}IN ([_{Thing}ROOM])])])])]$

There have been number of attempts by generative linguists to stipulate how the conceptual↔d-structure mapping is achieved, ranging from the rigid and simple to the flexible and complex. Within the first type we have Baker's UTAH (*Uniformity of Theta Asignment Hypothesis*) which claims that 'Identical thematic relationships between items are represented by identical structural relationships between those items at the level of d-structure'. For example, this would entail that in (51) the theme (= the entity undergoing a change or being located) must appear in the same d-structure position in (a) and (b), with the difference in surface position being the result of move-α.

(51) a. The window [*Theme*] broke.

b. Mark [*Agent*] broke the window [*Theme*].

---

[11] *Mark seems (that) got the job; *Mark thinks that himself got the job.

However this approach has largely been abandoned in favour of one or other form of *hierarchical* mapping theory in which the surface position of NPs can be determined directly on the following kind of assumption: if the argument structure of the verb only contains a theme then this is mapped onto the subject position; if it contains an agent and a theme then the former is mapped onto the subject position and the latter to the object position.

While there are, then, different accounts on offer, there is general consensus (Jackendoff, 2002, p. 143) that agents generally come first, followed by recipients, themes, locations, and finally predicate NPs. In his earlier work Jackendoff (1990, chapter 11) proposed the Principle of Argument Fusion, which governs how the conceptual structure of a phrase is derived by fusing the conceptual structure of each of the elements with co-indexed conceptual constituents. The hierarchical system he proposed is reproduced in (52).

(52)

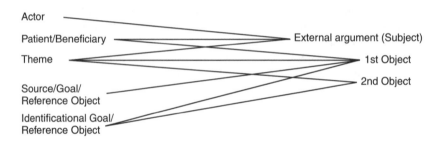

To simplify, the linking rules link, in turn, the highest available thematic role on the hierarchy with the unlinked grammatical relation that is highest on its own hierarchy (see Newmeyer, 1992, 4.1.2 for discussion). This deals with iconicity of distance straightforwardly: in so far as elements that are structurally distant from each other they are interpreted as conceptually distant. Iconicity of independence also falls out quite naturally because, if an incorporated element forms a constituent with another these two will inevitably have a close semantic relationship, on this scheme. Much the same things can be said about the iconicity of complexity; though these would seem to have a tautologous flavour. As iconicity of order depends upon difficult-to-explicate notions such as 'order or thought/experience' one is hard-pressed to say quite how this applies.

A tricky issue then arises with regard to the role of d-structure in this kind of process. If Jackendoff's analysis can be taken to apply to the interface between d-structure and the semantic systems then the division between functionalist and generative approaches is unequivocally maintained. However, as Jackendoff (1990, p. 246) points out himself, Foley and Van Valin (1984, pp. 27–35, 47–53) present an account of mapping roles to syntactic categories which is, like his own, one in terms of mapping ordered lists of theta roles onto ordered lists of syntactic roles. And given this, the *only significant* difference between the functionalist and the generativist acknowledgement of iconicity would seem to lie in the latter's positing of d-structure. So *this* spurs the question of how one is to differentiate the functionalist (*à la* Van Valin) treatment of iconicity from that to be found in minimalism, given that the latter does not contain a level of d-structure as a level of explicit representation.

This question cannot be resolved neatly, but one can at least say that while there is no d-structure in minimalism there is still a place within the grammar that is responsible for an interface with the lexicon (via merge and move) just as LF is the component of grammar that interfaces with logico-semantics, and PF is the component of grammar that interfaces with phonetics. It should also be borne in mind that move and merge are defined in entirely syntactic terms. Such notions are unintelligible without the assumption of syntactic autonomy, and nothing like them could be assimilated into Van Valin's approach without altering its fundamentally functionalist character. Moreover, there is, and probably never could be, any equivalent to move in RRG.

But however this issue is resolved, the fact remains that iconicity (of the kind covered in Newmeyer's first four properties) is something that functionalist and generative linguistics deal with in their own ways rather than a selling point for functionalism – as if it were unique in dealing with it, and thereby gaining 'psychological reality'.

The iconicity of categorisation raises different kinds of issue. Recall that Langacker founded his cognitive grammar on a 'cognitivising' of the syntactic categories. Thus, he distinguished between nouns and verbs (p. 357) in terms of the fact that nouns are 'nominal predicates' that refer to 'entities' ('a region in some domain') whereas verbs are 'relational predicates' that refer to temporal relations and processes – to 'an evolution of a situation over time'. There are two issues here: one local and one global.

The local one is whether Langacker's way of drawing the distinction really does not do the job intended for it. In fact, even linguists who are highly sympathetic to the procedures of cognitive grammar find fault with the distinction as presented. While Croft (1991, pp. 104–07), for example, defends Langacker's conception of a noun in terms of its 'autonomy' (see 'autonomy versus dependency' discussed earlier), as contrasted with the relational nature of adjectives and verbs, he asks how inherently relational nouns can exist within this scheme. Kinship terms, and words like *friend*, and words for mathematical concepts like *division* are obvious examples here. Moreover, he is sceptical about how Langacker's conception of verbs can be maintained in light of some difficult cases. For example, it may be recalled that Langacker's use of the term 'process' involved what he called 'sequential scanning' ('processing component states in series rather than in parallel, transforming one configuration into another' – see Figure 4.2.). And recall that Langacker insisted that this applied to stative verbs such as *resemble, have, want, know,* and *like* as plausibly as to any other (given that these stative predicates are 'plausibly interpreted as describing the perpetuation through time of a static configuration', 1987, p. 79). 'Unfortunately,' says Croft (1991, p. 107) that description applies better to *keep* than to *have*, to *yearn for* than to *want*, to *stay* rather than to *be (at)* and to *look at* rather than to *see*.[12] The first verb in each pair occurs naturally in the progressive, conceptualising the state of affairs as an 'inactive action', and contrasts with the second verb in the pair, which occurs in the simple present without [we say *I have an X* not *I am having an X*, JR] – the standard test for stativity. Thus it is not clear how Langacker's definition extends beyond true processes.

But let us assume for the sake of argument – turning now to the 'global' issue – that this cognitive characterisation of the noun–verb distinction is successful. The question then becomes whether such characterisations actually illuminate our knowledge of language. There is clearly a sense in which they do not, given that 'what a noun is', 'what a verb is', and so forth, are determined not (only?) by what kind of cognising they capture but by they way in which they interact with other syntactic entities. This returns us, of course, to the central issue of the autonomy of syntax. If syntax is an autonomous system then the computations that language users undergo/perform are formal ones *whatever* their cognitive archaeology can be said to be. Moreover, it is worth bearing in mind that children will not only become skilled speakers and comprehenders of language, but that they will also acquire the ability to regard linguistic operations as an object of knowledge, as it were, 'in the stream of behaviour'. How plausible is it to take this object as a set of cognitive categories, *à la* Langacker? Consider the question of how we say something. As Higginbotham (1987, pp. 125) puts it (previously quoted in 1.1.3):

> Suppose that I am on the point of speaking and that – recognising that what I am going to say would be ambiguous and therefore liable to misinterpretation – I switch at once to a more precise way of expressing myself. Then I have used my knowledge of language, even though nothing has happened than the auditors can detect.

What the generative linguist would deny here is that all that's involved in this 'switching' is pragmatics and cognitive categories. Rather, the language user has at her disposal (what Higginbotham calls) a *central resource* with many applications which is not in the service of any particular mechanism.

I will be arguing in the next subsection, however, that Langacker's work of cognitive archaeology is applicable in developmental work.

4.2.3 'External' explanation and development

First, it is necessary to explode the popular myth that Chomsky himself denied the existence or relevance of external influences on grammar. Not only is minimalism *constituted* by a concern with exactly these influences, but this was no change of heart (see Newmeyer, 1998, 7.1). To illustrate, in his *Reflections on language* (1975b) Chomsky, responding to John Searle's (1972/1974) philosophically functionalist objections to his theory, said that 'there are significant connections between structure and function' (1975b, p. 56). And in response to Searle's 'it is quite reasonable to suppose that the needs of communication influence [linguistic] structure', Chomsky replies 'I agree' (ibid., p. 58). Recall also Chomsky's description of the role of s-structure as expressing

---

[12] See Dahl, O, (1979) Case grammar and prototypes. *Prague Bulletin of Mathematical Linguistics.* 31, 3–24.

'such properties as topic-comment, presupposition, focus, specificity, new-old information, agentive force, and others that are often considered more discourse-oriented',
(p. 153 – in the long quotation). So while he certainly denied the functionalist
assumption that all aspects of syntactic structure will ultimately be seen to be non-
arbitrary, he thought there was no reason why the language faculty should not be
shaped by external influence.

And yet ... Bates and MacWhinney (1989, p. 5) are able to interpret Chomsky's
position in *Reflections on language* as an argument 'for a kind of autonomy of syntax
that would cut it off from the pressures of communicative functions. In the
Chomskyan vision, language is pure and autonomous, unconstrained and
unshaped by purpose or function'.

There should be, then, no real controversy over the question of whether external
forces influence syntactic structure. But there certainly is room for fundamental disagreement over whether appeals to such influence are explanatory – as we shall see.
Unfortunately for the developmentalist, it is questions about external explanations of
cross-linguistic differences and of syntax as it synchronically is which have dominated
the linguistic literature. But, as mentioned earlier, if externalist forms of explanation
work phylogenetically then there is some reason to believe that they will also work
ontogenetically. Given this, the functionalist might be led to posit a kind of 'dynamic
functionalism' in competition with Atkinson's (nativist) dynamic minimalism.
(Indeed, there is a sense in which this is what developmentalists such as Tomasello do
in fact, as we shall see in 4.3.) For this reason, then, it is certainly worth the developmentalist's while looking at the explanatory force of externalist accounts of syntax synchronically construed. (In 4.5 I shall be discussing language evolution directly.)

Newmeyer (1994, 1998) has constructed a strong case against the sufficiency of
externalist explanations of syntax, based on the fact that not only are there numerous candidates for being an external force but these frequently compete over the
explanation for a single syntactic character. This embarrassment of riches brings
with it the pressure to make a *language-independent* case for saying *which* of the
competing forces is operative in a particular syntactic case. Without this, the explanation will not go through. Nevertheless, functionalists are not coy about admitting
the role of competition. Haiman (1983), for example, describes the competition
between the functional demand for economy (reduce redundancy, avoid needless
structural complexity) and that for iconicity, arguing that when there are such competing demands '*apparent* arbitrariness results ... To the extent that different generalisations are possible, some arbitrariness is possible' (Haiman, quoted in Newmeyer,
1998, p. 139, my emphasis). But why must the arbitrariness only be apparent? To
show that it is only apparent, the functional linguist is free to tell a just-so story
about how the different demands interacted.

Moreover, functionalists are sometimes forced to acknowledge that *language-
internal* demands can also complete with external ones. For instance, Comrie (1984,
pp. 89–90), follows Greenberg (1963) in putting forward the following generalisation
about sentences that express volition or purpose: *a subordinate verbal form always
follows the main verb as the normal order* [e.g., *Jill wants to dress up/*Jill to dress up
wants*] except in those languages in which the nominal object always precedes the

verb [e.g., where the canonical word order is SOV]. So here we have a principle of iconicity (a desire precedes its coming to fruition) conflicting with a typological fact about basic word order. In fact, one might see this as an example of the simplicity/economy factor competing with iconicity given that 'It is simple to have a rule that the verb of the main clause follows all constituents irrespective of their semantics' (Comrie quoted in Newmeyer, 1998, p. 139) – and so form can win out over function.

Remaining with typology (= the study of structural similarity between the world's languages), Newmeyer (1998, 6.3.1) also gives the following example of a 'vacuous' appeal to functional motivation. Tomlin (1986) sought to explain the relative frequency of basic word orders in the world's languages (53) by appeal to three competing functional principles (54).

(53) a. SOV = SVO (most common)

　　　b. VSO

　　　c. VOS = OVS

　　　d. OSV (least common)

(54) a. *The Theme-First Principle*

　　　　　More thematic information tends to precede less thematic.

　　　b. *Verb-object bonding*

　　　　　In a transitive clause, the object is more tightly 'bound' to the verb than it is to the subject.

　　　c. *The Animated-First Principle*

　　　　　Animated NPs tend to precede other NPs

But the problem then becomes that of explaining why the lower ranking orders exist at all. Some languages, for example, put the thematic material last (cf. *The window broke*, where it is first). And, as mentioned before, one cannot *explain* ordering in terms of the relative 'strengths' of different external motivations *unless you are in possession of some independent account of why one motivation is stronger than another*. Tomlin does attempt to provide this for (54a) in terms of the cognitive principle of 'information flow', but the awkward fact remains that there are a significant number of languages that violate it.

Next, I consider a functional motivation that is linguistic in character whilst being external to *knowledge* of language, namely, *sentence parsing*. In this case, the functionalist argument runs that *what determines syntactic structure is pressure towards ease of extracting parses for perceived sentences*. In terms of Chomsky's (1964) well-known diagram (Figure 4.20) we explain B mechanisms in terms of A mechanisms, which are themselves explained functionally.

A situation that would bolster the functionalist case is one in which, when faced with an ambiguity in sentence interpretation, it is the grammatical rather than ungrammatical interpretation that is favoured. This would be consistent with grammaticality being, at least in part, a *function of what the parser finds natural*. This at least appears to be the case in so-called filler-gap constructions in which a movement or deletion rule creates a 'gap' in a sentence which must be associated with its correct filler (the moved constituent or antecedent of the deleted constituent).

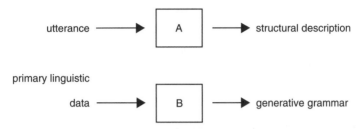

Figure 4.20 Chomsky's (1964) diagram showing the mechanisms of parsing and acquisition.

These constructions are frequently ambiguous, but the fillers and gaps must be correctly associated within the constraints defined by the grammar. 'It has been tempting' as Janet Fodor puts it, 'to view these constraints not as a further complication of the parser's task but as a simplification, in that *they crystallise within the grammar the parser's own inherent tendencies*' (Fodor, 1984, p. 17, emphasis added). (The italicised clause expresses very nicely one motivation for explaining B in terms of A in Chomsky's diagram.) Consider (55)

(55)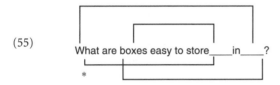

The *store boxes in what* (upper) reading of (55) is clearly preferable to the *store what in boxes* (lower) reading. In this case, the sentence contains two filler-gap dependencies; and something – perhaps something within the parser – must ensure that the associations are relatively easy to detect. There is a constraint operating in this case called the 'nested dependency constraint' (NDC) which requires that two dependencies can be nested or disjoint, but cannot be intersecting – *as they are in the lower portion of* (55). The functionalist account here is that a drive to ease-of-parsing would dictate that if there is any potential for ambiguity the parser will consistently plump for one or the other. In support of this view, we find cases in which an intersecting dependency is both naturally parsable and grammatical and where no ambiguity around possible parses is present (56). This suggests that the *NDC is there to avoid ambiguity*, and counterindicates the view that it is a straightforwardly grammatical constraint.

(56)

But we obviously need an explanation here for *why* it is the nested rather than the intersective reading that the parser prefers. These explanations have tended to be in terms of grammatical principles rather than in terms of processing ease. J. D. Fodor (1984) offers one in terms of c-commanding (see Steedman, 1984, for another).

Moreover, as Fodor (1984, pp. 19–21) illustrates clearly, there is a double dissoci-
ation (not her term) between ease-of-parsing and grammaticality: *we find troublesome
gaps that are grammatical and easy-to-parse gaps that are ungrammatical.* Thus, it is
easy to detect the gaps in (57) and (58), despite the sentences being ungrammatical.

(57) *Who were you hoping for ___ to win the game?

(58) *What did the baby play with ___ and the rattle?

Also, what is supposed to be making the gap in (59) hard to locate if the gap in
(60) is locatable?

(59) *John tried for Mary to get along well with ___.

(60) *John is too snobbish for Mary to get along well with ___.

And why should the gap in (61) be any harder to fill than the gap in (62)?

(61) *The second question, that he couldn't answer ___ satisfactorily was obvious.

(62) The second question, it was obvious he couldn't answer ___ satisfactorily.

'The data', as Fodor says, 'run exactly contrary to any functional considerations'
(ibid., p. 20). So what then is the role of the parser in relation to the grammar?
According to J. D. Fodor, the role of the grammar here is to assist the parser by
restricting the domain through which the parser must search for the gap it needs.
Sometimes the grammar determines a unique position for the gap, as in the control
(e.g., *John wants ___ to see the film*) and raising (e.g., *John seems ___ to be happy*)
sentences, discussed earlier. But sometimes there are a number of possible gap
positions, to the extent that we may have to wait till the end of the sentence for
disambiguation, as in (63).

(63) a. Which book did you read ___ to the children?

b. Which book did you read to the children from ___?

J. D. Fodor argues further that there is 'pressure', as it were, against the grain of the
grammar, coming from what she calls 'the expressor' ('whatever aspect of the language faculty concerns itself with protecting the expressive potential of the language'
– ibid., p. 11). To obtain the goal of expressive power it is worth paying some price
in ambiguity. The general position is – for J. D. Fodor – that the parser, far from
having its inherent tendencies *crystallised* in the grammar, requires some constraints
from the grammar in order to facilitate its task – which will involve some negotiation
with the expressor. Put this way, then, we can detect a role for functional considerations but no suggestion that grammar is no more than parsing exigencies crystallised.

We cannot really leave matters here. Questions about the sufficiency of functional
explanations for syntactic structure also need to be addressed within the wider context of language evolution; and this is what will be attempted in 4.5. Keeping within
our developmental perspective then, what can be said, before we turn to empirical
developmental questions, about the developmental import of the kinds of functionalist theories we have been considering in relation to generative theories?

First, if generatively-minded linguists such as Newmeyer are correct, then any
developmental theory has to accommodate (1) the autonomy of syntactic rules and

operations, (2) the fact that, as well as being ideally placed to explain the non-iconic aspects of syntax, generative approaches are also designed to handle the iconic aspects, (3) the fact that, because there are many possible external forces prevailing upon any one syntactic principle, appeals to external explanation for syntactic structure will tend not to be explanatory. Putting the three claims together we have the position that there are a set of deep principles and local rules operating within the native language that children must come to know and that are not a mere symbolised inventory of what they can do in cognition.

This position does not, as it stands, entail nativism. Indeed, as Newmeyer (1998) points out, there is no *logical* necessity that the set of parameters should not be learnable; though it is surely very likely that some of them are not learned inductively. Indeed, we should is bear in mind that, as Newmeyer (ibid., p. 363) puts it:

> In MP the computational system (that is the derivational aspect of grammar) is held to be subject to unparametrised economy principles, with parameters confined to morphological features of the lexicon, the particular choice of which has consequences for syntactic behaviour. Are the possible settings of these parameters held to be provided innately? There has not been a great deal of discussion on the topic. However, it seems to me that the idea that placing parameters in the lexicon further strengthens the case for individual parameter setting being learnable without demanding that the child literally choose from an innately-specified set.

But notwithstanding this, there is an onus on functionalist developmental psycholinguists to provide a theory of syntax learning. If syntax is difficult, if not impossible, to construe as an 'emergent property' of socio-cognitive development then some account must be forthcoming of how the child crosses the bridge into syntax.

The position emergent from these three conclusions is, however, congruent with dynamic minimalism, despite its not *entailing* nativism in itself. On this view, language development is driven forward by conceptual development, a process that is not reducible to 'concept development plus learning'. This is because children are taken to possess an innate ability to render conceptual advances in terms of autonomous syntactic operations; they have the ability to 'read' these advances in a *sui generis* code. Children do not have to learn from scratch how to form phrases and clauses by merging, and to produce surface forms by move.

This view, which can be thought of as replacing *autonomous development of syntax* position, might in fact gain some nutrition from cognitive linguistics. This is because theories of the kind constructed by Langacker *provide the developmentalist with imaginative accounts of the kind of conceptual advances that, on dynamic minimalism, spur syntactic development.* I will give just one sketchy example, for now, of how this might work.

Recall Langacker's claim that the conceptual distinction on which the noun/noun-phrase ('nominal') distinction is based is that between *types* and *instances*, respectively. It might be thought that the development of this conceptual distinction is something that can be studied using the kind of dishabituation designs employed by Mandler and McDonough (1993) or by Xu and Carey (1996, see Figure 2.30). Dynamic minimalism could predict that the use of determiners would follow 'shortly' on from the non-verbal manifestation of this distinction. Now for the bad news: a determiner system seems to be absent from children's productions (e.g., as tested by elicited imitation) before the early months of the third year of life (or the very end of the second year) with personal possessives making an early appearance (Radford, 1990, chapter 4, for discussion) while dishabituation techniques are insensitive when used with children over 12 months of age. Clearly, there is not only scope but *necessity* for new and sensitive paradigms for testing categorisation skills in older pre-school children – at least if the implicit claims of dynamic minimalism are to be tested.

Accordingly, if questions of this kind could frame the contours of a dynamic minimalist research programme, what form would one expect a functionalist research programme to take, in the light of sections 4.1 and 4.2?

In the first place, the developmental functionalist would gather data bearing on the question of whether syntactic acquisition reveals markers of the kind of systematicity discussed earlier – while predicting that it will not. Recall from our discussion that systematicity is one of the main considerations in favour of the autonomy-of-syntax thesis. Two related questions would be uppermost here. (1) Is there early appreciation of the way in which elements of the syntactic system are inter-dependent (e.g., auxiliaries and main verb forms) or does each facet develop in an independent manner like elements of an inventory? (2) When control of a certain syntactic rule is acquired (e.g., an argument structure for a verb) does this generalise rapidly to other examples of that rule, or is control of the rule specific to certain items in the lexicon, as it usually is for the phrase book user? Does, to borrow Wittgenstein's expression, 'light dawn gradually over the whole'? The functionalist predicts that it does *not*.

Next, data would be gathered on the question of whether syntactic development is as error-free as generatively-minded workers say it is. And the converse question would also be asked of whether apparently precocious control of syntactic rules can be explained in terms of imitation of the input, by the construction of local expressive formulae, or a mixture of both.

In the next subsection we will encounter examples of both of these concerns. I will first, however, place this work in context by describing the first wave of functionalist developmental work in the 1970s.

4.3 Explaining development: cognitive–functionalist theory and data – past and present

There have been two waves of socio-cognitive work on language development. The first – in the 1970s – was often ideologically driven, over-confident, overreaching, and, in some respects, wrong-headed. The second and continuing is data-driven, more sceptical than dismissive, often explicitly informed by the kinds of functional linguistics we have been discussing and by computational modelling. I will give a rather broad-brush and *ad hominem* treatment of the first and then report how things seem to stand at the moment with the second.

The 1970s was a time that spawned many fashions that embarrass us now, but these fashions were at least bold and distinctive. Theories of language development in those days were also bold and distinctive – and explicitly pragmatist, carrying copious references to action and social interaction, sometimes taking *gesture* to be the crucible of linguistic development (papers in Lock, 1978). But the analogy with fashion quickly breaks down when we turn to the question of motivation.

Whereas 1970s fashion was really a cartoonish extension of 1960s fashion, the developmental theories were an explicit and emphatic *reaction* to the dominant theorising of the 1960s – Chomsky's 'structuralism'. Indeed, papers published by functionalists of a social-reductionist stripe tended to begin with a nod to 'Chomsky (1965)' followed by a swift dismissal of this psychologically jejune theory plus an academically dressed laughing-up-the-sleeve at how misguided it managed to be. The cognitively-inspired practitioners tended to be more circumspect, given that their mentor Jean Piaget was himself a kind of structuralist; but their essential confidence was no less strong. They believed it was possible to explain the kind of structure possessed by grammar more or less directly in terms of cognitive structuring, sometimes arising from the child's knowledge of the physical world.

Before dealing first with cognitive reductions and social reductions, I should mention the painstaking and withering analysis of these approaches to be found in Martin Atkinson's book *Explanations in the study of language development* (1982), which looked back on a decade of socio-cognitive work. It was written at time when not only was the shallowness of the functionalist developmental research programme beginning to reveal itself, but when, as he put it, 'the most extensively-researched competence theory ... developed within transformational generative grammar [was seen to be] riddled with serious methodological problems' (Atkinson, 1982, p. 6). Yet while its bleak message was hard to take at the time, it makes for a rather positive read today, showing us, as it does, how *relatively* well-placed we now are, with P & P theory and its descendants, with connectionist modelling, with a smorgasbord of functional linguistic theories – *and with better data.*

4.3.1 Early cognitive reduction – 1970s and beyond

One of the services that Atkinson (1982) performed was the listing of necessary conditions on the adequacy of this kind of reduction. (He also listed two conditions which move in the direction of sufficiency, but as cognitively reductive theories struggle with the necessary ones I will not mention them.) There are three such necessary conditions.

1) The theoretical terms of the linguistic theory must be translatable into the theoretical terms of the cognitive theory. (For example, NP translated as 'entity', VP as 'event', and so forth.)

2) The formal operations of the linguistic theory must be identifiable in the cognitive theory. (For example, if the linguistic theory includes phrase structure rules then formal operations building hierarchical structures must appear in the cognitive theory; if the linguistic theory contains transformational rules, then the cognitive theory must include 'structure-dependent processes in the familiar sense' (Atkinson, 1982, p. 176).

3) The translations of theoretical terms and corresponding formal properties required for satisfaction of (1) and (2) must appear in the sequence of cognitive theories before they are recruited by a linguistic one. For example, if C is a cognitive theory held by the child and L is a linguistic one then we might see the 'collapsed' sequence C_1, C_2, L_1, L_2.

One of the best studies in this area was done by Patricia Greenfield and her colleagues (Greenfield, Nelson and Saltzman, 1972). These authors claimed to have unearthed a structural analogy between three forms of means-end behaviour in children between 11 months and 36 months and three grammatical structures. At the outset, they mention Chomsky's scepticism about the value of such analogies, but also cite him as accepting the possibility that 'the lack of analogy testifies to our ignorance of other aspects of mental function, rather than to the absolute uniqueness of linguistic structure' (Chomsky, 1968, pp. 77–78). While this sentence might seem encouraging to the cognitivist it also reminds us how little we actually know about the course of early cognitive development: we do not possess a body of secure knowledge about when certain concepts come on stream and in what form. (In 1972 there was something nearly approaching consensus around features of the Piagetian timetable (e.g., the course of object permanence), but this has been undermined by studies using more sensitive methodologies that reveal representational capacities undreamed of in Piagetian theory.)

The children were given five nesting cups and encouraged, by modelling, to nest them. The three dominant strategies ranged from the primitive ('pairing' A in B, C in D, E in F etc.) to the sophisticated ('subassembly' A in B which then goes into C), with the 'pot' strategy (A into B, then C into B, then E into B) being intermediate. The subassembly strategy was the one that was actually modelled. Between 11 and 16 months the pairing method dominated; between 20 months and 28 months the pot strategy dominated; and at 36 months seven out of eight children used the subassembly strategy at least once. The nature of the cognition-action analogy is outlined in (64).

(64) *Pairing method*

ACTOR	ACTION	ACTED UPON
cup a	*enters*	*cup b*
subject	verb	object

Pot method

ACTOR	ACTION	ACTED UPON
cup a	*enters*	*cup b*

and

subject	verb	object
ACTOR	ACTION	ACTED UPON
cup c	*enters*	*cup b*
subject	verb	object

Subassembly method

ACTOR	ACTION	ACTED UPON ------→
cup a	*enters*	*cup b*
subject	verb	object

	------→ACTOR	ACTION	ACTED UPON
	which	enters	cup c
	subject	verb	object

In their discussion, Greenfield *et al.* mention a similar study that was carried out with children living in Zincantan, a Mayan community in Southern Mexico. The outcome was very similar, despite the fact that the Mexican children were quite unfamiliar with nesting cups.

> When one considers that the language environment of these children was Tzotzil, a Mayan language totally unrelated to European languages, the possibility of universal innate competencies basic to language and other forms of behaviour is a very real one. Indeed the existence of action structures formally similar to grammatical structures may provide a cognitive base for learning language itself.

> (Greenfield et al., 1972, p. 308)

The lingering question, however, concerns where exactly the linguistic end of the structural analogy is supposed to reside. The descriptive sentences in (64) 'are not supposed to be in the child's head' (ibid., p. 305). In fact, the view the authors favour is what has been called an 'homology' position (Bates *et al.*, 1979), meaning that there is some more fundamental representational capacity underlying both arms of the structural analogy: 'The importance of the action-grammar analogy lies in the possibility that the same human capacities may be responsible for both types of structure' (ibid., p. 305). But why is there such a lag between the action and the language? Indeed it is so great that the authors report finding in a pilot study (ibid., p. 305) that linguistic commands to make the different types of structure could not be comprehended and acted on before adolescence; so college students had finally to be used.

With regard to Atkinson's three necessary conditions for cognitive reduction, (1) might be said to be fulfilled in so far as, while some verbs do not refer to actions, some subjects do not refer to agents, and some objects do not refer to acted upon objects, many *do* – a fact that may help to 'bootstrap' children into syntax (a possibility to which section 4.4 is dedicated). But bootstrapping is a far cry from reduction. Condition (2) might be seen to be fulfilled (formal operations of the linguistic theory in the cognitive theory), but, on closer inspection, is not. This is because the SVO structure is traditionally analysed hierarchically with verb and object forming sub-units of the higher-order unit VP. But, as Atkinson points out, there is no suggestion in the paper that the 'action + acted upon' is supposed to form a higher-order unit. The action structure is, unlike the grammatical structure, essentially *linear*. In fact, the imagination gives out when one asks what kind of structured action *would* evince this kind of formal hierarchy.

With regard to condition (3) what we see is not C_1, C_2, L_1, L_2, but C_1, C_2, C_3, then a very long wait and L_1, L_2, L_3. Moreover, with regard to the crucial requirement of (3) that the cognitive advance should precede the linguistic one, rather than the other way about, a somewhat later study by Greenfield and Schneider (1977) affords the interpretation than L can precede C. In their study, children between 3 and

11 years were given sets of sticks that could be fitted together to form a concrete hierarchy of the kind seen in mobiles. The mobile construction was modelled for them. What was of interest here was the order in which the sticks were combined. As the authors say, the more a subject interrupts the performance of a sub-unit to complete another one while keeping the whole unit 'in mind', the more hierarchical the thought. This way of proceeding necessarily involves working from the top down, whereas an uninterrupted strategy involves starting at the bottom and working upwards. There was found to be a shift in strategy around the age of seven (a very 'Piagetian' age). Six out of 10 6-year-old children started at the bottom and worked upwards using the 'minimally interrupted' strategy. Among the 7-year-olds, only one out of 10 did this. The 11-year-olds typically started at the top. Now 6-year-old children can surely be said to be able to control complex hierarchies on the linguistic level. We do not need to read the experimental studies on even younger children's acknowledgement of the binding constraints by workers such as Stephen Crain (see 2.5.4) to confirm this.

Finally, the authors assume, despite their references to Tzotzil, that SVO will be the beginning speaker's canonical ordering. However, there is evidence, reviewed by Bowerman (1973), that not only is SVO not the word order initially adopted by many children, but that young speakers do not universally follow the order of the adult language.

But the story does not end here. In more recent years Greenfield (1991) has extended this research programme toward neurobiological questions about the links between earlier hierarchical skills and grammar development. This has necessitated a move away from the rather simplistically reductive position just discussed to the view that it is only in very early development – before two years or so – that the hierarchical organisation of action and grammar share a representational format. After this, the two are assumed to have distinct, essentially modular, developmental trajectories. Using data from research on acquired aphasia (Grossman, 1980), developmental aphasia (Cromer, 1983), from studies of chimpanzee signing and tool use (Savage-Rumbaugh, et al., 1990), and, most provocatively, from the analysis of neural growth spurts as measured by EEG coherence (Thatcher, 1991) she has developed the following position. On the assumption that Broca's area (which is the key neural substrate for syntax) contains two subsections, one a manual object combination circuit linked to the manual motor area and the other a 'grammar circuit' linked to the orofacial area, she claims that these two become differentiated around two years of age. The advent of syntactic marking is hypothesised to stem from the addition of the anterior prefrontal area to the language production circuit, while there is a separate development of complex 'grammars' of object combination after this time. Two years of age is, as we shall later see, certainly a crucial age in syntactic development, but two caveats are worth bearing in mind about Greenfield's specific position. First, rather than an early form of cognitive growth 'handing over' to a later linguistic trajectory, the situation may be that general cognitive development sets limits on early linguistic development, after which, as it were, the brakes are released. As Richard Cromer put it:

> Cognitive limitations in younger (less mature) normal children prevent them from being able to interact with data that are crucial for grammatical change. For example, in recent

linguistic theories that view some aspects of language acquisition in terms of setting and changing particular 'parameters' certain 'parameters' remain fixed to particular values until the maturation of cognitive mechanisms makes it possible for the child to experience linguistic data that would act to set these parameters.

(Cromer, 1991, p. 78)

On this 'triggering problem' see Borer and Wexler (1987).

Second, ideas of this kind have to be considered in the context of acquired impairments in deaf signing patients. Broadly, it is found that such patients can become impaired on signing while performing normally on tests of learning and producing unfamiliar hand movements (Poizner, Bellugi, and Klima, 1990; Poizner and Kegl 1992). Thus even in praxis itself there is differentiation between the linguistic and the non-linguistic.

Stepping back a little, the 1970s Greenfield position seemed to partake of both of the views of the cognitive development/language development relationship which then had currency: (1) the cognitive and the linguistic developments paralleled each other because they both derived from the same underlying format (e.g., Bates *et al.*, 1979), (2) the developments in language succeeded their cognitive counterparts because language development somehow depended upon cognitive development (Cromer, 1974/91; MacNamara, 1972). The arena within which these alternatives were pitted against each other – in so far as they ever were – was entirely Piagetian. In particular, researchers debated the relation between language development and symbolic play (Nicholich, 1977), means-end behaviour, and object permanence. With regard to the latter, L. Bloom (1973) hypothesised a relation between object permanence and the onset of the vocabulary spurt/naming explosion,[13] while Bates *et al.* (1979) concluded that awareness of means-end relationships was more crucial to the onset of speech, while studying rather younger children.

A methodological difficulty with studies of this kind is that they depend upon measuring one variable (cognitive development) on an ordinal scale, where it is necessary to elicit specific behaviours in contrived situations, against another variable (language) which is assessed by recording spontaneous, naturally-occurring behaviour that cannot be measured on an ordinal scale. Bloom, Lifter and Broughton (1985) made this point and went on to present some longitudinal data on the relation between spontaneous play and the onset of the vocabulary spurt. They report that constructing novel, unobserved relations between objects (e.g. putting a peg, which had previously only been seen in a hole, into a bucket) either preceded or coincided with the vocabulary spurt.

The quest for the cognitive prerequisites of the naming spurt continued well into the 1980s; although it can hardly be said to be a lively research area today. Gopnik and Meltzoff (1987) report that object permanence and categorisation skills (e.g. sorting blocks and dolls into two separate piles) were related to the onset of the spurt, while – *pace* Bates *et al.* (1977)– means-end skill was not. In another study

---

[13] The criteria for this can vary: see P. Bloom (2000, pp. 39–43).

these authors (Gopnik and Meltzoff, 1986) suggest that object permanence skills and the production of utterances like 'Gone' bear a bootstrapping relationship to each other, in so far as one level of search appears just before the appearance of 'Gone' while a higher level of search appears just after it. More recently, they elaborated these findings in the context of their 'child as scientist' perspective on development (Gopnik and Meltzoff, 1997).

But such work spurs two kinds of sceptical thought. We can surely wonder, in the first place, about the generality and reality of the spurt phenomenon (on which see P. Bloom, 2000, pp. 38–43); and some have argued that it is no more than a function of statistical features of the input, given that one can obtain non-linear shifts in vocabulary without qualitative shifts in mechanism (Plunkett *et al.*, 1992). In the second place, so much *else* is coming to fruition at around the age of 18 months that the prospects for pinpointing a single cognitive prerequisite for the vocabulary spurt would seem to be bleak. In addition to those developments already considered we have symbolic play (Nicholich, 1977), the imitation of goal-directed actions (Meltzoff, 1995); mirror self-recognition (Bertenthal and Fischer, 1978), and medium-term location memory (Russell and Thompson, 2003). A traditional Piagetian would try to explain this confluence in terms of their all manifesting 'the symbolic function' or 'mental representation'. But while such terms have great resonance, trying to elaborate a common-denominator form of 'representational' advance as explanatory across so many domains (from pantomiming acts, to naming, to medium-term location memories) is surely going to prove a mug's game.

To bring us more fully up to date, Richard Cromer came to abandon his original 'cognition hypothesis' (Cromer, 1974) which was essentially the claim that certain grammatical forms will not come to fruition unless the corresponding cognitive abilities do so first. In what was to be his final statement on this issue (Cromer, 1991) he argued that (1) the existence of language itself can cause new concepts to be constructed (e.g., diary data from Bowerman, 1982), while (2) there are forms of developmental handicap in which syntactic development seems to run ahead of cognitive development. His work on a young lady named DH (reported in Cromer, 1991) persuaded Cromer that 'general cognitive mechanisms are neither necessary nor sufficient for the growth of language'[14] (Cromer, 1991, p. 135).

With further regard to Cromer's first point, there is no shortage of evidence that the linguistic input to the child can influence the timing of cognitive development. In the first place, cross-linguistic studies have been richly informative. Gopnik and Choi (1990) originally proposed that the reason there are so many object words in the vocabulary spurts of English-learning toddlers is that nouns are very prevalent and very salient in the input. Au *et al.* (1994) tested this idea by comparing the vocabulary spurts of English-learning and Korean-learning toddlers. First, they showed that many more verbs than nouns were present in salient positions in the Korean adults' speech to children; and the opposite was true for the English-speaking sample.

---

[14] See footnote 38 in Part 2 and associated text.

(Unlike English, Korean is not a canonically right-branching language, and so sentences are likely to end in verbs rather than nouns: SOV). Notwithstanding this, both the Korean- and the English-speaking toddlers produced more nouns than verbs, and the nouns were mainly object words. The authors interpret this as support for the idea that all children, irrespective of the language being learned, are biased towards taking words to refer to kinds of object.[15]

Choi and Gopnik (1995), meanwhile, produced completely different results. In their study they showed that Korean-learners showed an early verb-spurt that often preceded the object-naming spurt. This is not found in English-learning toddlers. Gopnik, Choi and Baumberger (1996) explain the divergence in terms of methodological differences between the two studies. For example, the mothers in the Au *et al.* study had to record the production of Korean verbs from a checklist translated from English. This would be likely to underestimate the number of verbs produced, because many Korean verbs have no English equivalents.

Gopnik *et al.* were also able to show (1) that Korean mothers emphasised actions while the US mothers emphasised names, and (2) that a kind of double-dissociation existed between the nature of sensorimotor development and the nature of vocabulary acquisition (see Table 4.1).

This suggests that the nature of the language being learned can influence cognitive development; though of course this is evidence of an influence on its *timing*, not evidence that cognitive development will not happen without language.

For example, in Korean, inflected verbs need only include information about actions and relations: they need not include information about subjects (or objects). Thus '*mek-ess-tay*' expresses 'eat-Past-Reported speech': in English 'Somebody said that somebody [identity retrievable from context] ate'. This fact about Korean may, therefore, lead adults to be more action-oriented in their speech and consequently lead their children to be more action-oriented in *their* speech, as well as relatively more developed in means-end behaviour than English-learning children. So the story goes.

We also have evidence of language input influencing young infants' ability to individuate objects. In a recent study, Fei Xu (2002) demonstrated that 9-month-olds

Table 4.1 The relation between language being learned and the timing of sensorimotor abilities (Gopnik *et al.*, 1996)

	Korean-learners	English-learners
Categorisation and the naming spurt	late	early
Means-end abilities and success/failure terms	early	late

---

[15] See the discussion of the 'special constraints approach' in 4.3.3 (i) below.

could use the presence of labels to help them represent two objects in a complex array as being distinct. But while labels aided object individuation, two distinct tones, two distinct sounds, and two distinct emotional expressions did not. There was something peculiar to the labels that was supporting the cognitive task of individuation.

It is clear, then, that there can be a two-way traffic between the onset of cognitive abilities and linguistic abilities, whether the latter are productive or receptive.

So we have moved a very long way from Atkinson's three necessary conditions for cognitive reduction, and from the researchers' original ambition that inspired them. The relation between cognitive development and language development is one that does not yield to any straightforwardly causal formulation – unsurprisingly. Part of the problem would appear to be that research in this area has been conducted with instruments as blunt as object permanence and the vocabulary spurt. Where else might we look? As I said earlier, one can view Langacker's cognitive grammar as a rich source of hypotheses about what forms of cognition children must be able to control if they are to acquire certain syntactic forms. In this case, the level of detail in which these ideas are elaborated would seem to be far more appropriate than those derived from Piaget's concerns.

But, summing up this subsection, attempts to reduce grammatical advances to cognitive ones in a Piagetian style simply did not get off the ground. And even if they had got off the ground, much harder work would then have needed to be done to convince us that cognitive structuring was sufficient for the development of syntactic abilities.

4.3.2 Early social reductions

The Oxford philosopher J. L. Austin (1911–1960) became something of a mentor to the group of theorists I will be considering in this subsection. His most influential idea was that certain utterances are neither descriptive nor evaluative, but count as *actions*. Thus to say 'I promise' is to *make* a promise, not to talk about one. To this we can add the *speech acts* of state, assent, describe, warn, welcome, comment, commend, order, request, criticise, apologise, censure, approve, and express regret. Later, he was to develop the concepts of *locutionary force* (what an utterance says or refers to), *illocutionary force* (what is intended by saying it) and *perlocutionary* force (what effects it has on others). It was inevitable that such notions should strike a chord with language researchers of a pragmatist cast of mind. In a commentary on Austin's work, John Searle (1969, p. 39, original emphasis) says:

> I think it is essential to any specimen of human communication that it involve a linguistic act. It is not, as has generally been supposed, the symbol or word or sentence or even the token of a symbol or word or sentence which is the unit of communication, but rather it is the *production* of the token in the performance of the speech act that is the unit of linguistic communication.

Social reductionists, as understood here, all subscribe to this position. But in the 1970s there tended to be a divergence between those who wished to expand the research programme of language acquisition towards the study of the transition from pre-linguistic acts of meaning in the child to meaning in sentences and those who believed that structured social action was in some sense the *origin* of grammatical structure. Within the first bifurcation we can place the work of John Dore (1975, 1978). Dore drew up a list of 'primitive speech acts' expressed by children at the one-word stage – labelling, calling, greeting, protesting, and so forth. These were not, for Dore, evidence of proto-linguistic structures, but rather tracks of the journey the child was taking toward true linguistic communication. The most direct trajectory between pre-grammatical vocalisation and syntax was by way of modality, something initially expressed as a communicative intention and later marked on – what would later be called – the inflection phrase. Interestingly, Dore explicitly rejected the claim that linguistic structures were underpinned by cognitive ones, and embraced the notion of innate linguistic universals, while expanding it towards the illocutionary. There were three main kinds of linguistic universals, in his view.

1) A set of innate communicative intentions (asserting, reporting, etc.). He cautions that although some forms of communicative intentions exist before language emerges 'linguistically expressed intentions are not isomorphic with pre-linguistic intentions. (It is difficult to imagine, for example, what would count as a prelinguistic "asserting" of a proposition.)' (Dore, 1975, p. 37).

2) Referring and predicating. He insisted that the speech act of referring is not reducible to any kind of non-linguistic experience: it is 'controlled by maturation and not by the child's prior experience … linguistic reference is discontinuous with earlier indicating behaviour'. Likewise, 'the predicating expression is emergent since there appears to be no convincing explanation of what could be the basis for the child's learning about predication' (ibid., p. 37).

3) The processes responsible for the *grammaticalisation* of 1 and 2.

I mention Dore's work because it serves as an 'existence proof' that pragmatism and empiricism can clearly dissociate in this area. He says (ibid., p. 38; original emphasis):

> Thus the general rationale for the speech act view of language universals is that while it is possible to explain how KINDS of referring expressions could be learned by inductive principles, it does not seem possible that a child ('initially uninformed' as Chomsky (1965) put it) could learn what a referring expression is (despite the claims made by many cognitive theorists about the derivability of reference from pre-linguistic gestures).

Moving to the other arm of the bifurcation (pre-linguistic communication as origin of syntax), the work of the linguist M. A. K. Halliday (1973, 1975), whose empirical basis was an analysis of the communicative functions of the utterances of his son Nigel from 10 months onwards, was radically social-reductive. His position defies crisp summary, but it is not unfair to say that his determination to analyse child (and adult) language entirely in relation to its social function bore similarity to the Skinnerian project of analysing 'verbal behaviour' in terms of its reinforcement history. Language was, for Halliday, social behaviour, and where Chomsky placed 'competence' Halliday placed the 'behaviour potential' which underpinned 'meaning potential'. And where some workers took Chomsky as their lodestar Halliday took the sociologist Basil Bernstein.

The work of Jerome Bruner – with whom, recall, Van Valin makes common cause – also lies on the more reductive arm of the bifurcation; though Bruner is an altogether more ambiguous and interesting theorist than Halliday, and was certainly a pioneer in many areas of developmental and cognitive psychology. The ambiguity arose both from Bruner's style of argumentation and from his employment of the term 'speech acts'. With regard to style, this was extraordinarily inclusive and difficult to pin down, to the extent that no positions were ever really rejected, while the position being argued for was protean. In a conference address in 1979,[16] Bruner spoke of his 'language acquisition system' (LAS = mother and child) as being something additional to rather than something that would replace Chomsky's language acquisition device (LAD) adding that they would 'interact'. (In his other work [Bruner *et al.*, 1966] he recruited the Chomskyan concepts of deep and surface in an attempt to illuminate concept acquisition in middle childhood.) While, at the same time, he was not unfriendly to strong reductive claims.

> A strong claim would be that the child comes to recognise the grammatical rules for forming and comprehending sentences by virtue of their correspondence to the conceptual framework that is constructed for the regulation of joint action and joint attention ... Such a view ... is attractive in some ways.

(Bruner, 1975, p. 17)

With regard to what Bruner meant by 'speech acts' (e.g., in his well-known paper of 1975 'The ontogenesis of speech acts') we find something far removed from Austin's (indeed from Dore's) concerns. What Bruner intended by the term was the physical action, most notably the reciprocal action between mother and child, which precedes the appearance of language proper. In any event, he certainly seemed to be assuming that what goes on in LAS is necessary – at least – to language development; and he was fairly explicit about the structural correspondences between pre-linguistic communicative acts, such as passing objects back and forth between mother and child, and grammatical structure. There are three kinds of correspondence: (1) the turn-taking, sequencing and segmentation in pre-linguistic play routines and conversation; (2) 'case' relations in pre-linguistic social action and in sentences; (3) early joint attention as related topic-comment and subject-predicate. With regard to (2) Bruner argues that the

Agent – Action – Patient – Recipient

action structure observed when a toddler learns, with much help from mother, to exchange plastic shapes and insert the vocalisation *Kew* (thank you) in the appropriate place, grounds, in some sense, the appreciation of word order in general and the SVO order in particular – pragmatic iconicity, in other words. But as we have seen, not only do many languages not have this basic word order, but sometimes children learning an SVO language begin with a different basic ordering. Bruner mentions, in

---

[16] British Psychological Society Developmental Section conference held in Edinburgh in that year.

support of his position, Slobin's (1966) observation that children learning Russian, which is a highly inflected language, sometimes impose the SVO order. But if so, they are doing something that is not helping them learn the surface forms of Russian.

This is how Bruner (1975, p. 17) summarises his position:

> The argument has been that structures of action and attention provide BENCH MARKS for interpreting the order-rules in initial grammar: that a concept of agent-action-object-recipient at the prelinguistic level aids the child in grasping the pre-linguistic meaning of appropriately ordered utterances involving such case categories as agentive, action, object, indirect object, and so forth. And by the same token, a grasp of the topic-feature structure of shared experience AIDS the child in grasping the linguistic relation inherent in topic-comment and subject-predicate. The claim is that the child is grasping initially the requirements of joint action at the pre-linguistic level, learning to differentiate these into components, learning to recognise the function of utterances placed into these serially ordered structures, until finally *he comes to substitute elements of the standard lexicon in place of the non-standard ones.* The process is, of course, made possible by the presence of an interpreting adult who operates not so much as a corrector or reinforcer but rather as a provider, an expander and idealiser of utterances while interacting with the child.

I have capitalised the expressions which cry out for explication and italicised the achievements which provoke the question 'But *how?*'

On the positive side however, we do not find Bruner expressing the radically pragmatist view which pervaded social-pragmatist work in the 1970s: that what of intention and meaning the child brings to this crucible interaction only really becomes intentional and meaningful when *interpreted* as such by the 'caregiver'. This idea was taken to have originated in the writings of the pragmatist G. H. Mead, with mother representing the 'generalised other'. It was mediated into developmental psychology by John Shotter (1973). In fact in a collection entitled *Action, gesture and symbol* (1978) edited by Andy Lock, one encountered a number of versions of the following idea: the child's contribution is 'biological' not psychological; these biological imperatives cause the child to act (smile, cry, reach, etc.); but these actions have no true purpose or meaning until the caregiver treats them as such; somehow (despite lacking any innate understanding of intention) the child is able to appreciate what is being mirrored and thereby becomes a member of the human intending-and-meaning society. From this point on, the ideas about language development itself were essentially Brunerian.

(I mention this now as a kind of *reductio* of a certain form of developmental pragmatist impulse.)

In Lock's collection, Martin Richards wrote 'if one believes that a behaviour pattern arrives with a ready-made meaning there is no room left for the development of autonomy and self-reflection by the infant' (Richards, 1978, p. 26). Meanings are '*negotiated*' by the infant and mother dyad, mother 'decides what [behaviours] mean', and this process constitutes 'the formation of the person' (op. cit.).

Well, something like this would appear to be the inevitable outcome if the highest item on one's intellectual agenda is the denial of internalism. Autonomy is not an intrinsic characteristic of the individual, but something gifted to him through the reflecting operations of others. For many of us this would seem to be something *other* than 'autonomy'.

4.3.3 Contemporary cognitive–functional research on syntactic development

The contemporary form of cognitive–functional work in language development could, in some respects, hardly be more different from this. For one thing it focuses upon the course of language development itself rather than upon its cognitive correlates and social precursors. But what it clearly shares with the approaches discussed in 4.3.1 and 4.3.2 is the deep conviction that language development is a far *simpler* process than dreamt of in Noam Chomsky's philosophy. Students of syntactic development will no longer need to know about subjacency, c-commanding, and all the rest of it; whole crate-loads of abstractions can be thrown overboard; and we can float within our common sense ignoring such fictions as 'trace'. And one cannot help but be reminded once more of Menard's (1997, p. xi) words on pragmatism's appeal: it feels to the reader as if some 'pressing but vaguely understood obligation' has suddenly been lifted from our shoulders, as if a final examination for which we could never have been properly prepared had just been cancelled.

Moreover, while the cognitive and social reduction is not as heavy-handed as it was in the 1970s, it is ineluctably there. 'My view,' writes Michael Tomasello (1999, p. 150), 'is simply that language is a form of cognition; it is cognitively packaged for the purposes of interpersonal communication (Langacker, 1987, 1991).' But this reduction is exercised, as I said, within the domain of what children say and comprehend rather than with regard to their extra-linguistic capacities and dispositions.

This research programme – it can tendentiously be said – is aimed at showing that syntactic development really is quite similar to the process of learning to use a phrase book, in the sense of an *inventory* of symbolic constructions passed on to us as the medium for framing our thoughts and expressing them to others.

The core rejection is the continuity assumption and the three core empirical claims are the following.

1) Syntactic development is a piecemeal affair rather than something in which the systematicity of human syntactic competence is manifest. And so we should find children mastering forms locally rather than expressing abstract principles across different contexts and contents.

2) Because language development is a species of 'cultural' or 'imitation' learning (Tomasello, 1999) the child's productions should closely resemble the speech input. Accordingly, the errors children make should, if they are not overgeneralisations, take the form of more or less slavishly reproducing adult forms in the wrong context. (For example, they might be prone to use infinitive forms as matrix verbs – recall the 'optional infinitive stage' – because they hear them so often in questions and commands like 'Do you want to go?'.)

3) Far from being almost error-free, syntactic development is strewn with errors, as one would expect if learning were taking place rather than the coming to fruition of innate knowledge.

My way of proceeding will again be somewhat *ad hominem* in so far as I will focus upon the work of two researchers – that of Michael Tomasello (initially in the USA and now in Germany) and Julian Pine (in the UK). The surface differences between them are that Tomasello is an evangelist for cognitive linguistics and for cognitive development as enculturalisation, while Pine's stance is that of data-driven scepticism about the view that syntactic development is anything more than gradualist learning from the input.

4.3.3(i) The non-systematic nature of early linguistic development

Tomasello's work on lexical development is only tangential to our concerns, but I shall briefly mention it for the sake of completeness, and as a lead-in to the work on syntax. Tomasello is broadly sceptical about the so-called 'special constraints' approach to word learning, meaning the position most closely associated with the work of Ellen Markman (1990) that the child has certain innate, constraining assumptions about how words refer to objects: the 'whole object' assumption (i.e., children assume that a word refers to a whole object not a part or property of it); the 'taxonomic' assumption that a word refers to a kind of thing – that words are not like people's names (Markman and Hutchinson's 1984); the 'mutual exclusivity' principle that one object cannot have two labels at the same semantic level (Markman and Wachtel's 1988).

For Tomasello, and for other researchers such as Dare Baldwin (1991, 1996), this undersells the role of social cuing by the adult speaker. Tomasello and Barton (1994), for example, showed that 24-month-old children do not have the simple rule 'map the new action word onto the next action the speaker produces'. If the subsequent action was performed unintentionally ('…Whoops!') they will ignore it and map the new word on to the intentional action that follows it. Social cues are also central to the child's decisions about whether a word refers to a thing or to an action. In a study by Tomasello and Akhatar (1995) the experimenter performed a sequence of actions on a novel object, then the target action plus the novel word 'modi', with the result that children took this to refer to the novel action, not the object; but when one action was performed on a series of objects then on a novel object as the word 'modi' was said, they took this to refer to the most recent object.

One should certainly assimilate the message of this work, though I think it is better to avoid the position (evident also in Bloom, 2000) that we have to *choose between* special constraints and social cuing and that we should pick the latter. Surely, both positions are likely to be true. For recent data in support of the 'special constraints', see Markman *et al.* (2003).

But Tomasello is certainly correct than the special constraints approach, as presently constituted at least, can tell us little about verb learning, whereas his social-pragmatic approach can. In fact, it is to verb learning – and more generally to syntactic development – that we now turn.

The message delivered by *First verbs* (1992), Tomasello's monograph in which he reported his daughter's (Travis) grammatical development between 1y 0m and 2y 0m years and set out the theoretical foundations of his programme, was that verb learning is not, in his own terminology (p. 254) 'systematic'. So let us remind ourselves what systematicity in syntax (as opposed to Fodor and Pylyshyn's cognitive systematicity) amounts to and then relate this back to Tomasello's developmental scepticism. Taking my cue from Newmeyer (1998), I took systematicity to mean two things:

> (A) the ability to control sentences exemplifying a given syntactic operation *across quite different semantic/pragmatic functions*;

plus

> (B) the ability to control the way in which *other* algebraic operations/constraints interact with this operation.

With regard to (A), for example, auxiliary-verb inversion signals a number of communicative functions, from questioning to making a conditional statement without *if*. With regard to (B), this inversion 'interacts' with the constraint that no more than one auxiliary can be involved. In our second example, the numerous functions performed by *wh*-phrases and the interaction of these with subjacency represent (A) and (B) respectively.

In fact, Tomasello (1992) has something rather more basic in mind in his use of 'systematic'; although it can be taken to count as a species of (A). We can, first of all, take 'sentences' to mean types of verb-argument structure – sentence frames. Some of these are shown in (65), in which ϕ = verb or verb stem.

(65) A ϕ B

A ϕ

ϕ B!

ϕ B with an X

A is ϕing

ϕ!

A ϕ B on the Y

Only some verbs can be represented in all of these frames, and so, to some degree, they constrain the semantic content of ϕ. Verbs such as *cut, draw, push,* and *pull* would fit, while *give, think,* and even *see* would not. What would, then, count as a systematic capacity here? It would be manifested in children who are able to control some, or at least one, of these frames with different verbs. Thus, if a child has both *cut* and *draw* as part of her productive vocabulary then using one of them in, say, three of these frames should raise the probability of her also using the other verb in them. This would be prima facie evidence of her hiving off syntactic structures (a set of verb-argument frames) from the meaning/use of the utterances.

Non-systematic, or what I am calling *phrase-book*, performance, on the other hand means an essentially bottom-up kind of learning in which children's use of a given verb in one kind of frame does not increase the probability of their using a different verb with a relevantly similar argument structure in this frame. They might produce, for example, 'cut on the table' and 'mummy cut the cake' but not produce 'draw on the wall' and 'mummy drew baby'. To say that children begin verb learning as phrase book users in what Tomasello calls *the verb-island hypothesis*. This states that (Tomasello, 1992, p. 23):

> Unless proved otherwise, we should assume that young children's early verbs and relational terms are individual islands of organisation in an otherwise unorganised grammatical system. In the early stages the child learns about arguments and syntactic marking on a verb-by-verb basis, and ordering patterns and morphological markers learned for one verb do not immediately generalise to other verbs.

Before digging deeper into the verb-island hypothesis it would be useful to consider some of the theoretical and methodological decisions that form the background to it. In the first place, Tomasello adopts a highly conservative position on what is to count as a child's having control of a word class or a relational category. In strong contrast to the continuity assumption, he argues that syntactic knowledge should only be ascribed when there is positive evidence for the categories in multiword production. This might take the form of category-general marking or the contrastive use of word order. To give Tomasello's examples, if a child only uses one word order with a given verb (see above) or if either of two orderings are used to mean the same thing (e.g., 'Hat off' and 'Off hat') then we cannot say that the child has syntactic control of the category in question. Moreover, if children use a word with an accusative marker they can only be said to be using that marker to represent case if that marker can be contrasted with its absence to create a different meaning.

The background to this kind of scepticism can be found in seminal monographs by Martin Braine (1976) and by Melissa Bowerman (1976). As Tomasello reminds us, Braine, in particular, cautioned, in contrast to the nativist analyses of early two-word utterance of David McNeill (1966), that when we see word pairs like 'bring truck', which have the appearance of being truncated verb phrases, we should always consider the possibility that these are no more than 'limited scope formulae' – meaning local forms tailored to express particular, domain-specific communicative functions. The child may, for example use the form '*more* + X' in cases when she desires increase or recurrence. But does this mean that 'X' plays the role of noun or that 'more' plays that of a relational term, as it does in adult speech? We should not assume so, argued Braine. In the case of his son, for example, the child began, when saying two words, by positioning the words *big* and *little* and then later *hot, cold* and *hurt* appropriately before nouns. This might suggest that he had control of the broad-scope fragment 'property + X'; but the child never used the word *wet* in this context, though it did appear in others. It is worth mentioning, however, that there are quite substantial individual differences within this trend. Bowerman (1976) reports data from one limited-scope-formulaic child but also data from another child who used the locatives *up, down, on, off,* and *back* productively almost as soon as she began pairing words. Some children show more systematicity than others then.

That said, Braine's scepticism would certainly seem to be appropriate, given the ever-present possibility that children may simply be parroting chunks of adult speech and thereby giving the impression of possessing syntactic capacities which they do not in fact possess. Though it is also reasonable to wonder how productive some *adult* speech would be judged to be on these stringent criteria – a point to which I will return.

In any event, Tomasello (1992) is actually more conservative than Braine. For he argues that even if a child uses contrastive word order (e.g., using 'A ɸ B' when A is the actor and 'B ɸ A' when it is the patient) this may still may not imply, as Braine is willing to accept, that the child has the productive semantic category of Actor. Such a contrastive ordering may reflect no more than the child's ability to form novel linguistic structures by concatenating words (a capacity which Tomasello links to the Piagetian notion of combining sensorimotor schemes). Alternatively, it may reflect no more than verb-specific knowledge. She might, for example, know that when hitting is being talked about the hitter precedes *hit* and the hitee succeeds it.

Well, is *this* degree of scepticism justified? The nagging doubt is essentially as follows (to recur remorselessly in this and the next section). While such a severe application of Lloyd Morgan's canon is likely to be appropriate in discussing linguistic comprehension in apes (as reported, for example, in Savage-Rumbaugh *et al.*, 1990) for the simple reason that the animals will never acquire English, its application to human children can begin to look like a case of putting off the evil day when either some account of adult competence has to be given – or the radical step taken to deny its existence.

In fact, Tomasello (1992) taps two further sources of scepticism; though they could not be more different. From Karmiloff-Smith (1986) he takes the view that linguistic structures can only be regarded as such when they become the *objects* of mental operations.

> As long as words are only operated *with* – they are the predicates doing the operating – there can be no question of word-class formation. This has particular reference to verbs because even if the child is speaking in short sentences the verb is still the main relational structure of the sentence and thus is still something the child is operating with, not on.

> (Tomasello, 1992, pp. 26–27; original emphasis)

Is this reasonable? Those who are friendly towards Karmiloff-Smith's 'representational redescription' view of development might think it is (see 3.5 for discussion of this). But those who are more sceptical, indeed even some of the friendly ones, may find this highly prescriptive view to be unmotivated – by itself. At the very least, such a high-level proposal needs to be tied down to specifics. In fact it evokes a debate that is almost as old as developmental psycholinguistics itself. Roger Brown (1973) originally proposed that very young children have the structure VP, employing arguments based on 'privileges of occurrence'. Thus, the privilege of occurrence of V + N pairs was found to be similar to those of V alone, suggesting that V + N is indeed a verbal unit. Meanwhile, Bowerman (1973) denied this on the grounds that the existence of a VP unit of analysis requires that the child use devices to *make reference* to a preceding VP. For example, if the possibility of the child's being given a bun is the VP in question, the child's uttering the command 'Do it' would count as such a reference. She pointed out that 'children do not use phrases like "do (so)" which might refer to the preceding VP' (Bowerman, 1973, p. 179).

This brings us directly to Tomasello's second source of scepticism. He takes a paper by Anat Ninio (1988), whose subject is the criteria for ascribing formal grammatical classes to beginning speakers, and selects and strengthens one of its more sceptical threads to produce the view that 'children should not have the word class of verb until they are treated as arguments by other predicates in, for example, sentences of the kind *I want to play* [latter verb an 'argument' of the former, JR]' (Tomasello, 1992, p. 27). He does, however, admit in a footnote that his reading of Ninio's position is 'slightly slanted'. In fact, it would be well to look at Ninio's actual argument in some detail, because it is a highly judicious and insightful reading of the issues – and right to the present purpose. This will enable us to place Tomasello's species of scepticism within a broader context.

Ninio cautions that, while it is obviously true that we should not ascribe all the categories and apparatus of adult competence to the very young child, when they have no morphological rules and produce utterances of only about two words long, we should not wish to be saddled with the view that there is simply *no* continuity between what they start out doing and what they end up knowing. In fact, her paper can be read as a cautious case for a modest form of continuity assumption!

She points out that

> It is logically impossible to point to a minimal set of features that has to be attained for a speaker to be credited with category knowledge … until children have mastered the whole of grammar, it will always be possible to find some feature or other of such category knowledge that children do not yet possess.

> (Ninio, 1988, p. 102)

The question should rather be about what kind of early knowledge of lexical (e.g., noun, verb) and functional (subject, VP) categories should be considered to be a *subset* of adult's knowledge of formal categories. Do they, for example, 'follow the same combinatorial rules as would govern the combination of the same items in the endstate language?' (ibid., p. 103).

Now the fact is that children typically, in their first word combinations, *do* generally follow adult combinatorial restrictions, while errors in doing so are rare in the languages studied; Ninio mentions Hebrew (Levy, 1988) and Finnish (Bowerman, 1973). So one might conclude that syntactic symbols like noun and verb do seem to be justified in very early child grammars 'in the minimal sense that different kinds of terms fit into different and mostly appropriate, syntactic environments' (ibid., p. 103). But how do we then accommodate the fact that, as Braine and Bowerman pointed out, children do not apply every combinatorial rule to every term in their vocabulary to which such a rule could apply? Sometimes the reasons for such restrictions may be entirely pragmatic (Ninio and Snow, 1988), *while lack of full productivity does not necessarily imply lack of competence.* But at the very least we should accept that 'in the early stages of language acquisition syntactic subcategory symbols such as verb and noun in children's rule systems *do not seem to have the adult range of application to concrete terms*' (ibid., p. 104; emphasis added).

In other words, we might cautiously credit them with the symbols whilst noting that these do not have the adult range of applicability. As to those such as Braine and Bowerman who wheel on Lloyd Morgan's canon at this point and deny that we should ascribe any subcategory symbols at all, Ninio would say that 'the notation should make prominent, rather than obscure, the basic continuity between child language and the endstate system' (ibid., p. 104). Thus, if one only wishes to give a *parsimonious description* – this term will be seen many times more – of child grammar then one will naturally balk at ascribing even semantic rules to them – only lexical ones. But these are creatures who, unlike chimpanzees, are on their way to adult competence; and so it surely 'a legitimate research strategy to plot the course of development in terms of its departure from the end state … to trace continuities between children's rule systems and endstate grammar as well as spot[ting] departures from it' (ibid., p. 105). Or as Maratsos (1982, p. 39) has put it 'the conscientious use of sceptical arguments … could prevent the analysis of the beginnings of such grammatical unification in subsets of the system or even prevent analysis of the completed system'.

Accordingly, rather than ascribing no more than limited-scope formulae to young speakers one might say that a child who, by parsimonious description, has '*want* + X' can be said to in fact be operating with

VP → V + NP

But that if the only verb that follows this rule is *want*, this can be noted by a lexical insertion rule attached to the phrase structure rule thus:

VP → V + NP   V ⇐ *want*

As Ninio puts it:

> The fact that children seem to acquire rules in a piecemeal fashion for the expression of individual predicate-argument relations and at best generalise these formal rules to other semantically very similar predicate-argument relations … *should not in fact be taken as evidence for their grammatical system being organised in ways alien to the organisation of the endstate system.*

> (ibid., p. 106; emphasis added)

We now come to the more *sceptical* strain within Ninio's paper. While individual learning of predicate-argument configurations is, she argues, not only a natural but a 'logically necessary' way of learning language, one should propose that it is only *when predicate-argument pairs are nested in higher-order constructions as phrases* that their 'abstractness as constructional units is required in grammar or for that matter can be thought of as developmentally possible' (ibid., p. 109). Thus, when we see a combination of one predicate (e.g., *hit*, *big*) with a set of arguments we can indeed say that the child has acquired the rule 'predicate + variable'; but the predicate element itself is not, for Ninio, an abstract variable but is 'concrete and tied to specific terms'. The child has done little more than learn the semantic restrictions on a set of predicates. 'In a real sense, the linguistic system is not generative on the level of individual predicates, and, regarding predicates, linguistic rules are concrete and item-bound rather than abstract' (ibid., p. 114).

What injects true generativity is the advent of multi-word utterances in which the 'predicate + argument' unit is embedded in the predicate slot of a higher-level 'argument + predicate' construct, as in (66).

(66) X + [hit Y]

this + [big X]

I-can't + [open + this]

want + [this + X]

According to Ninio, these combinations become possible because children realise that '*word combinations inherit the logical combinatorial properties of one of their terms, and with their formal (i.e., syntactic) privileges*'. In other words children are coming to understand what the two-word combinations they have been producing up to now actually mean – in the sense of gaining an insight into how combinations can be deployed in an utterance, rather than bare functional meaning. This can be called the acquisition of the predicate variable insight.

An hypothesis flows from this proposal, which is that once the predicate variable insight has been attained and the abstract nature of phrases, and ultimately sentences, comes to be appreciated, the child will begin to mark verb morphology. This was what Brown (1973) reports, in fact; as Ninio notes.

Tomasello's Travis also provides evidence for something like Ninio's hypothesis. So now we are back with Travis's verb-island-style productions, we can look in more detail at the evidence. As Tomasello (ibid., p. 239; emphasis added) says:

> A major line of evidence for systematicity would be consistency among the sentence patterns T [=Travis] expressed with different verbs. For example, if *as soon as* T used her first sentence expressing both actor and object she then *immediately* produced similar sentences with other verbs (ideally in the absence of adult models), this could be adduced as evidence that her verbs are in a single class (or alternatively that her arguments are verb-general categories).

In Table 4.2, I reproduce the table constructed by Tomasello in support of the claim that systematicity was *not* in evidence.

As Tomasello cautions, however, it is important not to confuse data of this kind with measures of the *complexity* of her sentences (on which see his Table 8.4, p. 240). For example, the verb *read* was used with a number of different argument types (actor, object, location) but always with only one argument at a time, whereas the verb *gave* was only used in one sentence frame, though often involving three arguments. In the case of *draw*, however, there was both a relatively wide range of sentence frames in evidence and numerous arguments. This is how Tomasello (ibid., p. 243) sums up the situation:

> Thus, although these two analyses [of number of accompanying arguments and of variety of sentence frames, JR] obviously do not provide conclusive evidence that T's language is organised around individual verbs – pragmatic factors influencing T's production played some role in determining some, though not all, of the observed patterns [these are certainly given full weight in the book, JR] – they certainly do not provide any support for the existence of more abstract linguistic structures. In all, it would be very difficult for a proponent of abstract rules to explain why T uses the verb *cut* (with one singular expression) in only

Table 4.2 The number of verbs Travis employed with different numbers of sentence frames (based on Tomasello's (1992) Table 8.5)

Age	16–18 m	18–20 m	20–24 m
Number of sentence frames			
one	20	61	29
two	3	29	31
three	—	11	18
four	—	7	11
five	—	—	11

one single-argument sentence frame throughout her second year of life, while she used the verb *draw* – learned at around the same time and involving a similar cognitive profile – in at least eight different sentence frames involving up to three arguments during the same period.

The final sentence of this passage clearly stands in need of comment. If it is what I have called *parsimonious description* that we are engaged in then we might indeed conclude that Travis is learning English on a word-by-word basis. But let us assimilate the message of the non-sceptical face on Ninio's (1988) paper. In this case, we attend to the fact that, because Travis will develop adult competence in English, we surely need a research strategy that will enable us to explain how she gets from here to there. So it becomes, as Ninio puts it, a 'legitimate research strategy' to plot development in terms of its departure from the end state and to trace continuities between children's rule systems and adult grammar in addition to noting departures from it. And recall the words of Michael Maratsos (1982, p. 39) who is somebody more usually appearing for the sceptics, that 'the conscientious use of sceptical arguments [may] even prevent analysis of the completed system'. From Ninio's perspective, then, we would credit Travis with adult grammatical symbols while cautioning that her ability to deploy them is severely limited by their being tied to the semantics of a particular set of predicates. Far from being surprising, and a challenge to the nativists, this is 'logically necessary'. I take Ninio to mean by this that learning will tend to move from the concrete to the abstract for a particular database (even if the learner has innate abstract knowledge of the kind of data base being learned).

It seems to me that this passage from Tomasello also serves to illustrate the gulf between the pragmatist and the rationalist cast of mind. In the former, one's framing premise is that the child will do what she needs to do, and no more, to get *this far* as a communicator; while in the latter case one assumes that the child has something within her that will drive her on from this position, and that this 'something' is related by form to the mature mind. In fact, if one really wants to adopt a thoroughgoing pragmatism and insist that adult 'competence' is a chimera and that language is really no more than a inventory of 'how to do things with words' then the Travis data will tell us that she is starting as she means to go on. But if *this* is your view of language then developmental data are not going to sway you one way or the other. If you can maintain your pragmatism in the teeth of the facts about adults, about the systematicity of our competence, then *nothing* children do will change your mind.

I now return to the way in which Tomasello utilises the more sceptical strain in Ninio's paper. We have seen that Tomasello's (as he admits 'slightly slanted') reading of Ninio's predicate variable proposal (child's 2+ word utterances allow analysis in terms of phrasal sub-units) is that the paradigmatic class of verb cannot be said to exist until we see them being used as the arguments of predicates (e.g., in *I can't open it*). This carries along with it the positive claim that the conditions for Travis having a subset of words that have attained the noun class are much more easily met, because her nouns appeared in argument slots. Thus, for Tomasello, once something has come to be treated as an argument of a predicate it has become, for the child, a 'mental object' – operated 'on' not 'with'. So, where Ninio writes of arguments operating as variables, Tomasello recruits the Karmiloff-Smith's redescription metaphor. Given this, he regards Travis's speech as supporting Ninio's hypothesis (suitably modified) that the noun class precedes the verb class. In line with this, there was productive morphology in evidence for nouns before 24 months (pluralisation, possessives), and she used pronoun substitution (e.g., *it* for a noun). By contrast, what little evidence there was for the morphological marking of verbs was taken to suggest that it had a verb-specific nature. For, although Travis had 24 past-tense forms and 23 present progressives, there were only four verbs that were used with *both*; while two-thirds of her 150+ words were never inflected at all. As we have seen, Ninio's position does indeed predict this; but for her it is the ability of produce utterances such as 'X + [hit Y]' and 'this + [big X]' which encourages verb morphological marking, not specifically treating verbs as the arguments of other verbs.

Tomasello also mentions that Travis had flexible use of newly learned nouns in novel sentential contexts and speculates that she would have passed the 'wug test' (Berko, 1958) before 24 months. (The wug test is a measure of productive, say, noun morphology in which a child is introduced to a novel creature called a 'wug' after which a context is presented in which the child might be encouraged to, for example, pluralise the word.) This lead later to some innovative experimental studies in which 24-month-olds were shown to have the category noun (Tomasello and Olguin 1993), but were shown to lack the verb category, in so far as they tended not to generalise a novel verb referring to a novel action beyond the argument frame (e.g., agent + verb) in which it had been modelled (Olguin and Tomasello (1993). Also see Tomasello *et al.* (1997) for a direct comparison of noun and verb productivity. More of this kind of work a little later.

Before leaving *First verbs*, however, it will be useful to look at how the work of Langacker and Van Valin is accommodated within this landmark monograph. Langacker's influence is most clearly in evidence in Tomasello's use of image-schematic diagrams to represent the meaning of early verbs, relational terms more generally (e.g., *more*), and words like *where, no, gone, again*, and many others. What is common to all the diagrams, as is it was for Langacker, is their representing temporal sequences with at least two windows, with the first being a static 'moment of attention', followed by some new state (desired or actual) with, perhaps, an intervening window negating the static state. There are a large number of these in the early chapters of the book, and they spur thoughts about the amount of common, superordinate structure they can be taken to possess. For, while much attention is given to the *differences* between kinds of image-schemas (e.g., for two senses of *where*, or for *have* versus *give*), one wonders what attention to *commonalities* between verbs of a similar argument structure would yield. If it indeed yielded second-order image-schemas with an interesting level of structure then attention might also usefully turn to questions about how this might interface with syntactic development. As it is, however, the image-schematic diagrams themselves have something of an island-like character. It is interesting to note (ibid., p. 36), by the way, that Tomasello's initial cognitive framework was Piagetian – replete as it is with domain-general logico-mathematical structures. The image-schematic approach was initially influenced by von Glaserfield (1972) and later by Langacker.

These do indeed capture the fine social grain that early utterances might have; but maybe they do so at the cost of losing deeper and wider cognitive structures that could be the armatures of syntactic development – however we wish to explicate that metaphor!

Van Valin, meanwhile, appears right at the end of the monograph in a section called 'Later development'. Here Tomasello reiterates that cognitive linguistics provides us with an approach preferable to the 'formalist' one because it '*allows us to describe the child's language in its own terms*' (ibid., p. 271, emphasis added). Having acknowledged the sure fact than generativists will think that this theoretical apparatus will not get the child up to adult competence, Tomasello counters that we should question whether we really do need their apparatus of transformations and all the rest of it. He notes, in support of this, that Travis framed questions very early on by fronting utterances with 'Whereda __?' and 'What's-da ___?' and did so with specific verbs 'suggesting once again some less than generalised movement rules' (p. 272). Adult questions could evolve from these. He does, though, accept that a broad-brush account of this kind 'is of no help … in the specifics of why particular structures in particular languages work the way they do'. (p. 272). Accordingly, he lists those cognitive linguists who 'work at the level of specificity: Lakoff on *there*, Langacker on transitivity, and Van Valin on question formation' (see 2.5.5), and one or two others. No single theory is, then, being advertised as an equal and opposite force to the Chomskyan research programme; and in this sense – at least – it differs from empiricist connectionism.

Since *First verbs,* Tomasello's empirical research programme has been directed towards revealing how conservative, unproductive, uncreative, and item-centred children's language is, up to the age of three or even four years. On the more theoretical front, in addition to a general championing of cognitive linguistics within developmental psychology and of the view that the notion of the grammar of a language is a 'myth' (Tomasello, 2003), he has presented the case against the continuity assumption from the perspective of a usage-based theory, has proposed an account of later syntactic development in terms of analogy making and 'structure mapping' (Tomasello, 2000a), and has elaborated the view that language acquisition is a form of 'imitative' or 'cultural' learning (Tomasello, 1999). I will first discuss the empirical project before turning to more theoretical matters. The business about imitation learning will lead naturally to the second prong of the cognitive–functionalist research programme: early speech as a reproduction of the input.

4.3.3(ii) Further evidence for the 'item-centred' nature of early syntactic development

First, using a technique that employs the basic rationale of the wug test, Tomasello and his co-workers have amassed a very substantial body of data showing that young children frequently fail to generalise novel verbs into sentence frames which they had not heard the experimenter use with that verb, but which they themselves can use with familiar verbs. For example, Tomasello and Brooks (1998) showed that young 2-year-olds are reluctant to generalise from an intransitive model like *The ball is dacking* to a transitive production, but that they were likely to do so when the model was transitive (e.g., *Jim is taming the car*). Utterances were evoked by questions of the form 'What's the AGENT doing?' Only 19 per cent of somewhat older children (mean of 2y 6m) produced a novel transitive utterance from an intransitive model. Similarly, Tomasello and Brooks (1999) found that children with a mean age of 2y 10m often (i.e., 78 per cent of the time) failed to generalise passive models to active, although they could do so from active to active. Having heard *Ernie is getting meeded by the dog* or *Bert is getting gorped by the cat*, they are, as above, asked what the agent is doing. A correct answer would be 'He's meeding Ernie' or 'He's gorping Bert'. These are production experiments, but a similar message holds for comprehension, in which children might have to follow instructions like *Make Cookie Monster dak Big Bird* (Akhtar and Tomasello, 1997).

In a review of this work Tomasello (2000a, p. 222) concludes from both the experimental and the naturalistic data that 'Before 3 years of age, only a few English-speaking children manage to produce canonical transitive utterances with verbs they have not heard used this way'. This of course naturally spurs the question of whether wug-style techniques dip deep enough into competence. For when a *preferential-looking* procedure is used, we get rather positive news of children's knowledge about the difference between transitive and intransitive sentence frames. An excellent example of this is afforded by a study by Letitia Naigles' (1990). In this, children with a mean age of 25 months were presented with videos of adults dressed as different kinds of animal performing actions together in parallel (intransitive) or on each other (transitive) as they heard sentences or injunctions from a central loudspeaker. In the test phase of the experiment there was a video clip played on either side of the child, with the question being which one they would attend to when they heard *Where's gorping now?* or *Find gorping!* In the initial 'teaching' phase of the experiment, a 'duck' and a 'bunny' were seen to perform actions which had *both* transitive and intransitive features. In one case, for example, the transitive feature consisted of the duck pressing down on the rabbit's head while they both performed the intransitive action of extending one arm. The half of the children who had been assigned to the transitive group heard the commentary on this complex action as '*Look! The duck is gorping* [head press] *the bunny*, while the intransitive commentary for the other half was *Look! The duck and the bunny are gorping* [arm extension]. After this, in the test phase, the video on one side of the child showed the transitive action *only* as the one on the other side of the child showed the intransitive action *only*, while they heard the injunctions to find gorping mentioned above. The children who has heard the transitive commentary attended to the transitive action and those who had heard the intransitive attended to the intransitive ($p < .001$).

Naigles' discussion of the data is cautious. She leaves open the possibility that, rather than representing the sentences as abstract, hierarchically-organised structures ([NP [V NP]]) they could have been parsed as particular combinations of predicates and arguments or as purely pragmatic structures composed of topics and comments: 'it would be premature to assume that the 25 month olds in this study were operating with full-blown syntax' (Naigles, 1990, p. 369). But it is nonetheless a strong possibility that they were picking up structural differences of *some* kind between transitive and intransitive sentence frames. Indeed Naigles takes her data to be supportive of the so-called *syntactic bootstrapping hypothesis* (Landau and Gleitman, 1985) which states that young children use the syntactic frameworks within which verbs appear to draw inferences about the verb's meaning (to be discussed further in 4.3.3 (vi)).

Needless to say, one would expect Naigles' children to fail Tomasello's wug-style tests of understanding the transitive form (Akhtar and Tomasello, 1997). For, by maternal report, just under a third of her subjects only produced two words at a time, with the rest producing around three. Tomasello's reaction to the study is to regard the outcome as artefactual (Tomasello, 2000a, p. 221, footnote). 'The problem,' he writes, 'is that children might very well have been using the word *and* [in *The Duck and the Bunny are gorping* – JR] as an indicator of a parallel-action picture'. This is possible, of course, but it should be borne in mind that preferences at test were also measured against preferences in a *control* phase, which came between the teaching and the test phases, in which the two different actions were presented as at test but with the children hearing the neutral *Oh! They're different now*. In this case, not only was there a clear preference for the matching videos in test over control ($p < 0.003$), but there was no interaction between type of sentence frame and difference scores, suggesting that the children *positively preferred* the transitive match at test, as compared to the control condition, no less than they preferred the intransitive match which Tomasello's account tried to explain away. Their preference for the *transitive* match at test more than in the control phase stands in need of explanation. Moreover, Naigles herself anticipates and answers Tomasello's objection in the paper (ibid., p. 367). She points out that even if we accept that the coordinate noun phase ('The Duck and the Bunny') could have motivated the children to look for the scene in which both characters are doing the same thing, a syntactic facility still stands in need of explanation. That is to say, the child is still faced with the task of spotting that the action described by the predicate is applicable to *both* characters in the subject position (i.e., that the sentence means *The duck is gorping and the bunny is gorping*. 'However', she writes, ' it is important to know whether the coordinate subject is the only type of intransitive frame that could yield this result'. 'More research needed', in other words.

In fact, this divergence between Tomasello's and Naigles' assessment of competence will have a familiar ring to those who have followed infancy research for the past fifteen or so years. Studies using looking time (dishabituation to 'impossible' scenes, not attention to matching ones, as in the present case) by Elizabeth Spelke, Renée Baillargeon and others has revolutionised and revitalised our collective view of object permanence development. As measured by looking-time, infants have a rich body of information about object occlusion and 'folk physics' even before they can organise visually-guided reaching and well over a year before the 'object concept' is acquired on the Piagetian criterion of searching for objects after their unperceived displacement. Looking time, it might be said, informs us about the representational format that is innately present and on which – for the minimalistically Piagetian (Russell, 1999) – executive development builds and from which 'full' object permanence comes to fruition. For the true pragmatist (the classical Piagetian) however, all representations have their origin in action ('thought is internalised action'); while for the representationalist (of either rationalist or empiricist stripe) action is the externalisation of representation. Accordingly, Tomasello, as a pragmatist, regards our mature representations of syntactic rules as originating in the child's active construction of inventories of local regularities and of later analogical synthesis of them (on which see below); while those of us who are not persuaded by the application of pragmatist principles to syntactic development suspect that looking-time studies will unearth evidence of rich grammatical capacities in very young children. But it remains, as ever, to be seen.

Tomasello's broadly sceptical analysis of early syntactic knowledge does not, however, depend entirely upon the kind of wug-like studies just described earlier. More recently, Abbot-Smith, Lieven and Tomasello (2001) looked at how young children respond to ungrammatical word orders. Previously, Akhtar (1999) had demonstrated that 4-year-olds will correct 'transitive' utterances such as *Gorped Elmo the cow*, whereas older 2-year-olds and even 3-year-olds behaved inconsistently. Meanwhile, Abbot-Smith *et al.* tested children with a average age of 2y 4m on 'intransitive' utterances such as *Meeked the duck* (where the duck was seen to be the agent) and found them to correct them less than half as often as did Akhtar's 2-year-olds who were only 4 months older. However some implicit acknowledgement of the grammaticality of one order was in evidence, in so far as these youngish 2-year-olds would use novel verbs learned in the grammatical order (SV) four times as often as they used novel verbs learned in the ungrammatical order (VS), while also showing some command of pronouns and progressive auxiliary like *He's VERBing it* for the novel verbs in the verb learned with the correct ordering.

As a further example of Tomasello's programme of inoculating us against the view that young children's utterances have any real syntactic complexity, I mention some work by Diessel and Tomasello (2001). In this case the authors examined the phenomenon, frequently discussed in the context of theory of mind development, of very young children's attaching complement clauses to main clauses, especially when the verb in the latter is of a mental state variety: *I think I'm go in there; I know this piece go; See I have teeth.* The ten children in the study were taken from the CHILDES data base (McWhinney and Snow, 1990). The authors base their conclusion that the main clauses did not really 'express a full proposition' on the fact that the use of these constructions was limited to only a few verbs used with a restricted set of complements. The logic is, then, a familiar one: if children are seen to be doing something which in adults would be called following a rule but only do so in the case of a few verbs in as few contexts then they are not really following a rule at all but exemplifying the verb island – now often called 'constructional island' – phenomenon. Thus expressions of the form *SUBJ + think/say/see/know/look/pretend/mean/guess/ tell/wish/hope/ wonder/bet/remember+ COMP* are in reality no more than epistemic markers, attention getters or markers of epistemic force. In the case of *know* for example, Diessel and Tomasello note that this very frequently took a *wh*-complement with a polar question. *(Do you) know X?* occurred in more than half of all the utterances in which *know* took a complement clause. The authors point out in the case of sentences like *Do you know what time it is?* the *Do you know* is semantically redundant; the complement clause is what is actually being expressed, with the *know* element merely being a polite form.

My final example is another naturalistic study – by Lieven, Tomasello, Behrens and Speares (in press). The authors made a very dense sampling of the speech of a 2-year-old girl over a 6-week period. Then, in order to assess her 'constructional creativity' they looked at all of the 500+ utterances she produced during the final hour of recording and examined their antecedents in what she had said before. Their conclusion was that this final set of utterances had been 'cut and pasted' from the child's earlier utterances, put together from a motley assortment of pre-existing linguistic units. There were, for example, many repetitions of established utterance schemas plus other linguistic material filled in or added on to beginning or the end of utterances; *Where's the X*, for example. Only a small minority of the utterances differed from things she has said before. Tomasello (2003) concluded that 'linguistic creativity occurs in the context of her already well-established item-based constructions'.

4.3.3(iii) The pragmatist case against the continuity assumption

I now turn, as promised, to Tomasello's (2000a, section 3) case against the continuity assumption, discussing it in the context of the scepticism about 'strong continuity' that already exists within the generative community. In order to spell out the implications of his position for the continuity assumption Tomasello takes the three versions of the continuity claim as listed by Clahsen (1996) and seeks to show why none of them works. These are 'versions' in the sense of being three ways of accounting for why children's language looks so different from adults' despite their putative possession of essentially the same body of innate, abstract linguistic knowledge.

1) The presence of full grammatical competence in young children is masked by lack of development in extra-linguistic ('external') areas, such as 'information processing' and 'pragmatic' areas.

2) The principles of universal grammar and most of the grammatical categories are known by the very young language user, but not all of these will be manifest at the outset because the ability to employ them will mature, i.e., appear develop by virtue of endogenous change rather than of learning from the data.

3) While knowledge of universal grammar is present at the outset, the child still has to learn the particular features of the language to which he or she is exposed. Innate abstract knowledge will interact with developing knowledge about (say) the lexicon.

Tomasello's answers are as follows. (I am paraphrasing and eliding.)

1) *Plus external development*: Some account must be forthcoming of how these 'performance' factors constrain children's productivity with novel verbs but not with novel nouns – one that is not merely post hoc. Why, more generally, do these performance factors bear upon forms they have *not* heard the experimenter say, but do not bear upon forms they have heard the experimenter say?

2) *Maturation*: Like the 'processing or pragmatics' of 1, this is a 'fudge factor' in so far as it is 'unconstrained' (Tomasello, 2000a, p. 230). That is to say, whenever new acquisition data arise 'maturational' factors can be invoked – at will. Moreover, with specific regard to Tomasello's data, what kind of genetic

timing mechanism leaves the ability to be productive with novel verbs till later? Why evolve this biological brake only to remove it?

3) *Role of language-specific knowledge*: For Tomasello, this essentially reduces to the same kind of empirical position as his own, non-nativist approach, namely, that children have to hear each new verb being used in all of its contexts before they can be contextually 'creative'. But Tomasello's position *wins on parsimony*. (He also raises under this heading some big questions about how nativist accounts explain the linking between innate abstract knowledge and the concrete elements of a human language. But this issue is so big I will devote all of section 4.4 to it.)

These points are well taken, but they must be placed in context. The fact is, what Tomasello is describing is a debate which has raged for decades within the *generative* community. There are indeed linguists and psycholinguists who argue for the so-called 'strong continuity hypothesis', but this is not even what *Chomsky* argued for, in so far as, when he touched on the actual course of acquisition, he came out as a maturationist. And it is the supporters of strong continuity such as Stephen Crain, Nina Hyams, Barbara Lust and others who spell out why this might be unsatisfactory. Accordingly, Chomsky (1988, p. 70) writes:

> It seems hard to explain these transitions without appeal to maturational processes that bring principles of universal grammar into operation on some regular schedule in a manner to be described and accounted for in a genetic way.

To this Lust (1994, p. xxv, emphasis added) replies that such a view

> Divides the real facts of development of language from linguistic theory ... as no independent theory of UG *change* exists in linguistic theory. [Indeed] no independent explanation at the level of biology or neuroanatomy currently exists, either, for a maturationally-staged UG.

(This really does – in passing – betray a striking lack of faith in theories of competence.) Similarly, Crain (1991) and Hyams (1994) argue for strong continuity fielding considerations rather similar to those found in Tomasello's point 2. For them, embracing maturationism allows the theorist too much explanatory leeway – too many 'degrees of freedom' – in the explanatory resources. Sticking with continuity, however, means facing the empiricist fire – bravely providing no moving target. To this, sceptics about strong continuity such as Atkinson (1996) point out that, viewed methodologically, this is a strange manoeuvre in so far as stating a fact about an organism without evidence for it (that very young children have 'full competence' while only being able to string two or three words together) will in turn draw fire from Lloyd Morgan's canon. Articles of faith generally do not make good science, though they can, of course, inspire it.

Indeed, it is to generative authors such as Atkinson (1996) that one turns for hard-hitting and remorseless scepticism about strong continuity – all the more so for its deploying technical arguments and arithmetic detail. So is there not a paradox here: pragmatists and rationalists agreeing that a seeming tenet of nativism should be jettisoned? No, because, for generativists, the alternative to strong continuity is not pragmatist nihilism about the psychological reality of a grammar plus a phrase-book-learner view of development but a *dis*continuity theory framed from within a generative account. On the one hand, strong continuity is seen to struggle, given that children really do seem to begin by lacking certain principles of UG. (For example, in Dutch (Wijnen and Bol, 1993) and Danish (Plunkett and Strömqvist, 1992) children undergo a phase in which their main-clause verbs are exclusively infinitival.) While on the other hand, brute appeals to endogenous change of one kind or another will remain unpersuasive unless they are backed up by talk of mechanisms; and yet still on this hand 'my biology is not up to much, but I have the sneaking suspicion that most biologists would probably view maturation as the norm in the development of complex biological systems' (Atkinson, 1996, p. 458). (In fact, the issues in this area are often debated in a theory-internal style, and are consequently highly technical; though they are sometimes centre around the kind of developmental evidence reviewed towards the end of Part 2. For both, see Lust [1984].)

But let us then pause to consider what a generative discontinuity theory looks like. One of the best examples of these is the '*structure-building*' approach of Andrew Radford. In his 1990 monograph *Syntactic theory and the acquisition of English syntax* Radford focused upon the language development of children between the ages of about 20 months and 24 months – just after the 'vocabulary spurt' and just before the 'syntax spurt'. He examined upwards of 100,000 spontaneous utterances recorded by himself and his co-workers in order to assess the possibility that during these months children acknowledge lexical-thematic categories (e.g., noun, verb, agent, patent), while not acknowledging functional categories (see Abney, 1987, for this distinction). Functional categories comprise determiners, auxiliaries, complementisers and inflection phrases. He does indeed conclude that these are absent during this period. But he does not deny that children of this age 'know' basic phrase structure of the X' kind. For example, a child of 20 months might say *Bottle juice* (= 'bottle of juice'), suggesting to Radford that she is projecting N upwards into N' by adding a nominal complement to a noun. Moreover *Mummy blue dress* and *Daddy new car*, from children of 20 months and 24 months, respectively, can be seen to be a projecting of N' into NP by the addition of a preceding possessive specifier.

I will touch on Radford's claim that these children lack inflection phrases (IP). (See pp. 96–98 for discussion of these). Basing his analysis on Chomsky (1988), Radford points out that if IP verbs are finite then they must take modal auxiliaries, as in *I'm anxious you should do it*, but that if the verb is infinitive then it will attract the *to + Infin* form, as in *I'm anxious for you to do it*. In a nutshell, children of this age tend not to produce either auxilars or the *to + Infin* form, even when explicitly encouraged to do so in an elicited imitation task. See (67a–b).

    (67) a. Want Teddy drink (= to drink). (20 months)

        b. Jem want mummy take it out. (24 months)

        c. Adult: Mr. Miller will try.

        Child: Miller try.

        [*Mr* might be regarded as a determiner]

        d. Adult: I can see the cow.

        Child: See cow.

        [Note absence of determiner *the*]

(Needless to say, this spurs the question of how a Tomasello-style account will explain why children neglect to use these forms. One would have thought that *can/ + familiar verb, want to + action* would be rather handy idioms to have in one's growing inventory of symbolic units.)

Why do we see this pattern? Having rejected, for essentially Fodorian reasons (see pp. 17–18) the view that functional categories are simply 'harder to learn', Radford adopts a maturationalist position (1990, p. 275). The debate around why functional categories are acquired after lexical ones has tended to centre upon the question of whether the lacking of functional categories may indicate an initially unmarked parameter setting. The possibility that some languages, such as Japanese, can be said to lack determiners and complementisers renders this plausible. But there has been mounting evidence against the view that some adult languages completely lack certain functional categories in more recent years (Lust, 1994) – thus rendering maturationism a better option.

In more recent years Radford (1994, 1996) has been looking at the language of children between two and three years of age, and in particular at the period – usually called 'the optional infinitive stage' – during which they alternate between untensed (infinitive) and tensed verb forms in finite clauses. His explanation for this phenomenon is within the spirit of recent minimalist proposals (Chomsky, 1995), in which tense is carried by a head T constituent (see p. 155) which projects to a tense phrase (TP). (See the previous discussion of Radford's minimalist developmental proposals in 2.4.4.) This in turn, Radford argues, is absent, because children during this period have an underspecified agreement (AGR) constituent (see pp. 155–156) – underspecified with respect to complement-selection properties. One advantage of this proposal is that it also accounts for why children also have agreement problems with case, producing sentences such as *Me can have an apple* (28 months). (The point here, by the way, is not to discuss the technicalities of the proposal, but to touch on how one examines developmental change from within a generative analysis.)

But to bring ourselves fully up-to-date we need to consider the impact of the minimalist programme on the continuity versus discontinuity issue. One impact is essentially theory-internal while the other is quite radical, and will be familiar to readers. In the first place, Atkinson (1996, section 7) points out that merger theory might be seen as having the effect of relaxing the distinction between strong continuity and structure-building. Recall from Part 2 that merge operates on lexical items construed as sets of abstract features. But it can operate, Atkinson reminds us, on items containing only partial sets of features as well as on the complete sets that exist in the adult system. Structure-building then becomes the successive acquisition of features, but with continuity around the fact of merge. This does not, of course, solve any deep developmental problems but it does help to render some theory-internal dilemmas less urgent.

The more radical, minimalist-inspired proposal is, of course, Atkinson's dynamic minimalism. This position is indeed maturationist; though rather than taking syntactic maturation to be autonomous, it is seen to be spurred on by 'external' conceptual developments. It is maturationist, as it were, at second hand. Does if fall foul of Tomasello's point 1 ('plus external development')? Not so long as one is precise about which conceptual advances are supposed to fuel which syntactic ones – rather than making vague references to information-processing constraints putting breaks on syntactic development. And note that it is *conceptual* development/maturation that is at issue here, not mere processing capacity. In this context, we might recall the earlier reference to Langacker's idea that the conceptual distinction between types and instances may underlie the use of determiners. Dynamic minimalism would predict that the use of determiners would follow 'shortly' from the non-verbal manifestation of this distinction. The big question, of course, is whether the other functional categories whose early absence Radford notes could conceivably wait upon similar external conceptual categories and distinctions coming on stream.

The general moral of this short discussion of the continuity hypothesis is that seeing it as problematic is hardly the exclusive prerogative of the kind of approach favoured by Tomasello. One can be a generativist and an opponent of strong continuity. As we have seen, *Chomsky* is.

4.3.3(iv) Later development by analogy and structure mapping

Tomasello argues that his extreme scepticism about the existence of pre-syntactic assumptions in young children saves him from the kind of accusation that is usually ranged at 'tadpole-frog' theories of grammatical development, which is that they begin by describing children as making false generalisations that they later have to abandon. They are cul-de-sac theories. Thus, to paraphrase Chomsky (and see Gleitman and Wanner, 1982), why have your children begin with purely semantic generalisations (e.g., agent-action rather than noun-verb) only to have them unlearn these and make syntactic ones?

> The current theory avoids this problem by positing that in the beginning children make virtually no linguistic abstractions [i.e., not even semantic ones, JR] at all (beyond something like 'concrete nominal'), only later attempting to zero in on adult-like categories and schemas.

> (2000a, p. 242)

His account of how they achieve this zeroing in process is very simple. They make a series of analogies of a progressively higher level of abstraction, and they combine early simple schemas into more complex ones. The first process can be seen as happening in three stages.

1) They construct verb islands around individual verbs by analogising across uses of the verb.

2) They construct analogies between verb islands to produce 'something like simple transitive constructs' (ibid., p. 242).

3) Given a stock of 'first order' constructs (transitives 'and other 'similar' ones') they will – by a process of 'second-order structure mapping' (Gentner and Markman, 1997) construct higher-order analogies – such as subject-predicate.

With regard to the latter process, the child – it is the younger child who is usually exemplified – might combine schemas such as 'Daddy's + X', ' See + X' and 'X + car' to produce 'See Daddy's car'.

We have already seen this processes described – in somewhat older children – in the context of Diessel and Tomasello's work on complementising with epistemic verbs (e.g., *think* plus COMP). Commenting on this Tomasello (2000a, p. 245, emphasis added) says: 'In all, it seems that these early complex sentences are not abstract embeddings, as they are treated by generative theorists, but *they are pastiches of well-learned linguistic patterns.*'

Well, if this is not a phrase-book conception of syntactic development I don't know what is.

4.3.3(v) Imitating the input but making errors

I am addressing the second and third features of this present approach together because, despite their being seemingly contradictory, they touch upon something essential to the kind of pragmatist approach that eschews syntactic theory – at least as being explanatory in early speech. On the one hand, in so far as acquiring syntax is supposed to exemplify 'cultural' or 'imitative' learning more generally (Tomasello, 1999, chapter 5) the well-formedness of children's early productions will be seen to be no more than a product of their attending to input patterns and reproducing them without insight into the rules that went into their construction (in so far as such rules exist at all for the pragmatist). But on the other hand, the kind of errors children make will be seen to be a function either of the high frequency of certain forms in the input or will be caused by children's blind cutting-and-pasting (see immediately above) of imitated fragments – a case of 'groping' (Braine, 1976) just beyond the range of their imitative capacity. In the first case, for example, the high incidence of injunctions expressed with infinitive verb forms in the input ('Go to sleep') may encourage them to use infinitives as main verbs; in the second case, the child may cut and paste '*the* = object of attention' to the unanalysed unit '*my ball*' and produce *the my ball.*

That this kind of approach is favoured will come as no surprise to the reader. But what I wish to stress at the moment is the interesting theoretical tension between linguists who study syntax from a functionalist-pragmatist perspective and theorise about acquisition, such as Robert Van Valin, and language development researchers, such as Julian Pine, who are sceptical about the whole idea of applying adult syntactic theory to development and prefer to regard acquisition as a matter of learning from the input plus un-insightful groping. In other words, this is a tension between pragmatists with a somewhat rationalist temper and those with a somewhat empiricist one. The former will tend to argue that early successes and failures are not a function of relatively blind imitation, but of children's early attempts to construct a *grammar* for their language – albeit not a Chomskyan one.

Let us consider, in pursuance of the Van Valin–Pine debate, the following kind of error English-learning children frequently make. In asking *wh*-questions, they will undergo a period of correctly inserting the *wh*-word at the head of the sentence while failing to invert the order of the auxiliary and the verb, thereby producing utterances like *what he can do*? (See above discussion of aux-verb inversion in the context of the systematicity issue – pp. 411–413.) In an analysis of these errors made by

Adam in Brown's (1973) corpus, Rowland and Pine (2000) draw our attention to the interesting fact that, rather than progressing smoothly from no-auxiliary to uninverted form to inverted form, once Adam began to use auxiliaries he was correctly inverting more than not, later progressing to rather a high proportion of uninverted forms. They explain this pattern as being *a function of mother's speech to Adam*, and demonstrate that the *wh* + aux combinations in Adam's data (e.g., *What are you doing?*) were of significantly higher frequency in the input to the child than the combinations that Adam used erroneously (e.g., **What he can do?*; from, *verb* + *what he can do* in the mother, e.g. *see what he can do*). The *wh* + aux combinations the child used were more frequent in the mother's input than those he failed to use ($p < 0.05$). They argued that 'children will only produce the correct, inverted *wh*-question when they have been able to learn the relevant *wh* + aux combination necessary to produce the question from the input' (Rowland and Pine, 2000, p. 177). Un-inversion errors, meanwhile, are caused by the kind of 'groping' just described: when the child has not learned the particular *wh*-word + auxiliary marker (e.g., *why don't, what can*) around which to base the question they simply cut and paste *wh* + a declarative fragment.

Van Valin (2002), however, objects to the idea that children are not using any kind of rule, and seeks to explain the developmental pattern by appeal to the principles of role and reference grammar (RRG). He claims that the errors children make can be analysed in terms of their failing to detect how IF (illocutionary force: declarative versus interrogative in this case) has to be signalled *by a tense-bearing morpheme* in English. In terms of the taxonomy of RRG, they have yet to learn that in declarative sentences tense appears 'core internally' (i.e., after the subject) but that it appears 'core initially' (i.e., before the subject) in interrogatives. (Note here the assumption that the young child is indeed learning something about syntactic regularity!) He or she also has to learn the presumably easier (because less 'structure dependent') principle that *wh*-words appear in the 'pre-core slot'. Van Valin argues that they learn the latter before they learn that auxiliaries carry tense – and thus the core-internal/core initial ordering rule in relation to IF.

Next, Van Valin points out that some auxiliaries clearly carry tense while others do not: *is, does, did, have* and *had* clearly do while modals like *can, should, may* and *might* are not so obviously tensed. In addition, if children are indeed following Slobin's (1979) 'operating principle A' of attending to the ends of words then they should have difficulty tensing auxiliaries with negative clitics (*can't, don't,* and the like), despite their bearing tense inherently. This then leads to the following prediction. If learning the signalling of IF by the relative position of auxiliary and verb requires knowledge of how tense-marked morphemes are positioned relative to verbs in the core *then young children will perform better with those auxiliaries that are more clearly marked for tense*. Accordingly, in *wh*-questions, children should be seen to initially place only those auxiliaries that are explicitly tensed in the core-initial position. Van Valin claims that Adam's data do indeed show this, and that therefore adult-grammar-driven analyses do a better job than do statistical, input-driven analyses.

In their reply to Van Valin, Rowland and Pine (2003, p. 201) accept, in fact, that 'Van Valin's theory seems to fit the summary data presented in R&P better than the input account'. However as a principled account of the Adam's developmental trajectory the RRG account is flawed, they say, because of 'a number of parameters that are added to the basic premise of the theory' (the 'premise' being that children must spot the link between IF and inversion). What troubles the Van Valin account, they argue, is that Adam should really be advancing quite discontinuously from using un-inverted to using inverted forms, when in fact the development is mixed and gradual. The following are the three 'parameters' which Rowland and Pine think will have to be imported: (1) the existence of early correct performance suggests that inversion as a cue to IF is known but is treated as being redundant and unnecessary; (2) 'the RRG account has to posit that inversion will come in only gradually, starting with auxiliaries that can easily be identified as tensed'; (3) it has to explain the relatively late inversion of *why*-questions. From where I sit, these problems look less than devastating; indeed (2) is *constitutive* of Van Valin's original account rather than an additional parameter. But this is not the kind issue upon which it is necessary to adjudicate.

Before further consideration of the work on Pine's group, it would be useful to pause to examine how more rationalist approaches tackle what Rowland and Pine call parameters (1) and (3) – optionality and *wh*-word specificity in development (e.g., the late development of correctly formed *why*-questions). This will enable us to place the intra-pragmatism debate, which we have just touched upon, in relation to more Chomskyan views. The nativist Virginia Valian and her colleagues (Valian, Lasser and Mandelbaum, 1992) present a movement-based analysis of these errors, which predicts just the kind of lexical specificity (inversion earlier with certain *wh*-words) of which Rowland and Pine make so much. Valian *et al.* argue that the young child has every reason to believe that inversion *is* optional in English rather than mostly obligatory. Here are two of Valian *et al.*'s reasons why. First in some languages (notably, Romance languages like French) there is optional inversion in main verb object questions (e.g., *Who did you see?/Who you did see?*); and if so then optionality of this form is a possible parameter which the young child's LAD initially considers. Second, the input to the child provides examples of un-inversion, such as subject *who*-questions (e.g., in *Who has left it here?* 'who' is in the subject slot) and in *how come* questions (e.g., *How come John has left this here?*). So what the child must learn, on Valian *et al.*'s analysis, is that particular *wh*-words have their own inversion properties – e.g., that inversion is obligatory with object *wh*-words (e.g., *What did John leave?*). See Rowland and Pine (2000, pp. 161–162) for some difficulties with this proposal.

Valian *et al.*'s first analysis captures a very distinctive feature of the rationalist approach, namely the premise that where we find errors in children's syntax these will frequently be caused by parameters being incompletely set. Given this, errors should *carry echoes of other human languages*. Some interesting examples of this have recently emerged from the laboratory of Stephen Crain and Rosalind Thornton (Crain and Thornton, unpublished data, Department of Linguistics, University of Maryland). In addition to showing, in a laboratory context, that English-learning children of about two years of age will tend to produce un-inverted forms of *why*-questions at a time when they do not do this for *how*-questions and others, (echoing the optionality found in Romance languages), they also show that children of this age produce German-like and Swedish-like errors. In the first place, as noted before in 2.5.1, they produce a so-called 'medial-wh' (de Villiers *et al.*, 1990), producing questions of the form *What do you think what she said?* In miminalist terms, the *wh*-trace is 'spelt out' in German where it is not in English. (For example, *Wen glaubst du wen sie getroffen hat?* = 'who think you who she met has?') In order to encourage children to produce questions of an 'epistemic verb + COMP' form, young children were shown a blindfolded teddy bear who sat by while some objects were put into boxes and some dolls were produced, and were told to ask the teddy what he thought was in front of him. One child asked the following three questions in a single session: *What do you think what is in that box?; What do you think what is in this box; Who do you think who this is?* And this needs to be set beside the fact that the forms of *wh*-word repetition *not* found in human language also seem to be *absent* from child language. For example, no languages, to our knowledge, allow questions of the form *Who do you want who to help you?*; and this was also a form that the Maryland team failed to observe in young children. In a laboratory setting, they found that children avoided this kind of question, saying instead things like *Who do you want … to get toothpaste out of your ear? Who do you want to brush your hair?* So it is not just a matter, then, of younger children being relaxed 'across-the-board' about repeating *wh*-words.

Now for an example of 'Swedish' errors, from Crain and Thornton. The domain this time is that of negation. In English, the present tense agreement morpheme [-*s*] is attached to the verb in affirmative sentences (e.g. *It fits*). But when the word *not* is inserted it attaches to the auxiliary *do* thus: *It does not fit*. In Swedish negation, however, the agreement morpheme [-*r*] affixes to the *verb* when the word *not* (*inte*) is introduced. See (68). In the laboratory set-up, children were encouraged to comment on Kermit's successes and failures as he tried to fit pieces onto a shape board. One child of 23 months, for example, said after witnessing one of Kermit's failures *It not goes there* – a kind of Swedish. However, just shortly after this she also said *That one doesn't go there.* Presumably, this was because the reduced form *-n't*] forces the insertion of *do*, as [*-n't*] cannot stand alone. (In passing, it is difficult to see how utterances like *It not goes there* could have occurred by virtue of 'cutting and pasting' from imitated fragments.)

(68) a. … om hon ha-*r* sett honom.

　　　whether she has seen him.

　　b. … om hon inte ha-*r* sett honom.

　　　whether she not has seen him.

Pine and his colleagues also direct their scepticism towards the claim that the high incidence of correct forms in early multi-word speech entails the presence of syntactic categories. For we have to ask whether these forms are anything more than rote-learned units and whether they are generated by anything more than by Braine's (1976) *limited scope formulae* (LSF). If they *are* more that this then these usages should be *productive*. To explain what this means, let us take the case of determiners such as *my, the, a, that* and so forth. The fact that a child attaches these words to a range of nouns and adjective + noun pairs might encourage us to think that they have done more than pick up useful little packages like 'my ball' 'the pussy' and so forth.

But Braine's notion of LSF allows for the fact that a range of different formulae will encode a range of meanings in the following way (where X could equal a noun or adjective + noun unit): that's a + X; in the + X; want my + X). If this analysis works just a well as a syntactic one then, as Pine puts it, 'the basis of current support for the syntactic position should be seen as conceptual rather than empirical' (Pine and Martindale, 1996, p. 376). (Of course one 'conceptual' consideration in favour of it might be the explanatory need for something more than, what I called above, parsimonious description.)

In an analysis of determiner use in seven children between 1y 11m and 2y 6m Pine and Martindale (1996) find reason to take issue with Valian's (1986) nativist conclusions drawn from her study of six syntactic categories (determiner, adjective, noun, noun phrase, preposition, prepospitional phrase) in the speech of six children of a similar age. Valian concluded that the children were operating with the determiner category essentially on the basis of the fact that they fulfilled the following criteria for correct usage: (1) inserting determiners in the correct order before nouns and adjective + noun pairs); (2) not producing free-standing determiners; (3) not producing more than two in sequence erroneously such as *kick the my ball, *that's a her car. In addition to taking issue with Valian's criteria for being an error, Pine and Martindale point out that it is necessary to take account of contexts in which instances of a category should occur *but do not*. Without this, we cannot assess the degree to which use of determiners was genuinely productive rather than being the product of LSFs. What needs to be recorded in this case is the degree of *overlap* in the use of particular determiners. That is to say, if a child knows that *a* and *the* are both determiners, then having control of one should bring in train the control of the other: their contexts of use should overlap. But if there is little overlap then we have every reason to assume that each determiner was supported by a specific linguistic armature; they are 'defined in terms of their position within the particular formulae of which they form a part' (ibid., p. 376).

Pine and Martindale's measure of overlap was confined to the definite and the indefinite articles, as these were the determiners which Valian had reported to be the most frequently occurring. Their measure of overlap was the following. They calculated the number of linguistic contexts (nouns or predicates[17]) in the pooled data for all the sample used with both definite and indefinite articles. With regard to article overlap with nouns, they computed the number of nouns that were used with both articles for each child as a proportion of the number of nouns from this pooled sample vocabulary that appeared in the child's individual corpus. Or:

> n. of individual child's noun use with both *a* and *the*
> --
> n. of nouns in child's vocabulary that also occurred in the vocabulary of the
> pooled sample with both *a* and *the*

---

[17] Verbs, prepositions and structures like *It's*.

(This is an ingenious measure, because defining the denominator in this way ensures that it consists only of nouns that do generally afford pairing with both kinds of article in children of this age.)

A similar analysis was also undertaken of the maternal[18] speech to the children, and samples were taken at two periods – 'Time 1' and 'Time 2' – for both the children and the adults. There was quite wide variability in the proportion of both noun and predicate overlap among the children. For noun overlap at Time 1, for example, the range was between 0 per cent (0/15) – this was the youngest child in the sample (1y 11m) – and 19 per cent (4/21), with a mean of 11.8 and 21 per cent at Times 1 and 2 respectively. As one would expect, the overlap percentages were significantly lower in the children than in the adults. But it has to be said that, in absolute terms, the differences were not overwhelming: the noun overlap proportion at Time 1 in the adults was 29.9 per cent – not a million miles from the 21 per cent at Time 2 in the children.

In addition, Pine and Martindale report that the children produced a number of utterances that, on Valian's criteria, would be judged to be correct, but which certainly did not seem very grammatical: *There's a blue*; *I think that's a funny*; *There's a don't know* (said twice).

The authors' discussion is judicious and circumspect, but they do suggest that 'at face value' at least these data

> seem to suggest that, in the early stages, children's knowledge about the behaviour of determiners is specific to the predicate frames in which they appear, and that the acquisition of a general syntactic determiner category may be a gradual process involving the progressive broadening of the range of predicate contexts in which different determiners appear.

> (ibid., p. 392)

The theme of gradation is taken up and amplified somewhat in a later paper by Pine and Lieven (1997). In this study the overlap criterion was different, being:

n. of noun types with which child used both *a* and *the*

----

n. of noun types with which child used either *a* or *the* in his/her 400-word sample

The study had a similar message to that of Pine and Martindale, concluding that (1) early determiner use can be explained as a combination of rote knowledge and knowing how particular determiners behave in lexically specific contexts, and, more theoretically (2) that 'the nativist's real motivation for attributing syntactic categories to young children is theoretical rather than empirical' (Pine and Lieven, 1997, p. 137), where 'theoretical' = 'with a commitment to the continuity assumption'.

It will, perhaps, be evident that there is, within this approach, potential for scepticism about early linguistic knowledge which goes deeper than that to be found in Tomasello's verb-island hypothesis (VIH). This potential is realised in a recent paper

---

[18] In two cases it was the speech of the investigator.

by Pine, Lieven and Rowland (1998). In this, the authors' analysis of early multi-word speech is not only in radical opposition to Valian's (1991) strong-continuity analysis (i.e., Valian's contra Radford's, 1990; see above), but it makes itself distinct from verb-island analyses. Two problems are raised for VIH, by these authors. One is that the only theoretical motivation for assuming the centrality of verb-frames to meaning and grammar, as Tomasello implicitly does, is that this carries the assumption that the noun-verb distinction captures the argument predicate distinction at the cognitive-semantic level (objects versus actions). But, argue Pine *et al.,* the lack of correlation between the verb-noun distinction and the object-action distinction in early speech (Maratsos, 1990) threatens this assumption. (This is, in fact, part and parcel of Pine's scepticism about attempts by both constructivists' and by nativists to ground early grammatical development in semantic categories.) The second difficulty raised for VIH is that we know little about whether island-like phenomena exist in structures other than verb frames, and that, given the first problem, it is essential that we look for them. Their paper fills this gap in our knowledge.

In their analysis of the speech of a sample of twelve children between the second half of the second year and the first half of the third year, Pine *et al.* show that while there was much evidence of the appropriate use of the following structures this usage was so *lexically specific* that one would naturally describe it as island-like: verb morphology (-ing; -ed; -s), auxiliary verb structures, pronoun case marking, and the use of SVO order. In each case an overlap quotient was calculated in a similar way to that described above. In the case of verb morphology, for example, two quotients were worked out: (1) the proportion of verb types marked with a particular morpheme that also occurred in the unmarked form, and (2) for each combination of markers (e.g., -ing and -ed) the proportion of verbs occurring with both as a proportion of those that occurred with either. This showed that category-general marking was rare, with there being little overlap between the verbs with which different morphemic markers were used. A majority of the children did, however, meet a productivity criterion for the progressive morpheme, while a minority met this for the regular past tense and the third-person singular morpheme.

However, when a similar analysis was performed for the frequently-occurring auxiliary forms *can, do, be,* and *have* none of the children met the productivity criterion of a score significantly greater than zero, although one child fell only marginally short. Children often seemed to be using Braineian 'formulae' such as *Can't + X* and *Don't + X*. Finally, a similar story can be told about use of the SVO form. While there was a very high number of constructions with SVO and fragments thereof, there was also a high degree of clustering around a small number of common lexical patterns, with the five most common of them, in each child's data, accounting for between 67 per cent and 90 per cent of all SV constructions – *Mummy + X; I + X; X is,* and so forth. The question of the degree to which children showed *contrastive* use of the SVO form was addressed by noting the number of different noun and pronoun types that occurred as subjects and objects of transitive verbs and then calculating the overlap score per child in terms of the proportion of transitive subject and object argument types that occurred as both subjects and objects of transitive verbs. Only three of the 12 children showed overlap scores of significantly greater than zero.

Pine *et al.* conclude that this lack of overlap in the verbs to which morphological markers were applied and with which different auxiliaries were used and in the words which served as subjects and direct objects of transitive verbs, not to mention (indeed I did not mention) the disproportionate use of the first-person singular pronoun 'I', tells us that lexical specificity in early language goes well beyond the verb frames of the VIH. 'Children's early language,' they say, 'is not organised around lexically specific verb structures, but around other high-frequency markers such as bound morphemes, auxiliary verbs, and case-marked pronouns' (Pine *et al.*, 1998, p. 895). They also stress the need to explain why some markers function as islands and others do not.

Having identified this developmental *archipelago*, Pine also advances beyond Tomasello's position on learning mechanisms, by calling for an information-processing account which explains these kinds of findings in terms of the interaction between the statistical properties of the input and the 'shape', as he calls it, of the child's language learning mechanism. In fact, he contributes to this himself in a series of collaborative papers (Gobet and Pine, 1997; Jones, Gobet and Pine, 2000; Freudenthal, Pine and Gobet, 2002a and 2000b).

The computational model used by these authors is a member of a general class of models called EPAM (elementary perceiver and memoriser). These were originally employed by H. A. Simon, E. A. Feigenbaum and others (see Feigenbaum and Simon, 1984) to model verbal learning data and related phenomena. Despite the fact that it is couched in terms of nodes and links, this class of models is not connectionist in nature, in so far as the nodal representations (called 'images') carry a symbolic form of information about features of the input. The representations are not 'in' the connections but 'in' the nodes. Two forms of learning are involved: *familiarisation* or *image-building* and *discrimination* (in which new branches are added to the nodes). These come into play whenever there is a mismatch between the contents of the input and of the network. Where Simon and others have used EPAMs to model access to long-term memory, Gobet and his colleagues have been attempting to model the creation of semantic memory and syntactic development in terms of images and links.

In Gobet and Pine (1997) and in Jones, Gobet and Pine (2000) the authors demonstrate the utility of EPAM and the EPAM-derivative MOSAIC (model of syntax acquisition in children) by feeding real maternal input into the performance-limited distributional learning mechanism and generating child-like utterances as output. The results enable them to claim that they are not only reproducing verb-island and other island-like phenomena but that they are contributing to an explanation of why some lexical items come to function as islands.

I now sketch how this works; see Figure 4.21. At the outset, there is only an 'empty' net containing no images and with a *root* node at the input which itself remains empty throughout all subsequent inputs. With the first word or word-sequence (and with every subsequent utterance) the network runs a 'test' to determine whether anything on the network matches the input. As nothing will match it at the outset, the twin processes of discrimination and familiarisation will result in new links, nodes and node contents (images) being constructed. Subsequently of

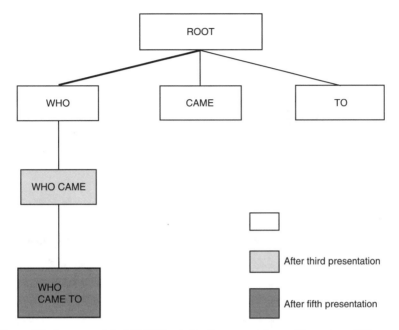

Figure 4.21 Structure of the MOSAIC net after five presentations of the sentence 'Who came to see you on the train'. Reproduced from Jones, G., Gobet, F. and Pine, J. M. (2000) A process model of children's early verb use. In L. R.. Gleitman and A. K. Joshu (eds) *Proceedings of the 22nd Annual Meeting of the Cognitive Science Society,* pp. 723–728. Lawrence Erlbaum, Mahwah, NJ, with permission of the publisher.

course, some of the inputs will result in matches to individual words or word sequences, but each time there is a mismatch to a sequence a new link and node will be created to represent the sequence 'below' the one with which it shares elements. The amount of information stored at the nodes increases then, as the distance from the root node increases, as each node contains the accumulated contents of all nodes traversed down to that point. Broadly, a sequence of words in an image within a single node will contain the same number of words as there are nodal layers between it and the root node. This is, then, a model of rote learning in which the complexity of an utterance is represented in terms of its distance from the input. But crucially, in addition to this *vertical* process there is also the *lateral* process of *contextual linking*. In this, lateral links are forged between words that are seen to be used in the same way, in the sense of sharing contents vertically linked beneath them; see Figure 4.22. In the clearest kind of case, there might be similar predicates shared by two arguments. Thus the arguments *cat* and *dog* will tend to share predicates like *sit, walk* and *chase*. The more the *overlap* then, the higher the chance there will be of a lateral link being forged.

Armed with these rote (vertical) and contextual (lateral) links between contents, the network is able to generate utterances based on the rote-learned and contextual associations thus formed. All that happens, essentially, is that the lateral links now become construed as *generative* links. To take Jones *et al*'s (2000) example, a network

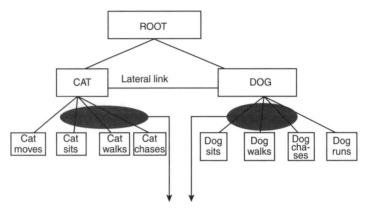

Contextual overlap which leads to lateral link formation

Figure 4.22 An example of how lateral links are created in MOSAIC. Reproduced from Jones, G., Gobet, F. and Pine, J. M. (2000) A process model of children's early verb use. In L. R.. Gleitman and A. K. Joshu (eds) *Proceedings of the 22nd Annual Meeting of the Cognitive Science Society*, pp. 723–728. Lawrence Erlbaum, Mahwah, NJ, with permission of the publisher.

which has heard about cats sitting, walking and chasing will be able to generate the novel utterance *cat runs* by virtue of its sharing these three predicates with *dog* and because it has heard *dog runs* (see Figure 4.22). Conversely, if it had also heard about cats moving it might also produce the novel utterance *dog moves*. (One might say that the reason the root node remains content-less is that it not only has to function as the input gateway but also has to function, in output, as the route from the conceptual-intentional systems that kick-start speech.) In practice, the degree of overlap being permitted before a lateral link is made is a parameter set by the programmer. If the minimum number of shared links is too low then an unacceptably large incidence of grammatical errors will result. For example in Gobet and Pine (1997, p. 5) a low setting of this parameter resulted in the outputs **I wrong* and **I road*.

Jones *et al.* (2000) tested MOSAIC on 33,390 utterance tokens from the mother of a child called Anne, setting the lateral overlap parameter at 15. They found that MOSAIC's utterances matched those of Anne more closely than they matched those of Anne's mother. Also, as one would expect, there was evidence of 'island' phenomena in the model's output. The authors defined an island as a lexical term acting as a 'frame' for at least ten different 'slot fillers'. There was a high number of verb islands, thus defined, but very few common-noun islands. There were also pronoun islands and proper-noun islands. This is certainly an intriguing outcome, but three caveats need to be entered: (1) These islands also existed in Anne's mother's input; (2) The notion of a verb island, as used here (as a landmark around which words cluster), is at variance with the original usage by Tomasello (1992) where it meant a verb whose mastered argument structure is not extended to grammatically similar words (e.g., *draw* to *cut*); (3) The reason for the scarcity of common-noun islands relative to verb islands *may* lie in the fact that the sequence verb + common noun was twice as common in the input than common-noun + verb (5.66 per cent versus 10.42 per cent), whereas this was not true of the pronoun/verb and the proper-noun/verb relationship. Given the architecture of MOSAIC, this would mean that there were more common nouns clustering in nodes beneath verbs than vice versa, and consequently more chance of these reaching the threshold for overlap with another verb's associated words.

In defence of MOSAIC, however, it can be noted that it also mimics certain kinds of frequently-observed production errors, such as the appearance of optional infinites (Freudenthal, Pine and Gobet, 2002a; on Dutch) and subject omission in English (Freudenthal, Pine and Gobet, 2002b). With regard to the latter, this mimicry is a simple consequence of the fact that utterance-final phrases have a high likelihood of being encoded in this model because they contain end-markers. MOSAIC can output partial utterances provided that the utterance-final element has occurred in a sentence-final position in the input. This explanation of subject omission is argued to be preferable to two competing nativist alternatives: (1) that the child's parameter-setter 'thinks' that a Romance language, in which subject omission is acceptable, may be the target (Hyams, 1986), and (2) the child knows that subjects are required, but performance limitations sometimes prevent them from being produced (Valian, 1991).

Let us, for the moment, accept that MOSAIC is modelling the fact that early speech is grounded in an essentially phrase-book-learning process in which frequently occurring strings are rote-learned and in which the generation of modestly novel utterances takes place through parallels being drawn between landmark lexical items in virtue of the overlap between the sets of items with which they co-occur, thus enabling old landmarks to be paired, in production, with new asssociates. (We have all done something similar in foreign restaurants, supposing that we are finally 'getting to grips' with the language.) Well and good, but then – this is a by-now familiar point – the theorist must then confront the following alternative: (1) adult linguistic competence is no more than this process writ large (i.e., with deeper nodal levels of rote learning and with more landmark items and more overlapping); or (2) something happens in development to transform the phrase-book learner into a competent speaker-hearer who has some recursively applicable but finite apparatus – an abstract tool kit – for expressing any well-formed thought in speech and for transposing any well-formed sentence into a thought and doing both without limit. In the first case, the theorist would be throwing *all* linguistics out of the window, simply ceasing to find relevant to his/her enterprise attempts to describe the target of acquisition and to explain how a system of this character is acquirable. Not only would generative linguistics be thus jettisoned but also that of Van Valin, Langacker, and many others within the functionalist camp. In the second place, the theorist is faced with a blank: the learning model designed to produce limited outputs guided by a theory *whose solitary goal is parsimonious description* lacks the resources for bootstrapping itself onto a higher explanatory level.

However a pragmatist does not have to abandon his or her rejection of syntactic nativism in order to take this second course, because it is always possible to look to the *cognitive-intentional* systems for an explanation for this transition – to argue, that is, that systematicity/compositionality/productivity is rooted entirely in cognitive-semantic competence and that MOSAIC-like learning processes are somehow able to interface with this. This is, in fact, a route that is explicitly rejected by Pine (e.g. Pine, Lieven and Rowland, 1998) who repudiates the idea that syntactic categories are semantically grounded, given that semantic and syntactic categories are found to diverge so clearly in early language (e.g., Maratsos, 1990).

In the next section, we examine attempts to embrace this second alternative. But before I get to this, I want to touch on how proposals of the kind covered in this section have been received within the developmental community.

4.3.3(vi) Some contemporary reactions to the Tomasello–Pine research programme

I will mention two recent critical papers here – one by Cynthia Fisher (2002) and the other by Letitia Naigles (2002). Michael Tomasello has replied to both: Tomasello and Abbot-Smith (2002) to Fisher and Tomasello and Akhtar (2003) to Naigles. My aim is not to give a blow-by-blow, point-by-point, study-by-study dispatch from the front, but rather to highlight some themes on which we have already touched in one way or another. At the end of the subsection, I will also discuss a cross-linguistic study which is naturally linked to the Naigles paper, and which seems to put pressure on the Tomasello–Pine position.

Fisher questions three of Tomasello's assumptions:

1) That if children have more-or-less adequate knowledge of the verb category, they should use new words in unattested constructions when prompted so to do. For example, they should use novel verbs transitively to which they have only been exposed in an intransitive context.

2) That it is lack of syntactic competence, and lack of this alone, that limits generalisation of novel verbs to novel forms.

3) That when young children hear a novel verb presented to them in what the experimenters assume to be a certain context of action (e.g., causally, for a transitive) then they too will interpret it in this way.

With regard to point 1, Fischer argues that because there are a number of English verbs that do not alternate transitive/intransitive (e.g., *fall, cry*[19]), and because children may well be aware of this, then they may simply be being appropriately conservative. I might add that this is indeed what we would expert from Berwick's subset principle; and indeed we would expect it too from the behaviour of Chang's (2002) connectionist production model.

Tomasello and Abbot-Smith's (2002, pp. 208–209) reply is illuminating. They say, in effect, that once the critic concedes that children have to learn which verbs alternate and which do not, then the game is up: the point has thereby been conceded that children must learn about verbs individually. In other words, the nativist is simply not allowed to countenance *any* language-specific learning, on pain of eroding her own position. Are there nativists of this kind? They field a quotation from Andrew

---

[19] Though sometimes they are either not aware of this or they decide not to be conservative: from Mellisa Bowerman's (1982) daughter, *You cried me* and *you falled it.*

Radford in which he, quite unexceptionally, says – and recall that Radford is a *discontinuity* ('structure building') not a continuity theorist – that children's parsing of a command as 'V + NP' will help them to 'infer' that verbs tend to precede their complements in English. They insist, following Mazuka (1996, p. 317), that one cannot believe both that development is by parameter-setting and that there is some lexically-specific learning. This is a version of Tomasello's point 3 (from 4.3.3 (iii)).

Well, is it not possible to believe (a) that children entering their second year know what the category verb consists in but that (b) they still have to learn about how individual verbs behave and (c) they are cautious producers in novel contexts?

I will also mention an issue raised by Fisher that bears variously on all three points. It is, to put it in my own terms, that the Tomasello–Pine (though more Pine than Tomasello) emphasis on the role of the input can be turned on its head in favour of the nativist critic. Recall, in this context, the studies by Pine's group showing that the maternal input to the child was sometimes found to itself have an archipelago-like character. Recall, in particular, the mother of the child Anne in Jones *et al.*, (2000) MOSAIC study, and Pine and Martindale's finding that the noun overlap (for *a* and *the*) proportion in the adults of 29.9 per cent at Time 1 was not strongly divergent from that of the children, at the 21 per cent at Time 2). Given this, the child's island-like output may be no more than a function of the island-like input; in which case it can hardly be used as evidence for lack of adult-like competence in the child.

Fisher mentions two relevant studies here. First, Naigles and Hoff-Ginsberg (1995) showed that verb use in mothers' speech to 2-year-olds bears a strong similarity to the speech of Tomasello's Travis at that age. As she puts it (ibid., p. 264) 'verbs in adult grammar differ in their syntactic privileges, each verb has a life of its own in adult usage as well'.

Second, with particular relevance to her point 3, it may well be the case that the structure of the information fixing the meaning of a verb is inherently more difficult to extract from a context of utterance than that defining the meaning of a noun. If so, it would explain, without any reference to lack of syntactic competence, why evidence for a systematic grasp of verb argument structure appears relatively late. After all, verbs can be seen to have a degree of inherent referential ambiguity (e.g., exhange? or giving? or getting?; knocking over? or falling?) that nouns lack. This difficulty is eloquently demonstrated in a study by Gillette, Gleitman, Gleitman, and Lederer (1999) on *adults'* ability to guess what mothers said while talking to their toddlers. Adult subjects were shown video clips of mother-child dyads, hearing only a bleep when the mother spoke the target word. They correctly guessed the meaning of 45 per cent of the nouns, but of only 15 per cent of the verbs. Indeed, 8 of the 24 verbs were *never* guessed correctly. The moral would seem to be then that children's lack of productivity could have been due to difficulties in extracting the meaning of the verb in the first place. Tomasello and Abbot-Smith (ibid., p. 210) quite reasonably respond to this that the studies did include control conditions in which children of the same age as the experimental children were seen to correctly generalise a novel transitive verb to a novel transitive context. So they must have been extracting something of the meaning in this case. But of course one is entitled to wonder whether their grasp of the meaning was sufficiently strong to encourage creative extension to a new syntactic context.

I turn now to Naigles' (2002) paper. Naigles says that we are confronted with the 'paradox' that infants seem to be better at coding syntactic form than do toddlers – and even young pre-school children. In support of this, she pits five studies of the kind we looked at in 3.3.3 on 'the algebraic infant debate' against five studies from Tomasello's group of the kind just discussed. In the former case, she mentions Saffran *et al.* (1996), Marcus *et al.* (1999), Gómez and Gerken (1999) and two others. In one of these additional ones, Shady (1996) showed that infants of 12–16 months preferred to listen to synthesised speech that followed English word order (e.g., *The kitten was hiding*) than speech which did not (**Was kitten the hiding*). In the other, Santelmann and Jusczyk (1998) showed that 15–18 month olds preferred to listen to passages in which the 'be + progressive aspect' rule was being 'followed': e.g., *She is running* versus **She can running*.

Naigles seeks to 'resolve the paradox' by saying that what challenges language-learning children is not pure syntactic form, but syntactic form when this has to be recruited to express a meaning. 'My conjecture,' she writes, 'is that the absence of any context of meaning in the infant studies provided the infants with the opportunity to display their knowledge of form without the added burden of meaning' (Naigles, 2002, p. 176).

The rest of the paper Naigles raises questions about whether the Tomasello and Pine data represent false negatives. In this case, there is a flurry of sceptical points being fielded – about, for example, Pine's sampling (p. 172), as well as worries similar to those voiced in Fisher's third point about the difficulty of extracting verb meaning from a context in the first place. She also makes some points about the relative ease of 'comprehension' versus production, to one of which I will shortly return.

Is there a paradox? As Tomasello and Akhtar (2003) rightly say, no there isn't. On the one hand, we have two studies of the extraction of statistical structure from artificial stimuli, two on the extraction of statistical structure from English, and one on the putatively algebraic capacities of infants with regard to non-linguistic stimuli. While these abilities will surely be recruited in the service of language learning, they are not, in themselves, capacities of a linguistic kind – as I argued in Part 3. As empirical support for this view Tomasello and Akhtar mention the fact, also touched on in 3.3.3, that tamarin monkeys perform similarly to Marcus *et al.*'s infants (Hauser *et al.*, 2002), and that Kirkham, Slemmer and Johnson (in press) have shown that infants demonstrate similar abilities to Saffran *et al.*'s (1996) children when sequentially presented *visual* stimuli, such as coloured lights turning on and off, are used. And one is also entitled to wonder whether it is justifiable to refer to the perception of canonical word order (in the Shady study) when there is supposed to be no meaning being processed: if there is no meaning then these are no linguistic stimuli at all.

Viewed in this light then, the infancy studies demonstrate the presence of processing capacities on which the evolution of human language seems to have capitalised, in much the same way in which the capacity for the categorical perception of auditory stimuli that we share with lower animals (Kuhl, 1981) is recruited by human languages. A defining character of syntax is that it serves the expression of meaning, so 'syntax without meaning' is the *true* paradox-or rather oxymoron. There is then no paradox present, in the sense of 'presence of early linguistic competence followed by later lack of linguistic competence'.

That said, the Naigles paper does succeed in pointing us towards the arresting tension between the success revealed in studies that employ the preferential looking technique and the failure evident in those, like Tomasello's, that employ production-based techniques (although her placing the former within the over-broad category of 'comprehension' studies does somewhat blunt their edge). Naigles herself was one of the pioneers here. Recall (pp. 448–449) her demonstration (Naigles, 1990) of how children with a mean age of 25 months can employ clues from the syntactic structure of the sentence in which a novel verb was presented to identify its meaning – 'gorp' = push someone's head down, or stick an arm out. Using a similar technique, Hirsh-Pasek, Golinkoff and Naigles (1996) claim to have demonstrated 17-month-olds' comprehension of canonical English word order. Children also saw two video clips side by side and heard one of two sentences: *Big Bird is tickling Cookie Monster* or *Cookie Monster is tickling Big Bird*. They looked longer at the clip that matched the sentence, even if they were not producing such word combinations in their speech. This result by itself, however, does not tell us that children as young as this could control SVO, because it is possible that they had acquired the Brainean LSF 'agent + *tickle*' and/or '*tickle* + patient' (either would be sufficient). Fisher (2000) tried to answer this point in a later study, by using invented verbs and actions; although her inclusion of additional prepositional phrases, as in *The duck is gorping the bunny up and down,* does inspire the sceptical response that the children merely had to interpret *bunny up and down* correctly to prefer the correct picture, without needing to extract any SVO information (Tomasello and Abbot-Smith, 2002, p. 211). What Tomasello and Akhtar (2003, p. 321) say here is well taken:

> … we simply point out that the most straightforward use of this methodology to test the questions being asked … has never been done. That is, no one has ever simply presented children with the sentence 'Ernie is gorping Bert' and two videos in one of which Ernie is doing something to Bert and in the other of which Bert is doing something to Ernie. This would be a direct test of English-speaking children's understanding of the transitive construction, including its characteristic ordering of agent and patient.

But while we wait for this direct test to be run we can reflect upon, and consider a recent empirical assessment of, the deep theoretical chasm over which the preferential-looking versus productive-extension debate is perched. It is more than a debate about the right methodology to use. There is a clear, symmetrical conflict between workers like Tomasello and Pine, who view syntactic knowledge as emerging gradually from item-based learning and those – most notably Lila Gleitman – who hold the opposite view, sympathetic to nativism, that children recruit syntactic knowledge in the service of learning the meanings of individual items – most notably verbs. As I mentioned before, the second is the position that Naigels (1990) took her data to be endorsing – what has become known as the *syntactic bootstrapping hypothesis* (Landau and Gleitman, 1985).

On the syntactic bootstrapping hypothesis, there are universal properties of the mapping between syntax and lexical semantics; and so, for the nativist, the child will know innately about how different kinds of verbs project into syntax, and conversely what syntax implies about the nature of the event the verb is encoding. For example, the child will naturally assume that if the lexical representation of a verb is '+ causative' (e.g., *push* versus *sleep*) then it will project into syntax as a transitive; while, 'reading backwards', she will use transitivity as a primary indicator of causativity. On the emergentist, item-by-item position, by contrast, the child learns about whether or not a verb takes one or two arguments on a verb-by-verb basis, with no prior assumptions being made about the linkages between causal events and transitive syntax.

Now whether or not the nativist element in syntactic bootstrapping is well motivated, there is a substantial amount of evidence, in addition to Naigles (1990), that toddlers are able to draw inferences about verb meaning on the basis of the structures in which they appear (e.g., Fisher, 1996; Fisher *et al.*, 1994; Gleitman, 1990; Landau and Gleitman, 1985; Naigles, Gleitman and Gleitman, 1993; Naigles and Kako, 1993). Moreover, we know that before children are able to control the '*make* X verb' construction, which turns non-causatives into causatives (e.g., *make me cry*) they sometimes erroneously employ the transitive frame to render a verb causative, as in *Daddy giggled me* (see footnote 19).

Naigles (Naigles, Fowler and Helm, 1992; Naigles *et al.*, 1993) has examined this phenomenon in the laboratory, by asking whether young children could be encouraged to interpret familiar non-causatives like *come* and *go* as causatives by having them act out double-argument sentences such as *Noah comes the elephant* and *The zebra goes the lion*. That is to say, will they take the first to mean *make come* and the second *make go*? They (mean age: 2y 9m) had little difficulty in interpreting these verbs transitively, suggesting that the causative-transitive linkage is a strong one for them This phenomenon has become known as *frame compliance*.

The question then becomes: Is this transitive-causative linkage something that children bring with them to language learning (Gleitman) or is it a generalisation children have built up by inductive distributional learning from the behaviour of particular verbs (Tomasello and Pine)? One way of answering this question is by looking at how children behave when learning a language in which transitive syntax is only a *weak* predictor of causative meaning, looking at whether they will *impose* a transitive-causative linkage. The Naigles act-out technique can be used to this end. This was done in a recent study by Lidz, Gleitman and Gleitman (2003).

Lidz *et al.* tested children learning a language called Kannada. This is a language spoken by some 40 million people in the south west of India; and crucially, it is a language in which the most reliable cue for causativity is not transitive syntax, but a *verbal affix*. (This might be compared to the English affix *–ise*, as in *magnetise*.) There are some inherently causative verbs in the language, but if the affix is used then causative meaning will be intended. Causative verb morphology is, therefore, a *sufficient but non-necessary* condition for causative meaning. The causative morpheme can be added to any verb.

There were three variables in the to-be-acted out sentences: one- versus two-argument frames (i.e., intransitive versus transitive); the inclusion of the causative morphology on the verb; the inherent transitivity (or 'valence') of the verb (e.g., *push* versus *hop*). The subjects in the first study were three years old. The syntactic bootstrapping, universalist position predicts that argument number ('two = causative') will be the principle determinant of causative acting out; while the emergentist, item-by-item approach predicts that verb morphology will determine causative acting out.

(69) *kudure hoDey-**is**-utt-ade.

   horse hit-CAUS-NPST-3SN.

   the horse hits.

   *kothi yeth-annu eer-utt-ade.

   monkey ox-ACC rise-NPST-3SN.

   'the monkey raises the ox'.

Examples of the stimuli are shown in (69). The causative morpheme is –*isu*, marked in bold. On the syntactic bootstrapping hypothesis, (68a) should be interpreted non-causatively despite the presence of the causative morpheme and (68b) should be interpreted causatively, despite the absence of the morpheme.

The data favoured the universalist position, as there was a strong main effect of argument number irrespective of verb morphology and valence. When adults were tested, however, they showed the opposite tendency, favouring verb morphology: they were 'verb compliant'.

Do these data favour the nativist over Tomasello's and Pine's learning based accounts? They are consistent with it. However both the data and their interpretation are open to criticism. In the first place (which the authors touch on in their footnote 7) it is possible that Kannada does afford the learning of transitive cues to causality perfectly well. That is to say, although the causative morpheme may be the more *reliable* cue to causative meaning in the sense that it is never misleading, it may actually be inferior to the transitive cue because it may predict fewer of the causative meanings in the input sample than the transitive syntax cue. Just because a cue is reliable, in the sense of being a sufficient condition, does not make it better than other cues. It is the case, for example, that some verbs in Kannadan, such as *lift*, can yield a causative sense without the causative morpheme but with transitive syntax. In fact, because we lack a detailed quantitative analysis of the properties of Kannadan we have no way of determining if causative morphology is a better cue to causal meaning than transitive syntax. Second, with regard to interpretation, it is worth bearing in mind that the causative-transitive linkage represents one of the cases in which syntax is a fairly transparent reflection of semantics; it is one of the forms of iconicity discussed in 4.2.2 – 'iconicity of categorisation' perhaps. Nothing could be less arbitrary and *sui generis* than placing an object-of-action after a causal action and not otherwise. So a sceptic might say, then, that the Kannada-learning children were behaving, unlike the adults, as semantic tadpoles.

To sum up this subsection: we clearly need a lot more studies of syntactic frames using the preferential looking technique, and we clearly need to pay more attention to the symmetrical conflict between the syntactic bootstrapping hypothesis and the pragmatism-based alternative.

Now we turn to another kind of bootstrapping, where the conflicts are no less marked.

4.4 Is semantic knowledge sufficient or only necessary? Semantic bootstrapping versus semantic assimilation

In this the final section on ontogeny, we find the path forking between to quite different kinds of pragmatist approach, one that veers off towards empiricism and one going in the direction of nativism (though not syntactic nativism of course). In the first, we see central roles for input regularities, for imitation learning and for detecting clusters about encapsulated elements and limited scope formulae, and we see learning metaphors of the 'cut and paste' variety as well as more elaborated learning algorithms of the kind formalised in MOSAIC. But in the 'path not (yet) taken' we see the process of syntactic development being grounded in richly structured semantic knowledge. It is at once a Piagetian path (reliance upon the process of 'assimilation') and a Fodorian one (an innate LOT is assumed). And it is a clear tribute to the intellectual fecundity of the late Martin Braine that his work forms a cornerstone of both approaches; though it is a far more substantial one in the second case.

The fundamental claim of this second approach (by now a familiar one from the work of Langacker and others) is that syntactic categories such as noun, verb, subject, and so forth, are in reality semantic categories (object, action, agent) and that, given this, the child's acquisition of grammar, though grounded in innate semantic knowledge, simply does not require her to possess innate syntactic knowledge. Superficially, this kind of approach might seem to evoke the 'semanticised' linguistic and psycholinguistic work of Ray Jackendoff. But if the reader glances again at my account of Jackendoff's position in Part 2 – of his tripartite parallel architecture (phonological, *syntactic*, semantic) for language processing (p. 169) and at my characterisation of the difference between Chomsky's thick-membrane view of the relation between semantics and syntax versus Jackendoff's thin-membrane view (p. 175–176) – it becomes immediately obvious that Jackendoff is not saying that formal categories are *really* semantic in nature (a no-membrane, no-need-for-one view). Indeed he explicitly argues against this position in his most recent book (Jackendoff, 2002, p. 126). (It has to be added, though, that he does categorise Van Valin's RRG as an 'elaboration' of his tripartite architecture – ibid., p. 127.)

Touching upon Jackendoff's *difficulties* with the standard Chomskyan architectures will, however, usefully focus our attention on a thought lurking beneath all discussion of the developmental relation between meaning and syntax: that while semantic knowledge may not be a sufficient grounding for syntactic development it may well be a *necessary* one. To explain – en route to describing Braine's theory – in (what Jackendoff calls) Chomsky's 'syntactocentrism', the construction of a 'semantic representation' or 'interpretation' takes place as the *final* step of the derivation process. Recall that in both of the Y-shaped architectures of the P & P theory and minimalism (in which there is a final bifurcation to PF and LF and in which the lexicon enters at the primary level) the interpretation of both PF and LF features happens at the final stage. In a metaphor owing to Ivan Sag 'it is as though syntax has to carry around two locked suitcases that it turns over at the checkpoint to the components that have the right key' (Jackendoff, 2002, p. 150).

But a moment's thought tells us that when we are concerned not with how the derivation takes place in a competent speaker-hearer but with children's learning about what are the actual nouns, verbs etc. in their native language 'late' semantic interpretation of this kind is not really an option. The late-unpacking metaphor might indeed have some foothold in those who can immediately analyse, say, *cow* as noun and *ate* as verb, but what of a child who *only* knows (1) what cows and eating are and who knows (2) that Human contains nouns and verbs. The latter innate knowledge of language cannot *by itself* tell such a child that *cow* is a noun and *eat* is a verb. Recall my discussion of Jane Grimshaw's (1981) solution to this problem in Part 2, based around the idea that children innately apply rule-of-thumb semantic characterisations of the form classes of the kind 'nouns are broadly objects', 'verbs are broadly actions'. I now reprise this.

While there is not a perfect mapping between the semantic and the syntactic – while, for example, all nouns are not object words, all verbs are not action words – there is a *partial* mapping. Accordingly, the child can *begin* by assuming that if it is an object word then it is a noun; if the word describes an action then it is a verb. Doing this will enable a substantial number of words to be correctly categorised, after which X-bar grammar or merge will to begin its work. Recall Grimshaw:

> Thus certain cognitive categories have what I call a *Canonical Structural Realisation* (CSR): CSR(object) = N, CSR(action) = V. LAD employs a CSR principle: a word belongs to its CSR, unless there is evidence to the contrary. Of course, the data will include many examples that cannot be analysed this way, but they are likely to occur in relatively complex sentences that probably do not form part of the real data-base at this point. In any event, should a sentence like 'NP *belongs to* NP' occur, *it will just have to be ignored*. LAD can construct phrase-structure rules for NP and VP by drawing on example sentences whose lexical items can be assigned category labels by CSR principles.

(ibid., p. 174–175, first and final italics mine)

This solution to the categorisation problem is one approved of by Chomsky (1986).

So while these rule-of-thumb assumptions are strictly false (*fun* can be noun, *own* is a verb, and so forth) they contain a grain of truth sufficient for the child to apply them, along with innate knowledge of phrase-structure formation, to parse some early sentences. Then, they can apply the parse-trees thus constructed to cases in which the generalisations do not hold (e.g., *The party will be your first, and you will have some fun*). Grimshaw continues (1981, p. 178), in fact:

> LAD will in effect be establishing a set of structural generalisations governing the distribution of N, V, and so on. These can be used as evidence for the analysis of any new categories (such as Det. or Modal) for which no CSR is defined. The rules will also make it possible to assign category labels to words like *belong*.*belong* is a verb because it behaves like one with respect to phrase structure rules [a role for distributional learning here? JR]. As for cases such as *destruction*, LAD will receive positive evidence about their categorisation.

Steven Pinker (1984, 1987) called this solution *semantic bootstrapping theory* (SBT). He added detail, explicated the basic idea step-by-step as a plausible developmental mechanism, and extended it towards the view that the child would also be making innate assumptions about the linkage between subjecthood and being an

agent and objecthood and being a patient. The latter is, in fact, far more problematic territory than the linkage between nouns and physical objects, which seems to
hold universally; because there are a number of languages in which subject properties reliably fall to patients (Maratsos, 1999). For such cases, Pinker (1984) argues
that an innately known 'parametric variation' will reliably enable children to classify
the language being learned as either agent-centred or patient-centred.

Imagine then that the child hears the sentence (Pinker's example) *the dog bit the
cat* (see Figure 4.23). Because *cat* and *dog* are each a 'name of a person or thing' and
because *bit* refers to 'an action or change of state' (Pinker, 1987, p. 408, Table 1) the
former are taken to be nouns and the latter is taken to be a verb. Additionally,
because the dog was the agent of the action and the cat was the patient, they are
assigned, respectively, to subject and object. Because the child is also assumed to
possess innate knowledge of X-bar theory she will consider projections above the
minimal N and V (N', N'', V', V''): 'X-bar theory leaves the child no choice but to posit
maximal projections of each of the major lexical categories' (Pinker, 1984, p. 70).
She will, moreover, place S [the sentence node] above V'' as X-bar theory also entails
that 'Subjects are the daughters of the node that dominates the maximal projection

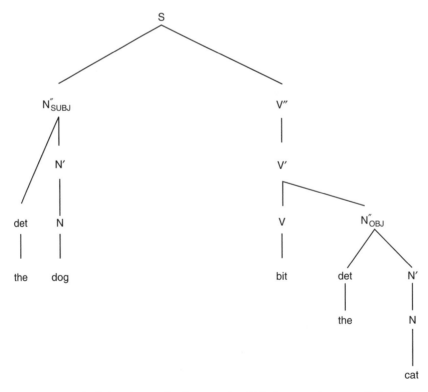

Figure 4.23 Pinker's (1987) example of sentence in which the semantics–syntax links hold.

of their predicates' (1984, p. 71) (i.e., the S node which necessarily dominates the maximal projection of V will also be linked to N''_{SUBJ}. Knowledge of X-bar will also ensure that the child will take the two instances of *the* to be specifiers, given that nounphrases require them. Finally, 'using the provisions of X-bar theory that states that arguments are attached as sisters of X and specifiers are sisters of X' the child completes the tree' (ibid., p. 71). To expand this latter statement: the argument of the head (i.e., *the cat* of *bit*) will be attached as the sister of the head, so N'' and V are on the same level, while N'' will be a daughter of V'. The child will attach V' to N''_{OBJ} and each determiner to the two N''s. This is what it means to say that subjects are 'tree-structure privileged' on this analysis: they are higher on the tree than objects in X-bar theory.

This would arm the child with the following rules:

$$S \rightarrow NP_{SUBJ} + VP$$

$$VP \rightarrow V + NP_{OBJ}$$

$$NP \rightarrow Det + N$$

Two sceptical thoughts are likely to enter the reader's mind at this point: (1) whether X-bar theory really is no more than what Van Valin (1992, p. 10) calls 'English constituent grammar' and therefore a poor candidate for being something innately specified in such formal detail, and (2) because minimalism essentially dispenses with X-bar theory as an innate template, will such an account not appear to be otiose to a contemporary Chomskyan? In tackling the second point we will also be tackling the first.

While minimalism eschews bar levels and has it that the result of merge can be no more than the content of the elements (the 'inclusivity principle'); while it even eschews the distinction between lexical items and their head projections (so an item can be both X^0 and XP) and while intermediate projections may not be relevant at the LF interface,[20] intermediate levels do emerge in the course of the derivation (described on pp. 143–144). What has happened is that merge retains the recursive power of X-bar theory without formalising the distinctions between levels of recursion. In other words, while minimalism avoids commitment to innately represented phrase structure templates, it nonetheless attempts to duplicate what X-bar achieves in a bottom-up style, replacing it with operations constrained by virtual conceptual necessity and legibility conditions.

Now recall also from Part 2 the proofs of how the following three central properties of merge exist in virtue of good design and legibility: (1) the binary nature of branching, (2) the asymmetry or 'headedness' of phrases, (3) that the targets of merge project. It seems to me that these three principles (existing by computational 'necessity' rather than as innate representations) would be sufficient to ensure that phrase structures would be computed on the basis of knowing the formal category of certain lexical items. Not only would branching be binary, but (2) would ensure that the resulting phrases would be either VPs or NPs and by (3) these would project

---

[20] As noted in Part 2, Chomsky (e.g., 2001) says this question is yet to be decided.

upwards to S. It might be thought that we would, however, lose the result that subjects are tree-structure privileged. But given the fact that in languages with the canonical word order of VSO subjects are not privileged in this way this is perhaps no bad thing. There is, indeed, some gain in flexibility. To explain, (1) ensures that the two noun phrases that are the arguments of the verb cannot both be sisters to the verb: there can be no three-way branching. That is to say, a parse like the one shown in Figure 4.24 cannot be made. Given this asymmetry, one of the noun phrases will have to be lower on the tree. In some languages this will be the patient and in some it will be the agent. This is something the child can learn from positive evidence alone guided by his or her inability to have branchings that are more than binary.

Back to SBT. As mother watches an episode of *The Teletubbies* with her small son it is unlikely that she will turn to him and comment '*The situation justified the measures*' (Pinker's example of a so-called *non-basic* sentence in which the semantic rules of thumb do not apply). In other words, the likelihood would appear to be high that much of the input to the child will contain many so-called *basic* sentences in which noun = thing, verb = action, and so forth. But even if this does not happen to be the case, it is open to the nativist to argue that young children will tend to *ignore* sentences on whose structure they cannot gain a grip by the use of semantic tags (see the first Grimshaw quotation above). Or more simply, they may not be able to *understand* nouns and verbs whose meaning cannot be accessed by way of concrete and immediate referents.

It is now time to consider Braine's (1992) alternative to SBT. It is seductively simple. He claims that there is no point at which action-words transform into verbs, at which object-words transform into nouns, and so forth. And more broadly, there is no point at which cognitive/semantic recursion becomes X-bar grammar. This is because verbs *are* action words, nouns *are* object words and there is only X-bar *semantics*. (I'll leave to later the shrilly nagging question about what then is the ontology of syntax.) After Ira Scheslinger (1988), Braine argues that children gradually expand their category of (say) action words from ones like *eat* and *chase*, to *look at*, to *see*, to *sleep*, to *sit* to *like* to *own* to *resemble*. Schlesinger calls this process *semantic assimilation*, and the parallel with Piagetian assimilation is clear enough. So in Piagetian terms, as the correlative mental process of accommodation proceeds, there is no point at which the scheme becomes qualitatively transformed from something semantic to something syntactic.

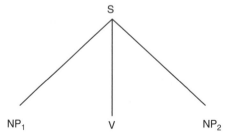

Figure 4.24 A tree analysis that should be impossible on MP.

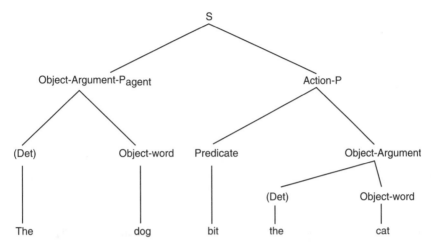

Figure 4.25 One of Braine's (1992) possible 'semantic' parsings of a basic sentence.

This means that children might initially assign a structure to a basic sentence of the kind shown in Figure 4.25 (from Braine, 1992). However, if they are learning a language in which 'object argument phrases with agents' (or 'subjects') are not privileged then the parse shown in Figure 4.26 might be constructed. Though note that this would not be possible on minimalist assumptions, as this assumes that branching cannot be greater than binary. (It has been claimed, as we have seen, that some languages lack verb-phrases; in which case such a parse, or something like it, would be the appropriate one.) Braine claims that either of these parse trees could cope with sentences of the '*The situation justified the measures*' kind – on an appropriately relaxed reading of 'object' and 'action' and 'agent'.

As noted earlier, in Braine's hands the semantic assimilation theory is nativist, in so far as he assumes an innate LOT, with categories such as object, place, time, event and proposition as well as the distinction between a concept and its instances (realised in language as the predicate-argument distinction) coming together to make an 'innate format for recording information' (Braine, 1992, p. 80). But a more empiricist-minded pragmatist who balked at this would not have to look far for an alternative account of how such categories come to be in the mind of the syntax-acquiring child. In the same year as Braine's paper appeared, Jean Mandler (1992) published a paper in which she argued that concepts such as 'animate' are derived not from some innate symbolic format but from the very young child's 'perceptual analysis' of events. This is her empiricist/pragmatist alternative to LOT.

Mandler's idea is that the infant, by a process of so-called *perceptual analysis* of events, abstracts a set of dynamic, analogue schemas of how objects can move, causally interact, and be spatially related to one another. These are called *image-schemas*. 'By perceptual analysis I mean,' she writes 'a symbolic process (probably

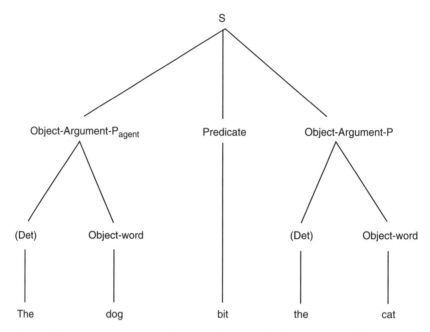

Figure 4.26 Braine's (1992) alternative semantic parse of a basic sentence in which agent-phrases are not 'privileged'.

conscious) by which one perception is actively compared with another' [Mandler, 1992, p. 595]. (Why 'symbolic' by the way?)

She sometimes talks of these image schemas as being derived from motor processes ('to a lesser extent' than perceptual), but has surprisingly little to say about the role of the infant's bodily interactions with objects. She writes of image-schemas as being 'condensed redescriptions' of perceptual experiences. These representations are certainly *not propositional*, unlike those of LOT; they are 'analogue' in the sense that they capture continuous rather than discrete states of objects.

Some examples of image-schemas are: PATH, UP-DOWN, CONTAINMENT, FORCE, PART-WHOLE, and LINK. Within the PATH set, for example, schemata differ in terms of how the path begins, the kind of trajectory it has, and how it ends. These are, then, three image-schemas embedded in the more general PATH schema. The nature of each of these three will determine the kind of moving thing that the infant will conceptualise. She argues that infants ground the concept ANIMAL by utilising such schemata:

> Thus, a first concept of animals might be that they are objects that follow certain kinds of path, that begin motion in a particular kind of way, and whose movement is often coupled in a specific fashion to the movement of other objects. Notice that several image-schemas have been combined to form the concept of animal.

(ibid., p. 592)

Animal PATHS can have at least the following characteristics.

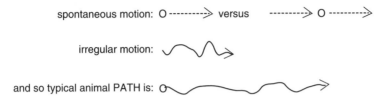

Moreover, the movements of animate entities are contingent upon the movements of other entities, which may themselves be animate. (For example, the infant sees two cats chasing each other in the garden or sees a cat playing with a ball of wool.)

She describes the various kinds of animate-object contingency in terms of the LINK image-schema. Thus

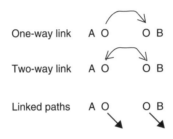

she adds: 'the contingency of animate movement not only involves such factors as one animate following another, as described by LINKED PATHS, but also involves *avoiding barriers*, and making sudden shifts in acceleration' (1992, p. 595, my emphasis). (See the discussion below of Gergely *et al.*, 1995.)

> These analyses are characterised as *redescriptions* of varied and exceedingly complex percep-
> tions into a few different kinds of trajectories … Such redescription could in principle be
> carried out from a very young age by analysis of spatial structure into image-schematic forms.
> It would provide the beginnings of a concept of (or theory of) what an animate thing *is*,
> above and beyond what it looks like.
>
> (ibid., p. 587; original emphasis)

The concept of an animal is, then, ultimately a compound of image schemas derived from perceptual activity.

Mandler makes explicit the implications of all this for language development: 'image schemas provide a foundation for language acquisition by creating an interface between the continuous process of perception and the discrete nature of language' (Mandler, 1992, p. 587). Is this account supposed to carry the full richness of Braine's LOT? Apparently, yes. Mandler is saying not only that this process enables children to pick out *instances* of ANIMAL when she sees them, but that it is the grounding of the 'concept of animacy' (ibid., p. 591). Something of this kind would reasonably be expected also to afford the presently crucial notions of agent, action, and inanimate object. Moreover, image schemas are spatially constructed, so they necessarily – if you like to think this way – bring spatial ideas in their train. And what of time? 'Temporal concepts', she writes, 'are at least partly derived from spatial ones' of which the image schema theory explains the construction. They are 'in the first instance represented as analogical extensions of spatial schemes' (ibid., p. 591, footnote). (Although advertised as an alternative to Piaget as well as to Fodor, Mandler's position is, in fact a kind of third-person version of Piaget in which the observation of agency events replaces the first-person *exercise* of agency.)

For our purposes in fact, it does not matter whether Braine's position depends upon the LOT doctrine. (We will, however, return to Mandler's image-schema theory in order to draw some general morals.) For at this point what is at issue is the question of how it is possible for Braine to argue as he does. I wish to suggest that the very surface plausibility of usurping SBT and replacing it with semantic assimilation is due to the fact that a crucial element of SBT *is nativist in the wrong way*: that it entails a highly questionable position on how lexical items map to basic-level concepts.

To explain: there is a view about concepts that SBT and semantic assimilation share. It is, in fact, the fault-line of SBT into which Braine's theory drives it wedge. The view is that, in order for a child to understand the lexicon of basic sentences – words like *cat* and *eat* – the concept expressed by the words *must be decomposed into a more abstract semantic format*. (Those who take this view frequently represent these concepts in capitals, so I shall do so.) Accordingly, to understand what the English word *eat* means the child must necessarily access a substratum of notions – 'meaning primitives' – such as ACTION, EVENT, SUBSTANCE (ingesting of). Just as understanding the word *kill* should be decomposed into the knowledge that it means CAUSE (TO DIE), and just as understanding the sentence *John entered the room* requires us to access the semantic nodes EVENT, OBJECT$_1$, PATH, PLACE, OBJECT$_2$, and just as understanding the word *keep* means to have a representation of the form CAUSE A STATE THAT ENDURES OVER TIME. For over 30 years Fodor (e.g., 1970; 1998), among others (e.g., Lewis, 1972[21]) has been an opponent of this kind of view, arguing that such decomposition does not actually get us any closer to explicating meaning *as we have no way to explicate the 'primitives' themselves*. Jackendoff (2002, p. 369) however, is its foremost champion, and he writes in its defence:

> My working hypothesis is that the meaning of the primitives is exhausted by (a) their capacity for combination with other primitives, (b) their use in triggering inference rules, individually and in combination. But I acknowledge that this remains to be demonstrated.

But what if we run with the *anti*-decompositionists' view and deny that when a child understands *eat* she is accessing the semantic feature ACTION? This is to deny

---

[21] 'Translation into Markerese is at best a substitute for real semantics ... The Markerese method is attractive in part because it deals with nothing but symbols ... But it is just this pleasing finitude that prevents Markerese semantics from dealing with the relations between symbols and the world of non-symbols - that is, with genuine semantic relations.' (Lewis, 1972, pp. 169–710; quoted in Jackendoff, 2002).

that 'denoting an action' is a property that eating has *in virtue of what it means*, that in order to understand the word the child must necessarily access the 'concept of action'. In other words, what the child needs to know is that *eat* means eating, and she may or may not consider further that eating is a kind of action.[22] The decompositionists get the cart before the horse. For Fodor (1998, p. 64), as far as the child is concerned the relation between eating and action may be a *contingent* one; and this is all that is required for the bootstrapping to work.

In fact, Fodor seems quite content to accept that bootstrapping may depend upon the child's utilising the concept of action, while only demurring at the idea that children's access to word meaning is secured *via* decomposition into 'primitives' like ACTION. His concern is with the cart being correctly positioned relative to the horse. It is possible, however, to go further with regard to the developmental story, and question whether semantic bootstrapping depends upon such high-level abstract primitives at all. I will now suggest that it does not: what's in the cart may be something with an essentially concrete and undecomposed semantics.

Whether or not Fodor's atomistic view of concepts is correct, it is possible to argue that language-acquiring children do not need to operate with concepts on the level of 'action', 'object' and 'agent'. (It is easy to slip into this way on thinking; and even the best undergraduates will produce essays on something called 'the infant's *concept* of object permanence'.) For an illustration of this denial let us consider two intriguing studies of infants' detection of agency from the laboratory of Georgy Gergely. Gergely takes the view that from at least 12 months of age infants operate within the principle of 'rational action', meaning that they assume that if somebody has a goal then he or she will, if it is possible, pursue the most direct means to achieving it. The first of these studies (Gergely, Nádaskty, Csibra and Bíró, 1995) employed the technique of dishabituation to surprising events. In the 'rational action' group, the babies watched a cartoon in which a big and a small blob were positioned either side of a barrier. The smaller one expanded and contracted slightly before approaching and retreating from the barrier and then finally jumping over it as if to achieve the goal of joining the big blob. To the adult eye it looked like a child trying and then succeeding in getting close to its mother. In the comparison condition ('non-rational' action), the little blob did the same thing but in the absence of a barrier. In the second phase of the experiment, the barrier was removed and the 'rational-action' group showed more surprise when the little blob continued to jump en route to the big one than when it travelled in a straight line: they were surprised at its performing, then, the *same* action. The high-level, decompositional, holist reading of this result is that infants were applying to this scenario the concept AGENT. Whereas on the alternative view, which I wish to recommend, they were operating with a concept of 'creature' (as including humans and animals), a relaxed conception into which blobs can be assimilated. (In future months they will be doing this on a daily basis – aka 'engaging in symbolic play'.) The distinction between the two views looks superficial but in fact it is fundamental.

---

[22] This way of putting it is owing to Eric Margolis, Fodor points out (Fodor, 1998b, p. 64).

The different levels of abstraction would quickly reveal themselves as such should anybody try to launch the notion of 'creature-phrase' or 'creature word' before a sceptical public. The category 'creature' might pick out cats, dogs, characters like Tom and Jerry and the Tellytubbies, as well mum and dad and self; and the net will catch in it the common characters of being an agent and also such things as being a walker and a sleeper. But it really would be getting the cart before the horse to say that the child has constructed this category in virtue of the members all being *agents* – a concept that we ourselves cannot adequately define. They *are* all agents in fact, but, for the child, it is likely – unless she is precociously philosophical – that this is only *extensionally* not *intensionally* so.

The next Gergeley study (Gergely, Bekkering and Király, 2002) focuses our attention on the contours of human action rather than upon agenthood more generally. The inspiration for the study was a deferred-imitation experiment by Meltzoff (1988) which showed that 14-month-olds will, after a delay of a week or over, imitate the counterintuitive means act of lighting up a pad on the table by touching it with the forehead rather than by the more direct route of using the hands. Gergely *et al.* (2002) showed that when a *rationale* is given for using the head (the model, pretending to be cold, wraps a blanket about herself) toddlers were more likely to use their hands than when it was made clear that the model's hands were free. This is an impressive result on any interpretation, but does it does not suggest that the children were parsing the event by accessing the meaning primitive ACTION, which itself means something like 'a bodily movement intentionally performed to bring about a desired effect with the greatest economy of effort'. Such a reading is hardly mandatory. The toddlers can, however, at least be said to have been displaying a sensitivity to how impedance can constrain goal-directed movement. Indeed, for both studies it would seem to be nigh impossible to describe what was going on without using the word 'goal', or a cognate term. While only agents can have goals, and while it has to be an action of some kind that brings a goal to fruition, we can just as well think of goals, on a lower level of abstraction, as being that which *creatures* have. Again, nobody is ever likely to coin the terms goal-word or goal-phrase. Although GOAL is one of the thematic (or theta) roles on P & P theory, there is not a set of words that intrinsically refers to goals, in the sense in which some intrinsically refer to things or actions.

By the same token, while they look synonymous, the phrases 'the object concept' (qua object permanence') and 'the concept of an object' are quite distinct notions. It is the latter that Pinker and Braine take children to be operating with and it is the existence of the latter in very young children about which one is entitled to be sceptical. *Extensionally*, mum and dad, the cat, teddy, the cot, and so forth, are all objects for the child in the sense that she takes them all to possess the properties of solidity, being subject to gravity, etc. But to accept this is very far from saying that the animate and inanimate furniture of the child's world are gathered together as such, *intensionally*, in virtue of them all being of the abstract kind OBJECT. We do not need to say that she conceptualises her mother and her cot as having objecthood in common. Of course one may be wrong about this: the point is that attributing this high-level conception is *not mandatory*, as it is on the decompositional view of meaning.

It is not hard, then, to see where all this is leading. Because Pinker assumes that children understand the meaning of the lexicon of basic sentences in terms of their *decomposition* into 'object-words', 'action-words' and so forth, theorists like Braine can hijack this representational level in order to do their X-bar *semantics*, denying, which Jackendoff does not, that syntax is *ever* bootstrapped into. There is also a moral here for empiricist-style just-so stories of the Mandler kind about the origins of concepts such as ANIMAL and the like. If we allow that we possess such concepts in virtue of a clutch of more primitive concepts involving agenthood, and also allow that this itself is a compound of still more primitive notions such as '+ uncaused trajectory' and '+ irregular path' (the kind of thing that be captured iconically) then the way is clear for reducing *these* to image schemas – and thus to perceptual experience. But this path is only clear for those who believe that words like *cat* and *dog* must be understood decompositionally.

My quarrel here is not so much with the decompositional theory of concepts – sometimes called the 'classical' theory – itself, but with its (implicit) deployment in semantic bootstrapping theory. For there are, after all, obvious advantages to decompositional accounts, not the least of which is that they allow us to retain our intuitions about analyticity and necessity as manifested in propositions like *The bachelor is an unmarried man*. One also accepts, of course, the necessity for some kind of syntactic bootstrapping theory. So the onus is on me to sketch – at least – what a bootstrapping theory bleached of decompositionalist assumptions would look like. I will do this before returning to Braine's position.

On this version of semantic bootstrapping, we assume that the child has an innate capacity (perhaps of the kind described by minimalism) for forming phrase structures, along with an innate tendency to categorise words into the major form classes – innate ideas of noun and verb at the very least. Furthermore, the child has an innately-specified capacity for identifying *Persons* (conspecifics), *Animals*, and *Things* (inanimate objects), which I will dub *PATs*. Finally, there is the innate tendency to take PATs to be nouns and to take the doings of PAs to be verbs. Adjectives are words telling us what PATs are like, adverbs tell us what the doings of PAs are like, determiners pick out PATs, and prepositions tell us where they are doing. It seems to me that a bootstrapping theory of this kind would do the work of the Grimshaw–Pinker account whilst being quarantined from Braine's kind of pragmatist revisionism. This is, of course, because notions such as object-word, action-word, and action-phrase have no place in it.

Needless to say, a proper working out of this account would have to specify how this identification process is supposed to work. For now: it would need to be something above the level of bare sensory resonating and yet below that of full conceptualisation. Perhaps we might consider the child in a Gibsonian light as being able to pick up the affordances (Gibson, 1979) of PATs and for picking up the difference between the doings of PAs and the physical fate of Ts. Certainly, the contemporary developmental journals are chock-full of dishabituation studies suggesting that this knowledge is specified in plenty of time for language acquisition.[23]

---

[23] See reviews by Johnson (2000) and Gergely and Csibra (2003).

To return to Braine (1992), by way of making a bridge between this section and the next (on evolution), he asks at the very end of his paper why, if syntactic categories are, at bottom, semantic in nature, children acquire them. This question, of course, answers itself: because languages have them, which is to say that languages contain categories whose extensions do not match those of the semantic categories 'which are the child's starting point' (idid., p. 96). So why do *languages* have syntactic categories? Braine gives four answers.

1) Because LOT boundaries are fuzzily drawn (e.g., 'event' versus 'state of affairs') different languages are 'free' to draw them in different ways.

2) While the syntactic categories through which we communicate are essentially orthogonal to one another in terms of semantic content, syntax does sometimes capitalise on semantic similarities; e.g., the grammaticalisation of spatial and temporal relations is similar, as is that between different kinds of transfer relations (of physical objects, information, etc.).

3) Because young children are good at categorising phonetically words whose semantic nature is various (e.g., French gender markings).

4) Because the available surface structure positions are fewer than the semantic categories expressed in the representation of a sentence.

It seems to me that the premise of 1 is questionable (conscious conception and LOT being at the same level?), that the relevance of 2 to the question of why syntactic categories exist at all is uncertain, that 3 gets matters the wrong way round (why not children being good at detecting the categories because they exist?), and that 4 is in essence the Chomskyan point about the C_{HL} being subject to external conditions from the A–P systems.

We will turn to the question of why syntactic categories exist at all in the final section of the book, but, in rounding off, it would be well to consider the status of a theory that *unlike Braine's* (which accepts the autonomy of syntax thesis while not mandating it; ibid., p. 98) says essentially that (a) syntactic categories do exist *externally* in languages but (b) we do not compute with them *internally*. In this theory we see – to misquote[24] William James (p. 60) 'the pragmatist temper regnant'. What would it mean, in fact, to say that we never do anything other than compute with semantic categories when we move between the thought systems and the sensorimotor systems? A moment's thought tells us that this would be a dog's breakfast of a computational system. Despite our speaking and hearing nouns and verbs we compute over object-words and action-words. The action-words will be coupled with auxiliaries and inflected for tense, object-words will take determiners, prepositions will really be about spatial location while metaphorically not being so (*on the grounds that* etc.), while phrases will have no formal status, being no more than collections of words about events, actions, and particulars. Why not just give up and accept that we use syntactic categories not only extensionally but also intensionally?

---

[24] He said 'empiricist' – referring to one face of pragmatism.

Here we might detect one reason why syntactic categories exist: *they do the computations so efficiently.*

4.5 Does an evolutionary perspective reveal the strengths of the pragmatist approach?

At this point a pragmatist may object in the following terms: rationalistic explanations push the deeper problems downstairs to evolution. For even if it *were* the case that some acquisitional trajectories are prima facie explicable in terms of is innately specified syntactic 'knowledge' we still have to give some principled account of how they came to be there in the first place. Surely syntactic nativists do not believe that that their nature – the 'linguistic universals' they reflect – is a matter of simple chance? 'We are all Darwinians now', and so the only remotely plausible account of how they came to be there, and came to take the form they do, is one in terms of their adaptive advantage. In other words, the use and usefulness of linguistic forms and of certain ways of parsing explains not only the constraints on cross-linguistic variation but on acquisitional trajectories. Hard evidence for innate linguistic universals is, in fact, hard to come by – indeed sometimes syntactic nativism is no more than a sceptical position about what is learnable – while nativists offer nothing in the way of developmental mechanisms to compete with connectionist models or even those of the MOSAIC kind. Indeed, even strong supporters of syntactic autonomy will leave the door open to the possibility that parameters, rather than being innately represented, are 'arrived at inductively by the child' (Newmeyer, 1998, p. 364). Given this, a successful attempt to explain why – let's call them for the sake of argument – 'linguistic universals' are the way they are in terms of functional variables such as ease-of-parsing will render an account of syntactic *development* couched in terms of the *canalisation of syntactic development by general information-processing constraints on parsing and by social–functional constraints on communicative fluency* that much more plausible.

My first task is to tackle the kind of issues raised in that objection. The weakness of the objection – we shall see – lies in the fact that the links between linguistic universals (or, more neutrally, constraints on cross-linguistic variation) and functional variables like parsing ease is not only one that is mindbogglingly difficult to uncover, but that when some uncovering work has been done, the results can favour the rationalist position rather than the functionalist one.

After this I will discuss a process (or *purported* process) of which functionalists make a great deal – *grammaticalisation*. Roughly speaking, this means the historical progression whereby forms within a language which originally had a clearly semantic function become bleached of meaning and acquire purely syntactic roles. One can dramatise the relevance of this to evolutionary questions in the following way. Let us assume that the neural substrate responsible for the human ability to acquire language has not evolved in the past – say – 30,000 years.[25] Language itself, by contrast,

---

[25] Foley (1996, pp. 96–109) estimates the end of genetically based evolution at 30, 000 years.

has 'evolved' in the course of human history in the general direction of acquiring progressively more semantically arbitrary features (subjacency, c-commanding, branching direction, headedness, and so forth) *for the learning of which the original and unchanging neural substrate has had to suffice*. Well, if this is so, it is simply not possible to argue that babies are able to acquire any of the world's languages in virtue of the fact that their brains represent the possible parameters within which these *historically* evolved syntactic principles can vary. Surely it is more plausible to argue that the massively semantic brain with which the human race kick-started the cultural process of grammaticalisation is the brain a child uses in 2004 to acquire a language more or less encrusted with the residue of this sociocultural process. The problem here – we shall see – is that 'the process of grammaticalisation' may prove to be something of a myth.

Third and finally I will discuss Chomsky's most recent statement on the evolution of the language faculty – not one in terms of 'a shower of cosmic rays', but of something far more down to earth. The possibility that the certain aspects of the language faculty evolved by exaptation rather than by simple adaptation will be explored.

4.5.1 The functional roots of linguistic universals?

It is hardly an eccentric view that human syntax evolved by natural selection. 'We are all Darwinians now' – as the pragmatist has just said. And so it should come as no surprise that a prominent nativist like Steven Pinker should be the first author of a paper arguing for the view that syntax, as it is described in P & P theory, evolved by the same kind of gradual, adaptive processes that were responsible for the evolution of the human eye (Pinker and Bloom, 1990). (Needless to say, explaining 'how the mind works' by reference to the adaptive function of its various 'modules' is highly fashionable nowadays, and Pinker is a standard-bearer of this 'evolutionary psychology'.)

Pinker and Bloom do caution, however, that there is every reason to believe that a 'functionalist theory of language acquisition can be true while functionalist theories of the acquisition of language can be false. From the very start children obey grammatical constraints that afford no immediate communicative advantage' (Pinker and Bloom, 1990, p. 719). But the functionalist accounts that they offer for the existence of principles such as subjacency would seem to provide plenty of succour to the pragmatist. Recall that subjacency describes a constraint on the movement of a *wh*-element in d-structure to the front of an s-structure, setting a limit on the amount of syntactic material (no more than 'one layer of structure') that can be traversed. To take Pinker and Bloom's own example, while it is acceptable to say *What does he believe they claimed I said?* [trace: *what*], the following is certainly not acceptable: *What does he believe the claim that I said?* [trace: *what*]. They suggest that the constraint exists because it is difficult to parse sentences with traces in any event, and so life is made easier for the listener by having structural constraints of some kind. They make reference to the pycholinguistic work of Berwick and Weinberg (1984) who argue that subjacency exists in order to rule out sentences in which the 'distance' between the *wh*-element in s-structure and the co-indexed trace is too long. (Recall my earlier discussion of J. D. Fodor's work on parsing and grammatical structure, work which – recall – denies the reducability to the grammatical to the easy-to-parse.) The LAD has responded to pressure to keep the distance down to a minimum. Accordingly, one would expect languages to vary in the degree to which distance between trace and co-indexed *wh*-element can disrupt parsing, and so – as we saw in Part 2 – Italian has a relatively relaxed interpretation of the principle, while in the Akan (from Ghana) it is freely violated. Viewing matters from the perspective of grammaticalisation then, the functionalist would say that subjacency should not be considered as a constraint on movement, innately represented as a parameter in case the target language has it, but rather should be seen as an emergent property of the demand to parse languages with a certain kind of structure. The rule is as 'external' as, say, the morphological cues to gender in German, not part of the I-language. What helps adults to parse will also help children.

Something in the same functionalist spirit can be said when we turn to typology (= the study of structural similarity between the world's languages). It is the case (Hawkins, 1983) that for all known languages the canonical appearance of verbs before objects (VO) is accompanied by the canonical use of *pre*positional forms,[26] while verbs regularly following objects (OV) is canonically accompanied by *post*positions (as in Japanese and Hindi). The working hypothesis for the functionalist would be that these constraints exist to facilitate parsing and fluency of expression.

We are now in a position to compare, in a more rigorous way, the nativist and the functionalist positions on the linkage between constraints on cross-linguist variation, acquisition and such aspects of language use as ease-of-parsing. In what follows I shall pay close attention to the work of Simon Kirby (1999). Kirby reminds us, first of all, that the deep division between the two approaches is rooted in their different explanatory priorities. For the nativist, the central question is about how children are able to acquire language from 'primary linguistic data' that contains insufficient – indeed the wrong kind of – information about how sentences are generated. Their answer is that children come equipped with an LAD. A subsidiary question for them is why there are clear constraints on cross-linguistic variation, to which they answer that it is *because these need to be there if the LAD is to be efficacious*. For the functionalist, by contrast, the typological rather than the developmental question is primary. Accordingly, their central question is why the constraints on cross-linguistic variation take the form they do, to which they answer that the constraints are a function of language use, in the sense of reflecting what humans find easier to parse and produce. To this, the acquisitional question is subsidiary, with their answer being that the linguistic data available to children are 'rich' enough for them to 'learn' syntax with general-purpose processing mechanisms.

Also following Kirby, one can see quite clearly what are the prima facie strengths and weaknesses of the two approaches. At one extreme, the nativist might regard himself as free simply to ignore questions about why human languages do indeed appear to be designed for the effective expression and communication of thoughts. Such considerations can be pooh-poohed as a lingering prejudice of iconicity – and structuralists should have no truck with *that*. But if so, are we then to regard the

---

[26] There are some *post*positions in English, such as *two years ago*.

good fit between structure and function as nothing more than a happy coincidence (the fortuitous arrival of Chomsky's 'shower of cosmic rays' perhaps)? Not only is this position verging on the wacky, but it cuts against Chomsky's attempt to describe the way in which the language faculty is the optimal solution to legibility conditions imposed at the interface with the thought systems.

But when we turn to functionalism we encounter a dilemma that is at least as pressing. As we saw when reviewing Newmeyer's discussion of iconicity, there is, in fact, a fundamental emptiness to the position that linguistic universals fit pressures imposed by language use. 'On its own,' writes Kirby (1999, p. 19) this does not constitute an explanation of anything'. He continues:

> The innatist approach links universals to acquisition, so that constraints on cross-linguistic variation are the *direct consequence* of constraints on the acquisition (and mental representation) of language. The functionalist approach fails to make the link between *explicans* and *explicandum*, leaving the real puzzle, the puzzle of fit, unexplained.

> (emphasis in original)

Thus, where the nativist posits an *explicans* – the LAD mechanism – for the explicandum (linguistic universals), the functionalist says, in effect, that *some process or other* ensures that structure will fit function. This is not to deny, however, that a research programme can be designed to explain how functional pressures give rise to universals in particular cases, and which asks whether this can be done without recourse to innate constraints. Indeed, this is Kirby's own research programme – addressing what he calls *the problem of linkage*, which is (ibid., p. 20)

> Given a set of observed constraints on cross-linguistic variation, and a corresponding pattern of functional preference, an explanation of this fit will solve the problem: how did the latter give rise to the former?

The main way in which Kirby tackles this question is by computer simulation, a full description of which would take us well beyond the domain of this book. I will, in fact, describe Kirby's treatment of the relation of some facts about typology and about parsing, while only touching on the computational work. This work alone is sufficient to give the functionalist pause for thought.

First, one can address questions about the 'fit' between processing (qua accessibility to the parser) and linguistic universals in terms of the relation between (1) hierarchies of accessibility and (2) the form and existence/non-existence of language types. Along these lines, Keenan and Comrie (1977) argued that what they call the relative clause *accessibility hierarchy* (AH) constrains possible languages. I give examples of Keenan and Comrie's relative clause accessibility hierachy, with the most accessible at the top (from Kirby, 1999), in (70).

(70) a. the band that plays the Jazz Joint (Subject)

　　 b. the band that I saw in the Jazz Joint (Object)

　　 c. the band that I gave five pounds to (Indirect Object)

　　 d. the band that I play guitar in (Oblique)

　　 e. the band whose songs are funky (Genetive)

　　 f. the band that few are bigger than (Object of Comparison)

It will be noted that the accessibility to relativisation depends upon the grammatical function of the resumptive pronoun within the relative clause (*that* or *whose* in this example: subject > direct object > indirect object > oblique > genitive > object of comparison.

From a cross-linguistic analysis, Comrie and Keenan (1979, p. 653) postulate two *accessibility hierarchy constraints*:

1) 'If a language can relativise any position on the AH with a primary strategy then it can relativise all higher positions with that strategy'.

2) 'For each position on the AH, there are possible languages which can relativise that position with a primary strategy, but cannot relativise any lower position with that strategy.'

In the 1977 paper Keenan and Comrie presented data from around 50 languages in support of their AH. For example, in Western Malayo-Polynesian languages only subjects can be relativised; in Welsh the primary strategy is for only subjects and direct objects to be relativised. In both English and Urhobo (spoken in the Western Niger Delta) the object of comparison can be relativised as, of course, can all points higher on the hierarchy: *the man who Mary is taller than* in English and the equivalent of *man the that Mary big than him* in Urhobo. French stops short (at genitive relativisation) of relativising the object of comparison. Also in the paper, some developmental evidence is fielded for the comparative ease with which children can comprehend relative clauses (Legum, 1975, on 6- to 8-year-olds' comprehending relative clauses with subjects more successfully than with objects).

More recently, MacWhinney and Pleh (1988) reviewed psycholinguistic studies showing that subject-relative clauses are easier to parse than object relatives, while additionally reporting their studies of Hungarian showing the same thing. With regard to relative clauses modifying subjects in the matrix clause (e.g., in sentences like *The man who saw me liked Cheddar* unlike the examples in (70) which have no matrix clause), Keenan and Hawkins (1987) report that ease of repetition declined down the hierarchy. While, as Kirby points out, this result tells us nothing about relative ease of sentence production or perception (and, of course, nothing about object relatives and about other languages) the data add detail to a familiar picture.

For Hawkins (1994) the fact that ease of parsing seems to decline as one travels down the AH implies, typologically, that each language must somehow be selecting a certain point on the hierarchy above which relativisation is grammatical and below which it is not. (As to what determines which actual point is selected, one supposes that 'structural' facts about the particular language must be determining this, as I argued above with regard to subjacency; though put like this the assumption is no more than a hand-wave.)

Kirby's computational work puts pressure on the simple assumption that the structural complexity of relative clauses in the hierarchy gives rise, in some direct fashion, to different languages settling on different points. (Structural complexity at different levels of the hierarchy is calculated by counting the number of nodes within the domain of relativisation – see Kirby, pp. 65–66.) His initial model showed that structural complexity by itself *cannot* give rise to the hierarchy. In this simulation, there was an initial comparison of subject and object relatives only. Essentially, what happened in the simulation was that, among other variables, utterances of the different types together with variables representing speakers of the four possible grammars SO, SO', S'O' and S'O (where prime means *lacking* that kind of relativisation) and variables representing 'acquirers' (without any grammar) interacted over a number of generations. The expected outcome was that SO, SO' and S'O' would emerge, but not S'O. In fact, what happened was that the 'evolution' converged nihilistically upon the type S'O'.

This problem was, however, rectified by adopting a *competing motivations* approach in which forms emerge due to different functional pressures conflicting with each other. Kirby nods towards Newmeyer's (1998) sceptical analysis of this approach (described on p. 421), but argues that Newmeyer's charge of vacuity will not stick in the present case. Kirby's actual justification is somewhat technical. But, for our purposes at least, one may say that the difference between the use of the competing motivations approach by somebody like Haiman and the present usage is that in Kirby's case these motivations are pre-hoc causal variables whose effect can be gauged in the computed outcome, whereas in the case of functional linguistics more generally the usage is post hoc and unconstrained.

What Kirby demonstrates is that the focus on parsing complexity (*p-complexity* as he calls it) ignores a converse functional pressure – from the speaker rather than the listener – called *m-complexity*, for morphological complexity (given two competing ways in which to produce some message the speaker will be more likely to produce the one that is less morphologically complex). So what helps the speaker may not help the listener, and vice versa. Both kinds of complexity were fed into the system, and it was found that there was a shifting in prominence between the two over time, which in the end resulted in dynamic situation in which the correct hierarchical pattern shifted across populations. By generation 25, examples of SO, S'O' and SO' clearly emerged. There was still a sprinkling of S'O, by this time, but this was the only grammar of the four whose frequency *reduced* dramatically in the early generations.

This is clearly a good result for the functionalist approach. But Kirby's next task is to spell out its limitations. Staying within the domain of relativisation, he discusses cases in which a phenomenon involving the relative ease of processing (a 'processing asymmetry' as he calls it) does *not* give rise to the expected kind of cross-linguistic 'asymmetry', as well as cases in which the typological asymmetries are related to processing asymmetries to which they should not be related on functionalist principles. He focuses on the kind of relativisation illustrated in (71) – taken from Kirby (ibid., p. 98) – in which there is both a subordinate and a matrix clause.

(71) (a) The man who found me saw Ruth. (matrix subject, subject relative – S^s)

   (b) The man whom I found saw Ruth. (matrix subject, object relative – S^o)

   (c) Ruth saw the man who found me. (matrix object, subject relative – O^s)

   (d) Ruth saw the man whom I found. (matrix object, object relative – O^o)

(In the notation X^y, X is the matrix element and Y the relative.) Now, generalising from the psycholinguistic work of Keenan and Hawkins (1987) just touched upon, we should be finding the following order of accessibility:

$\{S^s, O^s\} > \{S^o, O^o\}$

However, the first study on the ease of processing matrix plus subordinate relativising, by Sheldon (1974), resulted in the following order:

$\{S^s, O^o\} > \{O^s, S^o\}$

In other words, sentences were found to be easier to process if the matrix function of the head was paralleled by the grammatical function of the resumptive pronoun in the subordinate clause. Kirby calls this the role of *parallel function*. But it turns out, as Kirby shows in a review, that many subsequent studies using English and other languages produced results that were in conflict with this. Some of them, indeed, found evidence for the kind of accessibility effect discussed earlier. In any event, the conclusion drawn by Kirby is that accessibility effects as traditionally understood (from the AH) and parallel function effects both exist and are *in interaction*. See (72).

(72) (a) $S^s > O^s > O^o > S^o$ (accessibility > parallel function)

(b) $S^s > O^o > O^s > S^o$ (parallel function > accessibility)

Note, by the way, that where accessibility is construed by Hawkins and others as a matter of relative 'complexity', no such claims have been made for the parallel function. Be that as it may, Kirby assumes, as there is no reason to do otherwise, that *parallel function can be a functional selection pressure.*

Next step: just as we were able to move from the AH to claims about the kinds of languages that can exist (e.g., that S'O will not exist), so we should in principle be able to do much the same thing will parallel function (as a factor in p-complexity). Accordingly, if the situation can sometimes be

$\{S^s, O^o\} > \{O^s, S^o\}$

then by the same kind of logic used before, if there is a language with O^s or S^o then this language should also have S^s or O^o. Thus, expressing $(S^s, O^o) \rightarrow (O^s, S^o)$ as a conjunction we get $(S^s \vee O^o) \& \neg (O^s \vee S^o)^{27}$. In (73) I show the kind of language types that should exist, on this argument, together with a note on whether they do indeed exist.

(73) (a) $S^s \& \neg O^s$ [not found]

(b) $S^s \& \neg S^o$ [found; Iban (spoken in Malaysia)]

(c) $O^o \& O^s$ [not found]

(d) $O^o \& \neg S^o$ [not found]

As can be seen, three of the proposed language types do not exist; so there is no available evidence for parallel function being realised cross-linguistically.

---

[27] $\neg$ is the symbol for 'not' and v is the symbol for 'or'.

(Though with regard to non-existence, it must be borne in mind that one cannot prove a negative.) More generally, if parallel function had the same status as a functional pressure as accessibility then we should find:

1) Languages that allow subject relative clauses, unless they are in an object position in the matrix (S^s but not O^s); or

2) Languages that allow object relative clauses, unless they are in the subject position in the matrix (O^o but not S^o).

But neither of these appear to exist.

> This poses serious problems for the functional approach [...]. There is nothing in the theory that can explain why accessibility has cross-linguistic implications, but parallel function has not. It seems that the explanations put forward here suffer from being ad hoc, a common criticism of functional explanations.
>
> (Kirby, 1999, p. 102)

In a nutshell, the issue is this: Why do we not find languages that have the parallel-function relative clause without also having the non-parallel function relative clause? This would be the expression of the universal conjunction $(S^s \text{ v } O^o) \&\neg (O^s \text{ v } S^o)$. Specifically, why is it that for any language in which subject fragments like *the man who found me* is grammatical *the man whom I found* it is also grammatical?

In answering this question, Kirby draws our attention to another 'side of the coin'. That is to say, while we have so far been focusing entirely on links between heard sentences and the triggering experiences for syntactic development (e.g., p-complexity) and between developed competence and spoken utterances (e.g., m-complexity), we have been ignoring constraints on the linkage between the triggering experiences for syntactic development and the resultant competence. In other words, there may be *constraints within the child's acquisition device which ensure that children cannot get the parallel-function form without also getting the non-parallel one*. What Kirby seems to succeed in demonstrating is that, if we assume this acquisition device is structured rather as P & P theory takes it to be structured, this association can be explained.

This is how such a process (i.e., limitation on what can be acquired by the acquisition device) would work: why both non-parallel and parallel function forms must be acquired together. For a non-parallel fragment such as *the man whom I found*, P & P theory assumes that there is co-indexation between three elements: the head noun, the *wh*-element, and the trace of the *wh*-element at the end of the fragment. So two relations have to be considered: (1) between the trace and the *wh*-element (via movement) and (2) between the subordinate clause headed by the *wh*-element and the head noun (a process called 'predication'). In P & P theory, Kirby points out, the operations involved in these two are *informationally encapsulated*, thereby ensuring that any constraints on (1) would be independent of constraints on (2), and vice versa. However, if parallel function is to be realised cross-linguistically to produce $O^o \&\neg S^o$ or $S^s \&\neg O^s$ (i.e., having cases of parallel without non-parallel functions) any constraint on predication would need to be *dependent* on information about *wh*-movement, or vice versa.

> However, it is generally assumed that an operation like predication cannot be sensitive to the internal structure of the CP [the complement clause resulting from *wh*-movement, JR], and

similarly *wh*-movement cannot be restricted on the basis of structure outside the CP [i.e., of the determiner phrase, JR] … This means that, if these facts are mirrored in the LAD, these predicted language types are impossible to acquire or represent in the I-language domain.

(Kirby, 1999, pp. 107–108)

The LAD has, in effect no 'choice' but to make S^o grammatical if S^S is grammatical, given this encapsulation: competence is blind to the derivational history of the *wh*-element. The only other option is to make both forms ungrammatical. So, if an innate LAD can set limits on the emergence of relative clause universals, it is likely that we will find other mismatches between function and form; and so much the worse for the functionalist meta-theory.

It is likely that the functionalist would defend her position by saying that this is all too dependent upon the assumed psychological reality of parallel-function as a processing variable. Maybe it will turn out that it is no more than 'noise' serving only to obscure the substantive and universal operation of the accessibility hierarchy – similar to the pragmatic 'noise' one encounters in studies of children's acknowledgement of the binding and bounding constraints. Additionally, the functionalist might remind us that subscription to P & P theory is hardly compulsory; and indeed a minimalist or post-minimalist Chomskyan theory would perhaps not take such a hard line on informational encapsulation. Be that as it may, the kind of arguments and computational models fielded by Simon Kirby will surely guarantee that functionalists will be far more circumspect when talking about how 'ease of processing' gives rise to constraints on cross-linguistic variation; cf. the 'I get my constraints from evolution' line quoted earlier.

4.5.2 Grammaticalisation: is it a process that bolsters functionalism; is it a process at all?

In the cartoon description of grammaticalisation I presented earlier it was said to be the historical process whereby lexical items became drained of meaning while taking on a purely grammatical function (e.g., open-class words becoming closed-class, verbs becoming auxiliaries, pronouns becoming clitics, and so forth). I raise the topic now because, from a functionalist-evolutionary perspective, the existence of grammaticalisation can be taken to suggest that many of the grammatical functions whose acquisition Chomskyans explain by the operation of an innate LAD may in reality be little more than cultural conventions whose acquisition is explicable in terms of essentially domain-general processes. Here is Tomasello (2000b, p. 162):

Each of the 5000 or more languages of the world has its own inventory of linguistic conventions, including syntactic conventions, which allow its users to share experience with one another symbolically. This inventory of symbolic conventions is grounded in universal structures of human cognition, human communication, and the mechanics of vocal-auditory apparatus […] All the conventions and constructions of a given language are not invented all at one time, of course, and once invented they often do not stay the same for very long, but rather they evolve, change, and accumulate over time as humans use them with one another. This set of processes is called grammaticalisation, and it involves such well-attested phenomena as free-standing words evolving into grammatical markers, and loose and redundantly organised discourse structures congealing into tight and less redundantly organised syntactic constructions.

In minimalist language, one might say that, in reality, human languages only consist of interpretable features with a *sui generis* semantic character, legible at the interface with the thought systems, and that the uninterpretable, 'apparent imperfections' are no more than an historical accretion of symbolic conventions. If so, then the notion of an LAD, configured to deal with these uninterpretable features by 'checking' and so forth, cannot be sustained.

As far as I know, nobody has ever argued in quite this sweeping way; but it is a view which lurks in the functionalist shadows. In any event, it is fair to say that grammaticalisation is regarded by functionalists as (a) a *sui generis* unidirectional process about which one can theorise and (b) a process that undermines generativist linguistic theory.

Generativists such as Frederick Newmeyer (1998) argue that neither of these claims can be sustained. With regard to (a), rather than being a particular, determinate and measurable current of linguistic change (i.e., something like the sense in which acquisition is such a current) grammaticalisation is really a loose term used to describe an *epiphenomenon* of other independent processes of linguistic change. Much of what follows will be taken from that source.

Let us begin be setting out a more careful definition of grammaticalisation. Grammaticalisation is the '*loss of grammatical independence* of a grammatical structure or element' (Newmeyer, 1998, p. 227; emphasis added). That is to say, the appearance of this structure or element in a sentence becomes dependent upon which other structures or elements are present. Consider the way in which an auxiliary is dependent as compared with a verb, a pluralising affix as compared with a noun, and a clictic like –'s as compared with the word to which it is attached. Here are some examples of the move from less grammatical to more grammatical (put another way, from the lexical[28] to the less lexical – a process called *downgrading*). Moving from the more lexical to the less, a lexical category, such as a noun, can downgrade to a functional category. Whereas in modern French, for example, *pas* routinely follows *ne* to express negative force (becoming a functional category therefore), in Old French *ne* was reinforced by a number of semantically appropriate nouns of which *pas* (step) was just one. Some of the others included *point* (dot), *mie* (crumb), and *gote* (drop). With regard to the downgrading from functional category or pronoun to clitic, in Old Norse the third-person, accusative reflexive *sik* developed into the clitic *–sk*, which spread to other pronouns, also becoming a marker for voice.

As is evident from the *ne ... pas* example, these changes were frequently accompanied by what functionalists call a 'bleaching' of the original meaning. Thus, while *pas* still means 'step' in French, *ne ... pas* is not being used to say something about stepping. Indeed it is commonly claimed that the progressive loss of meaning is what caused the morphosyntactic 'reanalysis' (a term to which I will return). Accordingly, Heine and Reh (1984, p. 15) say:

> With the term 'grammaticalisation' we refer essentially to an evolution whereby linguistic units lose in semantic complexity, pragmatic significance , syntactic freedom, and phonetic substance, respectively.

---

[28] Lexemes are the units that are conventionally listed in dictionaries as separate entities.

Viewed in a more positive light, this bleaching can be seen as a strengthening of a metaphorical flavour – as in the evolution of the Old English *have* (meaning simple possession) to the sense of *have* (*have to* ...); as an obligation is something that we 'have' willy nilly.

Newmeyer's (1998) aim in his chapter is to 'deconstruct' the term 'grammaticalisation', by which he means to show (a) that it consists of a set of sub-processes that operate independently, and (b) that when these overlap then there is something that we might call grammaticalisation, but to do so is not to name a *sui generis* process. As he puts it (ibid., p. 295):

> Far from calling for a 'new theoretical paradigm', grammaticalisation appears to be no more than a cover term for a conjunction of familiar developments from different spheres of language, none of which require or entail any of the others.

This then is the charge of being an epiphenomenon of other changes. These changes are: (a) the reanalysis of a syntactic pattern (as having a different abstract syntactic structure from that which it had originally) in the direction of downgrading (i.e., of *increased* grammatical function), (b) semantic changes, (c) phonetic reduction.

I will deal with each of these in turn. First, the reanalysis of a syntactic pattern can be defined as the abstract syntactic structure of the expression changing without any accompanying changes in the order of the surface elements in the pattern. Newmeyer's argument is that one cannot have grammaticalisation without reanalysis but one *can* have reanalysis without grammaticalisation. For an example of the latter case we can return to the example of *let's* (a reduction of *let us*), for whose reduction – it might be recalled (p. 219) – Haiman argued that iconicity offered a better account than trace theory. Haiman argued that trace theory could not explain why, to take his example, Moses could not have said to the Pharaoh, as it were, *let's go* (= *let us go*). But perhaps one reason why *let's* cannot be addressed to somebody as an entreaty on behalf of a group is that the verb and the clitic now have such a degree of *cohesion* (as it is called) that the expression is more appropriately written as *lets* (minus the apostrophe). This is exemplified in expressions like *Lets make room for you*, as spoken by a single individual. In this case, there is no downgrading (*lets* is no more grammatical than *let's*; indeed less so if anything), but the expression has been *reanalysed* as one in which *let* and *s* have coalesced rather than functioning as verb-plus-clitic. (One might say that this is similar to what Pine claimed for young children's use of determiners and verb inflections!) In a similar vein, taking the example from Lightfoot (1979), the verb *like* could mean 'please' in Old English; so in the *Him liked the pears* and *The King liked the pears* the initial noun phrase was interpreted as the object, by taking the structure to be object-subject-verb. However, when SVO became the canonical word order for English, sentences such as *The King liked the pears* were reanalysed as SVO, with *liked* meaning 'was fond of' or 'enjoyed' – while sentences of the *Him liked the pears* kind dropped out of use. Note that here we see a change of lexical meaning but not in the direction of bleaching, while the change cannot be understood as a grammatical enriching/lexical downgrading. As a final example of reanalysis without grammaticalisation, one can take the example given by Haspelmath (1998; discussed on p. 259

of Newmeyer) from colloquial modern French. Here the post-verbial third-person pronoun *ti* is reanalysed as an interrogative particle to make, say, *Votre père parti* a question.

With regard to the independence of semantic change – (b) – Newmeyer gives examples of the way in which semantic change in the direction of acquiring a stronger metaphorical flavour can take place *independently* of grammaticalisation, *pace* the functionalists claim that 'Grammaticalisation may also be viewed as a sub-type of metaphor … a metaphorical shift to the abstract' (Matisoff, 1991, p. 284). Heine *et al.* (1991) have proposed a scale of metaphorical directionality of

> PERSON > OBJECT > ACTIVITY > SPACE > TIME > QUALITY

in which an entity on the left-hand can be used to conceptualise one on the right, but not vice versa. But such metaphorical extensions are found, Newmeyer points out, without grammaticalisation. For example the use of synecdoche is promiscuous (as in examples like *I've just read the latest Martin Amis*), in which a person is used to conceptualise an object. But this is not a case of grammaticalisation. While the evolution of the term *moon* to *month* (an object conceptualising a time) must likewise fail to be counted as grammaticalisation.

Third, in considering phonetic reduction – (c) – one can turn to cases where what looks like reduction as a sign of grammaticalisation turns out to be a case of regular phonological change occurring elsewhere in the language. Joseph (1996) has argued, for instance, that phonological reduction in the development of the modern Greek future marker *tha* out of the classical Greek *thelo* ('want') is a manifestation of regular sound change not of grammaticalisation. More generally, the phonological reductions found in grammaticalisation are frequently no more than a subset of the phonological changes at work in general in fast speech.

Newmeyer's position on the epiphenomenal nature of grammaticalisation is shown in Figure 4.27 (adapted from Newmeyer's own Figure 5.1).

Newmeyer also questions whether historical change is invariably in the direction of downgrading. To this end, he cites a number of examples of change in the direction of 'upgrading', i.e., *de*crease in grammatical content/increase in lexical content. Such phenomena, he says, are 'rampant' (ibid., p. 263). I now list some of Newmeyer's examples of historical upgrading.

- *The lexicalisation of affixes.* In this case, affixes can fuse with the root of a word. Thereby, the English *drench* has emerged from the two-morpheme form *drank-jan*, meaning 'cause to wet' (Ramat, 1992).

- *Inflectional affixes becoming words.* In Old English, there was a genitive case inflection *–(e)s*. During Middle English this became, by phonological accident, a homophone of *his*, with the initial *h* going unpronounced in some dialects. Eventually, the genitive affix came to be interpreted as the full lexical pronoun *his* (Janda, 1980). An echo of this is detectable in archaic forms such as *John Smith his book*.

- *Derivational affixes becoming words.* In Dutch, the derivational suffix *–tig* (a cognate of the English *–ty*) developed into the indefinite numeral meaning the

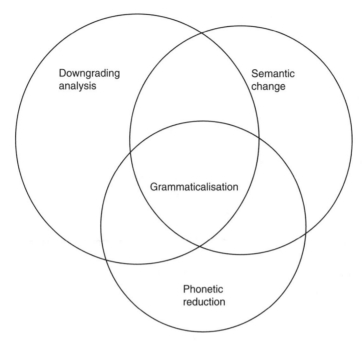

Figure 4.27 Newmeyer's (1988) illustration of how grammaticalisation is an epiphenomenon of other processes (permission sought).

equivalent of our 'umpteen' (Norde, 1997). It came to be pronounced as full vowel, unlike the reduced pronunciation of the suffix form.

- *Clitics becoming words.* In an Austonesian language spoken in the Phillipenes called Ilokano (Rubino, 1994) the enclitic form –*to* attached to the verb to mark the future tense became a free-standing, unbound word which can be used, in colloquial speech, to mean the equivalent of 'I'll do that'.

- *Functional categories (e.g., pronouns) becoming lexical categories (e.g., nouns)* The Old English word *man* was used, as it is in present-day German, to mean the equivalent of the English indefinite pronoun *one* (as in *One is not amused*). After swinging back and forth from indefinite pronoun to noun meaning male person, it was the latter, *less* grammatical usage that survived into Modern English.

I have presented, then, the bare bones of Newmeyer's exhaustive and tenaciously argued case against grammaticalisation being a determinate process and in favour of its being an epiphenomenon of independent processes that are well understood. It is not difficult to imagine, however, how functionalists might seek to rebut his conclusions. In the first place, they might say that downgrading analysis lies at the heart of grammaticalisation in a way that semantic change and phonetic reduction does not. Indeed they could say that grammaticalisation just is downgrading reanalysis *tout court*. The strong claims about semantic change causing downgrading analysis could be jettisoned, while a relaxed line on the presence of phonetic reduction could be adopted. As Newmeyer himself insists, there is never grammaticalisation without reanalysis. As for the claim that there can be reanalysis without grammaticalisation (e.g., *lets*, and the *partil* example above; and see Newmeyer, 1998, pp. 257–59) this is a far cry from establishing that there can be *downgrading* reanalysis without grammaticalisation. And even if this could be established, one can, as I said, drop the insistence that grammaticalisation must involve both semantic change and phonetic reduction. With regard to the evidence, just reviewed, for the converse process of *up*grading, functionalists can take comfort from Newmeyer's admission that the claim for the unidirectionality of re-analysis (i.e., its being in the downgrading direction) is 'almost true' in so far as 'a rough impression is that downgrading has occurred at least 10 times as often as upgrading' (ibid., pp. 275–76).

Moreover, functionalists can always insist that grammaticalisation 'emerges' as a *sui generis* phenomenon from the confluence of its three components; linguistic processes do not have to be additive; the true situation may be 'chemical'. In fact, there would appear to be a number of ways in which one could justify cleaving to grammaticalisation as a determinate process rather than a descriptive shorthand for a nest of complex historical changes. But even if it could be shown that Newmeyer is overstating his case against grammaticalisation-as-process, the phenomena investigated within the grammaticalisation research programme do not – I hope it has emerged from this brief review – reveal the evolution of the truly grammatical from the fundamentally semantic – the illegible from the legible. Much of what we find looks more like fiddling at the margins.

If there can be seen to be an essentially unidirectional process of downgrading analysis over historical time coupled, more or less, with some semantic bleaching and phonological reduction then it is, by any standards, a remarkably weak and conservative progression. For no one would seriously advance that the English of Chaucer was less grammatical than the English of Jonathan Franzen, or that a speaker of Old French who did indeed think 'no ... step' when she negated a sentence was less grammatically competent than a present-day Parisienne turning down a pass. Indeed, compared with other evolutions wrought within human culture (from superstition to science, from wax tablets to digital computers ...) syntactic evolution is very small beer indeed.

For the Chomskyan, this conservatism is easily explained; and likewise for somebody who takes seriously the arguments of Simon Kirby just described. One says that the child's LAD sets limits on the grammatical changes that can be assimilated by the next generation. Children sift out the syntactically outré.

4.5.3 Exaptation: that's the name of the game?

We do seem to need some position standing between the two stark alternatives of saying (1) that syntax evolved essentially because being a successful communicator aids reproductive fitness (don't confuse a potential mate by spouting a subjacency-violating word-salad!) and the view that (2) because syntax's being the 'optimal' conduit between the thought systems and the sensorimotor systems counterindicates its having evolved by the messy, hit-and-miss process of Darwinian selection it must have come about by some fortuitous, geophysical DNA-reorganising cataclysm. The first provides reams of blank sheets to just-so story writers, while the second sounds downright flaky.

A middle way between the two is provided by the notion of *exaptation*. This refers to cases in which a physical attribute or a capacity that has evolved for one function comes to be recruited by a species to fulfil a different function. Bird flight is thought to be an exaptation: the feathers from thermo-regulation, the wing structures from limbs evolved (more controversially) to facilitate climbing (Chatterjee 1997; Feduccia,1999). As applied to the evolution of syntax, one might suppose that, say, tool-making or numerical reasoning skills have been bolted on to a protolanguage (see p. 87) to produce a recursive syntactic system. By this route, one can retain one's Darwinian credentials while still denying that syntax evolved by the gradual, continuous, extension of pre-existing communication systems. One can deny functionalists their story while staying within a respectable evolutionary-biological ambit.

In this final subsection, I will consider three kinds of exaptationist story. They are variously unsatisfactory, but thinking about them does focus the mind on the fact that no matter how minimalist we strive to be there is an ineluctable kernel of something *sui generis* about syntax that resists dissolution or deconstruction. Here are the three positions.

1) Exaptation from the 'social calculus' and from ballistic movements' planning circuits (Calvin and Bickerton, 2000);

2) Exaptation from the 'tree-like' structure of the syllable to sentential structure (Carstairs-McCarthy, 1999);

3) Exaptation from non-linguistic recursive systems 'evolved to solve other computational problems such as navigation, number quantification, and social relations' (Hauser, Chomsky and Fitch, 2002).

Taking these in turn, no discussion of language evolution would be complete without reference to the work of Derek Bickerton. As is well known, his position is Chomskyan – generativist and nativist. In the present co-authored book, however, Bickerton seeks to out-minimilalise Chomsky (a sort of minimal minimalism), presumably with the intention of hammering out the syntactic material so thinly that it will stretch as far as the non-syntactic processes of the reciprocal altruism and throwing rocks at fast-receding rabbits. Within his kind of minimalism there are four basic 'mechanisms' (to which he adds movement and traces).

A Argument structure – the obligatory representation of one, two, or three (depending on the nature of the verb) arguments.

B The obligatory attachment of arguments to non-arguments, where non-arguments are verbs, prepositions, and case markers. (*Columbus discovered America* – verb; *Columbus's discovery of America* – case marker and preposition). This is acknowledged even in creoles.

C The binary attachment of constituents. This is essentially the same conception of merge as described in 2.3.3. Bickerton uses the term 'attachment' rather than 'merge', however, because merging is clearly what α (target) and β (non-target) do not do. Rather β gets attached to α (e.g., modifiers to heads) in such a way that the result is not a blend, intersection or union of the two, but an α-phrase.

D A hierarchy of thematic roles that determines the *order* in which attachment is performed at (in English) the left and right of the verb. We have, in fact, already discussed Jackendoff's proposals for a thematic hierarchy (actor > patient > theme > goal ... see (52) p. 416) in our discussion of how the generative approach accommodates some degree of iconicity (4.2.2). However more is at stake in the present case, for the following reason. The minimalist approach makes issues about order of attachment of crucial importance, in contrast to their place in P & P, because, recall, in minimalism there is assumed to be no pre-existing X' framework onto which to map theta roles: *the process is essentially bottom-up.* The serial, cumulative process of attachment/merge must progress in moves whose order must be constrained and motivated by *something* if not by a pre-existing phrase structure. For Bickerton, the thematic hierarchy fits the bill, as order naturally falls out of it. We need not dwell on the details of his proposal; but he argues for an hierarchy, similar to Jackendoff's, of AGENT/CAUSER > GOAL > THEME/EXPERIENCER, with the final attachment (AGENT) ending up at the highest point on the tree and with GOAL as the first attachment prior to THEME. As I understand it, this hierarchy, and its associated obligatory order in which elements have to be attached to ensure that the correct elements end up in the correct levels of the tree, is supposed to fill the vacuum left by X' and d-structure. It provides a syntacto-conceptual framework upon which move can operate.

So *does* this thinly hammered out syntactic material reach the supposed pre-linguistic evolutionary precursors? In the case of A (obligatory representation of one, two, or thee arguments for a verb) some might want to say 'yes'. This is the 'social calculus'. First, we can suppose that pre-linguistic man established the same kind of dominance hierarchies, cliques, food-sharing networks, and systems of reciprocal altruism more generally, that are found in modern-day chimpanzees. For these to operate effectively, the creatures would be required to (1) distinguish between individuals, (2) distinguish between types of action, and (3) carry around some more-or-less abstract memorial representation of the roles of the participants in these actions. Accordingly, Bickerton (ibid., p. 130–131) writes:

> We can suppose that every time primates record an event in memory they tag each participant in that event with the role of AGENT, THEME, GOAL (whom the action was directed towards) ... In other words, with that apparatus you have a mechanism powerful enough to detect cheaters and freeloaders and make reciprocal altruism work as a lynchpin of social life.

A little later, however, Bickerton raises the following issue: if protolanguage (with flat trees, see Figure 2.1 p. 86) was around for something like two million years and social altruism for still longer why was the evolution of syntax so delayed? Bickerton's co-author William Calvin offers an answer to this question, about which Bickerton says 'I knew that what he proposed just had to be right' (ibid., p. 150). The answer, as we have seen, is that the ballistic movement planner was exapted to become a sentence planner. (This kind of idea has certainly done the rounds, with Bruner [Bruner and Bruner, 1968], to name just one, also recruiting it.) The analogy is based on the idea that skilled action is hierarchically organised and that it is crucial that each subcomponent be engaged in the correct order. And yet, at the end of the chapter in which Calvin sets out this idea Bickerton (ibid., p. 167; emphasis added) sets out the kind of objections to this idea that linguists often field. They are worth quoting in full.

> I think we have to be a little careful here in the analogy between executing a throw and building a sentence. The things that you regard as embedded in the throw – arm movements, wrist movements, and the rest – differ from the phrases and clauses that are embedded in language in more than one way. First, an arm movement is not built up out of wrist movements, and a shoulder movement isn't built up out of arm movements: we're talking about

things which, while they share obvious commonalities, *are simply different in kind from one another*. However every clause is a collection of phrases, one or more of which will expand into a clause, which in turn consists of a collection of phrases, one or more of which may be expanded, and so on indefinitely, *the same kinds of things are used over and over*. Second, the number of units you use in a throw is finite and strictly limited – there are only so many parts of the body you can involve – whereas a sentence is potentially infinite, and certainly has no numerical limit.

And yet, later in the book (ibid., p. 193) Bickerton is clearly accepting that 'recip-rocal altruism's cognitive categories and ballistic movement's planning circuits are compatible with slow language improvement over a few million years'. This is not really self-contradiction, because one can accept a fundamental structural and func-tional divergence between a precursor and an evolved capacity without this debar-ring the claim that one evolved from the other. Lungs, to borrow one of the authors' examples, evolved from swim bladders – a breathing function from a flotation func-tion. The problem is not with contradiction but with 'compatibility' arguments – which bedevil the field of language evolution. So much is 'compatible' with this lan-guage improvement and so little isn't.

With regard to the other three mechanisms B, C, and D, it looks rather as if Bickerton believes that the theta role hierarchy is supposed to be rooted in the ballistic movement planner. In any event, he concludes:

> The fact that this [i.e., accounting for so much linguistic structure with only A, B, C, and D]
> is possible and that a grammar arising from research into the evolution of language
> combines such extensive coverage with such extremely restrictive principles, strongly suggests
> that language really did follow the paths that we have proposed in the body of this book
>
> (ibid., p. 246)

Well, many of us will still see a chasm hanging between the linguistic and social/ballistic domains, and will be left thinking 'Just how much imagination am I being expected to extend to bridging it? The less need for imaginative leaps (e.g., the swim bladder-to-lung transition), the better.'

The next kind of exaptationist theory to be considered certainly does not leave one complaining about the ambiguity of the message and the over-familiarity of the proposal. Carstairs-McCarthy's (1999) scenario is provokingly original. He asks why languages universally make a distinction between a sentential element at a higher level in the tree (usually a subject) and a verb phrase at a lower level, usually con-taining a grammatical object (broadly: [N[VN]]), when the same information can be conveyed by a NP alone. To take Chomsky's well-known example, *the enemy destroyed the city* and *the enemy's destruction of the city* not only share a similar X' structure, but they tell us more or less (see below) the same thing. Why do we use [N[VN]] when NP would so just as well?

Carstairs-McCarthy's answer is that the [N[VN]] structure of a sentence is an exaptation of the [Consonant [Vowel Consonant]] structure of the syllable. To explain, it is generally accepted that the internal syllabic structure is as shown in 4.28(b) rather than in 4.28(a).

There is a good deal of psycholinguistic evidence (about 'slips of the tongue') and cross-linguistic evidence (relative frequency of nucleus-coda constraints versus onset-nucleus constraints) which suggests that 4.28(b) is the correct analysis.

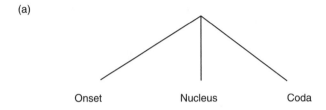

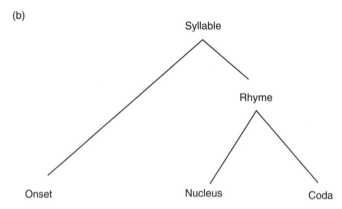

Figure 4.28 Carstairs-McCarthy's (1999) illustration of the true (b) nature of syllabic constituent structure: (a) is not the case.

What this view affords us – most strikingly – is way of relating early man's evolution of upright posture to language evolution. Walking upright is thought to have brought about a radical change in the shape of the passage between the larynx and the lips (Liberman, 1984) – a change which not only made humans the only mammals who cannot breathe while they eat and drink but made us able to articulate full syllables. In his own words the claim is this (Carstairs-McCarthy, 1999, pp. 147–148).

> So, since the syllable appeared as a unit of phonetic and phonological organisation as soon as the lowered larynx and other vocal tract changes made a more modern style of vocalisation possible, it is reasonable to conclude that the neural organisation underlying syllable structure was co-opted to provide a syntax for strings of 'words' when the need became pressing. This resemblance was neither accidental nor analogical, but rather homological in the evolutionary sense: that is, it came about because sentence structure had originally the same biological basis in neural organisation as syllable structure had.

It is perhaps easy to agree with Jackendoff (2002, p. 253 footnote) that this kind of proposal has 'the right sort of flavour'. But a couple of fairly obvious sceptical remarks need making. First, one may want to insist that the thoughts whose structure language evolved to express were intended to have a truth value. Sentences can, of course fill this bill; but NPs can do no more than secure *reference*. The assumption that the thoughts of early man made no distinction between truth and reference seems hard to sustain – particularly if we reflect upon what Bickerton calls the social calculus. Second, it is by no means clear how the property of recursion is supposed to emerge from such a process. It is to this which we finally turn.

Hauser, Chomsky and Fitch (2002) distinguish between the faculty of language in the broad sense (FLB) – this encompasses the sensorimotor and the conceptual-intentional systems – and the faculty of language in the narrow sense (FLN) whose core is the property of recursion that gives us the capacity for generating an infinite array of expressions from a limited set of elements. This allows the authors to take a gradualist, classically Darwinian view of language qua FLB while claiming that FLN is uniquely human and 'recently evolved'. Their proposal (Hauser *et al.*, 2002, p. 1573; emphasis added) is that

> FLN comprises only the core computational mechanisms of recursion as they appear in narrow syntax and the mappings to the interfaces. If FLN is really this restricted, this hypothesis has the interesting effect of nullifying the argument from design, and *thus rendering the status of FLN as an adaptation open to question...* By this hypothesis, FLB contains a wide variety of cognitive and perceptual mechanisms shared with other species, but only those mechanisms underlying FLN – *particularly its capacity for discrete infinity are uniquely human...* What is unique to our species is quite specific to FLN, and includes its internal operations *as well as its interface with other organism-internal systems of FLB.*

Needless to say, FLN is supposed to approximate an 'optimal solution' to the problem of linking the two external systems; and the authors add that many of the issues that have exercised linguists since the Chomskyan revolution, such as subjacency and *wh*-movement, are *by-products* of the solution 'generated automatically by the neural/computational constraints and the structure of FLB'. Moreover, the possibility is raised that

> The structural details of FLN may result from pre-existing constraints, rather than directly from the direct shaping by natural selection targeted specifically at communication. In so far as this proves to be true, such structural details are not, strictly speaking, adaptations at all

(ibid., p. 1574; emphasis added)

Unfortunately, the authors are vague about the evolutionary roots of recursion. Their hypothesis does, though, have the advantage of suggesting the testable hypothesis that we should be able to identify capacities in animals that are recursive in nature without being linguistic. They mention 'navigation' and 'social relationships'. I suppose many of us would have a favourite candidate for this extra-linguistic recursion. Mine would be coding transitive relationships, both in physical properties like size (or simply stacking objects) and in the social calculus (e.g., A deferred to B, and B deferred to C, so A would be expected to defer to C). Who knows?

4.6 Taking stock

I have displayed the pragmatist case encrusted with critical editorialising (aka 'sniping'); so it might be well now to nod towards a more positive assessment. I will give this in rough narrative order. Some of the points will have appeared before.

With regard to Langacker's cognitive grammar, first of all, rather than focusing on its shortcomings as a syntactic theory *vis-à-vis* Chomskyan theory, one might regard it primarily as a theory of the mental models that underlie different kinds of syntactic capacity. In this light indeed, it might be regarded as scoring over Chomsky. For while Chomsky is vague and metaphorical ('imposed at the interface' and the like) about the impact of cognition on syntax, Langacker can be said to be offering us quite precise accounts of the *representational conduits* between the two. What's more, as I said earlier, it offers hints on how the claims of dynamic minimalism might be tested.

Turning next to Van Valin, is it not grossly unfair to suggest, as I did (p. 405), that somebody sympathetic to the Chomskyan approach might be right to regard this theory as not even approaching descriptive adequacy, in so far as it offers us 'lowest common denominator' descriptions of 100 or so languages without giving a competence theory of any one of them that bears comparison to Chomsky's in terms of simplicity, elegance, and economy? For who says that the only conception of descriptive and explanatory adequacy must be the Chomskyan conception? Indeed, it is not strange to base a theory of universal preparedness for the syntax of 'Human' on the study of *English*, assuming, in essence, that, because all human children can acquire English, once we have a theory of what syntactic representational format is sufficient for learning English we have described something universally present; thus making it a subsidiary question what needs to be added and subtracted from this picture on the basis of cross-linguistic data. A disinterested observer, in fact, is likely to find Van Valin's conception of linguistic universals the more sympathetic one. On this view a linguistic universal is not something that one identifies essentially on the basis of the study of a single language – the theory still essentially trades in English phenomena – and for theory-internal reasons; it is something that cross-linguistic investigation reveals. Moreover, one might say that both Chomsky and Van Valin are now both travelling in the same minimalist direction, with Van Valin being some leagues in front. For example, many years before Chomsky abandoned the idea of X-bar grammar as being a representational template for phrase construction, Van Valin was dismissing it as 'English-style constituent analysis'(Van Valin, 1991, p. 10). Perhaps the next phase in the development of the minimalist 'research programme' will produce further jettisoning, to the extent of approaching Van Valin's stripped-down conception. And one might add the degree to which Van Valin is alive to empirical developmental matters, as contrasted with Chomsky's attitude of serene disinterest.

Turing now to 4.2, we can ask what threat to functionalism has really been demonstrated here. Of course, a generative linguist – Frederick Newmeyer in this case – will be able to produce examples of the way in which syntactic systematicity fails to reduce to functionalist motivations. But at the same time he acknowledges that the iconicity of which the functionalists make so much is real phenomenon, while describing the scope and need for bridging theories between semantic and syntactic structure (see (52) p. 416), some of the claims of which are not a million miles from those made by Van Valin. What really emerges in this section is the complexity and the subtlety of the issues rather than any vacuity in the functionalist approach.

With regard to my review of broadly pragmatist developmental psycholinguistics, many would find what Tomasello and Akhtar (2003, p. 321, emphasis added) say here to be highly sympathetic:

> In the beginning there are no abstract linguistic categories such as agent and patient, much less subject and object, that cut across all their language. *This is a genuine empirical discovery about children's early language*, and, following in the footsteps of Braine and others, we are proud to have contributed to it.

Perhaps there has been a lot of loose talk about 'abstract linguistic knowledge' not only in children but also in adults; while the standard objection to the 'inventory' conception of adult competence has been no more than a wheeling out of the 'phrase book' boo-word. As Van Valin argued with regard to linguistic universals, abstract knowledge must be demonstrated with data, not assumed for theory-internal reasons. Why should not, in William James' words, the 'empiricist temper' not be 'regnant' when it is indeed an empirical investigation on which we are embarking!

In 4.4, my argument that Braine's semanticist dissolving of semantic bootstrapping theory could be resisted if we reject the 'decompositional' theory of meaning will not impress people who are unconvinced by Fodor's atomistic rejection of semantic decomposition. As I mentioned, if one gives up on semantic decomposition, then one may also be forced to give up on the idea that some sentences are necessarily true. So why not stick with this – as Quine called it – 'dogma of empiricism' and maintain both that there is an analytic–synthetic distinction and that Braine's semantic assimilation theory is to be preferred to Pinker's semantic bootstrapping theory on the grounds of parsimony.

As for the final section on evolutionary questions, what most clearly emerges from this – the argument might run – is not the inadequacy of functionalist accounts in relation to generative ones but (a) just how complex, technical and subtle the issues are when approached seriously and (b) how right Chomsky was a few years ago when he called all hypotheses about the evolution of language 'mere hand-waving'. Moreover, taking sections 4.2 (Newmeyer's critique of functionalist accounts) and 4.5 (Kirby's work in particular) together, the thought occurs as to why the functionalist cannot claim, paralleling Chomsky in minimalism, that her position is in the nature of a 'research programme'. Accordingly, just as Chomsky assumes, as a defeasible working hypothesis, that syntax is the 'optimal' solution to external pressures, so the functionalist might regard the idea that all syntactic forms are more or less (often less) direct products of functional pressures. Neither the Chomskyan nor the functionalist claim will ever be secured, but can they not be afforded a similar status?

Well, as a pragmatist would say, 'that's one possible perspective on the issues'. It is not, however, mine. My difficulties with the pragmatist alternative resolve themselves into two, almost instinctual, reactions. First, thinking back to the discussion of pragmatism in Part 1, the reader is entitled to wonder what the ideas of a philosopher like Richard Rorty have to do with the kind of material covered in Part 4. What, most notably, does Rorty's rejection of the 'phallocentric metaphor of depth' have to do with (say) Julian Pine's painstaking analyses of children's use of the determiner? Well, in a way, quite a lot – if you stand back far enough to see the pattern.

The pragmatist-style empirical investigator does not feel the need to reach beneath the surface revealed by parsimonious description to consider, and to imaginatively construct, a dynamic competence driving development forward. Having the pragmatist temper will lead one to reject the idea that the phenomena we encounter in syntax and its development are really reflections of something that goes too deep for grasping by common sense and acute observation, that has to be understood by way of an imaginative project wrought from materials no less abstract than those we use to understand the physical universe. On the view that pragmatism rejects, an abstract imagination that conjures mechanisms whose work we only see as ripples on the surface is what has to guide theorising about the nature of our linguistic abilities and how they develop.

Now this may seem itself to be *over*-wrought! But a glance at any post-Chomskyan volume on syntax will reveal satisfying accounts of why sentences which common sense tells us should be grammatical are not – accounts that recruit abstract mechanisms going far deeper than consciousness. Are such projects based on an illusion, or on some blind anti-empirical drive to posit hidden mechanisms?

Pragmatism tells us: the depth, the complexity, the abstract mechanisms are not really there at all, things really are as they seem, and 'some final examination for which [you] could never have been properly prepared ha[s] just been cancelled' (p. 61). But in reality, 'the study of language acquisition is extraordinarily difficult' (Atkinson, 1982, p. vii) – something that, if nothing else, is borne out in the present book. The challenge to the imagination is a real one. What is most difficult of all is giving a satisfying account of how syntactic development is driven forward. Essentially, as we saw in 4.3, the pragmatist developmental theories of the present day fail to provide this, just as they failed in the 1970s. These focus on where children are *falling short* and then make hopeful gestures towards imitation learning, cutting-and-pasting, analogy making and spotting contextual overlap in predicates (in MOSAIC) to get the child up to our level. This stands in strong contrast to generatively-inspired accounts such as Andrew Radford's structure building and Martin Atkinson's dynamic minimalism in which specifically syntactic *motivations* and capacities are ascribed to the child. The child is given an engine to get from here to there, albeit at the cost of challenging common sense and our deep faith in the domain-general learning capacities and imitation.

This reference to motivation brings me to my second 'instinctual' point. To explain, the kind of nativism that Tomasello, Pine and others reject is something similar to the ancient doctrine of preformationism, within which it was believed, for example, that human spermatozoa contained tiny humans. But as we saw, the strong continuity assumption is rejected by many generativists; and even Chomsky himself opts for maturation. Rather, the kind of nativism that appears to have emerged intact from this book is one in which the child is credited with specifically syntactic motivations (e.g., to express the difference between types and instances by using articles and constructing noun phrases more generally) which do not reduce to the motivation to copy the input. The child-as-language-learner is not fundamentally mimetic – in contrast to the empiricist and pragmatist child. Perhaps the best illustration of this fact we have is the construction – not to be confused with the much-abused word 'constructionism' which has come to mean something like 'learning from the input' – of linguistic systems by children born profoundly deaf to hearing parents, and who in consequence were not exposed to sign language. They are language users without a language model.

Susan Goldin-Meadow and her colleagues have been investigating these children for over 25 years; and some of this work is excellently reviewed in her recent book *The resilience of language* (2003). These children will invent signing systems for themselves which express complex thoughts in primitively recursive structures – recursive in the sense of using rules that can be applied repeatedly to transform simple structures into complex ones. Not only this, but they will do something that looks awfully like reducing in surface structure by assuming null elements (as in *John₁ came and ____₁ stayed*). For example, one child expressed the propositions (1) the horse climbed into the house and (2) the same horse sleeps by signing *CLIMB SLEEP horse*. Because there was no language model these children showed no particular preference for reduction to the right (as in English) or reduction to the left (as in Japanese) – see 2.5.3 above. The model, had it been there, would only have canalised a process that was already under way.

References

Aaron, R. I. (1965) *John Locke.* Oxford University Press, Oxford.

Abbot-Smith, K., Lieven, E. and Tomasello, M. (2001) What preschool children do and do not do with ungrammatical word orders. *Cognitive Development,* **16**, 1–14.

Abney, S. P. (1987) The English noun phrase in its sentential aspect. Unpublished Ph.D. dissertation, MIT, Cambridge, MA.

Akhtar, N. (1999) Acquiring basic word order: evidence from data-driven learning of syntactic structure. *Journal of Child Language,* **26**, 339–356.

Akhtar, N. and Tomasello, M. (1997) Young children's productivity with word order and verb morphology. *Developmental Psychology,* **33**, 952–965.

Aksu, A. (1978) Aspect and modality in children's acquisition of the Turkish past tense. Unpublished doctoral dissertation, University of California, Berkeley.

Allan, L. G. and Jenkins, H. M. (1983) The effect of representations of binary variables on judgment of influence. *Learning and Motivation,* **14**, 381–505.

Allen, J. and Seidenberg, M. (1999) The emergence of grammaticality in connectionist networks. In B. MacWhinney (ed.) *The Emergence of Language,* pp. 115–151. Lawrence Erlbaum, Mahwah, NJ.

Altmann, G. T. M. (1998) Ambiguity in sentence processing. *Trends in Cognitive Sciences,* **2**, 146–151.

Altmann, G. T. M., Dienes, Z. and Goode, A. (1995) On the modality-independence of implicitly learned grammatical knowledge. *Journal of Experimental Psychology: Learning, Memory, and Cognition,* **21**, 899–912.

Anderson, S. C. (1979) Verb structure. In L. Hyman (ed.) *Aghen grammatical structure* (Southern Californian Occasional Papers in Linguistics 7), pp. 73–136. University of Southern California Press, Los Angeles.

Antinucci, F. and Miller, R. (1976) How children talk about what happened. *Journal of Child Language,* **3**, 167–189.

Ariel, M. (1988) Referring and accessibility. *Journal of Linguistics,* **24**, 65–87.

Atkinson, M. (1982) *Explanations in the Study of Language Development.* Cambridge University Press, Cambridge.

Atkinson, M. (1992) *Children's Syntax: an introduction to principles and parameters theory.* Basil Blackwell, Oxford.

Atkinson, M. (1996) Now hang on a minute. In H. Clahsen (ed.) *Generative perspectives on Language Acquisition: empirical findings, theoretical considerations, and cross-linguistic comparisons*, pp. 451–485. John Benjamins, Amsterdam.

Atkinson, M. (2000) Minimalist visions. Unpublished mss. Department of Linguistics, University of Essex, UK.

Au, T, K-F., Dapreto, M. and Song, Y.-K. (1994) Input versus constraints: early word acquisition in Korean and English. *Journal of Memory and Cognition*, **33**, 567–582.

Baker, M. (1988) *Incorporation: a theory of grammatical function changing.* University of Chicago Press, Chicago.

Baker, M. C. (2003) Linguistic differences and language design. *Trends in Cognitive Sciences*, **7**, 349–353.

Baldwin, D. (1991) Infants' contributions to the achievement of joint reference. *Child Development*, **62**, 875–890.

Baldwin, D. (1996) The ontogeny of social information gathering. *Child Developmentelopment*, **67**, 1915–1935.

Barnes, J. M. and Underwood, B. J. (1959) 'Fate' of first-list associations in transfer theory. *Journal of Experimental Psychology*, **58**, 97–105.

Barsalou, L. W. (1987) The instability of graded structure: implications for the nature of concepts. In H. Clahsen (ed.) *Concepts and Conceptual Development: ecological and intellectual factors in categorization*, pp. 101–140. Cambridge University Press, New York.

Barsky, R. F. (1997) *Noam Chomsky: A life of a dissent.* MIT Press, Cambridge, MA.

Bartsch, K. and Wellman, H. W. (1995) *Children Talk About the Mind.* Oxford University Press, New York.

Bates, E. and Elman, J. (1996) Learning rediscovered. *Science*, **274**, 1849–1850.

Bates, E. and MacWhinney, B. (1982) Functionalist approaches to grammar. In E. Wanner and L. Gleitman (ed.) *Language Acquisition: the state of the art*, pp. 203–367. Cambridge University Press, New York.

Bates, E. and MacWhinney, B. (1987) Competition, variation and language learning. In B. MacWhinney (ed.) *Mechanisms of Language Acquisition*, pp. 157–193. Lawrence Erlbaum, Hillsdale, NJ.

Bates, E. and MacWhinney, B. (1989) Functionalism and the competition model. In B. MacWhinney and E. Bates (eds) *Crosslinguistic Study of Sentence Processing*, pp. 3–73. Cambridge University Press, Cambridge.

Bates, E., Benigni, L., Bretherton, I., Camaioni, L. and Voltera, V. (1979) Cognition and communication from nine to thirteen months: correlational findings. In E. Bates (ed.) *The Emergence of Symbols: cognition and communication in infancy*, pp. 3–43. Academic Press, New York.

Bavin, E. (1989) The acquisition of Walpiri temporal system. Talk given at University of California, Davis (discussed in Van Valin, 1991.)

Bellugi, U., Wang, P. P. and Jernigan, T. (1994) Williams Syndrome: an unusual psychological profile. In S. H. Broman and J. Grafman (eds) *Atypical Cognitive Deficit in Developmental Disorders: implications for brain function*, pp. 23–56. Lawrence Erbaum Associates, Hillsdale, NJ.

Bengio, Y. (1996) *Neural Networks for Speech Recognition*. International Thompson Computer Press, London.

Berent, I. and Shimron, J. (1997) The representation of Hebrew words: evidence from the obligatory contour principle. *Cognition*, **64**, 39–72.

Berent, I., Everett, D. L. and Shimron, J. (2001) Do phonological representations specify variables? Evidence from the obligatory contour principle. *Cognitive Psychology*, **42**, 1–60.

Berko, J. (1958) The child's learning of English morphology. *Word*, **14**, 150–177.

Berman, R. (1985) The acquisition of Hebrew. In D. Slobin (ed.) *The Cross-linguistic Study of Language Acquisition*, pp. 67–89. Lawrence Erbaum, Hillsdale, NJ.

Berthenthal, B. I. and Fisher, K. W. (1978) Development of self-recognition in the infant. *Developmental Psychology*, **14**, 44–50.

Berwick, R. C. (1985) *The Acquisition of Syntactic Knowledge*. MIT Press, Cambridge, MA.

Berwick, R. C. and Weinberg, A. S. (1984) *The Grammatical Basis of Linguistic Performance*. MIT Press, Cambridge MA.

Bickerton, D. (1990) *Language and Species*. University of Chicago Press, Chicago, IL.

Bishop, D. V. M. (1997) *Uncommon Understanding: development and disorders of language comprehension in children*. Psychology Press, Hove, Sussex.

Bishop, D. V. M., Carlyon, M. R. P., Deeks, J. M. and Bishop, S. J. (1999) Auditory temporal processing impairment: neither necessary nor sufficient for causing language impairment in children. *Journal of Speech, Language, and Hearing Research*, **42**, 1295–1310.

Blackburn, S. (1984) *Spreading the Word: groundings in the philosophy of language*. Clarendon Press, Oxford.

Bloom, L., Lifter, K. and Broughton, J. (1985) The convergence of early cognition and language in the second year of life: problems in conceptualisation and measurement. In M. Barrett (ed.) *Children's Single Word Speech*, pp. 149–180. John Wiley, London.

Bloom, L. (1973) *One Word at a Time: The use of single-word utterances before syntax*. Mouton, The Hague.

Bloom, P. (2000) *How Children Learn the Meaning of Words*. MIT Press, Cambridge, MA.

Bloomfield, L. (1933) *Language*. Holt, Rinehart, and Winston, New York.

Borer, H. and Wexler, K. (1987) The maturation of syntax. In T. Roeper and E. Williams (eds) *Parameter Setting*, pp. 123–172. Reiden, Dordrecht.

Bowerman, M. (1973) *Early Syntactic Development: a cross-linguistic study with special reference to Finnish.* Cambridge University Press, Cambridge.

Bowerman, M. (1976) Semantic factors in the acquisition of rules for word use and sentence construction. In D. Morehead and A. Morehead (eds) *Directions in Normal and Deficient Child Language,* pp. 79–90. University Park Press, Baltimore, MD.

Bowerman, M. (1982) Reorganisational processes in lexical development. In E. Wanner and L. R. Gleitman (eds) Language acquisition: the State of the Art, pp. 45–68. Cambridge University Press, New York.

Braine, M. D. S. (1976) Children's first word combinations. *Monographs of the Society for Research in Child Development,* **41,** 164.

Braine, M. D. S. (1987) What is learned in acquiring word classes – a step towards an acquisition theory. In B. MacWhinney (ed.) *Mechanisms of Language Acquisition,* pp. 65–87, Lawrence Erlbaum, Hillsdale, NJ.

Braine, M. D. S. (1992) What sort of innate structure is needed to 'bootstrap' into syntax? *Cognition,* **45,** 77–100.

Braine, M. D. S. (1994) Is nativism sufficient? *Journal of Child Language,* 21, 9–31.

Braine, M.D. S. (1988) Modelling the acquisition of linguistic structure. In Y. Levy, I. Schlesinger and M. D. S. Braine (eds) *Cognitive processes in language acquisition,* pp. 217–259. Lawrence Eolbaum, Hillsdale, NJ.

Brandom, R. B. (1994) *Making it Explicit.* Harvard University Press, Cambridge, MA.

Brandom, R. B. (2000) Introduction. In R. B. Brandom (ed.) *Rorty and his Critics,* pp xi–xx. Basil Blackwell, Oxford.

Brill, E. (1992) A simple, rule-based part of speech tagger. In *Proceedings of the Third Conference on Applied Computational Linguistics,* pp. 152–155. Morgan-Kaufman, San Francisco, CA.

Briscoe, J., Bishop, D. V. M. and Norbury, C. F. (2001) Phonological processing, language, and literacy. a comparison of children with mild to moderate sensorineural hearing loss and those with specific language impairment. *Journal of Child Psychology and Psychiatry,* **42,** 329–340.

Brody, M. (1998a) The minimalist program and perfect syntax. *Mind and Language,* **13,** 205–214.

Brody, M. (1998b) Projection and phrase structure. *Linguistic Inquiry,* **29,** 367–398.

Bromberger, S. (2002) Chomsky's revolution. *New York Review of Books* **49**(7) 25 April,.

Brooks, L. R. and Vokey, J. R. (1991) Abstract categories and abstracted grammar: comments on Reber (1989) and Mathews *et al.* (1989) *Journal of Experimental Psychology: General,* **120,** 316–323.

Brooks, R. A. (1991) Intelligence without representation. *Artificial Intelligence,* 47, 139–159.

Brooks, P. and Tomasello, M. (1999) Young children learn to produce passives with nonce verbs. *Developmental Psychology,* **35,** 29–44.

Brown, R. (1973) *A First Language: the early stages.* Harvard University Press, Cambridge, MA.

Brown, R. and Hanlon, C. (1970) Derivational complexity and the order of acquisition in child speech. In J. R. Hayes (ed.) *Cognition and the Development of Language,* pp. 11–54. Wiley, New York.

Bruner, J. S. (1966) On the conservation of liquids. In J. S. Bruner *et al.* (eds) *Studies in cognitive growth,* pp. 3–32. John Wiley, London.

Bruner, J. S. (1975) The ontogenesis of speech acts. *Journal of Child Language,* **2,** 1–19.

Bruner, J. S. and Bruner, B. M. (1968) On voluntary action and its hierarchical structure. *International Journal of Psychology,* **3,** 239–255.

Bryant, P. E. (1974) *Perception and Understanding in Young Children.* Methuen, London.

Bryant, P. E. and Trabasso, T. (1971) Transitive inference and memory in young children. *Nature,* **232,** 456–485.

Calvin, W. H. and Bickerton, D. (2000) *Lingua ex Machina: reconciling Darwin and Chomsky with the human brain.* MIT Press, Cambridge, MA.

Carpenter, P. A., Just, M. A. and Schell, P. (1990) What one intelligence test measures: a theoretical account of the processing in the Raven Progressive Matrices Test. *Psychological Review,* **97,** 404–431.

Carruthers, P. (1997) *Language, Thought and Consciousness: An essay in philosophical psychology.* Cambridge University Press, Cambridge.

Carstairs-McCarthy, A. (1999) *The Origins of Complex Language: An inquiry into the evolutionary beginnings of sentences, syllables and truth.* Oxford University Press, Oxford.

Chalmers, D. (1990) Why Fodor and Pylyshyn were wrong: the simplest refutation. *Proceedings of the 12th Annual Conference of the Cognitive Science Society.* Lawrence Erlbaum, Hillsdale, NJ.

Chang, F. (2002) Symbolically speaking. *Cognitive Science,* 93, 609–615.

Chang, F., Dell, G. S., Bock, K. and Griffin, Z. (2000) Structural priming as implicit learning: A comparison of models of sentence production. *Journal of Psycholinguistic Research,* **29,** 217–229.

Chang, F., Griffin, Z., Dell, G. S. and Bock, K. (1997) Modelling structural priming as implicit learning. Presented at Computational Psycholinguistics, Berkeley, CA. August.

Chater, N. and Conkey, P. (1994) Sequence processing with recurrent neural networks. In M. Oaksford and G. D. Brown (eds) *Neurodynamics and Psychology,* pp. 269–295. Academic Press, London.

Chatlosh, D. L., Neunaber, D. J. and Wasserman, E. A. (1985) Response-outcome contingencies: behavioural and judgemental effects of appetitive and aversive outcomes with college students. *Learning and Motivation,* **16,** 1–34.

Chatterjee, S. (1997) *The Rise of Birds; 225 years of evolution.* John Hopkins University Press Baltimore, Maryland, USA.

Chien, Y.-C. and Wexler, K. (1990) Children's knowledge of locality conditions in binding as evidence for the modularity of syntax and pragmatics. *Language Acquisition,* 1, 225–291.

Choi, S. and Gopnik, A. (1995) Early acquisition of verbs in Korean: A cross-linguistic study. *Journal of Child Language,* 22, 497–530.

Chomsky, N. (1957) *Syntactic Structures.* Mouton, The Hague.

Chomsky, N. (1963) Formal properties of grammar. In R. D. Luce, R. R. Bush, and E. Galanter (eds) *Handbook of Mathematical Psychology,* volume 2, pp. 101–134. Wiley, New York.

Chomsky, N. (1964) *Current Issues in Linguistic Theory.* Mouton, The Hague.

Chomsky, N. (1965) *Aspects of the Theory of Syntax* MIT Press, Cambridge, MA.

Chomsky, N. (1966) *Cartesian Linguistics.* Harper and Row, New York.

Chomsky, N. (1968) *Language and Mind.* Harcourt, Brace, and World, New York.

Chomsky, N. (1970) Remarks on nominalization. In R. A. Jacobs and P. S. Rosenbaum (eds) *English Transformational Grammar,* pp. 184–221. Ginn and Company, New York.

Chomsky, N. (1973) Constraints on transformations. In S. Anderson and P. Kiparsky (eds) *A Festschrift for Morris Halle,* pp. 232–286. Holt, Rinehart, and Winston: New York.

Chomsky, N. (1975a) Recent contributions to the theory of innate ideas. In S. P. Stich (ed.) *Innate Ideas.* University of California Press, Berkeley, CA.

Chomsky, N. (1975b) *Reflections on Language.* Pantheon Books, New York.

Chomsky, N. (1979) *Language and Responsibility.* Pantheon, New York.

Chomsky, N. (1980a) Initial states and steady states. In M. Piattelli-Parmarini (ed.) *Language and Learning,* pp. 107–130.

Chomsky, N. (1980b) *Rules and Representations.* Basil Blackwell, Oxford.

Chomsky, N. (1981) *Lectures on Government and Binding.* MIT Press, Cambridge MA.

Chomsky, N. (1982) *Some Concepts and Consequences of the Theory of Government and Binding.* MIT Press, Cambridge, MA.

Chomsky, N. (1986) *Knowledge of Language, its Nature, Origin and Use.* Praeger, New York.

Chomsky, N. (1988) *Language and Problems of Knowledge: the Managua lectures.* MIT Press, Cambridge, MA.

Chomsky, N. (1993) A minimalist program for linguistic enquiry. In K. Hale and S. J. Keyser (eds) *The View from Building 20,* pp. 1–52. MIT Press, Cambridge, MA.

Chomsky, N. (1995) *The Minimalist Program.* MIT Press, Cambridge, MA.

Chomsky, N. (2000a) *New Horizons in the Study of Language and Mind.* Cambridge University Press, Cambridge, UK.

Chomsky, N. (2000b) Minimalist inquiries: the framework. In R. Martin *et al.* (eds) *Step by Step: Essays on minimalist syntax in honour of Howard Lasnik,* pp. 89–155. MIT Press, Cambridge, MA.

Chomsky, N. (2001) Derivation by phrase. In M. Kenstowicz (ed.) *Ken Hale: A life in language,* pp. 1–52. MIT Press, Cambridge, MA.

Chomsky, N. (2003) Reply to Gopnik. In L. M. Antony and N. Hornstein (eds) *Chomsky and his Critics,* pp. 316–325. Basil Blackwell, New York.

Chomsky, N. and Lasnick, H. (1977) Filters and controls. *Linguistic Inquiry,* **8,** 425–504.

Chomsky, N., Belletti, A. and Rizzi, L. (2002) *On the Nature of Language.* Cambridge University Press, Cambridge.

Christiansen, M. H. and Chater, N. (1999) Toward a connectionist model of recursion in human linguistic performance. *Cognitive Science,* **23,** 157–205.

Clahsen, H. (1996) Introduction. In H. Clahsen (ed.) *Generative Perspectives on Language Acquisition: empirical findings, theoretical considerations, and cross-linguistic comparisons,* Benjamins, Amsterdam.

Clark, A. (1989) *Microcognition: Philosophy, cognitive science and parallel distributed processing.* MIT Press, Cambridge, MA.

Clark, A. (1993) *Associative Engines: Connectionism, concepts and representation change.* MIT Press, Cambridge, MA.

Clark, A. (1997) *Being There: Putting brain, body, and world together again.* MIT Press, Cambridge, MA.

Clark, A. (1998) Magic words: how language augments human computation. In P. Carruthers and J. Boucher (eds) *Language and Thought: interdisciplinary themes,* pp. 262–283. Cambridge University Press, Cambridge.

Clark, A. and Karmiloff-Smith, A. (1993) The cognizer's innards: a philosophical perspective on the development of thought. *Mind and Language,* **8,** 487–519.

Clark, E. V. (1971) The acquisition of the meaning of 'before' and 'after'. *Journal of Verbal Learning and Verbal Behaviour,* **10,** 266–275.

Clark. A. (1987) The kludge in the machine. *Mind and Language,* **2,** 277–300.

Comrie, B. (1984) Language universals and linguistic argumentation: a reply to Coopmans. *Journal of Linguistics,* **20,** 155–164.

Comrie, B. (1988) Linguistic typology. In F. Newmeyer (ed.) *Linguistic Theory: Foundations,* pp. 447–461. Cambridge University Press, Cambridge.

Comrie, B. and Keenan, E. (1979) 'Noun Phrase Accessibility Revisited'. *Language,* **55,** 649–64.

Cosmedes, L. and Tooby, J. (1992) Cognitive adaptations for social exchange. In J. Barkow, L. Cosmedes and J. Tooby (eds) *The Adapted Mind: evolutionary psychology and the generation of culture,* pp. 163–228. Oxford University Press, New York.

Cottingham, J. (1984) *Rationalism.* Thoemmes Press, Bristol, UK.

Cottrell, G. (1985) A connectionist approach to word sense disambiguation. Unpublished Doctoral Dissertation, University of Rochester.

Crain, S. (1991) Language acquisition in the absence of experience. *Behavioural and Brain Sciences,* **14**, 597–650.

Crain, S. and McKee, C. (1985) The acquisition of structural restrictions on anaphora. In S. Berman, J-W. Choe and J. McDonoug (eds) *Proceedings of the North Eastern Linguistic Society,* pp. 94–110. GLSA, Amhust, MA.

Crain, S. and Thornton, R. (1998) *Investigations in Universal Grammar: a guide to experiments on the acquisition of syntax.* MIT Press, Cambridge, MA.

Croft, W. (1991) *Syntactic Categories and Grammatical Relations.* Chicago University Press, Chicago, IL.

Cromer, R. F. (1974/91) The development of language and cognition: the cognition hypothesis. In B. Foss (ed.) *New Perspectives in Child Development,* pp. 1–54 (reprinted) Penguin Books, Harmondsworth.

Cromer, R. F. (1983) Hierarchical planning disability in the drawings and constructions of severely aphasic children. *Brain and Cognition,* **2**, 144–164.

Cromer, R. F. (1991) The cognition hypothesis of language development. In R. F. Cromer *Language and Thought in Normal and Handicapped Children.* Basil Blackwell, Oxford.

Cutting, J. C. and Ferreira, V. S. (1999) Semantic and phonological information flow in the production lexicon. *Journal of Experimental Psychology: Learning, Memory, and Cognition,* **25**, 318–344.

Dalakakis, J. (1994) Familial impairment in Greece. In M. Matthews (ed.) Linguistic aspects of familial language impairment, *McGill Working Papers in Linguistics,* **10**, 216–227.

Damasio, H., Grabowski, T. J., Tranel, T., Hichwa, R.D. and Damasio, A. R. (1996) A neural basis for lexical retrieval. *Nature,* **380**, 499–505.

Davidson, D. (1986) A nice derangement of epitaphs. In E. Lapore (ed.) *Truth and Interpretation,* pp. 433–446. Oxford: Basil Blackwell.

Davis, H. (1992) Transitive inferences in rats (*rattus norvegicus*) *Journal of Comparative Psychology,* **106**, 342–351.

de Boysson-Bardies, B. and O'Regan, K. (1973) What children do in spite of adult hypotheses. *Nature,* **246**, 531–534.

De Villiers, J. and Roeper, T. (1995) Relative clauses are barriers to wh-movement in young children. *Journal of Child Language,* **22**, 389–404.

De Villiers, J., Roeper, T. and Vainikka, A. (1990) The acquisition of long-distance rules. In L. Frazier, and J. de Villiers (eds) *Language Processing and Language Acquisition,* pp. 257–297, Kluwer, Dordrecht.

Dell, G. S., Chang, F. and Griffin, Z. M. (1999) Connectionist models of language production: lexical access and grammatical encoding. *Cognitive Science,* **23**, 517–542.

Dennett, D. C. (1981) *Brainstorms*. Harvester Press, Sussex.

Dennett, D. C. (1991) *Consciousness Explained*. Penguin Books, Harmondsworth.

Dennett, D. C. (1993) Learning and labelling. *Mind and Language*, **8**, 540–548.

Devlin, A. M., Cross, J. H., Harkness, W., Chong, W. R., Harding, B., Vargha Khadem, F. and Neville, B. G. R. (2003) Clinical outcomes of Hemispherectomy for epilepsy in childhood and adolescence. *Brain*, **12B**, 556–566.

Dewey, J. (1938) *Logic: The theory of inquiry*. Henry Holt, New York.

Diessel, H. and Tomasello, M. (2001) The acquisition of finite complement clauses in English: a corpus-based analysis. *Cognitive Linguistics*, **12**, 97–141.

Diver, W. (1995) Theory. In E. Conti-Morava and B. S. Goldberg (eds) *Meaning as Explanation: advances in linguistic sign theory*, pp. 43–114. De Gruyter, Berlin.

Dore, J. (1975) Holophrases, speech acts and language universals. *Journal of Child Language*, **2**, 21–40.

Dore, J. (1978) Conditions for the acquisition of speech acts. In I. Markove (ed.) *The Social Context of Language*, pp. 87–111. John Wiley, London.

Durlach, P. J. (1983) Effect of signalling intertribal unconditioned stimuli in autoshaping. *Journal of Experimental Psychology: Animal Behaviour Processes*, **9**, 374–379.

Eisele, J. and Lust, B. (1989) Language competence and language performance: the truth about 'directionality effects'. Paper presented at the Society for Research in *Child Development*, biennial meeting Kansas City.

Elman, J. L. (1990) Finding structure in time. *Cognitive Science*, **14**, 179–211.

Elman, J. L. (1993) Learning and development in neural networks: the importance of starting small. *Cognition*, **48**, 71–99.

Elman, J. L. (1995) Language as a dynamical system. In R. Port and T. van Gelder (eds) *Mind as Motion*, pp. 195–225. MIT Press, Cambridge, MA.

Elman, J. L., Bates, E., Johnson, M. H., Karmiloff-Smith, A., Parisi, D. and Plunkett, K. (1996) *Rethinking Innateness: A connectionist perspetive on development*. MIT Press, Cambridge MA.

Evans, G. (1980) Pronouns *Linguistic Euqivy*, **xi**, pp. 337–362.

Evans, G. (1982) *The Varieties of Reference*, (ed. J. McDowell) Oxford University Press, Oxford.

Fauconnier, G. (1985) *Mental Spaces*. MIT Press, Cambridge Mass.

Feduccia, A. (1999) *The Origin and Evolution of Birds*. Yale University Press, USA.

Feigenbaum, E. A. and Simon, H. A. (1984) EPAM-like models of recognition and learning. *Cognitive Science*, **8**, 305–336.

Fersen, L. von., Wynne, C. D. D., Delius, J. D. and Staddon, J. E. R. (1991) Transitive inference formation in pigeons. *Journal of Experimental Psychology: Animal Behaviour Processes*, **17**, 334–341.

Field, H. (1978) Mental representation. *Erkenntniss*, **13**, 9–61.

Finch, S. and Chater, N. (1991) A Hybrid Approach to the Automatic Learning of Linguistic Categories. *Artificial Intelligence and the Simulation of Behaviour. CAISB Quarterly*, **78**, 16–24.

Finch, S. and Chater, N. (1994) Learning syntactic categories: A statistical approach. In M. Oaksford and G. D. A. Brown (eds) *Neurodynamics and Psychology*, pp. 296–322. Academic Press, London.

Fisher, C. (1996) Structural limits on verb mapping: the role of analogy in children's interpretation of sentences. *Cognitive Psychology*, **31**, 41–81.

Fisher, C. (2002) The role of abstract syntactic knowledge in language acquisition: a reply to Tomasello (2000) *Cognition*, **82**, 259–278.

Fisher, C., Hall, G., Rakowitz, S. and Gleitman, L. (1994) When it is better to receive than to give: structural and cognitive factors in acquiring a first vocabulary. *Lingua*, **92**, 333–376.

Fletcher, P. (1999) Specific language impairment. In M. Barrett (ed.) *The Development of Language*, pp. 349–371. The Psychology Press, Hove, UK.

Fodor, J. A. (1968) *Psychological Explanation*. Random House, New York.

Fodor, J. A. (1970) Three reasons for not deriving 'kill' from 'cause to die'. *Linguistic Inquiry*, **1**, 129–438.

Fodor, J. A. (1975) *The Language of Thought*. The Harvester Press, Hassocks.

Fodor, J. A. (1980) Fixation of belief and concept acquisition. In M. Piattelli-Parlmarini (ed.) *Language and Learning: The debate between Jean Piaget and Noam Chomsky*, pp. 142–163. Harvard University Press, Cambridge, MA.

Fodor, J. A. (1983) *The Modularity of Mind: An essay in faculty psychology*. MIT Press, Cambridge MA.

Fodor, J. A. (1987) *Psychosemantics*. MIT Press, Cambridge, MA.

Fodor, J. A. (1997) Connectionism and the problem of systematicity (continued): why Smolensky's solution still doesn't work. *Cognition*, **62**, 109–119.

Fodor, J. A. (1998a) Review of Jeff Elman *et al.*, *Rethinking innateness*. In *In a Critical Condition: Polemical essays on cognitive science and the philosophy of mind*. MIT Press, Cambridge, MA.

Fodor, J. A. (1998b) *Concepts: where cognitive science went wrong*. Clarendon Press, Oxford.

Fodor, J. A. (1998c) There and back again: A review of Annette Karmiloff-Smith's *Beyond modularity*, pp. 127–142. In *In a Critical Condition: Polemical essays on cognitive science and the philosophy of mind*. MIT Press, Cambridge, MA.

Fodor, J. A. (2000a) It's all in the mind: Noam Chomsky and the arguments for Internalism. Review of Chomsky (2000) *Times Literary Supplement*, *23* June, pp. 3–4.

Fodor, J. A. (2000b) *The Mind Doesn't Work That Way: The scope and limits of computational psychology*. MIT Press, Cambridge MA.

Fodor, J. A. (2003) *Hume Variations.* Oxford University Press, Oxford.

Fodor, J. A. and McLaughlin, B. P. (1990) Connectionism and the problem of systematicity: Why Smolensky's solution doesn't work. *Cognition,* **35,** 183–204.

Fodor, J. A. and Pylyshyn, Z. (1988) Connectionism and cognitive architecture: A critical analysis. *Cognition,* **28,** 3–71.

Fodor, J. D. (1984) Constraints on gaps: is the parser a significant influence? In B. Butterworth, B. Comrie, and O. Dahl (eds) *Explanations for Language Universals,* pp. 9–34. Mouton, Berlin.

Foley, R. A. (1996) An evolutionary and chronological framework for human social behaviour. In W. G. Runciman, W. G. Maynard-Smith and R. Dunbar (eds) *Evolution of Primate Social Behaviour Patterns in Primates and Man,* pp. 95–117. Proceedings of the British Academy, volume 88. Oxford University Press, Oxford.

Foley, W. A. and Van Valin, R. D. (1977) On the viability of the notion of 'subject'. In *Universal Grammar, Proceedings of the Annual Meeting of the Berkeley Linguistics Society,* **3,** 293–320.

Foley, W. A. and Van Valin, R. D. (1984) *Functional Syntax and Universal Grammar.* Cambridge University Press, Cambridge.

Frankfurt, A. (1958) Peirce's account of inquiry. *Philosophical Review,* **55,** 575–600.

Frantz, D. (1977) A new view of to-contraction. *Workpapers,* **21,** 71–76. Summer Institute of Linguistics (North Dakota Session).

Freudenthal, D., Pine, J. M. and Gobet, F. (2002a) Modelling the development of the Dutch Optional Infinites in MOSAIC. In W. D. Gray and C. D. Schunn (eds) *Proceedings of the 24th Annual Meeting of the Cognitive Science Society,* pp. 334–339. Lawrence Erlbaum, Mahwah, NJ.

Freudenthal, D., Pine, J. M. and Gobet, F. (2002b) Subject omission in children's language: the case for performance limitations in learning. In W. D. Gray and C. D. Schunn (eds) *Proceedings of the 24th Annual Meeting of the Cognitive Science Society,* pp. 328–333. Lawrence Erlbaum, Mahwah, NJ.

Fukuda, S. E. and Fukuda, S. (1994) Developmental language impairment in Japanese: In M. Matthews (ed.) Linguistic Aspects of familial language impairment, *McGill Working Papers in Linguistics,* 10, 150–177.

Garrett, M. F. (1981) Disorders in lexical selection. *Cognition,* 42, 143–180.

Gazdar, G., Klein, E. Pullum, G. and Sag, I. (1985) *Generalised Phrase Structure Grammar.* Harvard University Press, Cambridge, MA.

Geach, P. (1957) *Mental Acts.* Routledge and Kegan Paul, London.

Gelman, S. A. and Coley, J. D. (1999) The importance of knowing that a dodo is a bird: categories and induction in 2-year-old children. *Developmental Psychology,* **26,** 796–804.

Gelman, S. A., Coley, J. D. and Gottfried, G. M. (1994) Essentialist beliefs in children: The acquisition of concepts and theories. In L. A. Hirschfeld and S. A. Gelman (eds) *Mapping the Mind*, pp. 341–366. Cambridge University Press, New York.

Gelman, S.A. and Markman, E. M. (1986) Categories and induction in young children. *Cognition*, **23**, 183–209.

Gentner, D. and Markman, A. (1997) Structure mapping in analogy and similarity. *American Psychologist*, **52**, 45–56.

Gergely, G. and Csibra, G. (2002) Teleological reasoning in infancy: the naïve theory of rational action. *Trends in Cognitive Sciences*, **7**, 287–292.

Gergely, G., Bekkering, H. and Király, I. (2002) Rational imitation in preverbal infants. *Nature*, **415**, 255–259.

Gergely, G., Nádaskty, Z., Csibra, G. and Bíró, S. (1995) Taking the intentional stance at 12 months of age. *Cognition*, **56**, 165–193.

Gibson, J. J. (1979) *The Ecological Approach to Visual Perception*. Boston, Houghton Miffliva Co.

Gillette, J., Gleitman, H., Gleitman, L. and Lederer, A. (1999) Human simulations of vocabulary learning. *Cognition*, **73**, 135–176.

Gleitman, L. (1990) Structural sources of verb learning. *Language Acquisition*, **1**, 1–63.

Gleitman, L. and Wanner, E. (1982) Language acquisition: The state of the art. In E. Wanner and L. Gleitman (eds) *Language Acquisition: The state of the art*, pp. 123–153. Cambridge University Press, New York.

Gobet, F. and Pine, J. M. (1997) Modelling the acquisition of syntactic categories. In M. G. Shafto and P. Langley (eds) *Proceedings of the 19th Meeting of the Cognitive Science Society*, pp. 265–270. Lawrence Erlbaum. Mahwah, NJ.

Gold, E. M. (1967) Language acquisition in the limit. *Information and Control*, **16**, 447–474.

Goldin-Meadow, S. (2003) *The Resilience of Language: what gesture creation in deaf children can tell us about how all children learn language*. Psychology Press, New York.

Gómez, R. L. and Gerken, L.-A. (1998) Artificial language learning by one-year-olds leads to specific and abstract knowledge. *Cognition*, **70**, 109–135.

Gómez, R. L. and Gerken, L.-A. (2000) Infant artificial language learning. *Trends in Cognitive Sciences*, **4**, 178–186.

Gómez, R. L., Gerken, L.-A. and Schvanevelt, R. W. (2000) The basis of transfer in artificial learning. *Memory and Cognition*, **28**, 253–236.

Goodluck, H. (1991) *Language Acquisition: A linguistic approach*. Basil Blackwell, Oxford.

Goodluck, H. (1997) Islands, parsing, and learnability: a commentary on some experimental assessments of children's knowledge of island constraints. Paper presented at the 10th Annual CUNY Conference on Human Sentence Processing, Santa Monica, CA, 21 March, 1997. TS available from the Department of Linguistics, University of Ottowa.

Goodluck, H., Foley, M. and Sedivy, J. (1992) Adjunct islands and acquisition. In H. Goodluck and M. Rochemont (eds) *Island Constraints*, pp. 181–194. Kluwer, Dordrecht.

Gopnick, A. and Meltzoff, A. N. (1997) *Words, Thoughts, and Theories*. MIT Press, Cambridge MA.

Gopnik, A. (2003) The theory theory as an alternative to the innateness hypothesis. In L. M. Antony and N. Hornstein (eds)*Chomsky and his Critics*, pp. 238–254. Basil Blackwell, New York.

Gopnik, A. and Choi, S. (1990) Do linguistic differences lead to cognitive differences?: A cross-linguistic study of semantic and cognitive development. *First Language*, **10**, 199–215.

Gopnik, A. and Meltzoff, A. N. (1986) Relations between semantic and cognitive development in the one-word stage: the specificity hypothesis. *Child Developmentelopment*, **57**, 1040–1053.

Gopnik, A. and Meltzoff, A. N. (1987) The development of categorisation in the second year of life and its relation to other cognitive and linguistic developments. *Child Developmentelopment*, **58**, 1523–1531.

Gopnik, A., Choi, S. and Baumberger, T. (1996) Cross-linguistic differences in early semantic and cognition development. *Cognitive Development*, **11**, 197–227.

Gordon, P. (1985) Level ordering in lexical development. *Cognition*, **21**, 73–93.

Grant, J. A., Karmiloff-Smith, A., Gathercole, S. E., Paterson, S., Howlin, P., Davies, M. and Udwin, O. (1997) Phonological short-term memory and its relation to language in Williams Syndrome. *Journal of Cognitive Neuropsychiatry*, **2**, 81–99.

Greenberg, J. H. (1963) Some universals of language with special reference to the order of meaningful events. In J. H. Greenberg (ed.) *Universals of Language*, pp. 73–113. MIT Press, Cambridge MA.

Greene, J. (1972) *Psycholinguistics: Chomsky and psychology*. Harmondsworth: Penguin Books.

Greenfield, P. M., Nelson, K. and Saltzman, E. (1972) The development of rulebound strategies for manipulating seriated cups. *Cognitive Psychology*, **3**, 291–310.

Greenfield, P. M. (1991) Language, tools and brain: the ontogency and phylogeny of hierarchically organised sequential behaviour. *Behavioural and Brain Sciences*, **14**, 531–595.

Greenfield, P. M. and Schneider, L. (1977) Building a tree structure: the development of hierarchical complexity and interrupted strategies in children's construction activity. *Developmental Psychology*, **13**, 299–313.

Grice, P. (1975) Logic and conversation. In P. Cole and J. Morgan (eds) *Syntax and Semantics 3: Speech acts*, pp. 187–222. Academic Press, New York.

Grimshaw, J. (1981) Form, function and the language acquisition device. In C. L. Baker and J. McCarthy (eds) *The Logical Problem of Language Acquisition*, pp. 165–178. MIT Press, Cambridge, MA.

Grimshaw, J. and Rosen, S. T. (1990) Knowledge and obedience: The developmental status of binding theory. *Linguistic Inquiry*, **21**, 187–222.

Grodzinsky, Y. and Reinhart, T. (1993) The innateness of binding and the development of co-reference: a reply to Grimshaw and Rosen. *Linguistic Inquiry*, **24**, 69–103.

Grossman, M. (1980) A central processor for hierarchically structured material: evidence from Broca's aphasia. *Neuropsyschologia*, **18**, 299–308.

Hadley, R. F. (1994) Systematicity in connectionist language learning. *Mind and Language*, **9**, 245–272.

Haegeman, L. (1994) *Introduction to Government and Binding Theory*, second edn. Basil Blackwell, Oxford.

Haiman, J. (1983) Iconic and economic motivation. *Language*, **59**, 781–819.

Haiman, J. (1985) *Natural Syntax: iconicity and erosion*. Cambridge University Press, Cambridge.

Halford, G. (1984). Can the young child intergrate permises in transitivity and serial order tasks? *Cognitive Psychology*, **16**, 65–91.

Halliday, M. A. K. (1973) *Explorations in the Functions of Language*. Edward Arnold, London.

Halliday, M. A. K. (1975) *Learning how to Mean*. Edward Arnold, London.

Hamburger, H. and Crain, S. (1984) Acquisition of cognitive compiling. *Cognition*, **17**, 85–136.

Harman, G. (1965) The inference to the best explanation. *Philosophical Review*, **74**, 88–95; reprinted in Steven M. Cahn, editor, *Philosophy for the 21st Century*, Oxford: Oxford University Press, 2003; 249–53.

Harris, P. L. (1994) Thinking by children and scientists: false analogies and neglected similarities. In L. A. Hirschfeld and S. A. Gelman (eds) *Mapping the Mind: domain specificity in cognition and culture*, pp. 294–315. Cambridge University Press, New York

Haskell, T. R., MacDonald, M. C. and Seidenberg, M. (2003) Language learning and innateness: some implications of compounds research. *Cognitive Psychology*, **47**, 119–163.

Haspelmath, M. (1998) Does grammaticalisation need reanalysis? *Studies in Language*, **22**, 49–85.

Hauser, M. D., Weiss, D. and Marcus, G. F. (2002) Rule learning by cotton-top tamarins. *Cognition*, **86**, B15-B22.

Hauser, M. D., Chomsky, N. and Fitch, W. T. (2002) The faculty of language: what is it, who has it, and how did it evolve? *Science*, **298**, 1569–1579.

Hawkins, J. A. (1994) *A Performance Theory of Order and Constituency*. Cambridge University Press, Cambridge.

Heine, B. and Reh, M. (1984) *Grammaticalisation and Reanalysis in African languages*. Helmut Buske Verlag, Hamburg.

Heine, B., Claudie, U. and Hünnemeyer, F. (1991) *Grammaticalisation: a conceptual framework.* University of Chicago Press, Chicago, IL.

Higginbotham, J. (1987) The autonomy of syntax and semantics. In J. L. Garfield (ed.) *Modularity in Knowledge Representation and Natural Language Understanding,* pp. 119- 131.

Higginbotham, J. (1998) Visions and revisions: A critical notice of Noam Chomsky's The Minimalist Program. *Mind and Language,* **13,** 215–224.

Hinton, G. ed. (1991) *Connectionist Symbol Processing.* MIT Press, Cambridge, MA.

Hinton, G. E., & Shallice, T. (1991) Lesioning an attractor network: Investigations of acquired dyslexia.*Psychological Review,* **98,** 74–95.

Hirsh-Pasek, K., Golinkoff, R. and Naigles, L. (1996) Young children's use of syntactic frames to derive meaning. In K. Hirsh-Pasek and R. Golinkoff (eds) *The Origins of Grammar,* pp. 123–158.

Hirsh-Pasek, K., Treiman, R. and Schneiderman, M. (1984) Brown and Hanlon revisited: Mothers' sensitivity to ungrammatical forms. *Journal of Child Language,* **11,** 81–88.

Hofstadter, D. (1995) *Fluid Concepts and Creative Analogies.* Basic Books, New York.

Hollis, M. (1973) *The Light of Reason.* London: Fontana/Collins.

Hookway, C. (1985) *Peirce.* Routledge and Kegan Paul, London.

Hopper, P. J. (1987) Emergent grammar. *Berkeley Linguistic Society,* **13,** 139–157.

Hornik, K., Stinchcombe, M., and White, H. (1989) Multilayered feed-forward networks are universal approximators. *Neural Networks,* **26,** 359–366.

Huang, C-T., J. (1981) Move *wh* in language without *wh*-movement. *Linguistic Review,* **1,** 369–416.

Hudson, R. A., Rosta, A., Holmes, J. and Gisborne, N. (1996) Synonyms and syntax. *Journal of Linguistics,* **32,** 439–446.

Hume, D. (1739/1962) *A Treatise on Human Nature: Book One.* Edited by D. G. C. Macnabb, Fontana Library of Philosophy, Collins, London.

Hummel, J. E. and Holyoak, K. J. (1997) Distributed representations of structure: a theory of analogical access and mapping. *Psychological Review,* **104,** 427–466.

Hyams, N. (1986) *Language Acquisition and the Theory of Parameters.* Reidel, Dordrecht.

Hyams, N. (1994) VP, null arguments, and COMP projections. In T. Hoekstra and B.D. Schwartz (eds) *Language Acquisition: studies in generative grammar,* pp. 21–55. John Benjamins, Amsterdam.

Jackendoff, R. (1977) *X′ Syntax: A study of phrase structure.* MIT Press, Cambridge, MA.

Jackendoff, R. (1983) *Semantics and Cognition.* MIT Press, Cambridge, MA.

Jackendoff, R. (1990) *Semantic Structures.* MIT Press, Cambridge, MA.

Jackendoff, R. (1997) *The Architecture of the Language Faculty.* MIT Press, Cambridge, MA.

Jackendoff, R. (1999) Parallel constraint-based generative theories of language. *Trends in Cognitive Sciences,* **3**, 393–400.

Jackendoff, R. (2002) *Foundations of Language: Brain, meaning, grammar, evolution.* Oxford University Press, Oxford.

Jackendoff, R. (1993) *Patterns in the Mind.* Harvester/Wheatsheaf, New York.

Jacobs, R. A., Jordan, M. I. and Barto, A. G. (1991) Task decomposition through competition in a molecular connectionist architecture. *Cognitive Science,* **15**, 219–250.

Jacobson, R. (1965) Quest for the essence of language. *Diogenes,* **51**, 21–37.

Janda, R. D. (1980) On the decline of declensional systems: the overall loss of OE nominal case inflections and the ME reanalysis of *–es* as *his.* In E.C. Traugott, R. Labrum and S. Shapherd (eds) *Papers from the 4th International Conference on Historical Linguistics,* pp. 243–252. John Benjamins, Amsterdam.

Johnson, S. C. (2000) The recognition of mentalistic agents in infancy. *Trends in Cognitive Sciences,* **4**, 22–28.

Johnson-Laird, P. N. (1977) Psycholinguistics without linguistics. In N. S. Sutherland (ed.) *Tutorial Essays in Psychology* volume 1, pp. 34–56. Lawrence Erlbaum, Hillsdale, NJ.

Johnson-Laird, P. N. (1983) *Mental Models.* Cambridge University Press, Cambridge, UK.

Jones, E. (2003) Conceptual factors in children's sentential parsing. Unpublished M. Phil. thesis, University of Cambridge.

Jones, G., Gobet, F. and Pine, J. M. (2000) A process model of children's early verb use. In L. R. Gleitman and A. K. Joshu (eds) *Proceedings of the 22nd Annual Meeting of the Cognitive Science Society,* pp. 723–728. Lawrence Erlbaum, Mahwah, NJ.

Jones, M. and van der Lely, H. K. J. (1998) On-line lexical processing in normally developing and specifically language impaired children. Paper presented at the 23rd Annual Bostom University Conference on Language Development.

Jordan, M. I. (1986) An introduction to linear algebra in parallel distributed processing. In J. L. McClelland, D. Rumelhart and the PDP Research Group (eds) *Parallel Distributed Processing: foundations,* volume 1, pp. 365–422. MIT Press, Cambridge, MA.

Jordan, M. I. (1990) Motor learning and the degrees of freedom problem. In M. Jeannerod (ed.) *Attention and Performance XIII: motor representation and control,* pp. 171–190. Lawrence Erlbaum, Hillsdale, NJ.

Joseph, B. (1996) Where can grammatical morphemes come from? Greek evidence concerning the nature of grammaticalisation. Paper presented to the Formal Linguistics Society of Mid-America.

Just, M. A. and Carpenter, P. A. (1992) A capacity theory of comprehension: individual differences in verbal memory. *Psychological Review*, **99**, 122–149.

Kant, I. (1933/1787) *The Critique Pure Reason* translated by N. Kemp Smith. Macmillan.

Karmiloff-Smith, A. (1984) Children's problem solving. In M. E. Lamb, A. L. Brown and B. Rogoff (eds) *Advances in Developmental Psychology*, pp. 145–187.

Karmiloff-Smith, A. (1986) From meta-process to conscious access. *Cognition*, **23**, 95–148.

Karmiloff-Smith, A. (1992) *Beyond Modulanty: A Developmental Perspective on Cognitive Science.* MIT Press, Cambridge, MA.

Karmiloff-Smith, A. (1998) Development itself is the key to understanding developmental disorders. *Trends in Cognitive Sciences*, **2**, 389–398.

Karmiloff-Smith, A., Grant, J. A., Berthoud, I., Davies, M., Howlin, P. and Udwin, O. (1997) Language and Williams Syndrome: how intact is 'intact'. *Child Development*, **68**, 246–262.

Katz, J. J. and Fodor, J. A. (1963) The structure of semantic theory. *Language*, **39**, 170–210.

Kaufman, D. (1988) Grammatical and cognitive interactions in the study of children's knowledge of binding theory and reference relations. Unpublished doctoral dissertsation, Temple University.

Kayne, R. (1994) *The Asymmetry of Syntax.* MIT Press, Cambridge, MA.

Keenan, E. and Comrie, B. (1977) Noun phrase accessibility and universal grammar. *Linguistic Inquiry*, **8**, 63–99.

Keenan, E. and Hawkins, S. (1987) The psychological validity of the accessibility hierarchy. In E. Keenan (ed.) *Universal Grammar: 15 essays*, pp. 60–85. Croom Helm, London.

Kiparsky, P. (1982) From cyclic phonology to lexical phonology. In H. v. D. Hulst and N. Smith (eds) *The Structure of Phonological Representations*, pp. 131–175. Foris, Dordrecht.

Kirby, S. (1999) *Function, Selection, and Innateness: the emergence of language universals.* Oxford University Press, Oxford.

Kirkham, N. Z., Slemmer, J. A. and Johnson, S. P. (2003) Visual statistical learning in infancy: evidence for a domain-general learning mechanism. *Cognition*, **83**, B35–B42.

Koerner, E. F. K. (1995) Introduction. In E. F. K. Koerner and R. E. Asher (eds) *A Concise History of the Language Sciences from the Sumerians to the Cognitivists* pp. 2–23. Pergamon, London.

Körner, S. (1955) *Kant.* Penguin Books, Harmondsworth.

Kripke, S. A. (1982) *Wittgenstein on Rules and Private Language.* Basil Blackwell, Oxford.

Kuenne, M. (1946) Experimental investigation of the relation of language to Transposition behaviour in young children. *Journal of Experimental Psychology,* **36,** 472–490.

Kuhl, P. (1981) "Discrimination of speech by nonhuman animals: basic auditory sensitivities conducise to the perception of speech-sound categories,". *Journal of Acoustic Society of America,* **70,** 340–349.

Landau, B. and Gleitman, L. (1985) *Language and Experience: evidence from the blind child.* Harvard University Press, Cambridge, MA.

Langacker, R. W. (1969) On pronominalisation and chain of command. In D. A. Reibel and S. A. Schane (eds) *Modern Studies in English,* pp. 160–186. Prentice-Hall, Englewood Cliffs, NJ.

Langacker, R. W. (1987) *Foundations of Cognitive Grammar: Volume One, Theoretical prerequisites.* Stanford University Press, Stanford, CA.

Langacker, R. W. (1991) *Foundations of Cognitive Grammar: Volume Two, Descriptive application.* Stanford University Press, Stanford, CA.

Langacker, R. W. (1995) Raising and transparency. *Language,* **71,** 1–62.

Langacker, R. W. (1998) Conceptualisation, symbolisation, and grammar. In M. Tomasello (ed.) *The New Psychology of Language: cognitive and functional approaches to language structure.* Lawrence Erlbaum, Mahwah, NJ.

Lasnik, H. (2002) The minimalist program in syntax. *Trends in Cognitive Science,* **6,** 432–436.

Legum, S. (1975) Strategies in the acquisition of relative clauses. *Technical Note,* 2, 75, 10, Sountwest Regional Laboratory, Los Alamitos, California.

Leonard, L. (1994) Some problems facing accounts of morphological deficits in children with specific language impairment. In R. Watkins and M. Rice (eds) *Specific Language Impairments in Children,* pp. 91–105. Paul H. Brooks Publishing, Baltimore.

Leonard, L., Sabbadini, L., Leonard, J. and Volterra, V. (1987) Specific language impairment in children: a cross-linguistic study. *Brain and Language,* **32,** 233–252.

Leslie, A. M. (1987) Pretence and representation: the origins of 'theory of mind'. *Psychological Review,* **94,** 412–426.

Levelt, W. J. M. (1989) *Speaking: From intention to articulation.* MIT Press, Cambridge, MA.

Levelt, W. J. M. (1991) The time course of lexical access in speech production: A study of picture naming. *Psychological Review,* **98,** 122–142.

Levelt, W. J. M. (1999) Models of word production. *Trends in Cognitive Sciences,* **3,** 223–232.

Levy, Y. (1988) The nature of early language: evidence from the development of Hebrew morphology. In Y. Levy and I. M. Schlesinger (eds) *Categories and Processes in Child Language,* pp. 73–98. Lawrence Erlbaum, Hillsdale, NJ.

Lewicki, P., Czyzewska, M. and Hoffman, H. (1987) Unconscious acquisition of complex procedural knowledge. *Journal of Experimental Psychology: Leaning, Memory, and Cognition,* **13**, 523–530.

Lewis, D. (1972) General semantics. In D. Davidson and G. Harman (eds) *Semantics for Natural Language,* pp.169–218. Reidel, Dordrecht.

Liberman, P. (1984) *The Biology and Evolution of Language.* Harvard University Press, Cambridge, MA.

Lidz, J., Gleitman, H. and Gleitman, L. (2003) Understanding how input matters: verb learning and the footprint of universal grammar. *Cognition,* **87**, 151–178.

Lieven, E., Behrens, H., Speares, J. and Tomasello, M. (2003) Early syntactic creativity: A usage based approach. *Journal of Child Language,* **30**, 333–370.

Lightfoot, D. W. (1979) *Principles of Diachronic Syntax. Cambridge studies in linguistics 23.* Cambridge University Press, Cambridge.

Lloyd, P. and Fernyhough, C. (eds) (1999) General introduction to *Lev Vygotsky: critical assessments,* volume 1) Routledge and Kegan Paul, London.

Lock, A. Ed. (1978) *Action, Gesture, and Symbol: the emergence of language.* Academic Press, London.

Lust, B. (1977) Conjunction reduction in child language. *Journal of Child Language,* 4, 257–287.

Lust, B. (1994) Introduction. In B. Lust, M. Suñer, and J. Whitman (eds) *Syntactic Theory and First Language Acquisition: Cross-linguistic perspectives: volume 1, heads, projections, and learnability,* pp. i–xxx. Lawrence Erlbaum, Hillsdale, NJ.

Lust, B. and Chien, Y.-C. (1984) The structure of coordination in first language acquisition of Mandarin Chinese. *Cognition,* **17**, 49–83.

Lust, B. and Wakayama, T. (1979) The structure of coordination in first language acquisition in Japanese. In F. Eckman and A. Hastings (eds) *First and Second Language Learning,* pp. 101–143. Newbury House, Rawley, MA.

Lust, B., Chien, Y.-C. and Mangione, L. (1984) First language acquisition in Chinese: constraints on free and bound null anaphora. In S. Hattori (ed.) *Thirteenth International Congress of Linguistics,* pp. 1127–1130. Gakushuin, Tokyo.

Lust, B., Eisele, J. and Mazuka, R. (1992) The binding theory module: Evidence from first language acquisition for Principle C. *Language,* **68**, 333–358.

Lust, B., Loveland, K. and Kornet, R. (1980) The development of anaphora in first language: syntactic and pragmatic constraints. *Linguistic Analysis,* **6**, 359–391.

Lyons, J. (1970) *Chomsky.* Fontana Modern Masters, London.

Mackintosh, N. J. (1995) Categorisation by people and pigeons. *Quarterly Journal of Experimental Psychology,* **48B**, 193–214.

Mackintosh, N. J. (2001) Abstraction and discrimination. In C. Heyes and L. Huber (eds) *The Evolution of Cognition,* pp. 123–141. MIT Press, Cambridge MA.

MacNabb, D. G. C. (1966) *David Hume: His theory of knowledge and Morality.* Basil Blackwell, Oxford.

MacNamara, J. (1972) Cognitive basis of language learning in infants. *Psychological Review,* **79,** 1–13.

Macphail, E. M. (1982) *Brain and Intelligence in Vertebrates.* Clarendon Press, Oxford.

MacWhinney, B. (1978) The acquisition of morphonology. *Monographs of the Society for Research in Child Development,* 43, Whole number 1.

MacWhinney, B. (1987) The competition model. In B. MacWhinney (ed.) *Mechanisms of Language Acquisition,* pp. 157–193. Lawrence Erlbaum, Hillsdale, NJ.

MacWhinney, B. and Pleh, C. (1988) The processing of restrictive relative clauses in Hungarian. *Cognition,* **29,** 95–141.

MacWhinney, B. and Snow, C. (1990) The Child Language Data Exchange: an update. *Journal of Child Language,* **17,** 457–472.

MacWhinney, B., Leinbach, J., Taraban, R. and McDonald, J. (1989) Language learning: cues or rules. *Journal of Memory and Language,* **28,** 255–277.

Mandler, J. M. (1992) How to build a baby: II. Conceptual primitives. *Psychological Review,* **99,** 587–604.

Mandler, J. M. and McDonough, L. (1993) Concept formation in infancy. *Cognitive Development,* **8,** 291–318.

Mani, D. R. and Shastri, L. (1993) Reflexive reasoning with multiple instantiation in a connectinionist reasoning system with a type hierarchy. *Connection Science,* **5,** 205–242.

Manzini, R. (1995) From merge to move in form dependency. *University College London Working Papers in Linguistics,* **7,** 29–81.

Maratsos, M. P. (1982) The child's construction of grammatical categories. In E. Wanner and L. Gleitman (eds) *Language Acquisition: the state of the art,* pp. 23–46. Cambridge University Press, New York.

Maratsos, M. P. (1990) Are actions to verbs as verbs are to nouns? On the differential semantic bases of form, class, and category. *Linguistics,* **28,** 1351–1379.

Maratsos, M. P. (1999) Some aspects of innateness and complexity in Grammatical acquisition. In M. Barrett (ed.) *The Development of Language,* Psychology Press, Hove UK.

Maratsos, M. P. and Chalkley, M. A. (1980) The internal language of children's syntax. In K. Nelson (ed.) *Children's Language,* pp. 127–213. Gardner, New York.

Marcus, G. F. (1998) Can connectionism save constructivism? *Cognition,* **66,** 153–182.

Marcus, G. F. (2000) *Pabiku* and *Ga Ti Ga:* two mechanisms infants use to learn about the world. *Current Directions in Psychological Science,* **9,** 145–147.

Marcus, G. F. (2001) *The Algebraic Mind: integrating connectionism and cognitive science.* MIT Press, Cambridge, MA.

Marcus, G. F., Vijayan, S., Bandi Rao, S. and Vishton, P. M. (1999) Rule learning in seven-month-old infants. *Science*, **283**, 77–80.

Mareschal, D., Plunkett, K. and Harris, P. L. (1999) A computational and neuropsychological account of object-orientated behaviours in infancy. *Developmental Science*, **2**, 306–317.

Mareshal, D. and Shultz, T. R. (1996) Generative connectionist networks and constructive cognitive development. *Cognitive Development*, **11**, 571–603.

Markman, E. M. (1990) Constraints children place on word meaning. *Cognitive Science*, **14**, 57–77. *Cognitive Psychology*, **47** (2003) 241–275.

Markman, E. M. and Wachtel, G. F. (1988) Children's use of mutual exclusivity to constrain the meaning of words. *Cognitive Psychology*, **20**, 121–157.

Markman, E. M. and Hutchinson, J. E. (1984) Children's sensitivity to constraints on word meaning: taxonomic versus thematic relations. *Cognitive Psychology*, **16**, 1–27.

Marr, D. (1982) *Vision: a computational investigation into the human representation and processing of visual information*. Freeman, San Francisco, CA.

Marshall, J. B. (1999) A self-watching cognitive architecture for analogy-making and high-level perception. Unpublished Ph.D. thesis, University of Indiana.

Maskara, A. and Noetzel, A. (1993) Sequence recognition with recurrent neural networks. *Connection Science*, **5**, 139–252.

Mathews, R. C., Buss, R. R., Stanley, W. B., Blanchard-Fields, F., Cho, J. R. and Druhan, B. (1989) Role of implicit and explicit processes in learning from examples: A synergistic effect. *Journal of Experimental Psychology: Learning, Memory, and Cognition*, **15**, 1083–1100.

Matisoff, J. A. (1991) Areal and universal dimensions for grammaticalisation in Lahu. In E. C. Traugott and B. Heine (eds) *Approaches to grammaticalisation, volume 2: Focus on types of grammatical markers*, pp. 383–453. John Benjamins, Amsterdam.

Matthei, E. H. (1982) On the acquisition of prenominal modifier sequences. *Cognition*, **11**, 301–332.

May, R. (1985) *Logical Form*. MIT Press, Cambridge MA.

Mazuka, R. (1996) Can a grammatical parameter be set before the first word? Prosodic contributions to early setting of a grammatical parameter. In J. L. Morgan and K. Demuth (eds) *Signal to Syntax: bootstrapping from speech to grammar in early acquisition*, pp. 313–330. Lawrence Erlbaum, Hillsdale, NJ.

McCarthy, J. (1986) OCP effects: gemination and antigemination. *Linguistic Inquiry*, **17**, 207–263.

McClelland, J. L. (1989) Parallel distributed processing: implications for cognition and development. In R. G. M. Morris (ed.) *Parallel Distributed Processing: Implications for psychology and neurobiology*, pp. 9–46. Oxford University Press, Oxford.

McClelland, J. L. and Rumelhart, D. E. (1985) Distributed memory and the representation of general and specific information. *Journal of Experimental Psychology: General*, **114**, 159–188.

McClelland, J. L., McNaughton, B. L. and O'Reilly, R. C. (1995) Why there are complementary learning systems in hippocampus and neocortex: Insights from the successes and failures of connectionist models of learning and memory. *Psychological Review*, **102**, 419–457.

McDowell, J. (1984) Wittgenstein on following a rule. *Synthese*, **58**, 325–363.

McGonigle, B. and Chalmers, M. (1977) Are monkeys logical? *Nature*, **267**, 694–696.

McGonigle, B. and Chalmers, M. (1992) Monkeys are rational! *Quaterly Journal of Experimental Psychology*, **45B**, 189–228.

McLaren, I. P. L., Kaye, H. and Mackintosh, N. J. (1989) An associative theory of the representation of stimuli: applications to perceptual learning and latent inhibition. In R. G. M. Morris (ed.) *Parallel Distributed Processing: Implications for psychology and neurobiology*, pp. 47–67. Oxford University Press, Oxford.

McLaren, I. P. L. (1993) APECS: a solution to the sequential learning problem. *Proceedings of the Fifteenth Annual Conference of the Cogntive Science Society*, pp. 717–722. Lawrence Erlbaum, Hillsdale, NJ.

McNeill, D. (1966) Developmental psycholinguistics. In F. Smith and G. A. Miller (eds) *The Genesis of Language: a psycholinguistic approach*, pp. 35–51. MIT Press, Cambridge, MA.

Meltzoff, A. N. (1988) Infant imitation after a one-week delay. Long-term memory for novel acts and multiple stimuli. *Developmental Psychology*, **24**, 470–476.

Meltzoff, A. N. (1995) Understanding the intentions of others: re-enactment of intended acts by eighteen-month-old children. *Developmental Psychology*, **31**, 838–850.

Meltzoff, A. N. and Moore, K. M. (1998) Object representation, identity, and the paradox of early permanence. *Infant Behaviour and Development*, **21**, 201–235.

Menard, L. (1997) *Pragmatism: A reader*. Vintage Books (Random House), New York.

Migotti, M. (1999) Peirce's double-aspect theory of truth. *Canadian Journal of Philosophy (Supplementary Edition)*, **24**, 75–108.

Miller, G. A. and Chomsky, N. (1963) Finitary models of language users. In R. D. Luce, R. R. Bush and E. Galanter (eds) *Handbook of Mathematical Psychology*, pp. 293–329. Wiley, London.

Misak, C. (1999) Introduction to supplementary edition. *Canadian Journal of Philosophy*, **24**, 1–8.

Mishkin, M. and Ungerleider, L. G. (1982) Contribution of striate inputs to the visuospatial functions of parieto-preoccipital cortex in monkeys. *Behavioural Brain Research*, **6**, 57–77.

Mitchell, M. (1993) *Analogy-making as Perceptron: A computer model*. MIT Press, Cambridge MA.

Mitchell, M. (in press) Analogy-making as a complex adaptive system. In L. Segal and I. Cohen (eds) *Design Principles for the Immune System and other Autonomous Systems.* Oxford University Press, New York.

Moeser, D. S. and Bregman, A. S. (1972) The role of reference in the acquisition of a miniature artificial language. *Journal of Verbal Learning and Verbal Behaviour*, **11**, 759–769.

Mozer, M. and Smolensky, P. (1989) Using relevance to reduce network size automatically. *Connection Science*, **1**, 3–17.

Munakata, Y., McClelland, J. L., Johnson, M. H. and Siegler, R. S. (1997) Rethinking infant knowledge: Toward an adaptive process account of successes and failures in object permanence tasks. *Psychological Review*, **104**, 686–713.

Naigles, L., Fowler, A. and Helm, A. (1992) Developmental changes in the construction of verb meaning. *Cognitive Development*, **7**, 403–437.

Naigles, L. (1990) Children use syntax to learn verb meanings. *Journal of Child Language*, **17**, 357–374.

Naigles, L. R. and Hoff-Ginsberg, E. (1995) Input to verb meaning: evidence for the plausibility of syntactic bootstrapping. *Developmental Psychology*, **31**, 827–837.

Naigles, L. R. (2002) Form is easy, meaning is hard: resolving a paradox in early child language. *Cognition*, **86**, 157–199.

Naigles, L. R. and Kako, E. (1993) First contact in verb acquisition: defining a role for syntax. *Child Development*, **64**, 1665–1687.

Naigles, L. R., Gleitman, H. and Gleitman, L. (1993) Syntactic bootstrapping in verb acquisition. In E. Dromi (ed.) *Language and Cognition: a developmental perspective*, pp. 32–51. Ablex, Norwood, NJ.

Newmeyer, F. J. (1992) Iconicity and generative grammar. *Language*, **68**, 756–796.

Newmeyer, F. J. (1994) Competing motivations and synchronic analysis. *Sprachtypologie und Universalienforschung*, **47**, 67–77.

Newmeyer, F. J. (1998) *Language Form and Language Function*. MIT Press, Cambridge, MA.

Nicholich, L. M. (1977) Beyond sensorimotor intelligence: assessment of symbolic maturity through analysis of pretend play. *Merrill-Palmer Quarterly*, **23**, 201–235.

Niklasson, L. F. and Van Gelder, T. (1994) On being systematically connectionist. *Mind and Language*, **9**, 288–302.

Ninio, A. (1988) On formal grammatical categories in early child language. In Y. Levy and I. M. Schlesinger (eds) *Categories and Processes in Child Language*, pp. 99–120. Lawrence Erlbaum, Hillsdale, NJ.

Ninio, A. and Snow, C. (1988) Language acquisition through language use: the functional sources of children's early utterances. In Y. Levy and I. M. Schlesinger (eds) *Categories and Processes in Child Language*, pp. 11–30. Lawrence Erlbaum, Hillsdale, NJ.

Nissen, M. J. and Bullemer, P. (1987) Attentional requirements of learning: evidence from performance measures. *Cognitive Psychology,* **19,** 1–32.

Norbury, C. F., Bishop, D. V. M. and Briscoe, J. (2001) Production of English FINITE verb morphology: a comparison of SLI and mild-moderate hearing impairment. *Journal of Speech, Language, and Hearing Research,* **44,** 165–178.

Norbury, C. F., Bishop, D. V. M. and Briscoe, J. (2002) Does impaired grammatical comprehension provide evidence for an innate grammar module? *Applied Psycholinguistics,* **23,** 247–268.

Norde, M. (1997) Grammaticalisation versus reanalysis: the case of possessive constructions in Germanic. In L. van Bergen and R. M. Hogg (eds) *Papers from the 12th International Conference on Historical Linguistics,* pp. 61–78. John Benjamin, Amsterdam.

Norman, D. A. (1986) Reflections on cognition and parallel distributed processing. In J. McClelland, D. E. Rumelhart and the PDP Research Group (eds) *Parallel Distributed Processing: volume 2, Psychological and biological models,* pp. 531–546. MIT Press, Cambridge, MA.

Norman, D. A. and Shallice, T. (1986) Attention to active: willed and automatic control of behaviour. In R. J. Davidson, G. E. Schwartz and D. S. Shapiro (eds.) *Conscionsuers and Self-Regulation: Advances in Research: vol.4,* Plenum Press, New York.

O'Hara, M. and Johnson, J. (1997) Syntactic bootstrapping in children with specific language impairment. *European Journal of Disorders of Communication,* **32,** 189–206.

Oetting, M. L. and Rice, M. (1993) Plural acquisition in children with specific language impairment. *Journal of Speech and Hearing Research,* **36,** 1236–1248.

Olguin, R. and Tomasello, M. (1993) Twenty-five-month-old children do not have a category of verb. *Cognitive Development,* **8,** 245–272.

Otsu, Y. (1981) Towards a theory of syntactic development. Unpublished Doctoral Dissertation, MIT.

Peirce, C. S. (1902/1932) The icon, the index and the symbol. MS printed in C. Hartshorn and P. Weiss (eds) *Collected papers of Charles Saunders Peirce (Volume 2: Elements of logic),* pp. 156–173. Harvard University Press, Cambridge, MA.

Perlmutter, D. and Ross, J. R. (1970) Relative clauses with split antecedents. *Linguistic Inquiry,* **1,** 350–370.

Peterson, R. R. and Savoy, P. (1998) Lexical selection and phonological encoding during language production: Evidence for cascade processing. *Journal of Experimental Psychology: Learning, Memory, and Cognition,* **24,** 539–557.

Piaget, J. (1948) *The Psychology of Intelligence.* Routledge and Kegan Paul, London.

Piaget, J. (1952) *The child's conception of number.* Routledge and Kegan Paul, London.

Piatelli-Palmarini, M. (1989) Evolution, selection and cognition: from 'learning' to parameter setting in biology and in the study of language. *Cognition*, **31**, 1–44.

Piatelli-Palmarini, M. (ed.) (1980) *Language and learning: the debate between Jean Piaget and Noam Chomsky.* Harvard University Press, Cambridge, MA.

Pine, J. M. and Lieven, E. V. M. (1997) Slot and frame patterns and the development of the determiner category. *Applied Psycholinguistics*, **18**, 123–138.

Pine, J. M. and Martindale, H. (1996) Syntactic categories in the speech of young children: the case of the determiner. *Journal of Child Language*, **23**, 369–395.

Pine, J. M., Lieven, E. V. M. and Rowland, C. F. (1998) Comparing different models of the development of the English verb category. *Linguistics*, **36**, 807–830.

Pinker, S. (1984) *Language Learnability and Language Development.* Harvard University Press, Cambridge, MA.

Pinker, S. (1987) The bootstrapping problem in language acquisition. In B. MacWhinney (ed.) *Mechanisms of Language Development*, pp. 399–442. Lawrence Erlbaum, Hillsdale, NJ.

Pinker, S. (1994) *The Language Instinct.* Allen Lane, London.

Pinker, S. (1999a) *Words and Rules: The ingredients of language.* New York: Basic Books.

Pinker, S. (1999b) Out of the minds of babies. *Science*, **283**, 40–41.

Pinker, S. and Bloom, P. (1990) Natural language and natural selection. *Behavioural and Brain Sciences*, **13**, 707–784.

Plunkett, K. and Elman, J. L. (1997) *Exercises in Rethinking Innateness.* MIT Press, Cambridge, MA.

Plunkett, K. and Marchman, V. (1991) U-shaped learning and frequency effects in a multilayered perceptron: implications for child language acquisition. *Cognition*, **38**, 43–102.

Plunkett, K. and Strömqvist, S. (1992) The acquisition of Scandinavian languages. In D.I. Slobin (ed.) *The Crosslinguistic Study of Language Acquisition*, vol. 3, pp. 457–556, Lawrence Erlbaum Associates: Hillsdale, NJ.

Plunkett, K., Sinha, C. G., Müller, M. F. and Strandsby (1992) Symbol grounding or the emergence of symbols? Vocabulary growth in children and a connectionist net. *Connection Science*, **4**, 293–312.

Poizner, H. and Kegl, J. (1992) The neural basis of language and motor behaviour: evidence from American sign language. *Aphasiology*, 1992, **6**, 219–256.

Poizner, H., Bellugi, U. and Klima, E. S. (1990) Biological foundations of language: clues from sign language. *Annual Review of Neuroscience*, **13**, 283–307.

Pollack, J. (1990) Recursive distributed representations. *Artificial Intelligence*, **46**, 77–105. Reprinted in G. Hinton (ed.) (1991) *Connectionist Symbol Processing.* MIT Press, Cambridge, MA.

Postal, P. (1964) Limitations of phrase structure grammar. In J. Fodor and J. J. Katz (eds) *The Structure of Language: Readings in the philosophy of language,* pp. 137–152, Prentice Hall, New York.

Prince, A. and Smolensky, P. (1997) Optimality: from neural networks to Universal Grammar. *Science,* **275**, 1604–1610.

Radford, A. (1988) *Transformational Grammar: A first course.* Cambridge University Press, Cambridge.

Radford, A. (1990) *Syntactic Theory and the Acquisition of English syntax.* Basil Blackwell, Oxford.

Radford, A. (1994) Tense and agreement variability in child grammars of English. In Lust, M. Suñer, and J. Whitman (eds) *Syntactic Theory and First Language Acquisition: Cross-linguistic perspectives: volume 1, heads, projections, and learnability,* pp. 135–157. Lawrence Erlbaum, Hillsdale, NJ.

Radford, A. (1996) Towards a structure-building model of acquisition. In H. Clahsen (ed.) *Generative Perspectives on Language Acquisition: empirical findings, theoretical considerations, and cross-linguistic comparisons,* pp. 43–89. John Benjamins, Amsterdam.

Radford, A. (1997a) *Syntactic Theory and the Structure of English: A minimalist approach.* Cambridge University Press, Cambridge.

Radford, A. (1997b) *Syntax: A minimalist introduction.* Cambridge University Press, Cambridge.

Radford, A. (2000) Children in search of perfection: Towards a perfect acquisition model. Unpublished ms. Department of Linguistics, University of Essex, UK.

Ramat, P. (1992) Thoughts on degrammaticalisation. *Linguistics,* **30**, 549–560.

Reber, A. S. (1989) Implicit learning and tacit knowledge. *Journal of Experimental Psychology: General,* 118, 219–235.

Reddington, M., Chater, N. and Finch, S. (1998) Distributional information: a powerful cue for acquiring syntactic categories. *Cognitive Science,* **22**, 425–469.

Reinhart, T. (1986) Centre and periphery in the grammar of anaphora. In *Studies in the Acquisition of Anaphora, volume 1: Defining the constraints,* pp. 123–150. Reidel, Dordrecht.

Reinhart, T. and Reuland, E. (1993) Reflexivity. *Linguistic Inquiry,* **24**, 657–720.

Rice, M. Ed. (1996) *Towards a Genetics of Language.* Lawrence Erlbaum, Mahwah, NJ.

Rice, M., Wexler, K. and Cleave, P. L. (1995) Specific language impairment as a period of extended optional infinitive. *Journal of Speech and Hearing Research,* **38**, 850–863.

Richards, M. P. M. (1978) The biological and the social. In A. Lock (ed.) *Action, Gesture, and Symbol: the emergence of language.* Academic Press, London.

Rizzi, L. (1982) Violations of the *wh*-island constraint and the subjacency condition. In R. Rizzi (ed.) *Issues in Italian Syntax,* pp. 49–76. Foris, Dordrecht.

Rizzi, L. (1991) Residual verb second and the WH-criterion. *Technical Reports in Formal and Computational Linguistics, no. 2.* University of Geneva.

Robinson, E. J. (1983) Ambiguity and communication. In *Developing thinking: Approaches to children's cognitive development*, pp. 34–65. Methuen, London.

Roeper, T. (1972) *Approaches to acquisition theory, using a data from German children.* Doctoral Dissertation, Harvard University, Cambridge, MA.

Rogers, T. T. and McClelland, J. L. (in press) *Semantic Cognition: a parallel distributed processing approach.* MIT Press, Cambridge, MA.

Rorty, R. (1982) Method, social science and social hope. In his *Consequences of Pragmatism.* Harvester Press, Brighton.

Rorty, R. (2000) Universality and truth. In R. B. Brandom (ed.) *Rorty and his Critics*, p1–24, Basil Blackwell, Oxford.

Ross, J. R. (1967) Constraints on variables in syntax. Unpublished Ph.D. Thesis, MIT, Cambridge MA.

Rowland, C. F. and Pine, J. M. (2000) Subject-auxiliary inversion errors and *wh*-question acquisition: 'what children do know?' *Journal of Child Language*, **27**, 157–181.

Rowland, C. F. and Pine, J. M. (2003) The development of inversion in wh-questions: a reply to Van Valin. *Journal of Child Language*, **30**, 197–212.

Rubino, C. (1994) Against the notion of unidirectionality in lexeme genesis. *Linguistica Antlantica*, **16**, 135–147.

Rumelhart, D. E. and McClelland, J. L. (1986) PDP models and general issues in Cognitive science. In J. L. McClelland, D. Rumelhart and the PDP Research Group (eds) *Parallel Distributed Processing: foundations, volume 1*, pp. 110–156. MIT Press, Cambridge, MA.

Rumelhart, D. E., McClelland, J. L. and the PDP research group. (1986) *Parallel Distributed Processing: Foundations, volume One.* MIT Press, Cambridge, MA.

Russell, J. (1978) *The Acquisition of Knowledge.* Macmillan, Basingstoke.

Russell, J. (1984) *Explaining Mental Life: some philosophical issues in psychology.* Macmillan, London

Russell, J. (1987a) 'Can we say...?' Children's understanding of intensionality. *Cognition*, **25**, 289–308.

Russell, J. (1987b) Three kinds of questions about modularity. In S. and C. Modgil (eds) *Noam Chomsky: Consensus and Controversy.* Falmer Press, Brighton.

Russell, J. (1987c) Rule-following, mental models and the developmental view. In M. Chapman and R. Dixon (eds) *Meaning and the Growth of Understanding: Wittgenstein's significance for developmental psychology*, pp. 23–48. Springer, Berlin.

Russell, J. (1988) Cognisance and cognitive science. Part one: The 'generality constraint'. *Philosophical Psychology*, **1**, 235–258.

Russell, J. (1995) At two with nature: The role of agency in mental development. In J. Bermúdez, A. J. Marchel, and N. Eilan. *The body and the self.* Cambridge Mass.: MIT Press (Bradford Books).

Russell, J. (1996) *Agency: Its role in mental development.* The Psychology Press, Hove.

Russell, J. (1999) Cognitive development as an executive process – in part: A homeopathic dose of Piaget. *Developmental Science,* **2,** 247–295.

Russell, J. (2002) Current cogntiive models of autism – assessment. In A. Owen and J. Harrison (eds) *Cognitive Deficits and Brain Disorders,* pp. 295–323. Martin Dunitz, London.

Russell, J. and Thompson, D. (2003) Memory development in the second year: for events or locations? *Cognition,* **87,** B97–B95.

Russell, J., McCormack. T., Robinson, J. and Lillis, G. (1996) Logical (versus associative) performance on transitive reasoning tasks by children: Implications for the status of animals' performance. *The Quarterly Journal of Experimental Psychology,* **49**B, 231–244.

Ryle, G. (1949) *The Concept of Mind* Hutchinson's University Library, London.

Saah, K. K. and Goodluck, H. (1995) Island effects in parsing and grammar: Evidence from Akan. *The Linguistic Review,* **12,** 381–409.

Saffran, J. R., Aslin, R. N. and Newport, E. L. (1996) Statistical learning by 8-month-old infants. *Science,* **274,** 1926–1928.

Saffran, J. R., Johnson, E. K., Aslin, E. K. and Newport, E. L. (1999) Statistical learning of tone sequences by human infants and adults. *Cognition,* **70,** 27–52.

Santelmann, L. and Jusczyk, P. (1998) Sensitivity to discontinuous dependencies in language learners: evidence for limitations in processing space. *Cognition,* **69,** 105–134.

Savage-Rumbaugh, E. S., Sevcik, R. A., Brakke, K. E., Rumbaugh, D. M. and Greenfield, P. M. (1990) Symbols: their communicative use, comprehension, and combination by bonobos (*Pan paniscus*). In C. Rovee-Collier and L. P. Lipsitt (eds) *Advances in Infancy Research,* volume 6. Ablex, New York.

Schlesinger, I. M. (1988) The origin of relational categories. In Y. Levy, I. M. Schlesinger and M. D. S. Braine (eds) *Categories and Processes in Language Acquisition,* pp. 121–178. Lawrence Erlbaum, Hillsdale, NJ.

Searle, J. (1969) *Speech Acts: An Essay in the Philosophy of Language.* Cambridge University Press, Cambridge.

Searle, J. (1972/74) Chomsky's revolution in linguistics. In G. Harman (ed.) *On Noam Chomsky: critical essays,* pp. 2–33. Anchor Books, New York; originally published in *New York Review of Books,* 29 June, 1972, pp. 16–24.

Searle, J. (1984) *Minds, Brains, and Science: the Reiln Lectures 1984* Penguin Books, Harmonsworth.

Searle, J. (2002) End of the revolution. *New York Review of Books,* **49,** 28 February.

Seidenberg, M. and MacDonald, M. C. (1999) A probabilistic constraints approach to language acquisition and processing. *Cognitive Science,* **23,** 569–588.

Shady, M. (1996) Infant's sensitivity to function morphemes. Unpublished doctoral dissertation. State University of New York at Buffalo, Buffalo, NY.

Shanks, D. and St. John, M. F. (1994) Characteristics of dissociable human learning systems. *Behavioural and Brain Sciences*, **17**, 367–447.

Shanks, D. R. (1986) Selective attribution in the judgement of causality. *Learning and Motivation*, **17**, 311–334.

Shanks, D. R. (1989) Selectional processes in causality judgement. *Memory and Cognition*, **17**, 27–34.

Shanks, D. R. (1991) Categorzation by a connectionist network. *Journal of Experimental Psychology: Learning, Memory, and Cognition*, **17**, 433–443.

Shanks, D. R. (1995) *The Psychology of Associative Learning*. Cambridge University Press, Cambridge.

Shastri, L. and Ajjanagadde, V. (1993) From simple association to systematic reasoning: a connectionist representation of rules, variables, and dynamic bindings using temporal synchrony. *Behavioural and Brain Sciences*, **16**, 417–194.

Sheldon, A. (1974) On the role of parallel function in the acquisition of relative clauses in English. *Journal of Verbal Learning and Verbal Behaviour*, **13**, 272–81.

Shotter, J. (1973) Acquired powers: the transformation of natural into personal powers. *Journal for the Theory of Social Behaviour*, **3**, 141–156.

Shultz, T. R., Mareschal, D. and Schmidt, W. C. (1995) Modelling cognitive development on balance scale phenomena. *Machine Learning*, **16**, 57–88.

Shultz, T. R. (1999) Rule learning my habituation can be simulated in neural networks. In M. Hahn and S. C. Stoness (eds) *Proceedings of the twenty-fifth annual conference of the Cognitive Science Society*, pp. 665–670. Lawrence Erlbaum, Mahwah, NJ.

Siegelman, H. and Sontag, E. (1995) On the computational power of neural nets. *Journal of Computer and System Sciences*, **50**, 132–150.

Slobin, D. (1979) *Psycholinguistics*. Scott Foresman and Co, Glenview, IL.

Slobin, D. and Bever, T. (1982) Children use canonical English sentence schemas: a cross-linguistic study of word order an inflections. *Cognition*, **12**, 229–265.

Slobin, D. I. (1966) The acquisition of Russian as a native language. In F. Smith and G. A. Miller (eds) *The Genesis of Language*, pp. 68–85. MIT Press, Cambridge, MA.

Smith, B. C. (1998) Meaning and rule-following. In E. Craig (ed.) *Routledge Encyclopedia of Philosophy*. Routledge and Kegan Paul, London.

Smith, K. H. (1966) Grammatical intrusions in the recall of structured letter pairs: mediated transfer or position learning? *Journal of Experimental Psychology*, **72**, 580–588.

Smith, K. H. (1969) Learning cooccurrence restrictions: Rule learning or rote learning? *Journal of Verbal Learning and Verbal Behavior*, **8**, 319–321.

Smith, N. (1981) Consistency, markedness and language change: on the notion of 'consistent language'. *Journal of Linguistics*, **17**, 381–409.

Smith, N. (1999) *Chomsky: ideas and ideals*. Cambridge University Press, Cambridge.

Smolensky, P. (1988) On the proper treatment of connectionism. *Behavioural and Brain Sciences*, **11**, 1–23.

Smolensky, P. (1990) Tensor product variable binding and the representation of symbolic structures in connectionist systems. *Artificial Intelligence*, **46**, 159–216. Reprinted in G. Hinton (ed.) *Connectionist Symbol Processing*. MIT Press, Cambridge, MA.

Smolensky, P. (1995) Constituent structure and explanation in an integrated connectionist/symbolic cognitive architecture. In C. McDonald and G. McDonald (eds) *Connectionism: debates on psychological explanation*, pp. 78–94. Basil Blackwell, Oxford.

Sokal, R. R. and Sneath, P. H. A. (1963) *Principles of Numerical Taxonomy*. Freeman, San Francisco.

Sophian, C. and McCorgray, P. (1994) Part-whole knowledge and early arithmetic problem solving. *Cognition and Instruction*, **12**, 3–33.

Sougné, J. (1998) Connectionism and the problem of multiple instantiation. *Trends in Cognitive Sciences*, **2**, 183–189.

Spelke, E. and Kestenbaum, R. (1986) Les origins du concept d'objet. *Psychologie Francaise*, **31**, 67–72.

Spelke, E., Breitlinger, K., Macomber, J. and Jackobson, K. (1992) Origins of knowledge. *Psychological Review*, **99**, 605–632.

Sperber, D. and Wilson, D. (1986) *Relevance: communication and cognition*. Basil Blackwell, Oxford.

Spiegel, R. C. (2003) Human and machine learning of spatio-temporal sequences: an experimental and computational investigation. Unpublished Ph.D. thesis, University of Cambridge.

Spiegel, R. C. and McLaren, I. P. L. (2003) Abstract and associatively-based representations in human sequence learning. *Philosophical Transactions of the Royal Society, (Biological Sciences)*, 03TB020L.1-L.7.

St John, M. F. and McClelland, J. L. (1990) Learning and applying contextual constraints in sentence production. *Artificial Intelligence*, **46**, 217–257. Reprinted in G. Hinton (ed.) *Connectionist Symbol Processing*. MIT Press, Cambridge, MA.

Steedman, M. (1984) On the generality of the nested-dependency constraint and the reason for an exception in Dutch. In B. Butterworth, B. Comrie and O. Dahl (eds) *Explanations for Language Universals*, pp. 35–66. Mouton, Berlin.

Steedman, M. (2000) *The Syntactic Process*. MIT Press, Cambridge, MA.

Steeedman, M. (1999) Connectionist sentence processing in perspective. *Cognitive Science*, **23**, 615–634.

Stenning, K. (2002) *Seeing reason: Language and image in learning to think*. Oxford University Press, Oxford.

Stevenson, R. (1988) *Models of Language Development*. Open University Press, Milton Keynes.

Stowe, L. (1986) Parsing wh-constructions: evidence for on-line gap location. *Language and Cognitive Processes*, 1, 227–248.

Strawson, P. (1959) *Individuals: An essay in descriptive metaphysics*. Methuen, London.

Strawson, P. (1966) *The Bounds of Sense*. Methuen, London.

Stromswold, K. (1995) The acquisition of subject and object in WH-questions. *Language Acquisition*, **4**, 5–48.

Tallal, P., Miller, S. and Fitch, R. (1993) A case for the preeminence of temporal processing. In P. Tallal, A. M. Galaburda, R. R. Llinas and C. von Euler (eds) *Temporal Information Processing in the Nervous System: special reference to dyslexia and dysphasia. Annals of the New York Academy of Science*, **682**, 27–47.

Thatcher, R. W. (1991) Maturation of the human frontal lobes: physiological evidence for staging. *Developmental Neuropsychology*, 7, 397–419.

Thornton, R. (1990) *Adventures in long-distance moving: The Acquisition of complex* wh-*questions*. Doctoral Dissertations, University of Connedicut Storrs.

Thornton, R. and Wexler, K. (1999) *Principle B, VP Ellipsis and Interpretation in Children's Grammar*. MIT Press, Cambridge, MA.

Tomasello, M. (1992) *First Verbs: a case study in early grammatical development*. Cambridge University Press, Cambridge.

Tomasello, M. (1999) *The Cultural Origins of Human Cognition*. Cambridge MA: Harvard University Press.

Tomasello, M. (2000a) Do young children have adult syntactic competence? *Cognition*, **74**, 209–253.

Tomasello, M. (2000b) The item-based nature of children's early syntactic development. *Trends in Cognitive Sciences*, **4**, 156–163.

Tomasello, M. (2003) Introduction to the volume: Some surprises for Psychologists. In M. Tomasello (ed.) *The New Psychology of Language, volume 2: Cognitive and functional approaches to language structure*. Lawrence Erlbaum, Mahwah, NJ.

Tomasello, M. (ed.) (1998) *The New Psychology of Language: cognitive and Functional approaches to language structure*. Lawrence Erlbaum, Mahwah, NJ.

Tomasello, M., Akhtar, N., Dodson, K. and Rekau, L. (1997) Differential productivity in young children's use of nouns and verbs. *Journal of Child Language*, **24**, 373–387.

Tomasello, M. and Abbot-Smith, K. (2002) A tale of two theories: a response to Fisher. *Cognition*, **83**, 207–214.

Tomasello, M. and Akhtar, N. (1995) Two-year-olds use pragmatic cues to differentiate reference to objects and actions. *Cognitive Development*, **10**, 201–224.

Tomasello, M. and Akhtar, N. (2003) What paradox? A response to Naigles (2002) *Cognition*, **88**, 317–323.

Tomasello, M. and Barton, M. (1994) Learning words in non-ostensive contexts. *Developmental Psychology*, **30**, 639–650.

Tomasello, M. and Brooks, P. (1998) Young children's early transitive and intransitive constructions. *Cognitive Linguistics*, **9**, 379–395.

Tomasello, M. and Olguin, R. (1993) Twenty-three-month-old children have a grammatical category of noun. *Cognitive Development*, **8**, 451–464.

Tomblin, J. B. and Pandrich, J. (1999) Lessons from children with specific language impairment. *Trends in Cognitive Sciences*, **3**, 283–285.

Tomlin, R. S. (1986) *Basic Word Order: functional principles.* Croom Helm, London.

Uriagereka, J. (1998) *Rhyme and Reason: A introduction to minimalist syntax.* MIT Press, Cambridge, MA.

Valian, V. (1986) Syntactic categories in the speech of young children. *Developmental Psychology*, **22**, 562–579.

Valian, V. (1991) Syntactic subjects in the early speech of American and Italian children. *Cognition*, **40**, 21–81.

Valian, V., Lasser, I. and Mandlebaum, D. (1992) Children's early questions. Paper presented at the 17th annual Boston University Conference on Language Development.

van der Lely, H. K. J. (1994) Canonical linking rules: forward versus reverse linking in normally developing and specifically language-impaired children. *Cognition*, **51**, 29–72.

van der Lely, H. K. J. (1998) SLI in children: movement, economy, and deficits in the computational-syntactic system. *Language Acquisition*, **7**, 161–192.

van der Lely, H. K. J. (1999) Learning from grammatical SLI: response to J. B. Tomblin and J. Pandrich (1999) *Trends in Cognitive Sciences*, **3**, 286–287.

van der Lely, H. K. J. and Battell, J. (2003) Wh-movement in children with Grammatical SLI: a test of the RDDR hypothesis. *Language*, **71**, 153–181.

van der Lely, H. K. J. and Christian, V. (2000) Lexical word formation in children with grammatical SLI: a grammar specific versus an input-processing deficit. *Cognition*, **75**, 33–63.

van der Lely, H. K. J. and Harris, M. (1990) Comprehension of reversible sentences in specifically language impaired children. *Journal of Speech and Hearing Research*, **55**, 101–117.

van der Lely, H. K. J. and Stollwerck, L. (1997) Binding theory and grammatical specific language impairment in children. *Cognition*, **62**, 245–290.

van der Lely, H. K. J., Rosen, S. and Adlard, A. (in press) Grammatical language impairment and the specificity of cognitive domain: Relations between auditory and language abilities, *Cognition*.

van der Lely, H. K. J., Rosen, S. and McClelland, A. (1998) Evidence for a grammar-specific deficit in children. *Current Biology*, **8**, 1253–1258.

van Gelder, T. (1990) Compositionality: A connectionist variation on a classical theme. *Cognitive Science*, **14**, 355–384.

Van Hoek, K. (1995) Conceptual reference points: a cognitive grammar account of pronominal anaphora constraints. *Language*, **71**, 310–340.

Van Valin, R. D. (1987) The role of government in the grammar of head-marking languages. *International Journal of American Linguistics*, **53**, 371–397.

Van Valin, R. D. (1991) Functionalist linguistic theory and language development. *First Language*, **11**, 7–40.

Van Valin, R. D. (1993a) A synopsis of role and reference grammar. In R. D. Van Valin (ed.) *Advances in Role and Reference Grammar*, pp. 1–164. John Benjamins, Amsterdam and Philadelphia.

Van Valin, R. D. (2000) The acquisition of complex sentences: a case study in the role of theory in the study of language development. *Chicago Linguistic Society: The Panels*, **36**, 511–531.

Van Valin, R. D. (2001) *An Introduction to Syntax*. Cambridge University Press, Cambridge.

Van Valin, R. D. (2002) The development of subject-auxiliary inversion in English wh-questions: an alternative analysis. *Journal of Child Language*, **29**, 161–175.

Van Valin, R. D. (ed.) (1993b) *Advances in Role and Reference Grammar*. John Benjamins, Amsterdam and Philadelphia.

Van Valin, R. D. and LaPolla, R. J. (1997) *Syntax: Structure, meaning and function*. Cambridge University Press, Cambridge.

Visser, I., Raijmakers, M. E. J. and Molenaar, P. C. M. (2000) Reaction times and predictions in sequence learning: a comparison. In L. R. Gleitman and A. K. Joshi (eds) *Proceedings of the 22nd Annual Conference of the Cognitive Science Society*, pp. 971–976. Lawrence Erlbaum, Mahwah, N.J.

von Glaserfield, E. (1972) Semantic analysis of verbs in terms of conceptual situations. *Linguistics*, **94**, 90–107.

Wagner, S., Winner, E., Cicchetti, D. and Gardner, H. (1981) 'Metaphorical' mapping in human infants. *Child Developmentelopment*, **52**, 728–731.

Wanner, E. and Maratsos, M. (1978) An ATN approach to comprehension. In M. Halle, J. Bresen and G. A. Miller (eds) Linguistic theory and psychological reality, pp. 119–161. MIT Press, Cambridge, MA.

Weisler, S. E. and Milekic, S. (2000) *Theory of Language*. MIT Press, Cambridge, MA.

Wexler, K. (1994) Optional infinitives, head movement, and the economy of derivations. In D. Lightfoot and N. Hornstein (eds) *Verb Movement*, pp. 34–67. Cambridge University Press, Cambridge.

Wexler, K. (1996) The development of inflection in a biologically based theory of language acquisition. In M. Rice (ed.) (1996) *Towards a Genetics of Language*. Lawrence Erlbaum, Mahwah, NJ.

Whittlesea, B. W. A. and Dorken, M. D. (1993) Incidentally, things in general are particularly determined: an episodic-processing account of implicit learning. *Journal of Experimental Psychology: General*, **122**, 227–248.

Wiggins, D. (1999) Belief, truth, and going from the known to the unknown. *Canadian Journal of Philosophy* (Supplementary edition), **24**, 9–27.

Wijnen, F. and Bol, G. (1993) The escape from the optional infinite stage. *Papers in Experimental Linguistics*, pp. 239–248. University of Groningen.

Wilson, B., Mackintosh, N. J. and Boakes, R. A. (1985) Transfer of relational rules in matching and oddity learning by pigeons and corvids. *Quarterly Journal of Experimental Psychology*, **37**B, 313–332.

Wilson, R. and Peters, A. (1988) What you cookin' on a hot?: movement constraints in the speech of a three-year-old blind child. *Language*, **64**, 249–273.

Wimmer, H. and Perner, J. (1983) Beliefs about beliefs: representation and constraining function of wrong beliefs in young children's understanding of deception. *Cognition*, **13**, 103–128.

Wittgenstein, L. (1953) *Philosophical Investigations*. Basil Blackwell, Oxford.

Wittgenstein, L. (1956) *Remarks on the Foundations of Mathematics*. Basil Blackwell, Oxford.

Woodhouse, R.S. (1988) *The Empiricists*. Oxford University Press, Oxford.

Wright, B. A., Lombardino, L. J., King, W. M., Puranik, C. S., Leonard, C. M. and Merzenich, M. M. (1997) Deficits in auditory temporal and spectral resolution in language-impaired children. *Nature*, **387**, 176–178.

Wright, C. (1999) Truth: A traditional debate renewed. *Canadian Journal of Philosophy* (Supplementary edition), **24**, 28–41.

Xu, F. (2002) The role of language in acquiring object kind concepts in infancy. *Cognition*, **85**, 223–250.

Xu, F. and Carey, S. (1996) Infants' metaphysics: the case of numerical identity. *Cognitive Psychology*, **30**, 111–153.

Author Index

Subject Index

a (argument) movement 232
A′ (A-bar or non-argument) movement 189–91
abstract ideas (for the British Empiricists)
   31–3
accessibility and independence theses
   (in Peirce) 67
A/D (autonomy/dependence) relations in
   Langacker's cognitive grammar 360, 372
accessibility hierarchy (AH) 488–91
Acehese (a Sumatran language) 385–6
affirming the consequent 22, 326–67
agency (infant perception of) 481–3
agent versus 'undergoer' 382–3, 385, 387
agree 155–6
Akan language 221–2, 487
algebraic infant debate, the 289–96
Allen and Seidenberg's connectionist sentence
   production model 251–4, 272
  assessment of 254–9
analogy-making
  in development 346–7
  in the SARAH model 347–8
  in Tomasello's theory 454–5
anaphora
  forward and backward 201–2, 210–211
  pronominal (in cognitive grammar)
    378–8
anarchism (Chomsky's) 10–11
anti-representationism 61–2
APECS model, the 288–9, 295
argument from perception (Fodor's)
   179–82
articulatory-perceptual (A-P) systems 135,
   137, 140, 237, 267
artificial grammar learning 38–48, 293–4
array 140, 283
ascriptivism (of Dennett) 321
aspect marking by children 393–4
associative learning (in the laboratory)
  human 38–48
  animal 41–2, 50–1, 293–4
'associative foci' (for Braine) 47
Atkinson's conditions for cognitive-syntactic
   reduction 425–7
auditory deficits (in SLI) 234–7
autism research 224–5, 237
auto-association 291

autonomy of syntax
  for Chomsky 158–66
  for Newmeyer 406–13

back-propagation 52
'basic' sentences 473–7
behaviourism 278
belief (as construed within pragmatist
   theory) 67–8
Berkeley's views on abstraction 32–3, 308
Berwick's subset principle 362
  Van Valin's use of in an analogy 400–2
binary nature of branching 145–6, 475,
   476, 477
binding theory 122–5
  in parsing 177
  see also 'principles'
bound variable anaphora 211–12
bounding theory 125–7
  developmental work on 220–4, 230–1
Brandom's pragmatism 72–9
Brunerian ideas about speech acts 434–5

c-commanding 113–15, 124, 137, 140, 146, 421
Canonical Structural Realisation (CSR) of Jane
   Grimshaw 116–17, 296, 473–4
case marking (for Langacker) 370–2
case theory 127, 137
categorisation (for Langacker) 364–5
categories (in Peirce and Kant) 69–71
causative-transitive linkage 470–2
central-system cognition 28–9
chaining 137, 165–6
Chang's connectionist models of
   sentence production
  initial model 247–51
  assessment of 254–9
  latest model 337–45
checking theory 149–58, 239
CHILDES 186, 298, 319, 449
Chinese left-branching sentences 203–4, 213